Immigration and Asylum

From 1900 to the Present

Immigration and Asylum

From 1900 to the Present

Volume 1: Entries A to I

Matthew J. Gibney and Randall Hansen, Editors

Santa Barbara, California • Denver, Colorado • Oxford, England

Library of Congress Cataloging-in-Publication Data
Immigration and asylum : from 1900 to the present / Matthew J. Gibney and Randall Hansen, editors
p. cm.
Includes bibliographical references and index.
ISBN 1-57607-796-9 (hardback : alk. paper)—ISBN 1-57607-797-7 (ebook)
1. Emigration and immigration—Encyclopedias. 2. Asylum, Right of—Encyclopedias. 3. Immigrants—Encyclopedias. 4. Refugees—Encyclopedias. I. Gibney, Matthew J. II. Hansen, Randall.

JV6012.I56 2005
325'.09'0403—dc22

2005013788

ISBN-13 978-1-57607-796-2 ebook 978-1-57607-797-9
09 08 07 06 10 9 8 7 6 5 4 3 2

This book is also available on the World Wide Web as an eBook. Visit abc-clio.com for details.

ABC-CLIO, Inc.
130 Cremona Drive, P.O. Box 1911
Santa Barbara, California 93116-1911
This book is printed on acid-free paper.

Manufactured in the United States of America

For Arthur C. Helton
(1949–2003)

Contents

Contributors

Manolo I. Abella
International Labor Organization (ILO)
Chief, International Migration
Geneva, Switzerland

Chowdhur R. Abrar
University of Dhaka
Refugee and Migratory Movements Research Unit
Dhaka, Bangladesh

Howard Adelman
Princeton University
Woodrow Wilson School
Princeton, New Jersey

Madawi Al-Rasheed
King's College, University of London
Department of Theology and Religious Studies
London, United Kingdom

Peter Andreas
Brown University
Department of Political Science
Providence, Rhode Island

Nicola Ansell
Brunel University
Department of Geography and Earth Sciences
Uxbridge, West London, United Kingdom

Graziano Battistella
Scalabrini International Migration Institute
Rome, Italy

Jon Bennett
Oxford Development Consultants
Oxford, United Kingdom

Richard Black
University of Sussex
Sussex Center for Migration Research
Brighton, United Kingdom

Erik Bleich
Middlebury College
Department of Political Science
Middlebury, Vermont

Lúcia Bógus
Pontifical Catholic University of São Paulo
Department of Sociology
São Paulo, Brazil

Eberhard Bort
University of Edinburgh
Institute of Governance
Edinburgh, United Kingdom

Peter Braham
The Open University
Faculty of Social Sciences
Milton Keynes, United Kingdom

Cathrine Brun
Norwegian University of Science and Technology
Department of Geography
Trondheim, Norway

Kitty Calavita
University of California, Irvine
Department of Criminology, Law and Society
Irvine, California

Stephen Castles
University of Oxford
Refugee Studies Center
Oxford, United Kingdom

Max Jose Castro
Florida Atlantic University
Miami, Florida

Dawn Chatty
University of Oxford
Refugee Studies Center
Oxford, United Kingdom

B. S. Chimni
W.B. National University of Juridical Sciences
School of International Studies
Kolkata, India

Barry R. Chiswick
University of Illinois at Chicago
Department of Economics
Chicago, Illinois

Ryszard Cholewinski
University of Leicester
Leicester
United Kingdom

Joshua Comenetz
University of Florida
Department of Geography
Gainesville, Florida

Frederick J. Conway
San Diego State University
Department of Anthropology
San Diego, California

Susan Bibler Coutin
University of California, Irvine
Department of Criminology, Law and Society
Irvine, California

David R. Cox
La Trobe University
School of Social Work and Social Policy
Bundoora, Victoria, Australia

Randy Crisler
University of Arizona
Tucson, AZ

António Cruz
Migration Policy Group
Editor-in-Chief, Migration News Sheet
Brussels, Belgium

Mark Cutts
United Nations
Special Assistant to the High Commissioner, United Nations High Commissioner for Refugees
Geneva, Switzerland

Chris de Wet
Rhodes University
Grahamstown
South Africa

Mark R. Elliott
Samford University
Beeson Divinity School
Birmingham, Alabama

Anita H. Fabos
University of East London
Refugee Studies
London, United Kingdom

Patricia Weiss Fagen
Georgetown University
Institute for the Study of International Migration, School of Foreign Service
Washington, DC

Randa Farah
University of Western Ontario
Department of Anthropology
London, Ontario, Canada

Adrian Favell
University of California, Los Angeles
Department of Sociology
Los Angeles, California

Dean T. Ferguson
Texas A&M University—Kingsville
Department of History
Kingsville, Texas

Elizabeth G. Ferris
World Council of Churches
International Relations
Geneva, Switzerland

Joel S. Fetzer
Pepperdine University
Social Science Division
Malibu, California

Anthony J. Fielding
University of Sussex
School of Social Sciences and Cultural Studies
Brighton, United Kingdom

Keith Fitzgerald
New College of Florida
Department of Political Science
Sarasota, Florida

Nancy Foner
Hunter College, SUNY
Department of Sociology
New York, New York

Donna R. Gabaccia
University of Pittsburgh
Department of History
Pittsburgh, Pennsylvania

Romain Garbaye
Université Paris IV-Sorbonne
Institut d'Etudes Anglophones
Paris, France

Peter Gatrell
University of Manchester
Department of History
Manchester, United Kingdom

Andrew Geddes
University of Sheffield
Department of Politics
Sheffield, United Kingdom

Eagle Glassheim
Princeton University
Department of History
Princeton, New Jersey

Nathan Glazer
Harvard University
Department of Sociology
Cambridge, Massachusetts

Stella P. Go
De La Salle University
Behavioral Sciences Department
Manila, Philippines

Guy S. Goodwin-Gill
University of Oxford
All Souls College
Oxford, United Kingdom

Simon Green
University of Birmingham
Institute for German Studies
Birmingham, United Kingdom

Elspeth Guild
Radboud Universiteit
Nijmegen, The Netherlands

Virginie Guiraudon
CNRS
Political Science Department
Lille, France

James Hampshire
University of Sussex
Department of International Relations and Politics
Brighton, United Kingdom

Alec G. Hargreaves
Florida State University
Winthrop-King Institute for Contemporary French and Francophone Studies
Tallahassee, Florida

Barbara E. Harrell-Bond
American University in Cairo
Forced Migration and Refugee Studies Programme
Cairo, Egypt

Nigel Harris
University College London
Professor Emeritus, Development Planning Unit (Bartlett School)
London, United Kingdom

Arthur C. Helton†

Renée Hirschon
University of Oxford
St. Peter's College
Oxford, United Kingdom

James F. Hollifield
Southern Methodist University
Department of Political Science
Dallas, Texas

Agnès Hurwitz
International Peace Academy (IPA)
New York, New York

Stefan Ihrig
Freie Universität Berlin
Berlin, Germany

Christian Joppke
International University Bremen
School of Humanities and Social Sciences
Bremen, Germany

Ray Jureidini
American University of Beirut
Social and Behavioral Sciences
Beirut, Lebanon

Charles B. Keely
Georgetown University
Walsh School of Foreign Service
Washington, DC

Anne J. Kershen
Queen Mary College, University of London
Center for the Study of Migration
London, United Kingdom

Gaim Kibreab
South Bank University
Faculty of Humanities and Social Sciences
London, United Kingdom

Desmond King
Oxford University
Nuffield College
Oxford, United Kingdom

Jobst Köhler
University of Oxford
Nuffield College
Oxford, United Kingdom

Pål Kolstø
University of Oslo
Department of East European and Oriental Studies
Oslo, Norway

Khalid Koser
University College London
Department of Geography
London, United Kingdom

Tony Kushner
University of Southampton
Department of History and Parkes Institute
Southampton, United Kingdom

Sandra Lavenex
University of Bern
Institute of Political Science
Bern, Switzerland

Zig Layton-Henry
University of Warwick
Department of Politics and International Studies
Coventry, United Kingdom

Stephen H. Legomsky
Washington University School of Law
St. Louis, Missouri

Alana Lentin
Oxford University
Refugee Studies Center
Oxford, United Kingdom

Cathie Lloyd
University of Oxford
Oxford, United Kingdom

Sean Loughna
University of Oxford
Refugee Studies Center
Oxford, United Kingdom

Maryanne Loughry
University of Oxford
Refugee Studies Center
Oxford, United Kingdom

Leo Lucassen
University of Amsterdam
Center for the History of Migrants
Amsterdam, The Netherlands

Zdzislaw Mach
Jagiellonian University
Center for European Studies
Kraków, Poland

Hani Mansourian
Society for Protection and Assistance to Socially Disadvantaged Individuals
Tehran, Iran

David A. Martin
University of Virginia
School of Law
Charlottesville, Virginia

Philip L. Martin
University of California, Davis
Department of Agricultural Economics
Davis, California

Susan F. Martin
Georgetown University
Institute for the Study of International Migration
Washington, DC

Felix Masud-Piloto
DePaul University
Department of History
Chicago, Illinois

Rima Berns McGown
Independent Scholar/Writer
Toronto, Ontario, Canada

Syed Sikander Mehdi
University of Karachi
Departement of International Relations
Karachi, Pakistan

Peter C. Meilaender
Houghton College
Department of History and Political Science
Houghton, New York

Anthony M. Messina
University of Notre Dame
Department of Political Science
Notre Dame, Indiana

Kurt Mills
University of Glasgow
Department of Politics
Glasgow, Scotland

James Milner
University of Oxford
St. Antony's College
Oxford, United Kingdom

Francisco Javier Moreno-Fuentes
Universitat de Barcelona
Departament de Sociologia i Analisi de les Organitzacions
Barcelona, Spain

Karen Munk
Research and Documentation Center (WODC), Ministry of Justice
Department of Migration, Integration and International Affairs
The Hague, The Netherlands

Karma Nabulsi
University of Oxford
Nuffield College
Oxford, United Kingdom

Christian A. Nielsen
Independent Scholar
The Hague, The Netherlands

Gregor Noll
Lund University
Faculty of Law
Lund, Sweden

Pia A. Oberoi
University of Oxford
Oxford, United Kingdom

Rainer Ohliger
Humboldt University
Berlin, Germany

Wayne Patterson
St. Norbert College
Department of History
De Pere, Wisconsin

Susan Pattie
University College London
Department of Anthropology
London, United Kingdom

Sally Peberdy
Southern African Migration Project
Southern African Research Center, Queen's University and University of the Witwatersrand
Johannesburg, South Africa

Georges Prevelakis
Sorbonne University and the Fletcher School
Paris, France

Alexander V. Prusin
New Mexico Tech
Humanities Department
Socorro, New Mexico

Eric Reeves
Smith College
Department of English Language and Literature
Northampton, Massachusetts

Jeffrey G. Reitz
University of Toronto
Department of Sociology, and Munk Center for International Studies
Toronto, Ontario, Canada

Adam Roberts
Oxford University
Balliol College
Oxford, United Kingdom

Hiram A. Ruiz
Independent Scholar
Washington, DC

Saskia Sassen
University of Chicago
Department of Sociology
Chicago, Illinois

Andrew I. Schoenholtz
Georgetown University
Institute for the Study of International Migration
Washington, DC

Peter H. Schuck
Yale University
Yale Law School
New Haven, Connecticut

Ayelet Shachar
University of Toronto
Faculty of Law
Toronto, Ontario, Canada

Abbas Shiblak
University of Oxford
Refugee Studies Center
Oxford, United Kingdom

Marion Ryan Sinclair
South Africa

Ýbrahim Sirkeci
University of Bristol
Bristol, United Kingdom

Claudena Skran
Lawrence University
Government Department
Appleton, Wisconsin

John D. Skrentny
University of California, San Diego
Department of Sociology
La Jolla, California

Peter J. Spiro
University of Georgia School of Law
Athens, Georgia

Ronald Grigor Suny
University of Chicago
Department of Political Science and History
Chicago, Illinois

Heloisa Szymanski
Pontifical Catholic University of São Paulo
Doctoral and Master Programme in Educational Psychology
São Paulo, Brazil

John C. Torpey
University of British Columbia
Department of Sociology and Anthropology and Institute for European Studies
Vancouver, British Columbia, Canada

Takeyuki Tsuda
University of California, San Diego
Center for the Comparative Study of Immigration
La Jolla, California

David Turton
University of Oxford
Queen Elizabeth House
Oxford, United Kingdom

Emek M. Uçarer
Bucknell University
International Relations Program
Lewisburg, Pennsylvania

Nicholas Van Hear
University of Oxford
Center on Migration, Policy and Society
Oxford, United Kingdom

G. C. J. Van Kessel
Intergovernmental Consultations on Asylum, Refugee and Migration Policies in Europe, North America and Australia
Geneva, Switzerland

Joanne van Selm
Migration Policy Institute
Washington, D.C.

Ellie Vasta
University of Oxford
Center on Migration, Policy, and Society (COMPAS)
Oxford, United Kingdom

Guglielmo Verdirame
Corpus Christi College, University of Cambridge
Department of Law
Cambridge, United Kingdom

Steven Vertovec
University of Oxford
Institute of Social and Cultural Anthropology
Oxford, United Kingdom

Dita Vogel
University of Oldenburg
Interdisciplinary Center for Education and Communication in Migratory Processes (IBKM)
Oldenburg, Germany

Carmen Voigt-Graf
University of the South Pacific
Department of Geography
Suva, Fiji Islands

Christian Raitz von Frentz
Delegation of the European Commission to Bangladesh
Dhaka, Bangladesh

Bronwen Walter
Anglia Polytechnic University
Department of Sociology
Cambridge, United Kingdom

Wim Willems
University of Amsterdam
Institute for Migration and Ethnic Studies
Amsterdam, The Netherlands

Suke Wolton
Oxford University
Regent's Park College
Oxford, United Kingdom

Bernard P. Wong
San Francisco State University
Department of Anthropology
San Francisco, California

Monette Zard
Migration Policy Institute
Washington, DC

Aristide R. Zolberg
New School University
Department of Political Science
New York, New York

Alphabetical List of Entries

VOLUME 2

Preface

For millennia, people have moved, between cities, and across regions, countries and continents. For nomads, movement was not an unusual process but rather the foundation of their very way of life. Some migrated willingly—to escape poverty and disease or to pursue wealth, others unwillingly—fleeing war, genocide, or ethnic cleansing.

From 1900 until the new millennium, more people—hundreds of millions of people—moved than ever before. World War I led to the migration and displacement of more than 10 million people. In the 1930s, 400,000 Spaniards fled the Spanish Civil War and Franco, while 200,000 Jews fled Germany. After World War II, between 1945 and 1951, more than 10 million Germans were expelled from Central and Eastern Europe. Some 700,000 Jews migrated to Israel from 1948 until 1951, and during partition, 7 million Muslims fled India for Pakistan, while 8 million Hindus and Sikhs fled Pakistan for India. In the 1950s and 1960s, millions of guestworkers traveled to Germany, Austria, and Switzerland, traditionally nonimmigration countries, while millions of colonial migrants traveled to France, Britain, and the Netherlands. From the 1960s, Canada, Australia, and the United States, traditionally immigration countries already, opened their doors to non-European immigration, and their societies were transformed as a result.

Immigration is history, but it is also politics, and contemporary politics. Over the course of the 1990s, the United States alone accepted almost 1 million legal migrants per year, and it could not stop an unknown annual number—but one surely in the hundreds of thousands—of clandestine migrants. Despite instituting a formal stop to immigration in the early 1970s (one that is now being revised), the major European receiving countries—France, Germany, and the United Kingdom—all have net migrations in the hundreds of thousands. Nor is the South free from migration. Countries such as South Africa and India are not only a source of migrants—particularly skilled ones—but also a common destination country for economic migrants and asylum seekers. Of the world's 12 million refugees, only 10 percent are in Europe. The majority are in the south, often held in mass refugee camps.

These movements are bound up with domestic politics and foreign policy. In 2000–2001, whites became the minority in California, and migration patterns, especially of Latinos, indicate they will become a gradually shrinking minority. The implications of this demographic development for educational policy, for relations with other ethnic minorities (particularly African Americans), and for electoral behavior and political participation are immense. Although rarely discussed in the United States, migration also raises questions of class and race as a declining white population continues to dominate politics, business, and the liberal professions. California is only the starkest example of similar broad developments elsewhere. In Europe, migration is directly or indirectly linked with "race riots" in the United Kingdom; the rise of the far right in Denmark, Austria, and France; and right-wing violence in eastern Germany. Across northern Europe, migrants—with some notable exceptions—suffer from lower levels of educational attainment and higher levels of unemployment. In some countries—such as the Netherlands and France—they contribute to impassioned and at times tortured debates about national identity. Finally, across Europe, North America, the Middle East, the Indian subcontinent, and Asia, migration has become a question of security. The September 11, 2001, attacks on New York and Washington, D.C., changed migration politics forever. On the one hand, nations have begun to fear that migration channels are possible sources of terrorism; on the other, pro-migrant lobbies and citizens are concerned that these fears may be exaggerated to serve exclusionary ends. Migration has become, and will in all likelihood remain, a question of security.

Adopting a comparative and a historical perspective, this three-volume encyclopedia is an attempt to review and categorize migration over the past 100 years or so. We are the first to recognize that it is an ambitious, even arrogant, attempt. A quotable British politician Enoch Powell once said that all political careers ended in failure. The same might be said of academic enterprises. For how can a century of movement from hundreds of countries, from a complex myriad of linguistic and cultural groupings, and for an innumerable range of good and bad reasons possibly be captured in three volumes? And this is, of course, at most only half of the story. Migration is a process of leaving (emigration) and arriving (immigration). If the former is shaped by a multitude of causes, the latter is equally varied. The ways in which people who have moved interact with the new cultures, languages, and institutions in their country of destination; the structures they create to cope with their new world; and the ways in which and extent to which they integrate are all complex stories that deserve to be told. No one encyclopedia can do all of this, and as a result the process of inclusion is to an even greater extent one of exclusion.

What is included should at least be guided by some criteria. In drawing up a list of entries, we sorted them according to four themes. The first centers on the distinction between immigration and asylum. There are a number of ways of making this distinction. Immigrants might be said to want to migrate, while asylum seekers are forced to leave. Since 1951, when international rules governing the treatment of asylum seekers were adopted, asylum seekers have been defined as those who claim a right—namely, to apply for asylum and not to be returned to a country where their lives are threatened—whereas migrants are admitted or rejected at the behest of the destination state. Legally, a migrant is one who moves to another country and resides there for at least one year; an asylum seeker is one who applies for refugee status under the 1951 UN Convention Relating to the Status of Refugees; and a refugee is one who is granted that status.

The asylum/migration distinction runs through the encyclopedia, and at many points inevitably blurs. Two sets of entries can nonetheless be grouped under the asylum heading. The first concerns the legal definitions and statuses governing asylum (with entries on refugees, asylum, nonconvention status, and temporary protection) and the asylum process (asylum determination). These are in the main about the law and process that asylum seekers encounter when arriving in the West. An important subcategory, of particular importance since the early 1980s, is made up of the battery of measures designed to prevent asylum seekers from reaching Western soil and claiming rights accorded by international treaties and domestic courts and constitutions (safe country of origin/safe third country rules, carrier sanctions, and employer sanctions). The second set concerns the origin of asylum seekers. We have included entries on more than a dozen of the world's largest refugee-producing regions in recent history—Afghanistan, Angola, Armenia, Bosnia-Herzegovina, Burundi, Colombia, Croatia, the Democratic Republic of Congo, Eritrea, Kosovo, Somalia, and the Sudan. Although some of these are no longer mass refugee–producing regions, the entries both provide the political, social, and economic context of the actual refugee movements and isolate some of the dynamics common to the movement of refugees.

A second theme concerns major émigré groups in diaspora. There are entries on Armenian, Chinese, Colombian, Dominican Republican, Filipino, Greek, Indian, Iraqi, Irish, Japanese, Jewish, Korean, Polish, Russian, Sri Lankan, and Turkish emigrants. We selected these migrant groups according to three related criteria: size of the migrant group relative to the country of origin (Ireland, for instance, is an important case); overall size of the total diaspora; and size and political importance of the migrant group in one or more of the major North American or European destination countries (Australia, Canada, France, Germany, the United Kingdom, and the United States). As the migrants' experience cannot be separated from the country to which they immigrated, we have also included entries on these countries of immigration as well as on Israel, Italy, South Africa, and Spain.

The third thematic consideration is historical. Throughout the previous century—and into this one—mass movement was bound up with several key historical moments. The most striking was expulsion. The harnessing of bureaucratic rationality, on the one hand, and industrial and military hardware, on the other, to the pursuit of population policy was one of the most brutal features of a wholly brutal century. Literally millions of people were "cleansed" from territorial spaces for reasons of revenge (the Armenians from Turkey, the Germans from Eastern Europe), in pursuit of an ethnically and/or religiously "pure" society (Jews from Europe, Muslims from Serbia), and as the secondary effect of a shift in borders (Muslims from India, Hindus from Pakistan, and Germans, Serbs, Bosnians, and many others from their traditional homelands). In some cases, ethnic cleansing evolved from expulsion into genocide—the Jews of Germany, Poland, and the rest of Europe remain the starkest example, but to them should be added the Muslims of Yugoslavia and the Tutsis of Rwanda. The encyclopedia contains entries on these gruesome expulsions as well as on less violent, but politically still important, conflict-related migrations: Hungarians who fled their country after the Soviets crushed the 1956 uprising, for example, and Czechoslovakians who escaped west when the flowering of the Prague Spring ended in Soviet tanks and barbed wire in 1968.

The final category of entries is the broadest, and it is here that the boundaries are most fluid and the choice of inclusion and exclusion most difficult. We have attempted to convey a sense of the events, themes, and policies that are basic elements in what might very broadly be called the politics of migration. The main focus in these entries is on the United States, as the world's premier country of immigration. Some entries—covering, for instance, major U.S. legislation on immigration—are historical, but most are on contemporary issues and problems. Immigration is linked—inevitably, or because actors make a point of linking it—with social policy, with public health, and with issues of race and racism. Public opinion affects migrants and migration policy, and migrants may shape public opinion. They are shaped by the political process, and as citizens, lobbyists, and components of public opinion, they and their descendants shape the political process. Finally, in a post-9/11 world, migration raises issues of security. Policies of entry, integration, and, in some instances, detention and expulsion, govern these areas, and we have therefore included entries addressing, in whole or in part, each of them.

This preface began by suggesting that immigration is history and politics; it is also the future. Whether one supports or opposes migration, it is clear that it will not go away. Massive economic inequalities—which may be exacerbated by political instability and/or natural disasters—will continue to push migrants toward the West. At the same time, the West needs—and will need more and more—migrants. Europe, in this respect, is the clearest example of a broader development. Britain, France, Italy, and Germany all have birth rates below the replacement rate, and, all things being equal, face aging populations and probable population declines over the next fifty years. In the context of generous pension and health systems (the United Kingdom partially excepted), a migration-free Europe would face crippling financial crises. Demographers and other scholars are divided over how much migration can help avoid or temper population aging and decline, but it is clear that migration will need to be part of the solution. In the United States, population decline is not an issue—partly because of immigration, the U.S. population is predicted to increase while Europe's falls—but population aging is. In any case, history, sentiment, and the strength of migrant lobbies mean that U.S. policy is effectively locked into a pro-migration stance. Immigration is, of course, emigration, and the movement from source countries and through transit countries will continue to affect economies, polities, and societies. Finally, war, environmental degradation, and human rights violations, all compounded by economic inequalities, will continue to create refugee movements and mass influxes. One century of migration has given way to another.

Acknowledgments

Putting together an encyclopedia is a large task, and in completing it we have acquired many debts. Our greatest is to the editor at ABC-CLIO, Patience Melnik. Patience has the ideal first name for one who has to encourage and cajole contributors (and editors) who, as good academics, do not like to be rushed. Bob Neville, who has since left ABC-CLIO, first suggested the idea of an encyclopedia. In Oxford, Kate Prudden has provided essential and excellent research assistance. James Milner has provided extremely helpful advice and assistance in compiling the documents for volume three. We also owe many thanks to the members of the editorial board, who provided much-needed comments on entry lists and who never tired of suggesting possible contributors. Finally, we owe our gratitude to the contributors. The quality of their contributions made editing a fulfilling and informative job, and without them these volumes would of course not exist.

We should also say a last word about the contributor to whom this encyclopedia is dedicated. For two decades, Arthur C. Helton devoted himself to issues of refugees and displaced persons. He wrote more than eighty articles on the topic; founded and directed the Forced Migration Projects at the Open Society Institute; taught at New York University and the Central European University, Budapest; advocated in court and testified before Congress for the rights of asylum seekers; and served as the Director of Peace and Conflict Studies and Senior Fellow for Refugee Studies and Preventive Action at the Council on Foreign Relations. Although one of the senior figures in the field, he was never too busy to provide help and assistance to his junior colleagues. When one of the authors first met him as an earnest and unknown graduate student, in New York in 1996, Arthur found two hours out of his busy schedule to provide academic and professional advice. His commitment and enthusiasm made it clear that asylum and migration were worth a lifetime of study.

In the end, Arthur gave his life to the cause of improving the lives of others. He died in the August 19, 2003, bombing of the United Nations headquarters in Baghdad. UN Special Representative for Iraq Sergio Vieira de Mello, who was in a meeting with Arthur, was also killed, and another leading asylum scholar in the same meeting, Gil Loescher, was seriously wounded.

Arthur was a towering figure in the study and practice of asylum. He was a valued colleague, advisor, and friend, and he is sorely missed.

Matthew J. Gibney
Randall Hansen
Oxford, August 2004

Afghanistan and Refugees

During the 1980s and early 1990s, Afghanistan produced more refugees than any other country. Large numbers of Afghans first fled their homeland following the Soviet Union's invasion of Afghanistan in 1979. The Afghan refugee population peaked in 1991, when more than 6 million Afghans (nearly one-quarter of Afghanistan's entire population) were refugees in other countries, primarily Pakistan and Iran.

Some 1.4 million Afghans repatriated in the early 1990s, but refugee flows continued throughout the decade, not only into neighboring countries, but also further afield, including to Europe, where nearly 200,000 Afghans applied for asylum between 1992 and 2001. Hundreds of thousands of other Afghans became displaced within Afghanistan during this period. Although more than 1.8 million Afghan refugees returned home in 2002 after the United States ousted the Taliban regime, Afghans remain the world's second-largest refugee population.

Among the main causes of the flight of Afghan refugees have been Soviet efforts to impose social and economic reforms, ongoing fighting between Soviet and Afghan opposition forces, infighting among various Afghan factions following their defeat of the Soviets, and widespread human rights abuses at the hands of successive regimes and different factions, including the Taliban.

Besides giving rise to massive refugee flows, twenty-five years of endless conflict and violence have devastated Afghanistan and its people. Most of the population lives in poverty. Afghanistan has the world's highest infant mortality rate and its lowest life expectancy. Much of the country's infrastructure lies in ruins.

Soviet Occupation and Mujahideen Resistance

Afghan refugees first fled in notable numbers in 1978 after a pro-Communist group overthrew Afghanistan's king and took power. The new government quickly alienated Afghanistan's mostly rural, conservative population by trying to impose an unpopular agricultural reform program. Government forces killed an estimated 50,000 to 100,000 civilians who resisted the changes.

In late 1979, Soviet forces occupied Afghanistan. Fearing that the Soviets would enforce even more radical measures, as many as 600,000 Afghans fled to Pakistan and Iran within weeks of the invasion. In an effort to control the population, the Soviets embarked on a wave of terror. By the end of 1981, more than 1.5 million Afghan refugees had fled the country. Afghan opposition forces known as *mujahideen* ("struggler") quickly surfaced, largely from among the refugees.

In Pakistan, most of the refugees settled in camps in the two provinces nearest the Afghan border—Northwest Frontier Province and Baluchistan. It was the height of the Cold War, and the West, particularly the United States, showered the refugees in Pakistan, who had fled communism, with aid. Eventually, most of the refugees were able to find subsistence work or to rent land that they could farm, and their camps achieved an air of normalcy.

The international community was not as generous, however, to Afghan refugees who fled to Iran. Islamic fundamentalists had seized power in Iran in 1979, and just one month before the Soviet invasion of Afghanistan, Iranian students had taken a group of U.S. embassy officials hostage. The United States and its allies were not inclined to offer the Iranian authorities any assistance, even for Afghan refugees.

With financial support and political encouragement from outside sources as diverse as the United States, Saudi Arabia, and Pakistan (all seeking to advance their own geopolitical interests), the various mujahideen groups gathered strength. Throughout the 1980s, the mujahideen, which largely operated out of Afghan refugee camps in Pakistan, repeatedly attacked Soviet troops and weakened Moscow's resolve. Fighting between the Soviets and the mujahideen, and Soviet retaliatory measures against the civilian population, prompted even more Afghans to flee. By the late 1980s, the number of Afghan refugees outside the country had grown to more than 5 million.

The Soviet Union's occupation of Afghanistan proved costly both politically and financially. In 1989, the combination of international pressure, domestic dissent, and the mujahideen's persistence led Moscow to withdraw from Afghanistan. The Soviets left in power a Communist regime headed by Mohammed Najibullah that held on to power for three more years. The mujahideen intensified their efforts, and the number of Afghans fleeing the country increased yet again. According to the UN High Commissioner for Refugees (UNHCR), by 1990 some 6.3 million Afghans were refugees.

In April 1992, the mujahideen captured Kabul. Between April 1992 and late 1993, more than 1.4 million Afghans repatriated. But within months of their victory, the various mujahideen groups, unable to work out a power-sharing agreement, turned against each other. In Kabul alone, more than 50,000 people were killed as rival mujahideen factions battled for control of the city. The southern city of Kandahar descended into chaos, with warlords looting, raping, and killing at will. The new round of violence, together with decreased international funding for repatriation, brought the repatriation to a standstill.

The repatriation's funding problems reflected the West's diminished interest in Afghanistan and Afghan refugees following the end of the Cold War. In Pakistan, lack of international funding led the UNHCR and the World Food Program (WFP) to cut off food aid to most refugees in 1995. That prompted a large-scale migration of refugees from the camps into Pakistani cities, particularly Peshawar in western Pakistan, a move that the Pakistani authorities said led to increased crime and economic problems in the cities. The welcome that Afghan refugees had enjoyed in Pakistan for a decade and a half came to an end.

The Taliban

The lawlessness that existed in southern Afghanistan during the mid-1990s led to the emergence of a new group, the Taliban, that initially sought to bring order to the area. The group was guided by ultraconservative religious leaders from rural areas of Kandahar but was made up primarily of young returned refugees from Pakistan who had studied at religious schools in Pakistan that taught a strict, insular brand of Islam.

The Taliban (reportedly funded and largely manipulated by the Pakistani armed forces, which sought to expand their influence in Afghanistan) gained control of Kandahar and took a series of measures to establish order, including executing drug traffickers, burning opium fields, and disarming the warlords. But they also imposed their own brand of Islam. They commanded women to cover themselves from head to toe with *burqas* and banned them from working outside the home. They also ended education for girls.

The relative order that the Taliban managed to bring to Kandahar increased the group's popularity and attracted thousands of new recruits to its ranks. In 1995, the Taliban captured Herat, the largest city in western Afghanistan. The population of Herat did not welcome the Taliban, however. Most Taliban fighters were of a different ethnic group (Pashtun) than the locals, and their strict brand of Islam was not popular with many local people. Nevertheless, the Taliban continued to gather strength and in 1996 captured Jalalabad, the most important city in the east (and the gateway to Pakistan) and then the capital, Kabul. Its victories were costly, however. Thousands of civilians died as a result of the fighting. The Taliban's seizure of Kabul also led to yet another exodus of some 40,000 Afghans, mostly members of ethnic minorities and Kabul residents who opposed the Taliban's conservative social policies.

According to international human rights groups, the Taliban administered areas under its control like a police state. Observers reported killings of civilians, the destruction of homes and entire villages, the detention of civilians, and forced recruitment. The Taliban's restrictive policies toward women, including the ban on their working outside the home, the requirement that women be escorted by a male relative any time they left the house, and the ban on male doctors or nurses attending female patients, resulted in a health care crisis for women and left thousands of widows and their families destitute.

During the late 1990s, the Taliban continued its efforts to gain control of the north, the only region of the country still controlled by the opposition. In July 1998, the Taliban captured Mazar-e Sharif, Afghanistan's largest city and the opposition's de facto capital. Following their victory, Taliban fighters were said to have killed thousands of ethnic Hazara residents of Mazar-e Sharif and nearby areas. The fighting and subsequent massacres drove thousands more Afghan refugees, mostly Hazaras and members of other ethnic minorities, to Pakistan and Iran.

The Taliban launched another successful offensive in the north in mid-1999, this time in the Shomali Plains, an area just north of Kabul. More than 250,000 people fled the plains. Most went into the opposition-controlled Panjshir Valley, in northeastern Afghanistan, or to Pakistan. But the Taliban reportedly forced some 40,000 to move to Kabul. Continued fighting in northern areas during 2000, compounded by the effects of a drought of historic proportions, led to an exodus of another 172,000 refugees to Pakistan and to the displacement within Afghanistan of some 350,000 other people.

Afghan refugees fight for food being doled out by a private bankowner at the Kili Faizo temporary camp at the Chaman border. Thousands of Afghans have crossed into neighboring Pakistan, bringing few belongings and living in squalid conditions with little food. (Lynsey Addario/Corbis)

Afghan Refugees No Longer Welcomed

Some 10,000 Afghans who fled the fighting in the north in 2000 tried to seek refuge in Tajikistan but were refused entry by the Tajik authorities and Russian troops guarding the Tajik/Afghan border. Members of the group remained stuck at the border, enduring frequent attacks by the Taliban and receiving little international assistance.

Afghan refugees arriving in Pakistan in the late 1990s and early 2000s found a situation much changed from that experienced by those who had fled to Pakistan before them. The Pakistani authorities, frustrated by the continuing flow of Afghan refugees, had embarked on a campaign of harassment of Afghan refugees living in urban centers. Police stopped Afghanis in the streets and demanded bribes to set them free. They forcibly returned to Afghanistan thousands of Afghan men who could not afford to pay the bribes.

In November 2000, Pakistan officially closed its border to prevent more refugees from entering (a move that had little effect, since most refugees found other ways to enter the country). The authorities also blocked assistance to tens of thousands of Afghan refugees who had managed to enter Pakistan and had gathered at Jalozai camp, near Peshawar. By doing so, the Pakistani authorities sought to send a message to others inside Afghanistan that they would not be welcomed or assisted in Pakistan. The result was that by late 2000 conditions at Jalozai were described as among the worst of any refugee camp in the world.

Afghan refugees in Iran experienced similar problems. Since the mid-1990s, the refugees had lost many of the benefits they had previously enjoyed—for example, the ability to work in Iran. In late 1998 and early 1999, mobs demanding the deportation of the refugees attacked and in some cases killed Afghan refugees. In 2000, Iranian Revolutionary Guards swept through Afghan-populated areas, arrested Afghans on the street, confined them to camps, and deported as many as 50,000 of them. The Iranian authorities also blocked an unknown number of Afghans from entering Iran during 2000.

At the beginning of 2001, Afghanistan stood on the brink of catastrophe. Some 3.6 million Afghan refugees were outside the country; 375,000 other Afghans were internally displaced. The drought that had begun in 2000 had turned into the most severe drought to hit the country in more than thirty years. More than 4 million people were at risk. The Taliban did little to assist the displaced.

Tens of thousands more Afghans fled to Pakistan or became displaced within Afghanistan in early 2001. In Herat, more than 80,000 newly displaced persons gathered in a makeshift camp on a barren field outside the city. In late January 2001, a sudden cold snap hit Herat and killed more than 480 of the displaced, mainly children and elderly people. By August, an estimated 900,000 Afghans were internally displaced. Nearly half were located in areas of northern and central Afghanistan that were battered both by conflict and drought. The World Food Program reported that famine conditions existed in some areas. The international community's response, however, was limited.

The situation in Afghanistan changed dramatically after September 11, 2001. The terrorist attacks on the United States set into motion a series of events that once again thrust Afghanistan into the international spotlight and brought about momentous political change.

Post–September 11, 2001

Shortly after the September 11 terrorist attacks on the World Trade Center and the Pentagon in the United States, the U.S. government accused the Al Qaeda organization, and its leader, Osama bin Laden, based in Afghanistan, of masterminding and executing them. The U.S. government demanded that the Taliban turn bin Laden over to the United States, but the Taliban refused. On October 6, the U.S. Armed Forces launched a military campaign in Afghanistan aimed at rooting out Al Qaeda and removing the Taliban from power.

During the four-week period between September 11 and October 6, 2001, thousands of Afghan civilians fled Kabul and other cities likely to be targeted by U.S. and allied forces. Most remained within Afghanistan, largely because all of Afghanistan's neighbors kept their borders closed and refused to permit fleeing Afghans to enter. UN and nongovernment organization (NGO) personnel working in Afghanistan, including relief personnel, also left the country.

After U.S. air strikes began on October 6, hundreds of thousands of Afghans fled their homes, including an estimated 40 to 70 percent of the residents of the country's largest cities. Despite Pakistan's border closure, an estimated 160,000 Afghans made their way into Pakistan between September 11 and the end of the year, mostly by avoiding official border crossings and entering via remote mountain passes.

The Pakistani authorities, apparently fearing that millions of Afghans would try to enter if they did not take steps to deter them, kept their border sealed and blocked aid to the refugees who did manage to get into the country. The UNHCR and other refugee advocacy and relief groups criticized Pakistan's actions, but the Pakistani authorities remained unyielding.

The Iranian authorities, who also kept their border sealed, established two camps just inside the Afghan border for fleeing Afghans. They provided the displaced Afghans with little assistance, however, and conditions were said to be grossly inadequate.

The U.S. military action succeeded in ousting the Taliban from most of northern and western Afghanistan by mid-November. Taliban forces abandoned Kabul on November 13 and headed south toward Kandahar, the only region still largely under Taliban control. Anticipating that the Kandahar region would become the new focus of U.S. military action, tens of thousands of Afghans fled the area.

By the end of 2001, a new, interim Afghan government was in place in Kabul. International peacekeeping troops began to arrive, and relief agencies were able to get much-needed assistance to most of the estimated 1 million Afghans who were displaced throughout the country.

Unprecedented Repatriation

Tens of thousands of refugees made their own way back to Afghanistan during the last weeks of 2001 and first two months of 2002. Many were spurred by the fall of the Taliban. Others were encouraged by the international community's promise of massive aid to a post-Taliban Afghanistan. Donors meeting in Tokyo in late January pledged $1.8 billion for 2002 to assist in the reconstruction of the country. Several thousand Afghans were also forcibly returned to Afghanistan during this period, primarily from Iran.

It was only on March 1, 2002, however, that UNHCR began its program of assisted repatriation to Afghanistan. The speed and scale of the repatriation exceeded all expectations. During the first month of the organized return, some 150,000 refugees repatriated, mostly from Pakistan. By mid-June, the number of returned refugees from Pakistan and Iran surpassed the 1 million mark. Although the rate of repatriation slowed later in the year as winter approached, by late December 2002 more than 1.8 million Afghan refugees had repatriated, including 1.5 million from Pakistan and more than 250,000 from Iran. It was the largest repatriation taking place anywhere in the world in more than thirty years.

Besides the refugees who repatriated, another 400,000 internally displaced Afghans returned to their homes between December 2001 and December 2002. A majority, some 230,000, did so with assistance from the International Organization for Migration, UNHCR, and other organizations, but many returned by their own means.

Most observers welcomed the repatriation. They argued that it denoted a positive response to political developments since September 11, 2001, and reflected refugees' confidence in the future of their country. Others, however, expressed concern about Afghanistan's ability to absorb so many additional people. With the cities largely in ruins, the countryside still in the grips of drought, millions of people dependent on international assistance, sporadic fighting continuing around the country (both between U.S. forces and remaining Al Qaeda and Taliban fighters and among rival Afghan factions), and the new administration struggling to establish order, some relief groups argued that UNHCR should not encourage repatriation until conditions inside Afghanistan improved. Also during the course of 2002, a number of industrialized countries stopped accepting new asylum applications from Afghan nationals and began taking steps to return Afghan asylum seekers to their homeland, a move that concerned refugee advocates and that some viewed as premature.

Indeed, many of the refugees who returned found it impossible to return to their areas of origin because of drought, insecurity, or lack of assistance. At the end of 2002, nearly one-third of all the returnees were living in Kabul. Some were crowded into the homes of relatives or friends, but many were living in abandoned or partially destroyed buildings, and some only had tents for shelter. Although the international community provided Afghanistan substantial international assistance during 2002, donors did not provide the full $1.8 billion they had promised, an amount that would, in any case, only have scratched the surface of Afghanistan's many reconstruction needs.

A Hopeful but Uncertain Outlook

At the end of 2002, more than 2.7 million Afghan refugees remained outside the country and 700,000 Afghans were still internally displaced. Anticipating continued repatriation in the coming year, UNHCR launched an appeal for $195 million to assist the repatriation of another 1.5 million refugees in 2003.

There remained many obstacles to repatriation, however. The new Afghan administration that was put in place by Afghan leaders in June 2002 was weak. Despite substantial financial, political, and military support from the international community, the Afghan government remained woefully underfunded, had limited capacity to meet the country's many needs, and exerted little authority outside of Kabul. Powerful warlords who once terrorized vast regions of the country were once again in control in many areas, and widespread insecurity and human rights abuses continued.

Nevertheless, many observers both inside Afghanistan and internationally, as well as many ordinary Afghans, remained positive about the country's future and hopeful for an end to what has been one of the largest refugee crises in modern history.

Hiram A. Ruiz

See also: Border Controls; Civil Wars and Migration; Cold War; Internally Displaced Persons; Non-Refoulement; Refugee Camps; Repatriation; Return Migration; UN High Commissioner for Refugees

References and further reading:

Center for Economic and Social Rights. 2002. *Human Rights and Reconstruction in Afghanistan.* New York: Center for Economic and Social Rights.

Hassan, Yusuf. 2000. "The Crisis the World Forgot." *AINA UN Afghanistan Magazine.*

Human Rights Watch. 2001. *Crisis of Impunity: The Role of Pakistan, Russia, and Iran in Fueling the Civil War.* New York: Human Rights Watch.

Kaplan, Robert D. 2000. "The Taliban." *The Atlantic Monthly* (September).

Marsden, Peter. 1998. *The Taliban: War, Religion and the New Order in Afghanistan.* Hampshire, UK: Palgrave MacMillan.

Rashid, Ahmed. 2000. *Taliban: Militant Islam, Oil and Fundamentalism in Central Asia.* New Haven, CT: Yale University Press.

Rubin, Barnett. 2002. *The Fragmentation of Afghanistan, State Formation and Collapse in the International System.* 2d ed. New Haven, CT: Yale University Press.

Rubin, Barnett, Ashraf Ghani, William Maley, Ahmed Rashid, and Olivier Roy. 2001. "Afghanistan: Reconstruction and Peacemaking in a Regional Framework." *KOFF Peacebuilding Reports.* Bern: Swiss Peacebuilding Foundation.

Ruiz, Hiram. 2001. *Pakistan: Afghan Refugees Shunned and Scorned.* Washington, DC: U.S. Committee for Refugees.

United Nations High Commissioner for Refugees, http://www.unhcr.ch/.

———. 2000. *The State of the World's Refugees 2000.* Oxford: Oxford University Press.

United Nations Office for the Coordination of Humanitarian Affairs (OCHA), "Relief Web," http://www.reliefweb.org.

United Nations Security Council. 2002. *The Situation in Afghanistan and Its Implications for International Peace and Security: Report of the Secretary-General (A/57/487-S/2002/1173).* New York: United Nations.

U.S. Committee for Refugees. 2002. *World Refugee Survey 2002.* Washington, DC: USCR.

African Union

The Organization of African Unity (OAU) addressed three mammoth challenges during its thirty-eight-year history: coping with African migration and refugee flows, encouraging economic and social development, and preventing regional conflict. The OAU was established on May 25, 1963, in Addis Ababa, Ethiopia, against the backdrop of profound change in the international system, including the demise of European colonialism and the rise of the nonaligned movement of Third World states. It was succeeded by the African Union in 2002.

The organization embodied many of the aspirations of the Pan-African movement, which evolved in the mid–nineteenth

(L-R:) Zambian president Levy Mwanawasa, South African president Thabo Mbeki, Secretary General of OAU Amara Essy from Mali, and former South African president Nelson Mandela and his wife Graca pose for photographers at the International Conference Center in Durban, July 8, 2002. African leaders gave a state funeral to their Organization of African Unity (OAU) and attended the opening of a new African Union (AU), whose mission is to combat poverty, conflict, and corruption. (Reuters/Corbis)

century out of the concrete realities of the partition of Africa and the experience of slavery. It gradually developed into an organized force with political and cultural goals, gaining momentum after World War II. At its inception, thirty-two heads of state of newly independent African countries committed themselves to abide by the principles and objectives embodied in the charter of the organization. Although a vocal minority, including Ghanaian president Kwame Nkrumah, would have preferred to see these aspirations culminate in a "United States of Africa," the OAU Charter forged a compromise with those African leaders who were inclined to accept the boundaries established under colonial rule. Article II of the charter, which noted as OAU objectives both the promotion of "solidarity and cooperation" among African states and the "defense of their sovereignty and territorial integrity," graphically illustrated this compromise. A creature of its time, the charter cited the eradication of all forms of colonialism as a principal objective, in addition to the harmonization of policy in a number of spheres, including politics, economics, education, health, and defense, and the promotion of international cooperation, with due regard to the charter of the United Nations and the Universal Declaration of Human Rights (1948). The OAU Charter also noted a number of core principles, including recognition of the sovereign equality of all member states, the peaceful settlement of disputes, and the principle of noninterference in the internal affairs of states.

The OAU had fifty-three members, the most controversial of which was the Sahrawi Arab Democratic Republic (SADR), admitted to the organization in 1984; Morocco's consequent withdrawal presented the OAU with one of its most serious political crises ever. Throughout its short history, the OAU witnessed a period of immense and often turbulent change on the continent. Although the organization often played a positive role, for example, in the struggle and eventual defeat of apartheid in South Africa, it also presided over a continent that has been wracked by famine, genocide, and bloody conflict. The organization's strict adherence to the principle of nonintervention and its subordination to state interest, combined with chronic financial difficulties, often precluded the organization from asserting any form of moral authority or leadership in tackling some of Africa's chronic problems.

The problem of forced displacement was one such issue that challenged the OAU throughout its existence. The scale and complexity of the refugee problem faced by Africa has been enormous. The continent is host to an estimated 3.5 million refugees, 1.7 million internally displaced persons, and 0.9 million returnees (UNHCR 2000). A 1968 conference focused attention on the legal, economic, and social needs of refugees and led to the establishment of the OAU Bureau for the Placement, Education and Training of Refugees, followed a year later by the enactment of the 1969 OAU Convention Governing the Specific Aspects of Refugee Problems in Africa. The convention marked an important step forward in strengthening protection for those forcibly displaced on the continent. At the time of its adoption, African states were struggling to cope with mass influxes of refugees precipitated by the struggle against colonial occupation and wars of national liberation—a situation that highlighted the limitations of the individualized, persecution-based definition of refugees contained in the 1951 UN Convention Relating to the Status of Refugees. Though the OAU Convention retained the Convention's individual criteria for determining refugee status, it also introduced a new, expanded definition of who is a refugee, providing that: "The term refugee shall also apply to every person who, owing to external aggression, occupation, foreign domination or events seriously disturbing public order in either part or the whole of his country of origin or nationality, is compelled to leave the habitual place of residence in order to seek refuge in another place outside of the country of origin or nationality."

The OAU Convention was progressive in a number of other ways as well. It strengthened the principle of nonrefoulement, explicitly prohibiting measures such as rejection at the frontier, return, or expulsion that would compel a person to return to or remain in a territory where his life, physical integrity, or liberty would be threatened. Moreover, although there is no obligation to grant asylum under international law, the OAU Convention noted that "Member States shall use their best endeavors . . . to receive refugees and to secure the settlement of those refugees who, for well founded reasons, are unable or unwilling to return to their country of origin or nationality" (Article II[1]). Finally, the OAU Convention was the first international legal document to incorporate a provision on the principle of *voluntary* repatriation (emphasis added), providing, in Article V, that "no person shall be repatriated against his will."

The Bureau for the Placement, Education and Training of Refugees became the Division for Refugees, Displaced Persons and Humanitarian Assistance, a change that suggested an increasing awareness of the need to address the problem of internal displacement on the continent. The division was responsible for monitoring developments with regard to refugees and displaced persons, assisting member states with the implementation of the convention, coordinating with other international agencies, especially the UNHCR, and developing and improving the skills of refugees with a view to making them self-supporting. It also supported the work of the "Commission on Refugees," the principal policy-making organ of the OAU on all matters relating to refugees in Africa. This "Commission of 20," composed of ambassadors of OAU member states, was able to undertake fact-finding missions and to provide advice to governments regarding the management of their refugee populations as well as emergency financial assistance. Moreover, it undertook initiatives in a bid to shape the OAU's response to refugee issues. Over the years, the OAU developed and participated in a number of such initiatives, including the Pan African Conference on the Situation of Refugees in Africa (which produced the Arusha Recommendations of May 1979); two International Conferences on Assistance to Refugees in Africa, which took place in November 1980 and July 1984, known as ICARA and ICARA II, respectively; the Oslo Declaration and Plan of Action on the Plight of Refugees, Returnees and Displaced Persons in Southern Africa (SARRED) of August 1988; the Khartoum Declaration on Africa's Refugee Crisis of September 1990; the Tunis Declaration on the 1969 OAU Convention Governing the Specific Aspects of Refugee Problems in Africa of June 1994; the Addis Ababa Document on Refugees and Forced Displacements in Africa of September 1994; and the Declaration of Khartoum of December 1998.

An important additional source of protection for the refugee was provided by the 1981 African Charter on Human and Peoples' Rights (also known as the Banjul Charter). This charter prohibited forced exile and the collective expulsion of foreign nationals, including refugees. It also guaranteed every persecuted individual the right "to seek *and obtain* asylum"(emphasis added). The inclusion of a right "to obtain" asylum was a significant advance on the Universal Declaration of Human Rights, which merely provided the right to seek asylum. The charter was thus unique in creating an obligation on states parties to grant refugee protection through the asylum process.

The African Commission, a body of eleven human rights experts based in Banjul, the Gambia, monitored compliance with the Banjul Charter. The commission reported annually to the OAU Assembly of Heads of State and Government, which was responsible for the implementation of the commission's decisions and resolutions.

Finally, the OAU system also created important supplementary forms of protection for vulnerable groups amongst the forcibly displaced. The African Charter on the Rights and Welfare of the Child, which entered into force in November 1999, required parties to ensure appropriate protection and assistance to the child asylum-seeker or refugee (one below eighteen years of age.) Moreover, a Draft Protocol to the African Charter on Women's Rights sought to extend this protection to female refugees by committing states parties to "take all appropriate measures to involve women . . . in the local, national, subregional and international structures for the establishment and management of camps for refugees and displaced persons and for humanitarian assistance and aid" (Draft Protocol, Article 12[2]).

The OAU thus made important contributions to the development of the normative framework for the protection of refugees and forced migrants, although implementation of these norms was always a considerable challenge. The OAU also focused its attention on two new areas in the 1990s: first, conflict prevention and resolution, and second, economic development and integration, both of which have important implications for migrants and the forcibly displaced.

The creation of the OAU Mechanism for Conflict Prevention, Management and Resolution marked an important milestone in the evolution of the organization. In 1990, the OAU took the unprecedented step of committing itself to work toward the speedy and peaceful resolution of all conflicts in Africa, including those *within* states. This led, in June 1993, to a Declaration on the Establishment of a Mechanism of Conflict Prevention, Management and Resolution, adopted at the Cairo Summit. The Conflict Resolution Mechanism (CRM) had two objectives: to anticipate and prevent conflicts in Africa, and to plan and implement peace-making/peace-building functions where conflicts were already in progress. A central organ composed of representatives of member states was responsible for the overall direction of the CRM's activities.

Although it is tempting to view the creation of the CRM as a departure from the time-honored OAU commitment to the principle of noninterference in the internal affairs of member states, paragraph 14 of the Cairo Declaration made clear that the mechanism would be guided by the objectives and principles of the OAU Charter, including "the principle of noninterference in the internal affairs of States," and said the CRM would "function on the basis of the *consent and the cooperation* of the parties to the conflict" (emphasis added). This qualification raised doubts about the CRM's effectiveness, but it may have strengthened the ability of the OAU to foresee, prepare for, and prevent mass influxes on the continent.

From a migration perspective, perhaps the most interesting initiatives were those on the economic front. On June 3, 1991, the heads of state and government of the OAU signed the treaty establishing the African Economic Community (AEC). The treaty entered into force on May 12, 1994, following ratification by the requisite two-thirds of member states. Steps have been taken to implement the treaty and establish the structure and policy organs of the community.

The objective of the AEC was to promote the economic, social, and cultural development and integration of African economies as well as the mobilization of the human and material resources of Africa. To that end, AEC member states, which were also concurrently the member states of the OAU, undertook to ensure the liberalization of trade and the creation of free trade areas and customs unions at subregional and regional levels that will ultimately converge into an African common market. Member states thus committed themselves to the gradual removal of obstacles to the free movement of goods, services, capital, and, of course, people. Chapter VI of the treaty also committed member states to work progressively toward the attainment of free movement of persons within the region and rights of residence and establishment within the community for citizens of member states. The provisions on free movement of persons can already be found in the charters of a number of subregional organizations in Africa, including the Economic Community of West African States (ECOWAS), the L'Union Économique et Monétaire de L'Afrique de l'Ouest (UEMOA, West African Economic and Monetary Union), the East African Community (EAC), the Inter-Governmental Authority on Development (IGAD), and the Southern African Development Community (SADC).

The African Union, the successor organization to the OAU, had its first meeting at Durban, South Africa, in 2002. It has inherited much of the institutional structure and normative framework put in place by the OAU.

Monette Zard

See also: Asylum Determination; Border Controls; Civil Wars and Migration; Colonial Immigration; Economic Effects of Migration; Gender and Migration; Genocide; Humanitarian Intervention; Internally Displaced Persons; Mass Influx; Migrant Rights; Non-Refoulement; Open Borders; Refugees; Return Migration; Southern Africa; Southern African Development Community; Sovereignty and Migration; UN Convention Relating to the Status of Refugees, 1951

References and further reading:

Legum, Colin. 1988. *The Organization of African Unity at Twenty-Five.* Richmond, VA: Third World Reports.

Mathews, K. 1987. "The Organization of African Unity in World Politics." *Nigerian Journal of International Affairs* 13, no. 1: 48–90.

Naldi, Gino J. 1999. *The Organization of African Unity.* 2d ed. London: Mansell.

United Nations High Commissioner for Refugees. 2000. *News Country Updates* (May).

AIDS and Migration

Not only is Acquired Immune Deficiency Syndrome (AIDS) transmitted around the world by the movement of people across geographical boundaries, but people who move across those boundaries are particularly vulnerable to Human Immunodeficiency Virus (HIV) infection. In the early years of the epidemic, interest focused on the role played by migration in the spread of AIDS. Research tended to treat migrants as vectors of disease, and policy responses sought to restrict immigration by infected people. More recently, concern has switched to the way in which the situations migrants encounter often render them vulnerable to infection with HIV and make it difficult for them to access treatment and care for AIDS-related illnesses. There is also increasing awareness that migration takes place as a consequence of the epidemic, both in terms of the movement of people living with HIV/AIDS (PLWHAs) and in terms of migration by relatives of those who become sick or die from the disease.

Migration and the Transmission of AIDS

Within a decade of its identification in the 1980s, HIV had spread to all parts of the globe. The vast majority of the epidemic's transmission has been through the movement of people rather than through the movement of blood and blood products. Early studies of the epidemiology of AIDS focused on global transmission routes in an effort to identify a geographical source for the epidemic. Such research led to a focus on immigrants as bearers of the virus. In the early 1990s, for instance, 95.8 percent of the cases of HIV-2 identified in Europe were in people born in West or Central Africa (Cliff and Smallman-Raynor 1992). The global distribution of HIV prevalence today is extremely uneven, and in several countries nonnationals are disproportionately infected. For example, in the United Kingdom, though homosexual men account for the majority of infections, more than 80 percent of HIV-positive women are African, as are most HIV-infected babies (UNAIDS 2001).

In response to the perceived association of AIDS with migrants, many countries have sought to erect barriers to the transmission of the virus through their immigration laws. Sixty countries worldwide have laws restricting the entry of HIV-positive people, usually applying to long-stay visitors, migrant workers, and students (U.S. Department of State 2003). The restrictions imposed vary: Some require people to be tested before entering the country for stays as brief as fifteen days. In some cases, requirements for testing only apply to those entering to participate in particular occupations: food handling and patient or child care (Bahrain), prostitutes (Greece and Panama), entertainers (Korea), or mineworkers (South Africa), for example. Other countries exempt certain occupational groups, such as experts, teachers, and foreign missions workers (Yemen), or the spouses of applicants (Egypt), from the testing requirement. Some countries require testing only of the unskilled (Malaysia) or those on low salaries (Singapore). The particular form taken by entry restrictions and testing requirements in different countries needs to be understood in relation to the rationales they purport to serve.

There are two arguments advanced for requiring HIV screening of people applying to settle in a country. The first relates to the perceived public health risk: The presence of PLWHAs is thought to put the general population at greater risk of contracting the disease, especially when the migrants belong to particular occupational groups. This argument is not, however, accepted by bodies such as the World Health Organization (WHO). Although HIV is undoubtedly transmitted through the movement of people, it is not transmitted by casual contact, and there is no inherent public health risk in admitting HIV-positive people (Goodwin-Gill 1996; UNAIDS 2001). Furthermore, because there is a time lag between infection and the development of the antibodies that the HIV test detects, a test cannot prove that a person is not infected. It is also illogical, from a public health perspective, to test only those who intend to settle and not short-term visitors or returning citizens (Goodwin-Gill 1996). Migration only accounts for a very small fraction of those who cross international borders each year. The movement of tourists and military personnel has been shown to contribute to the spread of AIDS (Carballo and Siem 1996) yet is seldom restricted.

The second argument for testing relates to the potential cost to the public purse. This is why some countries exempt those people who are deemed capable of paying for their own treatment, but screen those on low incomes. Yet there are other medical conditions that are likely to impose as great a cost but for which no screening is required (Goodwin-Gill 1996).

Although testing of immigrants is sometimes performed to respond to their health needs (Carballo and Siem 1996), it is usually easier to understand screening as a political response to ill-informed public fears about contagion and potential costs to taxpayers (Goodwin-Gill 1996). Attitudes toward migration differ greatly from country to country: In some countries, migrants are seen as benefiting the local economy by filling demand for labor and contributing to the tax base, but there are many countries where migrants are viewed as an undesirable threat to traditional ways of life (Carballo and Siem 1996). Screening for HIV may thus reflect xenophobia more than practical attitudes toward the disease and how to address it.

Government policies of screening for HIV, in combination with the focus of epidemiological research on migrants as vectors of disease, contribute to the stigmatization of immigrants, the places they come from, and PLWHAs. Both immigrants and people with AIDS are commonly regarded as outsiders, and to draw connections between AIDS and immigration may doubly marginalize both groups. Those working in the field of migration have been reluctant to focus on AIDS for fear of compounding the stigmatization of migrant communities, a reluctance that has arguably exacerbated the tendency of the literature in this area to be dominated by epidemiology (Haour-Knipe and Rector 1996).

People from Africa and other Third World countries are often subjected to HIV testing on account of the presumption that they are more likely than others to carry the virus. In 1991, 19,000 Jewish Ethiopians airlifted to Israel were compulsorily tested for HIV, without pretest counseling, while immigrants from the USSR and the United States were not screened in this way (Sherr and Farsides 1996). Such differential treatment reinforces negative perceptions of migrants from Africa. Such presumptions also permeate research. HIV rates in Europe are often revealed to be higher among those who have lived in or visited countries with high prevalence rates, and associations are drawn with the sexual behavior of these individuals while overseas. That little consideration is given to people's sexual behavior in Europe itself reflects an unwarranted assumption that infection must have happened overseas (ibid.).

Routine screening also makes unhelpful assumptions about people with HIV, failing to take into account the fact that even if they test positive they might contribute to both receiving and source countries (Carballo and Siem 1996). Compulsory testing may make migrants more vulnerable by discouraging them from accessing prevention information, testing, and counseling (UNAIDS 2001). Furthermore, if migrant workers are sent home because they test positive, they are vulnerable not only to loss of livelihood, but also to discrimination at home (Haour-Knipe and Rector 1996).

Although overdrawing the association between migrants and AIDS is highly problematic, there is undoubtedly a close association between AIDS and mobility. Globally, HIV infection appears to be growing faster in areas where populations are particularly mobile. This includes the countries of Southeast Asia, between which migration is very high (Guinness and Kumaranayake 2002). Higher rates of infection are commonly found along transport routes and in border regions (UNAIDS 2001), and in many parts of the world HIV infection rates are higher among mobile people than among those who are less mobile.

Southern Africa has the world's highest HIV prevalence rates, and with its long history of labor migration also has a highly mobile population. Levels of infection are particularly high among migrants in the region, yet the prevalence of the disease does not map so straightforwardly onto spatial migration patterns as was the case in the past. There are several reasons for this, largely connected to the end of apartheid in South Africa, which brought about a decline in the employment of migrant male labor in the mining industry but also a wide range of alternative opportunities and reasons for migration. Trading, both formal and informal, increased across the region's borders, bringing growing numbers of long-distance truckers. These changes also increased the geographic mobility of women in the region. Moreover, South Africa has become a favored destination for asylum seekers from across the region (Williams et al. 2002). Yet, "while it is certain that migration has fuelled the epidemic of HIV in Southern Africa, infections are now so widespread that it seems likely that migration is no longer driving the epidemic" (ibid., 10).

The Vulnerability of Migrants to AIDS

It is increasingly recognized that migrants may be more vulnerable to HIV infection than are people who do not move (UNAIDS 2001). It is not simply that migrants carry infection from places of high prevalence to those where prevalence is relatively low, but that the processes of migration and resettlement increase the risks to which migrants are subjected (Carballo and Siem 1996). Being mobile is not a risk factor in and of itself; rather, the situations migrant people often encounter put them at risk of infection (UNAIDS 2001). Migrants with AIDS are also commonly less able to access treatment and care than are those who are settled. UNAIDS (2001) has argued that AIDS prevention, care, and support should target migrants before they leave home, as they travel, in their destination countries and communities, and once they return home.

Migrants are at risk as they travel. Places through which migrants transit, such as truck stops, train and bus stations, marketplaces, harbors, and customs zones, have all been identified as "risk zones" (ibid.). Some southern African border posts, for instance, close in the late afternoon and reopen in the morning, requiring those who wish to cross to spend the night at the border. Many such border post areas develop into informal settlements that attract street vendors and sex workers. In such areas, not only are travelers at heightened risk, but so also are the local populations (IOM 2000).

Migrants are at risk when they reach their destinations as well. They may be among the poorest in the society in which they live, and even if not particularly poor, they often live on the margins of society. This marginalization is exacerbated where people's cultures and sexual preferences are considered "different" (Carballo and Siem 1996). Poverty and marginalization both put migrants at risk of infection. Marginalized people are more likely to purchase sex and/or drugs than are those who are fully integrated into a community. If immigrants are poor or, as in South Africa, discriminated against in the labor market and unable to find regular employment, they may have few choices other than to engage in commercial sex work (Williams et al. 2002).

In many cases, it may be the separation involved in migration that makes people vulnerable (Sherr and Farsides 1996). Migration separates people from their families and from the social control that families, communities, and even wider social norms may exercise over sexual behavior (Carballo and Siem 1996). In the case of refugees and asylum seekers, family reunification may be prohibited by legal restrictions (Haour-Knipe and Rector 1996). Labor migration, too, is selective in who it recruits, commonly removing young and sexually active people from their families. Both men and women are involved, but seldom in the same location at the same time; hence, migration separates sexual partners (Carballo and Siem 1996). In their new homes, migrants may find themselves socially isolated, emotionally vulnerable, and more likely to engage in serial and high-risk sexual relationships (ibid.). In relation to the characteristic pattern of labor migration in southern Africa, the words of Mark Lurie are very apt: "If you wanted to spread a sexually transmitted disease, you'd take thousands of young men away from their families, isolate them in single-sex hostels, and give them easy access to alcohol and commercial sex. Then, to spread the disease around the country, you'd send them home every once in a while to their wives and girlfriends" (cited in UNAIDS 2001, 6).

Despite the evident risks, migrants in Europe and elsewhere often have relatively limited access to both information and health care. AIDS prevention programs have commonly neglected the needs of migrants, a situation particularly problematic in areas where migrants with a low level of HIV awareness arrive in a high-prevalence country (Haour-Knipe and Rector 1996). Migrants may find it difficult to access relevant information, care, and medical facilities, partly because they lack legal rights and partly on account of the cultural and linguistic barriers they confront (Guinness and Kumaranayake 2002; IOM 2000). Undocumented migrants are particularly vulnerable (IOM 2000). Migrants' health needs may not be addressed by national health programs (Haour-Knipe and Rector 1996). Italy, for instance, was until recently a country of net emigration and has simply failed to consider the needs of immigrants in its provision of health and social services (Carballo and Siem 1996). Sweden, by contrast, has provided special education and counseling to immigrants to help them address their own health needs (ibid.), and in London there is a growing recognition of the need to work with organizations of African migrants to provide appropriate health promotion information (McMunn et al. 1998).

Studies of the health impacts of migration have focused much more on areas that receive migrants than on the areas from which they originate (Williams et al. 2002). Yet in southern Africa the impacts on the rural communities that "send" migrants are significant. Women who are married to migrant mineworkers are more likely to become infected with HIV than others in southern Africa. Women whose husbands spend ten days or less at home each month are far more likely to be infected than those whose husbands are at home for more than ten days a month (IOM 2000). This statistic relates only in part to the direct risk of transmission from the migrant husband. Where women are left behind to fend for themselves and their children, high-risk sex work may be one of the few sources of employment available to them (Carballo and Siem 1996).

Sickness among southern African labor migrants also renders their home communities vulnerable. It deprives households of breadwinners and imposes costs in terms of health care, as well as having implications for the sexual health of partners. Similar problems have been identified for source communities in Southeast Asia (Guinness and Kumaranayake 2002). Income generation and literacy programs in source communities might help reduce the propensity to move, or ensure that those who move are better educated. This would also have the advantage of reducing the vulnerability of the community if breadwinners become sick (ibid.).

AIDS as a Cause of Migration

Migration is not only associated with vulnerability to AIDS but may be undertaken as a response to AIDS. Research in the United States, for instance, found that about 10 percent of people changed their place of residence between being diagnosed with AIDS and dying, half of them moving between states (Buehler et al. 1995). The reasons people move are varied. Some seek places with good medical care and the most up-to-date treatment; others choose to leave places where they experience discrimination or prejudice on account of their illness; and still others move away from people they know to preserve confidentiality (Sherr and Farsides 1996). It is common, however, in many parts of the world for PLWHAs to move to seek support from their parents (Ellis and Muschkin 1996; Knodel and VanLandingham 2003). Because a person with AIDS suffers prolonged illness prior to death, there is generally time to move to a preferred place to die (Urassa et al. 2001).

Many migrants who find that they have AIDS undertake return migration to their home communities, either because they are expelled from their places of work or in order to seek the support of their families (Carballo and Siem 1996). In Thailand, for example, many PLWHAs return to live with their parents to receive care. This in part reflects the absence of suitable care from hospices and the unwillingness of hospitals to provide long-term care. Most PLWHAs delay returning as long as possible, until their illness is severe (Knodel and VanLandingham 2003). Zimbabweans living with AIDS in the United Kingdom often wish, for cultural reasons, to be buried in Zimbabwe. Few, however, wish to leave until they are seriously ill, preferring to take advantage of the medical facilities available in the United Kingdom and to avoid having to admit to relatives that they have AIDS. There is, however, a danger in remaining too long, as the cost of repatriating a body greatly exceeds that of flying while alive.

The migration of PLWHAs has implications for the provision of medical care. In most countries, records of AIDS incidence reflect the location of diagnoses and fail to recognize that when symptoms are most severe and medical attention most needed, the people affected are likely to be resident elsewhere (Buehler et al. 1995; Knodel and VanLandingham 2003). In the United States, most people diagnosed with AIDS are residents of urban areas, but some subsequently move to nonmetropolitan areas. Although the absolute number of people needing HIV care in nonmetropolitan areas is small, it is swollen by around 50 percent as a result of migration from cities (Buehler et al. 1995). In Thailand, the prevalence of return migration among people with AIDS is such that the geography of demand for medical services is likely to reflect the high levels of labor out-migration in some remote areas of the country (Knodel and VanLandingham 2003).

It is not, however, only PLWHAs who migrate in response to the epidemic's effects. The sickness or death of an individual can result in the migration of other household members. Research in southern Africa has shown that many children move from home for a number of reasons associated with AIDS (Young and Ansell 2003). Some are sent to care for sick relatives resident elsewhere. Some move in direct response to the death of one or both parents in order to be cared for in another household. More often, however, children's migration is a response to increased poverty due to illness or death in the family. Finally, some children move from home when a widowed parent remarries. A study in Tanzania found that 44 percent of rural households dissolved following the death of the household head from AIDS, all household members having moved away (Urassa et al. 2001).

Nicola Ansell

See also: Assimilation/Integration; Border Controls; Economic Effects of Migration; Family Reunification; Migrant Rights; Migration Policy; Public Health; Public Opinion and Immigration; Push-Pull Factors; Return Migration; Skilled Migration; Southern Africa

References and further reading:

Buehler, James W., Robert L. Frey, Susan Y. Chu, and Brian Doyle. 1995. "The Migration of Persons with AIDS: Data from 12 States, 1985 to 1992." *American Journal of Public Health* 85: 1552–1556.

Carballo, Manuel, and Harald Siem. 1996. "Migration, Migration Policy and AIDS." Pp. 31–49 in *Crossing Borders: Migration, Ethnicity and AIDS.* Edited by Mary Haour-Knipe and Richard Rector. London: Taylor and Francis.

Cliff, Andy D., and Matthew R. Smallman-Raynor. 1992. "The AIDS Pandemic: Global Geographical Patterns and Local Spatial Processes." *Geographical Journal* 158: 182–198.

Ellis, Mark, and Clara Muschkin. 1996. "Migration of Persons with AIDS—A Search for Support from Elderly Parents?" *Social Science and Medicine* 43: 1109–1118.

Goodwin-Gill, Guy S. 1996. "AIDS and HIV, Migrants and Refugees: International Legal and Human Rights." Pp. 50–69 in *Crossing Borders: Migration, Ethnicity and AIDS.* Edited by Mary Haour-Knipe and Richard Rector. London: Taylor and Francis.

Guinness, Lorna, and Lilani Kumaranayake. 2002. *The Potential Costs and Benefits of Responding to the Mobility Aspect of the HIV Epidemic in South East Asia: A Conceptual Framework.* Bangkok: United Nations Development Programme, South East Asia HIV and Development Project.

Haour-Knipe, Mary, and Richard Rector, eds. 1996. "Introduction." Pp. 1–14 in *Crossing Borders: Migration, Ethnicity and AIDS.* London: Taylor and Francis.

International Organization for Migration. 2000. *Past, Present and Future Activities with Regard to HIV/AIDS: Migration in Southern Africa.* Pretoria: IOM Regional Office.

Knodel, John, and Mark VanLandingham. 2003. "Return Migration in the Context of Parental Assistance in the AIDS Epidemic: The Thai Experience." *Social Science and Medicine* 57: 327–342.

McMunn, Anne M., Roy Mwanje, Katie Paine, and Anton L. Pozniak. 1998. "Health Service Utilization in London's African Migrant Communities: Implications for HIV Prevention." *AIDS Care* 10: 453–462.

Sherr, Lorraine, and Calliope Farsides. 1996. "The Person behind the Virus: Migration, Human Factors and Some Moral and Ethical Questions." Pp. 70–85 in *Crossing Borders: Migration, Ethnicity and AIDS.* Edited by Mary Haour-Knipe and Richard Rector. London: Taylor and Francis.

UNAIDS. 2001. *Population Mobility and AIDS.* Technical Update. Geneva: UNAIDS.

Urassa, Mark, J. Ties Boerma, Raphael Isingo, Juliana Ngalula, Japheth Ng'weshemi, Gabriel Mwaluko, and Basia Zabal. 2001. "The Impact of HIV/AIDS on Mortality and Household Mobility in Rural Tanzania." *AIDS* 15: 2017–2023.

U.S. Department of State, "Human Immunodeficiency Virus (HIV) Testing Requirements for Entry into Foreign Countries," http://travel.state.gov/HIVtestingreqs.html (cited June 30, 2003).

Williams, Brian, Eleanor Gouws, Mark Lurie, and Jonathan Crush. 2002. *Spaces of Vulnerability: Migration and HIV/AIDS in South Africa.* Cape Town: Southern African Migration Project.

Young, Lorraine, and Nicola Ansell. 2003. "Fluid Households, Complex Families: The Impacts of Children's Migration as a Response to HIV/AIDS in Southern Africa." *Professional Geographer* 55, no. 4: 464–476.

Apartheid

See Southern Africa; Southern African Development Community

Armenia

See Armenian Diaspora; Ethnic Cleansing: Armenia

Armenian Diaspora

The numbers and nature of the Armenian diaspora changed dramatically during the twentieth century. Always diverse, the diaspora has become more radically dispersed and attained a greater sense of fragile permanence. The majority of Armenians in diaspora are not originally from the present Republic of Armenia but from what is called "western Armenia"—the descendants of survivors of the deportations and genocide at the end of the Ottoman Empire. Reliable figures are difficult to find, but probably more than half of Armenians in the world today live outside of Armenia, including those who are part of the "internal diaspora," that is, those living in other states of the former Soviet Union. According to some estimates, as many as 4 million or more Armenians are in diaspora, whereas only 2.5 million or so live in the Republic of Armenia itself.

For some 2,000 to 3,000 years, the Armenian world was firmly rooted in the lands between present-day eastern Turkey and the Caucasus. There has been an Armenian diaspora for more than 1,700 years. The earlier diaspora was in part trade-based, the result of fleeing successive invasions, or the result of forced migrations under various empires. In the early seventeenth century, for example, Shah Abbas transferred the skilled Armenian traders of Julfa in eastern Armenia to an area of Persia called New Julfa. When voluntary, earlier diaspora communities were often small outposts of family businesses. After the genocide of Armenians became more widely dispersed, more loosely connected, and more urban. In the last decades of the twentieth century, further troubles and waves of migration took Armenians from diaspora centers in Lebanon and Iran toward Europe, the United States, and elsewhere. Following *glasnost* and independence, perhaps half the population of Armenia migrated, primarily because of the economic problems the new state encountered.

Although life for many Armenians in diaspora appears comfortable today, there are always newcomers who remind the others of their precarious position. Some who have migrated to North America or Europe may move multiple times. Security is an issue in some countries, whereas in others assimilation is the greatest concern. Greater Los Angeles, with over 1 million Armenians, is the largest community of Armenians in diaspora. Approximate figures for other major population centers are as follows: the rest of the United States (Fresno, San Francisco, Boston, New York, New Jersey, and Detroit), 500,000–600,000; Canada (Toronto, Montreal), 50,000; South America (Argentina, Brazil), 100,000; France (Paris, Marseilles), 300,000; other European countries (Germany, Britain, Belgium, Holland, Sweden, Greece, Bulgaria, Cyprus), 200,000; Australia, 20,000; Lebanon (Beirut), 100,000; Syria (Aleppo, Damascus), 120,000; Turkey (Istanbul), 50,000; Iran (Tehran, Tabriz, New Julfa), 100,000; other Middle East nations (Egypt, Kuwait, Jordan, Gulf states, Iraq, Israel), 25,000. The largest dispersion from the state of Armenia itself is within the former Soviet Union, especially in Russia, and probably numbers more than 1.5 million people.

Both in the past and today, the Armenian communities around the world have developed in significantly different ways within the constraints and opportunities found in varied host cultures and countries. Though politically active Armenians have a strong desire for unity, there is in fact great variety among Armenians in diaspora, including several important internal divisions. The most significant politically has been between the Dashnaktsiutioune Party (Dashnak, or Armenian Revolutionary Federation [ARF]) and others, notably the Ramkavar Azadakan (Democrat Liberal) Party and the Hnchakian (Bell or Clarion) Party. Eastern and western Armenians (following the linguistic divide) speak of themselves as very different culturally, and other major divisions are based on further regional variation, age, economic status, and/or place of birth.

At the same time, there are strong ties, practical, symbolic, and emotional, that bind Armenians around the world to each other and to the idea of an Armenian people or nation. Webs of family networks, based on blood and marriage, pass on an attachment to the ethnic group, and institutional life, primarily through the national Armenian Apostolic Church, political parties, and some charitable and cultural groups, form transnational links and provide continuity in a fluid world. These institutions and the intellectual and/or politically active elite also construct a framework of ideas that informs private as well as public constructions of belonging. Moving from one country to another, an Armenian can find a familiar base from which to begin again, practical aid, and useful information. The local church often serves as a focal point for newcomers, a place to seek out others and to learn about the community. Key symbols of identity include the language (and alphabet), the national church, and a shared, long history.

Throughout Armenian history, including most of the twentieth century, there has been no single center and periphery regarding homeland and diaspora. Rather, there have been many centers with their own peripheries, changing over time, and often with several centers at the same time. It is only with the independence of the former Soviet Republic of Armenia in 1991 that there has been an increasingly widespread focus on one place as a symbolic

The Armenia-Diaspora Conference, Yereven, 1999. Participants include Armenian prime minister Vazgen Sarkisian and, far right, Armenian President Robert Kocharian. (Sivaslian Max/Corbis Sygma)

homeland. The Republic of Armenia is a small corner of the historic lands, and until recently, very few in diaspora were descended from that territory. Instead, thoughts of return were also directed at the lands lost during the deportations and genocide of the early twentieth century. Equally, many did not think of return at all but were pleased to be given a new start in countries where they felt more secure. These "western" Armenians speak (or spoke) the western dialect, and their recent ancestors lived in the Ottoman Empire.

The Armenian People

Although Armenians are not mentioned by name in documentary evidence until 518 B.C.E., there is linguistic evidence indicating that there were Armenian speakers well before this time. In the first century B.C.E., King Tigran the Great ruled an Armenian kingdom that stretched from the Mediterranean to the Caspian Sea. The people of the region, both then and now, have called themselves "Hai," the land "Hayastan," and the language *hayerane*. The language is Indo-European and shares root vocabulary most closely with ancient Greek and Persian. The alphabet was constructed around 400 C.E. by Mesrob Mashdots, a priestly scribe, and contains thirty-six letters. Read from left to right, it is basically phonetic. Classical Armenian (*grabar*) continues to be used in the church liturgy, and the vernacular language is divided today into two mutually intelligible dialects: eastern (primarily in the Republic of Armenia and Iran) and western. The many dialects of the different villages and regions have mostly faded out, but some continue to be spoken. King Trdat's conversion to Christianity, instigated by Gregory the Illuminator between 301 and 314, meant that the Armenians became the first Christian kingdom or nation. This encouraged a tendency to look toward Europe over the centuries. The theology and doctrine of the independent, autocephalos Armenian Apostolic Church is close to the Orthodox Church.

Armenians are often called a mountain people, and the land is a series of plateaus crosscut by mountain ranges. It is a volatile earthquake region but also serves as a land bridge between east and west. Consequently, competing empires have battled there over the centuries, with Armenians torn between them or living in a permanent buffer zone. They became minority peoples within successive empires, divided between east and west, and contact between Armenians living on either side of the shifting border was at times difficult.

At the turn of the twentieth century, the majority of Armenians in the Ottoman Empire were peasants. Crops included wheat and wheat products, fruits and vegetables, sericulture, cotton, and some tobacco. Sheep and goats were kept. A large number of people also lived in larger towns, such as Adana, Mersin, and Erzerum, where people worked in a wide variety of trades and skilled crafts. In Constantinople (now Istanbul), Armenians also worked in the civil service of the empire and as architects for the royal court. A network of Armenian traders and merchants retained family members in faraway commercial centers to facilitate trading. In the countryside and city, throughout the last half of the nineteenth century, Armenians became increasingly interested in educational opportunities for both boys and girls, and a significant number of young people went on to become doctors, nurses, and teachers.

Origins of the Present Diaspora

Ancient Roots

The Armenian diaspora before the twentieth century came about through forced migration under various empires, as a result of attacks by conquering tribes and armies, and because of families sending out representatives along trade routes. In the empires under which they lived, many Armenians became integrated to the point of taking on positions of power—for example, in the Byzantine Empire, rising to become commanders of military units and marry into royalty. Many Armenians living in the contemporary diaspora have their origins in the lands of what is now central and southern Turkey, Syria, and Iran, already outside the old lands. Their ancestors had migrated or been moved to these places by, for example, the Byzantines following wars with the Arabs. As trade networks blossomed and economic migration increased, a concept of diaspora developed. People living in such communities began to speak of themselves as living in exile, or colonies. The word for colony is the same as that used for local community (*gaghout*) and has only recently been replaced in common usage by *spiurk*, or diaspora.

The Ottoman Experience

The Ottoman Empire is crucial to understanding the present diaspora. The empire's "millet system" of organizing subject people by religion reinforced religious identity and extended the political power of the national Armenian church, and Constantinople, the capital of the empire, was a leading center of intellectual life for Armenians. Increasing insecurity toward the end of the empire, combined with new opportunities, propelled many Armenians to send boys and girls to national schools set up by the church and to those organized by Protestant missionaries. Though the Protestants were disappointed in the conversion rate, even among their own students, their influence was long-lasting and profound. New attitudes toward learning and leadership developed, Western influences and opportunities increased, and more Armenians traveled to Europe and the United States for educational purposes.

Genocide and Dispersion

By the late 1800s, sporadic massacres of Armenians in the eastern provinces were set against the backdrop of periodic attempted reforms of the central government. The empire's losses of other ethnic minorities' territories in the Balkans put Armenian political activity under a cloud of suspicion and encouraged the development of a pan-Turkic nationalism that excluded remaining minorities. In spite of this, most Armenians remained committed to the empire and even continued to enlist in the army. In late 1914, some Dashnaks and Hnchaks made declarations against the empire and set up guerrilla forces, symbolically significant far beyond their small numbers, both in terms of Ottoman and later Turkish rationalizations of the ensuing action and in terms of Armenian pride. The onset of World War I brought extreme and widespread violence against the Armenians. On April 24, 1915, Armenian intellectuals in Constantinople were rounded up and exiled or killed. Armenians were systematically driven from their homes and either killed or forced into death marches, mostly into the Syrian desert. Those who survived were often saved by Turkish, Kurdish, or Arab friends. Exact numbers of the dead and deported are difficult to ascertain, but evidence shows that probably three-quarters of the 2 million Armenians in the empire were uprooted. Of these, probably more than half died. In addition to resulting in physical decimation and dispersion, the genocide has overshadowed and pervaded most of twentieth-century Armenian life. Though there are many different kinds of reactions, nearly every family in the Western diaspora has been directly touched by the loss and trauma of that period. The psychological burden of the survivors was passed on to subsequent generations in a variety of ways.

Post-Genocide

During the troubles of the genocide period, many Armenians sought shelter in what is now Armenia. In 1918, though impoverished and famine-stricken, Armenia declared its independence. To the bitter disappointment of the Dashnak leaders of the young state, however, the country entered the Soviet system only a few years later. Repercussions were felt around the diaspora as there emerged a new version of the East/West divide, with the Dashnaks leading the anti-Soviet or pro-free, independent, unified Armenia movement. Ramkavars and

Hnchaks led a looser movement, more conciliatory toward the Soviets, accepting foreign rule as necessary for protection and aid. This opposition intensified as the political parties vied for control of the new diaspora communities.

Following World War II, a "repatriation" movement (*nerkaght*) was reestablished by Soviet Armenia. For most, it was a not a return to direct ancestral land but rather to another part of the old homelands. The repatriation movement was to have important consequences in both the short and long term for families and whole communities in diaspora. The communities left behind were affected by the scale of the migration, with some struggling to piece collective life back together. Armenian family life was such that very few would dream of that return alone, and negotiations took place between members torn in opposite directions. Usually, the young gave way to the old and repatriated but were among the first to return to the West when the opportunity later arose. Many, though not all, of the migrants were from lower economic levels and were attracted not only by ideology but by a promise of better opportunities. Instead, they found themselves on the fringe of an unexpectedly different, close-knit society where they encountered resentment from other Armenians who viewed them as a new burden on already scant resources. That said, the example of the first president of the new Republic, Levon Ter Petrossian, a child during the 1940s repatriation period, is enough to show that integration did occur, in spite of these initial difficulties.

Meanwhile, the diaspora passed on to another phase of more permanent settlement in the new environments. Repatriation continued sporadically until the early 1960s, but people understood that integration into Armenian society was not easy. Economic conditions in the diaspora improved for most, and people became increasingly "at home" in their adopted countries. In many, World War II further integrated the second generation into the mainstream through their war service to the host country.

Post–World War II

The Cold War years were marked by bitter and open rivalry between diaspora political parties and their sympathizers. The Dashnak party leadership feared the infiltration of the Soviet system into the hierarchy of the church. The supreme head of the church, or *catholicos,* was based in Etchmiadzin, Armenia, but an independent head, based in the diaspora, administered churches in the Middle East from Beirut. During the 1950s, the Dashnak Party consolidated its influence on this Holy See of Antelias, forming a parallel system of churches, the most important of which developed in the United States. Today, most Armenian communities in the United States have two churches, one affiliated with Etchmiadzin, the other with Antelias.

The anti-Soviet fervor of the Dashnak side was met with equally ardent sentiment against the Dashnaks themselves. The Ramkavars, Hnchaks, and other organizations took an opposite stand, believing Armenia should be supported no matter who ruled it. Though a few were Communists, the great majority was not. They maintained that the diaspora would soon die out through assimilation and physical threats and that the republic was the only viable solution for an Armenian future. These organizations regularly hosted guests from Soviet Armenia, including visiting artists, academics, and political speakers.

From the 1970s through the thawing of the Cold War, the two sides were less diametrically opposed and began to take similar stands, particularly regarding Armenia. In the late 1970s and early 1980s, the focus turned to genocide recognition, and a few small but very visible groups turned to terrorism in an attempt to draw attention to their cause. A number of Turkish diplomats were killed or wounded by the Justice Commandos or by the Armenian Secret Army for the Liberation of Armenia (ASALA). This ended with internal fighting and a diaspora divided over these methods. It has been suggested that these groups were equally motivated by the desire to awaken what they called a "sleep-walking" diaspora to political activism on a larger scale, working toward admission of the genocide by Turkey and restoration of certain of the old homelands.

All those who died during the genocide are commemorated annually on April 24. The events range from church Masses to evenings of speech, poetry, and music or protests and marches in front of Turkish embassies. In some communities, young people organize activities such as blood drives for current victims of ethnic cleansing and massacres. The purpose of commemorative events is threefold—to honor the dead, to put pressure on Turkey, and to try to forge ties among the dispersed Armenian people.

Today, few diaspora Armenians till the soil. Instead, they are known as merchants, traders, skilled artisans, and professionals. During the early twentieth century in the Middle East, Armenians were prominent in photography, and today they can be found in all the arts. Like other diaspora peoples, Armenians pursue a host of other mobile professions, increasingly varied as generations pass. In education, tension has emerged between the pressure for traditional Armenian-language-based schooling and a more Western-oriented, often English-based education, which is often seen as providing more sophisticated job opportunities and a deeper link with host countries.

As the twentieth-first century begins, Armenians speak of a sense that their culture is threatened on many fronts. In physically secure countries where there is little pressure on the group, assimilation is seen as taking a faster pace. Where physical insecurity looms, many people consider further immigration. The earthquake in Armenia in 1988, the independence of the republic in 1991, and the struggle for Karabakh (Artsakh) all had profound effects on the diaspora. In some cases, there has been a reawakening of connections and a mobilization of professional services previously unseen in community work. The outpouring of people from the republic following independence has also affected the diaspora and forced rethinking about the future.

The Armenian Community in North America

Though ethnic politics and state formulation of plural society differ in Canada, generally there are broad similarities with the United States. The diversity of the diaspora is clear even within the borders of one country, perhaps most obviously so in the United States. Regionally, there are marked differences between the east and west coasts. To some degree, this mirrors the differences perceived generally in U.S. culture, but it also reflects a much higher intake of the newest waves of immigrants in California since 1990. This development has redefined community profiles and priorities, instigating both regeneration of identity as well as resentments between the newcomers and the older families.

In spite of its smaller population, the east coast of the United States is the base of numerous cultural organizations and intellectual institutions. The first Armenian communities were in New England, and the Boston area alone is now home to Armenian newspapers, the National Association for Armenian Studies and Research (NAASR), the Armenian Library and Museum Association (ALMA), Project Save (a photographic archive), the Armenian International Women's Association (AIWA), and others. Washington, D.C., is the natural home for active lobbying groups such as the Armenian Assembly. The world's largest Armenian charity, the Armenian General Benevolent Union (AGBU), is based in New York City, though its membership is in local chapters around the world.

On the west coast, certain areas such as Glendale or Hollywood have a high percentage of Armenians and the language is often overheard on the street. Ararat Home, equipped for active and assisted retirement, is a popular institution. Compatriotic societies continue to link people with a local homeland ("the old country"), the most active perhaps being the Kessab Education Association, with an annual address directory and new social hall north of Los Angeles. Media publications include a unique English-language, *Time* magazine–like monthly, *Armenian International Magazine* (*AIM*), and popular television and radio programs. A number of Armenian day-schools serve the area. There are also Armenians serving time in jail, a fact that greatly distresses older Armenian American families. In California, Fresno was a center of Armenian agriculture and food production in the diaspora. It is also the birthplace of the most famous Armenian American writer, William Saroyan, and still maintains an active and large Armenian population.

In the United States, Armenian language skills are generally not retained beyond the second generation, and there is considerable exogamy. However, many express a desire to remain connected to other Armenians through family, institutions, life cycle events, attendance at camps or seminars, and annual regional and community events, such as the ARF or AGBU Olympics. Professional affiliations have also emerged both as aid agencies and as career and friendship networks. The churches (Apostolic and Protestant) remain the most meaningful link for many.

Contemporary Social and Institutional Life in the Diaspora

Family

Marriage among Armenians in diaspora was traditionally between two families as well as between two individuals. This practice resulted in the formation of mutual social obligations between the families that were potentially helpful in times of need, and it brought about a strong social network more generally. This tradition continues to some degree, and there is still pressure to choose an Armenian spouse, but not from a particular town or family as before. With increasing intermarriage, there is less chance of a household creating such connections. In the West, the emphasis on the individual is at odds with the earlier focus on the larger family unit. Higher education and professions also serve to encourage a focus on the individual and personal satisfaction. Ties with one's family become narrower, and with the community, more tenuous. The importance of family remains, however, and interdependence is encouraged.

The Armenian family of the early twentieth century is often portrayed as patriarchal. Certainly public life was and remains male-dominated. Many Armenians, however, speak of having been influenced by the strength of female relatives. When the home and family were agreed to be the focus of life, power was shared by women working within and men working outside of the home, and it was understood that both worked to promote the shared life of family. This attitude shifted radically with dispersion and uprooting and also with the rapid adaptation to modern life. The role of women within the home became secondary, as did the need for certain local knowledge and maintenance of family networks. Thus this source of power became greatly diminished. Increasingly, women around the diaspora are working outside as well as inside the home in a variety of careers.

Certain aspects of home life continue to anchor new generations in a sense of ethnic belonging—for example, food and the importance given to hospitality. Like others around the Middle East, Armenians welcome guests with a heavily laden table, and this practice continues in varying degrees around the diaspora. It is common to have visitors or houseguests from abroad, and children grow used to meeting many new people. Through them, they are introduced to political problems around the world in a very direct manner.

Institutions

"Cultural" organizations are often directly or indirectly associated with a political party. The Dashnak Party and cultural organizations in its circle, such as the Hamazkaine and the Armenian Youth Federation (AYF), have the largest membership. The AGBU, officially nonpolitical, is popularly thought of as non-Dashnak, and its many activities are primarily educational and charitable. Education remains a priority, and in the Middle East most children attend Armenian schools at least at the primary level. The Melkonian Institute in Cyprus and other secondary schools provide opportunities to continue, but elsewhere in diaspora, such schools are not widely available. Today the purpose of the Armenian school is to provide a specifically Armenian education, emphasizing language and history but also providing an environment the parents believe is "safer" from perceived new threats such as drugs and gangs in Western countries. The Armenian schools are also thought to slow the process of assimilation. At the level of higher education, individual scholars in the Middle East and Europe are pursuing Armenian studies. In the United States, a number of chairs of Armenian studies have been established in universities (for example, the University of California at Los Angeles and Fresno, the University of Michigan, and Harvard). E-mail and the Internet have ensured that many young people who would never subscribe to the ethnic press follow events regularly online. Equally important, new websites emerge daily on a wide variety of subjects, some representing organizations, others individuals.

The Armenian church remains a key symbol of continuity and survival for four main reasons: (1) it provides a link with the ancient past and preserves the classical language; (2) its political role continues; (3) it is a link to Europe through shared Christianity; and (4) the structure connects people throughout the diaspora and with Armenia. The church itself has been accused by some of focusing on the survival of the ethnic group rather than a particularly spiritual message. In Europe, secularization in general continues to grow, whereas in the United States a very different social environment prompts other changes, such as Christian education for children and the introduction of English into part of the Mass. The church is caught in a double bind, representing continuity and links with the past in its seemingly "unchanging" structure, while losing people who say it does not speak to their present needs. In addition, the needs (and opinions) of new waves of migrants are quite different from those of third- and fourth-generation Armenian Americans. It is important to note that there are two small but important religious minorities within the Armenian population: the Protestants and the Catholics.

Security versus Assimilation

Security remains a problem for Armenia, and events continue to occur that exacerbate such concerns. Political unrest in the Middle East, and the devastation caused by the December 1988 earthquake in Armenia, have contributed to a feeling of constant danger for the republic. Pogroms against Armenians in Azerbaijan during the same period presented yet another cause for alarm. Armenians in the diaspora have reacted to these dangers, seeing them as part of a larger configuration of threats to the Armenian people as a whole. Because of these issues, some see the Armenian population as an endangered people.

Living in the Middle East had allowed people to remain quite close to their original lands. They were familiar with the Arab and Turkish worlds and felt part of them, though connected to Europe. Further migrations from the Middle East, farther west, meant a transformation of the diaspora and a new form of insecurity. Assimilation, or, as the Armenians call it, "white massacre" (*jermag chart*), becomes the main concern in stable Western environments. During centuries of living with mostly Muslim neighbors, Armenians maintained friendly social relations, but religious differences prevented nearly all intermarriage. In Christian or secular settings, such barriers decreased.

In the Middle East, Armenians regularly speak several languages, but in many Western countries unilingualism is normal and Armenian is lost. Attending weekend schools or private day-schools helps, but even so, it remains difficult to practice the language on a daily basis. The number of readers and writers of Armenian literature is rapidly decreasing. Through political rhetoric, literature, and various media, the intellectual elite of the diaspora (of all political shades) has tried to counter the problems of dispersion and mobility by shaping a new identity that is not based on locale or kin. The "real" Armenian in this version is someone who speaks the language, knows the history, belongs to the Apostolic Church, and shows active commitment. This narrowing of identity has proven alienating to those who do not fit into the categories but do feel themselves to be Armenian.

Conclusions

In the Western Armenian case, there have been several visions of homeland, the most evocative having been the homes that were left behind in the genocide, now in eastern Turkey. Iran and Lebanon also have sentimental and historic importance for their Armenian citizens and their own diaspora. With the establishment of independent Armenia in 1991, however, the focus is changing to an idealized homeland on that soil. As with Israel and the Jewish diaspora, relations between Armenians in the homeland and those in diaspora reflect differences between their historical experiences, current political situations, and expectations of each other.

Following glasnost and the earthquake, diaspora funding has been channeled away from the diaspora's own institutions and toward Armenia. For some, the existence of a free Armenia means there is no further need for diaspora public life and that Armenia itself should serve as the anchor and focus of the culture. This view overlooks the very different historical and contemporary experiences of the Western diaspora and assumes that the political agenda and cultural attitudes of the state and its citizens are similar to those of the diaspora. Often they are actually quite far apart or even opposing. The September 1999 Armenia-Diaspora Conference, followed by a second conference, was an important symbolic event and could serve as a beginning for more formal, sustained attempts at cooperation and communication.

Diaspora life fits well with the mobility and flexibility required by globalization and modern life. The writer William Saroyan optimistically predicted that Armenians would continue to re-create themselves as a people wherever they are found and under whatever circumstances. Nationalists are scathingly skeptical, looking now toward an independent nation-state as salvation. Today, personal and collective belonging is constructed through multiple connections, and the nation-state is only one dimension of this process. For Armenians, the diaspora is the other—in all its diversity and richness.

Susan Pattie

See also: Ethnic Cleansing: Armenia; Polish Diaspora; Repatriation; Russian Diaspora; Russian Revolution; Transnationalism

References and further reading:

Armenia Diaspora, http://armeniadiaspora.com.

Bakalian, Anny. 1993. *Armenian-Americans: From Being to Feeling Armenian.* New Brunswick: Transaction.

Balakian, Peter. 1997. *Black Dog of Fate: An American Son Uncovers His Armenian Past.* New York: Basic.

Cilicia, http://www.cilicia.com.

Dadrian, Vahakn. 1995. *The History of the Armenian Genocide.* Oxford: Berghahn.

Deranian, Hagop, Martin. 1998. *Worcester Is America.* Worcester: Bennate.

Hovannisian, Richard, ed. 1997. *The Armenian People: From Ancient to Modern Times,* 2 vols. New York: St. Martin's.

Marsden, Philip. 1993. *The Crossing Place: A Journey among the Armenians.* London: HarperCollins.

Miller, Donald E., and Lorna Touryan Miller. 1993. *Survivors: An Oral History of the Armenian Genocide.* Berkeley: University of California Press.

Mirak, Robert. 1983. *Torn between Two Lands: Armenians in America, 1890 to World War I.* Cambridge: Harvard University Press.

Ormanian, Malachia. 1955. *The Church of Armenia: Her History, Doctrine, Rule, Discipline, Liturgy, Literature, and Existing Condition.* London: A. R. Mowbray.

Pattie, Susan Paul. 1997. *Faith in History: Armenians Rebuilding Community.* Washington, DC: Smithsonian Institution Press.

Suny, Ronald Grigor. 1993. *Looking toward Ararat: Armenia in Modern History.* Bloomington: Indiana University Press.

Tololyan, Khachig. 1999. "Textual Nation: Poetry and Nationalism in Armenian Political Culture." Pp. 79–108 in *Intellectuals and the Articulation of the Nation.* Edited by Ronald Grigor Suny and Michael D. Kennedy. Ann Arbor: University of Michigan Press.

Walker, Christopher. 1980. *Armenia: The Survival of a Nation.* London: Croom Helm.

Assimilation/Integration

Assimilation and integration are the two leading concepts referring to the process of settlement, interaction with a host society, and social change following immigration. Both are strongly contested terms politically, with shifting meanings, yet they have enjoyed a comeback in public policy debate and scholarly work in recent years.

The terms have their roots in Durkheimian functionalist sociology as core concepts pointing toward the unifying cohesion that functionalist theories believe any society must achieve—via the socialization of its members—in order to work properly. Applied to research, the concepts were popularized by the Chicago school of urban sociology in the early twentieth century before becoming familiar terms in public policy debates about the consequences of immigration. Both terms also promote a slippery metaphorical link between the social processes they describe and mathematical and/or biological theories that describe processes in the natural world using the same terms. Although applicable to any country of immigration, they are concepts that have been most developed, along rather distinct lines, in the United States and Western Europe.

"Assimilation," the more commonly used term in the United States, represents one pole in the debate over the degree to which new immigrants can and should strive to resemble average American middle- and upper-class norms and behavior as the path to successful settlement in the society. The most important theoretical formulation of how assimilation works in American society is the work of Milton Gordon (1964). He distinguished between various dimensions of assimilation in the society, identifying the need for structural assimilation—into the labor and housing markets, as well as language and education—as the most important element in immigrant success, ahead of racial, cultural, or moral (value) assimilation. Although a neutral typology, his framework is often equated (wrongly) with the conservative argument that new immigrants must conform to the norms and values of the dominant white majority in order to be accepted.

The idea of successful immigrant assimilation is clearly still today a vibrant part of the myth of the "American dream." Yet assimilationist assumptions about how America works as a society have led to numerous critiques that propose a more differentialist or multiculturalist view of society. In these, various minority or subordinate groups are viewed as able to assert their own cultural autonomy or distinctiveness from the white mainstream as a means to get ahead in American society. This view became an important position in the multiculturalist debates that have raged in the United States since the success of the civil rights movement in the 1960s and 1970s.

The term has enjoyed a comeback in recent years in response to heightened concern about the separatism latent in multiculturalist positions. It has been recognized that some set of shared norms and values are a likely precondition for the success of a genuinely pluralist nation of immigrants. Scholars have also sought to rehabilitate the term in the light of the clearly diverse (or "segmented") success rates of new immigrants from around the world since U.S. immigration policy reforms in the 1980s. Arguing that the concept need not be equated with the discredited white majority bias of earlier uses, Richard Alba and Victor Nee (1997) laid out an impressive research program documenting the continued importance of historically established patterns of assimilation to middle-class residential, educational, and occupational trajectories as the crucial precondition for the success of new immigrants in American society. Coming from a more multiculturalist position, Alejandro Portes and associates (Portes and Zhou 1993; Portes and Rumbaut 2001) have also used the term prominently to signal how less successful new migrant groups, with less "white" racial or cultural origins, often follow a path of downward assimilation to resemble the social profile of inner-city African American populations. A key part of this story has been an economic context in which the more stable industrial employment that immigrants used to seek has been replaced by far more precarious and low-paying opportunities in the new service industries.

All of these theories continue to adhere to an essentially functionalist vision of American society in which immigrant success or failure is charted against a set of taken-for-granted, mainstream American (white), middle- and upper-class norms bounded by the notion of American society as a wholly self-contained unit of social processes. There is thus little or no space here for a more transnational perspective on the social ties and networks of immigrants in which their complicated lives embody social structures that can span two or more continents economically, culturally, and politically. Moreover, the mainstream into which they are said to merge is never clearly defined, despite the fact that any majority of the population is likely to be riven by cultural, regional, political, and value differences. Beyond this, the assimilationist picture also renders invisible what is distinctly national about the characteristics of the American population. In the United States, folk ideology sees the mainstream culture rather blindly as a multinational, universal one, whereas in fact assimilation entails the complete renationalization of diverse immigrants into a new, nationally specific American culture that is far from universal in its attitudes about patriotism and cultural identity. Hyphenated U.S. identities (Italian-American, Danish-American, and so on) have rarely preserved any more than an ersatz element of the original homeland national culture in the face of the extraordinarily coercive power of the host society to absorb and transform newcomers into "Americans," particularly by the second generation. And, although in practice the new immigrant American identity has been open to all who embrace the American dream, there is still a lingering sense of exclusion hanging over the possibly "un-American" tendencies of more recent immigrants: for example, Muslims from the Middle East, whose culture and values—like the "Communists" before them—are seen now to be questionably compatible, or the vast population of Spanish-speaking Mexicans and other Latinos, who seem able to create a semiautonomous, bilingual society of their own in the big cities of the American Southwest, a space of flows and transactions that stretches out south across the U.S. border. These problems are shared by the rare examples of assimilationist studies in Europe—most notably in France (Tribalat et al., 1996)—in which immigrants' cultural and social features are evaluated in relation to average French norms, generalized from so-called *français de souche* (French citizens born of French-origin families) said to embody the universalist aspirations of French society. Such claims appear absurd when they are made about culturally specific, small European nations; it is only the sheer scale of the United States that enables it to be so blind to its own nation-building ideology.

The term "integration," however, is by far the more popular concept in a European context, including France. In recent years, it has been invoked prominently in public policy debates and in high-level policy formulations in Britain, France, the Netherlands, Germany, Italy, Denmark, Sweden, and Austria. In policy debates, it generally refers to a "middle way" between coercive conformism to national norms and values, on the one hand, and the threat of separatism, seen as latent in the excessive preservation of non-European cultures, on the other. In the United States, the term was mainly used to signify a goal in the black civil rights movement, that

Miss April Lou, teacher at PS 1, Manhattan, with six Chinese children, recent arrivals from Hong Kong and Formosa. Each holds up a placard giving his or her Chinese name (both in ideographs and in transliteration) and the name to be entered upon the official school records, 1964. (Library of Congress)

is, the opposite of segregation in schools and public services. Scientifically speaking, there are no satisfactory core definitions despite the growing number of national and cross-national projects (Favell 2003). Michael Banton (2001) referred to integration as a "treacherous metaphor" alluding to a two-way accommodation of host and immigrant groups, but he offered no clear criteria for operationalization and measurement. Crucially, this is because there is no clear measurement of how integrated modern societies are to begin to with.

The key historical background to ideas of integration in Europe is the consciously close relationship between these ideas and the long-standing narratives of nation-building and national identity that form the bedrock of European national politics. Each European nation has tended to narrate its history as a process of territorial and political integration of regional minorities and social classes, a process now seen to be played out with the new immigrants of the postwar period. A crucial part of this integration story has been the accession to citizenship of these new members, something that can be seen in terms of progressive legal, political, and social rights. This classic position evokes the work of Thomas H. Marshall (1950) and signals, too, the centrality of the building and preservation of the national welfare state as an essential part of this story. Residual concerns about the cultural and religious differences of immigrants remain, but in each national case the debate centers on how historical notions of the nation can be adapted to include new, culturally distinct immigrants, and conversely, which things these immigrants must change or adapt in their behavior to become integrated in the nation.

Debates in Europe have come to be increasingly focused around integrating Muslim-origin immigrants. These have often centered on issues such as schooling, the recognition and funding of mosques, the toleration of certain practices, or the position of women, but there has often been a lively debate in many countries about whether cultural or socioeconomic issues should be uppermost in immigrant reception policy. Some nations that opted initially for more culturally based differentialist or multicultural policies—such as the Netherlands and Sweden—have in recent years reverted to a more socioeconomic conception of integration (Fermin 1999). This approach usually includes a component of language learning and a presupposition that immigrants need to develop a knowledge of the host society as a precondition of success in education or the labor market. Far right parties, hostile to new immigration, often point to indicators of integration failure—such as immigrant unemployment, social tensions, or clashes over non-European practices—as an argument against immigration or in favor of repatriation. New issues have also arisen in connection with the integration of a growing number of asylum seekers in Europe, who have often not been able to follow the standard channel of integration through the labor market.

"Integration" is often used as an all-encompassing frame for a variety of other terms that pinpoint dimensions of the settlement process. Some writers prefer to write about "acculturation," "adaptation," "inclusion," or "incorporation," and there are other similar terms, but all are euphemisms for the same general process. "Integration" is useful as a term in that it goes beyond merely political issues, such as citizenship or participation, to encompass more difficult to specify social processes and moral problems. It also indicates that change is likely on both sides rather than presupposing that assimilation to the dominant culture is necessary. However, it is still strongly criticized by those coming from a more antiracist or conflict-theory vision of society, who tend to believe that discrimination is inevitable in all majority-minority relations, and that integration is thus a mask for specific relations of domination. What is clear is that like assimilation, integration presupposes the bounded nation-state society as the exclusive context for immigrant settlement processes. It upholds a nation-centered view of European societies that is hard to reconcile with the growing interdependence of European societies and the emerging transnational social organization of some migrant groups. Such migrants, indeed, often use links to their homeland and diasporic cultures as a buffer to integration pressures.

Some scholars have also sought to distinguish different patterns of social and/or political incorporation within the notion of integration. They point to different kinds of conscious strategies followed by immigrants in relation to the host society: either assimilation, differentialism, segregation, or marginalization (for example, Esser 1999). Again, these are bounded visions of how immigrants might interact with host societies and may overestimate how coherent, closed, and integrated Western societies are.

It seems likely that the use of the term "integration" will grow in future years. As immigration rises in political salience, ruling governments will be forced to reformulate policies in order to balance the rights of migrants with the popular pressure to close doors to new migrants. Although such policies may lead to a recognition of the permanence of immigrant settlement and to a reformulation of ideas of national culture, they presuppose a form of national closure and exclusion to some migrants who are seen as not belonging to the society. They also represent a form of rearguard action by agents of the nation-state who seek to preserve the fiction of bounded nation-state societies in an increasingly porous, interdependent world. The concept of assimilation has a more shaky future. Its use depends on the implicit blindness of American perspectives to the particularistic nation-building processes that the United States—like nations elsewhere—projects onto immigration issues in the name of a well-functioning society. America will need to look at itself in more comparative ways to reveal similarities between its debates about assimilation and debates in smaller European countries about integration and national identity.

The frontier for research in this field, therefore, lies in developing detailed comparative, cross-national studies that are able to explore how different dimensions of integration have affected migrants of different national origins in various countries. The research also needs to encompass transnational phenomena and to challenge the nation-building fictions that continue to portray nations as closed societies with coherent norms and values that immigrants must learn in a one-way fashion as a precondition of socioeconomic success. One way of breaking with this view is to take global/international cities or regions as the unit of comparison into which immigrants integrate (for example, Waldinger 2001). Such studies are now beginning to emerge tentatively in Europe, although large barriers remain owing to the very different means nations have of generating statistics and survey data about the migrant populations across continents.

Adrian Favell

See also: Citizenship; Migrant Rights; Multiculturalism; Muslim Immigration; Naturalization; Transnationalism

References and further reading:

Alba, Richard, and Victor Nee. 1997. "Rethinking Assimilation Theory for a New Era of Immigration." *International Migration Review* 31 (Winter): 826–874.

Banton, Michael. 2001. "National Integration in France and Britain." *Journal of Ethnic and Migration Studies* 27, no. 1: 151–168.

Bauböck, Rainer. 1994. *The Integration of Immigrants.* CMDG Report. Strasbourg: Council of Europe.

Brubaker, Rogers. 2001. "The Return of Assimilation? Changing Perspectives on Immigration and Its Sequels in France, Germany, and the United States." *Ethnic and Racial Studies* 24, no. 4: 531–548.

Esser, Hartmut. 1999. "Inklusion, integration und ethnische Schichtung." *Journal für Konflikt und Gewaltforshung* 1, no. 1: 5–34.

Favell, Adrian. 2001 [1998]. *Philosophies of Integration: Immigration and the Idea of Citizenship in France and Britain.* 2d ed. London: Macmillan.

———. 2003. "Integration Nations: The Nation-State and Research on Immigrants in Western Europe." *Comparative Social Research* 22: 13–42.

Fermin, Alfons. 1999. "Inburgeringsbeleid en burgerschap." *Migrantenstudien* 15, no. 2: 99–112.

Gordon, Milton. 1964. *Assimilation in American Life: The Role of Race, Religion and National Origins.* New York: Oxford University Press.

Marshall, Thomas H. 1950. *Citizenship and Social Class.* London: Pluto.

Portes, Alejandro, and Ruben Rumbaut. 2001. *Legacies: The Story of the Immigrant Second Generation.* Berkeley: University of California Press.

Portes, Alejandro, and Min Zhou. 1993. "The New Second Generation: Segmented Assimilation and Its Variants." *Annals of the American Academy of Political and Social Sciences* 530 (November): 74–96.

Tribalat, Michèle, Jean-Pierre Garson, Yann Moulier-Boutang, and Roxane Silberman. 1996. *De l'immigration à l'assimilation: une enquête sur la population étrangère en France.* Paris: INED.

Waldinger, Roger. 2001. *Strangers at the Gates: New Immigrants in Urban America.* Berkeley: University of California Press.

Waldrauch, Harald, and Hofinger, Christoph. 1997. "An Index to Measure the Legal Obstacles to the Integration of Migrants." *New Community* 23, no. 2: 271–286.

Asylum

Asylum has become one of the most controversial issues in the immigration politics of states in recent years. In contemporary terms, "asylum" refers to the sanctuary or refuge given to foreigners, usually refugees, by any sovereign state. Most recent controversy, particularly in the West, has focused on the category of the "asylum seeker"—individuals who claim at the border or within a state to be in need of asylum, but whose claim is either in doubt or, more commonly, yet to be confirmed as valid. Most immigration and refugee scholars believe that the availability of asylum, and thus protection for individuals fleeing human rights abuses and persecution, is in deep crisis because of measures that states, particularly the richer ones, have implemented to prevent asylum seekers from gaining protection. Although the reality is a little more complex, current state practices in relation to asylum are characterized by a large and growing gap between the rhetoric of states and their actual behavior.

The Idea of Asylum

The word "asylum" derives from the Greek *asylos,* meaning that which is inviolable or that may not be seized. Throughout Western history there have been many variations in the forms asylum has taken corresponding to the different types of social and political organizations with the power to offer protection (Schuster 2003). There is, for example, a long history of religious buildings (temples, churches, and so on) serving as sanctuaries for individuals fleeing prosecution or persecution. More generally, most human societies have offered refuge to at least some outsiders in need, at least temporarily. In doing so, they have reflected the teachings of the world's major religions, each of which, though not always as explicitly as Islam with its idea of *djiwar* (protection) for the stranger, articulates a duty to some foreigners in need (Plaut 1995).

In its contemporary form, however, the idea of asylum is firmly wedded to the emergence of the sovereign territorial state. The Peace of Westphalia in 1648 brought forth the modern system of independent states, each with sovereign jurisdiction over the territory it ruled. A corollary of this exclusive (territorially delimited) power was that states had the right to grant asylum to whomsoever they wished and to have that right respected by other states. The right is one that, though qualified by explicit agreements (such as extradition treaties), adheres in states to this day.

But if the state's right to grant asylum can be seen as an outgrowth of territorial sovereignty, so was a duty to provide asylum to those in need, at least when doing so did not exact heavy costs. Early normative defenders of the system of independent states needed to square this division of the globe with the traditional Christian view, expressed by the seventeenth-century philosopher John Locke, that God gave the world "to Mankind in common"(Locke 1964 [1698], Book II, chapter 5). To make a convincing normative argument for the advantages to human well-being of dividing the globe, defenders of territorial states were under pressure to make allowance for the protection of those who possessed no state of their own, or whose own state persecuted them.

Virtually all the early theorists of international law, including Hugo Grotius, Emmerich Vattel, Christian Woolf, and Samuel Pufendorf, thus recognized states as having a responsibility, stemming from natural law, to grant asylum to those in great need. The position was perhaps best expressed by Immanuel Kant in his work "Perpetual Peace" of 1795: "Hospitality means the right of a stranger not to be treated with hostility when he arrives on someone else's territory. He can indeed be turned away, if this can be done without causing his death, but he must not be treated with hostility. . . . The stranger cannot claim the right of a guest. . . . He may only claim a right of resort, for all men are entitled to present themselves in the society of others by virtue of their right to communal possession of the earth's surface. Since the earth is a globe, they cannot disperse over an infinite area, but must necessarily tolerate one another's

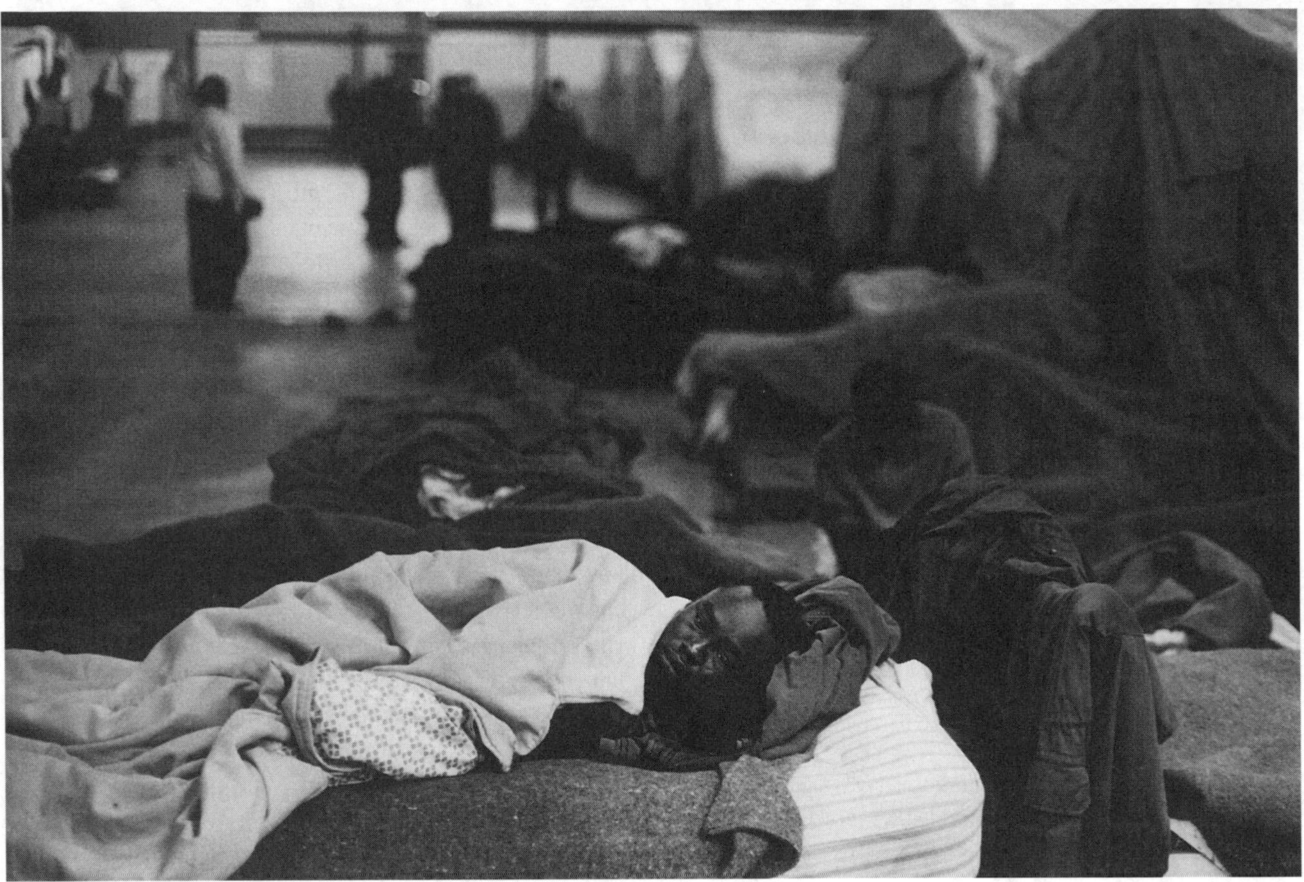

Asylum seekers at the Sangatte Red Cross center on the outskirts of Calais in France, 2002—many hoping to enter Britain. (Howard Davies/Corbis)

company. And no-one originally has any greater right than anyone else to occupy any particular portion of the earth" (Kant 1991 [1795], 105–106).

Asylum in International Law

If natural law recognized a duty to grant asylum, the translation of this moral responsibility into international law has historically proven less than complete. Although the right of states to grant asylum is usually undisputed under international law, "the individual," as Guy Goodwin-Gill has noted, "has no right to be granted asylum" (Goodwin-Gill 1983, 121). Indeed, in international law the term "asylum" tends to be both vague and ill-defined. The word does not, in fact, appear at all in the most significant universal treaty relating to the protection of refugees, the UN Convention Relating to the Status of Refugees of 1951. The nearest the treaty comes to an obligation to allow refugees entry is through the principle (in Article 33) of "nonrefoulement," an obligation not to return a refugee (an individual facing persecution on one of the grounds enumerated in the Convention) back to a place where he or she would face persecution. Because this article can be respected by actions that fall short of allowing entry and residence in the state at which a refugee arrives (by, for example, arranging for him or her to receive protection in another safe country), it is not equivalent to a duty to grant asylum. Other international legal agreements, including the Organization of African Unity Convention of 1969, also fall short of articulating an individual right of asylum.

There have, however, been attempts to specify duties of asylum in other parts of international law. The Universal Declaration of Human Rights (1948) proclaims the right of individuals "to seek and enjoy asylum," though this still falls short of creating an obligation on the part of any individual state to grant it. In 1977, there was an international attempt to rectify the gap in international law by creating a universally applicable right to asylum with a correlative obligation on the part of individual states. This United Nations Conference on Territorial Asylum ended, however, in "abject failure" (Goodwin-Gill 1983, 111).

Domestic law has scarcely proven more fertile ground for an entitlement to asylum. Although a number of countries recognize—at least in principle—a right of asylum for foreigners, only in Germany has this entitlement proved to have significant implications for state behavior. The Basic Law of the German Constitution of 1949, written in the aftermath of the country's experience with Nazism, provides, under Article 16, a right of asylum for individuals who have been politically persecuted. However, faced with huge numbers of asylum seekers, this uniquely wide-ranging entitlement was effectively neutered in 1993 by a constitutional amendment enabling officials to return most applicants to other countries (Gibney 2004; Joppke 1999a). Germany has now joined the ranks of other states, such as France, in having a constitutional right of asylum that is in large part nominal.

Asylum in Practice

The absence of a right of asylum in international law has not meant that states have refrained from granting protection to refugees and other individuals deemed in need of it. Throughout much of the past century, however, when and where refugees have received asylum have been determined less by legal principle than by state interests and felt obligations to specific groups. Significant developments occurred in the evolution of asylum between 1900 and 1945, with the emergence of large numbers of refugees—Russians from the Bolshevik Revolution, Armenians from genocide in Turkey, and Jews from Nazi Germany—and the first awkward steps were taken toward an international regime for the protection of refugees in the formation of the (short-lived) League of Nations High Commissioner for Refugees. Events from this period, especially guilt from the failure of Western states to offer asylum to Jews fleeing the Nazis in the 1930s, hung like a dark cloud over the post–World War II world.

Asylum since 1945

Unregulated Regionalism: 1945–1965

The sense of guilt over the fate of Jews denied access to Western countries helps to explain the incredible period of institutional and international legal innovation that marked the years immediately after 1945. Within six years of the end of World War II, the United Nations High Commissioner for Refugees (UNHCR) had been established (1950) and the Convention Relating to the Status of Refugees had been signed (1951). As the problem of those displaced by the war dissipated in the late 1940s, another rationale for responsiveness to refugees by Western states became salient. With the beginning of the Cold War, the provision of asylum became a foreign policy tool to be offered by states to those who fled or refused to be repatriated to Communist countries. The term "refugee" increasingly became interchangeable with "defector," and asylum became an inclusive West's reward for individuals who voted with their feet against Communist regimes.

The limits of Western inclusivity were never really tested during the 1950s and 1960s, however. The tight controls on exit practiced by most Communist states generally kept demands for asylum low throughout much of the period. Numbers did rise from time to time, reflecting the ebbs and flows of East/West conflict: More than 200,000 fled Hungary in 1956, and an additional 80,000 fled Czechoslovakia in 1968 (Loescher 1993). These movements, however, had no systematic quality. They were experienced in the West as occasional eruptions, events that could be tolerated or even welcomed. When refugees arrived, their integration was facilitated by the needs of booming postwar industrial economies, such as those in Germany and Australia, for cheap and plentiful labor. Even that economic laggard, Britain, accepted around 100,000 people from Latvia, the Ukraine, and Yugoslavia to work in labor-starved sectors of the nation's economy after 1946 (Rees 1982, 81–82). It is no exaggeration to say that the economic requirements of capitalist production almost rendered superfluous distinctions between immigrants, asylum seekers, and refugees in the period up to the 1960s.

In the twenty years between 1945 and 1965, the provision of asylum was generally seen across the West as a European affair. The fact that almost all refugees were Europeans reduced (but did not eliminate) the potential for cultural friction in host states (Loescher and Scanlon 1986; Divine 1957; Gibney 2004). Moreover, the fact that Western states were defined by a commitment to common values formed, to some extent, by hostility to communism helped create a measure of interstate solidarity that facilitated burden sharing in the aftermath of key refugee-generating events, such as the revolt in Hungary in 1956 (UNHCR 2000).

The view that the refugee issue was primarily a regional one was also built into the infrastructure of the new refugee regime. Responsibilities under the 1951 UN Refugee Convention were limited to refugees generated by events before 1951 occurring *within Europe.* It was in response to refugee events in the heart of Europe, specifically with the Hungarian refugee crisis in 1956, that UNHCR established its usefulness to donor states (Loescher and Scanlon 1986). In sharp contrast, neither Western states nor UNHCR played any real role in assisting the enormous numbers of displaced persons generated in the aftermath of the partition of India and Pakistan after 1947. Indeed, debates over the role of UNHCR in world affairs explicitly excluded consideration of the refugees created by partition. This kind of indifference to refugees in certain regions of the globe (especially when the interests of Western states were not at stake) was possible because the likelihood of refugees coming from these regions to the West was slim. The seemingly natural boundaries of geography allowed Western states to remain insulated from refugee events in other parts of the world.

Incipient Globalism: 1965–1979

The relative lack of controversy in Western states over the issue of asylum was not to last, however. Almost all of the factors that underpinned the relative tranquility of the immediate postwar period were undermined from the 1960s onward by a set of changes that placed the asylum policies of Western states in a global context.

The first of these was the escalation in refugee-producing events in Asia and Africa, most of them directly or indirectly related to the experiences of decolonization. In Africa, the Algerian War of Independence from the late 1950s, indigenous struggles for self-determination in Zaire and Rwanda in the 1960s, and events in the Sudan, Uganda, and Kenya in the 1970s all gave rise to significant refugee movements. The breakup of Pakistan in the early 1970s and the devastation of the Vietnam War, culminating with the fall of Saigon in 1975, proved that Asia, too, could be at the center of movements of forced migrants. Together these events dramatically called into question the widespread assumption that refugees were an intra-European phenomenon. More than this, they signaled the increasing prominence of a transformed international order, one in which the newly formed southern states were demanding a voice. Notwithstanding their funding base in the West, United Nations organizations such as the UNHCR could not ignore the regional shift in demand for their services (UNHCR 2000).

A second development, the geographical expansion of the UN definition of a refugee, reflected the new origins of refugee-producing events and changes in the international order. A 1967 Protocol was added to the UN Refugee Convention lifting the geographical limitation on who could count as a refugee. The sphere of those to whom Western states were legally obliged to give asylum was thus extended. Western states committed themselves to universally applicable standards for asylum just at the time that technological innovations in communications and transportation were eclipsing the distance between First and Third World countries (Brubaker 1990, 384; Suhrke 1997).

A third factor in the globalization of asylum pressures was the end of policies of labor migration by the countries of Western Europe in the early 1970s. Demand in Western states for cheap migrant labor ended abruptly with the downturn in the economic fortunes of the OECD countries in the early 1970s. By the time of this change in demand, however, most of the states of Western Europe had, in response to their expanding labor needs, tapped into the huge and seemingly flexible labor supplies of southern countries. Germany, for example, had recruited unskilled and semiskilled laborers from Turkey and the Maghreb. Many Western states were thus deeply implicated in a global migration system that traded on steep income and employment differentials between advanced industrial states and poorer ones. Unsurprisingly, their attempts to end South/North migration were mostly unsuccessful. Unfavorable economic conditions in the countries of emigration and a demand for illicit labor in the West meant that economically motivated migration did not stop; it simply took another form, evident in increasing pressure on asylum systems for entry.

A final change fueled the globalization of asylum. With the spread of film, television, and telecommunications, by the end of the 1960s differences in income, employment, and lifestyles across countries were better advertised than ever before. This was a process driven in large part by the trading and investment needs of the capitalist economies of the West. Moreover, relatively fast and cheap modes of intercontinental commercial transportation—particularly but not exclusively by air—had begun to come within the reach of a significant proportion of the world's denizens. The effect of these changes on asylum in the West began to be felt by the early 1970s as asylum seekers from Africa and Asia began to arrive by jet in European capitals. Advancements in communications and transportation signaled that the traditional connection between geographical proximity and responsibility for asylum seekers was at an end. Though many factors, including lack of resources, opportunity, and time, would continue to confine refugee movements within specific regions, the possibility of intercontinental movement was becoming real for many more asylum seekers than in the past.

Engineered Regionalism: 1980 to the Present

Asylum was profoundly changed by these developments. In combination, they suggested the prospect of a truly globalized system of asylum seeking, driven as much by economic disparities between North and South as by refugee-generating events, strictly defined. Ugandan refugees were now able to claim asylum in London, Sri Lankans in Amsterdam, and Chinese in New York. Moreover, the prospects of improved access to asylum did not apply to refugees alone. Government elites expressed concern that North-South inequalities were becoming a reason for migration in their own right. The British prime minister, John Major, warned his European Union (EU) colleagues in 1992 that "we must not remain open to all comers, simply because Paris, Rome and London seem more attractive than Algiers."

Some evidence for such a transformation could be found in a sharp rise in asylum applications. Asylum claims across Western Europe rose from about 13,000 annually in the 1970s to 170,000 by 1985, and to 690,000 by 1992. Between 1985 and 1995, more than 5 million claims for asylum were lodged in Western states (UNHCR 1997). The numbers were, however, also buoyed by the end of the Cold War. Emigration restrictions on the citizens of Eastern and Central Europe were lifted, and a brutal war broke out in the former Yugoslavia. But Western governments now lacked their traditional rationale for offering asylum—the desire to support those fleeing Communist regimes.

These changes, along with low rates of acceptance for refugee status in most European countries, transformed public and official attitudes toward those seeking asylum. Increasingly, asylum seekers were characterized in public discourse as "economic refugees," people taking advantage of the asylum route to escape normal immigration control, or as immigrants in pursuit of the benefits of the welfare state at the expense of citizens. Increasingly after September 11, 2001, asylum seekers were viewed as a security threat, possible terrorists working the asylum system to gain entry to Western countries. Many of these views were unfounded and a thin veil for xenophobic attitudes and vote winning. Yet they did point to real changes. Economic migration and movements of refugees fleeing conflict had become increasingly entangled (Van Kessel 2001); the incentives for people with implausible claims to asylum were strong, given that the chances of being removed if their claim was unsuccessful were exceedingly low (Gibney and Hansen 2003); and there were a number of high-profile events in the United States and Great Britain where asylum seekers were directly linked to terrorist activities (Zolberg 2001). It was not surprising, then, that asylum became mired in political controversy in countries as different as the United States, the Netherlands, Italy, and Germany.

Restriction is not the whole story. Countries of immigration such as Canada, the United States, and Australia resettled a total of more than 1 million refugees during the 1990s through orderly entrance schemes. Nonetheless, many observers have noted that the amount of asylum offered in Western countries pales to insignificance when considered against those countries, usually in the South, that border refugee-generating conflicts. As reports from UNHCR show, by the end of the millennium the states with the largest asylum burdens relative to gross domestic product (GDP) and population size were almost all in Africa and Asia (Castles 2005). Indeed, the top asylum providers—Armenia, Guinea, Tanzania, Zambia, Congo, and the Democratic Republic of Congo—read like a roll call of some of the world's poorest and least stable states. By the end of 2000, Pakistan and Iran alone hosted a combined total of almost 4 million refugees.

In recent years, Southern countries have railed against their role as large-scale asylum providers. They have repatriated refugees (sometimes forcibly), attempted to seal their borders, and become more vocal in expressing the political and economic difficulties of providing haven to such large numbers of refugees. Some have pointed to the security implications of accepting refugees, noting that camps for refugees often serve as a launching pad for the continuation of the hostilities that originally forced people to flee (Milner 2000). A palpable sense of injustice at the current inequalities in asylum burdens between South and North often lies behind their complaints: Why should they fulfill their duties to refugees when the richest countries of the world do not? In Asia, where the majority of countries have not signed the 1951 Refugee Convention, restrictive asylum practices by Northern countries are simply seen as evidence of the hypocrisy of the countries that have.

By the middle of the 1990s, the number of asylum applicants in Western countries had started to decrease. This was partly a result of a reduction in refugee-generating events and partly the result of a range of measures Western states had put in place to deter or prevent the arrival of asylum seekers. The range of these measures was truly remarkable, as was the speed with which virtually all Western states came to implement them. There were measures to prevent asylum seekers from accessing state territory (visa regimes and carrier sanctions); to deter potential asylum claims (detention, limitations on the right to work); and to limit the amount of time asylum seekers and refugees spent in the state (faster processing for claims deemed unfounded, temporary forms of asylum) (Gibney and Hansen 2005). States also began to cooperate with each other to a greater extent in regional forums, such as the EU, to manage (or prevent) the arrival of asylum seekers. Multilateral and bilateral agreements, such as the Canada/U.S. Safe Third Country Agreement of 2002, began to enter into force.

The success of Western states in reducing avenues for entry made it hard to avoid the conclusion that other states were being left to pick up the tab. A number of observers have argued that restrictive policies in the West "contain" refugees to the regions of the world that they came from, and indeed, to some of the poorest states therein (Castles 2002; Chimni 1998). Although no one knows how many of the world's refugees would move outside their immediate region if the opportunity presented itself, it is clear that refugees seeking to move outside Asia and Africa face steep hurdles. Increasingly, they need to rely on the dubious help of traffickers and smugglers (Morrison and Crosland 2001).

Western states seemed, by the end of the 1990s, to have limited the "globalization of asylum," at least for the time being. They have done so by creating new penalties and disincentives for intercontinental movement by refugees and asylum seekers, thus countering the potentially liberating effects of globalization. Asylum has been re-regionalized. However, unlike in the early post–World War II period, when geography allowed refugees from Asia and Africa to be ignored, the regional confinement of most refugees is now dependent on the active intervention of Western states: It is a regionalism that is engineered.

Asylum's Future

What, then, is the future for asylum? For the time being, little seems likely to change. States in close proximity to refugee flows, mostly in Asia and Africa, are likely to remain the main (albeit reluctant) sources of asylum for most of the world's refugees. Most of these governments will face practical difficulties in sealing their borders against large-scale movements of refugees desperate for protection.

The asylum issue is unlikely to go away in the West, either. The recent decrease in the number of asylum seekers arriving in richer states reflects in part a more general decline in the number of the world's refugees. If refugee numbers rise again, so will pressures on Western asylum systems. Western states are entangled in a range of international and domestic legal commitments, notably the 1951 Refugee Convention, that, if not explicitly demanding that they accept asylum seekers, do require them not to return them to countries that would persecute or harm them. Indeed, in a development that cuts against the trend toward more restrictive practices regarding asylum seekers, the number and scope of such agreements have increased in recent years. The European Convention on Human Rights (1950) and the UN Convention against Torture and Other Cruel and Degrading Treatment (1987) have been incorporated, for example, into the domestic laws of many states. More fundamentally, Western states cannot publicly renounce the principle of asylum without bringing into question their self-identity as places where human rights are respected.

In the long run, it is possible that the insecurity and instability generated by the maldistribution of asylum may give the world's richest states an incentive to create a more just and equitable international regime for responding to refugees and asylum seekers. That said, it is not at all clear what this regime would look like and how it could be made politically viable. Until then, the responses of Western states will most accurately be described, to borrow a term used in a different context by Stephen Krasner, as "organized hypocrisy" (1999). States will continue, that is, to trumpet the importance of asylum for refugees while enacting policies aimed at preventing the arrival of as many asylum seekers as possible.

Matthew J. Gibney

See also: Asylum Determination; Border Controls; Burden Sharing; Clandestine Migration; Cold War; Economic Determinants of International Migration; Economic Effects of Migration; Indian Partition; League of Nations; Migrant Rights; Migration between Northern and Southern Countries; Migration Policy; Non-Refoulement; Refugees; Repatriation; Safe Country, Safe Third Country; Temporary Protection; Trafficking; UN Convention Relating to the Status of Refugees, 1951; UN High Commissioner for Refugees

References and further reading:

Brubaker, William Rogers. 1990. "Immigration, Citizenship and the Nation State in France and Germany: A Comparative Historical Analysis." *International Sociology* 5, no. 4: 379–407.

Castles, Stephen. 2002. "The International Politics of Forced Migration." In *Fighting Identities: Race. Religion and Ethno-Nationalism, The Socialist Register 2003.* Edited by Colin Leys and Leo Panitch. London: Merlin.

——— and Sean Loughna. 2005. "Trends in Asylum Migration to Industrialized Countries: 1990-2001." In *Poverty, Immigration and Asylum.* Edited by George J. Borjas and Jeff Crisp. London: Palgrave.

Chimni, B. S. 1998. "The Geopolitics of Refugee Studies: A View from the South." *Journal of Refugee Studies* 11, no. 4: 350–374.

Divine, Robert A. 1957. *American Immigration Policy, 1924–1952.* New Haven, CT: Yale University Press.

Gibney, Matthew J. 2004. *The Ethics and Politics of Asylum: Liberal Democracy and the Response to Refugees.* Cambridge: Cambridge University Press.

Gibney, Matthew J., and Randall Hansen. 2003. "Deportation and the Liberal State." UNHCR New Issues in Refugee Research Working Paper 77 (February). Geneva: UN High Commissioner for Refugees.

———. 2005. "Asylum Policy in the West: Past Trends, Future Prospects." In *Poverty, Immigration and Asylum.* Edited by George J. Borjas and Jeff Crisp. London: Palgrave.

Goodwin-Gill, Guy S. 1983. *The Refugee in International Law.* Oxford: Clarendon.

Joppke, Christian. 1999a. "Asylum and State Sovereignty: A Comparison of the United States, Germany and Britain." In *Challenge to the Nation State: Immigration in Western Europe and the United States.* Edited by Christian Joppke. Oxford: Oxford University Press.

———. 1999b. *Immigration and the Nation State: The United States, Germany, and Great Britain.* Oxford: Oxford University Press.

Kant, Immanuel. 1991 [1795]. "Perpetual Peace: A Philosophical Sketch." In *Kant: Political Writings.* Edited by Hans Reiss. Translated by H. B. Nisbet. Cambridge: Cambridge University Press.

Krasner, Stephen D. 1999. *Sovereignty: Organized Hypocrisy.* Princeton: Princeton University Press.

Locke, John. 1964 [1698]. *Two Treatises of Government.* Edited by Peter Laslett. Cambridge: Cambridge University Press.

Loescher, Gil. 1993. *Beyond Charity: International Cooperation and the Global Refugee Crisis.* New York: Oxford University Press.

Loescher, Gil, and John A. Scanlan. 1986. *Calculated Kindness: Refugees and America's Half-Open Door, 1945 to the Present.* New York: Free Press.

Milner, James. 2000. "Sharing the Security Burden: Towards the Convergence of Refugee Protection and State Security." Refugee Studies Centre Working Paper 4. Oxford: University of Oxford.

Morrison, John, and Beth Crosland. 2001. "The Trafficking and Smuggling of Refugees: The End Game in European Asylum Policy?" UNHCR Working Paper 39 (April). Geneva: UN High Commissioner for Refugees.

Plaut, Gunther W. 1995. *Asylum: A Moral Dilemma.* Westport, CT: Praeger.

Rees, Tom. 1982. "Immigration Policies in the United Kingdom." In *Race in Britain: Continuity and Change.* Edited by Charles Husband. London: Hutchinson.

Schuster, Liza. 2003. *The Use and Abuse of Political Asylum in Britain and Germany.* London: Frank Cass.

Suhrke, Astri. 1997. "Uncertain Globalization: Refugee Movements in the Second Half of the Twentieth Century." In *Global History and Migrations.* Edited by Wang Gungwu. Boulder: Westview.

United Nations High Commission for Refugees (1997). *State of the World's Refugees.* Oxford: Oxford University Press.

United Nations High Commission for Refugees (2000). *State of the World's Refugees 2000.* Oxford: Oxford University Press.

Van Kessel, Gerry. 2001. "Global Migration and Asylum." *Forced Migration Review* 10: 10–13.

Zolberg, Aristide R. 2001. "Introduction: Beyond the Crisis." In *Global Migrants, Global Refugees: Problems and Solutions.* Edited by Aristide R. Zolberg and Peter Benda. New York: Berghahn.

Asylum Determination

Asylum determinations are decisions made by sovereign states as to whether an individual's claim for refugee status is valid. Generally, a grant of asylum enables a refugee to remain in the host country, often permanently. To qualify for asylum, an asylum seeker must meet the requirements of the refugee definition set forth in the 1951 UN Convention Relating to the Status of Refugees and its 1967 Protocol as implemented by domestic laws. Procedures governing these individualized determinations vary among states and include both adversarial and nonadversarial proceedings and appeals.

The substantive and procedural law of asylum is complex, making the process a very challenging one for those asylum seekers who do not have legal representation. They may experience the proceedings through translation, may fear interactions with government officials generally, and may be held in detention. The challenges to decision makers are also considerable. They must understand the human rights conditions in the countries from which asylum seekers flee, and they also need detailed information on the persecution feared or experienced by the asylum seeker. Many states have faced significant problems in operating fair and efficient asylum systems, particularly when they receive very large numbers of applications. The European Union (EU), for example, received an annual average of 564,000 asylum applications throughout the 1990s, with 858,000 applications in 1992 alone (UNHCR 2001, 60). The United States faced a backlog of more than 425,000 cases in the mid-1990s (U.S. INS 2000, 7). Despite these numbers, reforms have enabled certain states to develop systems that reasonably balance the refugee's interest in protection and the state's interest in minimizing abuse. Until recently, only developed states had asylum determination systems in place, but this has begun to change.

The Initial Asylum Determination

In assessing whether an individual has a well-founded fear of persecution on account of race, nationality, religion, social group, or political opinion, decision makers examine both objective conditions in the country of origin and the individual's particular situation. Decision makers need access to current human rights information to understand country conditions. They also need to obtain information from the asylum seeker about his or her fear of persecution. This can be a challenging task, since refugees often have to leave their countries precipitously and thus rarely bring with them documentation of their plight. If applicants occasionally produce such documentation, it is often difficult for the decision maker to determine its authenticity. As a result, the credibility of the asylum seeker often becomes the critical issue in determining eligibility for refugee status.

Influenced strongly by national traditions, first-instance procedures may be informal or formal. Though many states have a specialized administrative body in charge of these proceedings, others, such as Spain and Greece, do not. The degree of independence that the responsible government agency holds in relation to immigration law enforcement varies from country to country. In most states, an officer of the specialized agency conducts a personal interview. Some states use a type of triage system, where adjudicators conduct informal interviews with asylum seekers, generally grant the stronger cases, and refer others to more formal, sometimes adversarial hearings conducted by administrative judges. In such hearings, more formal rules of evidence govern the proceedings, and a government attorney represents the state. Asylum seekers may or may not be represented.

Credibility

Establishing proof of the claimant's fear of persecution is one of the major challenges in asylum determinations. Unless the asylum seeker is a high-profile dissident, newspaper accounts concerning her political activities likely do not exist. Women raped as part of a policy of ethnic cleansing are unlikely to have medical records of any posttraumatic hospitalization. The claimant's testimony is most often the major factor in determining eligibility for refugee status. Decision makers, faced with figuring out whether that testimony is credible, often look for sufficient and plausible details that support the claim and make sense in relation to the human rights situation in a particular country. But what does it mean if the claimant provides different dates for certain important events described? What if the claimant relates his or her history in a halting manner? Or doesn't look the decision maker in the eye when providing testimony? Are these indicators of untruthfulness? Some decision makers interpret these actions as such; others do not. Considerable cultural knowledge is needed to interpret the behavior of asylum applicants, who come from all over the world. Difficulties in remembering dates are a common problem for victims of persecution.

Appeals

Developed-nation asylum systems have traditionally permitted some degree of review of the initial asylum decision to ensure consistency, guard against error, and encourage thoughtful decision making in the first instance. Most countries use an administrative appeals process initially. After the administrative appeal is exhausted, some states permit a judicial appeal. The appeals models differ in two important ways: the degree of independence of the adjudicators, and the substantive role they play.

The degree of independence of the administrative bodies varies considerably. The French appellate commission, the Commission de recours des réfugiés (the Refugee Appeal Committee), provides a model with considerable independence. Its members sit in panels of three, composed of a judge, a member of the board of the French Refugee Office (the office that makes first-instance decisions), and a representative of the UN High Commissioner for Refugees (UNHCR). The judge who chairs the panel may be a member of the Conseil d'état (the Council of State), the Cour des comptes (the Court of Accounts), an administrative appeals court, or an administrative tribunal.

The German administrative appeals model provides for considerable, but not complete, independence. Asylum applicants are entitled to appeal their claim to a single judge of the German Administrative Court. These judges are appointed for life but selected and promoted to higher courts by the minister of justice.

In the U.S. model, the administrative appellate decision makers who review asylum claims serve at the pleasure of the attorney general, who appoints them and can remove them. Thus, the members of the Board of Immigration Appeals (BIA) are not independent of the chief law enforcer in the United States. BIA asylum decisions may be appealed by right to the U.S. federal courts, where judges are appointed for life and are completely independent of law enforcement and any executive branch agency. Although no hard data is regularly published regarding the exercise of this right, one study estimated that appeals of BIA decisions increased from around 5 percent to 15–20 percent after 1999, when the attorney general instructed the BIA to issue summary affirmances without explanations (Dorsey and Whitney 2003, Appendices 24, 26). Approaches differ considerably with regard to the substantive role of the review adjudicators. The French Commission commonly questions appellants and has the power to ask for supplementary information. Until recently, the U.S. administrative appeals body had the power to conduct de novo review, that is, they could make factual as well as legal findings based on the record. A third model, such as in Canada, places considerable resources into the initial determination on the assumption that such a front-end system will require less of a review process. An adverse decision in the first instance is possible only if both members of the Convention Refugee Determination Division panel reject the claim. Consequently, the appeals focus is largely on issues of law rather than fact. Moreover, at the judicial level there is no guaranteed appeal, only a discretionary one.

The recent trend in the United States has been to limit very significantly the role of the review function in the asylum system. The 1999 decision to authorize summary affirmances in certain circumstances was only one of several major changes made to the administrative review process in order to address an increasing caseload and backlog. Changes initiated by Attorney General John Ashcroft in 2002 went considerably further to speed up the adjudication process, requiring the administrative appeals members to clear their current backlog of about 55,000 cases within 180 days. Each appellate judge had to decide thirty-two cases every workday, or one every fifteen minutes (Human Rights First 2002).

Professionalization of the Decision Makers

For most of the advanced Western nations, signing the 1951 Refugee Convention or its 1967 Protocol did not immediately translate into an infrastructure blessed with well-trained, capable decision makers, an efficient yet fair process, and resources adequate for the challenges of asylum. Most countries had their migration or border personnel in place to handle cross-border movements. The idea of creating a specialized corps of professional asylum officers came later.

The UNHCR Executive Committee noted in 1977 that only a limited number of parties to the convention or protocol had established procedures for the formal determination of refugee status. The committee recommended two basic requirements related to decision makers. First, it called for the regular immigration or border-control authorities to refer asylum seekers to higher-level decision makers, determining that "the competent official (e.g. immigration officer or border police officer) to whom the applicant addresses himself at the border or in the territory . . . should be required to act in accordance with the principle of *nonrefoulement* and to refer such cases to a higher authority." Second, decision making in the first instance, the committee said, should reside with "a clearly identified authority, wherever possible a single central authority" (UNHCR 1977).

Where governments have developed their adjudicatory staff as an independent, dedicated asylum corps, they have done so through recruitment and training. Recruitment has helped states develop professional asylum systems in two ways. First, governments have used recruitment opportunities to hire adjudicators with either appropriate educational backgrounds or work experience in the field. Such special asylum agencies exist in several of the major receiving countries, including Austria, Belgium, Germany, France, Italy, Switzerland, and the United States.

In response to markedly increasing caseloads, governments have also recruited significant numbers of such adjudicators. Together with computerization, significantly increased staff resources have enabled states to issue decisions in months rather than years. Demonstrating efficiency in the asylum system has helped states address public concerns about government control and send a deterrent message to those who would otherwise abuse the system.

Training of asylum adjudicators, both initially and as developments occur, is a second means some states have used to make their systems more professional ones. In addition to government experts, trainers may include experts from universities, UNHCR, and nongovernmental organizations (NGOs). The best training programs focus on both substantive and procedural knowledge and skills: asylum law; relevant international human rights law; country condition information; cultural awareness; sensitive issues such as gender, torture, posttraumatic symptoms, and child development; interview techniques; working with interpreters; and analytical decision-making techniques. To ensure that asylum adjudicators learn about newly evolving events in a particular country, understand how cultural factors affect particular ethnic groups applying for asylum, and keep abreast of new legislative and major case law developments, some states provide regular and up-to-date training.

Human Rights Documentation Centers

One of the key human rights developments in the second half of the twentieth century has been the documentation of conditions in most of the world's countries. These records of human rights violations have become a major source of information for asylum decision makers.

In 1992, UNHCR's Centre for Documentation and Research (CDR) responded to an increasing need for current, reliable country-of-origin information by collecting a full range of sources on country conditions and human rights. In 1996, CDR published the first edition of *Refworld,* a collection of databases, including databases on country conditions. The databases come from international, governmental, and nongovernmental sources. CDR established information exchange agreements with documentation centers in Canada, Switzerland, and the United States as well as with such NGOs as Amnesty International, Human Rights Watch, the Lawyers Committee for Human Rights, and the U.S. Committee for Refugees. Today, comprehensive information on country conditions and asylum law is available on the UNHCR website (http://www.unhcr.ch).

Several states that are major contributors to the UNHCR database, including Canada, Switzerland, and the United States, have developed sophisticated national information centers. Information is gathered from a variety of sources, including national and international governmental and nongovernmental organizations, human rights monitors, academics, publications, and online news services, to ensure that the information is accurate, balanced, and corroborated and that the most comprehensive picture possible is given of conditions in the countries of origin of asylum seekers. In addition to maintaining a database of information, certain of these national information centers disseminate regular news summaries regarding country conditions to their state's asylum adjudicators.

Women and Children Asylum Seekers

Women and children face particular challenges in asylum proceedings that international organizations and states started to address in the 1990s. In July 1991, UNHCR issued "Guidelines on the Protection of Refugee Women." These guidelines focused especially on protection issues for refugee women in camps but also addressed gender-related persecution and recommended procedures to make the refugee adjudication process more accessible to women. The guidelines discuss the fact that women who arrive as part of a family unit are sometimes not interviewed about their experiences even when they have been the targets of persecution. The guidelines also focus on the special problems that women face in telling adjudicators about various forms of sexual assault they may have suffered. In October 1993, the UNHCR Executive Committee recognized that asylum seekers who have suffered sexual violence should be treated with particular sensitivity, recommending the establishment of training programs designed to ensure that those involved in the refugee-status determination process are adequately sensitized to issues of gender and culture. Both Canada and the United States have adopted official guidelines on the analysis of gender-related claims to asylum. Both efforts were developed collaboratively after consultations with interested governmental and nongovernmental experts.

The international community has recognized as well that refugee children have different needs from adult refugees when seeking refugee status. In 1996, Canada established special procedures to make the asylum process more sensitive to the unique needs of children. UNHCR published guidelines on unaccompanied children seeking asylum in 1997, and the United States issued guidelines for children's asylum claims on Human Rights Day in 1998.

These guidelines acknowledge that children may not be able to articulate their claims to refugee status in the same way as adults, establish special procedures for adjudicating children's claims, and often adopt the best interests of the child as the relevant standard for assessing a child's claim. Specifically, the guidelines address evidentiary issues as well as the designation of a representative. The guidelines recognize that human rights violations against children can take a number of forms, such as abusive child labor practices, trafficking in children, rape, and forced prostitution. Special attention is paid to "child soldiers," children under the age of fifteen who are recruited into military operations. The guidelines also recognize that children experience persecution differently from adults and have special needs when it comes to presenting testimony at the asylum interview.

To ensure that the child's best interests are met, the guidelines allow a trusted adult to accompany and participate with the child at the asylum interview. The guardian's role is to bridge the gap between the child's culture and the asylum interview, to assist the child psychologically, and to serve as a source of comfort and trust for the child. The guidelines encourage the asylum officer to allow the trusted adult to help the child explain his or her claim; at the same time, they ensure that the child has the opportunity to express him- or herself. The guidelines were developed after consultation with international, national, local, and legal organizations involved with refugee children.

Lack of Representation

The asylum process in any state is very difficult to navigate for the untrained, let alone for individuals who often do not speak the language of the adjudicators and come from very different legal cultures. Moreover, the law itself, with developments from gender-related claims to the UN Convention against Torture and Other Cruel and Degrading Treatment (1987), is complex. Expertise on human rights conditions in many of the world's countries is needed. In the United States, for example, claims are made annually bearing on conditions in some 175 countries (Martin and Schoenholtz 1999, 595).

The data show just how significant representation is. First, represented claims are much more likely to be approved than pro se claims. In fiscal year 1999, for example, the U.S. immigration courts granted asylum claims four to six times as often in cases where the claimant was represented (Schoenholtz and Jacobs 2002, 743). Second, more than 80 percent of those who failed to appear at their hearings lacked representation (ibid., 742, 766). Many adjudicators and practitioners believe that when aliens are represented in proceedings, cases move more efficiently, economically, and expeditiously through the system. Issues presented for decision by the administrative courts and on appeal are more readily narrowed. Simply put, these observers argue, when aliens in proceedings or on appeal have legal representation, the system works better.

There are two different models of representation, and each has its problems. In the U.S. model, asylum seekers placed in proceedings are guaranteed the privilege of being represented by an attorney or other qualified legal representative, but at no expense to the government. Unfortunately, this system results in many claimants without representation: Two out of every three asylum seekers are unrepresented in the first instance (before an asylum officer), and still one out of every three lacks representation in formal proceedings before immigration judges (ibid., 742). Experts maintain that the current system has created great expense and delay for the federal government because cases are often continued for lengthy periods while aliens try to find pro bono counsel or counsel they can afford. Detention has had a particularly deleterious effect, as it is much more difficult for detained asylum seekers to obtain effective representation. The U.S. Congress continues to consider legislation that would provide legal representation for unaccompanied children.

In a second model, one used by several European states (Denmark, France, Netherlands, Sweden), lawyers are appointed to take up cases at government expense. Where legal aid is provided, however, free legal advice may be limited to the first instance or to the appeal, or the amount that the state may spend on legal aid may be wholly inadequate. The European Council on Refugees and Exiles, an umbrella organization of refugee NGOs, advocates that legal aid payments should reflect the time and disbursements required for competent representation and should be administered by a body independent of the executive arm of government. In both models, the quality of representation is very mixed.

Legal Information Programs

Given the complexity of asylum law and process, administrative judges are often hesitant to proceed in the absence of representation. The efficiency of asylum determination systems suffers when unrepresented individuals have to seek repeated continuances to find counsel, when extra time is required to identify and narrow the relevant legal issues, and when hearing times are extended because of unfamiliarity with the court procedures. Studies have now shown that facilitating access to legal advice and representation can improve the efficiency of proceedings while strengthening administrative courts' commitment to due process.

The studies to date have focused on immigrants and asylum seekers detained in the United States during their proceedings. More than 80 percent of these detainees were unrepresented in fiscal year 2003, for example, largely owing to poverty and the remote locations of detention sites (EOIR 2004). These individuals, often with limited education and proficiency in English, must navigate the labyrinths of U.S. immigration and asylum law alone. Many are confused about their rights, options, and prospects. Some unnecessarily delay their cases even though they are not eligible for relief, while others with meritorious claims erroneously waive their rights and are wrongly deported.

In 1989, the Florence Immigrant and Refugee Rights Project created a model legal orientation program at the government's Florence, Arizona, detention center. The program consisted of a live presentation for all detainees before or at the time of their initial administrative court hearing, with follow-up screening and case assessment for those without private counsel. Additional legal assistance, referral, or representation was provided when available. During fiscal year 1998, the U.S. Department of Justice (DOJ) funded a pilot project to document the benefits of such programs. Based on case data from the pilot, DOJ evaluators found that legal orientations saved both time and money for the government while also benefiting detainees. In addition, they found that such programs were useful management tools that "strengthen the capability of [the government] to operate safer detention facilities" (U.S. DOJ 1998, ii). In conclusion, the evaluators recommended that the government expand legal orientations to all U.S. immigrant detention facilities. The U.S. Congress has provided initial funding for such programs at several detention facilities. Experts believe that this model can also address the information needs of undetained asylum seekers and help make the asylum system more efficient.

Deterring Abuse

All the major receiving countries found themselves unprepared in the 1980s for the large increase in the flow of asylum seekers, resulting in lengthy processing times and large backlogs. These problems encouraged abuse and left the public with the sense that the government was failing to deal with a major problem.

Key reforms concerning the process, asylum benefits, and staff and computer resources have enabled certain states to address these challenges. One successful streamlining model involved triage: identifying the clearer cases that merited a grant of asylum quickly and referring the rest for more formal adjudication. Reasonable time constraints and incentives have been placed on adjudicators to ensure that decisions are completed within six months. Where benefits, such as work authorization, appeared to have attracted increased claims, reform has delinked such benefits from the asylum application. In such instances, the benefits have been provided only after the adjudicators have granted the claim, unless they were not able to make that decision in a timely fashion. Finally, states have significantly increased the number of adjudicators and dedicated greater computer resources to the asylum system.

Where these reforms have been applied comprehensively and seriously, they have resulted in effective systems that minimize abuse and grant asylum within six months to bona fide refugees. Accordingly, the success rates in such systems have been relatively high (50–60 percent of decisions on the merits), since many of those who previously abused such systems no longer had any incentive to do so.

Time Limits on Applications

To discourage abuse, states sometimes impose time limits for individuals to file asylum claims. Turkey requires that applications be lodged within ten days of entering the country. Pursuant to a 1996 law, the United States accepts applications filed within one year of the claimant's arrival in the country. Exceptions are granted only in cases involving changed circumstances that materially affect the applicant's eligibility for asylum or extraordinary circumstances relating to the delay in filing. Those who object to such time limits internationally argue that genuine refugees often have good reasons for failing to file their claims immediately or soon after arrival. Many refugees are traumatized. Unless they are in countries that provide them with food and shelter, their first priority is survival—finding relatives, friends, or others who will help them. Language barriers, as well as ignorance of the law, hinder compliance with such limits. Perhaps most important, filing a considered asylum application is extraordinarily difficult without help from a lawyer or other professional who specializes in asylum.

Cost

The most readily measurable impact of asylum is the cost to taxpayers to maintain an asylum adjudication process and to detain and/or care for and maintain asylum seekers. Governments complain of these costs, but relatively little documentation is available of the actual numbers. A 1995 study of fiscal impact focusing on Austria, Denmark, Finland, Germany (partial data), Norway, Sweden, and Switzerland estimated that the total annual state costs, including both processing and care and maintenance, amounted to almost $2.7 billion (not counting Germany) (Jandl 1995, 15).

Care and maintenance costs accounted for 93 percent of the total costs (ibid., 16). These costs included the cost of reception centers established to house asylum seekers until (1) a decision was made on their case or, (2) if granted status, they moved into their own accommodations. They generally also included social assistance and health care. Total care and maintenance costs varied greatly by country depending on the number and characteristics of asylum seekers and those granted some other form of protection. Average costs also varied, generally by the type and duration of aid. The duration, in turn, was dependent on the average processing time, the average time those who were granted asylum status were allowed to continue to remain in reception centers or otherwise receive assistance, work authorization, and other similar factors.

The processing costs accounted for $167 million, or 6 percent of total costs (ibid.), and included the funding of admissibility procedures (first instance and subsequent appeals), the legal representation of asylum seekers, and the return of rejected applicants. The proportion of costs attributable to processing varied by country, with Norway spending 13 percent of its costs on processing and Denmark and Finland spending less than 3 percent on these activities (ibid.).

Andrew I. Schoenholtz

See also: Asylum; Border Controls; Canada; Dublin Convention; Expedited Removal Procedures, U.S.; Gender and Migration; Migrant Rights; Migration Policy; Non-Refoulement; Readmission Agreements; Refugees; Safe Country, Safe Third Country; Schengen Agreement; UN Convention Relating to the Status of Refugees, 1951; UN High Commissioner for Refugees; U.S. Immigration; U.S. Immigration Legislation: Post-1945

References and further reading:

Beyer, Gregg A. 1992. "Establishing the United States Asylum Officer Corps: A First Report." *International Journal of Refugee Law* 4, no. 4: 455–486.

———. 1994. "Reforming Affirmative Asylum Processing in the United States: Challenges and Opportunities." *American University Journal of International Law* 9, no. 4: 43–78.

Boeles, Pieter, and Ashley Terlouw. 1997. "Minimum Guarantees for Asylum Procedures." *International Journal of Refugee Law* 9, no. 3: 472–491.

Dorsey and Whitney. 2003. *Board of Immigration Appeals: Procedural Reforms to Improve Case Management.*

European Council on Refugees and Exiles. 1999. *Guidelines on Fair and Efficient Procedures for Determining Refugee Status.* London: ECRE.

Harvey, Colin. 1997. "Restructuring Asylum: Recent Trends in United Kingdom Asylum Law and Policy." *International Journal of Refugee Law* 9, no. 1: 60–73.

Immigration and Refugee Board of Canada. 1996a. *Guideline 3. Child Refugee Claimants: Procedural and Evidentiary Issues. Guidelines Issued by the Chairperson Pursuant to Section 65 (3) of the Immigration Act.* Ottawa: Immigration and Refugee Board of Canada.

———. 1996b. *Guideline 4. Women Refugee Claimants Fearing Gender-Related Persecution. Guidelines Issued by the Chairperson Pursuant to Section 65 (3) of the Immigration Act. Updated Version.* Ottawa: Immigration and Refugee Board of Canada.

Jandl, Michael. 1995. *Structure and Costs of the Asylum Systems in Seven European Countries.* Vienna: International Centre for Migration Policy Development.

Lambert, Helene. 1995. *Seeking Asylum: Comparative Law and Practice in Selected European Countries.* Boston: Martinus Nijhoff.

Legomsky, Stephen. 1996. "The New Techniques for Managing High-Volume Asylum Systems." *Iowa Law Review* 81: 671.

———. 2000. "An Asylum Seeker's Bill of Rights in a Non-Utopian World." *Georgetown Immigration Law Journal* 14: 619.

Martin, Susan, and Andrew I. Schoenholtz. 2000. "Asylum in Practice: Successes, Failures, and the Challenges Ahead." *Georgetown Immigration Law Journal* 14: 589.

Schoenholtz, Andrew I., and Jonathan Jacobs. 2002. "The State of Asylum Representation: Ideas for Change." *Georgetown Immigration Law Journal* 16: 739.

United Nations High Commissioner for Refugees. 1991. *Information Note on UNHCR's Guidelines on the Protection of Refugee Women.* UNHCR Sub-Committee of the Whole on International Protection, 42nd Session, U.N. Doc. EC/SCP/67. Geneva: UNHCR.

United Nations High Commissioner for Refugees. 1977. ExCom Conclusion No. 8.

United Nations High Commissioner for Refugees. 2001. *State of the World's Refugees 2001.* Oxford: Oxford University Press.

———. 1997. "Guidelines on Policies and Procedures in Dealing with Unaccompanied Children Seeking Asylum." Geneva: UNHCR.

U.S. DOJ, EOIR. 1998. *Evaluation of the EOIR-Funded Rights Presentation Pilot Project.*

U.S. Immigration and Naturalization Service. 1995. *Considerations for Asylum Officers Adjudicating Asylum Claims from Women.* Memorandum from Phyllis Coven, Office of International Affairs. Washington, DC: U.S. INS.

———. 1998. *Guidelines for Children's Asylum Claims.* Memorandum from Jeff Weiss, Acting Director, Office of International Affairs. Washington, DC: U.S. INS.

———. 2000. *Asylum Reform: 5 Years Later.* Washington, DC: U.S. INS.

Wallace, Rebecca. 1996. *Refugees and Asylum: A Community Perspective.* London: Butterworths.

Weidlich, Sabine. 2000. "First Instance Asylum Proceedings in Europe: Do Bona Fide Refugees Find Protection?" *Georgetown Immigration Law Journal* 14: 642.

Widgren, Jonas, ed. 1994. *The Key to Europe—A Comparative Analysis of Entry and Asylum Policies in Western Countries.* Vienna: International Centre for Migration Policy Development.

Aussiedler

See Ethnic Germans

Australia

Australia has been a land of immigrants since the beginning of British colonization in 1788. The early colonial period was marked by genocide, dispossession, and racism against the Aboriginal population, while at the same time the colonies were integrating into the British Empire as suppliers of raw materials. Britain took an active role in providing workers through convict labor, assisted passages, and the encourage-

A family gets information about emigration to Australia from an official at the Department of Immigration at Australia House, the Australian High Commission in London. December 26, 1953. (Hulton-Deutsch Collection/Corbis)

ment of free settlement. In the mid–nineteenth century, Australian employers sought cheap labor in China, India, and the South Pacific Islands. Hostility from the Australian labor movement toward Chinese and other workers led to the White Australia Policy established by the Immigration Restriction Act—one of the first laws passed by the new Federal Parliament in 1901. Between 1901 and 1945, poor economic conditions led to low levels of immigration. Most immigrants came from Britain, but smaller groups came from Italy, Spain, and other European countries. During this period there emerged a distinctive sense of Australian nationhood as an outpost of British culture.

After World War II, domestic industrial expansion was an urgent priority. The Labor government pursued a policy of developing secondary industries in order to reduce Australia's need for imports and to eliminate too heavy a reliance on primary product exports. Australian industry was compelled to rely on dramatic increases in immigrant labor, mostly semiskilled and unskilled. The policy was to draw on permanent, family immigration, since both workers and consumers were needed. Another motive behind the race to increase the Australian population was the fear of invasion from Asia, which gave rise to the popular slogan "Populate or perish."

From the 1950s to the early 1970s, Australia experienced sustained economic growth, close to full employment, and price stability. Migrant labor was directed into infrastructure projects or heavy industry, with southern European workers highly concentrated in manual manufacturing jobs. Asian workers were considered unsuitable by a broad spectrum of Australian society, and even when the White Australia Policy was officially abandoned in the mid-1960s, Asian migration was at first restricted to a small number of middle-class people. In order to help migrants settle, a policy of assimilation was pursued. Multiculturalism was introduced in the early 1970s when it became evident that migrants were not assimilating as planned. In the mid- to late 1970s, Asian immigration began to increase, starting with the arrival of boat people from Indochina.

From the mid-1970s to the early 1990s, there was a consensus between the major political forces on a nondiscriminatory immigration policy and multicultural policies for ethnic communities. Immigration remained relatively high, with family reunion as the largest component of entries. In the 1980s, the Australian Labor Party (ALP) government emphasized the need to recognize cultural diversity as a basis for Australian social policy, citizenship, and identity. However, anti-immigration and antiminority sentiments began to grow throughout the 1980s based on fear of the growth in Asian immigration and a rise in unemployment. Some began to call for a curb on Asian immigration. In 1996, with the election of a new conservative government, Australian immigration policy was to enter a new era, with a weakening of multiculturalism, cuts in family reunion, and draconian measures against asylum seekers. The rise of the right-wing political party One Nation, and the increase in the number of boat people arriving on Australia's northern shores, also brought about a change in Australia's social and political landscape (Collins 1991; Castles et al. 1992; Jupp 2002).

Recent Immigration Patterns

Migration Flows

Australia started its postwar immigration program in 1947 with a plan to recruit permanent settlers from the United Kingdom and the rest of Europe. Today, migrants come from all over the world, and permanent settlers are expected to become citizens. They can apply for naturalization after two years—the shortest qualifying period anywhere. As well as permanent settlers, Australia now has many foreign temporary workers. At the same time, as many as 800,000 Australian citizens currently work abroad.

Entries of permanent immigrants have varied over the years depending mainly on economic and political factors. There were high intakes in boom years such as 1950 (185,000) and 1989 (145,000), but relatively low numbers in recession periods, such as in 1976 (53,000) and 1984 (69,000). An average of about 90,000 a year for the 1990s represents a slight decline in numbers compared with previous decades. But the target figures for 2002–2003, 100,000–110,000, indicated a return to higher levels.

Entry Categories

In Australia, permanent immigration has two components: the Migration Program, with categories for Family Stream and Skill Stream entrants; and the Humanitarian Program, for refugees and others admitted on humanitarian grounds. In addition, New Zealand citizens can enter and remain freely. Since 1996, the government has been reducing Family Stream arrivals relative to Skill Stream arrivals. In 1995–1996, the last year of the Labor government, family entrants made up 69 percent of all nonhumanitarian entrants, while skilled entrants constituted only 29 percent. By 2000–2001, family entrants were down to 45 percent and skilled entrants were up to 53 percent. At the same time, the number of New Zealanders has grown rapidly in response to economic conditions in both the sending and receiving countries. In December 2002, it was estimated that 450,000 New Zealand citizens were present in Australia, of whom 84 percent were in the labor force.

About 80 percent of those accepted in the Family Stream are spouses or fiancé(e)s of Australian citizens or residents (who may be earlier immigrants). The next largest categories are children and parents of existing citizens or residents. It is very hard for other relatives, such as siblings, nephews, or nieces, to enter as dependents. Until 1996–1997, members of this group who entered to take up employment were counted in the Family Stream as "Concessional Family," although they were still measured against the Points Test, which assesses employability according to a set of criteria including age, education, professional experience, and English-language knowledge. Since 1997–1998, this group has been counted in the Skill Stream. The program proposed to admit 60,700 in the Skill Stream and 43,000 in the Family Stream in 2002-2003.

Humanitarian Program targets have been fairly constant at around 12,000 since the early 1990s. Australia remains one of only about ten countries in the world that have resettlement programs to select refugees in countries of first asylum in collaboration with the UNHCR. The Humanitarian Program has two main components. The first part is an Offshore Resettlement Program, which includes two subcomponents: the Refugee Program, covering refugees as defined by the 1951 UN Convention Relating to the Status of Refugees, and the Special Humanitarian Program (SHP), for people who suffer gross human rights violations but would not qualify under the 1951 convention. The second main component is the Onshore Protection Program for people who seek asylum after they arrive in Australia, including boat people.

Since the mid-1990s, the number of Refugee and Special Humanitarian entrants has declined, while the number of Onshore Protection permits has increased. Some of these visas were granted to people who arrived by plane on a visitor visa and then claimed asylum, but increasing numbers went to boat people, mainly from Afghanistan, Iraq, and Iran. This trend has now been reversed, with Onshore Protection figures falling to 3,885 in 2001–2002. The number of persons arriving in Australia without permission averaged only a few hundred per year up to the late 1990s, but it went up to 920 in 1998–1999, 4,175 in 1999–2000, and 4,141 in 2000–2001 (Crock and Saul 2002, 24). Although asylum-seeker numbers in Australia are still very low compared with the figures from other parts of the world, especially Europe, some see the growth as undermining the tradition of strict government control of entries, which has hitherto been possible because of Australia's remote location.

Immigration and Population

Australia's immigration program has significantly altered the size and composition of the population. The 1947 census counted 7.6 million people, of whom 90 percent had been born in Australia, and most of those born overseas had come from the United Kingdom and Ireland. By the 1996 census, the population had more than doubled, to around 17.9 million, of whom 3.9 million (22 percent) were overseas-born. The 2001 census put the overseas-born population at 4 million, 23.1 percent of a total population of 18.8 million.

In 1971, 85 percent of the immigrant population came from Europe, half of this group from the United Kingdom. By 2001, the European share had fallen to 52 percent, with only 25 percent of the total immigrant population coming from the United Kingdom. Meanwhile, the share of immigrants to Australia born in Asia and the Middle East was up to 29 percent. People born in New Zealand made up 9 percent, a proportion that was quickly increasing. There were also 400,000 Aboriginals and Torres Strait Islanders (2.2 percent of the total population)—the only true "nonimmigrants" in Australia. However, apart from the Italians (1.4 percent of the total population), no group of non-British origin makes up more than 1 percent of Australia's population. The Australian people today consist of an Anglo-Australian majority and a large number of relatively small ethnic groups.

The dramatic impact of immigration on the size and composition of the Australian population is further illustrated by census data on second-generation Australians (children of immigrants). In 2001, 23 percent of the population was born overseas, and about a quarter of the population had at least one overseas-born parent. First- and second-generation Australians together made up about half of the population.

Institutional and Legal Frameworks

Institutional Structures

The importance of immigration for Australia is reflected in its institutional structures. In 1945, the ALP government set up a Department of Immigration, which had the task of organizing the postwar immigration program. There has been an immigration minister ever since. Despite many changes in name, the main function of the department (currently named the Department of Immigration, Multicultural and Indigenous Affairs, DIMIA) throughout this half century has been to plan and manage the immigration program. The broad lines of policy are laid down by the prime minister and cabinet.

Program implementation is the responsibility of the department in Canberra and its immigration officers, who are stationed in Australian high commissions and consulates around the world. Prospective immigrants (up to 1 million each year) apply to the nearest of these and may be interviewed and given medical and occupational tests. Decisions are made centrally by DIMIA, which issues visas to successful applicants. DIMIA is responsible for combating "people smuggling" and stemming unauthorized entry to Australia. This function of control and repression is reinforced by DIMIA's responsibility for a chain of detention centers to implement the mandatory detention of all persons who enter illegally (including asylum seekers). Some centers are in remote areas like Port Hedland (in northwestern Australia) and Woomera, a former rocket range in the South Australian desert that in April 2003 was quietly closed after strong resistance to living and social conditions by inmates and by their supporters outside. However, actual management of the camps is subcontracted to the private company Australasian Correctional Management, a subsidiary of a U.S. security corporation (Castles and Vasta, 2003).

Legal Structures

The main legislative basis for Australian immigration is the Migration Act of 1958. All foreigners who wish to enter Australia, with the exception of New Zealanders, have to apply for visas in advance. The 1973 Trans-Tasman Agreement lays down reciprocal rights of free entry for Australians and New Zealanders. There are few illegal entrants. However, in 2001 there were estimated to be 60,103 "overstayers"—people who entered legally but remained after their entry visas had expired. About three-quarters had been in Australia for over one year, and many worked illegally. It appears that DIMIA makes little effort to detect and remove overstayers, a sharp contrast with official reactions to boat people. This may be because many overstayers are from the United Kingdom, the United States, and other developed countries (Crock and Saul 2002, 23).

Once accepted for entry as permanent settlers, immigrants enjoy a range of rights that are denied in many other countries of immigration. Permanent settlers have access to all employment-related social security and medical benefits. However, in January 1993, the ALP government decided to deny unemployment and medical benefits to immigrants for the first six months after arrival. In 1996, the Liberal-National Party government sharply increased the waiting period for most welfare benefits to two years for new entrants. This policy has led to increased poverty among some new immigrants who discover they cannot find employment.

The centerpiece of Australia's approach to incorporating immigrants is easy access to citizenship. Historically, citizenship was closely linked to British identity. Australia has been considered an independent nation since 1901, but it did not have its own citizenship until 1949. Before that date, all persons born, registered, or naturalized in Australia were considered British subjects. The Nationality and Citizenship Act of 1948 created Australian citizenship, but it still defined Australians as British subjects. Naturalization required five years of residence, an oath of loyalty to the British monarch, and evidence of cultural assimilation. Such conditions deterred many immigrants. As ethnic diversity increased, the pressure grew for a more inclusive notion of citizenship. By 1984, the law had been renamed the Australian Citizenship Act, the waiting period had been reduced to two years, the English language requirements were relaxed, dual citizenship was permitted for immigrants seeking naturalization, and the oath of allegiance was to "Australia and its people" rather than the British queen. In 2002, the law was further amended to allow Australians living abroad to take another citizenship without losing their Australian one—recognizing the emergence of a global Australian diaspora (Cronin 2001). This change in the meaning of citizenship can be seen as one of the most important impacts of migration on Australian society. It is closely bound up with the rise of multiculturalism.

Settlement Policy: From Assimilation to Multiculturalism

Australia's postwar immigration policy was intended to create a culturally homogeneous, cohesive, white society. As it became apparent that not enough British immigrants wanted to come, recruitment was broadened to other parts of Europe, including Italy, Greece, and Spain. In its determination to maintain cultural homogeneity and to allay popular fears, Australia turned to assimilationism, the doctrine that immigrants could be culturally and socially absorbed and rapidly become indistinguishable from the existing Anglo-Australian population. During the 1950s and 1960s, this approach helped immigrants find work, settle, and become citizens. However, labor-market segmentation and residential segregation, together with inadequate schooling and experiences of racism, provided the conditions for community formation and cultural maintenance. It was in this context that the ALP government of 1972–1975 developed the policy of multiculturalism, a new model for managing ethnic diversity. Successive governments continued with multicultural policies, though reformulating them in accordance with specific political agendas.

Multiculturalism, however, is a policy for immigrants, not for indigenous Australians. Aboriginal people regard all other Australians as immigrants, arguing that their long history on the continent gives them native title to the land. Otherwise, they believe they have similar rights as other Australians as regards citizenship, the law, and social justice.

There have been four main phases of multiculturalism. The first phase, from 1972 to 1975, was concerned with migrant rights and participation. The ALP government aimed to redress class and ethnic minority disadvantages by improving educational facilities and social services and ensuring immigrant access to these. Two factors were vital to the reform of social policy: recognition of cultural difference and a willingness to work with ethnic community associations. For the first time, migrants were involved in the planning and implementation of relevant policies. Ethnic communities, community-sector associations, trade unions, and sections of the ALP called for full participation of immigrants in society and argued that it was the duty of the state to provide the conditions needed to achieve this.

The second phase, from 1975 until the mid-1980s, saw the development of the "ethnic group model." Multiculturalism was seen as a way of achieving national identity (usually referred to as "social cohesion") in an ethnically diverse society. The Liberal-Country Party Coalition's strategy was to redefine multiculturalism with an emphasis on cultural pluralism and the role of ethnic organizations in the provision of welfare services. There were problems with this approach. The funding structures locked ethnic organizations into dependency on the government. The official concept of the ethnic group was based on a reductionist and static view of culture emphasizing language, tradition, and folklore. There was a predilection for supporting ethnic cultural and social associations, but these organizations were generally led by men and often ignored the needs of women, children, youth, and other minorities in their communities.

A third phase, from the mid-1980s until 1996, moved toward a "citizenship model" of multiculturalism. The ALP government used the concept of "productive diversity" to argue that a multicultural population was better placed to respond to the challenges of increased international trade and communication, and above all to provide the opening to Asia, which was seen as crucial to Australia's future. "Mainstreaming" was introduced as a general principle for restructuring government services so that specific migrant services would be integrated into all government agencies and accessible to all (Castles 1997).

The most significant statement of this approach to multiculturalism was the *National Agenda for a Multicultural Australia* published by the Office of Multicultural Affairs (OMA) in 1989. Multiculturalism was essentially seen as a system of cultural, social, and economic rights and freedoms. These rights, however, were limited by an overriding commitment to the nation and a duty to accept the constitution and the rule of law, basic principles such as tolerance and equality, English as the national language, and equality of the sexes. The program OMA set forth was based on the recognition that some groups were disadvantaged by lack of language proficiency and education as well as by discrimination based on race, ethnicity, and gender.

The current phase marks a restricted and skeptical view of multiculturalism. During and after the March 1996 election, the Liberal-Coalition government declared that the needs of "ordinary Australians" (by implication a sort of Anglo-white mainstream) should be put above minority needs. It seemed initially that Australia's leaders would abandon multiculturalism and move back to the assimilationist approaches of the 1950s. The realities of Australia's culturally diverse society, however, made this step impossible, and the government decided to water down multiculturalism and redefine it yet again. In 2001, the Department of Reconciliation and Aboriginal and Torres Straight Islander Affairs was absorbed within a new Department of Immigration, Multicultural and Indigenous Affairs.

In December 1999, the government launched *A New Agenda for Multicultural Australia* (DIMIA 1999), which stated its clear support for the retention of the term "multiculturalism" to describe Australia's cultural diversity. Although the *New Agenda* largely endorsed the principles of the ALP's 1989 *National Agenda,* it reworked the core values as "civic duty, cultural respect, social equity and productive diversity." It argued in favor of multiculturalism as an inclusive concept in terms of nationhood and identity "for all Australians," stressing the importance of the links between multiculturalism and citizenship as a set of rights and obligations by citizens toward the state. This approach fitted well with the coalition's social policy of "mutual obligation" for welfare recipients.

An important message of the *New Agenda* lies in its attempt to counter the antiminority backlash that had been encouraged by the government's hostility to multiculturalism and its failure to effectively combat racism in the 1996–1999 period. The *New Agenda*'s attempt to support cultural respect through the notion of "inclusiveness," without coming to grips with the increasing social inequality and exclusion in Australian society, is unlikely to have much effect. This new version of multiculturalism is quite compatible with a return to the insular values of the 1950s and with exclusionary immigration policies. For many, this is a retrograde step, given that Australia, from the early 1970s to the mid-1990s, was often considered a world leader in terms of its multicultural policies for immigrants and minorities (compare Jupp 2001, 2002).

Immigration and Racism in Australia

The colonization of Australia as a British settler society, the establishment of the White Australia Policy, and various forms of cultural and institutional racism have created an atmosphere of resistance and struggle for successive waves of migrants. From the early 1970s until the early 1990s, Australia enjoyed a period of progressive politics with an interest in justice and equality. Despite this, there remained an underlying fear of difference and of change. Over the past ten years, two major events have shaped the Australian response to immigration. The first was the rise of a new political party—One Nation—and the second was the Tampa affair.

During the March 1996 federal election, conservative candidates criticized provision of special services for minorities. In one Queensland electorate, the Liberal Party candidate, Pauline Hanson, attacked services for Aboriginal people in such an extreme way that she was disendorsed as a candidate by her own party. Despite this, she won the seat as an Independent in one of the biggest anti-Labor swings in the country. This was widely taken as a signal that antiminority discourses were now seen as acceptable by a large share of the population. After the election, there was a trend toward racist politics and a rise in racist attacks in Australia. Hanson quickly set up the One Nation party, which sought to build on such feelings. In her inaugural speech in Federal Parliament, Hanson attacked Aboriginal people, called for an end to immigration and the abolition of multiculturalism, and warned of "the Asianization" of Australia (Hage 1998; Vasta 1999).

There are two underlying problems behind these feelings of grievance, shared by many Australians. One is that economic restructuring and globalization have severely affected workers, families, and communities. A second is that attempts to redress the disadvantages experienced by Aborigines, many migrants, and refugees have been misunderstood as "handouts" (Brett 1997). As a result, at the everyday level and in local communities the problems these groups faced became "ethnicized," so that migrants and indigenous Australians suffered an increase in personal abuse. In the 2001 federal election, the Howard government swept back into office on a tide of anti-immigration feeling, and Pauline Hanson complained bitterly that Howard had stolen her policies and her voters. By this time, One Nation was a spent force.

The rise of One Nation was a prelude to the very public rejection of asylum seekers in Australia since 2000, both by the government and by the Australian people. In the late 1990s, boat people began to arrive on Australia's northern shores. These were mostly Iraqis and Afghans being brought in from Indonesia, usually by fishing boats chartered by people smugglers. Numbers were not high by international standards, never going much above 4,000 in a year, but they provoked media campaigns and popular outrage. The reaction of the government was to modify Australia's refugee and asylum policy to such an extent that it has been accused of contravening the 1951 Refugee Convention (McMaster 2001).

Asylum issues came even more into the spotlight in August 2001, when the Norwegian freighter *MV Tampa* picked up more than 400 asylum seekers (mainly originating in Afghanistan and Iraq) from a sinking boat off northern Australia. The Australian government refused the captain permission to land the asylum seekers, and the *Tampa* anchored near the Australian territory of Christmas Island. This was the start of a saga involving international diplomacy, heated public debates in Australia, and feverish political activity. A country previously noted for its openness to refugees rapidly adopted a set of draconian laws designed to exclude asylum seekers. Australia exported the asylum seekers to its Pacific neighbors, Nauru and New Guinea—and spent vast sums of money to do so.

Events since 1996 have tarnished Australia's reputation as an open and tolerant society and as a "good international citizen." However, a political movement against the new intolerance seems to be emerging. Led by the churches, humanitarian groups such as Amnesty International, and elements of the ALP and the trade unions, it gives some hope that the pendulum will once again swing to more open policies in the future (Castles and Vasta 2003).

Conclusion

Australia has pursued a carefully planned and managed immigration program since 1945. Public opinion, political leaders, migrants themselves, and global changes have all influenced the shape of immigration and settlement policies. Against its original aims, Australia's immigration program has given birth to one of the world's most ethnically and culturally diverse societies, leading to major changes in culture, national identity, and citizenship. Because of its remoteness, Australia has been able to maintain tight controls on entry levels. This is changing, however, owing to global forces encouraging greater mobility. Politicians and the public are finding it hard to come to terms with such changes, as the recent disproportionate reaction to the growth in asylum-seeker arrivals reveals. The fears of loss of sovereignty and identity have also spilled over into the realm of social policy, leading to a questioning of multiculturalism. These are matters that will continue to concern Australia well into the twenty-first century.

Ellie Vasta

See also: Assimilation/Integration; Citizenship; Colonial Immigration; Dual Nationality; Economic Effects of Migration; Family Reunification; Multiculturalism; Naturalization; Public Opinion and Immigration; Resettlement; Skilled Migration; White Australia Policy

References and further reading:

Brett, Judith. 1997. "John Howard, Pauline Hanson and the Politics of Grievance." In *The Resurgence of Racism: Howard, Hanson and the Race Debate.* Edited by Geoffrey Gray and Christine Winter. Monash Papers in History 24. Melbourne: Monash University.

Castles, Stephen. 1997. "Multicultural Citizenship: A Response to the Dilemma of Globalisation and National Identity." *Journal of Intercultural Studies* 18, no. 1: 5–22.

Castles, Stephen, Bill Cope, Mary Kalantzis, and Michael Morrissey. 1992. *Mistaken Identity—Multiculturalism and the Demise of Nationalism in Australia.* Sydney: Pluto.

Castles, Stephen, and Ellie Vasta. 2003. "Australia: New Conflicts around Old Dilemmas." In *Controlling Immigration: A Global Perspective.* Edited by Wayne Cornelius, Phillip L. Martin, and James F. Hollifield. 2d ed. Stanford, CA: Stanford University Press.

Collins, Jock. 1991. *Migrant Hands in a Distant Land: Australia's Post-War Immigration.* Sydney: Pluto.

Crock, Mary, and Ben Saul. 2002. *Future Seekers: Refugees and the Law in Australia.* Sydney: Federation Press.

Cronin, Kathryn. 2001. "The Legal Status of Immigrants and Refugees." In *The Australian People: An Encyclopedia of the Nation, the People and Their Origins.* Edited by James Jupp. Cambridge: Cambridge University Press.

Department of Immigration and Multicultural Affairs. 1999. *A New Agenda for Multicultural Australia.* Canberra: AGPS.

Department of Immigration, Multicultural and Indigenous Affairs (Australia), http://www.immi.gov.au/.

Hage, Ghassan. 1998. *White Nation: Fantasies of White Supremacy in a Multicultural Society.* Sydney: Pluto.

Jupp, James. 2001. *The Australian People: An Encyclopedia of the Nation, Its People and Their Origins.* Cambridge: Cambridge University Press.

———. 2002. *From White Australia to Woomera.* Cambridge: Cambridge University Press.

McMaster, Don. 2001. *Asylum Seekers: Australia's Response to Refugees.* Melbourne: Melbourne University Press.

Office of Multicultural Affairs (Australia). 1989. *National Agenda for a Multicultural Australia.* Canberra: AGPS.

Vasta, Ellie. 1999. "Multicultural Politics and Resistance: Migrants Unite?" In *The Future of Australian Multiculturalism.* Edited by Ghassan Hage and Rowanne Couch. Sydney: RIHSS. Sydney University.

B

Bangladesh and India

Population movements have been an integral part of state-formation processes in Bangladesh and India, and the politics of partition and separation have been the primary factors triggering large-scale population movements. The "Great Calcutta Killing" of August 1946 and the riots of Bihar and Noakhali culminated in the Punjab carnage of March 1947. The violence and the subsequent division of India into two states in August 1947 resulted in the migration of about 8 million Sikhs and Hindus from the territory of the newly created state of Pakistan and, in addition, of 6 million to 7 million Muslims from various parts of India to Pakistan. The governments and peoples receiving these refugees supported them generously, and they soon became integrated into their newly adopted states.

Bangladesh

Bangladesh's acquisition of statehood in 1971 was marked by one of the largest refugee movements of the twentieth century, with 10 million people seeking refuge in India. Bengalis took shelter in the neighboring Indian states of Assam and West Bengal to escape massacre for their political and religious beliefs. The Indian government granted refugee status to millions and, along with the international community, mobilized resources to assist the refugees. Within nine months, Bangladesh was liberated and the refugees were back home. Their repatriation and rehabilitation processes were facilitated by international assistance.

Since independence, Bangladesh has experienced several rounds of refugee movements. It received more than half a million ethnic Rohingya Muslims in two waves from Burma, while tens of thousands of its own citizens, the people of the southern district of Chittagong Hill Tracts (CHT), crossed the border to Tripura, India. All these events have made Bangladesh both a refugee-producing country and a country of first asylum.

The refugee influxes from Burma, Bangladesh's eastern neighbor, occurred in 1978 and again in 1991–1992. The Rohingyas claim that the democratic government of U Nu in Burma recognized them as a separate ethnic group; however, this status was rejected by subsequent military governments, who viewed all Muslims of northern Arakan as recent arrivals from the adjacent Chittagong region of Bangladesh. As a result, the Rohingyas faced unfavorable conditions that ultimately forced many of them to leave Arakan. These conditions included the withdrawal of citizenship, institutional restrictions on movement, forced labor, and forced relocation of villages. Rohingyas were also subjected to religious persecution and various kinds of discrimination that ensured their exclusion from civil and military jobs.

The 1978 influx was preceded by Operation Dragon King in Burma, which aimed to "scrutinize each individual living in the State, designating citizens and foreigners in accordance with the law and taking actions against foreigners who have filtered into the country illegally"(Human Rights Watch 1996). The operation was accompanied by widespread human rights abuses and caused about 250,000 Rohingyas to seek refuge in Bangladesh. Following a bilateral agreement between the two governments, the refugees were sent back home within sixteen months of their arrival.

The next outflow of Rohingyas from the Arakan region of Burma began to take place after November 1991, when they began to arrive in Bangladesh in small batches. These numbers grew quickly, however, and were quite high between February and June 1992. At the peak of the refugee influx, a total of 270,000 were taking shelter in Bangladesh. The government of Bangladesh admitted the refugees and eventually accommodated them in twenty camps. International nongovernmental and UN agencies, including the office of the United Nations High Commissioner for Refugees (UNHCR), were invited to engage in refugee assistance programs. At the

Carrying their belongings, East Pakistanis trudge along at Satkhira as they flee to the Indian border in a bid to escape the fighting between Bangladesh troops and regular Pakistani forces. India recognized the East Pakistani rebel Bangladesh government as fighting continued between India and the forces of the Pakistani military government. (Bettmann/Corbis)

peak of the refugee situation, there were as many as thirty-two nongovernmental organizations (NGOs) working in the camps.

A major policy consideration for the government of Bangladesh had been the "quick and safe return" of the refugees to their country of origin. Bangladesh authorities considered the refugee problem to be a short-term one and signed a memorandum of understanding with Burma on April 28, 1992. Following a separate agreement between the UNHCR and the Burmese government, a repatriation process gained momentum. By the end of August, 204,000 Rohingyan refugees had been repatriated (UNHCR 1996).

By 2003, the bulk of the refugees had been repatriated. However, about 21,000 are still living in camps in Bangladesh under difficult conditions. The repatriation process has virtually come to a standstill. The number of children being born in the camps now exceeds the number of refugees repatriated.

A series of measures put into place by the government of Bangladesh have prevented the refugees from gaining any sense of belonging in the host country. It was not until mid-1996 that the government allowed formal schooling in some camps. In 2000, the distribution of vegetable seeds and chickens among vulnerable households was unofficially approved. The freedom of movement of the refugees has been restricted, and they are not permitted to seek employment or engage in any activities outside the camps.

The government of Bangladesh from the very beginning insisted that asylum for these refugees was temporary and encouraged their immediate return. However, several factors have prompted the UNHCR to suggest the (temporary) settlement of the Rohingyan refugees in Bangladesh. These include the unwillingness of the Burmese authorities to accept the repatriation of those refugees remaining; the reluctance of a large section of the refugees to return to a country where the incidence of forced labor and the violation of rights is still rampant; and the lack of enthusiasm on the part of donor agencies to continue to fund the Rohingya operation for an indefinite period without any durable solution in sight. The UNHCR's proposed policy of temporary integration would entail dismantling the camps and allowing refugees to engage in income-generating activities. The Bangladesh government has so far refused to consider any proposal that allows refugees to move out of camps, pointing to the fact that, as one of the most densely populated countries of the world with major resource constraints, Bangladesh can ill afford any such scheme. It further argues that such a measure could trigger a fresh influx of Rohingyas from across the border. With little prospect for repatriation to their country of origin in dignity in the foreseeable future, the Rohingya refugees indeed face a bleak future.

The hill people of the Chittagong Hill Tracts are the only significant group of Bangladesh citizens who are ethnically different from the majority community. Of the thirteen ethnic groups of the hills, the Chakmas are numerically the largest. The first forced displacement of Chakmas took place in the mid-1960s when the government of Pakistan constructed a dam on the Karnaphuli River as part of a hydroelectric-power project. Several thousand Chakmas migrated in response to the state of Arunachal in India. Bengali settlers started coming to the hill districts in the wake of the construction of the Kaptai Dam. Their numbers swelled as the then military government encouraged the migration of the Bengalis to offset the demographic imbalance generated by the departure of the hill people. By the 1980s, a full-scale insurgency ensued in the hills that led to a sharp buildup in the state security apparatus. Counterinsurgency operations by the Bangladeshi forces were accompanied by massive violations of human rights that soon became a matter of international concern. By 1987, refugee camps were set up to provide shelter to 60,000 hill refugees in the Indian state of Tripura. Following a series of negotiations with successive governments, during the tenure of the Awami League government a cease-fire was negotiated between the authorities and the political wing of the hill insurgents. Within a short period, most of the refugees returned, but many of the provisions of the peace accord remain to be implemented.

Discriminatory practices and fear of persecution by the majority community has also led to out-migration of the members of the Hindu community from Bangladesh. The Bangladesh Census record of 1991 estimated that the country's population included some 11.2 million Hindus, and a natural growth rate would put the figure at 16.5 million (Barkat, Zaman, and Poddar 1996). According to the same source, however, the 1991 figure represented a decline of 5.3 million Hindus since 1964. Two laws, the Defense of Pakistan Ordinance of 1965 and the Bangladesh Abandoned Property (Control, Management and Disposal) Order of 1972, are generally blamed for creating situations of fear and insecurity for the minority community and forcing its members to leave for India.

India

India has been a host nation of refugees from several bordering countries. Tibetans from Tibet, Bengalis from (what was then) East Pakistan, Tamils from Sri Lanka, Chakmas from independent Bangladesh, and Chins from Burma are some of the major refugee groups that have taken shelter in India.

The escape of the Dalai Lama and exodus of some 100,000 Tibetans took place soon after the establishment of Chinese rule in Tibet in 1959. Persecution and widespread human rights abuses (torture, forced sterilization, destruction of family units, and confiscation of property) by the Chinese authorities contributed to the exodus, as did the replacement of traditional Tibetan values and institutions by the Communists. More than 98,000 Tibetan refugees were successfully resettled in several Indian states. These refugees have been provided assistance to build houses. Infrastructural support, educational institutions, and civic amenities were also created for their rehabilitation.

In 1971, India was faced with the mammoth task of providing shelter to 10 million refugees from Bangladesh who were fleeing massacre by the Pakistani forces. The refugees were mostly hosted in camps set along the bordering districts of West Bengal, Tripura, and Assam. With the support of the international community, India mobilized a massive relief operation. After Bangladesh became independent, most of the refugees voluntarily repatriated within a year of their arrival.

Tension between the majority Sinhalese population and the minority Tamils has over time led to a series of Sri Lankan Tamil outflows from the island nation. Geographical proximity and ethnic affinity have made the south Indian state of Tamil Nadu a safe haven for many fleeing Sri Lankan Tamils. They arrived in India in different phases, but in all cases the flows were linked to the Sri Lankan Army's operations in areas controlled by the Liberation Tigers of Tamil Eelam (LTTE). In January 2002, there were 63,941 Tamils accommodated in 111 camps spread throughout Tamil Nadu. The Indian government's Sri Lanka policy also had major ramifications for the refugees. The competitive nature of Tamil Nadu politics and the central government's decision to arm the Tamil militants led to the establishment of a large number of militarized camps in the state (Suryanarayan 2003, 42). Over time, the Tamil Tigers emerged as one of the most effective guerrilla fighting forces in Asia. However, the assassination of Rajiv Gandhi by Tamil guerrillas in May 1991 brought about a major change in India's treatment of the refugees. The LTTE was outlawed, and the state government demanded immediate repatriation of all Tamil refugees. The central government responded by exerting pressure for repatriation and by curtailing some of the entitlements of the refugees.

India also hosts a good number of Burmese refugees. Soon after the military crackdown on the pro-democracy movement in August 1988, thousands of students and other political activists crossed into the bordering northeastern states of Manipur and Mizoram. Over the years, the two states have become safe havens for the persecuted ethnic communities of the Chin and Arakan states of Burma. The U.S. Committee for Refugees has estimated the number of Chin refugees in India at between 20,000 and 40,000 (USCR 1996, 104). In most cases, these refugees have fended for themselves. Recent improvement in the relations between India and Burma, exemplified by a joint commitment to curb and contain insurgency in the border region and the opening of cross-border trade between the two countries, may have adverse repercussions for the Burmese refugees (Datta 2003, 131).

India's treatment of refugees is not uniform but varies greatly across groups. The Tibetans have been the only refugees encouraged to settle permanently, for example. India has always insisted on the temporary nature of protection offered to other refugee groups. Tamil refugees enjoy free housing, medical care, and education; clothing and utensils are provided free of cost, and rice and kerosene are supplied at a subsidized rate. The state government also permits Tamil refugees to take up work outside the camps, a privilege not accorded to any other refugee group. Compared to other refugees in India, the Chakmas and Chins have received the least favorable treatment. The UNHCR has been given a very limited mandate in India and is permitted to assume responsibility for only 9.3 percent of all refugees in the country (Lama 2000, 38). Although the agency has been allowed to set up an office in New Delhi, it has not been granted access to any of the refugee groups or camps. It was only after an international outcry that UNHCR was allowed a nominal presence in the departure centers for Sri Lankan Tamil refugees.

In the absence of formal legal structures and procedures, the Supreme Court of India and the National Human Rights Commission have played a key role in safeguarding and promoting the rights of the refugees. In quite a few instances, these two institutions have restrained the government from forcibly expelling refugee groups and repatriating individual refugees.

The Need for Refugee Law

The complexity and magnitude of the problem of refugees and migratory movements are creating major tensions among the South Asian states. The blurring of the distinction between refugees, who are fleeing persecution and threats to their lives and liberty, and economic migrants is another major issue of concern. Neither Bangladesh nor India has signed any international agreements concerning refugees (including the 1951 UN Convention Relating to the Status of Refugees and its 1967 Protocol), nor does there exist any regional instrument governing their treatment in South Asia. The absence of refugee-specific legislation leads to ad hoc administrative measures under which asylum seekers run the risk of being deported to their countries of origin where their lives might be at risk. To safeguard the interests of those who flee persecution, states must make a distinction between genuine asylum seekers and those who cross the border for other (economic) reasons. It is only by developing a proper administrative structure through national legislation, or by acceding to the Refugee Convention, that such a distinction may be drawn and lasting protection accorded to the former.

Chowdhury R. Abrar

See also: Assimilation/Integration; Asylum; Civil Wars and Migration; Deportation; Development-Induced Displacement; Indian Partition; Mass Influx; Migrant Rights; Muslim Immigration; Pakistan and Refugees; Refugee Camps; Refugees; Repatriation; Return Migration; UN High Commissioner for Refugees

References and further reading:

Abrar, Chowdhury, ed. 2000. *On the Margin: Refugees, Migrants and Minorities.* Dhaka: Refugee and Migratory Movements Research Unit.

Barkat, Abul, Shafique uz Zaman, and Obhijit Poddar. 1996. *Impact of Vested Property Act on Rural Bangladesh, Dhaka* (mimeo). Dhaka: Association for Land Reform and Development.

Datta, Sreeradha. 2003. "Myanmarese Refugees in India: An Enquiry into Their Conditions and Status." In *The Elsewhere People: Cross Border Migration, Refugee Protection and State Responsibilities.* Edited by Omprakash Mishra and Anindyo J. Majumdar. New Delhi: Lancer.

Human Rights Watch Asia. 1996. "The Rohingya Muslims: Ending a Cycle of Exodus?" *Human Rights Watch/Asia* 8, no. 9 (September).

Lama, Mahendra P. 2000. *Managing Refugees in South Asia.* Occasional Paper 4. Dhaka: Refugee and Migratory Movements Research Unit.

Mishra, Omprakash, and Anindyo J. Majumdar, eds. 2003. *The Elsewhere People: Cross Border Migration, Refugee Protection and State Responsibilities.* New Delhi: Lancer.

Suryanarayan, Venkateshwaran. 2003. "Humanitarian Concerns and Security Needs: Sri Lankan Refugees in Tamil Nadu." In *Missing Boundaries: Refugees, Migrants, Stateless and Internally Displaced Persons in South Asia.* Edited by Padmanabha Ranga Chari, Mallika Joseph, and Suba Chandran. New Delhi: Manohar.

United Nations High Commissioner for Refugees. 1996. *Update: Voluntary Repatriation and Reintegration: Bangladesh/Myanmar Situation.* Geneva: UNHCR.

U.S. Committee for Refugees. 1996. *World Refugee Survey, 1996.* Washington, DC: U.S. Committee for Refugees.

Basic Law (Germany)

Germany's Basic Law (*Grundgesetz*) was the prime example of a constitutionally entrenched right of asylum. Following Germany's total defeat and near-total physical destruction in

Turks protest the recent killing of a Turkish family by neo-Nazi arsonists. Turks are unable to obtain German citizenship despite living in the country for many years. 1993. (David Turnley/Corbis)

World War II, the founders of the fledging Bonn Republic sought to develop a constitution that would avoid both the total centralization of National Socialism (1933–1945) and the unstable decentralization of the Weimar Republic (1919–1933). One provision, thought to be symbolic at the time, concerned asylum. Article 16 of the German constitution included a clause granting the right of asylum to anyone claiming political persecution. According to it, *"Politisch Verfolgte geniessen Asylrecht,"* or, in translation, "Persons persecuted on political grounds shall enjoy the right of asylum" (Basic Law 1977). The significance of the clause flowed from the fact that the right to asylum was entrenched in domestic law, not simply international law. A right to asylum in international law is the right of the state to grant it; a right to asylum in domestic law is the right to receive it. It was the most generous asylum law in the West, before or since.

The article was part of a postwar revulsion against the Nazi treatment of minorities and a recognition that Germans persecuted by the regime had been granted asylum elsewhere in Europe. The clause was added at a time when the German economy (and Germany itself) was only beginning to recover from total devastation. Most European refugees at the time (displaced persons) were either Germans themselves (expelled from former German territories in Eastern Europe) or direct or indirect victims of Nazi crimes against Europe; for the latter, Germany would not have been a preferred choice. Few would have predicted that Germany would ever be a destination for asylum seekers. From 1953 to 1978, asylum applications to Germany averaged 7,100 per year.

From the late 1970s, however, applications sharply increased; they passed the 100,000 mark in 1980. Applications reached 193,000 in 1990; 256,000 in 1992; and a record 438,200 in 1992. Pressure for a reform of the asylum law became irresistible. As the article was part of the constitution, the main political parties had to agree to the reform. Pressure was only intensified by a series of horrific attacks on foreigners, resulting in deaths in Rostock and Mölln. In December 1992, the Social Democrats reluctantly acceded to the Christian Democrat/Christian Socialist demand for change, and applicants coming from safe third countries and safe countries of origin were excluded from Germany's asylum provisions. The debate about asylum policy, however, did not end in 1993. Each new discussion of changes in immigration policy brings debate about asylum reform.

Jobst Köhler

See also: Asylum; Asylum Determination; Berlin Wall

References and further reading:

Basic Law of the Federal Republic of Germany. 1977. Bonn: Press and Information Office of the Federal Government.

Kaanstroom, Daniel. 1993. "Wer sind wir wieder? Laws of Asylum, Immigration, and Citizenship in the Struggle for the Soul of the New Germany." *Yale Journal of International Law* 18, no. 1: 155–210.

Münch, Ursula. 1992. *Asylpolitik in der Bundesrepublik Deutschland.* Opladen, Germany: Leske and Budrich.

Berlin Wall

The Berlin Wall was both a symbol of a divided Europe and a physical structure. The wall surrounded West Berlin, sealing it off from East Berlin and the adjacent areas of East Germany, during the period from 1961 to 1989. It cut thousands of Berliners, tens of thousands of Germans, and millions of Europeans off from the West. The barrier was erected in response to growing numbers of East Germans fleeing from East to West Germany. In the years between 1949 and 1961, some 2.5 million East Germans, including steadily rising numbers of skilled workers, professionals, and intellectuals, had made this passage (Borowsky 1993, 227), and their loss had threatened to destroy the economic viability of East Germany.

With the closure of the border between East and West Germany in 1949, following the "Berlin crisis" of 1948, West Berlin became the principal escape route for these refugees from the East. The East German Volkskammer (People's Chamber) took notice and decided to close off the last passage to the West. On the night of August 12–13, 1961, East German authorities blocked the main access routes from East to West Berlin with barbed wire and cinder blocks. They soon replaced these fences with a series of concrete walls (up to 5 meters high) topped with barbed wire and guarded by watchtowers, automated shooting devices, and mines. By the 1980s, this system of fortification extended 45 kilometers through Berlin, dividing the two parts of the city, and 120 kilometers around Berlin, separating it from the rest of East Germany.

The Berlin Wall became the symbol of the Cold War, dividing not only East and West Germany but also Eastern and Western Europe. About 5,000 East Germans managed to cross over to West Germany after the wall was constructed, often by adventurous means such as hot air balloons, tunnels, and the like. Another 5,000 failed in the attempt to do so and were captured by East German authorities. Ninety-one more were killed while attempting to cross. During the 1970s, a network of treaties, based on the Four-Power Agreement of 1971, progressively eased relations between the Eastern and Western blocs, increasing freedom of movement for West Berliners and Western visitors. From 1961 to 1988, 616,051 people from East Germany visited West Germany (Bade 1992, 402–403).

In 1989, the number of crossings began to rise dramatically. Large-scale migration in the summer of that year via Hungary (which had already begun dismantling its border controls) and mass demonstrations in Leipzig, Dresden, and elsewhere in the German Democratic Republic brought about the collapse of the Communist regime just after the ruling elite celebrated the fortieth anniversary of the East German state. More than 340,000 East Germans crossed the border into West Germany that year (ibid., 402–403). On November 9, the East German government opened the state's border with West Germany, making it possible for East Germans to travel freely to the other side of the wall. Almost immediately, people began hacking off pieces of the wall, and within a year it was almost gone. Today, there are only a few strips left in the city.

The opening of the Berlin Wall marked the end of the Cold War and the beginning of a new era of more intense East-West migration. Ironically, however, just when Eastern Europeans gained their freedom of movement, new barriers began to be erected along the eastern border of the European Union. Along with the Mexican border to the United States, the eastern border of the newly united Germany has become one of the most intensely guarded in the world. Considerable financial resources have been invested in border control. From 1992 to 1997, the German government increased the budget of the German border police from 1.9 billion to 3.05 billion German marks (Alt 1999, 234). Most of the investment went into personnel and more sophisticated technology for policing illegal migration. Although the physical barriers to free movement disappeared with end of the Cold War, new, less visible walls have been erected in the post–Cold War period.

Jobst Köhler

See also: Asylum; Border Controls; Cold War; Germany

References and further reading:

Alt, Jörg. 1999. *Illegal in Deutschland.* Karlsruhe, Germany: Von-Loeper-Literaturverlag.

Bade, Klaus. 1992. *Deutsche im Ausland, Fremde in Deutschland: Migration in Geschichte und Gegenwart.* Munich, Germany: C. H. Beck.

Bornemann, John. 1991. *After the Wall: East Meets West in the New Berlin.* London: Collins.

A group of West Germans peers over the infamous Berlin Wall (Library of Congress)

Borowsky, Peter. 1993. *Deutschland, 1945–1969.* Hannover, Germany: Fackelträger.
Gelb, Norman. 1986. *The Berlin Wall.* London: Michael Joseph.
Muenz, Rainer, and Ralf Ulrich. 1997. "Changing Patterns of German Immigration, 1945–1994." In *Migration Past, Migration Future: Germany and the United States.* Edited by Klaus J. Bade and Myron Weiner. Oxford: Berghahn.

Boat People

See Haiti and Refugees; Vietnamese Boat People

Border Controls

All states claim the sovereign authority to control who and what crosses their territorial borders. In order to monitor and regulate border crossers and to distinguish between citizens and noncitizens, states have over time created an expansive system of surveillance and identification involving passports, ID cards, and so on. Indeed, a border-control apparatus is a core attribute of what defines a modern state, and the right to refuse entry to noncitizens is a basic principle of international law. State restrictions on exit have historically also been of great importance, but with the spread of liberal democratic forms of government, freedom of exit has become the norm. The fall of the Berlin Wall and the demise of the Iron Curtain brought to an end the twentieth century's most famous state efforts to restrict exit. Cross-national population flows have increased in recent decades, however, the practical reality is that the vast majority of the world's inhabitants are not mobile and face formidable state-imposed obstacles to crossing national borders. These obstacles include restrictions against freedom of entry that limit, for example,

Border patrol agent Alan Marshall stands high atop a signal tower shining a searchlight into freight cars and grain gondolas as a slow-moving freight train pulls into Niagara, New York, on January 21, 2002, from Canada. Since the events of September 11, trains are searched coming and going along this route for any suspicious items coming into the United States as well as for possible terrorists trying to escape the country. Border patrol agents have been brought up from the southern border to help with increased security measures on the northern border. (UPI)

global labor migration. Even though global labor migration involves about 120 million people, this figure represents only about 2.3 percent of the world's population.

A popular view is that border controls are becoming outmoded in an age of "globalization," with some commentators even suggesting the idea of an emergent "borderless world." Greater economic integration and interdependence, it is often assumed, necessarily leads to a relaxation of state restrictions over cross-border flows. However, rather than simply eroding in the face of growing transnational pressures, the border regulatory apparatus of the state in many places is being recrafted and redeployed through ambitious and innovative attempts to regulate the transnational movement of people. This includes an infusion of more border-control personnel, the development of more sophisticated inspection technologies and more forgery-resistant border-crossing documents, reliance on carrier sanctions to encourage transport companies to self-police, and greater harmonization of visa policies and asylum laws.

The effort to tighten border controls is especially evident where advanced industrialized and less developed countries meet, such as the southern border of the United States and the eastern and southern borders of the European Union. Although there has been a general trend toward stricter controls over cross-border population flows in both places, there has been considerable variation in the particular form of such controls, reflecting distinct regional political and institutional contexts. Whereas border controls in the United States reflect a unilateral reassertion of national sovereignty, in Europe they represent a multilateral "pooling" of sovereignty. This has taken the most concrete form through the 1985 Schengen Agreement, which calls for the abolition of internal EU border inspections within "Schengenland" and at the same time a harmonization and tightening of external border inspections. What were once viewed exclusively as national borders and national controls have now become part of a new European space of free movement insulated by a hardened external border. EU border controls must therefore be understood within the broader institutional framework and process of European integration. Also, U.S. controls are largely concentrated along the southern border, whereas EU controls extend more deeply into society. In many European countries, this includes the use of national identity cards and more extensive regulation and monitoring of the workplace. EU controls also reach further outward than in the U.S. case: Neighboring countries to the east increasingly cooperate with Western European immigration-control objectives as part of the price of future formal incorporation into the European Union.

Though border controls take different forms in the United States and the European Union, border enforcement officials in both places nevertheless face the same basic conundrum: how to turn their borders into more secure barriers while also assuring that they remain business-friendly bridges. Today's borders are expected to serve as filters that "weed out" undesirable flows while also encouraging desirable ones. Mounting domestic political pressure has necessitated that U.S. and EU leaders signal their commitment to stricter border controls and project at least the appearance of securing their borders. Economic realities, however, necessarily limit the degree to which they can truly seal their borders. Balancing the policy objectives of simultaneously *facilitating* ever-increasing cross-border economic exchange and *enforcing* border controls will continue to be an inherently cumbersome and politically sensitive task in an increasingly integrated world.

Peter Andreas

See also: Berlin Wall; Carrier Sanctions; European Union; Passports; Schengen Agreement; Visas

References and further reading:

Anderson, Malcolm. 1996. *Frontiers: Territory and State Formation in the Modern World.* Cambridge: Polity.

Andreas, Peter, and Timothy Snyder, eds. 2000. *The Wall around the West: State Borders and Immigration Controls in North America and Europe.* Lanham, MD: Rowman and Littlefield.

Torpey, John. 2000. *The Invention of the Passport: Surveillance, Citizenship, and the State.* Cambridge: Cambridge University Press.

Bosnia-Herzegovina

See Bosnia-Herzegovina and Refugees; Ethnic Cleansing: Bosnia-Herzegovina

Bosnia-Herzegovina and Refugees

The post–Cold War period was marked by the reemergence of ethnic conflicts in several regions of the world. Those in the former Yugoslavia, and particularly in Bosnia-Herzegovina, had significant implications for European and world politics, not least of which concerned refugee-protection policies. Responses to killings and detentions in concentration camps on a scale unseen in Europe since World War II included the creation of "safe areas" and the development of temporary protection policies in Western Europe. These responses were also a reflection of the ongoing process of European integration, coming at the exact moment when formal harmonization of asylum and immigration policies across the European Union (EU) was being formulated as a new goal, and at a time when the role of the United Nations High Commissioner for Refugees (UNHCR) and the relevance of the 1951 Convention Relating to the Status of Refugees were coming into question.

Background

On February 29 and March 1, 1992, a referendum on independence was held in Bosnia-Herzegovina. Sixty-three percent of Bosnians turned out to vote—many of them Bosnian Serbs, although the Serb nationalist party had called for a boycott. More than 99 percent of the voters opted for full independence. The republic had, along with Croatia, Macedonia, and Slovenia, requested recognition from the European Community (EC) in late December 1991. The referendum had been one condition set by the EC, which in January had considered the risk of ethnic conflict in the republic to be too high for it to qualify for EC recognition. On March 3, 1992, the republic declared itself independent, and on April 6 the EC Foreign Ministers meeting in Luxembourg recognized that independence as starting from April 7. Fighting intensified in the days preceding the recognition of the independence of the republic. According to some reports, Yugoslav National Army snipers and Serb nationalist militants opened fire on crowds demonstrating for peace between the three communities. "Ethnic cleansing," a practice that had become commonplace during the preceding year in other republics, particularly Croatia and Serbia, saw hundreds of thousands driven from their homes. In a state television interview, Bosnian Muslim leader Aliya Izetbegovic advocated the evacuation of the wounded, elderly, and ill from the city of Zepa. There were, he said, worse things than ethnic cleansing, namely ethnic killing. But the ethnic cleansing, and the refugee and displacement crisis to which it gave rise, provided perhaps the more complex political challenges for Western European states.

In 1991, Bosnia-Herzegovina, one of the six constituent republics of Tito's Yugoslavia, had almost 4.5 million inhabitants. Slav Muslims constituted the largest group within the republic and made up 44 percent of the population. Bosnian

Civilians flee the riots in Vitez with the assistance of British UN troops during the Yugoslavian Civil War. Conflict among the Croats, Serbs, and Muslims in Bosnia began when Bosnia declared independence in early 1992, several months after other regions of Yugoslavia entered into war. (Patrick Robert/Sygma/Corbis)

Serbs made up 31 percent, and Bosnian Croats 17 percent. Tito's reconstitution of the country saw Bosnia-Herzegovina restored to its pre-1918 borders in a state in which overt manifestations of nationalism were proscribed and strict limits imposed on the practice of religion. With Tito's death in 1980, the nonethnic, nonreligious grip of the Communist Party on power began to slip. The slippage was complete when Slobodan Milosevic, who sought to recentralize Yugoslavia under a single, powerful leader, putting an end to the system of a rotating presidency among federal republics, rose to power within Serbia. Slovenia was the first republic to attempt to leave the federation. It did so peacefully; Croatia's departure in 1991, however, saw serious fighting and the beginning of ethnic cleansing campaigns. With Slovenia and Croatia recognized as independent states, the leadership of Bosnia-Herzegovina was virtually forced to take the steps leading to the referendum of 1992. At that point, the war came to Bosnia-Herzegovina, and the ethnic cleansing became institutionalized.

Ethnic Cleansing and Displacement

Human Rights Watch reported that the Serb forces occupying territory in Bosnia-Herzegovina were removing non-Serbs from these areas in order to make them ethnically homogeneous. This "cleansing" involved executions, detentions, confinement to ghetto areas, and forcible displacement or deportation of Muslims (the majority) or Croats (Helsinki Watch 1992, 63). In some cases, non-Serbs were taken by commandeered bus to international border-crossing points and expelled from the country. The non-Serbs were required to show documentation, including a passport, however, in order to leave the country. They were also required by the expelling authorities to provide proof that they had purchased a ticket for transportation out of the country. The non-Serbs would pawn the few remaining valuables they had in order to honor the deportation or expulsion notice rather than risk death. As the war developed, Bosnian Muslim and Croat forces carried out the same practice.

People were leaving the country for a variety of reasons, in a variety of ways, and, where possible, to a range of destinations. Those with long-standing international connections and sufficient resources left the country through fear of a conflict, which was all but inevitable, given that the divisions of Yugoslavia were all based on ethnic lines and that this multiethnic republic had never been an independent state. Then people started to leave their homes while battles were taking place, as a result of the ethnic cleansing, or because of other impacts of the war on the civilian population. Those who were not deported were sometimes able to reach the homes of family members or friends or large refugee centers in the other former republics of Yugoslavia. Croatia, for example, was described at the time by some as becoming a giant refugee camp, while Bosnia-Herzegovina became a giant war zone. Some tried to seek safety in more distant Western states or waited in Croatia or Slovenia for opportunities for resettlement to the United States, Canada, or Australia.

By summer 1992, one in every three inhabitants of Bosnia-Herzegovina was homeless (some 1.5 million people). A total of 2.3 million people had been displaced by the conflicts in the Balkans, and 1,885,000 of them remained in the former Yugoslavia. Some 850,000 of these were internally displaced in Bosnia-Herzegovina, many of them trapped in enclaves that would become "safe areas"; 628,000 were internally displaced or refugees in Croatia (including in the Serb-occupied zones); 382,500 refugees were registered in Serbia; 48,500 in Montenegro; 31,000 in Macedonia; and 70,000 in Slovenia. A significant number of refugee arrivals showed up in other European countries—particularly those neighboring Yugoslavia or with long-standing Yugoslav communities from earlier economic migrations. Some 200,000 claimed refugee status in Germany; 60,000 in Hungary; 50,000 in Austria; 44,000 in Sweden; and 12,200 in Switzerland. Italy had received 7,000 refugees, and the United Kingdom 1,100.

"Safe Areas"

The international community shied away from organizing the movement of people out of Bosnia-Herzegovina, though it might have saved lives, on the grounds that any such resettlement could play into the hands of the ethnic cleansers. As newly independent states, neither Slovenia nor Croatia had developed an asylum system. These neighboring countries nevertheless began to offer what they called "temporary refuge" to people leaving Bosnia. Slovenia, later backed by Croatia, also started to push the wider international community to establish havens within Bosnia in which people would be assisted and protected. A "safe haven" had already been attempted in northern Iraq in the early 1990s as a means of protecting Iraqi Kurds from Saddam Hussein's regime. The UN High Commissioner for Refugees, Sadako Ogata, was highly critical of the idea, however, saying it would be unworkable. In the meantime, internal displacement rose constantly. José Maria Mendiluce, a senior UNHCR official in the Balkans, later admitted that the UNHCR had chosen "to have more displaced persons and refugees, rather than more dead bodies."

Venezuela picked up the safe haven initiative in the UN Security Council, proposing a resolution (on which it and Pakistan ultimately abstained) that in its final iteration toned down all language on military protection for the areas to be established. In 1992, before any "safe area" had been declared, General Philippe Morillon, trapped by a clearly desperate population and under the eye of the world's TV networks, declared that the town of Srebrenica would come under UN protection. Those images and the general's words led to higher expectations for this first formally declared safe area than for the others established in Bihaæ, Tuzla, Zenica, Zepa, Gorazde, Sarajevo, and Mostar. These safe areas concentrated the vulnerable populations in easy target centers. Although, as long as they remained accessible, they allowed more effective distribution of aid by the UN and nongovernmental organizations (NGOs), they also provided visible and concentrated targets for the Serbs, and it was feared that access would be cut off or attacks orchestrated against them.

The fact that symbolic protection was all that was on offer became tragically apparent in July 1995, when Serb forces easily took Srebrenica from a small Dutch battalion, killing at least 7,000 Bosnian males from the enclave and displacing the entire remaining population. Shortly afterward, Zepa also fell. A report by the Dutch Institute for War Documentation, finally published in April 2001, led the Dutch government of the day to resign. The report found that the Dutch battalion had been sent on a mission without a clear mandate to a place still not clearly defined in international agreements or Dutch law. They were given the task of keeping a nonexistent peace with no specific training for the task, no intelligence support, no air support, and no exit strategy. Under such circumstances, the soldiers could hardly protect themselves, never mind protect tens of thousands of displaced persons. Of concern to many analysts at the time was also the fact that the soldiers seemed to be in place to protect Western European states from having to deal with an influx of refugees as much as to protect people on the ground.

Temporary Protection

Although various forms of what could be called temporary protection had existed in European states for decades, real political debate about temporary protection in the form in which it is understood in Europe at the start of the twenty-first century really emerged in response to the movement of Bosnian refugees. As the conflict in Bosnia progressed, following as it did from the one in Croatia, European Union member states started to impose visa restrictions. Croatia refused entry to Bosnians who could not offer proof that they intended to transit through the country—and without a visa, such proof was difficult to provide. Croatia and Slovenia started to offer temporary refuge. Given that many of the people who fled Bosnia appeared to want to return to their homeland, and as countries in the region were facing a potentially enormous influx, governments in the European Union started to offer temporary protection rather than full UN Refugee Convention status to those who arrived. Despite the beginnings of EU integration on asylum matters, European states created different policies.

Statistical criteria for documenting arrivals from Bosnia varied enormously across European states. In some cases, all Bosnians were counted as "former Yugoslavs" and grouped together. This method sidestepped the question of ethnic cleansing. In other cases, temporary protection policies prevented recognition of asylum claimants. And in still other cases, former Yugoslavs who had been in a Western European country for years suddenly became counted as "refugees" from the conflict. It is therefore difficult to make statistical comparisons. Nevertheless, to some extent it is possible to determine how refugees from the crisis were dispersed.

In 1992, according to the *World Refugee Survey* published by the U.S. Committee for Refugees, Germany sheltered 220,000 former Yugoslavs; Sweden 74,000; Austria 73,000; Italy 17,000; the Netherlands and Denmark 7,000 each; the United Kingdom 4,900; Spain 4,600; and France 4,200. Belgium, Finland, and Luxembourg each received between 1,000 and 3,500. Norway accepted 3,700 former Yugoslavs, Switzerland 70,000. Hungary sheltered 40,000. By the end of 1995, there were 320,000 Bosnians in Germany; 50,000 in Austria; 10,000 each in France and the Netherlands, and several thousand in Sweden, United Kingdom, Denmark, and Belgium. Italy sheltered 59,000 former Yugoslavs. Apart from the neighboring states of Italy and Austria, the major receiving countries in the European Union were Germany and Sweden. The simple fact that the member states were each facing different pressures in terms of the numbers of arrivals (varying from just dozens to tens of thousands) led to a lengthy discussion on "burden" or "responsibility" sharing across Europe.

The European states not only had different conceptions of what "temporary" meant (for example, should it last for two years, three years, or five years?) but also paid various levels of attention to the desire for the "refugees" to return or to integrate. Some focused on gradual integration, but all explicitly said the protection would be short-term—many then highlighting return as the desired outcome. The conflict, however, went on for so long, and was ended with such uncertainty, that the majority of "temporarily" protected Bosnians remained in Western Europe.

Return

Although states and refugees focused on return, when the end of the conflict came with the Dayton Accords in 1995 it was not clear that return would be possible for all refugees, at least in the sense of being able to go back to the homes they had occupied prior to the conflict. Bosnia-Herzegovina was in a state of unofficial partition: For many people a real return "home" would mean a return to an area in which they belonged to a minority group, with all the fear this would entail.

The UNHCR started overseeing returns to Bosnia with a phased approach, wishing first to see the internally displaced go back to their towns and villages, then those who were in neighboring states, especially Croatia and Slovenia, and finally those who had gone further away. Some states stood in the way of this plan, enforcing the return of Bosnians by putting them on aircraft or "encouraging" their return through the removal of status and welfare benefits. When Germany sought to return a large group of Bosnians by involuntary means in 1996, the United States, architects of the Dayton Accords, stepped in to resettle the refugees, sure that they would not yet be safe in Bosnia.

The return process progressed slowly but eventually showed signs of success, if success can be measured in numbers alone. On February 6, 2003, UNHCR announced that more than a million people had returned to their prewar homes in Bosnia. Some 390,000 of these had returned to "minority areas," thereby reversing the ethnic cleansing of the war. Seventy percent of all property that could be reclaimed in Bosnia had been reclaimed, according to the refugee agency.

The Legacy of Bosnia

The conflict in Bosnia-Herzegovina scarred the landscape of the country and the lives of its people. It also marked distinct changes in approach to refugee protection, particularly in the European context. "Safe areas" proved, in retrospect, to be poorly protected, unsafe enclaves, and though the approach of creating safe areas has been tried since, it has largely been discredited. Temporary protection proved not to be as temporary as states wished it to be, and the concept gradually became refined as an administrative tool for mass influx situations—although its legacy lives on in the gradual undermining of the UN Refugee Convention and the limitations put on forms of subsidiary protection. Some countries, the Netherlands being the first, even made *all* protection for refugees temporary in the first instance, with a move to permanent status becoming possible only after three years when no change can be observed in the situation in the country of origin that caused the problem. "Ethnic cleansing," or attempted genocide, proved virtually impossible to counter or prevent, and forced displacement used as a weapon of war continues to present a moral challenge to the international community. However, one of the lessons of the Bosnian returns is that refugees often can and do return when the time is right, and that ethnic cleansing, to some extent, can thus be reversed.

Joanne van Selm

See also: Asylum; Civil Wars and Migration; Deportation; Ethnic Cleansing: Bosnia-Herzegovina; Ethnic Cleansing: Croatia; European Union; Genocide; Germany; Humanitarian Intervention; Internally Displaced Persons; Refugee Camps; Refugees; Resettlement; Temporary Protection; UN Convention Relating to the Status of Refugees, 1951; UN High Commissioner for Refugees

References and further reading:

Glenny, Misha. 1992. *The Fall of Yugoslavia: The Third Balkan War.* London: Penguin.

Helsinki Watch. 1992. *War Crimes in Bosnia Hercegovina.* New York: Human Rights Watch.

Hyndman, Jennifer. 2003. "Preventive, Palliative, or Punitive? Safe Spaces in Bosnia-Herzegovina, Somalia and Sri Lanka." *Journal of Refugee Studies* 16, no. 2: 167–185.

Johnston, Russell. 1993. "Information Document: The Yugoslav Conflict—Chronology of Events from 30th May 1991 to 8th November 1993." Information Document to the Defence Committee, 39th sess., Western European Union, A/WEU/DEF (93) 14, Paris, November 29.

Mendiluce, José Maria. 1994. "War and Disaster in the Former Yugoslavia: The Limits of Human Action." In *World Refugee Survey 1994.* Washington, DC: U.S. Committee for Refugees.

Nederlands Instituut voor Oorlogsdocumentatie (NIOD). 2002. *Srebrenica: A Safe Area. Reconstruction, Background, Consequences and Analyses of the Fall of a Safe Area.* Amsterdam: NIOD, http://www.srebrenica.nl/en/a_index.htm April 2002.

Riedlmayer, Andras. 1993. *A Brief History of Bosnia-Herzegovina.* The Bosnian Manuscript Ingathering Project, www.kakarigi.net/manu/briefhis.htm.

Van Selm-Thorburn, Joanne. 1998. *Refugee Protection in Europe: Lessons of the Yugoslav Crisis.* The Hague: Kluwer.

World Refugee Survey. 1993. Washington, DC: U.S. Committee for Refugees.

World Refugee Survey. 1994. Washington, DC: U.S. Committee for Refugees.

World Refugee Survey. 1995. Washington, DC: U.S. Committee for Refugees.

World Refugee Survey. 1996. Washington, DC: U.S. Committee for Refugees.

Brazil

The arrival and settlement of immigrants in Brazil is linked to a set of economic, social, and demographic transformations still under way in Europe that started halfway through the twentieth century. These transformations have been called a "demographic transition" and are usually attributed to the spread of capitalism in Europe and around the world as well as to major political trends (Bassanezi 1995, 3). Indeed, throughout this period intense social change led to population excess in several regions of the globe, especially in Europe and Asia, which in turn caused interoceanic migration on a large scale.

In Brazil at the end of the nineteenth and the beginning of the twentieth century, the expansion of agricultural exports and the ensuing appearance of an industrial estate in the city of São Paulo attracted investments to the regions concerned, generating the need for free labor, slavery having been abolished. In addition, the immigration policies taken up by the Brazilian government were largely linked to the ideology of whitening the population among those who saw the European immigrant as the ideal medium through which to achieve this aim. There was a certain degree of resistance to Asian immigration among the elite, who may have feared the social and cultural implications these population groups would have for a society already strongly marked by the African blacks, who had been enslaved for three centuries. Some segments of Brazilian society also perceived a need to strengthen their European ethnic and cultural foundations. Around 1902, however, the Italian government's decision to ban the subsidized emigration of laborers to Brazil, due to the appalling living conditions that the immigrants had to endure, led the authorities to accept Japanese immigrants to work on the coffee plantations, which at that time were going through a boom. But industrial firms were also enjoying a boom, especially in São Paulo, and it was the internal migration of coffee plantation workers to the cities to work in factories that created conditions encouraging the arrival of immigrants of Asian stock.

Although completely reliable data are not available, it is known that between 1836 and 1968 the largest contingents of immigrants to Brazil were Portuguese and Italian, totaling 3.38 million people. This group was followed by Spanish, German, and Japanese immigrants, who together accounted for 1.22 million, and a third group, comprising Russians, Austrians, Turks, Poles, and French immigrants, totaling 400,000. In all, there were 5 million people hailing from different parts of Europe and Asia. Some cultural diversity was thus counterbalanced by a clear European prevalence. Most of these immigrants headed for the rich regions of southeastern and southern Brazil. In the southeastern states of São Paulo, Minas Gerais, and Rio de Janeiro, they were housed on the coffee farms, where they worked and received salaries. In the southern states—Paraná, Santa Catarina, and Rio Grande do Sul—they typically settled on land of their own.

After World War II, this flow was supplemented by new waves of immigrants, especially from Arab countries, who headed off to regions of rubber production in the north of

Families searching for a better life immigrate by bus, with all of their belongings, to undeveloped territories of the Amazon such as Rondonia and Acre. (Stephanie Maze/Corbis)

Brazil (the Amazon region). Since then, many Syrians and Lebanese immigrants have settled in Brazil's urban areas, where they have engaged in retail business, especially in the textile industry. Many of them came to Brazil only because restrictive U.S. immigration policies prevented them from entering the United States, their first choice of destination. In the 1970s, the profile of foreign immigrants changed once again as company executives and qualified professionals, employees of multinational corporations, began to arrive in greater numbers.

From the 1980s, there was a significant decline in registered immigration to Brazil. Demographers started to consider Brazil a "closed population," that is, a population in which the entry and exit of immigrants showed only a residual importance in population growth rates. At that time, internal migration, which had started in the mid-1950s and gained momentum in the 1960s and 1970s, still seemed to predominate, albeit with less intensity than in the past. This migration was caused both by expulsion factors, such as the great droughts in northeastern Brazil, and the resulting poverty, and by the attraction generated by job opportunities in the southeast, especially in São Paulo and Rio de Janeiro (Singer 1973). An enormous labor contingent came from several parts of the country to work in the building boom that took place in the new capital, Brasília, and many of these workers remained, giving rise to numerous satellite towns. In the São Paulo metropolitan area, the growth of the industrial estate, and especially of the construction sector, became the main factor attracting national migrations. In the late twentieth century, millions of workers were attracted to this urban area. Other national metropolises and medium-sized cities were also points of attraction during this period, changing Brazilian society from rural to predominantly urban, so much so that by the end of the century 81 percent of the Brazilian population was living in cities.

The world economy has had a significant impact on migratory flow in Brazil, causing it to decrease. This impact was particularly harmful to the migrant working population, which started to make up an impoverished and discriminated contingent now seen in large Brazilian cities. Even so, in the 1990s internal migratory flow was still important in all regions of the country, and between 1991 and 1996, according to a population count carried out by the Brazilian Institute of Geography and Statistics (IBGE 1996), about 2.7 million Brazilians moved from one region to another within the country.

The 1991 census showed that Brazil was no longer a closed population. Indeed, it revealed significant migratory movement, both because of Brazilians going abroad and because of foreigners entering the country. Immigration to Brazil continues, even if on a smaller scale than at the start of the twentieth century (Carvalho 1996). Some analysts have expressed a worry, however, that government policies favor the immigration of big investors over the common worker (Milesi and Contini 2001). The policies have been criticized as being "highly restrictive and discriminatory" because they privilege "a minority of specialized immigrants" and "the transfer of financial and technological resources to specific sectors," excluding those who might "come to fill the needs in less skilled sectors, such as sewing" (Silva 2001, 499).

Concerns have also been expressed about the large influx of Latinos from neighboring countries (Bolivia, Peru, Paraguay, Chile, Uruguay, and Argentina). The Latino presence became more intense during the 1980s and more firmly established in the 1990s, especially in São Paulo, in other large urban centers, and in towns near the national borders. A large number of these immigrants have been illegal. In 1996, the various consulates estimated that there were 80,000 Bolivians, 4,000 Peruvians, 40,000 Chileans, 20,000 Paraguayans, 10,000 Uruguayans, and 11,500 Argentinians in the city of São Paulo (Silva 2001, 490). Slave labor is commonly found, often in commercial outlets or small production firms owned by their compatriots, not only among Latinos but among Chinese and Korean immigrants. This disrespect for human rights has often been denounced by the Catholic Church and other groups in Brazilian society and has resulted in some cases in amnesty, legalization of immigrants, and advances in immigration law.

The foreigners welcomed to Brazil have also included refugees, mostly from Angola and other African and Asian countries, fleeing war and political or religious persecution. Some refugees have come from Latin American countries such as Cuba, Peru, and Argentina. The 2,731 people living in Brazil who have been granted refugee status come from a total of forty-eight countries, of which 80 percent are African. In several cases, they arrived without knowing where they had landed, as they were escaping a home country on the first boat that would take them in, or in containers with an unclear destination. In spite of the small number of refugees who have taken up residence in Brazil, the country's legislation on the issue is one of the most advanced in the world, allowing the concession of work documents and free access to the labor market. In addition, Brazilian legislation has extended the concept of refugee to include victims of general human rights violations. On top of this, the CONARE (*Comité national para os refugiados,* the National Committee for Refugees) was set up.

By the end of the twentieth century, the immigration situation in Brazil had undergone a complete reversal from what had existed at the end of the nineteenth century. Instead of receiving people from other countries, the nation had started to export labor to the developed nations of North America and Europe as well as to Japan. This phenomenon is part of the process of the globalization, productive restructuring, and "flexibilization" of work relationships (Sassen 1988). This process has driven immigration by limiting job opportunities, especially for the young in their country of origin, leading them to seek better opportunities and living conditions abroad (Piore 1992; Bógus 1995, 1997; Sales 1999). Those affected are primarily young people who have attained an educational level higher than the national average, and in the countries of destination they end up carrying out activities well below their professional qualifications.

It is estimated that around 1.8 million Brazilians currently live outside the country, mostly in the United States (about 800,000), mainly in the Boston area, and in Japan (about 220,000). The other outflows headed mainly to Germany (about 60,000), Portugal (about 51,000), Italy, Switzerland, and France. At present there has been a greater presence of Brazilians in Portugal, as the language makes settling there easier than in other countries, and also because of the greater difficulties imposed on immigrants by the United States and other European countries. A bilateral agreement signed in 2003 between the Brazilian and Portuguese governments legalized the situation of thousands of Brazilians living in Portugal, allowing their entry into the labor market. The emigration of qualified labor nevertheless is a great loss to Brazil.

The mobility of the labor force in today's globalized environment is greater than at any other period of history. Brazil has both benefited and suffered from the economic trends of the twentieth century, and immigration trends have followed suit. Key political, social, and economic events, and above all the exigencies of capital, will continue to influence Brazilian demographic changes in the twenty-first century.

Heloisa Szymanski and Lúcia Bógus

See also: Clandestine Migration; Italian Migration Worldwide; Japan; Migration between Northern and Southern Countries; Refugees

References and further reading:

Bassanezi, M. A. B. 1995. "Imigrações Internacionais no Brasil: um panorama histórico." Pp. 1–38 in *Emigração e Imigração no Brasil contemporâneo.* Edited by Neide Lopes Patarra. São Paulo: FNUAP.

Bógus, Lúcia. 1995. "O Brasil no contexto das Novas Migrações Internacionais." *Travessia a revista do migrante* 7, no. 21: 5-8.

———. 1997. "Globalização e Migração Internacional: o que há de novo nesses processos." Pp. 165–174 in *Desafios da Globalização.* Edited by L. Dowbor et al. Rio de Janeiro: Vozes.

Brazillian Institute of Geography and Statistics (IBGE). 1996. Contagem de População.

Carvalho, J. A. M. 1996. "O Saldo dos Fluxos Migratórios Internacionais do Brasil na Década de 80: Uma tentativa de estimação." Pp. 227–238 in *Migrações Internacionais: Herança XX, Agenda XXI.* Edited by Neide Lopes Patarra. São Paulo: FNUAP.

Milesi, Rosita, and Nadir Contini. 2000. *Migrantes e Refugiados no Brasil: Realidade e Desafios.* www.migrante.org.br/artigo3outubro.doc

Piore, M. J. 1992. *Birds of Passage: Migrant Labour in Industrial Society.* Cambridge: Cambridge University Press.

Sales, Teresa. 1999. *Brasileiros Longe de Casa.* São Paulo: Ed.Cortez.

Sassen, Saskia. 1988. *The Mobility of Labour and Capital.* Cambridge: Cambridge University Press.

Silva, Sidney. 2001. "Hispano-Americanos no Brasil: entre a cidadania sonhada e a concedida." Pp 489–501 in *Migrações Internacionais: Contribuições para políticas.* Edited by M. G. Castro. Brasília: Comissão Nacional de População e Desenvolvimento.

Singer, Paulo. 1973. *Economia Política da Urbanização.* São Paulo: Brasiliense.

Britain

See United Kingdom

Burden Sharing

Burden sharing is the mechanism through which the diverse costs to a state of granting asylum to refugees are more equitably divided among states. The obligation of nonrefoulement, inscribed in the 1951 UN Convention Relating to the Status of Refugees, generates highly uneven refugee burdens. Germany and Tanzania, for instance, received a hugely disproportionate share of their regions' refugees in the 1990s. Although no binding obligation to engage in burden sharing exists under international law, the desirability of burden sharing (also referred to as "responsibility sharing") has been expressed in a number of international agreements and has been codified in some regional instruments. Historically, burden sharing has been successfully undertaken on an ad hoc basis. In recent years, however, a perceived lack of burden sharing has led some states to restrict asylum. This tension has resulted in a renewed debate on the desirability of more formalized burden-sharing arrangements. There is also a growing recognition of the need to address the diversity of burdens that may be associated with the presence of refugees in host states, including environmental, social, economic, and security burdens.

The importance of burden sharing is outlined in paragraph 4 of the preamble to the 1951 Refugee Convention, which states that "the grant of asylum may place unduly heavy burdens on certain countries, and . . . a satisfactory solution . . . cannot therefore be achieved without international cooperation." Similar statements have been repeated in other international declarations, most notably in Article 2(2) of the 1967 Declaration on Territorial Asylum and in several conclusions set forth by the Executive Committee (EXCOM) of the UN High Commissioner for Refugees (UNHCR). Although these statements suggest the desirability of burden sharing, they do not constitute binding obligations. International refugee law clearly states that the primary responsibility for protecting and assisting refugees rests with the country of asylum.

Some regional agreements, such as Article II(4) of the 1969 Organization for African Unity Convention, do bind member states to burden-sharing obligations. Nevertheless, historically the most significant burden-sharing arrangements have been ad hoc and situation specific. Agreements such as the Comprehensive Plan of Action (CPA) and the Plan of Action of the 1989 International Conference on Central American Refugees (CIREFCA) are the most prominent examples of large-scale, coordinated approaches to burden sharing. These arrangements, involving a wide range of states and organizations, were developed in response to specific crises and included elements of temporary protection, financial assistance, and refugee resettlement.

Recent crises, especially in the Great Lakes region of Central Africa, have illustrated the limitations of an ad hoc approach. In response to an absence of sufficient international support, a number of host states, especially the poor states of the South, have adopted more restrictive asylum policies. This trend has rekindled the debate on the desirability of more formalized burden-sharing mechanisms.

In academic circles, much debate has been generated by the work of the Reformulation Project (Hathaway and Neve 1997). The findings of the project were premised on the understanding that, given recent changes in the international political landscape, ad hoc burden-sharing arrangements are only possible in increasingly rare circumstances. The project authors argued that refugee protection advocates must actively seek solutions in line with state interests and premised on a more "robust" understanding of temporary protection. They further concluded that the institutions of the international refugee regime need to be "retooled" to "promote and coordinate a process of collectivized responsibility," to ensure confidence among states. Burden sharing would be more effectively administered if it took place in the context of prenegotiated undertakings within groups of states and organizations with common interests. Many academics and practitioners have been critical of the reformulation approach. It has been argued, for example, that prenegotiated arrangements to deal with refugees will not work because states would see it in their best interest to shift the burden to others (Suhrke 1998).

In international politics, developments toward more organized burden-sharing arrangements have generally been slow. There has been an express reluctance on the part of northern states to enter into such arrangements. When burden sharing was discussed at the forty-ninth session of EXCOM in 1998, there was widespread support among states for the concept of burden sharing and for greater cooperation for advocacy and fundraising, but not for new global burden-sharing mechanisms. Regional developments have proven more promising, however, especially within the European Union. A European Council decision in September 2000 created a European Refugee Fund that provides financial assistance to member states "in receiving and bearing the consequences of receiving refugees and displaced persons." A total of EUR216 million was released to allow for the establishment of the new fund, with appropriations to be made annually.

Recent discussions have also led to developments in the way burden sharing is understood. There is a growing consensus that traditional approaches to burden sharing do not effectively address the range of burdens refugees may impose on countries of asylum. It is now widely recognized that host states may face economic, environmental, social, and security burdens when hosting refugees. Comprehensive approaches to burden sharing are increasingly likely to address issues beyond protection, assistance, and durable solutions to include broader development, peacekeeping, and peacebuilding activities.

James Milner

See also: African Union; Asylum; Comprehensive Plan of Action; Economic Effects of Migration; European Union; Non-Refoulement; Temporary Protection; UN Convention Relating to the Status of Refugees, 1951; UN High Commissioner for Refugees

References and further reading:

Anker, Deborah, Joan Fitzpatrick, and Andrew Shacknove. 1998. "Crisis and Cure: A Reply to Hathaway/Neve and Schuck." *Harvard Human Rights Journal* 11: 295–310.

Hathaway, James C., ed. 1997. "Reconceiving International Refugee Law." *Nijhoff Law Specials* 30. London: Martinus Nijhoff.

Hathaway, James C., and R. Alexander Neve. 1997. "Making International Refugee Law Relevant Again: A Proposal for Collectivized and Solution-Oriented Protection." *Harvard Human Rights Journal* 10: 115–211.

Milner, James. 2000. "Sharing the Security Burden: Towards the Convergence of Refugee Protection and State Security." RSC Working Paper 4. May. Oxford: Refugee Studies Centre, University of Oxford.

Shuck, Peter J. 1997. "Refugee Burden-Sharing: A Modest Proposal." *Yale Journal of International Law* 22: 243–297.

Suhrke, Astri. 1998. "Burden-Sharing during Refugee Emergencies: The Logic of Collective versus National Action." *Journal of Refugee Studies* 11, no. 4: 396–415.

Thieleman, Eiko R., ed. 2003. "European Burden-Sharing and Forced Migration." Special issue. *Journal of Refugee Studies* 16, no. 3.

United Nations High Commissioner for Refugees. 1998. *Annual Theme: International Solidarity and Burden Sharing in All Its Aspects: National, Regional and International Responsibilities for Refugees.* UN Doc. A/AC.96/904. September 7. Geneva: UNHCR.

Burundi and Refugees

With neighboring Rwanda, the nation of Burundi has shared a tortuous history of escalating ethnic violence exploding at intervals—in 1965, 1972, 1988, and 1993—resulting in the deaths of countless ethnic Hutu and Tutsi and the displacement of hundreds of thousands of refugees of both ethnic groups. The consequence of this violence has been the solidification of ethnic hatreds and the emergence of a continuous state of civil war that has destabilized this Central African nation since 1994.

Burundi's countryside, rising from the coastal plains of Lake Tanganyika to the continental divide, retains much of the charm that led early European observers to liken it to an equatorial Switzerland. On its densely populated hillsides graze herds of long-horned cattle, while its volcanic soils are cultivated in banana groves, manioc, and beans for local consumption and coffee and tea for export. Since independence in 1963, however, a succession of ethnic confrontations and genocidal reprisals has left a legacy of unforgettable horror, and for many Burundians, permanent displacement. This pattern of periodic repression and consequent dispersal of populations separated by periods of tense anticipation has, since 1993, given way to a more consistent and ongoing experience of attack, reprisal, and flight common to centers of conflict around the world.

Refugees from Burundi's turmoil, however, quite unlike those in Somalia, Yugoslavia, or most noticeably Rwanda, have remained relatively invisible to the international media. Perhaps for this reason, Burundi's displaced populations have never been fixed in the world imagination as archetypal refugees. Nonetheless, as a host nation, taking in refugees from neighboring states, and as the point of origin for hundreds of thousands of refugees fleeing to Tanzania, Congo, and Rwanda, the refugee experience has been central to the solidification of ethnic identities in Burundi and to the emergence of a state of near-permanent hostilities between Tutsi and Hutu, the two dominant ethnic groups in this densely populated nation.

"Tribal Warfare" in Burundi—A Western Construct?

Contrary to Western conceptions, tribal identities and ethnic hatred are not immutable features of Burundi's history;

Hutu refugees who have fled the interethnic massacres in Burundi live in precarious conditions packed into very basic camps around Butare, Rwanda. 1988. (Alain Nogues/Corbis Sygma)

rather, "tribal" loyalties have only gradually acquired the concrete form that they exhibit today. Western journalists and policy makers have unfortunately simplified conflict in Rwanda and Burundi as a centuries-old hatred between physiologically and culturally distinct tribal groups. The Tutsi are thus described as the tall, slim, graceful, and haughty descendants of Nilotic herdsmen and warriors who some 500 years ago descended upon and rapidly subjugated the short, thickset Hutu cultivators and their predecessors in the area, the Twa. A Belgian census completed in 1934, which serves as the benchmark for all later discussions of ethnic representation, classified the population as 84 percent Hutu, 14 percent Tutsi, and 1 percent Twa.

In fact, these numbers belittled the shared language and traditions of all three groups and disguised a number of alternative social divisions, reifying the Tutsi and Hutu confrontation. The experience of colonial rule under Germany (1899–1916) and Belgium (1919–1962) contributed in important ways to hardening the Tutsi-Hutu dichotomy as European administrators, informed by theories of racial superiority, strengthened the Tutsi monarchy. Following independence in 1962, the failure of Burundi's new monarch, Mwami Mwambutsa (1916–1965), and of the traditional institutions of monarchy to balance dynastic interests, intra-Tutsi rivalries with regional and historic roots, and ethnic competition led to the collapse of the kingdom and the end of Burundi's relative ethnic harmony.

From the "Rwandan Revolution" to the Coup of 1965

Nothing so galvanized Tutsi anxieties or heightened Hutu political expectations as did the Rwandan Revolution and the consequent flood of Tutsi refugees into Burundi. Beginning in 1959, Rwandan Hutu intelligentsia engineered the overthrow of the Rwandan mwami and united a divergent Hutu populace around an ideology of Hutu nationalism reinforced by periodic repression of the Tutsi minority. Rwandan Tutsi fled the country, resettling in Burundi, Uganda, Tanzania, and the Congo. By 1966, nearly 54,000 Tutsi had taken refuge in Burundi, grouped primarily in camps in the eastern part of the country (Hamrell 1967, 14). The presence in Burundi of Rwandan Tutsi introduced a new measure of urgency to the country's simmering ethnic politics. The specter of the Rwandan model, and the encouragement of Rwandan refugees, inspired certain Burundi Tutsi to consider the possibility of preemptive measures to forestall Hutu aspirations in Burundi. The assassination of Hutu moderate Pierre Ngendandumwe in 1965 carried out by a Rwandan Tutsi refugee with the backing of a hard-line Burundi Tutsi faction illustrates this coalescence of interests. Rwandan refugees also heightened existing interethnic competition for positions in education, civil service, and the army. Comparatively well-educated Rwandan Tutsi rapidly rose to positions of importance within the educational bureaucracy, private business, and civil service. Their very presence reduced the opportunities available to native Hutu, and their influence within these institutions increased inequities and outright hostility to Hutu political and occupational aims.

In 1965, electoral successes by Hutu political candidates signaling a heightened Hutu political consciousness, and a failed coup attempt by Hutu army officers, ultimately resulted in the collapse of the Burundi monarchy—Mwami Mwambutsa fled the country in fear—and tragically to the collapse of Burundi's traditions of ethnic compromise. Following the coup attempt, virtually every Hutu leader faced imprisonment, some eighty-six were sentenced to die, and between 2,500 and 5,000 Hutu throughout the country were summarily executed (Lemarchand 1970, 418). An untold number left the country for haven in surrounding states. By July 1966, a junta of army commanders, led by Captain Michel Micombero, overthrew and exiled Mwambutsa's successor, Charles Ndiziye, establishing a republic on the fragile foundations of Tutsi political and military supremacy. Under the First Republic, intra-Tutsi political rivalries, coupled with the continued politicization of intertribal relations, ultimately resulted in the genocide that Hutu remember simply as "1972."

1972: "Selective Genocide" and Diaspora

The critical watershed in Burundi's postcolonial history remains the abortive rebellion, instigated by Hutu refugees based in Tanzania, that threatened Burundi's southern provinces in late April 1972, and the disproportionate reprisals unleashed as a result by the Burundi government upon Hutu civilians throughout the country. The death toll in the former conflict, perhaps as many as 2,000 Tutsi, was primarily localized in Bururi province, where the provincial governor, President Micombero's brother-in-law, was among those killed (Kay 1982, 5). The rebellion, however, was crushed in its first days and never received widespread Hutu support. Conservative estimates of the number killed in the ensuing military reprisals range from 80,000 to 150,000 (ibid.). Others, including the U.S. ambassador to the country at the time, suggested that as many as 250,000 may have died (Melady, cited in Malkki 1995, 33).

Hardly indiscriminate assaults on the Hutu population, these reprisals took on the character of what René Lemarchand has called a "selective genocide," targeting for extra-judicial arrest and execution Hutu intellectuals, clergy, schoolteachers, secondary school and university students, small businessmen, civil servants, medical personnel, and other potential Hutu leaders (Lemarchand and Martin 1974, 15). The entire Hutu contingent in Burundi's cabinet, nearly all of the Hutu military, and more than half of the nation's primary and secondary school teachers perished in this campaign of targeted terror. As crippling as this decapitation of the Hutu leadership proved to be, the long-term implications for Hutu families were equally severe. Socially aspiring Hutu parents were forced to make a choice between allowing promising children to go to secondary school at the eventual risk of their lives or having them remain at home and forfeit future social and economic opportunities.

The 1972 massacres precipitated a Hutu diaspora of at least another 5 percent of the population, or 150,000 people (Lemarchand 1990, 104). By mid-1973, some 6,000 Hutu had fled north, despite the fact that the Hutu majority population governed Rwanda (Kay 1982, 10). In larger numbers, Burundi refugees instead crossed into Zaire, where nearly 35,000 settled on the Ruzizi plain or in the provincial cities of Bukavu and Uvira (ibid.). Poorly organized relief efforts hampered by the endemic corruption of the Mobutu government and local Zairean authorities discouraged many Hutu from taking permanent residence in Zaire. By 1980, the majority of Hutu refugees who had crossed into Zaire had voluntarily returned to Burundi.

Most of Burundi's Hutu refugees, reacting to repression in central and southern Burundi, fled to nearby Tanzania. There, the availability of land and a long-standing relationship with the Ha people (who speak a language related to Kirundi) made resettlement a more permanent proposition. The government of Tanzania, the UN High Commissioner for Refugees (UNHCR), and the Tanganyika Christian Refugee Service, affiliated with the Lutheran World Federation, cooperated to settle these refugees, first setting up reception centers and later transporting the refugees from the border region to inland sites away from Lake Tanganyika. These settlements are still among the largest refugee camps in the world.

Ulyankulu, the first of the resettlement camps, covers an area of over 1,000 square kilometers and held more than 50,000 refugees by the end of 1975 (Malkki 1995, 38). The Tanzanian government settled a comparable number of Hutu refugees at Katumba between 1973 and 1976. Following an assessment of the available resources at Ulyankulu, and faced with increasing numbers of Hutu refugees settling on their own in the Kigoma region, the government of Tanzania determined to move more than 27,000 Burundi Hutu to a new site, known as Mishamo, located in an isolated area of Rukwa province in western Tanzania (ibid., 39). At Ulyankulu, Katumba, and Mishamo, Hutu refugees quickly developed their own civic structures and, with the aid of donor agencies, established primary and secondary schools, health centers, dispensaries, and agricultural cooperatives. These refugees continue to make up the majority of Burundi's refugee population abroad. Despite the general amnesties granted in 1974 and 1976 by President Micombero and his successor, Jean-Baptiste Bagaza, few Hutu who fled the country in 1972 returned to Burundi. Neither did later liberalization efforts reduce Hutu refugees' level of mistrust in the Burundi government.

Within Burundi's borders a no less significant and equally permanent population displacement occurred that would pay dividends in blood in later years. Tutsi who had once coexisted civilly in rural areas alongside predominantly Hutu populations no longer felt at ease and began to migrate to urban centers. In Bujumbura itself, Tutsi moving in gradually replaced the Hutu population, which dispersed to the surrounding shantytowns and to the hillsides overlooking the capital. The consequences of this population displacement have proven significant to the persistence of hostilities in later years.

The refugee diaspora also fostered a number of pro-Hutu rebel movements. Following the 1972 massacres, Gérard Rushishikara founded Tabara, or "Come to My Rescue," an offshoot of the Burundi political party Mouvement des Étudiants Progressistes du Burundi (MEPROBA, the Movement of Progressive Students of Burundi). Two years later, disaffected members of Tabara formed Palipehutu (Parti pour la Libération du Peuple Hutu, or Party for the Liberation of the Hutu People), which until 1996 stood as the symbol of Hutu resistance. Until 1993, however, pro-Hutu rebel groups had little impact within the country, serving primarily to justify ongoing repression due to Tutsi paranoia about the possibility of refugee-led rebellion.

1988: The World Pays Attention

While 1972 features in the collective memory of the Hutu masses and refugee population and in the official amnesia of the Tutsi governments that succeeded the rule of Michel Micombero, it was only in 1988 that Burundi's ethnic violence began to attract the attention of the international media. The contradictory aims of two successive governments—establishing national unity while at the same time securing Tutsi hegemony—ultimately contributed to the explosion of a second tragic episode of massacre and reprisal. From November 1976, when a coup led by Lieutenant Colonel Jean-Baptiste Bagaza toppled the Micombero government, and September 1987, when Bagaza was replaced by Major Pierre Buyoya, Tutsi elements continued to secure the machinery of power, exiling missionary and church groups involved in educating and proselytizing among the Hutu population and establishing control in the countryside by regrouping rural populations—primarily Hutu—in a program of "villagization." Buyoya's administrative agenda promised a liberalization of these policies, raising the hopes of Hutu exiles and the anxieties of Tutsi hardliners, without effecting any real redistribution of power in the countryside.

In the provinces of Kirundo and Ngozi, along the border with Rwanda, the presence of relatively prosperous coffee producers, mostly Hutu, as well as a critical mass of Rwandan Tutsi refugees, contributed to a localized outbreak of renewed interethnic violence. Mounting tensions in the region led Hutu to organize to prevent a repetition of the 1972 massacre. Groups of Hutu, armed with bows, arrows, machetes, clubs, and axes, downed trees across roadways and destroyed bridges as they endeavored to slow military patrols. Following an incident in the town of Ntega, where a Tutsi merchant fired upon and killed six Hutu in a crowd threatening his residence, Hutu bands began to indiscriminately attack Tutsi residents, prompting many to flee to local mission stations. As in 1972, however, military reprisals far exceeded the scale of the initial violence. Perhaps 15,000 Hutu, including many women and children, died at the hands of the Burundi army. Another 50,000 avoided reprisals by fleeing to nearby Rwanda (Lemarchand 1994, 126). Unlike the situation in 1972, when a larger number of casualties and much greater human displacement occasioned mostly international disinterest, the massacres of 1988 resulted in widespread condemnation. European governments, Amnesty International, the World Bank, and even the government of the United States, which had studiously avoided involvement in 1972, weighed in with public and official expressions of dismay. In the end, the effect of this pressure would be the introduction of democratizing reforms that promised a new era of national unity and, perhaps, an end to the cycle of ethnic violence afflicting the country.

1993: Reaping the Whirlwind—Assassination and Its Aftermath

On June 1, 1993, as a result of these reforms, Burundi held the first democratic election in the nation's history. Melchior Ndadaye received over 65 percent of the vote, becoming the first Hutu politician to hold the nation's presidency. Pierre Buyoya, Burundi's third president and the figure most responsible for initiating liberalizing reforms that had made the election possible, supervised what appeared to be the first peaceful transfer of power in the country's thirty-year history as an independent nation. Scarcely five months later, however, Ndadaye's assassination by members of the Burundi military initiated a cycle of violence and civil war that hardly subsided in the subsequent decade. After Ndadaye's murder, the countryside exploded as angry Hutu peasants unleashed a murderous vengeance upon rural Tutsi. For a brief time in Burundi's history, the number of Tutsi dead equaled those of their Hutu counterparts. The Tutsi innocent included a group of schoolchildren burned to death at Kibimba in an incident since commemorated by Tutsi hardliners as evidence of the ruthlessness of Hutu *genocidaires.* Swift reprisals carried out by Tutsi soldiers and youth gangs, however, rapidly restored the status quo. In all, between 30,000 and 50,000 Burundians, of both ethnicities, were killed before the world's attention shifted to the genocide that erupted in Rwanda in April 1994 (Human Rights Watch 1998, 15).

Burundi's Hutu population, remembering the ferocity of killing in 1972 and 1988, fled the country in greater numbers in 1993 than in either of these earlier outbreaks of violence. More than 600,000 Hutu (Human Rights Watch 1998, 8) left the country between October 1993 and May 1994, only to be drawn into the wider regional refugee crisis. Perhaps 300,000 Burundi Hutu fled to Rwanda (Lemarchand 1999, 198), where some undoubtedly took part in the Rwandan genocide. Most of these refugees would then become part of the Hutu exodus from Rwanda in advance of the Tutsi Rwandan Patriotic Front (RPF). With the collapse of Hutu power in Rwanda, Burundi's rebel movement also acquired manpower and training, along with a degree of international opprobrium, from the support of Rwandan Hutu militia, the infamous *interahamwe,* and the former Rwandan armed forces. As a result, pro-Hutu rebel forces increased their presence throughout the Burundi countryside.

The violence that erupted in 1993 also occasioned a massive displacement of both Hutu and Tutsi within the country. By late December 1993, up to 700,000 persons had fled their homes (U.S. Committee for Refugees 1998, 34). As many as 200,000 Tutsi evading attacks from Hutu neighbors sought refuge in camps protected by the Burundi military (ibid.). The success of pro-Hutu rebels after 1994 only increased the insecurity of rural Tutsi and encouraged their displacement to these protected enclaves or to urban areas, a continuation of processes begun in 1972 that have resulted in a sort of ethnic cleansing of the countryside. Ethnic Hutu, by contrast, scattered to the hills, swamps, and forests to escape reprisals by soldiers and armed militia. Relief workers estimated that as late as 1995 the number of internally displaced persons (IDPs) remained high, perhaps as many as 450,000 scattered unevenly across the countryside (ibid.). After the reestablishment of Pierre Buyoya's government in 1996, the status of the internally displaced has become an increasingly politicized matter. Ethnic Tutsi under military protection have been designated by the government as IDPs and made eligible for international food assistance, while ethnic Hutu who have fled their homes, or who have been forced into regroupment camps, are classified as "dispersed" and receive little in the way of institutional aid.

Since 1994: An Ongoing Refugee Crisis

Burundi has been enmeshed in an intractable civil war with devastating implications for the country's rural populace since 1994. The Burundi army still has the upper hand throughout the countryside and has been responsible for continuing reprisals against Hutu communities. However, quite unlike earlier periods in Burundi history, Hutu rebels have escalated their attacks on Tutsi military and civilian targets. After the paroxysm of killing that followed Ndadaye's assassination subsided, the violence abated only briefly. From an estimated 400 to 500 deaths a month in 1994, by 1996 Burundians were being killed at a rate of perhaps 15,000 a year (U.S. Committee for Refugees 1998, 31). Though hardly united—Palipehutu has since 1996 been superseded by the Forces for the Defense of Democracy (*Forces pour la défense de la démocratie,* FDD) and the Front for National Liberation (*Front de liberation nationale,* FLN)—Hutu rebels have managed to effectively disrupt commerce and administration in many areas of the country; they have infiltrated Hutu neighborhoods of Bujumbura, attacked military installations, and assassinated Tutsi officials. As of 2004, reports from Bujumbura described regular shelling of the capital by rebel forces. To support their operations, rebel groups routinely tax Hutu civilians and raid civilian households, stealing food and livestock. Hutu thus feel beset by the Burundi army, which perceives them as rebel supporters, and by the rebels themselves. In an effort to cut off rebel support and prevent the spread of local rebellions, the Buyoya government has since 1996 embarked on a strategy of forcing Hutu peasants into regroupment camps. Human rights organizations have accused army units and Tutsi militia of systematically employing intimidation, torture, rape, and summary execution of those resisting forced relocation. In addition, Hutu charge the military and Tutsi militia with burning and looting the abandoned homes of Hutu villagers.

One of the consequences of Burundi's thirty-year politicization of ethnicity and the resulting violent confrontations has been the development of an immutable dichotomy of what now may be clearly seen as tribal confrontations. It must be said that the constitution of these binary oppositions has, at least in part, developed in the context of the refugee experience. Whether the influence of Rwandan Tutsi refugees upon their Burundi counterparts after 1959, or the Hutu experience of exile in Tanzanian refugee camps and the gradual emergence of Hutu narratives of victimization and pro-Hutu ideology, at the heart of emerging tribal identities in Burundi and within the Hutu diaspora is the refugee experience.

Dean T. Ferguson

See also: Civil Wars and Migration; Ethnic Cleansing; Genocide; Internally Displaced Persons; Racism and Racially Motivated Attacks; Refugee Camps; Refugee Warriors; Resettlement; Return Migration; Rwanda and Refugees; Zaire/Democratic Republic of Congo and Refugees

References and further reading:

Daley, Patricia. 1991. "Gender, Displacement, and Social Reproduction: Settling Burundi Refugees in Western Tanzania." *Journal of Refugee Studies* 4, no. 3: 248–266.

Eller, Jack David. 1998. *From Culture to Ethnicity to Conflict: An Anthropological Perspective on International Ethnic Conflict.* Ann Arbor: University of Michigan Press.

Greenland, Jeremy. 1976. "Ethnic Discrimination in Rwanda and Burundi." Pp. 95–134 in *Case Studies in Human Rights and Fundamental Freedoms: A World Survey* 4. Edited by Willem A. Veenhoven. The Hague: Martinus Nijhoff.

Hamrell, Sven. 1967. *Refugee Problems in Africa.* Uppsala: Scandinavian Institute of African Studies.

Human Rights Watch. 1998. *Proxy Targets: Civilians in the War in Burundi.* New York: Human Rights Watch.

———. 1999. *In the Name of Security: Forced Round-Ups of Refugees in Tanzania* 11, no. 4 (A). New York: Human Rights Watch.

———. 2000a. *Emptying the Hills: Regroupment in Burundi* 12, no. 4 (A). New York: Human Rights Watch.

———. 2000b. *Neglecting Justice in Making Peace* 12, no. 2 (A). New York: Human Rights Watch.

Janzen, John M., and Reinhild Kauenhoven Janzen. 2000. *Do I Still Have a Life: Voices from the Aftermath of War in Rwanda and Burundi. Kansas University Monographs in Anthropology,* no. 20. Lawrence: University of Kansas.

Kay, Reginald. 1982. *Burundi since the Genocide.* London: Minority Rights Group.

Lemarchand, René. 1970. *Rwanda and Burundi.* London: Pall Mall Press.

———. 1990. "Burundi: Ethnicity and the Genocidal State." In *State Violence and Ethnicity.* Edited by Pierre L. van den Berghe. Denver: University Press of Colorado.

———. 1994. *Burundi: Ethnic Conflict and Genocide.* New York: Woodrow Wilson Center Press and Cambridge University Press.

———. 1999. "The Fire in the Great Lakes." *Current History* 98, no. 2: 195–201.

Lemarchand, René, and David Martin. 1974. *Selective Genocide in Burundi.* Report no. 20. London: Minority Rights Group.

Malkki, Liisa H. 1995. *Purity and Exile: Violence, Memory and National Cosmology among Hutu Refugees in Tanzania.* Chicago: University of Chicago Press.

U.S. Committee for Refugees. 1998. "Burundi: A Patchwork of Displacement." In *The Forsaken People: Case Studies of the Internally Displaced.* Edited by Roberta Cohen and Francis M. Deng. Washington, DC: Brookings Institution Press.

C

Canada

Canada is a "nation of immigrants" and today has a nondiscriminatory policy for admission of permanent immigrants in three categories—economic, family reunification, and refugees—virtually immediate access to all major institutions of society, and an easy pathway to full citizenship.

Throughout its history, Canada has sought immigration to expand the population, boost the economy, and develop society (Reimers and Troper 1992; Simmons and Keohane 1992; Green 1995; Li 2002; Reitz 2004). Major waves of immigration to Canada have corresponded to economic needs (Green and Green 1999). In the nineteenth and early twentieth centuries, agricultural development was a key to exploiting Canadian economic opportunities, so immigrants were recruited to settle the West. In the 1880s, construction of the Canadian Pacific Railway produced a significant wave of immigration, while the 1900s began with renewed agricultural development and thirty years of substantial immigration. Following World War II, Canada resumed an expansionist immigration policy that continues to be a major part of policy today.

Two major shifts in the economic objectives of Canadian immigration reflected changing requirements of the Canadian economy. First, a shift from rural to urban development accompanied industrialization. When large-scale immigration resumed in the postwar period, it consisted largely of unskilled laborers required for urban industrial employment, who entered the economic hierarchy at its lower levels and progressed from this starting point. The second shift, from low- to high-skilled immigration, accompanied the transition to a postindustrial economy. During the 1960s as well, Canada eliminated origins-based selection criteria, and in 1967 introduced a points-based system for selecting so-called "independent" or economic immigrants to ensure maximum employability in an economy in which skilled labor was a priority. Since then, immigration selection has become a form of human resource management.

The federal government's responsibility for immigration policy has been reinforced in successive legislative actions (1976, 2001), but in recent decades, the largely French-speaking province of Quebec has acquired significant powers for the selection and settlement of immigrants. Beginning in the late 1990s, other provinces also have reached agreements with the federal government regarding immigration policy. Immigrant settlement and integration is a shared responsibility of all levels of government.

Managerial issues, politics, and economics have all helped to shape Canadian immigration policy. Policy has also at times been an outgrowth of social impacts in linguistic, cultural, and racial dimensions. Finally, there are several emerging issues that will impact Canadian immigration policy in the years to come.

Managerial Issues

Since the policy reforms of the 1960s, Canada has maintained a "managerial" stance and focused on the size of the program and numbers of immigrants, the evolution of "economic" immigration, and the reduction of overall program costs.

Managing Numbers and Demographics

For most of the past decade, Canada has admitted between 200,000 and 250,000 immigrants per year, with a maximum of just over 250,000 in 2001. Current government policy is to raise this to 1 percent of population per year, or about 300,000. The 1996 Canadian census showed that about 17 percent of the population was foreign-born.

The Immigration Act of 1976 formalized immigration principles and processes and provided parliamentary authority for setting numbers of immigrants, which previously had been set through administrative regulation. The act authorized the government to set annual numerical targets for immigration in relation to its analysis of economic need and other priorities.

Today's immigrants are concentrated in the largest urban areas, particularly Toronto, Montreal, and Vancouver. In the five-year period prior to 1996, Toronto attracted 42.6 percent of all immigrants, Vancouver 18.5 percent, and Montreal 13.2 percent. Of Toronto's population of about 5 million, well over a third are of non-European origins as a result of immigration. The largest groups are the Chinese (8.0 percent), South Asian (7.5 percent), and African (6.6 percent). Thus, race has become a significant element in the social, cultural, economic, and political life of Canada's major cities (Reitz and Lum, forthcoming).

Overall population growth in Canada has been boosted significantly by immigration. The exact extent of this contribution is difficult to measure precisely, but it has been estimated that of the 26.4 percent population growth between 1971 and 1991 (from 21.6 million to 27.3 million, a 5.7 million increase), Canada's 2.8 million immigrants contributed 27 percent (McVey and Kalbach 1995, 87–90). Hence between 1971 and 1991 the population grew 7 percent from immigration. As the Canadian birthrate has declined, immigration has become increasingly important to population growth. The 2001 census showed that over the previous five-year period immigration had contributed more than 50 percent to population growth.

Managing Economic Immigration

The points system for the selection of independent or "economic" immigrants, and the associated effort to maximize the proportion that this category represents relative to the "family class" and other noneconomic categories, has evolved into the principal policy tool for ensuring that the flow of immigrants meets the needs of the Canadian economy. Under points-based selection, applicants are awarded points toward admission based on criteria such as education, occupational skills, and knowledge of one of the official languages, English or French. The underlying assumption has been that immigrants who are successful in employment make a more positive contribution to the economy and society: They buy more goods, pay more taxes, start more businesses, create more jobs, and use fewer social services. They will not take jobs from native-born workers, nor undercut their wages.

Over time, selection standards have been raised. The initial 1967 points system presented a fairly low hurdle. Occupational skills, including those based on education, were considered, but applicants could meet the required points total based on other criteria: meeting age and language requirements, showing proof of a job offer, stating a willingness to settle in an area of strong labor demand, such as Toronto, or at the discretion of the immigration officer. By 1985, the number of required points for economic immigrants had increased (from 50 to 70 out of 100), with minimum requirements in job experience and occupation categories. Revisions in the points system increased the importance of occupational qualifications and reduced the importance of age and "personal suitability" requirements (Reitz 1998, 74–79). The version in place in December 2001 allocated 34 points for education and training, 15 for language ability, and 10 for being between twenty-one and forty-four years of age and smaller amounts for other categories.

To strengthen the economic component of immigration, three categories of "business immigrants" were added in the 1980s: entrepreneurs, the "self-employed," and investors. In the business categories, the points-system criteria are altered to allow the admission of persons expected to start businesses and create jobs, who will undertake self-employment in key fields such as agriculture, or who will invest a specified amount of capital (currently $400,000) in the economy. These programs remain relatively small: In 2000, 13,645 business immigrants, or 6.9 percent of the total, were admitted.

Canada's temporary foreign worker program fills a range of needs for workers who may be in short supply in the domestic workforce, including seasonal labor in the agricultural sector, domestic workers, and high-tech workers. It also allows for management transfers in multinational businesses. In 1998, about 250,000 temporary residents were authorized to live in Canada, of whom over one-third were Americans. Employers who wish to hire foreign workers on a temporary basis must apply for an Employment Authorization (EA), which is validated by a labor-market testing process developed by Human Resources Development Canada (HRCD). Federal policy has attempted to increase the opportunity for temporary work visas, and the increased admission of temporary workers, with their potential for conversion to permanent status, has been heralded as part of the move to a "knowledge economy," which, unlike earlier policies, targets high-skilled occupations and those with specific job offers.

Managing "Noneconomic" Immigration and Overall Program Costs

Policy has also focused on reducing the family-class proportions of total immigration; reducing settlement and social services costs; and addressing problems of the refugee-determination process. Family-class immigrants are not the immediate dependents of principal applicants but more distant family members "sponsored" by Canadian residents. Some are "assisted relatives," who have family ties to residents but

German immigrants arrive in Topley, Canada, circa 1910. (Corel)

must meet certain points criteria. A long-held perception of family-class immigrants as economic liabilities has been supported by published studies showing that skilled workers out-perform both family-class immigrants and refugees (Citizenship and Immigration Canada 1998).

Despite the theoretic importance of family ties in promoting social and economic integration, data from the Longitudinal Immigrant Database (IMDB) support minimizing the size of the family-class stream. Yet while policy makers seek to choose immigrants based on human capital considerations, each economic immigrant represents a potential source of perhaps three or four subsequent family-class applicants. The only way to avoid the implications of this fact is to reduce or delay family-class eligibility, which may be opposed by already-resident immigrants, and may also reduce Canada's attractiveness as a destination.

Immigrant settlement programs providing counseling and language training are supported by the federal immigration program and topped up by provincial governments. While the federal immigration department accepts a degree of responsibility for immigrant settlement, it aims to reduce costs. One justification for a large economic class of immigrants is the expected reduction in all types of settlement costs. Immigrants are now charged for entry into Canada in an effort to make the program self-financing: Each principal applicant and dependent nineteen years or older pays $500; those under nineteen pay $100; business applicants, $1,000; and a "right-of-landing" fee of $975 is imposed.

Social services such as education, health care, unemployment compensation, and social assistance are available for immigrants. While Canada has implemented changes to social welfare policies to save money, legal immigrants have not been targeted in a major way. However, in Ontario social assistance payments for sponsored immigrants were reduced by $100 per month where sponsors were not providing support.

Refugees are accepted with an acknowledgment that economic criteria are secondary, but the potential abuse of the refugee-determination system is a concern. The system of hearings and appeals consumes considerable time, during which claimants establish themselves in Canada and acquire additional claims to residence. Large backlogs have accumulated, resulting in highly publicized cases in which the process of coping with years of litigation in itself became a legal basis for claims to residence rights.

Politics of Immigration

Public Opinion

Public opinion polls show comparatively strong support for immigration in Canada (Simon and Lynch 1999). In most years since 1970, a majority has supported existing or increased levels of immigration. The proportion of the general public wanting reduced immigration has fluctuated at between 30 and 46 percent, with a high point of 55 percent reached only in 1982, at the height of a recession when immigrants were more likely to be seen as presenting competition for jobs. Even in the early 1990s, when Canada was in recession and immigration levels remained high, the proportion wanting to lower immigration levels never reached a majority. Majorities have occasionally agreed that "overall there is too much immigration to Canada," but the proportion who disagreed with this statement reached a majority of 54 percent in 2000.

Political Discourse among Leaders and Parties

Public discussions of immigration in Canada remain strongly supportive. There are no prominent anti-immigrant politicians, and with certain variations, all major political parties support immigration, as do labor unions and employer groups. The governing federal Liberal Party has the most pro-immigration record of any political party and is committed to raising immigration levels to 1 percent of population per year. To its left, the labor-oriented New Democratic Party (NDP) endorses the 1 percent target while criticizing the government for failing to reach it. The labor union movement, with which the NDP is affiliated, is supportive of immigration and regards the emphasis on economic migration as "elitist." Parties to the right, and business representatives such as the Canadian Chamber of Commerce, while supportive of immigration, temper their enthusiasm by not mentioning specific numerical targets and by including proposals to make the program more cost-effective. The lack of specific targets has been interpreted by some as a sign that these groups favor a reduction in immigration, though they do not say this publicly. The Alliance Party, the largest party on the right, is definitely more hard-nosed on immigration, calling for stricter enforcement of sponsorship obligations for family-class immigration and immediate deportation of "bogus refugees and other illegal entrants." The Alliance would "severely penalize those who organize abuse of the system."

Economic Impact

In Canada it is widely assumed that in the current era, better-educated immigrants have a more positive economic impact than less-educated ones because of their higher earnings and greater economic independence. Economists generally agree, although they lack consensus on methods for estimating this impact. Unlike the low-skilled immigration of the 1950s and 1960s, immigrants arriving in Canada since 1970 generally possessed high educational levels because of the points-based selection program that had gone into effect. Earlier immigrants, particularly those from southern Europe, averaged eight years of education or less and worked in unskilled occupations—for example, Italians in construction and other groups in certain manufacturing industries. Over time, as the selection criteria have risen immigrant educational levels have increased substantially. The 1996 census showed that working-age immigrants arriving in the most recent five-year period had an average of fourteen years of education, and nearly 30 percent had university degrees (Reitz 2001b, 610). Although the level of education among immigrants has been high, however, they face stiff competition in the labor market from young, urban, native-born professionals, who in many cases boast even higher educational achievements.

In the years immediately following the introduction of points-based selection, immigrants to Canada achieved considerable economic success in relation to the native-born population. At the same time, immigrants also encountered a degree of labor-market adversity, or difficulty in securing work matching their high level of qualification. Concentrations of immigrants in certain occupations, such as Chinese immigrants in scientific and technical fields, or black West Indian immigrants in health occupations, often represent a downward trend from previous employment or an entrance into the labor market at a point below the appropriate level of qualification. High rates of immigrant self-employment, particularly in certain groups, may reflect frustration with opportunities in the mainstream labor market.

Immigrant earnings in Canada have been higher than for their counterparts in the United States. Part of this difference is related to unskilled Mexican immigration in the United States, which does not occur in Canada. However, even immigrants from origins in Asia and the Caribbean have more favorable relative earnings in Canada. As George Borjas (1990) has pointed out, the skill selectivity of immigration policy plays its intended role. However, despite Canadian immigration selectivity, immigrants in Canada from Asian origins are actually less well educated than their American counterparts. It appears that immigrants in Canada have received an important assist from the late development of Canada's educational system. After the immigration reforms of the 1960s, the most important reason for higher immigrant earnings in Canada was the lower educational level of the native-born workforce, which enabled immigrants to gain comparatively easy access to middle-class occupations (Reitz 1998). Canadian labor markets also allocate relatively high wages to workers in low-skill occupations, including many immigrants.

Nevertheless, since the 1970s there has been a downward trend in the employment rates and earnings of newly arriving immigrants (Reitz 2001b). Immigrants arriving in a period of high unemployment may be expected to encounter difficulty, as would any other labor-market entrants, particularly those lacking local connections and experience or handicapped by minority status. But Jeffrey G. Reitz (2001b) has shown that a significant part of the decline has been based on the rapid rise in education in the native-born population: Although the educational levels of immigrants have increased as a consequence of upgraded selection criteria, native-born levels have increased more rapidly. This creates greater obstacles for immigrants, and as immigrant qualifications tend to be discounted in the workforce, any increase in the emphasis on such criteria further widens the immigrant/native-born earnings gap.

High levels of earnings for immigrants have been a key "selling point" for the entire immigration program, underscoring a presumed positive contribution to the economy, and a downward trend in that success might be expected to undermine the program in political terms. As yet, economic problems for newly arriving groups have not significantly affected the overall tone of intergroup relations. Largely on the basis of the high income levels more prevalent in the past, simulations of the impact on public finances show positive contributions (Akbari 1995). Still, high poverty rates are now reported in some groups. There has been increased attention to the problem of immigrants working below the skill level for which they were selected—a so-called "brain waste" (Watt and Bloom, 2001; Reitz 2001a). Skilled immigrants may find that employers do not recognize their credentials as being equivalent to similar qualifications of native-born Canadians seeking the same employment situations.

Social Impact: Language, Multiculturalism, and Race
Understanding immigrant social and cultural integration in Canada requires attention to three circumstances that create challenges for policy management. First, immigration in Canada must be managed in relation to the country's linguistic balance and the relations between its two founding linguistic communities, English-speaking and French-speaking citizens. Second, Canada's official "multiculturalism," heralded within the country as a force promoting effective integration of immigrant groups, requires assessment. Third, racial divisions generated by recent immigration raise questions about the immigrant integration process.

Immigrants and French-English Relations in Canada
As immigration has increased the population (McVey and Kalbach 1995, 87–90), a new ethnic and cultural mix has affected the traditional English-French balance. On the one hand, up to the mid-1960s linguistic assimilation of immigrants occurred largely into the English-speaking community. On the other, among French-speaking Canadians, a higher birthrate helped maintain relative population size. In 1871, 61 percent of the Canadian population was of British origin, 31 percent French, and all others made up 8 percent. By 1951, these figures were 48, 31, and 21 percent, respectively; by 197, they were 45, 29, and 27 percent.

Even in Quebec, immigrants historically have tended to become integrated into the English-speaking, or "anglophone," community rather than the French-speaking, or "francophone," one. In 1971, among persons residing in Quebec with a mother tongue other than English or French, transfers to English outnumbered transfers to French by more than four to one (Lachapelle 1980, 33). Hence, immigration in large numbers has reduced the demographic significance of the French language in Quebec and in Canada as a whole.

Since the "Quiet Revolution" of an awakening ethnic and national consciousness in Quebec beginning in the early 1960s, the Quebec government has taken a degree of control over language and addressed the impact of immigration on the province. Through a series of agreements negotiated with the federal government, Quebec acquired substantial control of immigrant selection and settlement to ensure that, while contributing to economic development, immigration would not threaten the cultural or linguistic independence of Quebec within Canada. Administratively, all matters related to immigration and integration of immigrants within Quebec are centralized within the Ministère des Relations avec les citoyens et de l'Immigration (MRCI).

Since 1970, Quebec has thus set numbers of immigrants into the province and designated their main characteristics. The current agreement provides that Quebec should receive a number of immigrants corresponding to the province's percentage of the Canadian population, with the right to exceed this figure by 5 percent. As well, Quebec should receive refugees in proportion to its overall percentage of immigrants. Quebec administers its own selection system even though Canada retains the right to issue visas (and conducts background checks related to health and security issues). This system gives priority to persons fluent in French as well as to persons with higher levels of education, particularly in the French language. A 1991 agreement provides some provincial responsibilities for aspects of refugee selection and for the short-term stay of temporary foreign workers. The Quebec government has also expressed an interest in increasing its involvement in the temporary foreign worker program (Black and Hagen 1993).

The fact that so many immigrants to Quebec leave for other provinces underscores a critical weakness in provincial selection schemes and undermines the Quebec government's efforts to control the linguistic balance. Interprovincial migration of immigrants favors the high-immigration provinces of Ontario and British Columbia, as shown by the Citizenship and Immigration Canada study of interprovincial migration (CIC 2000) among tax filers tracked in the IMDB. This study showed that Ontario and British Columbia experienced net gains as a result of interprovincial migration, whereas Quebec lost the largest absolute numbers.

Canadian Multiculturalism
Although Canadian political leaders proclaim that Canada has always been a "multicultural" nation, throughout much of its history Canada had an assimilationist immigration policy, that is, immigrants were chosen for their perceived capacity for social and cultural accommodation in the mainstream populations. The earliest preferences were for persons of British or northern European origins, and initially admission of others, such as eastern and southern Europeans, was forced mainly by market pressures. Federal multiculturalism policy was officially launched in 1971, largely as a product of the French-English conflict. Because of pressure to protect the French language, the federal government initiated a policy of bilingualism and biculturalism but abandoned the latter in favor of multiculturalism in the face of protests from cultural groups other than English and French, notably Ukrainians.

Upon its introduction, multiculturalism policy was immediately embraced by all parties and at all levels of government. It has rapidly become regarded as a cornerstone of Canadian society, and it was entrenched in Canada's Charter of Rights and Freedoms in 1982. Multiculturalism in Canada represents cultural tolerance, a "live-and-let-live" mentality, but also a positive recognition of the value of cultural diversity. It also has become an important national symbol of the metaphoric contrast between a Canadian social "mosaic" and an American "melting pot."

Immigrant integration is, in Canadian mythology, supposed to be assisted by multiculturalism, but no government funds have been allocated for "program evaluation," reinforcing the impression that the policy is largely symbolic. Nevertheless, symbols matter. Analysis of higher rates of naturalization in Canada compared to the United States suggests that they may be a result in part of the symbolic feeling of acceptance that immigrants feel as a result of multiculturalism (Bloemraad 2001).

"Visible Minorities" and Race

Because of the predominantly European population base of Canada's nonaboriginal population up to the 1960s, and the sheer size of Canada's continuing immigration program relative to the existing population, the impact of cultural and racial changes has been profound. In 1971, racial minorities (other than aboriginal peoples) constituted less than 1 percent of the Canadian population; by 1996, as a result of immigration, they constituted 10 percent. Consequently, race has become an important issue in Canada. Experience with previous European immigration, with the trickle of U.S. blacks, and with issues of French-English relations and the status of aboriginal populations may have helped prepare Canadian citizens for this new racial diversity. But Canada has invented a new term, "visible minorities" (to avoid speaking of "race"), complete with its own legal framework, suggesting there are problems (see Henry et al. 1998).

Although most Canadians deny that they harbor racist views, they express preferences regarding the racial composition of groups in their neighborhoods or workplaces (Reitz and Breton 1994). Environics Focus Canada polls show large majorities reject the proposal that "non-whites should not be allowed to immigrate to Canada" (93 percent in 2000; Esses et al. 2002, 72). Yet the same polls show that a majority, 53 percent, agrees that "Canada accepts too many immigrants from racial minority groups" (in 1990, 1991, and 1992).

Canada's policies addressing race tend to be ambiguous and ineffective. The federal "employment equity" legislation, introduced in 1986, is a case in point: "Visible minorities" are included as one of four groups designated for attention (the others being women, native peoples, and the disabled), but the law covered only about 5 percent of the workforce and included no effective monitoring or enforcement mechanism (Lum 1995). New employment equity legislation passed in 1995 authorizes the Canadian Human Rights Commission to enforce compliance through the conduct of onsite employer audits but covers only 8 percent of the national workforce and restricts Human Rights Commission jurisdiction over systemic discrimination in employment.

As racial issues have grown, some racial minorities have begun to oppose multiculturalism on the grounds that it assigns minorities a marginal status (Bissoondath 1994). Others oppose it because it is said to underpin identity politics that support the rights of certain minority groups, supposedly at the expense of either majority rights or the rights of other minority groups (Kay 1998). Still others view multiculturalism as an attempt to maintain a traditional ethnic hierarchy. Multiculturalism, it is argued, socially constructs cultural identities but does little to recognize and remedy inequalities based on race. Such criticisms have prompted governments to look hard for ways to cut the already small multicultural budgets or to abandon the program altogether while still being politically correct. For example, as a result of a 1994 Federal Program review, funds allotted to multiculturalism have been reduced by 28 percent and reoriented from program to project funding. In short, the growth of racial minority populations is changing the role of multiculturalism, making it less a socially cohesive force than a rallying point for demands for potent public policy to address issues of equality and human rights.

Emerging Issues

Canada's immigration policy faces an uncertain future: Controlling immigration and its impact may pose greater challenges in the future than it has in the past (see Reitz 2004).

Having developed from a rural to an urban industrial nation, Canada is—or aspires to be—a postindustrial society with a knowledge-based economy actively confronting globalization. For immigration policy, the challenge posed by this juxtaposition of circumstances is whether large numbers of immigrants can be recruited to fill highly skilled occupations. It would be politically damaging for immigrants to be seen as struggling economically or representing a potential threat to the viability of social services. Hence, the declining economic position of new immigrants, particularly the large numbers arriving during the recession of the early 1990s, has been a major policy focus. The Immigration and Refugee Protection Act 2001 (Bill C-11) took effect in June 2002 and includes provisions to facilitate immigrants' economic roles. It provides "in-Canada" application for permanent residency for temporary workers, spouses and partners, and students with a permanent job offer who have been working in

Canada; this points to the role envisioned for temporary workers in high-skill knowledge-economy jobs. And it introduces a new multiyear planning process to provide greater continuity in immigration policy-making. The key feature of the new policy is the upgrading of skill selection for permanent immigrants, with greater emphasis on education and language knowledge, and less on specific occupational skills. The plan originally was to make the new selection criteria retroactive—that is, many who applied and paid their fees under old rules would now be considered under the more stringent new rules. In response to criticism, the government backtracked on retroactivity, but it is holding to the long-term goal of a dramatic upgrade in selection criteria. Should these efforts fail, Canada could be forced to curtail immigration significantly, as Australia has done, forgoing its developmental potential, or to opt for a more laissez-faire, U.S.-style approach, allowing immigrants to assume whatever economic role they can attain.

The integrity of the refugee determination process presents a second major issue in current immigration policy. Refugees represent between 10 and 20 percent of all immigrants. The rate of recognition of asylum applications is high, and Canadian policy has granted rights protections to applicants as they would to citizens, but substantial numbers are in immigration detention, about 450 at any one time. Because refugees are admitted for humanitarian purposes rather than economic criteria, because of uncertainty about the integrity of the refugee-determination process, and because large backlogs have plagued the system and compromised its capacity for effective claim adjudication, some fear that the refugee system allows Canadian generosity to be abused. In the wake of the terrorist attacks on September 11, 2001, the new Immigration Act contained provisions to tighten access to the refugee-determination system. These provisions included more extensive initial screening of claimants, more explicit policies regarding detention, limitations in the appeal processes, and other legal opportunities to speed the deportation of those suspected of serious crimes.

Jeffrey G. Reitz

See also: Asylum; Multiculturalism

References and further reading:

Akbari, Ather H. 1995. "The Impact of Immigrants on Canada's Treasury, circa 1990." Pp. 113–127 in *Diminishing Returns: The Economics of Canada's Recent Immigration Policy.* Edited by Don J. DeVoretz. Toronto: C. D. Howe Institute.

Bissoondath, Neil. 1994. *Selling Illusions: The Cult of Multiculturalism in Canada.* Toronto: Penguin.

Black, Jerome, and David Hagen. 1993. "Quebec Immigration Politics and Policy: Historical and Comparative Perspectives. In *Quebec: State and Society.* 2d ed. Edited by Alain-G. Gagnon. Scarborough: Nelson Canada.

Bloemraad, Irene. 2002. "The North American Nationalization Gap: An Institutional Approach to Citizenship Acquisition in the United States and Canada." *International Migration Review* 36, no. 1: 194–229.

Borjas, George. 1990. *Friends or Strangers: The Impact of Immigrants on the U.S. Economy.* New York: Basic.

Citizenship and Immigration Canada. 1998. "The Economic Performance of Immigrants: Immigration Category Perspective." IMDB Profile Series. Ottawa: Citizenship and Immigration Canada.

———. 2000. *The Interprovincial Migration of Immigrants to Canada.* IMDB Profile Series. Ottawa: Minister of Public Works and Government Services.

Esses, Victoria, John Dovidio, and Gordon Hodson. 2002. "Public Attitudes toward Immigration in the United States and Canada in Response to the September 11, 2001, 'Attack on America.'" *Analyses of Social Issues and Public Policy,* no. 2: 69–85.

Green, Alan. 1995. "A Comparison of Canadian and U.S. Immigration Policy in the Twentieth Century." Pp. 31–64 in *Diminishing Returns: The Economics of Canada's Recent Immigration Policy.* Edited by Don J. DeVoretz. Toronto: C. D. Howe Institute.

Green, Alan, and David Green. 1999. "The Economic Goals of Canada's Immigration Policy, Past and Present." *Canadian Public Policy/Analyse de Politiques* 25, no. 4: 425–451.

Henry, Frances, Carol Tator, Winston Mattis, and Tim Rees. 1998. *The Colour of Democracy: Racism in Canadian Society.* 2d ed. Toronto: Harcourt Brace.

Kay, Jonathan. 1998. "Explaining the Modern Backlash against Multiculturalism." *Policy Options* (May): 30–34.

Lachapelle, Rejean. 1980. "Evolution of Ethnic and Linguistic Composition." Pp. 15–43 in *Cultural Boundaries and the Cohesion of Canada.* Edited by Raymond Breton, Jeffrey G. Reitz, and Victor Valentine. Montreal: Institute for Research on Public Policy.

Li, Peter. 2002. *Destination Canada: Immigration Debates and Issues.* Toronto: Oxford University Press.

Lum, Janet M. 1995. "The Federal Employment Equity Act: Goals vs. Implementation." *Canadian Public Administration* (Spring): 45–76.

McVey, Wayne W., Jr., and Warren E. Kalbach. 1995. *Canadian Population.* Toronto: Nelson Canada.

Reimers, David M., and Harold Troper. 1992. "Canadian and American Immigration Policy since 1945." Pp. 15–54 in *Immigration, Language, and Ethnicity: Canada and the United States.* Edited by Barry R. Chiswick. Washington, DC: American Enterprise Institute.

Reitz, Jeffrey G. 1998. *Warmth of the Welcome: The Social Causes of Economic Success for Immigrants in Different Nations and Cities.* Boulder: Westview.

———. 2001a. "Immigrant Skill Utilization in the Canadian Labour Market: Implications of Human Capital Research." *Journal of International Migration and Integration* 2, no. 3: 347–378.

———. 2001b. "Immigrant Success in the Knowledge Economy: Institutional Change and the Immigrant Experience in Canada, 1970–1995." *Journal of Social Issues* 57, no. 3: 579–613.

———. 2004. "Immigration and Canadian Nation-Building in the Transition to a Knowledge Economy." In *Controlling Immigration: A Global Perspective.* 2d ed. Edited by W. A. Cornelius, P. L. Martin, J. F. Hollifield, and T. Tsuda. Stanford: Stanford University Press.

Reitz, Jeffrey G., and Raymond Breton. 1994. *The Illusion of Difference: Realities of Ethnicity in Canada and the United States.* Toronto: C. D. Howe Institute.

Reitz, Jeffrey G., and Janet M. Lum. 2003. "Immigration and Diversity in a Changing Canadian City: Social Bases of Inter-group Relations in Toronto." In *Inside the Mosaic.* Edited by Eric Fong. Toronto: University of Toronto Press.

Simmons, Alan B., and Kieran Keohane. 1992. "Canadian Immigration Policy: State Strategies and the Quest for Legitimacy." *Canadian Review of Sociology and Anthropology* 29, no. 4: 421–452.

Simon, Rita J., and James P. Lynch. 1999. "A Comparative Assessment of Public Opinion toward Immigrants and Immigration Policy." *International Migration Review* 33, no. 2: 455–467.

Watt, Douglas, and Michael Bloom. 2001. *Exploring the Learning Recognition Gap in Canada. Phase 1 Report. Recognizing Learning: The Economic Cost of Not Recognizing Learning and Learning Credentials in Canada.* Ottawa: Conference Board of Canada.

Carrier Sanctions

Initially intended as a universal mechanism of entry control, applied even in Communist countries, the practice of fining air and sea carriers for transporting insufficiently documented passengers, regardless of negligence or criminal intent, has now become in developed countries yet another instrument of preventing the arrival of asylum seekers, alongside entry visa requirements and readmission agreements. Since 1986, almost all European countries have adopted the practice, which has been increasingly extended to all carriers, including interstate coaches and even taxis operating in border regions. In most cases, fines are levied almost automatically, carriers being assumed "guilty" unless the contrary is proven, and lorry drivers unable to pay have had their vehicles seized. The number of asylum seekers, however, has not dropped. On the contrary, in the United Kingdom, the country where carrier sanctions are most severely applied, the number of asylum seekers has, since the law was introduced in 1987, increased by a factor of twenty. Some claim that the practice has shifted immigration control responsibilities to carriers. Others have raised questions about the compatibility of the sanctions with human rights instruments, such as the 1951 UN Convention Relating to the Status of Refugees and the 1950 European Convention on Human Rights. Finally, carrier sanctions have led inevitably to discrimination against bona fide travelers of non-European origin and have indirectly contributed to the booming human smuggling trade.

The adoption on June 27, 2001, of the European Union (EU) Directive on the harmonization of legislation on carriers' liability obliged two member states which had not yet done so, namely Ireland and Sweden, to fall in line before the end of 2002. The Irish law on carriers' liability finally came into force on September 19, 2003. In Sweden, a new asylum bill containing carrier liability provisions was submitted in December 2003, but the reasons for the delay are still very valid. The governing Social Democrats, as in their previous mandate period, do not have a parliamentary majority to push the bill through. Their allies, the Greens and the Left Party, will certainly vote against it, and the only way out is to gain the support of the opposition Conservatives, who are split on the bill, with many specifically against a carriers' liability law Given that other European countries with very close ties to the EU, namely Norway, Iceland, Liechtenstein, and Switzerland, along with some in Eastern and Central Europe aspiring for EU membership, must adopt similar legislation, the directive will eventually take effect throughout Europe.

Carriers wishing to avoid fines have taken on increasing responsibilities related to immigration control. They collaborate with governments in weeding out would-be passengers judged as "risky" or considered to be potential asylum claimants. The carriers are assisted by "airline liaison officers," immigration officials of developed countries who work onsite in the major countries of origin of asylum seekers.

As to whether the practice is compatible with the 1951 Refugee Convention, only the Austrian Constitutional Court, in its decision of October 29, 2001, has found it questionable. The German Constitutional Court, by contrast, rejected the complaints of two airlines on February 11, 1998.

The British House of Lords was expected to rule on the issue but only insofar as it applied to lorry drivers. Fifty lorry drivers or haulage firms contested the fines, and their complaints were upheld by the High Court on December 5, 2001. Challenged by the home secretary, the Court of Appeal confirmed, on February 22, 2002, that the carriers' liability law, as it applied to lorry drivers, infringed the 1950 European Convention with respect to presumption of innocence, right to a fair trial, and peaceful enjoyment of property. However, it supported the home secretary's argument that the liability law did not, as ruled by the High Court, infringe EU law on the free movement of goods and the right to provide haulage services. Instead of pursuing the matter further before the House of Lords, the government complied partially with the High Court ruling and introduced, on December 10, 2002, a new penalty regime allowing the fines to vary in accordance with the degree of responsibility. Fines unpaid until December 9, 2002, were canceled, whereas fines paid were not reimbursed, on the grounds that the drivers or firms concerned in the latter group had "accepted liability."

These cases illustrate how governments have interpreted the 1951 convention—that is, that it obliges them to grant protection to refugees, but not to facilitate their entry into their territory.

Having only a few minutes to check in passengers, airline workers have inevitably discriminated against bona fide travelers, sometimes denying them boarding rights. Discrimination lawsuits involving huge sums are still rare in Europe, with the exception of the United Kingdom, where victims have so far accepted out-of-court settlements.

Human smugglers have likely benefited from the sanctions. Analysts suspect that more "clients" are opting for land routes and that more are willing to pay much higher fees for air routes. Smugglers are always one step ahead, not lacking in imaginative means of deceiving airline staff and airline liaison officers.

António Cruz

See also: Border Controls; Employer Sanctions; Readmission Agreements; Visas

References and further reading:

Cruz, António. 1995. *Shifting Responsibility: Carriers' Liability in the Member States of the European Union and North America.* Stoke-on-Trent, Staffordshire, UK: Trentham.

Gilboy, Janet. 1993. "Gatekeepers: International Airlines as Third-Party Enforcers in Immigration Inspections." Internal document of the American Bar Foundation.

International Civil Aviation Organisation. 1995. *Report of the Eleventh Session of the Facilitation Division, Montreal, April 18–27, 1995.* Doc. 9649, FAL/11 (1995).

Cartagena Declaration

The Cartagena Declaration offers an innovative and wide-reaching conceptual framework for refugee protection in Latin America. It was devised by representatives and experts from ten Latin American countries between November 19 and 22, 1984, in Cartagena, Colombia. Although the Cartagena Declaration was based upon the 1951 UN Convention Relating to the Status of Refugees and its 1967 Protocol, it is broader in scope, building upon earlier, related initiatives in Latin America in an effort to specifically address the migration crisis Central America was experiencing at the time. The Cartagena Declaration was the first document to set forth guidelines for those states in the region faced with mass inflows of refugees, and it extended entitlement to protection to victims of generalized violence, internal armed conflict, and massive human rights abuses.

Historical Context

Latin American countries have espoused the concepts of asylum and refuge throughout their histories as independent states. The legal status of asylum in Latin America dates back to 1889 (Arboleda 1994, 3) and was borne in response to the political instability experienced by numerous countries in the region and a willingness to protect victims of political persecution. However, these earlier definitions only recognized persecution for political reasons and not for reasons of religious or ethnic affiliation.

In the early 1980s, Central American countries were experiencing massive influxes and outflows of displaced people as a result of internal conflict, civil strife, widespread human rights abuses, economic turmoil, and natural disasters. As in Africa, the 1951 Refugee Convention proved inadequate in addressing the problems posed by the movement of millions of uprooted people in the region. Those seeking refuge across national borders differed in their makeup from previous groups fleeing repressive regimes in Latin America: They were not primarily urban dwellers, nor did they consist mainly of members of the social or political elite, such as politicians, labor leaders, and intellectuals. Instead, these refugees originated from rural areas and were mostly ethnically mixed. In the case of El Salvador and Guatemala, entire communities were fleeing their countries of origin en masse (ibid., 6). From a strictly legal perspective, many of these people would have been unlikely to qualify as refugees under the convention definition, and to process these asylum claims on an individual basis was impractical.

It was against this background that the Colloquium on Asylum and International Protection of Refugees in Latin America was held in Mexico City from May 11–15, 1981. It was organized by the Mexican Secretariat of Foreign Affairs, in cooperation with the Institute for Legal Research of the National University of Mexico, under the auspices of the UN High Commissioner for Refugees (UNHCR). It sought to discuss the regional crisis in Central America and address the limitations of international and national refugee laws. An outcome of the colloquium was the recognition that local traditional, social, and economic contexts were relevant considerations in determining refugee and asylum law, and a broad and encompassing definition of a "refugee" in Latin America resulted. Although the colloquium was limited in its focus to the Central American situation, the definition (as in the Cartagena Declaration that followed) was made applicable to all of Latin America. The outcomes of this colloquium provided crucial input into a second one held three years later.

The prolonged severity of conflict and displacement in Central America led to another regional meeting from November 19–22, 1984. Experts and representatives from ten governments (Belize, Colombia, Costa Rica, El Salvador, Guatemala, Honduras, Mexico, Nicaragua, Panama, and Venezuela) met for a colloquium in Cartagena, Colombia. The event was sponsored by the Regional Centre for Third World Studies and the UNHCR and held under the auspices of the Colombian government. The Cartagena Declaration resulted from this colloquium and remains the most encompassing definition of a refugee to have emerged from Latin America. The definition adopted is very similar to that proposed by the Inter-American Commission on Human Rights to the General Assembly of the Organization of American

States in 1981–1982, and it was adopted by the General Assembly in 1985.

Significance and Limitations

The Cartagena Declaration defines a refugee in a very similar way to that enacted by the Organization of African Unity (OAU) in the Convention Governing the Specific Aspects of Refugee Problems in Africa (1969), or the OAU Convention. In addition to the types of protection delineated in the 1951 convention, the Cartagena and OAU agreements extend protection to "persons who have fled their country because their lives, safety, or freedom have been threatened by generalised violence, foreign aggression, internal conflicts, massive violations of human rights or other circumstances which have seriously disturbed public order" (UNHCR 1995, 208). However, unlike the OAU Convention, the Cartagena Declaration is legally nonbinding. It is also more restrictive than the OAU Convention, in that in order to be regarded as a refugee, individuals must demonstrate that "their lives, safety or freedom have been threatened." This stipulation is similar to one enshrined in the internationally accepted definition within the 1951 Refugee Convention, which requires that individuals be able to demonstrate that they personally are at risk of persecution. No such requirement was added to the OAU Convention.

The Cartagena Declaration has become the basis for refugee policy in Latin America and has created customary legal rules for defining refugees across the region. It has been repeatedly endorsed by the General Assembly of the OAS. Most Latin American states apply the Cartagena Declaration's broader definition of a refugee over the one spelled out in the 1951 Refugee Convention, and several countries have even incorporated the Cartagena definition into their national legislation. The Cartagena Declaration has also made the governments of Latin American countries more sensitive to the need to eliminate the root causes of large-scale displacement of people from their countries of origin.

It has been argued that the Cartagena Declaration's definition of refugee status might be best viewed as making "something of a compromise between the Convention standard and the very broad OAU conceptualisation" (Hathaway 1991, 21). Although it extends the Refugee Convention's understanding of persecution to include those abused as a result of sociopolitical unrest, it also limits the obligation to provide protection to cases where a real risk of harm can be proven, which is similar to the burden of proof placed on an asylum claimant under the Refugee Convention. In practice, however, the requirement of proof seems to have been loosely interpreted, and the definition of "refugee" has been widely applied, which is more in keeping with the OAU Convention's approach (Arboleda 1994, 13).

Like the OAU Convention, the Cartagena Declaration uses terminology not normally used in international refugee law. The use of terms such as "generalised violence," "internal conflict," and "massive violations of human rights" goes further and is more inclusive than even the terminology used in the OAU Convention. The declaration affords protection to those fleeing foreign aggression; accepts the notion of group determination without the need to determine the identity of the respective perpetrator; extends nonrefoulement (under Article 33 of the 1951 Refugee Convention) from those with an individualized fear of persecution to persons fleeing widespread human rights abuses; and calls upon the international community to recognize the need to provide protection and assistance to internally displaced persons. Other important aspects of the Cartagena Declaration include its recognition of: the need to find durable solutions to refugee crises, including family reunification; the importance of local integration of refugees in their country of asylum, with the assistance of the international community, in order to protect their physical and mental well-being; and the benefit of cooperation between the OAS and the UNHCR in their efforts to protect and assist refugees.

The Cartagena Declaration set out the legal groundwork for resolving the refugee crisis in Central America. In August 1987, the leaders of the five countries of Central America signed the Esquipulas II accords, which formed the basis for peace negotiations and efforts to address the causes and consequences of conflict in the region. The International Conference on Central American Refugees (CIREFCA), held in May 1989 in Guatemala City, began a process that stretched over several years and which sought political solutions to displacement and economic and social development in the region. CIREFCA has given greater legitimacy to the Cartagena Declaration by addressing various issues raised during the drafting procedure, such as the importance of addressing the developmental needs of refugees who repatriate as well as of those who integrate in the country of asylum. Although the continued validity of the Cartagena Declaration has been challenged by some Central American states in recent years because of the altered contemporary context, it continues to play an important role in integrating and informing universal principles, regional values, and state practices.

Sean Loughna

See also: African Union; Central American Refugees; Civil Wars and Migration; Development-Induced Displacement; Internally Displaced Persons; Nonconvention Status (1951 UN Convention); Non-Refoulement; Refugees; UN Convention Relating to the Status of Refugees, 1951; UN High Commissioner for Refugees

References and further reading:

Arboleda, Eduardo. 1991. "Refugee Definition in Africa and Latin America: The Lessons of Pragmatism." *International Journal of Refugee Law* 3, no. 2: 185–207.

———. 1994. "The Cartagena Declaration of 1994 and Its Similarities to the 1969 OAU Convention on Refugees—A Comparative Perspective." Paper presented at the Symposium on Refugees and Forced Population Displacement in Africa, Addis Ababa, Organization of African Unity and UN High Commissioner for Refugees.

Cuéllar, Roberto, Diego García-Sayán, Jorge Montaño, Margarita Diegues, and Leo Valladares Lanza. 1991. "Refugee and Related Developments in Latin America: Challenges Ahead." *International Journal of Refugee Law* 3, no. 3: 482–499.

Hathaway, James C. 1991. *The Law of Refugee Status.* Toronto: Butterworths.

United Nations High Commissioner for Refugees. 1982. *Asilo y Protección Internacional de Refugiados en América Latina.* Mexico: UNHCR.

———. 1995. *Collection of International Instruments and Other Legal Texts Concerning Refugees and Displaced Persons.* Vol. 2: *Regional Instruments.* Geneva: Division of International Protection, UNHCR.

Central American Refugees

Between 1979 and 1985, some 2 million Nicaraguans, Salvadorans, and Guatemalans were displaced by political violence occurring in their countries (UNHCR 1993, 117). Although most of the displaced remained within the borders of their own countries, hundreds of thousands sought safety in neighboring countries and in the United States. Most of those uprooted did not return to their communities of origin until the late 1980s and early 1990s when political settlements brought an end to the large-scale violence. The International Conference on Central American Refugees (CIREFCA) in 1989 represented a unique collaborative effort by governments in the region, UN agencies, and donor governments to provide durable solutions for the region's displaced.

The Context and Causes of Displacement

The flood of Central American refugees fleeing the violent conditions in their countries took place in the context of long-established Latin American migration patterns, strong regional traditions of political asylum, and dramatic changes in the nature of political violence in the region. Traditionally Central American borders had been relatively open to labor migration from neighboring countries, particularly in areas where ethnic communities lived on both sides of the border. Thus, thousands of Guatemalans migrated to southern Mexico every year to work in the coffee harvests. Long-established routes for labor migration also existed between Central America and the United States. In light of this tradition of extensive cross-border migration for economic reasons, it was perhaps inevitable that the political violence of the late 1970s and early 1980s would result in far higher numbers of Central American refugees crossing borders in search of protection and assistance.

The breakdown of traditional political systems in Central America dates from the late 1970s with the development of a full-scale revolutionary movement in Nicaragua, but the roots of the violence lie in the serious inequalities within the region. The successful Nicaraguan insurrection in 1979 broke the pattern of traditional politics in Central America. The revolution's success was made possible by a combination of unique factors, including the alienation of the working and middle classes by President Anastasio Somoza's greed in the aftermath of the 1972 earthquake and the unexpected military successes of the anti-Somoza rebels, the Sandinistas, which embarrassed the government and emboldened the opposition. Prodded by U.S. president Jimmy Carter's human rights policies, the Somoza regime attempted modest reforms through sporadic openings to the moderate opposition, but these reforms were interspersed with increasingly repressive measures. In a cycle that was repeated in El Salvador and Guatemala, governmental repression was directed to peasant populations suspected of harboring guerrillas. The repression radicalized the peasant populations, which led in turn to even more brutal repression, triggering the cycle once again. In Central America, both governments and revolutionary movements learned from the successful Nicaraguan insurgency that the countryside is the key to revolution.

In El Salvador, historic patterns of economic inequality and political exclusion of the majority of the population were the context for the development of revolutionary movements. Cynthia Arnson (1982, 7) reported that between 1961 and 1975, the number of landless peasants increased from 11 to 40 percent of the rural population. After the 1969 closing of the safety valve of migration to Honduras, conditions in El Salvador worsened. The formation of mass popular organizations to protest unjust social structures was paralleled by the rise of anti-Communist paramilitary groups known as death squads. The Frente Farabundo Martí de Liberación Nacional (FMLN), formed in the early 1970s, became the principal revolutionary organization in the country by the end of the decade. In October 1979, a group of reformist junior officers overthrew the military government of General Carlos Humberto Romero. But repression continued, the press remained censored, the university remained closed, and the violence continued to escalate. The death squads operated with impunity, causing perhaps 1,000 casualties per month (Berryman 1983). On March 24, 1980, right-wing sharpshooters assassinated Salvadoran archbishop Oscar Romero as he was saying Mass. For the next five years, El Salvador was engulfed in full-scale war.

Since 1954, military governments have alternated with fraudulent elections to provide uninterrupted repressive rule

Miskitu Indians, who had been forcibly displaced to relocation camps during the U.S.-led Contra war, pack up their belongings for their return to their homeland along the Nicaraguan northern coast. (Bill Gentile/Corbis)

in Guatemala. The rise of popular organizations, the awakening of Catholic movements in support of social change, and the development of mass organizations led to increasing repression on the part of the government and to the emergence of death squads. Amnesty International (1979) reported that between 1966 and 1976, 20,000 people died at the hands of the death squads. In 1982, General Efraín Rios Montt seized power, retaliated against the guerrillas, and oversaw campaigns directed against civilian populations judged guilty of supporting armed revolutionaries. Massive relocation programs intended to move indigenous population groups to villages, where they could be protected from enemy action, accompanied the formation of civilian defense patrols.

As revolutionary movements gathered strength in both El Salvador and Guatemala, the governments concentrated their operations in rural areas. Counterinsurgency campaigns designed to intimidate rural populations from aiding the guerrillas led to high civilian casualties. This led to increasingly polarized situations where moderate leaders of popular organizations and centrist political movements were killed or forced underground. Some fled into exile abroad. Governments turned to "pacification" techniques: increased military operations in the rural areas, scorched-earth policies, and the development of protected villages. In both El Salvador and Guatemala, the governments created "civilian patrols" to keep the peace in local communities and at the same time serve as a check on the loyalty of peasant populations.

The wars in Central America had serious economic consequences. The violence in El Salvador and Guatemala sharply diminished both agricultural and industrial production. Declining production, growing unemployment, and the climate of uncertainty limited growth and investment, causing even further hardship on the people. The economic difficulties of the Sandinista regime in Nicaragua were compounded by U.S. government funding of the contra insurgency, which kept Nicaragua in a permanent state of war and had an extraordinarily high economic and human cost.

These conflicts forced millions of Nicaraguans, Salvadorans, and Guatemalans to leave their communities in search of safety and assistance.

The Refugees

Large-scale displacement reached its peak in the early 1980s in El Salvador and Guatemala. Between 1981 and 1982, some 17 percent of the total Guatemalan population fled their communities, at least temporarily. Around 1.5 million were internally displaced at some point, and an estimated 250,000 to 350,000 Guatemalans fled the country between 1978 and 1983, with some 200,000 going to Mexico (Ferris 1993, 207). The internally displaced persons (IDPs) in Guatemala tended to move to other rural communities and were reluctant to seek out assistance from the government, nongovernmental organizations (NGOs), or churches. The displaced were often afraid that they would be suspected of guerrilla sympathies if they identified themselves to authorities. Governmental assistance to the displaced was minimal, and other organizations found it difficult to establish assistance programs for people who were more comfortable in hiding. The government responded to the massive population displacement by developing programs of model villages and "development poles" to encourage those displaced by the violence to return. Although internal displacement was a dynamic process, with people returning periodically to their lands, people did not return to their communities of origin in large numbers until political settlements were reached.

The arrival of large numbers of Guatemalans on the Mexican border created problems for the Mexican government. Limited efforts were made to provide assistance and some form of legal status for those in the border areas. The Guatemalan refugees arrived in Chiapas, one of the poorest regions of Mexico, following long-established traditions of labor migration. Security concerns were paramount to the Mexican government, and the border was violated on several occasions by Guatemalan military forces in pursuit of rebels. In response, the Mexican government relocated some 19,000 refugees to camps in Campeche and Quintana Roo, but an additional 27,000 recognized refugees lived in 127 dispersed camps in Chiapas. However, far larger numbers of refugees lived without any legal status on the margins of Mexico City and other urban centers (Coordinadora 1983, 2). Estimates in the mid-1980s were that as many as 385,000 refugees lived in Mexico (250,000 Salvadorans, 110,000 Guatemalans living outside the camps, and at least 25,000 Hondurans and Nicaraguans) (Ferris 1993, 207). Many of the Central American refugees were presumed to be in transit to the United States.

The violence in El Salvador displaced an estimated 1 million people—20 percent of El Salvador's population. About half remained within the country as internally displaced people, about 100,000 crossed into Honduras, and many more sought safety in Mexico and the United States. Salvadoran refugees began entering Honduras in 1980; by June they numbered 40,000 (U.S. Senate 1983, 2). The Honduran government viewed the refugees with suspicion, seeing them as either guerrillas or supporters of guerrillas. Camps were established for the refugees near the border and were kept under close military surveillance. In November 1981, 11,000 refugees were forcibly relocated from the border to Mesa Grande camp, while about 9,000 refugees remained in the camps of Colomoncagua and San Antonio near the border (Ferris 1987, 102). As in Mexico, large numbers of Salvadoran refugees lived outside the camps in Honduras without legal status.

CONADES (National Commission for Assistance to Displaced Persons), the Salvadoran government agency charged with relief to displaced persons, assisted some 250,000 people. The International Committee of the Red Cross aided approximately 80,000 other displaced persons, mostly in the guerrilla-controlled areas (Lawyers' Committee 1984, 95). As in Guatemala, Salvadoran displaced populations were often afraid to register for assistance with the government. However, unlike the displaced in Guatemala, the displaced in El Salvador tended to go to cities, where they lived with other members of their communities. The existence of the IDPs was officially recognized and assistance was organized. Camps were created for them, and both governmental and NGO initiatives were undertaken to provide relief. As many of the displaced were in cities, it was easier for NGOs and churches to provide alternative channels of relief.

In Nicaragua, the military campaigns of the contras and Sandinista policies toward indigenous groups led to the displacement of some 40,000 Nicaraguans, including indigenous groups fleeing persecution, Nicaraguans fleeing the violence of the bitter border wars and the increasingly inclusive government conscription, and the families and supporters of the contra insurgents who took up arms against the Sandinista government. In 1981, the Nicaraguan government forcibly relocated 12,000 indigenous people into settlements further from the border. In response to this displacement, some 14,000 Miskitus, Sumu, and Rama fled into neighboring Honduras in 1982 (Ortiz 1983, 466–470). The governments of the host countries, as well as the UN High Commissioner for Refugees (UNHCR) and NGOs, assisted Nicaraguan refugees in Honduras and Costa Rica.

By 1985, there were large numbers of Central American refugees throughout the region, most of whom had no legal recognition from their host governments. Even for those who were formally recognized by the host governments as refugees, there were difficulties, as neither Honduras nor Mexico were then signatories to the 1951 UN Convention Relating to the Status of Refugees.

The number of Central Americans arriving in the United States steadily increased as the violence in the region intensified. By the mid-1980s, an estimated 10 percent of El Salvador's 5 million people lived in the United States, along with growing numbers of Guatemalans and Nicaraguans. Central Americans fleeing war followed traditional routes of economic migration and were concentrated in U.S. cities with high Central American populations, such as Los Angeles, Washington, D.C., and New York. Estimates of the number of Salvadorans living in the United States in the early 1980s range from 300,000 to 500,000 (Berryman 1983, 3). The U.S. government argued that as most of the Central Americans arriving at its borders had left their country of first asylum (Mexico), they should not be granted asylum in the United States. Moreover, the government maintained that refugee status is reserved for those who can prove they have been individually singled out for political persecution, not those who are victims of generalized violence. The vast majority of the Central Americans who came to the United States were not officially recognized as refugees under U.S. law. Throughout the 1980s and 1990s, approval rates were below 5 percent for Guatemalans and Salvadorans. According to one analyst, "Even in the case of Nicaragua during the period of the Sandinista government, the asylum approval rate, although higher than for other Central American countries (as high as 30 percent in some years) was lower than the overall average" (Keely 1995, 227).

In 1982, a group of clergy and laypeople in Tucson, Arizona, began a national grassroots movement of providing protection to Central American refugees by declaring public sanctuary. Tracing their roots to biblical practices and to English common law, the U.S. churches declared their protection of the refugees in defiance of U.S. immigration law. By the mid-1980s, more than 300 churches and other groups were offering sanctuary to Central American refugees.

While the presence of refugees in Central America, Mexico, and the United States became a significant political issue, there were also economic consequences to their presence. By the late 1980s, Segundo Montes (1989, 213) estimated that remittances from Salvadorans in the United States to their families in El Salvador was US$1.4 billion and provided 60 percent of the income of the recipients. The importance of these remittances was a major factor influencing the return of the refugees. Even when political settlements were reached in El Salvador and Guatemala, the governments were reluctant to receive back all of the refugees living in the United States, for fear of the destabilizing impact of large-scale returns, but also because of the economic effects of losing the remittances.

Return

The Central American refugees and IDPs were displaced because of political violence; their return was only possible as governments in the region took steps to ensure peace and stability. In August 1987, the five Central American presidents signed the Esquipulas II accords, which laid down plans for a firm and lasting peace in the region and recognized that the issues of peace, development, political reform, and population displacement were inseparable. This opened the doors to some refugee returns, although formal peace agreements were not signed until later. The peace agreement in El Salvador was signed in December 1991. A UN-brokered agreement in 1992 in Guatemala ended the years of conflict, although the final peace accord was signed on December 29, 1996. During the years when governments and armed groups were involved in negotiations in search of political solutions, the refugees began to return.

Different patterns of repatriations were carried out in the region, some beginning before peace agreements had been reached. In 1986, in expectation that the refugees would be returning as a result of the restoration of civilian government in Guatemala, the Guatemalan government established the Comisión Especial para la Asistencia a Repatriados (CEAR) to facilitate the return of refugees. In 1988, the Guatemalan refugees living in camps in Mexico organized the Comisiones Permanentes, which developed a set of conditions under which they would return; these conditions served as a basis for negotiations with the government. Many of the collective returns were well-organized by the refugees themselves. For example, in the repatriations of Salvadoran refugees from Mesa Grande, Colomoncagua, and San Antonio in Honduras, the refugees themselves planned the routes, received delegations, and identified return sites. Far from being passive objects of others' decisions, they were active participants in the repatriation process, which often put them into conflict situations with the government. Many other refugees returned spontaneously, without assistance from UNHCR and without the political support of the organized refugee collectives. The return of the refugees was paralleled by the return of internally displaced people to their communities of origin, a process called the *repoblación* movement in El Salvador.

The principal concerns about return of both IDPs and refugees were security, property, assistance, and documentation. Since paramilitary groups, often outside of governmental control, had carried out much of the violence, government assurances that conditions for the returnees would be safe were viewed with suspicion by the refugees and displaced. Even after peace agreements were signed, sporadic violence occurred, which sometimes led to further displacement. Sometimes returnees were viewed with suspicion by governments. Returning refugees and the displaced sometimes had difficulty in reasserting their rights to their land and homes, as others had moved in during their absence. The need for assistance to reestablish themselves was acute. Finally, there were difficulties in securing identity cards and birth certificates for children born in exile—difficulties which dragged on for years.

In recognition of the complex factors surrounding the repatriation process, a coordinated international response was needed that would involve both the countries of origin and the host countries as well as donor governments, UN agencies, and NGOs.

CIREFCA

The International Conference on Central American Refugees, CIREFCA, was convened in Guatemala City in May 1989 under the cosponsorship of the UN secretary general, UNHCR, and the UN Development Programme (UNDP). The conference was organized to analyze the situation of refugees, returnees, and internally displaced people and to formulate concrete plans for resolving the problem. The governments of the region prepared detailed studies of the population movements that had taken place in the region and drew up project profiles that were presented to the conference.

The plan of action agreed on the following objectives: First, refugees would be encouraged to return voluntarily under conditions of safety; second, refugee-hosting countries of the region agreed to assist in settling and integrating those refugees who were unable to return to their countries of origin; and third, the plan included a commitment to the implementation of development programs that would benefit refugees, returnees, and IDPs. The region's refugee camps were formally closed down, and some 70,000 Nicaraguans, 32,000 Salvadorans, and 15,000 Guatemalans voluntarily returned to their own countries with some assistance from the international community. But many thousands of other refugees decided to stay in the countries to which they had fled (UNHCR 1993, 117).

According to UNHCR's *State of the World's Refugees* (1995, 50–51), the success of CIREFCA was due to a number of factors, particularly to the political will exhibited by the governments and the broad consensus and intensive dialogue between the seven countries of the region, UN agencies, and NGOs. But until hostilities were ended, the process was fragile. The development programs implemented as a result of CIREFCA built trust and contributed to reconciliation through their work on the grassroots level among all those affected by the conflicts—displaced people, refugees, demobilized soldiers, and so on. CIREFCA attracted substantial financial support—US$425 million in total, with an additional US$115 million contributed by the Italian government to a related program. Finally, the process was characterized by cooperation among various actors; although the UNHCR played the leading role until 1993, after that point the lead agency role shifted to the UNDP.

In 1993, the "collective" returns of Guatemalan refugees in Mexico began with 3,800 refugees. The permanent commissions had been negotiating with the Guatemalan government and UNHCR for collective returns since 1990. In October 1992, the Guatemalan government acceded to the main demands: collective returns, security guarantees, access to land, and freedom from forced conscription. Although the collective returns received considerable publicity, some 50,000–100,000 unregistered Guatemalans remained in Mexico, and in 1993 the Mexican government deported about 130,000 Central Americans arriving at its borders (USCR 1994, 164).

In 1999, the voluntary repatriation program from Mexico to Guatemala officially ended with more than 43,000 refugees having returned since 1992. In 2000, UNHCR officially declared an end to its activities to help Guatemalans returning from Mexico. Some 23,000 Guatemalans, half born in Mexico, remained in Mexico. By the end of 2000, some 8,000 had become Mexican citizens. Many more were already permanent residents, and others were in the process of becoming permanent residents and citizens (USCR 2001, 288). On four occasions in the 1990s, Costa Rica declared amnesties that permitted more than 150,000 undocumented persons, mostly Nicaraguans, to obtain legal residence.

Although many Salvadoran, Guatemalan, and Nicaraguan refugees returned from the United States following the conclusion of peace agreements, most remained. Some were able to take advantage of an amnesty program in 1986, others pursued asylum applications, and many chose to remain in undocumented status. Economic and political conditions in the countries of origin remained difficult, and Central Americans living in the United States were able to assist their families back home by sending remittances. Forced deportations of Central Americans from the United States were restrained for several years in order to prevent the destabilizing impact of large-scale returns.

Elizabeth G. Ferris

See also: Cartagena Declaration; Civil Wars and Migration; Internally Displaced Persons; U.S. Immigration Legislation: Post-1945

References and further reading:

Amnesty International. 1979. *Memorandum Presented to the Government of the Republic of Guatemala, Following a Mission to the Country from 10–15 August 1979.* London: Amnesty International.

Arnson, Cynthia. 1982. *El Salvador: A Revolution Confronts the United States.* Washington, DC: Institute for Policy Studies.

Berryman, Angela. 1983. *The Central American Refugees: A Survey of the Current Situation.* Philadelphia: American Friends Service Committee.

Coordinadora de Ayuda a Refugiados Guatemaltecos. 1983. *Boletín Informativo,* no. 2 (March).

Ferris, Elizabeth G. 1987. *The Central American Refugees.* New York: Praeger.

———. 1993. *Beyond Borders: Refugees, Migrants and Human Rights in the Post-Cold War Era.* Geneva: World Council of Churches.

Keely, Charles B. 1995. "The Effects of International Migration on U.S. Foreign Policy." Pp. 215–243 in *Threatened Peoples, Threatened Borders.* Edited by Michael S. Teitelbaum and Myron Weiner. New York: W. W. Norton.

Lawyers Committee for International Human Rights and Americas Watch. 1984. *El Salvador's Other Victims: The War on the Displaced.* New York: Lawyers Committee for Human Rights and Americas Watch.

Manz, Beatriz. 1988. *Repatriation and Reintegration: An Arduous Process in Guatemala.* Washington, DC: Center for Immigration Policy and Refugee Assistance, Georgetown University.

Mitchell, Christopher, ed. 1992. *Western Hemisphere Migration and United States Foreign Policy.* University Park: Pennsylvania State University Press.

Montes, Segundo. 1989. *Refugiados y repatriados: El Salvador y Honduras.* San Salvador: Universidad Centroamericana José Simeon Canas.

Ortiz, Roxanne. 1983. "Miskitus in Nicaragua: Who Is Violating Human Rights?" Pp. 466–470 in *Central America in Revolution.* Edited by Stanford California Action Netword. Boulder: Westview.

United Nations High Commissioner for Refugees. 1993. *State of the World's Refugees.* Oxford: Oxford University Press.

———. 1995. *State of the World's Refugees.* Oxford: Oxford University Press.

U.S. Committee for Refugees. 1994. *World Refugee Survey.* Washington, DC: USCR.

———. 1995. *World Refugee Survey.* Washington, DC: USCR.

———. 2001. *World Refugee Survey.* Washington, DC: USCR.

U.S. Senate Committee on the Judiciary, Subcommittee on Immigration and Refugee Policy. 1983. *Refugee Problems in Central America.* Washington, DC: Government Printing Office.

Washington Office on Latin America. 1989. *Uncertain Return: Refugees and Reconciliation in Guatemala.* Washington, DC: WOLA.

Zolberg, Aristide R., Astri Suhrke, and Sergio Aguayo. 1989. *Escape from Violence: Conflict and the Refugee Crisis in the Developing World.* New York: Oxford University Press.

Chavez, Cesar E.

Cesar Estrada Chavez (1927–1993) is the best-known Mexican American: More U.S. schools and streets are named for Chavez than any other Hispanic. Chavez was born in Arizona in a family that lost its farm and became migrant farm workers during the 1930s. He left a job registering voters in the Sal Si Puedes (lit., "get out if you can") barrio of San Jose in 1962 to found, in the farm-worker city of Delano, what became the United Farm Workers (UFW) union.

Chavez was drawn into a labor dispute in 1965 that involved an AFL-CIO-chartered union that went on strike against table grape growers. The dispute grew out of the end of the 1942–1964 Bracero program, which admitted 4.6 million Mexican workers for seasonal employment on U.S. farms. After the program ended, farmers had to pay the few guest workers still available \$1.40 an hour to pick grapes, and they elected to pay the U.S. workers \$1.25 an hour. The U.S. workers went on strike, and Chavez and his organization supported the strike. Growers refused to recognize the union or raise wages (Martin 1996).

Unlike previous unionization efforts, Chavez kept up the pressure in the off-season on several grape growers that were subsidiaries of conglomerates. He enlisted the help of churches, unions, and others to mount a boycott of Schenley liquor products because Schenley's grape farm refused to recognize the union and raise wages. Sympathetic politicians held hearings on the boycott, and in March 1966 Chavez led farm workers and sympathizers on a heavily publicized 300-mile march to the state capital. During the march, Schenley agreed to recognize the union and to increase wages by 40 percent, from \$1.25 to \$1.75 an hour (ibid.).

The UFW found it hard to get other grape growers to recognize the union and increase wages and decided to launch a boycott. This became one of the most successful union-called boycotts in labor history. Between 1968 and 1970, an estimated 18 percent of Americans avoided table grapes; most grape growers signed contracts with the UFW. The UFW then switched to organizing lettuce workers. It reached a high-water mark in March 1973, when it claimed 67,000 members working under 180 contracts. However, as these contracts expired, most of the lettuce and grape growers signed contracts with the rival Teamsters union rather than renegotiating contracts with the UFW. By the end of 1973, the UFW had only 12 contracts, while the Teamsters, the largest U.S. union at the time, had 305 contracts with farmers (ibid.).

The UFW got a second chance to organize farm workers in 1975, when California approved a state law, the Agricultural Labor Relations Act (ALRA), that gave farm workers organizing and bargaining rights—farm workers are excluded from federal labor relations laws. The UFW won most of the 418 elections held in 1975 under the ALRA but was unable to convert many of these election victories into union contracts.

In 1979–1980, as the first contracts signed under the ALRA were expiring, the UFW demanded another 40 percent wage increase, which would have raised entry-level wages from \$3.75 to \$5.25 an hour; the federal minimum wage was \$3.10 in 1980. Growers resisted, knowing that Mexican workers were readily available in the Imperial Valley next to Mexico, where the UFW first went on strike. After months of wrangling, some growers agreed to the 40 percent wage increase but then went out of business, leaving the UFW in the early 1980s with fewer than 25 contracts and fewer than 10,000 members (ibid.).

Cesar Chavez, United Farm Workers union leader, July 1972 (National Archives)

During the 1980s, the UFW tried to organize table grape workers again, with Chavez fasting to call attention to efforts to persuade growers to recognize the UFW and raise wages. However, the UFW had no table grape contracts when Chavez died in 1993; his son-in-law became the UFW's president and launched a campaign to organize strawberry pickers, with very limited success.

There are four major explanations for the rise and fall of the UFW: union leadership failures, political leadership changes, farm employer changes, and immigration. Chavez was a charismatic leader able to articulate the hopes of farm workers but was unable to administer the organizations he wanted to operate on their behalf, such as UFW-run hiring halls to organize and deploy workers and UFW-run health and pension funds. ALRA was administered under pro-worker Democratic appointees between 1975 and 1982, under Republican appointees between 1983 and 1998, and under Democratic appointees since 1999.

Two economic explanations focus on the rise of intermediaries such as farm labor contractors, who organized workers into crews in competition with the UFW, and rising illegal immigration. Contractors are often ex–farm workers who arrange a series of jobs for the crews they assemble, and the workers in these crews are often more loyal to the contractor than to a union trying to represent them. The UFW and other farm worker unions were most successful when illegal immigration was lowest. According to the Immigration and Naturalization Service *Statistical Yearbook* from various years, there were 1.6 million Mexicans apprehended in the United States during the 1960s, 8.3 million during the 1970s, 12 million in the 1980s, and 14 million in the 1990s.

Philip Martin

See also: Mexican Immigration

References and further reading:

Martin, Philip. 1996. *Promises to Keep: Collective Bargaining in California Agriculture.* Ames: Iowa State University Press.

Ong, Paul, and James Lincoln, eds. 2001. *The State of California Labor.* Berkeley: Institute of Industrial Relations, University of California.

Rural Migration News, http://migration.ucdavis.edu (cited September 18, 2001).

Taylor, Ronald B. 1975. *Chavez and the Farmworkers.* Boston: Beacon Press.

United Farm Workers, "Biennial Report for the Constitutional Convention," www.ufw.org (cited September 18, 2001).

Chinese Diaspora

Although the number of Chinese living abroad is great, it was not until the mid-nineteenth century that China became a source of significant immigration worldwide. The reason for the lack of Chinese interest in overseas migration was found in Confucian ideology. Such strong feeling existed about the ancestral land as the "Middle Kingdom," and China's cultural superiority to neighboring countries, that it was thought degrading for anyone to live among foreign "devils and barbarians" (Morse 1918; Tien 1953; Hsu 1971; Wong 1979, 1982). Under the Ching Dynasty (1644–1912), stiff penalties were applied to anyone who left the country: Until 1894, it was a capital offense for any Chinese to leave the shores of the Middle Kingdom (Morse 1918). Nonetheless, adventurous Chinese began to leave the motherland in increasing numbers.

The first substantial wave of international migration from China began in the early nineteenth century during the rule of the Manchus, whom the Han Chinese regarded as "foreign" rulers. For a considerable period of time, the Chinese government did not have any representatives overseas to protect their citizens abroad. Any Chinese who went overseas did so at their own risk. It is no secret that the Chinese "coolie" and railroad laborers faced severe racism and unfair punishment for perceived crimes or breaches of law once out of their country. China did not have any kind of extraterritorial rights in the United States. This resulted in the need for mutual reliance among the Chinese immigrants for protection (MacNair 1926; Wong 1979, 1998) and for the development of a unique network system abroad for the overseas Chinese.

In addition to legal difficulties and emotional stress, there was the hardship of travel by junk boat or steamboat. Traveling conditions for the Chinese contract laborers were so horrendous that many Chinese laborers died en route to their destinations. In most cases, there was no compensation of any form to the families left behind in China. In one case, more than 200 laborers died on one such migration to Peru (Morse 1918; Tien 1953; Wong 1979, 1982, 1998). Going abroad was equivalent to putting one's life at risk, and the Chinese had to weigh the dangers involved in such a difficult journey. Having survived the perilous and uncertain passage, the new immigrants were then faced with new challenges of surviving in a strange land with little if any knowledge of the foreign language, laws, and customs, not to mention overt discrimination.

Despite these hardships, many individuals decided to go abroad. Far more serious and numerous problems existed in their homeland. The Taiping Rebellion of 1840, during the reign of the infamous Empress Dowager, had a devastating effect on China's economy (Cheng 1923; Tien 1953; Wong 1998; Wu 1958). Losses resulting from war and natural calamities ruined the livelihood of many. Besides political strife tearing apart the country, the economic pressures (Cheng 1923; Wong 1988; Wu 1958) of poverty and overpopulation were so great that many Chinese were forced to look elsewhere for their livelihood and fortunes.

Overseas opportunities were available, especially to those in the coastal regions of Fujian and Guangdong. Possessing a historic seafaring tradition, it was natural that Chinese along the coast should look seaward for solutions. The Pacific Islands, Southeast Asia, Latin America, and the United States became the major regions to which the Chinese migrated in increasing numbers. At the same time, groups from certain regions of China or with particular group identities clustered in certain areas of the world. Traditionally, Southeast Asia had been a favorite place for the Fujianese, Tiochew, and the Hakka to migrate (Amyot 1960; Tien 1953), while the Cantonese from Chung San and Nan Hai went to Latin America (Ho 1959, 1967; Wong 1978, 1979). Chinese from Sze Yap and Sam Yap districts south of Canton migrated to the United States (Heyer 1953; Lee 1960; Wong 1978, 1988; Wu 1958).

The Chinese tended to emigrate to regions where a Chinese community was already established, and the strength of these overseas Chinese communities was based upon a shared sense of personal ties and obligations. The network of personal and social alliances in the Chinatowns abroad encouraged migration. Once established in a new country, this network of fictive kinship, in turn, allowed one to sponsor others to come abroad. Friends and relatives who spoke the same dialect and who were from the same district in China gathered in the same locale. It was not uncommon for residents of a Chinatown to be related by blood or fictive ties of kinship; indeed, anyone from the same rural village in China was often looked upon and treated as "kin." The phenomenon of "paper sons," whereby young boys not necessarily related by blood were brought into the United States as fictive kin to already emigrated men, became an established practice in San Francisco and Honolulu. Thus, once emigration began from a given location, it tended to continue.

Since the people from the provinces of Guangdong and Fujian were the first to emigrate, they established the patterns and were the principal constituents of the traditional overseas Chinese communities. From the nineteenth century to the middle of the twentieth, the overseas Chinese communities were organized under principles of social organization that had originated in their home communities. These principles, which bound people together along lines of consanguine kinship, clanship, friendship, locality of origin, and similarity of dialect (Wong 1988), were the foundation of the social structure of Chinese diaspora communities around the world. Family name or clan associations, friendship networks, regional and local associations, dialect associations, and political parties oriented to the old country were visible in many overseas Chinese communities. Additionally, in each overseas community there was a prominent association, such as the Chinese Consolidated Benevolent Association or the Chinese Six Company. These organizations, together with the various other associations, formed the visible social structure.

It is not surprising that much of the social, cultural, political, and even economic life of the Chinese was conducted wholly within the rubrics of these associations. As a result, there was a certain predictable pattern of social organization among the Chinese émigrés. Ideologically, many of the traditional immigrants in the nineteenth century were culturally oriented to China. Migration was a practical solution to economic difficulties at home. They aspired to get rich and return home to lead an elegant retirement, believing that with the wealth accumulated, they could purchase land and provide support for their families. In doing so, they could "glorify their ancestors and forebears" in the true Confucian manner. Thus, many of the old immigrants were "sojourners" who were not committed to their host countries. However, this situation has undergone important changes in the contemporary era.

The early Chinese immigrants were recruited principally to work as laborers, miners, and railroad builders in many colonies of the Western powers. Today, the paths of the new immigrants deviate from those of the nineteenth century. The overseas Chinese now live in 135 countries of the world and had in 1990 a total population of 35 million (Poston, Mao, and Yu 1992). Eighty-eight percent reside in Asia, 9 percent in the Americas, 2 percent in Europe, 1 percent in Oceania, and less than 1 percent in Africa.

Outside of Asia, countries that have large Chinese populations today include Canada, Peru, the United States, and Australia. In all these countries, the annual growth rate in the Chinese population is 9 percent or more. This increase is not due solely to natural growth of the local Chinese population (Poston, Mao, and Yu 1992). Rather, it is due largely to continued immigration. This is particularly the case of the Chinese in the United States since passage of the Immigration Act of 1965, which abolished quotas that had been in place for decades.

The United States, Canada, and Australia still attract Chinese immigrants for a number of reasons: (1) perceived political and economic stability; (2) educational opportunities for their children; (3) the existence of established Chinese communities; (4) kinship and friendship connections; (5) the enticements inherent in the visa allocation systems for skilled and educated immigrants; and (6) the availability of investment visas. In terms of the latter, the United States is the most expensive, requiring an investment of US$1 million or more. Canada and Australia require the equivalent of only about US$180,000. As a result, in Canada and Australia there are more new Chinese immigrants arriving with investment visas than in the United States, where the majority of Chinese immigrants enter in accordance with immigration laws that give preference to family reunion.

The recent face of Chinese immigration into the United States has a new profile, however. In addition to the large number of family reunification visa holders, there has been a surge in the number of H1B (temporary skilled and business) visa holders. Highly educated scientists and technical personnel swell the ranks of immigrants entering the country on work visas. Foreign students from China, Hong Kong, Macao, and Taiwan and from overseas Chinese communities in Southeast Asia and South America constitute a major group of technical workers. After graduation in the United States, many have stayed on to work in high-tech industries. Due to substantial demand, some Chinese high-tech workers were even recruited from Canada and England to work in the United States, particularly in such areas as the Silicon Valley in California (Wong 2002). Chinese high-tech immigrants in the United States today are drawn from all over the world. The diversity is seen in their use of language. Some use Spanish as their mother tongue, while others speak Chinese dialects such as Cantonese, Mandarin, Shanghainese, or Taiwanese, or even English, as their primary language.

History of the Chinese Diaspora in the United States

The question of when the Chinese first came to America is an intriguing one. Some claim evidence for the Chinese presence in North America in the fourth century C.E., long before Christopher Columbus (Fang Zhongpu 1980, 65). Others claim that the Chinese arrived even earlier—more than a thousand yeas ago (de Guignes 1761). According to reliable historical records, however, the first large influx of Chinese immigrants to the United States dates from the 1850s (Wong 1982). The number of immigrants steadily increased over the years and peaked in 1890 with a population of 107,488. Discriminatory legislation, such as the Chinese Exclusion Act of 1882, the anti-Chinese Scott Act of 1888, and the Geary Act of 1892, were designed to prohibit the entry or reentry of Chinese immigrant laborers. Racism and fear of economic competition from Chinese immigrants were the principal factors contributing to this discriminatory legislation. By 1920, there were only 61,639 Chinese still accounted for in the United States. It was not until after World War II that Chinese immigration recommenced, although a significant influx did not manifest itself until the passage of the 1965 immigration legislation. By 1990, the Chinese population in the United States had grown to 1,645,472. The census data of 2000 indicated that there were 2.43 million Chinese Americans in the United States (Wong 2001, 2002).

In the 1850s, the Chinese settled on the West Coast, where they found jobs as railroad workers, miners, farmers, and domestic servants. They have been a presence in California ever since. Upon completion of the Central Pacific Railway in 1869, at the same time that many mining companies were in the process of closing, Chinese and white laborers alike sought employment elsewhere in California. Economic competition with whites led to various anti-Chinese campaigns and the passage of discriminatory legislation in California as well as in other parts of the United States. One example of anti-Chinese legislation was the Sidewalk Ordinance of 1870 in California. It was customary for the Chinese coolies to carry heavy loads balanced on a pole resting on their shoulders, with the pole as a fulcrum. They used this method to carry laundry or in peddling vegetables. However, some city dwellers protested that this practice was a nuisance as it inhibited free movement of citizens on the sidewalks. The Sidewalk Ordinance, which outlawed the Chinese pole method of carrying goods, was directed specifically against the Chinese; non-Chinese people used wagons or carts to peddle their goods. There were also ordinances prohibiting Chinese from working in federal, state, county, or municipal government, and even barring them from the fishing industry (Wong 2001). Discriminatory laws prohibited the education of Chinese children in public schools and from testifying against white defendants in court (Wong 1982).

The Chinese responded to these legislative and discriminatory acts by establishing ethnic businesses, such as Chinese restaurants and laundries, which were not in direct competition with white enterprises. They organized interest groups and protective societies. Many moved to the major metropolitan areas of San Francisco, Los Angeles, Chicago, Boston, New York City, and Honolulu, where they could attract a larger clientele for their ethnic businesses. As a result of this movement, Chinese enclaves, known as "Chinatowns," developed. From the 1880s to 1965, the Chinese depended almost entirely on ethnic businesses for their survival. In these Chinatowns, they developed an ethnic economy that catered to both Chinese and non-Chinese customers. The social organization in the enclaves consisted of associations based on kinship, friendship, locality of origin, trade, dialects, and political parties. Through these associations, the Chinese mediated their own disputes, promoted their own economic interests, and fought against discriminatory practices emanating from the larger society. By 1940, there were twenty-eight Chinatowns in the United States. As discrimination against the Chinese diminished and they became more accepted by the larger society, the Chinese were able to move out of these Chinatown ghettos and pursue other economic activities. By 1955, there were only sixteen Chinatowns still in existence in the United States. With the influx of new immigrants after 1965, the existing Chinatowns in the United States got a boost to their populations. It was most common for new arrivals to move into established Chinatowns, drawn there by the strong local ethnic community and support network already in operation.

The passage of the 1965 immigration law and the Equal Employment Opportunity Act of 1972 significantly changed the social landscape of the Chinese in the United States. Many Chinese who now come to the United States, unlike their predecessors, are educated men and women holding advanced degrees, many from prestigious universities such as Harvard, Stanford, the University of California at Berkeley, and the Massachusetts Institute of Technology (MIT). These highly skilled scientists, educators, engineers, accountants, and others constitute an important labor force, easily finding employment and working as professionals within the parameters of the establishments and business organizations of the larger, dominant American society. They also work in the high-technology sectors in places such as Silicon Valley and for prestigious high-profile companies like NASA, IBM, CISCO, or Hewlett Packard (Wong 2001).

Before 1965, the Chinese in the United States were a rather homogeneous group in terms of their occupational, linguistic, social, and economic background. Most of the immigrants came from the rural area of Guangdong province in southern China, particularly the Sze Yap and Sam Yap districts. The lingua franca of the Chinese communities in the United States was the Taishan dialect. Before 1965, many immigrants were merely sojourners, temporary migratory workers with no intention of staying in America permanently. Very few had families in the United States. Indeed, as stories about the California Gold Rush reached China, their very rationale for coming to the United States was to make fortunes quickly "in the land paved with gold." Once they had made enough money in America, they would return to China to become entrepreneurs or lead blissful lives in retirement. However, the reality of their lives in America was far from what they had expected. Most never made a fortune, and many never made it back home, spending decades apart from their families and homeland. The forlorn graves of old nineteenth-century Chinese immigrants in the West are silent witness to broken dreams and forgotten sufferings.

After 1965, the population characteristics of the Chinese in America changed significantly. Some are U.S. citizens by birth—the ABC, or American-born Chinese. Among the newer immigrants, there is great diversity and heterogeneity.

Living and working in various places, and from diverse social and economic backgrounds, they negate former stereotypes labeling Chinese immigrants as the "refuse" of society, "welfare recipients," "illiterates," "unsophisticated villagers," or "burdens on American society." The majority are self-sufficient and resourceful, and to a great extent, their economic success in America has been due to their ability to create opportunities or to utilize the existing structures of the larger society along with their own economic, educational, and cultural resources (Wong 1998, 2001). Roughly speaking, half of the Chinese working force in America today still depends on the enclave business, while the other half works as professionals. An important shift in goals has taken place: While the old immigrants were mostly "sojourners," hoping to pass through as migrant laborers, the new immigrants seek to make America their permanent home. New immigrants' attitudes toward the United States are reflected in the phrase *Lo Di Sheng Gen,* "after reaching the land, grow roots."

Globalization and Americanization

Today, there is a tendency for Chinese professionals to be better educated or trained than professionals in other ethnic groups. U.S. census statistics indicate that the Chinese have a disproportionate number of university degrees relative to other ethnic groups. However, this does not mean that they are free from discrimination. A number of Chinese professionals have experienced social barriers based upon racism that hinders advancement in their chosen field. It could be said that the Chinese, as well as other Asian groups in America, have to excel simply to get employment, and furthermore, that employment does not guarantee success or promotion. It is a myth of the "model minority" that Asians have it easy in America and always do well financially. Many Chinese complain that they are paid less than other Americans doing comparable jobs. Many also experience difficulty in receiving promotions. The "glass ceiling" is frequently cited by the Chinese as an obstacle preventing them from advancing to higher career positions within their companies.

Some Chinese professionals feel that because of the real but subtle level of prejudice against them present in the United States, their opportunities are limited if they work in companies run by non-Chinese. As a result, some professionals prefer to start their own businesses. In Silicon Valley alone, there are about 2,300 Chinese-run high-tech companies (Wong 2002). Some new immigrants look for business opportunities overseas in China, Taiwan, South Africa, and Latin America. Instead of confining themselves to one location, they conduct business on a global scale (Wong 1998). Due to intense competition and scarcity of space in the few universities in Taiwan and Hong Kong, many believe their children will have a better chance of getting into universities in the United States. This practice of leaving children behind in the United States and flying back and forth for professional opportunities has become a noticeable trend. Journalists have described these global businessmen/workers as "astronauts." The *New York Times* (February 21, 1995), *Time* magazine (November 21, 1994), and other periodicals have reported on this phenomenon. The *San Jose Mercury News* (August 1, 1993) estimated that 30 percent of the Taiwanese immigrant engineers who work in the Silicon Valley eventually return to Taiwan for better economic opportunities.

The devastating recession of 2001–2002 that hit the IT industry, causing many layoffs in Silicon Valley, has propelled many Chinese immigrant professionals to make a U-turn and return to mainland China and Taiwan in search of business opportunities (Wong 2002). This trend of global commuting between the United States, Canada, and Australia to Asia in search of better employment opportunities and quick riches is a dramatic reversal of the historic traditional immigration patterns of the nineteenth and early to mid–twentieth century. In the past, it was the man as breadwinner and fortune-seeker who went overseas to America while his wife and extended family remained at home in China. It was not uncommon for these men to return to China only once every few years, having just enough time, perhaps a month or so, to get reacquainted with their estranged wives, children, and other relatives, make a new baby, and then return to a life of loneliness and grueling labor in the United States. Now, a Chinese American man is much more likely to return to Asia for long-term employment, leaving behind wife and family in the United States for extended periods of time. A similar phenomenon has occurred in Canada, particularly Vancouver. However, returning to Asia to find better employment and economic opportunities does not imply that such professional Chinese are abandoning America. On the contrary, it is their commitment to life in the United States that explains why they leave spouses and children behind.

The majority of the Chinese transnational migrants to the United States are strongly committed to the *Lo Di Sheng Gen* ideology of establishing roots in their new home. This commitment is evident in their willingness to participate in American politics. Chinese Americans have been quite active in establishing citizenship, voting, and supporting candidates of Chinese descent. Some actively seek political office. Prominent Chinese Americans active in politics include Elaine Chao, secretary of labor in the Bush administration; Gary Lock, governor of the state of Washington; and David Wu, U.S. congressman representing Oregon. Hiram Fong of Hawaii made his mark as the fiftieth state's first Chinese American senator. At the local level, Julie Teng, Leslie Teng, Michael Chang, and Leland Yee are prominent Chinese American politicians in northern California.

Community and Social Organizations

In the Chinatowns of the United States, Chinese Americans still rely on the traditional Chinese Consolidated Benevolent Association and other associations. The Chinese Chamber of Commerce, labor unions, and immigrant social services are also found in these enclaves. However, outside of Chinatown, most of the Chinese American associations parallel those of the larger society in organizational characteristics. There are political associations such as the Organization of Chinese Americans, the National Alliance of Chinese Americans, the Committee of One Hundred, and others. Chinese Americans are also developing coalitions with other Asian ethnic groups in their push for equal opportunities and in the battle against racism. The Cross-Cultural Community Services Center of Silicon Valley and Asian Americans for Community Involvement are two examples of such coalition groups.

In terms of educational affiliations, Chinese alumni, professional, and business associations are abundant. The Taiwan University Alumni Association, Beijing University Alumni Association, Tsing Hua University Association, Asian American Manufacturing Association, Chinese American Semiconductor Professional Association, and Monte Jade Science and Technology Association are examples of active groups. Chinese immigrants living in the suburbs have established many Chinese ethnic-based churches, such as the First Chinese Christian Assembly in Cupertino, the United Methodist Church in Fremont, or the San Jose Chinese Catholic Church. The social organizations of the Chinese Americans outside of ethnic enclaves assume a modern outlook, and their patterns of election and membership activities closely resemble those of the dominant U.S. society.

Contribution of Chinese Americans to U.S. Society

The emphasis on education has been a contributing factor in the success of many Chinese Americans. Success stories of Chinese Americans exist in all walks of life, especially education, medicine, architecture, arts, and computer science. Three Chinese Americans have been awarded the Nobel Prize in scientific fields: Dr. Chen Ning Yang in physics in 1957; Dr. Samuel C. C. Ting in physics in 1976; and Dr. Yuan T. Lee in chemistry in 1986. Notable Chinese Americans who have made significant contributions in various fields include I. M. Pei in architecture; David Ho in medicine; Chang-Lin Tien in education; Winston Chen in computer manufacturing; Yo-Yo Ma in music; Maya Lin, creator of the Vietnam War Memorial; and John Lone and Joan Chen in cinema for their roles in *The Last Emperor* (1987). This list is far from complete. Chinese Americans have served in politics as cabinet members, governors and lieutenant governors, judges, members of Congress, and mayors of many cities across America. Suffice it to say that the Chinese in America, through their active participation, have contributed a lion's share in enriching American society.

The economic condition of Chinese Americans overall has improved, and a relatively large group of professionals are visible as high wage earners. However, numerous immigrants from China still toil in the traditional, labor-intensive, ethnic enterprises of Chinatown, such as restaurants and garment factories. The income of these immigrants is meager in comparison with that of their affluent cousins in Silicon Valley. There are also elderly immigrants and poor families who depend on the U.S. welfare system, although the size of this group is quite small. Even with these divisions, the average income of Chinese Americans appears to be better than that of many other ethnic groups. "Racial profiling" of Chinese Americans still exists, and it is not just in employment that they sometimes encounter discrimination. A notorious case in recent years was that of Wen-Ho Lee, who was accused in 1999 of being an industrial spy for China, based on his Chinese ethnicity, and there are others who have been falsely accused of being spies. Economically, the restaurants, gift shops, laundries, and "sweat shops" are still lifelines for many Chinese immigrants. There is still much room for improvement in the financial health of the Chinese American community. Nevertheless, over the years legislative means have been responsible for the gradual elimination of social, legal, and economic injustices, helping to foster Chinese participation in American society.

Chinese Culture Retention

Although the majority of Chinese immigrants are committed to life in the United States and want to participate in the resource distribution of the larger society through participatory democracy, they retain many Chinese cultural traditions. Chinese cultural retention does not occur at the same rate among all the Chinese in America. There is great diversity in terms of cultural identity: Some adhere closely to Chinese cultural traditions, some are in favor of assimilation, and still others want the development of a hybrid identity (that is, the Chinese American identity). In terms of attitudes toward the motherland, there is a similar division. Because of their history, some Taiwanese are pro-Kuomintang (Nationalist Party); some from the People's Republic of China (PRC) are loyal to the current regime in mainland China; and others are more committed to establishing roots in the United States. Some want to see a unified China, with Taiwan and mainland China as a single political entity. Others would prefer to have an independent Taiwan nation separate from mainland China. Increasingly, Chinese residing in America are becoming less interested in the politics of their motherland and participating more actively in the social, political, and economic life of America.

The recent emphasis on diversity and multiculturalism in America encourages the celebration of one's ethnic roots and traditions. Some Chinese want to be wholeheartedly accepted by the larger society but retain their cultural heritage as Chinese. This tendency to emphasize ethnic pride while at the same time wanting to be accepted by the larger society has generated difficulties in practical application. First, there is the problem of a lack of education about Chinese culture. Many second-generation Chinese are so concerned with economic mobility and social acceptance in the United States that they have not paid attention to learning the Chinese language and culture. In recent years, some of the American-born Chinese are taking ethnic studies and Chinese-language courses to remedy this situation. Nonetheless, their knowledge of the Chinese language and culture tends to be limited. Second, new immigrants residing in Chinatown are often more comfortable speaking Chinese and feel more at ease following the Chinese patterns of interaction than the American ones. These immigrants are so busy trying to make ends meet that they have no interest in the multiculturalism movement. Third, what exactly constitutes Chinese culture is also being debated in the Chinese community. Some argue that there are separate and distinct Hong Kong, Taiwan, and mainland Chinese cultures.

Nevertheless, there are traditional customs and festivals that are universally recognized as important by Chinese, whether they be in the United States, China, Taiwan, Hong Kong, Cuba, Peru, Canada, or Australia. The major festivals observed by most Chinese around the world include the Chinese New Year, Ching Ming (Festival of the Tombs), Chungyang (Festival of the Kites), the Dragon Boat Festival, and the Mid-Autumn Festival. By far, the most popular and important is the Chinese Lunar New Year Festival, which plays an important role in the maintenance and recognition of Chinese tradition abroad. Chinese New Year's parades attract thousands of tourists in New York and San Francisco. The second most important event is the Mid-Autumn Festival, celebrated by eating moon cakes in many Chinese families. One can see these special treats, available only once a year, displayed enticingly in Chinese markets as the seasonal festivals approach.

First-generation Chinese may speak one of several Chinese dialects, including Mandarin, Cantonese, Fujianese (Min Nan Hua), or Taisanese. Mandarin and Cantonese are by far the most popular dialects used among the Chinese in America. Owing to historical immigration patterns, Cantonese remains the lingua franca of residents of Chinatowns in New York, San Francisco, Honolulu, and Vancouver, whereas Mandarin is the language of Chinese immigrant professionals in Silicon Valley and in many fields of academia.

The forces maintaining cultural heritage among the Chinese Americans include: (1) the Chinese-language ethnic press; (2) Chinese-language schools; (3) the various traditional associations, such as the family-name, locality, district, and regional associations; and (4) the various Chinese cultural centers established to promote the perpetuation of Chinese culture in America. These are found in cities with major Chinese populations such as New York, San Francisco, Los Angeles, Boston, and Chicago.

Conclusion

The Chinese diaspora worldwide has undergone many changes in its development over the past 200 years. The initial impetus for mass emigration from China in the nineteenth century was economic need. Ironically, the reverse flow immigration of Chinese Americans to the ancestral land in the twenty-first century is based upon the same premise of finding one's fortune abroad. Regardless of their origin, educational level, or language, the overseas Chinese have come to be a visible presence in major industrial countries, including the United States, Canada, England, and Australia. They bring with them a respect for authority and education, the drive to succeed with hard work and perseverance, loyalty to family and community, and a business acumen that makes them seize opportunities for economic and social improvement that others fail to see. Overcoming racism and discrimination, the Chinese in America have made many important contributions in a wide range of fields, from science to the arts, medicine, technology, and politics. But perhaps the greatest contribution comes from the less visible members of the Chinese community—the educators, businessmen and -women, and parents who quietly instill in the youth important social values.

The history of the Chinese diaspora is still being written in the twenty-first century. There is a tendency for the modern overseas Chinese to establish roots in the land of their destinations. The rate of participation in local affairs depends on both social, economic, and political conditions and the level of acceptance the Chinese encounter in host societies. Thus, instead of speaking of a single Chinese diaspora, it is more accurate to say that there are, in fact, many Chinese diasporas. It will be interesting to see how the overseas Chinese, who have made a name for themselves in their adopted countries, now turn their energies toward improving their host countries as well as their homeland.

Bernard P. Wong

See also: Diaspora; Family Reunification; Korean Diaspora; U.S. Immigration Legislation: Post-1945; U.S. Immigration Legislation: Pre-1945

References and further reading:

Amyot, Jacques. 1960. "The Chinese Community of Manila: A Study of Adaptation of Chinese Familism in the Philippine

Enlivenment." Research Series Monographs, No.2., Philippine Study Program, University of Chicago.
Cheng, Ta. 1923. *Chinese Immigration with Special Reference to Labour Conditions,* no. 340. Washington, DC: U.S. Bureau of Labor Statistics.
De Guignes, Joseph. 1761. *Researches sur les Navigations des Chinois du Cote de L'Amerique.* Paris: Academie des Inscriptions.
Fang Zhongpu. 1980. "Did Chinese Buddhists Reach America 1,000 Years before Columbus?" *China Reconstructs* (August): 65.
Heyer, Virginia. 1953. "Patterns of Social Organization in New York's Chinatown." Ph.D. dissertation. Ann Arbor: University Microfilms.
Ho, Ming Chung. 1959. *Overseas Chinese Enterprises in South America.* Taipei: Chung Kuo Chiu She Hui.
———. 1967. *Manual de la Colonia China.* Lima: Man Shing Po Press.
Hsu, Francis L. K. 1971. *The Challenge of the American Dream.* Belmont, CA: Wadsworth.
Lee, Rose H. 1960. *Chinese in the United States of America.* Hong Kong: Hong Kong University Press.
MacNair, H. F. 1926. *The Chinese Abroad.* Shanghai: Commercial Press.
Morse, Hosea B. 1918. *The International Relations of the Chinese Empire.* London: Longman, Green.
Poston, Dudley, Michael Xinxing Mao, and Neu-Yu Yu. 1992. "Patterns of Chinese Global Migration." Paper presented at the Luo Di Shen Gen International Conference on Overseas Chinese, San Francisco.
Tien, Ju-Kang. 1953. *The Chinese of Sarawak.* London: London School of Economics and Political Science.
Wong, Bernard P. 1978. "A Comparative Study of the Assimilation of the Chinese in New York City and Lima, Peru." *Comparative Studies in Society and History* 20, no. 3: 335–358.
———. 1979. *A Chinese American Community: Ethnicity and Survival Strategies.* Singapore: Chopman Enterprises.
———. 1982. *Chinatown: Economic Adaptation and Ethnic Identity of the Chinese.* New York: Holt Rinehart and Winston.
———. 1988. *Patronage, Brokerage, Entrepreneurship and the Chinese Community of New York.* New York: AMS Press.
———. 1998. *Ethnicity and Entrepreneurship: The New Chinese Immigrants in the San Francisco Bay Area.* Boston: Allyn and Bacon.
———. 2001. "From Enclave Small Businesses to High-Tech Industries: The Chinese in the San Francisco Bay Area." Pp. 111–130 in *Manifest Destinies.* Edited by David Haines and Carol Mortland. Westport, CT: Praeger.
———. 2002. *The Chinese in Silicon Valley.* Stanford: Stanford University Press.
Wu, Cheng-Tsu. 1958. "Chinese People and Chinatown in New York City." Ph.D. dissertation. Ann Arbor: University Microfilms.

Citizenship

In its classic sociological formulation, described by Thomas H. Marshall, the concept of citizenship is entirely unrelated to migration, denoting instead equal civil, political, and social rights that became successively applied to all individuals and groups in domestic society (especially workers). However, further consideration of the circle of includable individuals and groups leads ultimately to a second, external dimension of citizenship that Marshall's internal, rights-centered account simply took for granted: citizenship as a status denoting formal membership in a state. Citizenship is thus profoundly dualistic, "internally inclusive" in terms of the same rights and duties bestowed equally on all domestic individuals and groups, but "externally exclusive" with respect to excluding from its provisions all "foreigners" (see Brubaker 1992).

International migration after World War II, which postdated Marshall's classic account, has opened up three new vistas on citizenship. The first is citizenship as a mechanism of closure, distinct from the rights dimension, by means of which nation-states reproduce themselves as "relatively closed and self-perpetuating communities" (Brubaker 1992). The second new vista, perhaps best encapsulated in Yasemin Soysal's (1994) notion of "postnational membership," concerns the fact that many of the typical rights of citizenship (especially the right of residence and social rights) are increasingly being divested from citizen status and made available for certain noncitizens. In this sense the entire citizen construct has become devalued. Finally, a third new vista is "multicultural citizenship," where the thrust is not universalistic but particularistic, setting immigrants apart as members of protected ethnic groups (Kymlicka 1995).

Citizenship as Closure

A classic study of nationality law defined citizenship (in the German sense of *Staatsangehoerigkeit* [state membership]) as a "status," that is, "a condition to which certain rights and duties are connected" (Makarov 1947, 23). Defining citizenship as a status has an important implication: It is irrelevant *which* rights and duties are connected with that status. In this sense, Gerard-Rene de Groot (1989, 5) characterized state membership as a "legal-technical coupling notion (*Kopplungsbegriff*) without an essential content." Interestingly, the former Communist states went further than this, prosecuting expatriation for violating the socialist creed. The impossibility of expelling citizens in today's nontotalitarian states proves the "abstract character" (Makarov 1947, 32) of citizenship as state membership notionally decoupled from rights and identity. Viewing citizenship as a status has an interesting implication: As the presupposition for having rights, it cannot itself be a right. As de Groot (1989, 15) observed, the inclusion of state membership as a "human right" in Article 15 of the UN Universal Human Rights Declaration of 1948 is, strictly speaking, "the guarantee of a surprise package" because this membership can take on many a content.

If citizenship as state membership isn't a right, neither is it an identity. To build on William Rogers Brubaker's (1992) seminal comparison of Germany and France, the two principal mechanisms of attributing state membership, through birth in the territory (*ius soli*) or filiation (*ius sanguinis*), are sometimes construed as reflecting a "civic" or "ethnic" understanding of nationhood. Although this association is empirically possible, there is nothing necessary about it. In the shadow of Brubaker's agenda-setting analysis, it has been forgotten that ius sanguinis had been the quintessentially modern mechanism of citizenship attribution at birth, whereas ius soli was once tainted by its feudal origins. First introduced in the French Civil Code of 1803, ius sanguinis citizenship became the model of modern citizenship throughout nineteenth-century continental Europe.

The German *Reichs- und Staatsangehoerigkeitsgesetz* of 1913, archetype of an "ethnic" citizenship law, is significant not for being based on ius sanguinis but for rigorously discarding any ius soli element. This emphasis was driven by the desire to keep eastern Jews and Poles out of the citizenry. However, the "'blood' in the principle of 'ius sanguinis' was formal and instrumental, not substantial" (Gosewinkel 2001, 326)—it did not privilege a development toward an ethnic, or even a biological, race identity. Ius sanguinis is at heart a formal-legal concept indifferent to the nature and quality of the "blood" transmitted by it. For instance, under the 1913 German Citizenship Law one became a German at birth by being born to a German citizen, and as long as naturalization was in principle possible (as it always was), German ethnicity was not a prerequisite. Moreover, an interpretation of the 1913 law in terms of a pre-statal "ethnonational" identity (Brubaker 1992) overlooks some state-national principles that were built into it. For instance, this law prescribed the general loss of German citizenship when naturalizing abroad (as part of the worldwide campaign against dual citizenship at the time), and it even prescribed the expatriation of *Auslandsdeutsche* in the case of draft dodging. These were important limitations of the ethnonational principle.

Conversely, ius soli citizenship, now considered more modern because of its greater inclusiveness of foreign migrants, could well go along with racial exclusion—as it did in the English-speaking settler states, which inherited territorial citizenship from feudal England and then deliberately blocked its integrative potential by imposing racial barriers on naturalization into the mid–twentieth century. In short, rather than reflecting particular visions of "nationhood," ius soli and ius sanguinis are flexible legal-technical mechanisms that allow multiple interpretations and combinations, and states (or rather, the dominant political forces in them at a given point in time) have generally not hesitated to modify these rules if they saw a concrete need for or interest in it.

An important recent development across Western states has been the liberalization of the access to citizenship. Three elements of this trend stand out. The first is an increasing addition of ius soli and *ius domicili* (right of residence) elements to the continental European norm of ius sanguinis. Most European Union states today have citizenship laws that combine ius sanguinis with ius soli/domicili elements, granting as-of-right citizenship to second-generation immigrants (see Hansen and Weil 2001; Weil 2001). There is a simple reason for this: the need to be inclusive of growing foreign migrant populations. This "need" certainly comes with a historical index: the weakening of nationalism and the strengthening of the principle of liberal democracy, which has become the signature of the North Atlantic world after World War II. Liberal democracy demands congruence between the subjects and objects of rule, irrespective of the ethnic composition of the population (reflecting the very meaning of "liberal" in liberal democracy) (see Rubio-Marin 2000). In a context of massive international migration, ius soli citizenship is the *via regia* to bring this congruence about, at least for domestic-born migrant populations. Conversely, in moments and places where nationalism prevails over liberal democracy, the opposite response to the presence of foreign migrant populations is likely to occur. Germany's ethnic citizenship law of 1913 is a case in point, and the disturbingly "ethnocultural" citizenship laws in some successor states of the Soviet Union, which were meant to exclude the former Soviet-Russian colonizers, provide a more recent example of the same principle. Interestingly, the latter could be deflected under the influence of international (especially European) norms and organizations, leading one jurist to conclude that "increasingly . . . international law has subtly reinforced territorial/civic conceptions of nationality" (Orentlicher 1998, 312). Underlying the turn toward ius soli citizenship is a liberal rejection of ascriptive group markers as a criterion of citizenship attribution—the rise of a liberal nondiscrimination norm after World War II has been the most fundamental normative evolution in the entire citizenship domain.

However, the trend is not from purely ethnic to purely territorial citizenship, but from *exclusively* ius sanguinis to *mixed* regimes that combine ius sanguinis and ius soli elements. The recent European trend toward territorial citizenship does *not* emulate a pure ius soli regime like that found in America, where the mere fact of being born on U.S. territory suffices for becoming a life-long citizen. Instead, the territorial attribution of citizenship has been linked to (the length of) a parent's legal residence or his or her place of birth (as in the so-called "double ius soli"), or, in a combination of ius soli with ius domicili, to a minimal residence period of the citizenship candidate following birth in the respective state. This approach reflects the idea that an unconditional ius soli system is as much at odds with a reality of international migration as a pure ius sanguinis system, being as overinclusive as the latter is underinclusive. Since the famous 1955 Nottebohm decision of the International Court of Justice, it has been generally thought that nationality should reflect a "genuine link" between an individual and a state. Pure ius sanguinis and pure ius soli systems may equally fall short of that ideal because no additional attachment to the state is required by either. It is therefore no contradiction that some formerly pure ius soli states, such as Portugal and Britain, added elements of ius sanguinis to their citizenship laws in the early 1980s, while some ius sanguinis states, such as Belgium and, most spectacularly, Germany, moved in the opposite direction of incorporating ius soli elements at about the same time—both movements are part of the same trend toward mixed citizenship regimes that approximate the "genuine link" requirement in an age of migration.

A second important liberalization of access to citizenship has occurred with respect to naturalization, that is, the voluntary acquisition of citizenship. Most states now grant a "right" to naturalization if certain prerequisites (most notably a minimal residence time) are fulfilled, and they abstain from making cultural assimilation an individually tested condition of citizenship acquisition. Accordingly, an individual-rights logic has entered into a domain that had previously been a prime reserve of the sovereign state. This change has been especially drastic in Germany, where naturalization had traditionally been an always-exceptional act of grace by the state, commanded by "public interest" only, and excluding any consideration of the interest of the citizenship applicant. Since 1992, there is as-of-right naturalization for long-settled foreigners and their children, and the demanding, individually applied cultural "assimilation" test has been replaced by a weaker, generic "integration" requirement (which now includes proved German language competence and a commitment to the principles of the constitution).

The case of Germany represents a larger trend toward curtailing state discretion in post-birth citizenship acquisition. Belgium, for instance, first mellowed its integration requirement from factual to intentional integration (that is, from *idoneite* to *volonté d'intégration*) in 1985, and later even abandoned any "integration" requirement. Only French nationality still officially asks for the "assimilation" of citizenship applicants. The Conseil d'Etat, France's highest administrative court, however, has narrowly interpreted assimilation in terms of "sufficient knowledge" of the French language (and further made its determination dependent on a person's educational level and social standing), and it has repeatedly reined in overshooting magistrates who have refused citizenship requests by Muslim immigrants on capricious grounds, such as wearing a veil. In general, abstaining from a cultural assimilation requirement in citizenship acquisition epitomizes an abstention of the contemporary liberal state from "high modernist" nation-building (Scott 1998), that is, the forging of culturally homogeneous citizenries in which individuals were mere replicas of a national standard.

Finally, a third liberalizing trend has been an increasing toleration of dual citizenship (see Hansen and Weil 2002). Dual citizenship breaks with the segmentary logic of the classic nation-state, according to which an individual could belong to only one state at a time. Conversely, it may be interpreted as contagion by the functionally differentiated subsystems of society, which include all individuals as "free" and "equal" in a nonexclusive, cumulative way (see Luhmann 1995). Though also reflecting a changed geopolitical situation, in which interstate hostility is no longer the default mode of world politics, the more relaxed attitude to dual citizenship is most directly motivated by the need to integrate growing migrant populations. This linkage is explicitly made in the Council of Europe's new Nationality Convention of 1997, which justifies the departure from its 1963 predecessor's strict prohibition of dual nationality in reference to "labour migrations between European States leading to substantial immigrant populations [and] the need for the integration of permanent residents" (Council of Europe 1997, 23).

The toleration of dual citizenship has a reverse side—the maintenance of links with conationals abroad. If, from the point of view of *receiving* states, dual citizenship reflects a de-ethnicization of the state, in which a functional logic of multiple membership replaces the old segmentary logic of exclusive membership, from the point of view of *sending* states dual citizenship signifies a re-ethnicization, that is, a reinforcement of the state as an intergenerational membership unit. For instance, major migrant-sending states such as Turkey, Mexico, or the Dominican Republic have recently allowed their emigrants to keep their original citizenship (at least a reduced "nationality" status) when they naturalize elsewhere in the interest of retaining materially and politically valuable ties with their expatriates. This trend is not limited to traditionally poor migrant-sending states, however. In an age of technologically induced time-space compression and increasingly circular, short-term migration, there is a growing sense that spatial distance and residence abroad matter less than before for retaining links with one's country of origin. Australia, for instance, until recently had taken a peculiarly asymmetric stance on dual nationality, tolerating dual citizenship for immigrants, but prohibiting it for emigrants. At the behest of the growing expatriate community, especially in California, the Australian Citizenship Amendment Act of 2002 made the dual-citizenship option available for emigrants also. The list of states bolstering transgenerational ties with their expatriate communities could be easily expanded. Contemporary globalization and transnationalization provide a rhetoric and rationale for the de- *and* re-ethnicization of the state, bringing into sharp relief the state's dual nature as a territorial *and* membership unit.

However, the state's territorial vocation and the contemporary liberal norms that frame the inclusion of nonnationals set limits to any parallel desire to be ethnically inclusive with respect to conationals abroad. A little-noticed but highly significant side-effect of the recent introduction of ius soli elements in the German citizenship reform of 1999 was to limit the transmission of German citizenship outside the country, *iure sanguinis.* Previously, there had been no generational stopping point whatsoever to this transmission abroad (except for the loss of citizenship in the case of voluntarily acquiring another citizenship). The new law introduced such a stopping-point in terms of the second generation born abroad. The German citizenship of this group is no longer automatic, but conditional upon the parents' declaration of the fact of birth to a German consulate or embassy, and this within a tight time limit. With this reform Germany adjusted to the "genuine link" requirement of citizenship under international law. Because the state is ineradicably tied to a territory, a "genuine link" obviously thrives more easily within than beyond state borders.

Postnational Membership

Famously deplored by Hannah Arendt as a condition of utter human depravation, the lack of citizenship no longer implies a total absence of rights and protection. Since the 1970s, there has been a veritable revolution of alien rights. As a result, the Marshallian equation of civil, political, and social rights with the institution of citizenship has become questionable—many of these rights are now available independently of a person's citizenship, and citizenship has inevitably lost much of its previous value.

In Soysal's (1994) evocative formulation, today's migrant rights are rights of "personhood" legitimated by a global human rights regime outside the confines of nation-states. There is much to this view, particularly its capacity to explain a convergence of expanding migrant rights across European states. However, it needs to be nuanced. First, there never was a golden age of citizenship, and certain civic and social rights have always been tied to some other statuses (such as, indeed, an individual's abstract personhood, or age or labor-market status) (see Ferrajoli 1994). The rise of national welfare states clearly coincided with the national closure of the positive rights and benefits granted by them, but this closure has always been incomplete and countered by the principle of territoriality, on which most social insurance schemes have been based since their inception in Bismarckian Germany.

Second, conceiving of alien rights in terms of universal human rights would suggest that these are the same rights everywhere and for every alien. In reality, an alien's rights are highly stratified, depending on, among other things, the initial conditions of entry (illegal versus legal; temporary versus permanent) and the purposes of stay (tourism versus work, protection from persecution, and so on). In important respects, these diverse statuses are created and manipulated by receiving states, and they are an integral part of states' migration control efforts (see Morris 2001). Alien "rights" in the strict sense, which states have to respect against their own interests and preferences, are the result of constitutional politics, which has become the hallmark of Western democracies after World War II. In light of the early twentieth-century experience of totalitarianism, especially in Europe, most Western states have written constitutions that protect elementary human rights independent of citizen status. Autonomous domestic courts have mobilized these constitutional human rights clauses whenever vulnerable individuals faced overbearing state administrations—as did European "guestworkers" after the 1973 oil crisis, who were very much wanted out by the same states that had recruited them at an earlier point.

In their aliens decisions, constitutional courts walked a thin line between respecting an elementary sovereignty of the state vis à vis aliens as differently situated persons without a right of entry and stay, and protecting an especially vulnerable category of people, those of a different nationality, from the enormous police powers of the modern state (see Joppke and Marzal, forthcoming). Depending on the state and category of the alien in question, this balancing act fell out differently. In the United States, the so-called "plenary power" doctrine has immunized the federal government from any judicial constraint in broadly defined immigration matters, and the alien rights revolution remained largely confined to prohibiting subfederal state governments from discriminating against (legal or illegal) resident aliens in employment, welfare, or schooling. In Europe, no such similar immunities of national governments from court intervention exist, and courts have more aggressively curtailed these governments' detention, expulsion, or attempted rotation practices.

With respect to categories of aliens, the main distinction is between providing an increased level of protection for long-term residents, whose status has indeed been approximated to citizen status (with the notable exception of political rights), and, conversely, guarding wide-reaching state prerogatives over the regulation of first-time entrants, who have lesser rights everywhere. An interesting intermediate terrain in this respect is family unification, which falls under both rubrics at the same time, and in which the rights of long-term residents often clash with the migration-control interest of the state. In some European countries, such as Britain, the fight against unwanted migration (in terms of "white marriages") has gone so far that even citizens' marriage rights have been restricted, and citizens in such states, curiously, now enjoy more family rights under European Community regulations than under national law.

Despite such cross-national and cross-sectional variations, the trend to expanded alien rights is undeniable. If one combines this trend with the increasing liberalization of the access to citizenship, one cannot but conclude that the value of citizenship has much decreased. This has gone along with a transformation of the meaning of "rights," from positive to negative. The rights of citizens were once "positive" rights securing a decent life for all members of a nationally bounded society, and they were conceded through the blood of war, the sweat of work, and the tears of reproduction. If everybody has rights, as is the thrust of the alien rights revolution, the content of rights is bound to become "negative" and procedural only, for citizens and noncitizens alike. The liberalized access to citizenship is part of this same trend. Turning the access to citizenship into a "right" (which is paradoxical from the point of view of the classic theory of nationality law, but part of the alien rights revolution) is intrinsically connected to the hollowing out of the content of citizenship, particularly of its redistributive side. The nexus between inclusive citizenship and procedurally thinned rights for everyone is unsurpassedly expressed in the Fourteenth Amendment of the U.S. Constitution, which pairs a maximally inclusive ius soli definition of citizenship with a list of negative "due process" and "equal protection" rights for all "persons" independent of their citizenship status. This was a glimpse of the neoliberal future, which is marked by the decay of positive citizen rights and the rise of negative rights for everyone.

Multicultural Citizenship

If the thrust of the alien rights revolution was universalistic, that is, to abolish discriminations on the basis of alienage, the reverse thrust of multicultural citizenship is particularistic, that is, to carve out and perpetuate immigrants as protected ethnic groups. It is not alienage per se that is the basis of such groupness, but the ethnic or religious origins or affiliations of migrants, which further divide the latter into a multiplicity of groups. The rights implications and impact of multiculturalism on citizenship have been vastly exaggerated, however, at least with respect to migrants. Migrant multiculturalism has mostly been the side effect of other concerns, such as the accommodation of national minorities or of the legacy of black slavery, and it has been strongly counteracted by a general sense that people who have left their place of origin voluntarily and as individuals have no claim to be resurrected as a "group" in the receiving society. According to a prominent theorist of multiculturalism, migrants have "waived" the right to groupness through the act of migration (Kymlicka 1995).

Certainly, all Western states have embraced multicultural rhetoric, assuring newcomers that the whole point of "integration" is not "assimilation," so that in their private and associational lives migrants can cherish their particular ways as they see fit. However, at no point has the strongest form of group rights, in which groups are given autonomy over their members, been given to an immigrant group. And the weaker form of group rights, in which individuals who share certain characteristics are given special benefits or prerogatives, has been applied mostly remedially, in the intent of abolishing a discrimination, its thrust being universalistic and thus opposite from the group-building and -maintaining impulse of multiculturalism. In the liberal state, the protection of migrants' ethnicity and religion has not occurred in terms of group rights, but in terms of constitutionally guaranteed family and religious rights, which are the same for all individuals. Courts have again played a prominent role in this process, balancing, for instance, the mandate of the state to enhance the autonomy of future citizens with the rights of parents to a protected family life, which includes a religious education for their children.

One author has argued that large immigration, open citizenship, and official multiculturalism policies are mutually supportive (Kymlicka, forthcoming). Although this may be so in theory (or in a world of free lunches), in the real world especially the link between large immigration and official multiculturalism is not so obvious. For instance, as Europe is preparing itself for an economically and demographically motivated opening for new migration at the onset of the new millennium, there has been a marked withdrawal from official multiculturalism policies in the few states that had been prominently committed to them, such as Britain or the Netherlands. Instead, there has been a renewed emphasis on citizenship and civic education in order to contain the centrifugal forces of pluralizing immigrant societies. Since its origins in the Greek polis, citizenship has been a device to transcend one's primordial attachment to family, clan, or tribe. In light of this, the call for "multicultural citizenship" is paradoxical, and perhaps even destructive of the universalistic essence of the citizenship construct.

Christian Joppke

See also: Colonial Immigration; Commonwealth Citizenship and Immigration (UK); Dual Nationality; European Citizenship; Ius Sanguinus; Ius Soli; Postnationalism

References and further reading:

Aleinikoff, Alexander, and Douglas Klusmeyer. 2002. *Citizenship Policies for an Age of Migration.* Washington, DC: Carnegie Endowment for International Peace.

Brubaker, William Rogers, ed. 1989. *Immigration and the Politics of Citizenship in Western Europe.* New York: University Press of America.

Brubaker, William Rogers. 1992. *Citizenship and Nationhood in France and Germany.* Cambridge: Harvard University Press.

Council of Europe. 1997. *European Convention on Nationality and Explanatory Report.* European Treaty Series 166. Strasbourg: Council of Europe Publishing.

De Groot, Gerard-Rene. 1989. *Staatsangehoerigkeitsrecht im Wandel.* Cologne: Carl Heymanns Verlag.

Ferrajoli, Luigi. 1994. "Dai diritti del cittadino ai diritti della persona." In *La cittadinanza.* Edited by Danilo Zolo. Rome and Bari: Laterza.

Gosewinkel, Dieter. 2001. *Einbuergern und Ausschliessen.* Goettingen: Vandenhoeck and Ruprecht.

Hansen, Randall, and Patrick Weil, eds. 2001. *Towards a European Nationality.* Basingstoke: Palgrave Macmillan.

———. 2002. *Dual Citizenship, Social Rights, and Federal Citizenship in the U.S. and Europe.* Oxford: Berghahn.

Joppke, Christian, and Elia Marzal. Forthcoming. "Courts, the New Constitutionalism, and Immigrant Rights." *European Journal of Political Research.*

Joppke, Christian, and Ewa Morawska, eds. 2003. *Toward Assimilation and Citizenship: Immigrants in Liberal Nation-States.* Basingstoke: Palgrave Macmillan.

Kymlicka, Will. 1995. *Multicultural Citizenship.* Oxford: Oxford University Press.

———. 2003. "Immigration, Citizenship, Multiculturalism." *Political Quarterly* 74: 209-214.

Luhmann, Niklas. 1995. "Inklusion und Exclusion." In *Soziologische Aufklaerung.* Vol. 6. Opladen: Westdeutscher Verlag.

Makarov, Alexander. 1947. *Allgemeine Lehren des Staatsangehoerigkeitsrechts.* Stuttgart: Kohlhammer.

Marshall, Thomas H. 1950. *Citizenship and Social Class.* London: Pluto.

Morris, Lydia. 2001. "Stratified Rights and the Management of Migration." *European Societies* 3, no. 4: 387–411.

Orentlicher, Diane. 1998. "Citizenship and National Identity." In *International Law and Ethnic Conflict.* Edited by David Wippmann. Ithaca, NY: Cornell University Press.

Rubio-Marin, Rut. 2000. *Immigration as a Democratic Challenge.* Cambridge: Cambridge University Press.

Scott, James C. 1998. *Seeing Like a State.* New Haven, CT: Yale University Press.

Soysal, Yasemin. 1994. *Limits to Citizenship.* Chicago: University of Chicago Press.

Weil, Patrick. 2001. "Access to Citizenship." In *Citizenship Today.* Edited by A. Aleinikoff and D. Klusmeyer. Washington, DC: Carnegie Endowment for International Peace.

Civil Wars and Migration

The topic of civil war and migration raises issues concerning the changing nature of warfare, internal displacement, international law and institutions, and humanitarian intervention.

The changing nature of warfare has had profound impacts on population displacement. In the early twenty-first century, most humanitarian crises have stemmed from internal ethnic and separatist wars in which combatants have deliberately sought to engage in displacement by design. There are approximately 25 million persons internally displaced by such conflicts around the world. This compares to approximately 12 million refugees abroad who fear persecution upon return to their home countries (Helton 2002, 276).

Ethnic- or communal-identity-based conflicts became prominent in Africa, Asia, southeastern Europe, and the former Soviet Union. A typical pattern emerged in which dominant ethnic majorities repressed minorities, which in turn engendered and reinforced group identity and perceptions of injustice. But such repression also inspires resistance and frequently leads to armed conflict, usually internal to a country. Crises in Africa, the southern Balkans, and Indonesia have been illustrative. A large number of states, particularly in Africa and Eurasia, have the makings of such conflicts.

One of the outcomes of these new forms of conflict has been internal population displacement. At the beginning of the twenty-first century, there have been more than twice as many internal exiles as there have been refugees crossing national borders to flee their home countries. Huge dislocated populations are present in places such as Afghanistan, Angola, Azerbaijan, Burundi, the Democratic Republic of Congo, the Russian Federation, and the Sudan. These are uniquely vulnerable individuals who risk and suffer serious harm by virtue of their immediate proximity to conflict and because they are targeted by warring factions. These harms typically include direct physical attacks, sexual violence, dislocation, forced labor, compulsory military service, loss of employment, and denial of access to health care, education, and other basic services. The recent causes of displacement are many and varied and have come to include international military actions against nonstate terrorist networks. Although there is some evidence indicating that the number and intensity of internal conflicts may be decreasing, it seems certain that such humanitarian catastrophes will remain a prevalent phenomenon for the foreseeable future.

To deal with the growing phenomenon of internal displacement, the United Nations has promulgated guidelines on the protection of internally displaced persons that articulate principles derived primarily from international human rights and humanitarian law. These guidelines address chronologically the phases of displacement; protection from displacement; protection during displacement; humanitarian assistance; and then resettlement, return, and reintegration. Eschewing a doctrinal definition, the guidelines instead offer a description of the affected populations as "persons or groups of persons who have been forced or obliged to flee or to leave their homes or places of habitual residence, in particular as a result of or in order to avoid the effects of armed

Rwandan refugees leave the Biaro camp south of Kisangani, Zaire. The refugees were forced to flee to the rain forest when Alliance soldiers and locals attacked the camp, killing and maiming many. (Howard Davies/Corbis)

conflict, situations of generalized violence, violations of human rights or natural or human-made disasters, and who have not crossed an internationally recognized State border" (OCHA 1998, 2). In addition, the UN Office for the Coordination of Humanitarian Affairs seeks to harmonize international institutional mandates and programs to deal with internal displacement in countries around the world by providing humanitarian aid and promoting the protection of affected individuals.

There have been a series of efforts by outside governments and international organizations to protect and assist people before they cross a national border to flee a country in conflict. There have been increased efforts to assist civilians in the midst of armed conflict with humanitarian aid, for example. The motivations for this new activism, of course, are not always benign, and such efforts could be potentially intrusive. Many states have been less welcoming of new arrivals, seeing asylum seekers as uninvited migrants.

These new humanitarian deployments may involve military personnel and include complex and multifaceted emergency responses. They are often characterized by interactions between soldiers and civilian humanitarian workers and may result in a kind of culture clash in international operations. In general, there is little or no advance planning across the military-civilian divide. Yet, after initial friction, operational coordination typically evolves in more or less workable ways in different settings.

The new trend toward humanitarian action has produced new kinds of casualties. One of the harsh outcomes associated with the deployment of humanitarian workers in the midst of conflict has been the killing and abuse of aid workers. The result is an outcome deeply disruptive of the efforts to provide assistance to countries affected by conflict and crisis. Access by agencies trying to minister to vulnerable populations can be effectively blocked by attacks on aid workers, which are tantamount to attacks on the system of humanitarian assistance itself.

Multifaceted deployments and humanitarian actions are increasingly reflected in international responses to humanitarian catastrophes. These new, complex emergency responses by governments and international organizations, involving political, security, and humanitarian components, have characterized international efforts mounted over the past decade. This has included, most notably, forceful intervention for humanitarian purposes with military deployments in Somalia in 1994 and the air campaign in Kosovo in 1999. The most contentious debates concern the use of military force for humanitarian ends, particularly when resort to such means occurs without an authorizing resolution from the United Nations Security Council. Whether these endeavors represent an emerging norm of forcible intervention for humanitarian purposes or an aberration in international affairs, however, remains to be seen.

Arthur C. Helton

References and further reading:

Childers, Erskine, and Brian Urquhart. 1991. *Strengthening International Responses to Humanitarian Emergencies.* New York: Ford Foundation.

Cohen, Roberta, and Francis M. Deng. 1998. *Masses in Flight: The Global Crisis of Internal Displacement.* Washington, DC: Brookings Institution Press.

Crocker, Chester, and Fen Hampson, eds. 1996. *Managing Global Chaos: Sources and Responses to International Conflict.* Washington, DC: U.S. Institute of Peace Press.

Danieli, Yael, ed. 2001. *Sharing the Front Line and the Back Hills. International Protectors and Providers: Peacekeepers, Humanitarian Aid Workers and the Media in the Midst of Crisis.* Amityville, NY: Baywood.

Gurr, Ted Robert. 2000. "Ethnic Warfare on the Wane." *Foreign Affairs* 79, no. 3: 52–64.

Helton, Arthur C. 2000. "Forced Displacement, Humanitarian Intervention, and Sovereignty." *SAIS Review* 20, no. 1: 61–86.

———. 2002. *The Price of Indifference: Refugees and Humanitarian Action in the New Century.* Oxford: Oxford University Press.

Horowitz, Donald D. 2000. *Ethnic Groups in Conflict.* Berkeley: University of California Press.

United Nations Office for the Coordination of Humanitarian Affairs. 1998. *Guiding Principles on Internal Displacement.* New York: UNOCHA.

Clandestine Migration

Clandestine migration occurs when a person enters and stays in a country other than his own in contravention of its immigration laws and regulations. The term is normally used with reference to entering another country surreptitiously without valid authorization such as a visa, or not registering with the appropriate authorities upon entry or shortly afterward. It also pertains to situations where someone stays beyond an authorized period without informing the immigration authorities. Since most countries recognize the basic right of their citizens to leave as well as to return, "clandestine migration" is not normally applicable to exit or emigration from or return to one's own country. Illegal employment is usually distinguished from clandestine migration in that it can occur even when a person's admission into a country is perfectly legal. This is the case, for instance, with many who enter the United States legally as tourists or as students but who undertake paid employment in violation of the conditions for their admission. However, the association between the two terms is strong because clandestine migration is usually for the purpose of employment. For this reason, the terms "clandestine migrants" and "illegal migrants" tend to be used interchangeably in the literature.

There has been much concern in recent years over the growth of clandestine migration in many regions, notably to the United States, some parts of Europe and Asia, and South Africa. The extent of clandestine migration is, of course, inherently difficult to estimate, but it probably accounts for 15 percent of all migration movements today. Despite the billions of dollars spent by the U.S. government in securing its southern borders with Mexico, the clandestine flow of migrants from Mexico to the United States still averages more than 300,000 a year. The U.S. Census of 2000 indicates that there may be as many as 4.5 million undocumented Mexican migrants in the United States. In the European Union, the inflows in recent years of clandestine migrants have varied from 250,000 to 500,000, the level in any given year evidently influenced by the economic situation. In Asia, some 5 million Afghan refugees were said to have entered neighboring Pakistan and Iran to escape the violent conflicts that have ravaged the country since the 1970s, and Thailand and Malaysia each discovered about a million clandestine migrants within their borders at the start of the Asian financial crisis in 1997.

Where national authorities do not, or cannot, police their borders, the phenomenon of clandestine migration may be the rule rather than the exception. This is the case, for instance, in the movements of people across Brazil's long borders, across those of the Congo in Africa, and between Malaysia and Indonesia. Indeed, in some of these regions the movement would be best described as "informal" rather than clandestine, since they are not unknown to the authorities but tolerated for lack of capacity to restrict them or because they serve the interest of groups or communities on both sides.

Clandestine migration to countries that strictly control their borders is increasingly being organized by people smugglers (whose involvement ends once the prospective migrant is inside the destination country) or by traffickers (who also profit from subjecting the migrant, directly or indirectly, to some form of forced labor or servitude in the destination country). According to the U.S. Department of State, between 45,000 and 50,000 people, primarily women and children, are trafficked to the United States annually. In

These Mexican farm laborers are wading the Rio Grande River at Juarez to seek U.S. farm jobs after a recruiting plan collapsed. The U.S. Immigration Service abandoned efforts to halt the illegal entry of Mexican farmworkers and instead opened the border wide to thousands of the braceros. *(Bettmann/Corbis)*

Africa, the trafficking of children for sexual exploitation and for work on agricultural plantations is a serious problem, particularly in West and Central Africa. In Cote d'Ivoire, for example, some 15,000 boys from Mali were reported to be working on plantations. The same is true in Asia. In Thailand alone, some 200,000 children were reported in 1999 to have been "trafficked" from neighboring Burma, Laos, Cambodia, and Vietnam for purposes of cheap labor in construction, small factories, fishing and agriculture, sex work, and the footwear industry.

The growth of migration pressures has been attributed to the widening disparities in income around the world, the loss of employment in countries where traditional sources of livelihood in agriculture and industry have been dislocated by increased competition from abroad, the ease of obtaining information thanks to the Internet, and the decline in the real cost of travel. People also resort to clandestine migration because of the restrictive immigration policies of the industrialized countries that seem inconsistent with the evident shortages in the labor market. Any restriction naturally involves violations. It is clear that migration pressures would find release wherever there are outlets, legal or illegal, and clandestine migration will increase if no other avenues exist.

People who migrate clandestinely risk exploitation because their irregular status makes it unlikely that they would seek protection from national authorities. Many so-called "illegals" work under very difficult conditions, often paid well below prevailing wages; have no recourse to medical services in case of injuries or illness; and are reluctant to seek the assistance of police authorities even in cases of physical or sexual harassment, lest they be discovered and deported. Abuse occurs in all countries, even in the most developed ones. For example, many irregular Mexican agricultural workers in America are known to suffer treatment in violation of U.S. labor laws. When employers are reluctant to employ clandestine migrants directly because of penalties imposed against the hiring of foreign workers without work permits, they are hired instead by labor contractors, who often cheat them out of wages they have earned.

Suppressing clandestine migration has been the subject of international treaties and conventions. Up until 2000, the main international instrument was the UN Convention on the Suppression of the Traffic in Persons and of the Exploitation of the Prostitution of Others, adopted by the General Assembly in 1949. With respect to the migration of workers, the International Labour Organization (ILO) adopted in 1975 the Migrant Workers Convention C.143, which asked member states to commit themselves to taking measures against clandestine migration. Following years of development at international and regional levels, the Convention on Transnational Organized Crime was adopted in 2000 by the United Nations at a special meeting in Palermo (henceforth to be called the Palermo Convention), together with the Protocols against Smuggling of Migrants by Land, Sea or Air and to Prevent, Suppress and Punish Trafficking in Persons, Women and Children.

Even before these international agreements went into effect, individual states had already developed a variety of policy measures to curb clandestine or illegal migration. Aside from border controls, these measures have included:

- Information campaigns in origin countries
- Repatriation agreements with origin states
- Detention of clandestine migrants upon discovery
- Criminalization of smuggling and trafficking of people and prosecution of violators
- Labor inspection
- Employers' sanctions
- Workers' sanctions

Because of the growing incidence of people smuggling, the Australian government, in cooperation with the Chinese authorities, launched a campaign in 2000 to disseminate information throughout the Fujian province about the hazards of getting involved with criminal syndicates promising easy entry into Australia. Similar efforts have been undertaken by the Spanish authorities with the help of the Moroccan government to dissuade potential migrants from risking their lives in crossing the dangerous waters of the Straits of Gibraltar.

Repatriation agreements have become an important instrument in dealing with clandestine migration, since it has become increasingly difficult for destination states to send clandestine migrants caught by authorities back to their origin countries. It is common for clandestine migrants, especially those being smuggled in, to destroy any evidence of their nationality so that they cannot be sent back. Repatriation agreements enable destination-country authorities to work with origin-country authorities in establishing identities and arranging repatriation.

Internal measures, or those taken to control the employment and stay of foreigners after they have already gained entry into the country, have also been tried. These measures have included monitoring their activities; requiring mandatory registration of all nonnationals with local authorities; instituting campaigns to discourage would-be employers; imposing workplace inspections by immigration or labor ministry authorities; legislating sanctions against workers, recruiters, and employers, including stiff fines or jail sentences, or even withdrawal of business licenses, in the case of repeated offenses, and exclusion from public contracts; and offering various tax rebates or exemptions from social charges when employers hire only documented foreign workers in certain industries or occupations.

There has not been enough documentation and research to permit an assessment of each of these measures. What is clear from experience is that illegal migration has grown in all parts of the world, particularly in countries with robust economies. Variations in the growth of illegal migration among countries, however, may be a reflection not only of economic reality but also of the differential effects of internal and external measures to limit such migration. Consistent policies backed up by strong political will and efficient administration are necessary ingredients to success.

Employer sanctions are fines and penalties imposed on employers who are caught with undocumented workers at their workplace. Sanctions raise the potential cost of hiring such workers in two ways: first, they cause a loss in production time if the undocumented workers are discovered, and second, the employer must pay financial penalties if they are found guilty of violating the law. Such sanctions thus discourage employers from hiring undocumented alien workers unless the benefits of hiring them in terms of lower wages outweigh the risks. The deterrent power of employer sanctions therefore depends on two features of the policy: the probability of being caught and the severity of the penalties.

Sanctions were established in France as far back as 1946, but there was little effort to enforce them until the 1970s. Some industries with "well entrenched traditions of utilizing illegal alien labor and with political clout have been exempted from enforcement of employer sanctions" (Miller 1986). The penalty in 1985, up to three years in prison and/or a fine of approximately 25,000 francs, was later raised to 30,000 francs per alien irregularly employed. Criminal penalties, however, have very rarely been imposed because the wrongdoing must be demonstrated to have been committed by an individual rather than by a firm. Of 705 sanctions cases prosecuted in France in 1983, only one principal was sent to jail; 530 received fines greater than 2,000 francs; 106 were required to pay between 600 and 2,000 francs ($80 to $270); and 68 paid fines of under 600 francs.

In the United States, the Immigration Reform and Control Act of 1986 imposed a graduated set of penalties ($250 to $2,000 per worker for the first violation; $2,000 to $5,000 per worker for the second violation; and $3,000 to $10,000 for the third and subsequent violations). Criminal penalties were imposed on violators who engage in a "pattern or practice" of knowingly hiring unauthorized aliens. The act also made it criminal to transport anyone into or within the United States with the intention of concealing, harboring, or shielding them from detection by authorities. However, for the whole of 1998, only 6,500 investigations of employers were completed, or about 3 percent of the country's estimated number of employers of unauthorized aliens. Although many are caught, very few actually get prosecuted, and fewer still get convicted.

There has been a notable trend in some countries to address the problem of undocumented workers as one of labor exploitation and to rely on labor-standard laws and enforcement machineries to control abuse. Employers of the undocumented often violate minimum-wage laws with impunity, threatening to report foreign workers to immigration authorities if they complain. In the United States, researchers found evidence of lower compliance with minimum-wage requirements among those employing illegals (Ashenfelter and Smith 1979). The objective of policy is to reduce the economic incentive to employ illegal workers. Labor ministries that undertake inspections of workplaces to check on violations against labor and safety standards may at the same time pressure enterprises not to rely on cheap, undocumented labor. Labor inspectors do not usually check on work permits or immigration documents, but it is their business to verify whether employers are paying the minimum wage and providing decent working conditions.

To reinforce the legal order, to prevent exploitation of alien workers, and to avoid creating a dual labor market, states faced with growing numbers of clandestine migrants have set up systems, both permanent and ad hoc, to regularize or give legal status to undocumented migrants. In Switzerland, an employer can seek the regularization, at any time, of an undocumented foreign worker through a regular procedure involving judgment by the courts. In many countries, however, this permanent procedure fails to deal satisfactorily with the problem of large numbers; as a result, ad hoc measures such as amnesties are sporadically invoked. In giving the foreign workers legal status, these measures are expected to improve their wages and working conditions, protect the jobs and wages of native workers who would otherwise suffer from competition with them, and shore up the country's legal procedures and system for dealing with immigration and integration.

The assumption behind the policy of regularization is that unless given regular status, clandestine foreign workers are stuck in the underground or shadow economy where wages are low and work conditions unregulated or unprotected. Regularization opens the way for them to find better-paying jobs and occupations in an open market and to have access to social security programs that benefit them and their families. There is little doubt that the workers are better off after being regularized than before, but the impact does not become immediately apparent. In the United States most have tended to stay for some time in their prelegalization jobs, receiving the same wages as before. Occupational mobility depends more on language skills and experience than on legal status. Even the undocumented can be occupationally mobile if they have skills needed in the market. There is nonetheless evidence that legal status has enabled many to acquire language proficiency and to take advantage of opportunities for skills training. Indeed, the rate of human capital accumulation for most groups more than doubles with the achievement of legal status (Kossoudji and Cobb-Clark 2002), and there is evidence of some mobility from farm-sector jobs to low-wage manufacturing and on to service work following legalization This was also noted in France, where legalized foreign workers tended to leave the farms for the cities.

Amnesties and regularizations inevitably send an undesired message, however: that it is better to enter a country clandestinely than to let the official application procedures take their normal course. Illegal immigrants are rewarded, while those waiting patiently outside are not. For this reason, some countries have avoided using or repeating amnesties and regularization programs.

There is an economic argument that regularization has a positive impact on fiscal revenues, since income taxes can be collected from legal workers but not from unauthorized or illegal ones. The assumption frequently made is that clandestine or undocumented workers employed in the underground economy do not pay taxes and social security contributions. Legalization should therefore have the positive effect of raising tax revenues and social security contributions. The actual impact, however, has been mixed. In the United States, studies have shown that to avoid detection two-thirds of undocumented workers paid social security contributions, often in the name of other people whose cards they were using. Taxes were also usually deducted from their wages. In addition, any increase in tax revenues would be offset by greater use among immigrants of social services provided by the state once they are allowed to bring in family members, including children who need schooling, and particularly of health-care services.

What are the factors influencing successful legalization drives? Several years ago, the ILO examined this question with the participation of experts from several countries. Summarizing the major lessons drawn from the ILO studies, W. R. Bohning (1996) drew a distinction among three types of irregularity. First, institutional irregularity occurs when aliens become irregular because of a lack of explicit policies in the country they enter, ambiguous laws, or administrative inefficiency. Second, statutory irregularity arises where nonnationals violate restrictions imposed on them that contravene customary international law. Third, proper irregularity, the pure form of irregularity, occurs when nonnationals violate national laws and regulations that are compatible with basic human rights. Bohning argued that to be successful, regularizations must:

- have broad political support;
- institute fixed cutoff points for eligibility to prevent more border crossings by individuals attempting to take advantage of the measure;
- have maximum response from the target population;
- create eligibility rules for regularization based on the principle of equal treatment; and
- assure postregularization status.

From these, Bohning derived the components of a successfully implemented program. First, a sustained and well-targeted information campaign is very important. Second, the cutoff date to qualify for regularization must not exclude or disqualify a large proportion of the undocumented. Third, the conditions set for qualifying must not be onerous. And finally, there must be a clear advantage in acquiring legal status, such as some guarantee of being allowed to stay.

Some regularization campaigns have failed to induce the undocumented to declare themselves. In Australia, only 8,614 out of an estimated 50,000 to 60,000 illegals came forward in the amnesty of 1976. In nations where the undocumented are concentrated in agriculture, it is necessary to carry out an information campaign that reaches the remote rural areas. Similarly, attention must be paid to the best way to reach women migrant workers working in individual households. Canada was more successful with its regularization of 1973 because the effort was accompanied by an intensive publicity campaign, including advertisements in 600 newspapers, particularly the ethnic press.

Regularization programs frequently require proof of previous or current employment. In Italy, a legalization campaign was launched in 1990 to correct the mistakes of a 1986 effort that brought out fewer than 120,000 undocumented foreigners out of an estimated half a million. For the second campaign the government simply required applicants to show evidence that they had lived in Italy before the end of 1989. Some 220,000 were regularized, among whom only 21,000 declared themselves to be wage earners. The vast majority, 180,000, were looking for jobs (Reynieri 2001). In the 1996 regularization, employment was again made a qualification for acquiring legal status. Interviews showed that in order to meet this condition, many seeking legal status arranged for false jobs or had to buy labor contracts, even for nonexistent jobs, just to have evidence to show the authorities. Even when the undocumented aliens actually had jobs, the employers frequently refused to admit the matter for fear of being penalized.

Immigration policies should establish realistic deadlines for fulfilling paperwork requirements. A two-stage implementation tried out in Greece in 1998 was successful. It included an initial registration phase, which ran from January 1 to May 31, followed by a second phase, when a residence card of limited duration (from one to three years), or "green card," was issued. For the green card, the applicant had to demonstrate that he or she had earned an income equivalent to forty days' pay for an unskilled worker over the period from January 1 until July 31. The card was renewable, depending on the occupation and economic conditions, and made one eligible for family reunification. Of about half a million estimated undocumented aliens, some 373,196 had registered by the end of the initial phase.

Finally, for regularization programs to be successful, the undocumented must see an advantage to becoming regularized. If they see that regularization only means giving oneself up to the authorities for eventual deportation, then it is unlikely that many would voluntarily register. In Canada, much effort was put on assuring the migrants that the Canadian public would not support the deportation of those who had already successfully settled in the country. For this strategy to succeed, the immigration officers themselves had to be convinced of the objectives of the regularization program. Moreover, in the administration of the program the burden of proof for refusing an application was placed on the immigration officer.

Manolo I. Abella

See also: Border Controls; Citizenship; Migration Policy

References and further reading:

Abella, M. 1995. "Policies and Institutions for the Orderly Movement of Labour Abroad." ILO International Migration Papers 5. Geneva: ILO.

Ashenfelter, Orley and Robert S. Smith 1979. "Compliance with the Minimum Wage Law." *The Journal of Political Economy.* 87, 2: 333–350.

Bohning, W. R. 1996. "Employing Foreign Workers: A Manual on Policies and Procedures of Special Interest to Middle- and Low-Income Countries." Geneva: ILO.

Chiswick, B. R. 1999. "The Economics of Illegal Migration for the Host Economy." Paper presented at an International Expert Meeting on Irregular Migration: Dynamics, Impact and Policy Options, Jerusalem, August 29–September 2.

Cornelius, W. A., P. Martin, and J. Hollifield. 1994. *Controlling Immigration: A Global Perspective.* Stanford: Stanford University Press.

Garson, J. P. 2000. "Where Do Illegal Migrants Work?" *OECD Observer,* March 8, http://www.oecdobserver.org.

Jordan, Bill, and Franck Düvell. 2002. *Irregular Migration: The Dilemmas of Transnational Mobility.* Cheltenham, UK: Edward Elgar.

Kossoudji, S., and Deborah Cobb-Clark. 2002. "Coming Out of the Shadows: Learning about Legal Status and Wages from the Legalized Population." *Journal of Labor Economics* 20 (3).

Martin, P. L., and M. J. Miller. 2000. "Employer Sanctions: French, German and US Experiences." ILO International Migration Papers. Geneva: ILO.

Martin, Susan. 1998. "Politics and Policy Responses to Illegal Migration in the US." Paper presented at Conference on Managing Migration in the 21st Century, Hamburg, June 21–23.

Meissner, D., D. Papademetriou, and D. North. 1987. *Legalization of Undocumented Aliens: Lessons from Other Countries.* Washington, DC: Carnegie Endowment for International Peace.

Miller, M. 1986. "Employer Sanctions in Western Europe." Occasional paper. New York: Center for Migration Studies.

Reynieri, E. 2001. "Migrants' Involvement in Irregular Employment in the Mediterranean Countries of the European Union." ILO International Migration Papers 41. Geneva: ILO.

Stalker, Peter. 2000. *Workers without Frontiers: The Impact of Globalization on International Migration.* Geneva: ILO/Lynne Rienner.

Class

Migrations to the economic core countries of North America (the United States and Canada), Western Europe (mostly the European Union countries), and Northeast Asia (especially Japan) in the post–World War II period from periphery nations have in general followed certain principles and patterns as regards social and economic class issues. Although exceptions to these patterns abound, it is nevertheless useful to define how issues of class affect and may be affected by migration.

Three general assertions form the basis of class and immigration theories. First, social class is central to an understanding of the causes, the character, and the consequences of immigration (Savage et al. 1992). Without class analysis, "immigration" becomes a "chaotic concept." Second, class position determines the choices individuals have when engaging in migration. Location in a higher class gives one more choice about leaving, more choice about destination, and more choice about the manner of insertion into the destination society. Finally, class position before migration is typically different from class position after migration. Indeed, often the purpose of migration is to change one's (or one's family's) class position (for example, "to better oneself"). The shift from class before to class after migration is often mediated by a change in institutional status—for example, enrolling as a university student in a foreign country or entering into an international marriage.

Class before Migration: The Class Specificity of Emigration

Four broad generalizations may be made regarding class status before migration. First, it is generally not the poorest who emigrate. This is partly due, of course, to their inability to pay for a successful migration. The exceptions to this rule, however, are important. They include forced migrations due to civil war, ethnic cleansing, or environmental disaster and migrations conducted under noncapitalist social relations, such as debt-bondage (for example, sex-worker slavery). Second, other members of the working classes may have good reason to emigrate and the means to do so—for example, through the pooling of family resources to pay traffickers—but their contribution to receiving countries is constrained by immigration policies favoring people with high-level qualifications and/or wealth over the unskilled and poor. Third, members of the middle classes have a strong incentive to emigrate—the higher wages that they can obtain for the same work they are doing already and the better prospects they might gain for their children. But their migration often implies downward social mobility and a significant loss of status and power (for example, no servants). Finally, for holders of substantial capital, emigration is generally not a problem. Most countries of immigration have special schemes to allow the immigration of those who arrive accompanied by significant wealth.

Class after Migration: The Social Mobility of Immigrant Minorities

Seven broad generalizations apply to the question of class after migration. First, there is a big difference between intragenerational and intergenerational social mobility. First-generation immigrants are often confined to the working-class jobs they take on arrival or achieve modest upward mobility through the small-business sector. Second- and subsequent-generation immigrants often achieve upward social mobility into professional occupations through the acquisition of formal qualifications. Second, however, members of immigrant minorities show a high vulnerability to downward social mobility into unskilled working-class jobs and unemployment. Third, in comparison with social class and social mobility in the host population, immigrant minorities tend to be very strongly represented in the petty bourgeoisie, and the small-business sector plays a major role in upward social mobility. Fourth, a key role in the upward social mobility of immigrant minorities into professional and managerial jobs is played by cultural capital (especially language skills). Those lacking such cultural assets tend to be confined to working-class jobs or to an "ethnic enclave" in the small-business sector. Fifth, gender relations inherited from the countries of origin are often important in determining whether members of immigrant minorities enter into the white-collar or the blue-collar working class. For example, in cases where a very strong family system is linked with patriarchal gender relations, women tend to work in blue-collar jobs in family-owned businesses. Sixth, ethnicity is extremely important in determining rates of social promotion. Thus, immigrant groups arriving at the same time and sharing similar class backgrounds are nevertheless likely to experience different social-class trajectories in the country of destination. And finally, class location in the destination country is affected by the migrant's legal status. The range of categories includes the invited key worker immigrant (middle class), the "permanent resident" and "co-ethnic returnee" (stable working class) and the overstayer, the refused asylum applicant, and the illegal entrant (underclass).

Class Structures and Countries of Emigration

There are six main generalizations that can be made with respect to emigration for countries of origin. First, the loss of capitalists/capital holders (along with their wealth) may rob the country of origin of desperately needed capital for development and of significant business leadership. Second but equally important is the loss of professionals. Third, and often overlooked in the literature, is the loss of future middle-class members of society through student emigration. Fourth, the loss of skilled manual workers (and some petty commodity producers) can also have detrimental economic effects, although the remittances sent back by the emigrants can sustain or advance the class locations of family members who remain (as well as financing further family-member emigration). Fifth, there tends to be a growth of the petty bourgeoisie in the country of emigration through return migration (and the remittance wealth that they have accumulated). Finally, countries of emigration sometimes benefit from the growth of foreign settlement associated with the retirement migration (or part-year migration) of members of the core countries' (former) middle classes (for example, in the Caribbean, in Mediterranean countries, or in Southeast Asia).

Class Structures and Countries of Immigration

Four broad generalizations may be made about the effects of immigration on the class structures of receiving countries. First, immigration typically implies additions to both the top and the bottom of the class structure, so that the net effect of immigration is social-class polarization. This is true even if the majority of migrants are "gap-fillers," since the gaps that need to be filled are both those at the bottom of the social structure (those involving danger, dirt, and drudgery) and those at higher levels for which there is a shortfall of domestic recruitment (for example, public-sector professionals and high-technology workers). Second, the intersection of social class and race/ethnicity results in widespread, but often partially hidden, social exclusion on grounds of nationality. This result in turn leads to the formation of an underclass of immigrant workers and their families. (The opposite applies in migration from rich to poor countries, where the immigrant often enjoys elite status regardless of his or her class location in the country of origin.) Third, the intersection of class and gender means that in patriarchal societies the underclass is often predominantly female. (The exception is migration from high-gender-role-segregation societies to low-gender-role-segregation societies, which can lead to significant improvement in the class location of women.) Finally, there are major differences in the social-class implications of immigration to advanced capitalist countries between the early postwar "Fordist" period of immigration (1950–1975) and the more recent "post-Fordist" period (1975–present).

In the earlier period, international migration was dominated by the state-orchestrated mass migration of (initially male) manual workers to meet the labor shortfalls (and to undermine labor militancy) in manufacturing industries (for example, textiles, cars, consumer durables, and electrical goods) and public-sector services (for example, transportation and health services). After 1975, with the emergence of a new international division of labor, much of this manufacturing industry was transferred to low labor-cost countries (for example, in Latin America and East and Southeast Asia), and many of the public-sector services were privatized. Thus, the social-class nature of immigration changed sharply—much more of the migration was conducted by middle-class professionals, managers, and technical staff, often posted to foreign countries by their transnational company employers. But the rest was a highly complex mixture of unregulated, individualistic migrations that resulted in an immigrant presence in many class locations, albeit with a bias toward the least attractive, secure, or rewarding jobs (for example, domestic service, hotel and restaurant work, sweatshop industries, and the less regulated parts of the construction industry). Added to this mix was family reunification immigration, which became a major component of migration in the United States after 1965 and in much of Europe after 1970. Family migrants' class position in the receiving country depends on their skills, on their cultural capital, and on the structure of women's power within the sending country and their own families. At the same time, much of the migration became temporary, uncertain, and irregular (for example, farm-based labor).

Social Class "Escalator Regions"

At the same time that the scale of social relationships has expanded from the subnational to the national and now to the global, some features of international migration have grown out of subnational factors. This is true of the feminization of migration, but it is also true for the social-class compositions of migration flows (where the service class of professionals and managers is becoming increasingly important) and for the social class causes and consequences of migration. This means that demographers are witnessing a new relevance of internal migration theory for an understanding of international migration.

An example of this trend is the usefulness in an international migration context of the "escalator region" concept, that is, the idea that some regions enable people to move up a social-class "escalator." These regions must meet three conditions. First, young, single, able, ambitious adults must migrate to them from the periphery. Second, these regions, always core countries with global cities (such as in the United States, the United Kingdom, and Japan), must have higher than average rates of upward social mobility into middle-class jobs. And finally, a significant proportion of older adult, married migrants with children and successful careers behind them must migrate during or at the end of their working lives from the core back to the periphery. The migration to the core country is akin to stepping onto the escalator; the lifelong career takes one up the escalator; and the return to the country of origin is like stepping off the escalator. This conceptual scheme takes into consideration both globalizaton and individual achievement as well as much of what demographers know about class and immigration in the contemporary world.

Anthony J. Fielding

See also: Ethnic Cleansing; Family Reunification; Gender and Migration; Skilled Migration

References and further reading:
Berger, John, and Jean Mohr. 1975. *A Seventh Man: The Story of a Migrant Worker in Europe.* Harmondsworth: Penguin.
Castles, Stephen, and Godula Kosack. 1973. *Immigrant Workers and Class Structure in Western Europe.* London: Oxford University Press.
Cohen, Robin. 1987. *The New Helots: Migrants in the International Division of Labour.* Aldershot: Avebury.
Fielding, Anthony J. 1995. "Migration and Social Change: A Longitudinal Study of the Social Mobility of Immigrants in England and Wales." *European Journal of Population* 11: 107–121.
Modood, Tariq, et al. 1997. *Ethnic Minorities in Britain: Diversity and Disadvantage.* London: Policy Studies Institute.
Phizacklea, Annie, ed. 1983. *One Way Ticket: Migration and Female Labour.* London: Routledge and Kegan Paul.
Piore, Michael. 1979. *Birds of Passage: Migrant Labour and Industrial Societies.* Cambridge: Cambridge University Press.
Portes, Alejandro, ed. 1995. *The Economic Sociology of Immigration.* New York: Russell Sage Foundation.
Rex, John, and Robert Moore. 1967. *Race, Community and Conflict: A Study of Sparkbrook.* London: Oxford University Press.
Sassen, Saskia. 1998. *Globalization and Its Discontents: Essays on the New Mobility of People and Money.* New York: The New Press.
Savage, Michael, James Barlow, Peter Dickens, and Tony Fielding. 1992. *Property, Bureaucracy and Culture: Middle Class Formation in Contemporary Britain.* London: Routledge.

Cold War

On June 12, 1945, William Phillips, special assistant to the secretary of state and President Franklin D. Roosevelt's representative to India, testified in closed session before the Committee on Immigration and Naturalization of the U.S. House of Representatives. The purpose of the testimony was to underscore the support of the Truman administration for a bill to permit people from India to enter the United States as immigrants and to attain citizenship. The significance of this testimony lies in the reasons given by Ambassador Phillips. He expressed fear that India would look to the Soviet Union as a model not only for economic development but also for addressing the vast multiplicity of nationality, ethnic, and religious groups. His testimony, and accompanying testimony by Representative Clare Boothe Luce, portrayed the Soviet Union as a dangerous rival. The split in the wartime Allies was already having repercussions, and immigration policy was an integral part of the contest between East and West from the beginning.

Winston Churchill's Iron Curtain speech followed on March 5, 1946. Also at the beginning of 1946, the United Nations Relief and Rehabilitation Agency (UNRRA), which had been established during the war to repatriate refugees and displaced persons after the end of fighting, hit a major snag (UNRRA 1944). The Soviets, relying on the Potsdam Agreement, insisted that all displaced persons be repatriated. About 5 million of the 7 million displaced during the war in Europe were returned by this time. Many of the remaining 2 million refused to be sent back to places where they feared persecution, punishment, and even death. Many were convinced that countries under Soviet hegemony would punish those who fled before the Soviet forces, or that captivity itself would be a source of suspicion because captives were perceived as quislings or as having been "turned" in some way. Western countries, often pressured by their constituents, agreed that forced repatriation was not acceptable in light of suicides by displaced persons (DPs), as well as evidence of deportations to gulags and even executions among those already repatriated. So the Intergovernmental Committee on Refugees (IGCR), given the mandate during the war to oversee refugee matters, phased out the UNRRA, which was not organized to carry out overseas resettlements. A new agency, the International Refugee Organization (IRO), was established to integrate or resettle the remaining refugees in Europe (Holburn 1956).

Between June 26, 1948, and May 12, 1949, Allied air forces conducted the Berlin Airlift in response to the Soviet Union's closing land and water access to West Berlin. On June 25, 1948, the United States adopted the Displaced Persons Act, further amended on June 16, 1950, which authorized a combined 415,744 DPs from Europe to enter the United States. The purpose of this legislation, along with the Refugee Relief Act of 1953, the Year of the Refugee, was to empty the DP camps of Europe. The objective was not just or even primarily humanitarian but also political, to rebuild a stable Europe. Communist electoral victories in France, Germany, and Italy had important security implications for the Atlantic Alliance.

Meanwhile, the partition of India was accompanied by massive displacement and population exchanges without an agency to supply international protection or assistance; a Communist government took over Czechoslovakia in 1948; the USSR and Yugoslavia had a very public dispute in 1949–1950; and the People's Republic of China came on the scene in 1948, also without a UN agency to provide protection or assistance for refugees. The creation of the state of Israel and the consequent issue of Palestinian refugees led to the creation of the UN Relief and Works Agency for Palestinian Refugees (UNRWA) in December 1949, which has had its mandate consistently renewed, currently through 2005. The Korean conflict began in 1950. In December of that year, the UN Korea Reconstruction Agency was established; it was operated until 1957 and assisted in refugee and displaced person issues (Holburn 1975).

Against this backdrop the issue of refugees was debated in the United Nations between 1948 and 1951. The Soviet Union and its Eastern bloc allies stayed out of the debate, insisting

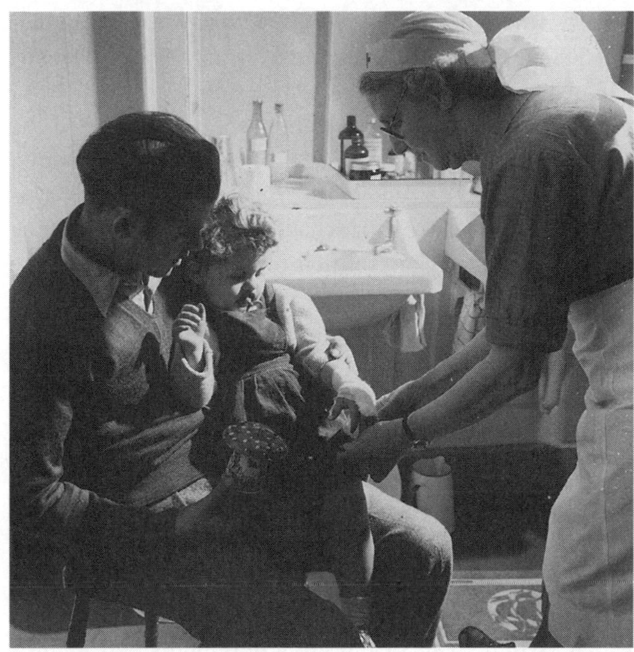

A Red Cross nurse tends to a toddler's injured arm in a sick bay at Domington Hall. The hall serves as a hostel for refugee families who have fled the 1956 uprising in Hungary. (Hulton-Deutsch Collection/Corbis)

that the Potsdam Agreement required repatriation and that resettlement of DPs was an exploitation of refugees for political purposes and an infringement on state sovereignty. The structure and operation of international collective action to protect refugees and seek durable solutions were addressed by Western countries, generally divided between Europe, on the one hand, and settlement countries, led by the United States, on the other.

The position of the overseas resettlement countries was that a new refugee agency should be temporary; have a limited purpose—international protection only; be nonoperational; operate within the IRO definition of a refugee—basically European DPs; and be a part of the UN Secretariat, not a separate agency. First-asylum countries in Europe generally took an opposite position, that the UN High Commissioner for Refugees (UNHCR) should be a permanent agency with a range of responsibilities; use a broad definition of refugee; and function independently of the Secretariat with a strong high commissioner.

The UNHCR was established in 1951 as a temporary agency needing reauthorization, with a major mandate of protection, to be nonoperational, and to focus on European refugees. The 1951 Convention Relating to the Status of Refugees originally applied only to pre-1951 refugees in Europe, but the 1967 Protocol dropped these limitations. The agency was separate from the Secretariat, with the high commissioner elected by the UN General Assembly. The UNHCR, however, concentrated on European refugees, including developing programs with the Ford Foundation funding training and integration projects (Keely and Elwell 1981).

In 1956, UNHCR provided assistance for Hungarian refugees on the putative basis that their displacement could be traced to events prior to 1951. Although all parties stressed that repatriation was the preferred solution, the UNHCR insisted that no Hungarian refugee would be forced to repatriate.

The situation of Chinese refugees in Hong Kong in 1952 led to the development of the concept of the "good offices" of UNHCR. For countries that recognized the People's Republic of China, refugees in Hong Kong fit the UNHCR statute definition, even if not the convention definition with its requirement that refugees be produced by events prior to 1951. For countries that did not recognize the People's Republic, there was no basis for refugee recognition in international law. The concept of using the high commissioner's good offices was invoked to assist in finding permanent solutions for refugees in Hong Kong. The same concept was invoked in 1959 in the case of Algerians when France objected to their recognition as convention refugees. It has been used since to allow protection and assistance when the member states of the General Assembly or the Security Council want a rapid and capable response to a humanitarian crisis.

In 1962, UNHCR opened its first branch office outside Europe (excepting the Hong Kong office in the British Crown Colony), in Burundi, to deal directly with refugees. This may be taken as the date when the activities of the UNHCR developed a decidedly non-European focus. The late Prince Sadruddin Aga Khan expanded UNHCR activities in Third World countries, especially Africa, during his tenure as high commissioner.

In many countries, refugee production accompanied the process of political development following independence (Zolberg, Suhrke, and Aguayo 1988). Part of the instability in postindependence countries and other developing countries was a mix of nationalities vying for political power and over ideological differences, particularly along the divide between Marxist-Leninist varieties of socialism and Western-style capitalism (Keely 1996). Ideological contests were part of a larger conflict between East and West, led by the Soviet Union and the United States, respectively. This contest was carried out with each side seeking client governments and backing government or rebel forces according to their ideological stances. Proxy wars took place around the world as part of a process of colonial liberation, national identity building, state building, and geopolitical alliance making that reflected superpower politics. Vietnam, Angola, the Horn of Africa, Cuba, Afghanistan, El Salvador, and Nicaragua are but a few of a long list of refugee-producing countries partly caught up in Cold War, superpower rivalry. While mutually assured destruction kept nuclear weapons at bay, the maelstrom of civil war was visited on politically weaker and poorer developing countries during the postwar period until the collapse of the Soviet Union (1989 to 1991).

During the Cold War, after the DPs from World War II were repatriated or resettled, two refugee regimes developed (Keely 2001). The UNHCR regime was generally confined to refugee protection and assistance in the Third World, and UNHCR was considered a Third World relief agency, becoming more operational in fact, despite its original mandate. Although the nature of the prolonged proxy wars made repatriation often a fond hope and rather sporadic, it remained the preferred durable solution. The UNHCR operated in the same manner as prior efforts on behalf of refugees since their beginning in 1921, providing protection, supporting first asylum, organizing assistance, and seeking a permanent solution, with repatriation as the preferred outcome.

Meanwhile, Western powers organized a second refugee regime as part of their Cold War strategy. Western industrial countries put in place a regime of asylum and resettlement for those "escaping" from Communist governments. In Europe, the major focus was on those leaving the Soviet Union and Eastern Europe for the West. This included regular flows from the German Democratic Republic until the building of the Berlin Wall in 1961. It included pulses from Hungary in 1956, Czechoslovakia in 1968, and Poland in 1981, as well as a small but steady stream of defectors. These asylum seekers were welcomed as escapees to freedom by an elaborate reception system, followed by permanent residence in Western Europe. There was no question of repatriation because living under communism was considered persecution enough.

The United States, along with Canada and Australia, focused more on a pattern of resettlement of those escaping from communism. They took many of the escapees from Eastern Europe as part of their partnership in opposition to the Soviets. They also took many from Third World countries with Communist governments, including Cubans beginning in 1959, Vietnamese in 1975–1976, Southeast Asian boat people beginning in 1979, and some Central Americans, notably Nicaraguans, in the 1980s.

This policy of accepting refugees from communism differed from the Third World regime dominated by the UNHCR, an agency that had little hand in the Western industrial regime. The anti-Communist regime encouraged refugee flows. It was predicated on small, controlled movements because of the no-exit policies of Communist governments, along with periodic outbursts, such as from Hungary, from Cuba from time to time, and from Vietnam. A steady stream with occasional spurts was considered an acceptable price for the propaganda effect of people voting with their feet. Refugees "escaped" Communist countries, while few attempted to travel in the opposite direction.

The Western countries established and supported the UNHCR regime, which is based on the idea of first asylum, temporary protection and assistance, and preferably repatriation. Yet these very countries had no legal basis for granting temporary first asylum in their own countries during the Cold War. For them the operative refugee regime in their region of the world was permanent settlement for opposition members from Communist countries who left often under great threat.

The disjuncture between the two regimes began to become glaringly apparent in the early 1980s. In 1983 and 1984, the number of asylum seekers in Europe took a large jump and continued to rise in the immediately following years. One source of the initial increase was Iranian dissidents coming through Turkey. This signaled the beginning of a period in which asylum seekers came from developing and, significantly, non-Communist countries into Europe. European governments started to feel overwhelmed and threatened. The kind of refugee who was supposed to be handled by the UNHCR regime was penetrating the anti-Communist regime.

Thus began the long and continuing political debate about asylum in Europe and, it turns out, also in North America and Australia, which also were target destinations for an increasing number of asylum seekers from non-Communist, developing countries. Western industrial states maintained that their refugee system was designed for the Cold War and they were not to be major destinations of refugees from civil turmoil in the developing world. They maintained that the basic refugee regime represented by the UNHCR was to reemerge as the dominant model. Refugees were to be given first asylum, protected and assisted, and preferably repatriated. Local integration in first-asylum countries, as part of a policy to regionally contain refugees, is decidedly the second choice of Western governments operationally. Resettlement in a highly developed Western country was to be the exception, not the rule. The post–Cold War debates around temporary protection, safe third countries, safe areas, safe return, carrier sanctions, asylum shopping, the Dublin Convention, and the Schengen Agreement ensued. Governments have divided constituencies concerning asylum and refugee policies. Some citizens perceive too many economically and culturally threatening asylum seekers. Others see hypocritical governments playing on racist fears and proposing double standards about human rights.

The policy and practice of dual-refugee regimes of the Cold War era are currently exacting a political price from the countries that established and maintain international protection and assistance for the politically persecuted. Many of the pieces are in place for a post–Cold War refugee regime, and adaptations to new challenges in an unsettled geopolitical environment have even taken place. The UNHCR, for example, has continued its role in the developing world while playing important roles in the Balkans. Many nongovernmental organizations (NGOs) continue to assist, protect, and advocate on behalf of refugees. They have also addressed new issues, such as humanitarian personnel safety, roles for the military in humanitarian emergencies, and the implications of neutrality in war-torn areas and refugee camps dominated by military elements. Internally displaced persons, generally absent during the Cold War because an integralist view of sovereignty reigned in international relations, have been added to the humanitarian agenda.

Whether the anti-Communist refugee regime contributed to the demise of the Soviet Union will be debated. Its role was probably of symbolic importance for keeping anti-Communist sentiment alive in the West. The full outline of a post–Cold War refugee regime is not yet in place. The international response to refugees in a post–Cold War world is a subject of great contention within and among countries, and the current disarray is partly a result of the divided responses to refugees reflected in the dual-refugee regimes of the Cold War.

Charles Keely

See also: Berlin Wall; Comprehensive Plan of Action; Dublin Convention; Resettlement; Safe Country, Safe Third Country; Schengen Agreement; UN Convention Relating to the Status of Refugees, 1951

References and further reading:

Holborn, Louise W. 1956. *The International Refugee Organization: Its History and Work, 1946–1952.* London: Oxford University Press.

———. 1975. *Refugees: A Problem for Our Time: The Work of the United Nations High Commissioner for Refugees, 1951–1972.* Metuchen, NJ: Scarecrow.

James, Robert Rhodes, ed. 1983. *Winston S. Churchill: His Complete Speeches, 1897–1963.* New York: Atheneum.

Keely, Charles B. 1996. "How Nation-States Create and Respond to Refugee Flows." *International Migration Review* 30, no. 4 (Winter): 1046–1066.

———. 2001. "The International Refugee Regime(s): The End of the Cold War Matters." *International Migration Review* 35, no. 1 (Spring): 303–314.

Keely, Charles B., and Patricia J. Elwell. 1981. *Global Refugee Policy: The Case for a Development-Oriented Strategy.* New York: The Population Council.

United Nations Relief and Rehabilitation Agency. 1944. *Organization, Aims, Progress.* Washington, DC: UNRRA.

U.S. House Committee on Immigration and Naturalization, 79th Congress. Records of the House of Representatives, Record Group 233, folder HR79A-F.16.2.

Zolberg, Aristede, Astri Suhrke, and Sergio Aguayo. 1988. *Escape from Violence.* New York: Oxford University Press.

Colombian Diaspora

More than half a century of internal conflict, politically motivated violence against civilians, and widespread human rights violations in Colombia have generated a level of displacement, both internal and external, that is beyond measure. Beginning in the 1940s, and following in periodic waves since then—the most recent beginning in the 1980s—conflict-related displacement has devastated Colombia. By 2003, one in every thirteen Colombians was uprooted, making Colombia the country with the "highest rate of forced migration in the Western Hemisphere and one of the highest in the world" (Loughna). Some 2.5 million Colombians were internally displaced and, even by conservative estimates, more than 400,000 others had fled the country and were refugees or in refugee-like circumstances, most without legal status (some observers say the number of Colombians who have fled abroad is in the millions) (*World Refugee Survey* 2003, 241).

La Violencia

A first wave of conflict and displacement during the period referred to as *La Violencia* (The Violence), which lasted approximately from the late 1940s through the mid-1960s, left an estimated 200,000 dead and displaced more than 2 million others (Kirk 1993, 1). Most of the displacement was within Colombia, but many also migrated abroad. Politically engendered displacement diminished during the late 1960s, but hundreds of thousands of Colombians migrated abroad during that period for economic reasons, primarily to Venezuela.

Between 1948 and 1953, competition for power between Colombia's two dominant political parties—the Partido Social Conservador (Conservative Party), which favored a strong central government and was supported by wealthy landowners and the Roman Catholic hierarchy, and the left-leaning, federally oriented, more secular Partido Liberal (Liberal Party)—engulfed the country in widespread violence. Entire towns and villages were burned to the ground and their residents murdered by supporters of the warring parties.

In 1958, the conservative and liberal parties signed a power-sharing pact that largely put an end to their conflict but effectively excluded all political opposition (some violence between supporters of the groups continued until the mid-1960s, but at a reduced level). The two parties' arrangement lasted officially until 1974 and unofficially into the mid-1980s.

It is estimated that La Violencia displaced more than 2 million Colombians. Many fled from rural areas to the cities, where large shantytowns sprang up. Others fled to less populated regions of the country such as Meta, lower Cauca,

Colombian policemen stand alongside alleged members of the left-wing guerrilla group FARC (Revolutionary Armed Forces of Colombia) in Villavicencio, in the Meta province, September 20, 2002. Violence and threats from either FARC, the Colombian government, or right-wing paramilitaries have forced many Colombians to flee the country. (Reuters/Corbis)

Magdalena Medio, and Putumayo. Many left the country altogether. Most went to Venezuela, but others fled as far afield as the United States.

In the 1960s, new leftist insurgent groups took up arms against the established powers. They sought to reverse some of the country's deep-rooted social, political, and economic problems, such as the government's near abandonment of most of the rural population and the concentration of land in the hands of a small number of wealthy landowners. A case study of displacement in Colombia described the factors that gave rise to insurgencies and conflict there as "the enormous disparities in the distribution of land and wealth, a loss of government legitimacy, the ineffectiveness of established institutions . . . the inaccessibility of power for the majority of Colombians, [and] the physical absence of the state in many regions" (Obregon and Stavropoulou 1998, 401).

The Fuerzas Armadas Revolucionarias de Colombia (Revolutionary Armed Forces of Colombia, FARC) emerged in 1964, an outgrowth of peasant self-defense groups that developed ties with the Communist Party and leftist intellectuals. The Cuban-inspired Ejército de Liberación Nacional (National Liberation Army, ELN) also arose in 1964 in Colombia's Middle Magdalena region. A smaller group, the Ejército Popular de Liberación (Popular Liberation Army, EPL), that began operating in the Caribbean coastal area of Cordoba in 1967 had a Maoist orientation. During this same period, economic decline led hundreds of thousands to emigrate, particularly to then oil-rich Venezuela, but also to the United States and elsewhere. By the early 1970s, Venezuelan officials reportedly estimated that more than 500,000 Colombians were living in that country, and the Colombian exodus became what one author called "the largest human migration in South America's history" (Gall 1971).

During the 1970s, the Colombian military pursued an aggressive counterinsurgency campaign that often targeted civilians in rural areas and that had the opposite effect of what it intended: Support increased for the guerrillas, who often delivered basic social, economic, and legal services that the government failed to provide.

By the 1980s, political violence was again causing large-scale displacement. The guerrilla groups increasingly turned to abusive tactics to intimidate the population into supporting them. They killed or threatened local officials, civic leaders, and business owners, whom they perceived as opposing them. Most often, their actions caused civilians to flee. FARC's recruitment of children also cost them support and caused many families to flee. The 17,000-member FARC funded its insurgency through kidnapping and by taxing wealthy individuals, businesses, coca growers, and narco-traffickers in areas under its control.

During the 1980s and into the 1990s, government forces were also responsible for widespread human rights violations. During that period, however, a new armed faction joined the fray and began to do much of the military's dirty work for it. Peasant militias armed by wealthy landowners and drug traffickers to protect them and their property from the guerrillas grew into independent, right-wing, paramilitary groups. The "Autodefensas" Unidas de Colombia (United "Self-Defense" Groups of Colombia, AUC), an umbrella organization for these paramilitary groups, has said that its aim is to rid Colombia of the guerrillas, but the organization has many other interests. Colombia's Ministry of Defense has said that paramilitaries intend "not only to eradicate the guerrillas from certain areas, but also to expel other land owners . . . with the aim of appropriating their lands."

Since 1995, paramilitary groups have been responsible for a greater amount of violence directed against civilians—including an increasing number of massacres—than the guerrillas or the armed forces. The AUC has tripled in size since 1988 and now reportedly has as many as 15,000 fighters. Colombian and international human rights groups have repeatedly charged that many in the Colombian military either facilitate or directly participate in paramilitaries' activities. According to the U.S. State Department, there are "credible allegations of cooperation with paramilitary groups, including instances of both passive support and direct collaboration by members of the public security forces, particularly the army" (*Human Rights Reports 2002*). The FARC is active throughout the country. In 1999, it carried out operations in 1,000 of Colombia's 1,085 municipalities.

Colombia's burgeoning narcotics industry, which for decades has had an impact on virtually every aspect of Colombian society—including politics and government—and from which both guerrillas and paramilitaries profit, has fueled the conflict, and drug-related criminal activity has added to the spiral of violence in the country.

Not surprisingly, Colombia has become one of the most violent and dangerous places on earth, with more murders and kidnappings than any other country. In 1995, the Colombian Catholic Bishops' Conference said, "Violence has profoundly altered the way of life of the Colombian people. It has not only left its destructive stamp on individuals, but has also penetrated the institutions and the very core of [Colombian] society" (Ruiz 1998, 6).

In May 2002, Colombia elected a new president, Alvaro Uribe Vélez, whose father was killed by the FARC in 1983 and who promised to get tough with the insurgents and bring security to the country. Within days of taking office, Uribe declared a "State of Internal Disturbance" that permitted the government to carry out generalized arrests, tap telephones, and restrict civilians' right to movement.

Internal Displacement

One of the most widespread consequences of the conflict and political violence in Colombia has been the massive internal displacement and refugee flight it has engendered. Between 1984 and 1994, some 600,000 Colombians became internally displaced. By 1997, more than 1 million were displaced. Over the next five years, the number of displaced jumped another 150 percent, to 2.5 million by the end of 2002 (*World Refugee Survey* 2003).

Internal displacement in Colombia is a phenomenon that affects the entire country. According to the Colombian government, although approximately half of all displaced persons originate in one of three departments (Antioquia, Bolivar, and Choco), Colombians have been displaced from 29 of Colombia's 32 departments; 30 of the 32 departments host internally displaced persons.

A disproportionate number of the displaced are Afro-Colombians and indigenous people. Although these groups represent less than 20 percent of Colombians, they comprise one-third of the displaced population. Widows whose husbands have been killed by one or the other side head a disproportionate number of households.

Most displaced Colombians live in shantytowns surrounding Colombia's largest cities. Nearly 50 percent of them are unemployed. Those who do find work usually find poorly paid daily or temporary work in construction or road-building crews. Many work for even less than the standard low wage, which generates resentment on the part of other local poor people. The displaced often turn to the informal economy, buying fruit and vegetables, cigarettes, or other products from markets and wholesalers and then selling them on street corners or house to house.

Lacking official papers, most displaced Colombians find it impossible to vote, to work in the formal sector, to own property, to drive, to send their children to public schools, or to receive treatment at public hospitals. According to the U.S. Department of State, only 34 percent of displaced Colombians have access to health care, and only 15 percent of displaced children attend school. The United Nations reports that the displaced evince moderate and in some instances acute malnutrition.

The International Committee of the Red Cross and the government provide limited emergency assistance to displaced persons during the first ninety days of their displacement. Even this emergency assistance reaches only a minority of the newly displaced, however. After ninety days, the displaced must fend for themselves. Colombian NGOs, the Catholic Church, and other private organizations provide very limited assistance to longer-term displaced persons. The government has enacted laws and issued several decrees that outline its responsibilities to the displaced. However, its record on implementing those has remained poor.

In 1999, the government transferred responsibility for assisting the displaced to yet another bureaucratic entity, the Red de Solidaridad Social (Social Solidarity Network, hereafter "the Red"). The Red is a loose-knit network of national and regional governmental agencies that, at the time it was assigned its new role with the displaced, most observers regarded as ineffective.

Beyond Colombia's Borders

Although most Colombians who become uprooted owing to political violence remain internally displaced, in recent years Colombians have increasingly sought refuge in other countries, both within the region and in Europe and North America. Most of those who flee to neighboring countries are, like most internally displaced Colombians, farmers or residents of small towns and villages that have been targeted or threatened by guerrillas, or, more often, by paramilitary groups (Ruiz 2001). Most Colombians who seek refuge in North America and Europe are professionals and white-collar workers who have been subjected to or fear kidnapping or extortion or who seek to escape the conflict and violence in Colombia. In recent years, guerrilla groups, in particular, have increasingly targeted residents of the country's large cities.

As the number of refugees increases, many countries have taken steps to limit Colombians' entry. Since 2000, Venezuela, which hosts a long-standing Colombian migrant community of more than 1.5 million, many of them undocumented, has taken steps to restrict and discourage the entry of Colombian asylum seekers in recent years. Venezuelan authorities promptly return groups of Colombians attempting to escape conflict in their home country without permitting them to apply for asylum. Venezuela also routinely denies the UN High Commissioner for Refugees (UNHCR) access to the would-be refugees.

The Venezuelan government took over responsibility for processing asylum claims in 1999 from UNHCR. It enacted an Organic Law on Asylum and Refugees in 2001 but had not taken steps to implement it by the end of 2002. The approximately 1,000 Colombians who have managed to apply for asylum since 1999 have not had their claims adjudicated and remain without protection. According to UNHCR, they risk being "indiscriminately deported in contradiction with international and national refugee law" (UNHCR 2003). In February 2002, some 3,000 Colombians fleeing fighting entered Venezuela through the town of La Grita, in Tachira state, but Venezuelan authorities returned the group to Colombia the following day in violation of its obligations under the 1951 UN Convention Relating to the Status of Refugees.

Panama has also denied entry to Colombian asylum seekers and forcibly returned others who have sought refuge there, including persons whom the Panamanian authorities had granted temporary humanitarian status (THS). It first did so in 1987, and then again in 2003. In the 2003 incident, Panamanian National Guard and immigration officials arrived in Punusa, where the refugees were living, and forcibly removed them, making the refugees leave all their belongings behind. The refugees—a large majority of them children—were then taken to a place near the border, from where they made their way into Colombia.

The Panamanian authorities established THS, which permits Colombians to remain in Panama temporarily, in 1998, ostensibly to provide protection to Colombians who might not meet the criteria for refugee status. However, Decree 23, the legislation that established THS, does not clearly define the eligibility criteria for THS or the rights accorded its grantees. The government restricts freedom of movement of THS beneficiaries and sometimes does not provide them documentation as to their status. The authorities also harass, abuse, and detain them, often accusing them of having links to Colombian paramilitary or guerrilla groups.

Often the Panamanian authorities grant individuals THS to deny them access to the regular asylum process and the full protections of refugee status. Even those Colombians who do manage to apply for asylum often find their claims rejected. Decree 23 does not recognize fear of persecution by nonstate agents as grounds for asylum. Since a large majority of Colombians who flee to Panama do so to escape persecution, threats, or violence perpetrated by paramilitary and guerrilla groups, they are routinely rejected.

In April 2001, Spain, too, joined the 170-plus countries worldwide that require Colombian nationals to obtain entry visas. Spain hosts some 350,000 to 400,000 Colombians, approximately half of them without legal status, and received some 5,000 asylum applications from Colombians between 2000 and 2002. Spain's action angered many Colombians and prompted a number of prominent Colombians, including Nobel laureate Gabriel Garcia Márquez and renowned painter Fernando Botero, to vow not to visit Spain "as long as it submits us to this humiliation" (Garcia 2001). Costa Rica, one of the few remaining countries that Colombians could still enter without a visa, also instituted a visa requirement in 2002.

As of April 2001, the United States has required entry visas of Colombians planning to transit through the United States. U.S. immigration authorities took the action after large numbers of Colombians en route to Europe and other destinations began to apply for asylum at U.S. airports. More than 1,000 applied at the airports in the last quarter of 2000 alone.

Despite efforts by many in the international community to keep Colombian asylum seekers at bay, the International Organization for Migration estimated that between 1998 and 2002, more than 1.2 million Colombians left the country—both to escape violence and persecution and for economic reasons—and did not return. A 1999 Gallup poll found that 54 percent of Colombians had considered leaving the country, and Colombian government passport offices are unable to keep up with the volume of requests for passports. In 2001, Colombian immigration authorities reported that of the approximately 1 million Colombians who left the country in 2000, 225,000 did not return.

Only a minority of Colombians who flee abroad seek or receive recognition as refugees. According to the U.S. Committee for Refugees (USCR), nearly 59,000 Colombians were granted formal refugee status in 2002 or were in formal proceedings for it at the end of that year. These included some 9,000 refugees in Ecuador; 7,500 in Costa Rica; and about 1,000 each in Panama and Venezuela. Approximately 24,100 Colombians were either granted asylum or had asylum claims pending in the United States at the end of 2002; another 4,200 were in Canada as refugees or with asylum claims pending, and more than 12,000 Colombians applied for asylum in European countries (mostly in Spain and the United Kingdom), Australia, and New Zealand during the year (*World Refugee Survey* 2003, 241).

In addition, USCR reported that in 2002, "more than 325,000 Colombians were living abroad in refugee-like circumstances, including at least 150,000 in the United States, about 75,000 in Ecuador, an estimated 50,000 to 75,000 in Venezuela, some 20,000 to 50,000 in Costa Rica, and more than 20,000 in Panama" (ibid.). Many more Colombians who may have left their country due to the conflict are living abroad with some legal status other than that of a refugee, or without documentation and thus subject to deportation to Colombia if found. The largest number is in the United States and Venezuela.

Estimates of the number of Colombians living in the United States vary significantly. Some sources estimate that a majority of the approximately 200,000 Colombians who have migrated in the past few years have gone to the United States. *Migration News* reported in August 1999 that as many as 1.5 million Colombians were in the United States, more than 800,000 of them in the New York City area (*Migration News* 1999). In 2003, the Colombian embassy in the United States reported that some 500,000 live in the United States legally, but according to several Colombian newspapers, more than 2 million Colombians live in the United States. Researchers at Florida International University (FIU) have estimated that some 500,000 Colombians seek entry to the United States every year and that some 250,000 to 450,000 Colombians live in South Florida, as many as half of whom may be undocumented (Colombian Diaspora Project 2001).

Most of the tens of thousands of Colombians who seek refuge in the United States every year arrive with tourist visas and remain in the country without documentation after their visas expire. They usually join the informal economy, where they are often subject to exploitation. Most do not apply for asylum fearing rejection and deportation. In U.S. fiscal year 2002 (October 1, 2001–September 30, 2002), U.S. immigration officers received some 10,800 asylum applications from Colombians, and immigration judges received some 12,400 (some of which were not new applications but referrals from immigration officers). Immigration officers approved 45 percent of the claims they reviewed, and the judges approved 37 percent (*Refugee Reports* 2002, 7).

The FIU study found that there have been two waves of Colombian migration to the Miami area since the late 1970s. The first, from the late 1970s through the mid-1990s, comprised Colombians of all social classes, mostly urban, many of whom "were escaping [the growing] drug-related violence and security threats," while some were associated with that very drug trade (Colombian Diaspora Project 2001). The study detailed a second wave of migration beginning in the late 1990s and continuing into the early 2000s that includes a disproportionate number of middle-class and professional Colombians who left their country "to escape the increasing violence and personal security threats (extortion, kidnapping, murder, etc.) to themselves and their families from the Colombian guerrillas, paramilitaries, common criminals, and government security forces." Although most Colombians in South Florida said they would return to Colombia if security improved, the study concluded that "whether or not they returned would depend on how well established they were in the United States" and that "like other migrants to the United States, Colombians are likely to stay" (ibid.).

Colombians in several U.S. cities have organized to petition the U.S. government to grant temporary protection status (TPS) to nationals of Colombia, permitting them to remain and work in the United States legally until it is safe for them to return home. A number of American nongovernmental organizations and religious groups have supported Colombians' calls for TPS. According to Bishop Thomas Wenski of the Roman Catholic Archdiocese of Miami, "For people in that situation, TPS would be very useful" (*Refugee Reports* 2001, 13).

In October 2002, UNHCR declared that many of the Colombians who flee abroad are probably refugees in need of international protection and urged governments to extend them this protection through whatever mechanisms they had available.

Hiram A. Ruiz

See also: Central American Refugees; Deportation; Repatriation

References and further reading:

Colombian Diaspora Project, Colombian Study Institute. 2001. "The Colombian Diaspora in South Florida." Miami: Florida International University.

Gall, Norman. 1971. "Los Indocumentados Colombianos," http://www.normangall.com/venezuela_art3.htm.

Garcia, Maria Isabel. 2001. "U.S., Spain Restrict Entry by Colombians." Inter Press Service, http://www.latnn.com/2001/April/News-US_Latino242.html (cited July 10, 2003).

Human Rights Reports 2002. 2002. Washington, DC: U.S. Department of State.

Kirk, Robin. 1993. *Feeding the Tiger.* Washington, DC: U.S. Committee for Refugees.

Loughna, Sean. FMO Research Guide Colombia, Forced Migration Online, http://www.forcedmigration.org.

Migration News. 1999. "Central/South America." August. University of California at San Diego, http://migration.ucdavis.edu/mn/more.php?id=1877_0_2_0 (cited February 15, 2005).

Obregon, Liliana, and Maria Stavropoulou. 1998. "In Search of Hope: The Plight of Displaced Colombians." In *The Forsaken People.* Edited by Roberta Cohen and Francis Deng. Washington, DC: Brookings Institution Press.

Refugee Reports. 2001. Washington, DC: Immigration and Refugee Services of America. Vol. 22, no. 1.

———. 2002. Washington, DC: Immigration and Refugee Services of America. Vol. 23, no. 9.

Ruiz, Hiram. 1998. *Colombia's Silent Crisis: One Million Displaced by Violence.* Washington, DC: U.S. Committee for Refugees.

———. 2001. "The Crisis of Internal Displacement." Crimes of War Magazine, http://www.crimesofwar.org/colombia-mag/displace01.html (cited July 10, 2003).

United Nations High Commissioner for Refugees, Branch Office, Caracas, Venezuela. 2003. Correspondence to Hiram Ruiz, U.S. Committee for Refugees, February.

World Refugee Survey. 2003. Washington, DC: U.S. Committee for Refugees.

Colonial Immigration

In the twentieth century, immigration to Europe and North America has generally been of four types: spontaneous labor migration (especially to the United States until 1924 and after 1965); recruited permanent and temporary migration (such as to postwar Canada and Germany, respectively); family migration (to all countries that experienced a wave of primary migration); and colonial migration. Colonial migration blurs with the other categories in that colonial migrants arrived spontaneously for work, were recruited by companies, and came as family members. Two factors, however, made colonial migrants distinct from other types of migrants.

The first, and most obvious, was geography: Colonial migrants traveled from present or past colonies to the present or past imperial metropole. Current and ex-colonials took advantage of established transportation links, knowledge of the colonizer's language, and a generally false assumption of affinity and welcome in the metropole. Like migrants everywhere, colonial migrants were particularly attracted to great imperial capitals—London, Paris, and to a lesser degree, Brussels and Amsterdam. The second factor is legal: Colonial migrants were generally able to avail themselves of migration and/or citizenship privileges. These were briefly the most generous in the United Kingdom: From 1948 until 1962, the United Kingdom extended full British citizenship to all members of the British Empire, that is, to a population numbering in the hundreds of millions. After a Labour government ended this right in 1962, colonial migrants had access to colonial quotas until 1971.

France presents a slightly more complicated story. Until Algerian independence in 1962, Algeria was formally not a colony but rather an integral part of France. Today, Martinique, Guadeloupe, French Guiana, and Réunion have a similar status as *départments* (departments, but really states or provinces) of France. Although widely thought of as colonial migrants, Algerians moving from Algiers to Paris were doing nothing more dramatic than an American moving from New York to Los Angeles. Sub-Saharan French colonies had a citizenship status closer, but not identical, to that of Algeria in matters of nationality and citizenship. The juridical status of each territory, whether or not it was legally French, was crucial in determining the extent to which French *ius soli* applied to people born there (Hargreaves 1998). Thus, neither Morocco nor Tunisia had privileged access because, unlike Algeria, they were juridically classified as protectorates, so never officially French territory.

The Dutch case is broadly similar to that of the French. For those colonies that gained full independence, the Netherlands, though attempting to retain the essentially European core of Dutch nationality, allowed variable degrees of access to Dutch citizenship (Jacobs 1998, 49–51). When Indonesia (formerly the Dutch Indies) gained its independence in 1949, "native" Dutch citizens (loosely "ethnic" Indonesians) became Indonesian. The non-Dutch "nonnative" Dutch subjects—usually residents of Chinese descent in Indonesia—could opt for Dutch

African women migrants, carrying their babies on their backs, shop for produce at a market in the Barbes-Rochechouart neighborhood in Paris. 1993. (David Turnley/Corbis)

citizenship. Elsewhere, Dutch subjects who did not obtain local citizenship continued to enjoy Dutch citizenship (for instance, certain groups of Javanese residing in Surinam) (ibid.). It was also possible to opt for Dutch citizenship during a transitional period. Thus, residents of Surinam became, at independence, Surinamese citizens, but they would be entitled to a one-year period in which they could regain Dutch citizenship. For all other groups, those who left the Netherlands before the independence of Surinam retained their Dutch citizenship. Until then, all Dutch (the Surinamese included) had the right to travel freely within the Dutch Kingdom; thus, at the moment of independence, more than 100,000 people of Surinamese origin resided in the Netherlands and retained Dutch citizenship (ibid.).

In contrast with France and the Netherlands, Belgium never considered the residents of its possessions (the Belgian Congo, the protectorate of Rwanda) citizens, and they had no privileged access to Belgium. For this reason, Belgium has had many fewer colonial migrants than France, Britain, or the Netherlands, and its population is correspondingly less ethnically diverse.

As a sort of historical irony ("The Empire Strikes Back," as one Schadenfreude-filled volume on the United Kingdom put it), the major colonial migrations occurred just before or after independence, just as the countries sought to divest themselves of links with their colonies and to close the book on their imperial past. At the same time, colonial citizenship structures determined the origin of migration and channeled it, but it was not the underlying cause of the migrations themselves. Germany lost its colonies after World War I, but its postwar economic boom led to the arrival of hundreds of thousands of migrants, mainly from Turkey. Today, Germany faces challenges and opportunities in migration-related areas that are similar in almost all respects to those faced by France, Britain, and the Netherlands.

Both France and Britain illustrate the tenuousness of the distinction between colonial and labor-market migrants. In the United Kingdom, France, and the Netherlands, colonial migrants were drawn to the imperial centers by an economic boom and attendant labor shortages. In France, companies directly recruited colonial migrants (from the former colonies or from within France itself) and then legalized them through France's guestworker schemes; the country was thus a blending of guestworker and colonial migration regimes. At the same time, France, Britain, and the Netherlands also operated guestworker schemes; in fact, the inability of France to compete with more generous offers found in Switzerland and Germany partly accounts for its decision to look to its former and then-current colonies.

In both France and the United Kingdom, the impending end to free migration heralded a surge in migration: Between 1954 and 1962, France's Algerian community increased in size from 7,000 to some 300,000 (Hargreaves 1998, 37); from 1948 until 1962, some 500,000 Commonwealth migrants moved to the United Kingdom (Hansen 2000, 265). These colonial migrants, though numerically small relative to the ethnic minority populations in those countries today, were crucial because they ensured that these nations developed into multicultural societies. Those who migrated were in the main young men. They later brought their wives, children, and other family members with them; thus, every young male colonial migrant who arrived in the former imperial centers ensured the eventual arrival of three to four more migrants. All attempts to limit family reunification (such as in France in the 1960s) or to encourage return (France and Britain in the 1970s) only solidified migrants' desire to remain and bring their families. Thus, by the 1980s there were 800,000 Algerians in France (Hargreaves 1998, 37–38), and more than 2 million New Commonwealth (nonwhite) migrants in the United Kingdom (Hansen 2000, 3–4).

The reception of colonial migrants cannot be separated from their status as nonwhite individuals. Although West Indians enjoyed some minority support in the upper echelons of the British government in the 1950s, migrants from the West Indies, the Indian subcontinent, and West, East, and North Africa encountered racism and discrimination in lodging, employment, and the provision of social services. West Indians in 1950s' London walked past boardinghouse after boardinghouse festooned with "no coloureds" signs. Most fell into the hands of unscrupulous landlords who charged them exorbitant rents for squalid properties. In France, many North Africans could find no housing whatsoever and found themselves pushed into shantytowns on the outskirts of Paris and other French cities. To this day, North Africans may find themselves turned away from Parisian nightclubs.

Their status as colonial migrants nonetheless distinguished them in one respect: It offered a greater degree of legal protection. As all Commonwealth migrants before 1962 (and, in a more complicated sense, before 1981) arrived as citizens, there was never any question of deporting them. Indeed, this fact in part encouraged the United Kingdom to adopt immigration controls more quickly than other European countries. Likewise, Algerians migrating before 1962 and the children of those migrating thereafter, under double ius soli (people born of someone born in France are French), were citizens and also free from deportation. The same was true of Dutch colonial subjects who took advantage of privileged naturalization channels. Their status as citizens, in turn, granted them a further right to family reunification. All states find it difficult to deport migrants of any nationality, and the United Kingdom responded to citizenship-generated constraints by removing a right to family reunification for all citizens. Nonetheless, colonial migrants were free from even the threat of deportation, and they avoided the waiting periods imposed, for instance, on Turkish migrants bringing family members to Germany.

The degree to which former colonial migrants enjoy privileges in the former imperial centers varies by country. The United Kingdom ended almost all privileges for Commonwealth citizens in 1981, with two main exceptions: people with British grandparents, mostly white, and residents of the Falkland Islands. The latter's patriotism, their role in ensuring Margaret Thatcher's 1983 election victory, and their grant of a new lease on life to a jingoistic strain of British self-definition gained them full British citizenship in 1983. In addition, East African Asians with no other citizenship waited on a queue to enter the United Kingdom according to a yearly quota; it wasn't much of a privilege but was somewhat better than statelessness. Residents of Guadeloupe, Martinique, French Guiana, Réunion and Mayotte islands in the Indian Ocean, French Polynesia, New Caledonia, the Pacific islands of Wallis and Futuna, and Saint Pierre and Miquelon all have full French citizenship. To this day, residents of the Dutch Antilles (that is, the Dutch West Indies—Dutch Antilles, Aruba, Bonaire, and Curaçao) all enjoy Dutch citizenship.

Southern European countries had relatively little colonial immigration in the first three decades of the postwar period (their citizens were themselves migrants to France and Germany), but Portugal granted full Portuguese nationality to citizens of Macao in the 1980s. The most recent form of (loosely) colonial migration has been the movement of Argentineans, and other Latin American nationals escaping economic uncertainty, to Spain.

Beyond questions of legal entitlement, colonial migrants have both indelibly altered European societies and internationalized them. As an extensive literature on transnationalism has emphasized, colonial migrants and their descendants retain links in the sending countries, and many move comfortably between both societies. They ensure that Europe is tied, socially, economically, and therefore politically, to its former colonies.

Randall Hansen

See also: Citizenship; Commonwealth Citizenship and Immigration (UK); France d'Outre-Mer; Germany; Guestworkers, Europe

References and further reading:

[Author's note: I am grateful to Alec Hargreaves and Romain Garbaye for assistance on France, and to Dirk Jacobs for assistance on the Netherlands and Belgium.]

Hansen, Randall. 2000. *Citizenship and Immigration in Postwar Britain.* Oxford: Oxford University Press.

———. 2002. "Globalization, Embedded Realism and Path Dependence: The Other Immigrants to Europe." *Comparative Political Studies* 35, no.3: 259–283.

Hargreaves, Alec. 1998. "Algerians in Contemporary France: Incorporation or Exclusion?" *The Journal of Algerian Studies* 3: 31–47.

Jacobs, Dirk. 1998. *Nieuwkomers in de politiek.* Gent: Academia Press.

Weil, Patrick. 2002. *Qu'est-ce qu'un Français? Histoire de la nationalité française depuis la Révolution.* Paris: Grasset.

Commonwealth Citizenship and Immigration (UK)

The British Commonwealth of Nations, an outgrowth of the British Empire, was linked together by one of history's most open citizenship and immigration regimes. From 1948 until 1962, some 600 million Commonwealth citizens had the right to enter the United Kingdom; from 1962 until 1981, Britons and "colonial" British subjects shared the same citizenship.

Until World War II, there was no such thing as British or Commonwealth citizenship. Britons, nationals of independent Dominions (Canada, Australia, New Zealand, and South Africa), and residents of the British colonies were "British subjects." Following the famous *Calvin* case of 1608, British subjects were ones born within the sovereign's realm and who otherwise owed their allegiance to the monarch.

For some 350 years, all British subjects had the formally unrestricted right to enter the United Kingdom, though few did in practice. Britons traveled to all corners of the globe; Dominion citizens traveled to the United Kingdom; and a trickle of nonwhite British subjects moved through the empire. The latter group often faced restrictions in spite of their small numbers: The Dominions sought power over immigration control to limit Indian migration, and they enacted Chinese Exclusion Acts limiting Asian migration.

Commonwealth citizenship emerged as the by-product of Dominion nationalism. After the war, Canada, tired of enjoying only subject status in nationality, announced that it would unilaterally create its own citizenship. Although seemingly unremarkable today, the action shocked the British government, which held that a common nationality, in the form of British subjecthood, was the main means to binding the empire together. Under Canadian legislation, Canadians would remain British subjects, but their subject status would derive from their Canadian citizenship. The British extended this logic to the whole empire: British subjects would obtain subject status in virtue of Commonwealth citizenship. In this vein, the British Nationality Act of 1948 created two categories of citizenship: Citizenship of the United Kingdom and Colonies (CUKC) for Britons and colonial British subjects, and Citizenship of Independent Commonwealth countries (for Canada, Australia, New Zealand, later for India and other newly dependent countries) (Hansen 1998). Commonwealth citizenship was an umbrella category for both nationalities and from 1945 was interchangeable as a term with "British subject."

The British Nationality Act was adopted at a time when the British economy was ravaged by war, when intercontinental travel was expensive, and before any significant colonial migration had begun. An unintentional result was that CUKC became the legal basis for a mass, nonwhite migration to the United Kingdom. By the early 1950s, the British economy had recovered; the country faced a labor shortage; and transportation infrastructures had expanded. The result was a migration of workers from the Commonwealth. Between 1951 and 1961, some 500,000 "New Commonwealth" (nonwhite) migrants traveled to the United Kingdom, first from the West Indies and later from the Indian subcontinent. Their reception was frosty: Racism and lingering postwar housing shortages made accommodations difficult to find ("no coloureds" signs hung in London houses), and slumlords exploited the new arrivals. Paul Rachman, a London property owner, for example, became infamous for profiting from West Indian migrants.

British governments were concerned about public opposition to Commonwealth migrants but could not bring themselves to restrict their entry until 1962 (Hansen 2000, 80–99). Politicians briefly attempted to slow entry informally, warning migrants of inhospitable weather, high prices, and inadequate housing. They eventually conceded the case in favor of migration control. "Race Riots" in Nottingham and London's Notting Hill (in which West Indians were attacked by white thugs) in 1958 increased anti-immigrant pressure. After further delay, the Conservatives finally responded with the Commonwealth Immigrants Act of 1962. The legislation, setting up a work permit scheme, was the first formal restriction on the immigration of British subjects. A centuries-old tradition had come to an end.

For those who wished to prevent the emergence of a multicultural Britain, the decision came too late. A substantial presence of Commonwealth migrants attracted, through family reunification and chain migration, more migrants to the United Kingdom. In 2001, a half-century after the creation of Commonwealth citizenship, 3.25 million UK residents (5.7 percent of the population) had a community background in Africa, the Caribbean, or the Indian subcontinent (Hansen 2000, 3–4). For supporters of Commonwealth immigration, postwar migrants enriched Britain culturally, economically, and socially, and as such they stand in a long tradition of prewar European migration to the United Kingdom. For critics, Commonwealth migrants, arriving without the consent of the British population, altered the United Kingdom in a manner opposed by Britons. Both camps agree that issues of immigration, race, and ethnic minority participation play a central role in contemporary British politics.

Randall Hansen

See also: Citizenship; Colonial Immigration; East African Asian Expulsions; France d'Outre-Mer; United Kingdom

References and further reading:

Hansen, Randall. 1998. "The Politics of Citizenship in 1940s Britain: The British Nationality Act." *Twentieth Century British History* 10, no. 1: 67–95.

———. 2000. *Citizenship and Immigration in Postwar Britain.* Oxford: Oxford University Press.

Spencer, I. R. G. 1997. *British Immigration Policy since 1939.* London: Routledge.

Commonwealth of Independent States Conference

An international process emerged in 1996 to address the needs of those uprooted in the Commonwealth of Independent States (CIS), an organization of twelve nations including the Russian Federation and nearby countries of the former Soviet Union. Since 1989, approximately 9 million people have moved from country to country within the region (Helton and Voronina 2000, ix). Ethnic Russians and Russian speakers migrating to the Russian Federation, sometimes under the pressure of severe discrimination, make up about a third of the CIS displacements. Others have been caused by armed conflicts in the Caucasus and Central Asian regions, as well as within Russia itself.

A Regional Conference to Address the Problems of Refugees, Displaced Persons, and Other Forms of Involuntary Displacements and Returnees in the Countries of the Commonwealth of Independent States and Relevant Neighboring States, known as the CIS Migration Conference, took place in May 1996. But the Russian Federation had begun calling for a world conference on migration in the UN General Assembly

Queen Elizabeth at Westminster Abbey, London, for a service to celebrate the Commonwealth. She is greeted by a crowd made up of Commonwealth representatives holding their national flag. (Corbis Sygma)

The leaders of eleven ex-Soviet states (L–R): Leonid Kuchma of Ukraine, Imomali Rakhmonov of Tajikistan, Askar Akayev of Kyrgyzstan, Eduard Shevardnadze of Georgia, Haydar Alyev of Azerbaijan, Vladimir Putin of Russia, Alexander Lukashenko of Belarus, Robert Kocharyan of Armenia, Nursultan Nazarbayev of Kazakhstan, Petru Lucinschi of Moldova, and Islam Karimov of Uzbekistan sit during a news conference in Minsk December 1, 2000. The heads of CIS countries hold a summit on Friday expected to focus on finding an antidote to religious and political extremism, which they say is threatening the Commonwealth of Independent States. (Reuters/Corbis)

as early as 1993. In 1994 the Russian foreign minister wrote to the United Nations High Commissioner for Refugees (UNHCR) and the International Organization for Migration (IOM) urging those agencies to organize a conference to deal specifically with ethnic Russians migrating to the Russian Federation.

The Geneva-based CIS Migration Conference was held under the auspices of UNHCR, IOM, and the Organization for Security and Cooperation in Europe (OSCE) and was attended by representatives of eighty-seven governments, twenty-seven international organizations, and seventy-seven nongovernmental organizations (NGOs). The conference adopted a nonbinding program of action divided into sections addressing an institutional framework for dealing with the displacements, an operational framework, prevention, cooperation, and follow-up plans. The conference also agreed upon innovative definitions for a number of categories of affected persons in the region, including externally displaced persons, repatriants, involuntarily repatriating persons, formerly departed persons, and "ecological migrants." The last category represented one of the first times such migrants had been defined in an international instrument.

The CIS conference initially appeared to offer significant advances in dealing with regional problems of displacement. But donor governments were reluctant to make contributions, and the conference process produced no more than $50 million of funding (Helton and Voronina 2000, 79). Perhaps the most notable accomplishment was the impetus given to the development of local NGOs. This is so even though NGO involvement in the preparation of the conference was controversial and limited. The conference follow-up program thus devolved into a largely technical-assistance exercise by donor governments concerned that borders in the region were too porous and a modest effort to support the work of NGOs. While explicitly launched in the name of prevention, the CIS

Migration Conference ultimately was characterized by meager results and lost opportunities.

Arthur C. Helton

See also: Internally Displaced Persons; UN High Commissioner for Refugees

References and further reading:

Helton, Arthur C. 1996. "The CIS Migration Conference: Lost Opportunities in the Former Soviet Union." *Oxford International Review* 59:59–64.

Helton, Arthur C., and Natalia Voronina. 2000. *Forced Displacement and Human Security in the Former Soviet Union: Law and Policy.* New York: Transnational Publishers.

Comprehensive Plan of Action

The Comprehensive Plan of Action (CPA) was the collective response to the Indo-Chinese refugee crisis adopted by the international community in 1989. The CPA was the culmination of efforts to respond to mass flight from Vietnam, Cambodia, and Laos since 1975. It focused on preventing clandestine departures from countries of origin, assurances of temporary protection by regional states, individual refugee status determination procedures, resettlement to Western states for those recognized as refugees, and return to countries of origin for those who were not. The overall response to the Indo-Chinese refugee crisis, primarily through the CPA, resulted in the resettlement of almost 2 million refugees to more than fifteen Western countries and is regarded as a successful example of burden sharing. Critics highlight the inconsistency of individual status determination procedures, low standards of care for asylum seekers, incidences of forced return, the conditionality of asylum, and the creation of an asylum market system as limitations of the CPA.

The consolidation of Communist Southeast Asian regimes in 1975 resulted in an estimated 3 million people fleeing Vietnam, Cambodia, and Laos in the following two decades. Most fled in small boats, and many died in shipwrecks or were targeted by pirates. Humanitarianism, coupled with the geopolitical interests of the United States, motivated Western states to recognize the "boat people" as refugees prima facie and to resettle them. More than 550,000 Indo-Chinese sought asylum in Southeast Asia between 1975 and 1979, of which 200,000 were resettled (UNHCR 2000).

As arrivals continued to exceed resettlement quotas, regional states declared in June 1979 that they had "reached the limit of their endurance and decided that they would not accept new arrivals" (ibid.). This reluctance, and reports of regional states pushing boats carrying asylum seekers away from their shores ("push-backs"), led to an International Conference on Indo-Chinese Refugees in July 1979. States agreed that worldwide resettlement quotas would be doubled, that the boat people would be recognized as refugees prima facie, that illegal departures would be prevented, and that regional processing centers would be established. The result was a formalized quid pro quo: resettlement to Western states in exchange for assurances of first asylum in the region.

The immediate results were positive. Resettlement increased, push-backs ended, and arrival rates fell dramatically as heavy penalties were imposed on clandestine departures. By 1988, however, the number of asylum seekers began to rise dramatically as promises of resettlement resulted in a dramatic pull factor. Believing that these new arrivals no longer warranted automatic refugee status, Western countries introduced selective criteria and reduced resettlement quotas. In response, regional asylum countries returned to earlier policies of preventing arrivals, including push-backs.

In light of this new reality, the UN General Assembly called for a Second International Conference on Indo-Chinese refugees (A/RES/43/119). The conference, convened in June 1989, adopted the CPA, which contained five mechanisms through which the countries of origin, countries of first asylum, and resettlement countries would cooperate to resolve the refugee crisis in South Asia.

First, clandestine departures were to be reduced by penalizing individuals organizing boat departures and through the implementation and promotion of an Orderly Departure Program (ODP).

Second, regional countries agreed, in exchange for substantial economic aid, to provide temporary asylum to all new arrivals, "regardless of their mode of arrival" (CPA, II.C), until their status was determined and a durable solution was found.

Third, individual refugee status determination (RSD) mechanisms—applying the criteria of the 1951 UN Convention Relating to the Status of Refugees and its 1967 Protocol in a "humanitarian spirit" (CPA, II.D.b)—were established in all countries of asylum. UNHCR was charged with the difficult task of ensuring that RSD was carried out in a consistent manner throughout the region.

Fourth, twenty Western states committed themselves to two resettlement programs: a Long-Stayer Resettlement Programme for "all individuals who arrived in temporary asylum camps prior to the appropriate cutoff date" (CPA, II.E.1), and a Resettlement Programme for Newly Determined Refugees to "accommodate all those who arrived after the introduction of status-determination procedures and are determined to be refugees" (CPA, II.E.2).

Finally, it was agreed that "persons determined not to be refugees should return to their country of origin in accordance with international practices" (CPA, II.F). A Memorandum of Understanding (MOU) between UNHCR and Vietnam later facilitated the safe return of rejected asylum seekers to Vietnam. As such, the CPA was "one of the first examples of a situation where the country of origin became a key player . . . in helping resolve a major refugee crisis" (UNHCR 2000).

The CPA is seen to have generally achieved its objectives of reducing the number of clandestine departures and finding extra-regional, durable solutions for recognized refugees. In 1989, roughly 70,000 Vietnamese sought asylum in Southeast Asia. By 1992, this number had fallen to 41 (ibid.). At the same time, more than 1.95 million refugees had been resettled by the end of the CPA in 1995—1.25 million to the United States alone. On this basis, the CPA is seen by many as a success and a dramatic example of the possibilities of burden-sharing arrangements to address refugee crises.

The CPA has, however, been criticized for a number of reasons. First, RSD procedures in the region varied considerably, were often inadequate, and were premised on the assumption that the "boat people" were predominantly economic migrants, not refugees. Second, the low standards of care and maintenance in asylum centers were reported to frequently violate international standards motivated by a desire to deter future asylum seekers. Third, scholars have argued that the conditionality of asylum for resettlement runs contrary to the principles of international law. Fourth, incidences of forced return of failed asylum seekers were frequently denounced by human rights organizations (Robinson 1998). Finally, it has been argued that the CPA created a "market system" where immigration and political considerations overshadowed asylum considerations (Suhrke 1998).

James Milner

See also: Burden Sharing; Resettlement

References and further reading:

Bari, Shamsul. 1992. "Refugee Status Determination under the Comprehensive Plan of Action (CPA): A Personal Assessment." *International Journal of Refugee Law* 4, no. 4: 487–511.

Robinson, W. Courtland. 1998. *Terms of Refuge: The Indochinese Exodus and the International Response.* London: Zed.

Suhrke, Astri. 1998. "Burden-Sharing during Refugee Emergencies: The Logic of Collective versus National Action." *Journal of Refugee Studies* 11, no. 4.

United Nations High Commissioner for Refugees. 2000. "Flight from Indochina." In *The State of the World's Refugees: Fifty Years of Humanitarian Action.* Oxford: Oxford University Press.

———. "International Conference on Indo-Chinese Refugees: Report of the Secretary General [Annex: Declaration and Comprehensive Plan of Action (CPA)]," http://www.unhcr.ch (cited March 1, 2002).

Contract Labor

See Skilled Migration

Courts, International

See European Court of Human Rights; European Court of Justice

Crime and Migration

In many countries, citizens have become fearful that they are now being invaded not by armies and tanks but by migrants who speak different languages, worship unfamiliar gods, and belong to other cultures. They fear that these migrants will take their jobs, occupy their land, live off their welfare system, and threaten their way of life, their environment, and even their polity (Weiner 1995, 2). They are concerned as well that an influx of migrants may increase the crime rate in their cities. Whether these fears are justified has been a matter of debate, however.

Europe may be seen as a laboratory for analyzing the contentious link between migration and crime. Whereas countries such as Australia, Canada, and the United States have a long history of immigration, European countries became immigration countries only in the twentieth century. Southern European countries experienced the turnaround from emigrant to immigrant nations only in the last decades of the period (King 1998,125). The vast majority of migration in postwar Europe was confined to intra-European flows from south to north (guestworker migration) due to economic shifts. As border regimes and immigration laws were tightened in the wake of the industrial and labor-market crises since the 1970s, illegal immigration, including the "abuse" of the asylum system, has increased. The fall of the Cold War border allowed for a substantial increase of East-West migration flows, and the countries of an enlarged European Union began to try to find a common response to these phenomena.

Legal versus Illegal Immigration

By the end of the twentieth century, people smugglers and traffickers were flourishing. Clandestine criminal groups lured migrants by promising help in overcoming the barriers of "fortress Europe," while anti-immigration groups lamented "sieve Europe," noting that international borders were too porous and no longer offered protection against the "waves" of immigrants crossing them (Bigo 1998, 153–157). Therefore, when it comes to crime and migration, the first distinction must be between legal and illegal migration. Illegal migration occurs when migrants find loopholes or otherwise violate the immigration laws of the country of destination. Legal migrants may be economic migrants exercising their freedom to move and take up work (for example, in the EU single market), migrants who have obtained a work permit, or asylum

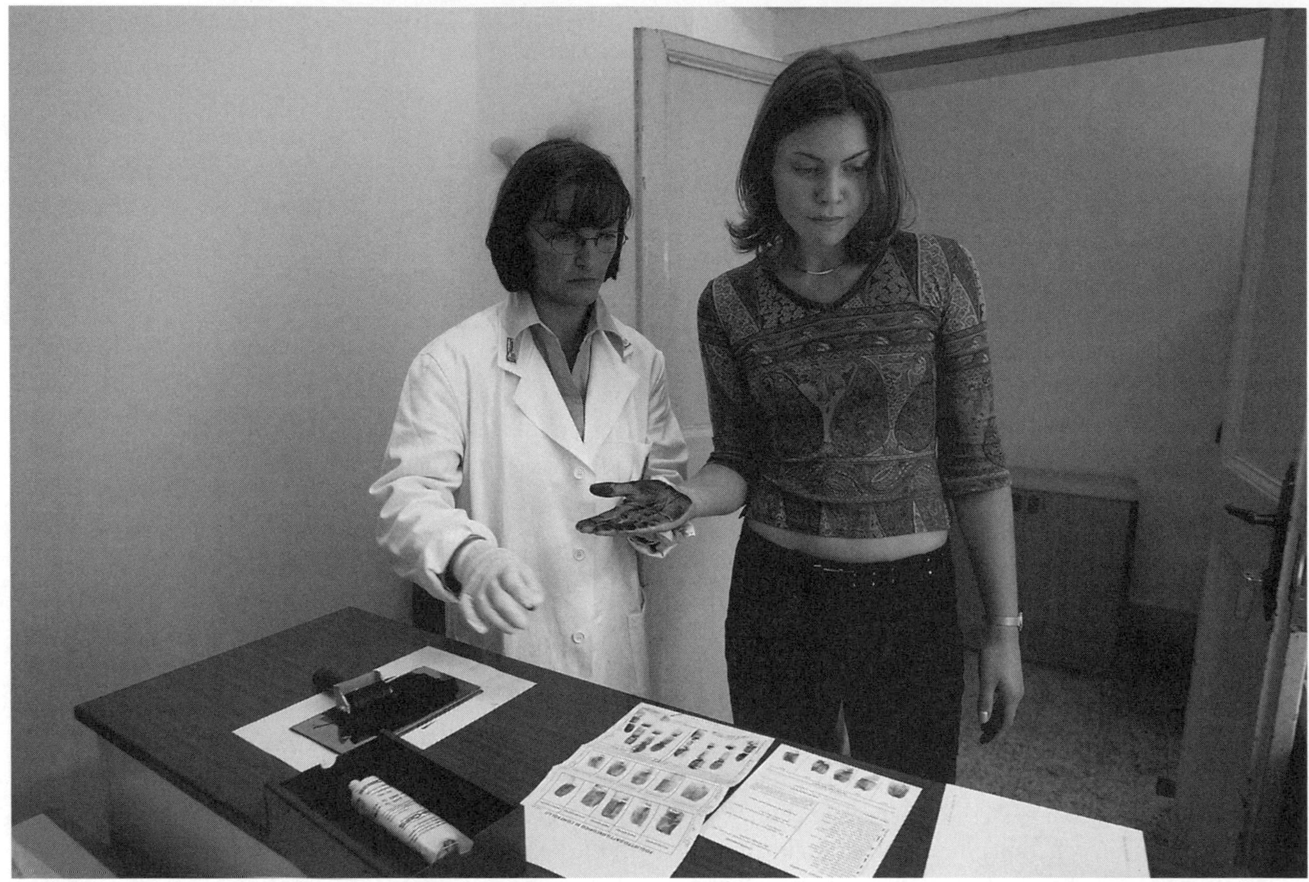

Rome, September 18, 2002. Mirroring tough new laws already passed in Britain and Denmark, Italy is now forcing foreigners to be fingerprinted if they want to live in Italy. While Italy has a relatively small immigrant community, polls show Italians fear excessive immigration and link illegal immigrants with crime. (Reuters/Corbis)

seekers and refugees protected by national or international refugee laws.

Lack of Reliable Data

The complex nexus between immigration and crime is further complicated by the absence of complete and reliable data concerning numbers of illegal migrants as well as on crimes committed by them. The clandestine nature of illegal migration itself presents problems: As two criminology researchers have noted, "The entire field of criminology is plagued by data quality problems. Indeed, these limitations make it quite difficult to feel very confident about the extent of crime and delinquency in general, let alone the extent of migrant crime in particular" (Borowski and Thomas 1994, 649). The claim of a strong connection is often used by anti-immigration platforms and parties to support populist, if not outright xenophobic, attitudes and to bolster resistance against multicultural and multiethnic trends. Crime and migration, in this context, are both seen as threats that in combination can produce an explosive cocktail of irrational responses.

Statistics in Europe generally support a link between migration and crime—that is, they support the conclusion that immigrants produce a higher percentage of crime than nationals. Immigrants are overrepresented in penal institutions, for example (see Table C-1). Statistics from Australia and Canada, both "classic" immigrant societies, however, present a different picture. Immigrants in both countries have a lower crime rate than nationals, and they are underrepresented in prisons and penitentiaries (ibid.).

Moreover, it is difficult to say whether migrants commit more crimes than other vulnerable, excluded groups of society, such as, for example, blacks or Hispanics in the United States or Aborigines in Australia (Carcach and Grant 1999, 6). Some have speculated that immigrants have become the "blacks of Europe." It is not only enforcement agencies that are prone to disproportionately target immigrant communities; courts tend to favor prison sentences for foreigners over suspended sentences or community sanctions, which seem to be the preserve of nationals (Wacquant 1999). And many of the offenses that brought immigrants behind bars, such as

Table C-1 Percent of Foreigners in the Prison Population in Countries of the European Union

Country	*1988*	*1991*	*1997*	*Latest Available Figures*	*Foreign Population*
Austria	9	22	27	30 (2000)	9 (1999)
Belgium	30	34	38	40 (2000)	8 (1999)
Denmark	—	12	14	17 (2000)	5 (1999)
England/Wales	—	—	8	10 (2001)	4 (1997)
France	26	30	26	21 (2003)	6 (1999)
Germany	15	15	34	34 (1999)	9 (1999)
Greece	19	22	39	45 (2001)	2 (1997)
Italy	9	15	22	30 (2001)	2 (1997)
Netherlands	20	25	32	30 (2001)	4 (1999)
Portugal	—	—	11	12 (2002)	2 (1999)
Spain	12	16	18	24 (2002)	2 (1999)
Sweden	22	20	26	27 (2002)	6 (1999)
Australia			22 (1988)	24 (1998)	24 (1998)
Canada			12 (1991)		17 (1998)
USA			25 (1995)	50 (1999)	10 (1998)

Sources: Council of Europe, Strasbourg, 1999; International Center for Prison Studies, King's College, London, 2003; Eurostat, Brussels, 2001; OECD, Paris, 2001; D. Thomas, 1993; Carcach and Grant, 2000.

falsification of papers and other violations of immigration law, are linked to their status.

The uncertain database makes judgment on such matters difficult. But the difference between Australia and Canada vis à vis Europe would suggest that even open societies with "generous" regulatory regimes—that is, those that make efforts at welcoming and integrating immigrants (not assimilating, but accepting, if not cherishing, differences)—produce different outcomes. Since the late 1990s, there has been a dramatic change toward a hardline immigration policy in Australia that over time might provide further clues about this nexus. But the link is perhaps not so much between crime and migration as between crime and law enforcement. How law-enforcement agencies and the criminal-justice system treat minorities seems to play an important role in the level of crime attributed to immigrants. One analyst has concluded that "the risk of criminality increases whenever individuals are unable to feel part of and genuinely accepted by the larger society" (Plecas et al. 1995, 24).

Organized Human Trafficking

Although it is unclear whether immigrants are producing more crime in general than nationals, there is no doubt that migration and crime are linked when organized smugglers of human beings come into play. According to Interpol, criminal networks smuggling human beings are gaining increasing control of the flow of migrants across international borders. Up to 50 percent of illegal immigrants could now be trafficked by organized criminal syndicates (Budapest Group 1999), and these syndicates have become a global multibillion-dollar business. Trafficking out of China alone was estimated, in 1995, as being worth US$3.5 billion (Savona 1996, 13). The number of people smuggled into Europe in the past few years could be as high as 500,000, according to the International Organization for Migration (IOM). Freedom of movement without border controls inside "Schengenland" (the free movement area in Europe established in 1994 by the Schengen Convention) is cited as an additional attraction for human traffickers (Savona 1996, 11). Still, illegal migrants as a rule are victims of criminal behavior rather than acting criminals.

Illegal migration can be linked to four different kinds of crimes. First, illegal migrants violate immigration law and border regulations through their illegal entry into a state. Their crossing often involves falsified personal documents, bribes for corrupt border guards, or clandestine border crossing. The second category is made up of the criminal transnational organizations specializing in human smuggling and trafficking. Generating "business" by making false promises about the opportunities available in the destination country, they sometimes force women into prostitution, abduct children for adoption, or worse. Third, illegal migrants might commit property crimes in their country of origin in order to pay the human smugglers their fee (in 2004 between US$2,000 and $12,000 per person). They might also be forced into criminal activity to pay the fee after having been successfully smuggled to their destination country. Practically all European states—but especially those in the southern part of the EU—have a large contingent of illegal immigrants working in the informal economy (for example, the *sans papiers* in France). These immigrants are violating both immigration and employment laws (Baldwin-Edwards

2001, 1). Finally, they are vulnerable in their illegal state to racist attacks, intolerance, discrimination, and exploitation. Asylum seekers have also been criminalized (that is, constructed as criminals), and genuine criminals may claim refugee status. This all adds up to a complex relationship between illegal migration and crime.

A special category of migration-related crime is made up of persons who cross borders (legally or illegally) in order to commit crimes, from run-of-the-mill burglaries to organized crime and highly specialized terrorist activities (as highlighted by the September 11, 2001, attacks on New York and Washington). These should not be confused with immigrants who are seeking to escape from persecution and/or trying to pursue a better life for themselves (Plecas et al. 1995, 121–122).

Policy Options

In responding to migratory pressures, states generally look to four different policy options. First, as the reason for illegal migration is often to be found in underdevelopment, lack of economic and social perspective, poverty and hunger, crisis, war, and oppressive regimes, developmental policies attempt to address and improve the situation in the countries of origin so that fewer people will be forced to emigrate. Exporting stability, in the long run, is the best antidote to importing instability. This, of course, is not a quick-fix option. It requires substantial redistribution of resources, restrictions on weapons sales to crisis regions, and intervention against regimes known to have ongoing human rights violations. This last method is highly contentious because it may destabilize entire regions. And because affluence increases exit possibilities, it can increase migration in the short or medium term. Second, regulatory policies, a "more intelligent immigration policy" (Baldwin-Edwards 2001), focus on granting refuge and asylum where necessary and offering generous quotas for legal immigration to reduce the temptation to migrate illegally. The third option is to increase measures for integrating immigrants—not to pursue assimilation, but to foster acceptance based on respect and tolerance of difference—so that they do not feel excluded, stigmatized, vulnerable, and exploited. Although this type of approach would not reduce clandestine migration, it would help to break the link between immigration and crime. Finally, coordinated efforts among neighboring countries are needed to combat organized criminal traffickers and their slave trade. The main components of this approach are increased cooperation between law-enforcement agencies across frontiers to crack down on criminal syndicates and a marked punitive deterrent for criminal traffickers. Another important component is an information campaign about options for legal immigration as well as about the dangers involved in illegal immigration.

EU Policies

In the 1980s and 1990s, migration issues and crime—both organized and transfrontier—were increasingly grouped together by national governments and supranational organizations such as the EU. As one scholar has observed, "Migration was linked with security: innocent people (whose only 'crime' is their poverty and keenness to migrate to improve their lot) were bracketed with terrorism and the smuggling of arms and drugs" (King 1998, 120). This trend corresponded to a rise in the number of refugees and asylum seekers, particularly in Europe, and to growing success among racist and anti-immigration parties on the hard right at the polls (for example, Jean-Marie Le Pen in France, Jörg Haider in Austria, and Pim Fortyn in the Netherlands). Whereas the Schengen Agreement of 1985 and the Dublin Convention of 1990 had mixed the issues of illegal migration and organized crime, the 1999 Tampere Declaration marked a departure away from the priority previously given to repression of criminal threats and prevention of immigration toward a greater emphasis on human rights and integration (Anderson and Bort 2001, 180). Since then, the EU has tentatively worked toward a common policy on asylum and immigration, envisioning an area of freedom, security, and justice. Particular emphasis is given to the European Convention on Human Rights (1950) and the EU Charter on Fundamental Rights (2000). The first stage of the Tampere Declaration includes:

- Minimum standards on asylum procedures
- Regulation as to which member state is responsible for the examination of an asylum application
- Minimum standards on the qualification of third-country nationals as refugees and for persons who otherwise need international protection (again, specifically invoking the 1951 UN Convention Relating to the Status of Refugees and its 1967 Protocol, the 1950 European Convention on Human Rights, the 1987 UN Convention against Torture and Other Cruel, Inhuman and Degrading Treatment or Punishment, and the 1976 International Covenant on Civil and Political Rights)

The EU is determined in its efforts to regulate migration flows associated with international crime and trafficking in human beings, especially for the purposes of prostitution. Harmonization of visa policy, information exchange and cooperation between member states' law-enforcement agencies, aliens and criminal law, and return and readmission policy are areas of priority.

A Framework Decision agreed upon in 2001 entails "active operational cooperation," "information campaigns" and the provision of assistance for victims of criminal traffickers, and higher penalties for traffickers—"not less than eight years' imprisonment if the offence is committed in circumstances endangering the life of the victim, against a victim who was particularly vulnerable, by the use of serious violence or has caused particularly serious harm, or within the context of criminal organisation" (EU 2002, 29–33).

The Barcelona process, inaugurated at the Barcelona Conference of 1995, focuses on closer economic cooperation across the Mediterranean to ease migratory pressure. With the Barcelona and Tampere regulations in effect, it remains to be seen whether Europe is finding a happier—and more efficient—balance between U.S.-style, restrictive anti-immigration policy and Canadian-style cooperative and integrative policy.

Conclusion

There is no denying that immigrants are sometimes criminals, and there is a clear link between organized illegal immigration and crime. Yet, as argued by the authors of one recent work on migration and crime, "fears about the impact of immigration on crime are not justified. Immigrants, although themselves individually at greater risk of exclusion, marginalization and exploitation, do not necessarily represent a greater risk of crime for the host society" (Plecas et al. 1995, 38). Policy choices concerning regulation, border management, access to labor markets, and access to the justice system increase or decrease that risk.

Eberhard Bort

See also: Asylum; Clandestine Migration; Dublin Convention; Schengen Agreement; UN Convention Relating to the Status of Refugees, 1951

References and further reading:

Anderson, Malcolm, with Eberhard Bort. 2001. *The Frontiers of the European Union.* Basingstoke: Palgrave.

Baldwin-Edwards, Martin. 2001. "Crime and Migrants: Some Myths and Realities." Paper presented to the International Police Association, Samos, Greece, May 4.

Bigo, Didier. 1998. "Frontiers and Security in the European Union: The Illusion of Migration Control." Pp. 148–164 in *The Frontiers of Europe.* Edited by Malcolm Anderson and Eberhard Bort. London: Pinter.

Borowski, Allan, and Derrick Thomas. 1994. "Immigration and Crime." Pp. 631–652 in *Immigration and Refugee Policy: Australia and Canada Compared.* Vol.2. Edited by Howard Adelmann, Allan Borowski, Meyer Burstein, and Lois Foster. Toronto: University of Toronto Press.

Bort, Eberhard. 2002. "Illegal Migration and Cross-Border Crime." Pp. 191–212 in *Europe Unbound: Enlarging and Reshaping the Boundaries of the European Union.* Edited by Jan Zielonka. London: Routledge.

Budapest Group. 1999. *The Relationship between Organised Crime and Trafficking in Aliens.* Warsaw: Budapest Group.

Carcach, Carlos, and Anna Grant. 1999. "Imprisonment in Australia: Trends in Prison Populations and Imprisonment Rates, 1982–1998." *Trends and Issues in Crime and Criminal Justice* no. 130.

———. 2000. "Australian Corrections: Main Demographic Characteristics of Prison Populations." *Trends and Issues in Crime and Criminal Justice,* no. 150.

European Union. 2002. *Annual Report on Human Rights.* Luxembourg: European Communities.

King, Russell. 1998. "The Mediterranean: Europe's Rio Grande." Pp. 109–134 in *The Frontiers of Europe.* Edited by Malcolm Anderson and Eberhard Bort. London: Pinter.

Plecas, Darryl, John Evans, and Yvon Daundurand. 1995. *Migration and Crime: A Canadian Perspective.* Vancouver, BC: The International Centre for Criminal Law Reform and Criminal Justice Policy.

Savona, Ernesto U. (in cooperation with Andrea di Nicola and Giovanni da Col). 1996. "Dynamics of Migration and Crime in Europe: New Patterns of an Old Nexus." TransCrime Working Paper 8. Trento, Italy: University of Trento.

Thomas, Derrick. 1993. "The Foreign Born in the Federal Prison Population." Paper presented at the Canadian Law and Society Association Conference, Carleton University, June 8.

Wacquant, Loic. 1999. "'Suitable Enemies': Foreigners and Immigrants in the Prisons of Europe." *Punishment and Society* 1, no. 2: 215–222.

Weiner, Myron. 1995. *The Global Migration Crisis: Challenges to States and to Human Rights.* New York: HarperCollins.

Croatia

See Ethnic Cleansing: Croatia

Cuban Migration

Motivated mostly by political and economic factors, Cubans have been migrating to the United States for more than 170 years. Each group of migrants, regardless of the length of their stay, has made important contributions to all sectors of American society. These contributions can be best appreciated in the contemporary Cuban community in the United States, the result of the largest and longest of the migrations. Concentrated mainly in Miami, Florida, since the 1960s, Cuban migrants have become leaders in local, state, and national politics, business, education, sports, and the arts. Cubans currently head all social indicators among Latin American immigrant groups in the Unites States, a remarkable achievement for a first generation of political exiles.

The first significant Cuban community in the United States was established in Key West, Florida, in the 1830s. The pioneers of that community were cigar manufacturers who went to Key West mainly to avoid the excessively high tariffs imposed by the U.S. government on their products. However, the cigar-factory owners and their workers also engaged in political activities and conspiracies aimed at ending Spain's imperial control over Cuba.

Cuban refugees wait for U.S. Immigration officials aboard the shrimp boat Big Babe *at Key West early April 23, 1980, after arriving from Cuba. (Bettmann/Corbis)*

The relocation of an important sector of the cigar industry from Havana to Key West was both an economic and political act that triggered a migration of several thousand skilled workers and their families. As the Cuban population in Key West grew, so did the political organizations advocating Cuban independence. José Martí, the political, organizational, and inspirational leader of Cuba's final and decisive offensive against Spain in the 1890s and founder of the Cuban Revolutionary Party in New York, considered Key West one of the revolution's most important strongholds. He visited the city often to raise funds for the war and was grateful to the immigrant cigar workers for their important monetary contributions to the cause.

The political activism and economic prosperity of the Key West Cuban community expanded in 1869, when one of its most prominent businessmen, cigar manufacturer Vicente Martínez Ybor, moved his operations to Tampa, Florida. Like Key West, the Tampa Cuban community grew quickly and became just as involved in the struggle for Cuban independence as its precursor. Perhaps even more involved, since as the Cuban insurrection spread to all parts of the island, so did Spanish repression, and tens of thousands were forced into political exile in the United States.

By the time Cuba finally won its independence from Spain in 1898, after a long and bloody thirty-year war, the Cuban population in the United States had grown to well over 100,000. With independence, many Cubans returned home to play important roles in the nation's government and society, or simply to help with the mammoth reconstruction efforts of a country devastated by war. Most, however, remained in the United States; today, both Key West and Tampa still preserve the flavor of the Cuban communities that once flourished there during much of the nineteenth century.

The United States as a Haven for Cuban Political Exiles

During the first five decades of the twentieth century, smaller groups of Cuban migrants went to the United States to escape political instability and repression in Cuba. In the late 1920s and early 1930s, groups of political and student activists opposed to dictatorial president Gerardo Machado found refuge in Miami and New York City. After Machado's overthrow, most of them returned to Cuba and were replaced in exile by Machado loyalists and the former president himself, who would later die and be buried in Miami. The same cycle was repeated, almost without variance, during the presidencies of

Fulgencio Batista (1940–1944; 1952–1958), Ramon Grau San Martín (1944–1948), and Carlos Prío Socarrás (1948–1952). It must be noted, however, that the United States was usually reluctant to grant political asylum to Cuban political leaders and activists. It did so on the assumption that their stay in the country would be brief.

During the 1950s, Cubans sought political asylum in New York City, Chicago, and Philadelphia, but Miami, owing to its geographical proximity to Cuba and mild climate, became the favorite place for political conspirators and freedom fighters. Even Fidel Castro, while in exile in Mexico, visited Miami several times to recruit fighters for his struggle against Batista and to raise funds for the war. Castro's 26 of July movement was very popular among the exiles, who, like their ancestors in the nineteenth century, looked forward to the day when they could return to Cuba to build a better nation.

Castro, the United States, and Migration

When the rebel movement led by Castro defeated Fulgencio Batista's U.S.-trained army on January 1, 1959, Cuba entered a very different political era that quickly transformed society in a most radical way, straining relations with the United States like never before. These two factors set the tone and the stage for the new Cuban migration to the United States. Once again, the United States, and especially Miami, Florida, became the choice place of asylum for those who fell out of grace or became disaffected with the new government. As was often the case before, among the first to go into exile were a few hundred close collaborators of the deposed government. By the end of 1959, more than 25,000 Cubans had requested and received political asylum in the United States.

Reacting to Cuban social reforms that damaged business and political interests on the island, the United States broke diplomatic relations with Cuba on January 3, 1961. Fearing the consequences of a war with the United States, more Cubans opted for exile. Ironically, both governments saw the break as a political opportunity. The Cuban government believed that the departure of disaffected citizens would allow a quicker and smoother consolidation of the revolution. The U.S. government felt that welcoming refugees from Cuba would accelerate the revolution's demise. At a minimum, the departure of thousands would embarrass the revolution at home and abroad. The United States hoped the brain drain caused by the exodus would strangle the Cuban economy, and better yet, that the new exiles could be organized into an invading army against the revolution.

The political objectives of both governments were played out in April 1961, when a force of 1,500 Cuban exiles, armed and trained by the U.S. government, invaded Cuba at the Bay of Pigs. The invasion, which was easily defeated in seventy-two hours, had profound repercussions for all parties involved. For the Cuban government, the victory over the exile army concluded the consolidation process. For the United States, the defeat meant not only an embarrassment for the Kennedy administration but also the loss of momentum for and confidence in the military option. For the 135,000 Cubans living in the United States since 1959, the Bay of Pigs fiasco brought the painful realization that their exile would be prolonged.

Alarmed by the increase in the number of Cuban refugees pouring into Miami (49,000 in 1961), and hoping that the Cuban migration would end soon, the Kennedy administration moved to create a Cuban Refugee Program to provide financial, medical, and employment assistance for the newcomers. The program, which remained in operation for fifteen years, helped more than 700,000 Cubans at a cost of more than $1 billion. The administration also provided funds to establish an airlift from Havana to Miami for those who were able to get the Cuban government's permission to travel or emigrate permanently. The Cuban Refugee Program is by far the longest-running and most expensive aid program for refugees from Latin America ever established by the United States.

In September 1965, the Cuban migration took an unexpected and unprecedented turn. The Cuban government, forced by the effects of a sharp economic decline and public pressures for migration venues, decided to open the port in the city of Camarioca to exiles willing to collect and transport their relatives to the United States. Castro announced his unilateral decision directly to the Cuban people during a speech and, within a few days, hundreds of boats from Miami arrived in Camarioca to transport the refugees. Since the United States and Cuba did not have diplomatic relations, the United States was faced with a difficult dilemma. It could exercise its sovereignty by refusing to accept the unauthorized migration, but that would mean closing the doors to refugees from a Communist country. The Cuban government correctly assumed that the United States would not refuse those who decided to accept Castro's offer. After all, it had served as a haven for all those who had defected from the revolution. As it turned out, seasonal bad weather limited the boatlift to only six weeks. The lift did, however, pave the way for a bilateral agreement by Cuba and the United States to create the Cuban Airlift, popularly know as the "Freedom Flights." The flights, sponsored by the U.S. government, operated for seven years and transported more than 260,000 Cubans to exile in the United States. The flights remain the longest and largest refugee operation in U.S. history.

The Camarioca boatlift and the Cuban Airlift led to passage of the Cuban Adjustment Act by the U.S. Congress in 1966. This act placed Cubans in a privileged and prioritized position over all other immigrant groups. Under the act, any Cuban who arrives in the United States, legally or illegally, can qualify for permanent residency after living in the country for one year and a day. The average wait for all other immigrants is five years.

Dramatic as the Camarioca boatlift and subsequent airlift were, the most dramatic episode in the current Cuban migration to the United States took place in 1980, after a diplomatic dispute over the custody of asylum seekers who had invaded the Peruvian embassy in Havana. When the Peruvian government refused to surrender the asylum seekers, the Cuban government responded by withdrawing its guards from the embassy compound and publicly inviting anyone who wanted to leave the country to go to the Peruvian embassy to receive exit visas. As more than 10,000 would-be refugees jammed the embassy compound for forty-eight hours, Cuban officials unilaterally announced the opening of the port in the city of Mariel for another Camarioca-style boatlift. In a repetition of events fifteen years earlier, Cubans in Miami responded eagerly to Castro's offer. This time, however, the boatlift went on for five months, and the strictly maritime and private operation transported 125,000 Cubans to the United States.

Throughout the duration of the frantic boatlift, exaggerated and often false stories about Castro's attempts to pack the boats with the worst criminal and undesirable elements of Cuban society appeared often in the U.S. media. In reality, less than 5 percent of the new arrivals had criminal records or serious illnesses. Nonetheless, the bad press resulted in the stigmatization of everyone who arrived in the boatlift. "Marielito," the label applied arbitrarily to all the boatlift entrants, implied that they were all social deviants, criminals, or otherwise dishonest. The false label tarnished the image and reputation of the new refugees and of the Cuban community in general.

Despite two boatlifts and an expensive airlift, the U.S. government continued to view Cuban migration as a temporary affair, so it did not make any attempts to normalize immigration from Cuba. On the contrary, after 1980 Cubans wishing to emigrate to the United States were left with few options: (1) going through the long, complicated, and expensive process of acquiring exit visas; (2) risking their lives at sea; (3) seeking asylum in foreign embassies; or (4) defecting while traveling abroad on official business.

Cuban Migration after Mariel

The Mariel boatlift was extremely expensive for the United States. In addition to the more than $100 million in detention and relocation costs during the five months of the boatlift, the federal government had to continue spending tens of millions a year for the detention and processing of the 2,800 Mariel entrants considered "excludable" by the Immigration and Naturalization Service (INS) upon arrival because of their criminal records in Cuba. The high costs and the lack of control over immigration made the United Sates realize that in the absence of full diplomatic relations with Cuba, it would be greatly beneficial and much more economical to normalize, or at least regulate, the migratory flow from Cuba.

In December 1984, after a series of secret negotiations, the United States and Cuba signed an immigration agreement that would, among other things, result in the repatriation of all "excludables" and the issuance of 20,000 U.S. visas per year to Cubans who qualified for permanent residence in the United States. Both governments welcomed the accords, but, as had often been the case since 1959, politics got in the way. In May 1985, the Reagan administration approved funds for Radio Martí, a radio frequency used to broadcast to Cubans the truth, in Washington's view, or enemy propaganda, in Havana's. To protest the broadcasts, the Cuban government canceled the 1984 migration agreements. The cancellation effectively closed the doors to the United States for Cubans hoping to emigrate for family reunification, economic, or political reasons. Expectedly, the closing of the only legal channel for emigration led to an increase in the number of Cubans attempting to reach the United States in rafts or in hijacked commercial planes and ships. The number of those who died trying also increased, even as the accords were resumed in 1987.

During the 1990s, Cuba experienced the worse economic crisis in its history. Brought about by a series of long-term domestic problems, the crisis was accelerated and deepened by the political crises that led to the collapse of the Socialist governments of Eastern Europe and the disintegration of the Soviet Union. Within a few months, Cuba lost 75 percent of its general trade, and its capacity to import was reduced by 80 percent. As a result, the already troubled Cuban economy went into an uncontrollable downward spin. As the economic crisis deepened, the number of Cubans leaving the country illegally by sea increased dramatically, from 567 in 1990 to 3,656 in 1993.

The depth of the Cuban economic crisis, coupled with the worldwide crisis of socialism, seemed to set the perfect stage for the end of the Cuban Revolution and Castro's government. Hoping to speed up that process, in 1992 the U.S. Congress, responding to the strong Cuban American lobby in Miami and U.S. interests in a post-Castro Cuba, passed the Cuban Democracy Act (CDA). The CDA was designed to tighten the U.S. economic embargo against Cuba and to strengthen the prospects for democracy in the island. Among other things, the bill prohibited trade with Cuba by U.S. subsidiaries in third countries and blocked access to U.S. ports for ships that had recently visited Cuban ports. The Cuban Democracy Act hurt the Cuban economy, but not enough to achieve its main objective of toppling Castro's government. On the contrary, it led to a government crackdown on the internal opposition movement that was accused of being influenced and financed by the United States. More than anything else, the CDA made life even more difficult for the Cuban people.

The Summer of 1994: Another Wave of Uncontrolled Cuban Immigration

More than 30,000 Cubans arrived in the United States aboard or hanging on to extremely dangerous and precarious homemade floating devices, loosely described as rafts, in the summer of 1994. The causes for the uncontrolled migration were many, but chief among them were the economic hardships brought on by the collapse of socialism in Eastern Europe and stronger American economic pressure, as well as the increase in political repression applied by the Cuban government against its internal opposition. Those harsh realities led many to head north on anything that floated.

With the number of rafters increasing daily, on August 5, 1994, Fidel Castro addressed the Cuban people to explain the causes for a small riot in Havana earlier that day. He also discussed his concerns over a series of embassy invasions and ship hijackings by Cubans seeking to emigrate to the United States. He angrily accused the United States of not complying with the 1984/1987 immigration accords by failing to issue the 20,000 visas per year that the two countries had agreed to. He pointed to the fact that from 1985 to 1995, the United States had issued 11,222 visas, only 7.1 percent of the 160,000 that should have been allotted for that period of time. Castro finished the speech by declaring that, in the light of the long history exhibited by the United States of encouraging illegal emigration, and the events he had outlined earlier, his government would stop putting obstacles in the way of people wishing to leave the country.

Castro was true to his words, and Cubans interpreted them accurately as a green light to head north in whatever way they could. From August 13 to 25, the U.S. Coast Guard rescued 13,084 rafters. On August 23, a single-day record 2,886 Cubans were rescued in the Florida Straits, and the total for the month of August alone was 21,300. The high rate of arrivals in this new, unsolicited migration alarmed the Clinton administration into taking action. On August 19, the president ordered the Coast Guard to continue rescuing Cuban rafters, but said that instead of transporting them to the United States for processing, as it had done for the previous twenty-five years, the Coast Guard would begin taking them to the U.S. Naval Base at Guantanamo Bay, Cuba, where they would be detained indefinitely.

President Clinton's order to stop the Cuban rafters and detain them off U.S. shore represented a complete reversal of a thirty-five-year-old immigration policy designed to welcome, as political refugees, almost any Cuban claiming to be escaping Fidel Castro's repression. Cubans, who had had the doors to the United States opened since 1959, were suddenly not only denied entry but taken to what they came to call "concentration camps." Once there, they were technically out of danger, but they were denied the right to claim political asylum in the United States. Despite its harshness, the president's action failed to discourage those attempting to make the crossing, and the migration continued unabated.

The rafters' crisis officially ended in May 1995 after a long series of talks between the United States and Cuba resulted in what may be the most important immigration agreement between the two countries since 1959. Under the new accords, the United States agreed to return to Cuba all Cuban migrants rescued by its Coast Guard at sea and help them apply for legal immigration to the United States. The accords kept the number of visas for Cubans at 20,000 per year and created a visa lottery for people who did not have relatives in the United States. Cuba agreed to peacefully discourage would-be illegal migrants, to refrain from arresting those who were sent back, and to encourage them to apply for legal emigration to the United States through the new channels established under the 1995 accords.

The accords were historic on several counts: (1) It was the first time since 1959 that the United States and Cuba agreed to collaborate on a long-term basis to regulate the Cuban migration to the United States; (2) for the first time since World War II, the United States agreed to return refugees to Cuba, signaling the end of the particular status of Cuban refugees; and (3) Cuba decriminalized emigration (and the desire to emigrate) to the United States.

Cuban Migration Today

Both the United States and Cuba hoped that the rafters' crisis of 1994 was the last time that they would have to cope with an uncontrolled migration. They also hoped that the immigration agreement of 1995 would work and lead to a more normal migratory process. As it happened, politics got in the way once again. In February 1996, the U.S. Congress approved the Cuban Liberty and Democratic Solidarity Act (also known as the Helms-Burton law). In addition to further tightening the U.S. economic embargo against Cuba, it threatened to retaliate against foreign businesses investing in Cuba and gave Cuban nationals residing in the United States the right to sue the Cuban government in U.S. courts to recover lost property in Cuba.

The Helms-Burton law increased the hostile environment between Cuba and the United States. It was a clear reminder that the cold war between the two nations was far from over. As long as that environment existed, it would be extremely difficult, if not impossible, to have a normal migratory flow between Havana and Miami. In fact, even before the enactment of the Helms-Burton law, a new, unwritten immigration policy affecting only Cubans had come into being: the "wet feet vs. dry feet" policy. That is, any Cuban rescued or stopped by the U.S. Coast Guard before reaching U.S. soil—those with wet feet—would be immediately returned to Cuba in accordance with the 1995 immigration agreements. Any Cuban who arrived undetected by the U.S. immigration authorities—those with dry feet—would automatically gain the right to apply for political asylum.

The wet/dry feet policy has developed into an extremely dangerous and often fatal cat-and-mouse game between the U.S. Coast Guard and private *lancheros* (high-speed boat operators) in the Florida Straits. According to Coast Guard estimates, from October 1998 to April 1999, more than 1,000 Cubans arrived illegally in Florida aboard high-speed boats. Each passenger paid at least $2,000 and up to $10,000 to improve his or her chances of arriving in the United States with dry feet. In accordance with U.S. immigration regulations affecting only Cubans, and in contradiction with the U.S. Refugee Act of 1980, all arrivals are granted political asylum, regardless of whether they have a "well-founded fear" of political persecution at home. In addition, because the Cuban Adjustment Act of 1966 is still in effect, those who make it can apply for permanent resident status one year and one day after their arrival.

The Cuban Adjustment Act and the wet/dry feet policy continue to keep the Cuban migration to the United States in a peculiar, yet privileged situation vis-à-vis migrants from the rest of the world. A recent and notorious case was that of Elián González, the six-year-old Cuban boy found floating off the coast of Fort Lauderdale, Florida, on November 25, 1999, after his mother, stepfather, and eight others drowned trying to reach the United States with dry feet. Little Elián met all the requirements to be sent back to Cuba: He was found at sea with "wet feet," and his natural father in Cuba requested his return seventy-two hours after his rescue. Instead of returning the boy to his father, U.S. authorities granted custody to his grand uncle in Miami, who quickly turned Elián into a symbol of the exile community's political war against Fidel Castro and the Cuban government. Not to be outdone, the Cuban government also turned Elián into a political symbol of its war against the Cuban community in Miami and U.S. imperialism.

Elián González's case was disputed in U.S. courts for nearly seven months, and although the boy's father came to the United States to claim his son and won the legal battle for custody, the case was finally settled when U.S. Justice Department armed guards forcefully removed Elián from his grand uncle's home in a midnight raid. Elián finally returned to Cuba with his father in the summer of 2000.

The Elián González case was a reminder of how passionate Cuban exile politics are and how much they influence U.S. policy toward Cuba. It also showed that the United States and Cuba are very far from having a normal migratory process. In the meantime, Cuban migrants continue risking their lives aboard dangerous rafts and high-speed boats hoping to arrive in the United States with dry feet in order to benefit from the peculiar Cuban immigration policy still in place.

Felix Masud-Piloto

See also: Central American Refugees

References and further reading:

Engstrom, David W. 1997. *Presidential Decision Making Adrift: The Carter Administration and the Mariel Boatlift.* Lanham, MD: Rowman and Littlefield.

Fernández, Damián J. 2000. *Cuba and the Politics of Passion.* Austin: University of Texas Press.

García, María Cristina. 1996. *Havana USA: Cuban Exiles and Cuban Americans in South Florida, 1959–1994.* Berkeley: University of California Press.

Grenier, Guillermo J., and Lisandro Pérez. 2003. *The Legacy of Exile: Cubans in the United States.* Boston: Allyn and Bacon.

Hamm, Mark S. 1995. *The Abandoned Ones: The Imprisonment and Uprising of the Mariel Boat People.* Boston: Northeastern University Press.

Levine, Robert M. 2001. *Secret Missions to Cuba: Fidel Castro, Bernardo Benes, and Cuban Miami.* New York: Palgrave.

Masud-Piloto, Félix. 1996. *From Welcomed Exiles to Illegal Immigrants: Cuban Migration to the United States, 1959–1995.* Lanham: Rowman and Littlefield.

Pérez, Louis A. 1999. *On Becoming Cuban: Identity, Nationality, and Culture.* Chapel Hill: University of North Carolina Press.

Porter, Bruce, and Marvin Dunn. 1984. *The Miami Riots of 1980: Crossing the Bounds.* Lanham, MD: Lexington.

Rieff, David. 1993. *The Exile: Cuba in the Heart of Miami.* New York: Simon and Schuster.

Rodríguez Chávez, Ernesto. 1999. *Cuban Migration Today.* Havana: Editorial José Martí..

Roy, Joaquín. 2002. *Cuba, the United States, and the Helms-Burton Doctrine: International Reactions.* Gainesville: University Press of Florida.

Stepick, Alex, Guillermo J. Grenier, Max Castro, and Marvin Dunn. 2003. *This Land Is Your Land: Immigrants and Power in Miami.* Berkeley: University of California Press.

Torres, María de los Angeles. 1999. *In the Land of Mirrors: Cuban Exile Politics in the United States.* Ann Arbor: University of Michigan Press.

Czechoslovakian Refugees

The largest movement of refugees out of Czechoslovakia in the postwar period occurred in the aftermath of the "Prague Spring" of 1968. The Prague Spring was a period of economic, political, and social liberalization in the Communist state of Czechoslovakia that led to public optimism and cultural flourishing. It was crushed by Warsaw Pact tanks, lead-

August 25,1968. Prague, Czechoslovakia. Black smoke fills the street as a Czech youth climbs aboard a Russian tank during a demonstration near the Prague radio station. (Bettmann/Corbis)

ing to a rush of refugees out of the country and making it clear that the Soviet Union would tolerate little divergence from its own rigid view of communism.

As in Hungary in the 1950s (leading to the 1956 Soviet invasion) and the 1980s (contributing to the Velvet revolution), reform in 1960s' Czechoslovakia emerged from within the Central Committee of the Communist Party of Czechoslovakia. Alexander Dubcek, an unknown Slovak Communist, replaced Antonin Novotny as the first secretary of the Communist Party of Czechoslovakia in January 1968. Key officials connected with the Novotny government were gradually replaced, and Novotny himself resigned on March 28, 1968. Ludvik Svoboda, the postwar defense minister, became the Czechoslovak president, and on April 8 a new government, headed by Oldrich Cernik, was appointed.

Dubcek initiated a set of ambitious and (with hindsight) dangerous economic and political reforms. In many cases, these were efforts to reconcile official policy with developments that had already occurred at the grassroots level. In April 1968, the Communist Party Central Committee of Czechoslovakia criticized past economic dogmas and offered a renewed commitment to respecting human rights. In contrast with the generally farcical proclamations in postwar Central Europe, there was at least some hope that this commitment was genuine.

As political reform moved forward, intellectuals contributed—as they would again in 1989—to the momentum of change. Ludvik Vaculik published a piece entitled "Two Thousand Words" in the literary weekly *Literarni noviny,* and in the dailies *Prace* and *Zemedelske noviny.* The article issued a public call for civic participation and resistance. For a few months, Communist Prague recalled Weimar Berlin. Jazz music, pop concerts, cabaret, and poetry readings sprung up. Milan Kundera and other Prague-based writers enjoyed an international audience, and the Czechoslovakian film industry thrived. In the use of light in theater and an early form of the music video, Czechoslovakia surpassed the West.

Soviet condemnation, echoed by its puppet regimes in Eastern Europe, became increasingly loud and hostile. Like the leaders in Hungary twelve years earlier, Dubcek and the

Czechoslovakian government, intoxicated by their country's success, responded with blithe indifference. On the night of August 20–21, it all came to an end. Warsaw Pact forces invaded Czechoslovakia, crushing resistance and beginning a twenty-year period of occupation and "normalization." Touching, pathetic pictures of Czechoslovakian citizens resisting Soviet tanks were flashed across the screens of a world that briefly felt the small country's pain, though it did nothing. In one of many declarations of unfathomable hypocrisy, the Soviets insisted they had been invited to invade the country by loyal Czechoslovak Communists seeking "fraternal assistance against the counterrevolution." The Soviets soon brought Alexander Dubcek and the other Prague Spring leaders to trial. After a week of "talks," a Moscow memorandum insisted on Czech and Slovak agreement to the temporary presence of Soviet troops on Czechoslovakian territory. Only one member of the delegation, Frantisek Kriegel, refused to sign the memorandum. The Prague Spring was over. Thousands of people were purged from their jobs, the country's liberal intellectuals were imprisoned or consigned to menial labor, and there were mass expulsions from the Communist Party. A young philosophy student, Jan Palach, burned himself to death in protest on Wenceslas Square in January 1969. Many in the West felt that if the world needed another illustration of how bankrupt Soviet communism had become, it had one (though the Soviet Union continued to enjoy sympathy from some Western university professors into the 1980s).

As life in Czechoslovakia became constrained and more miserable (despite the reformers' best efforts), some 150,000 Czechoslovakian citizens fled to the West, including 12,000 to Canada (CBC 2004); 11,000 to Austria (Austria 2004); and 6,000 to Australia (Yorck 2003). Thousands also fled to Germany, the United States, and France. Among other writers, Milan Kundera, in Paris, told the world, through his novel *The Unbearable Lightness of Being,* of his country's suffering. In Prague itself, dissident intellectuals, including Vaclav Havel and Jan Patocka, formed "Charter 77," a group of pro-democracy writers and intellectuals, in response to intensified state censorship.

Those who escaped Czechoslovakia were in the main educated and skilled, and they integrated easily into their new countries. As their plight was a powerful symbol of Communist repression and of Western superiority, they were popular and welcomed. In 1968, over 90 percent of them were accepted as asylum seekers, a figure that stands in sharp contrast with current asylum acceptance rates of less than 10 percent. Like Hungarians in 1956, and the occasional Soviet ballet dancer or Olympic athlete throughout the postwar period, the Czechoslovakians' arrival illustrated a postwar blurring of the category of "refugee" with that of "defector." It was in many ways the pillar on which the postwar refugee regime was founded. When the Cold War ended, the political and ideological basis of the refugee regime largely disappeared, and with it went Western generosity toward and sympathy for refugees.

Randall Hansen

See also: Cold War; Hungarian Revolution; UN Convention Relating to the Status of Refugees, 1951

References and further reading:

Austria, http://countrystudies.us/austria/64.htm (cited January 31, 2004).

CBC Radio One, www.cbc.ca/thecurrent/2003/200302/20030226.html (cited January 31, 2004).

Williams, Kieran. 1997. *The Prague Spring and Its Aftermath.* Cambridge: Cambridge University Press.

York, Barry. 2003. *Australia and Refugees, 1901–2002. Annotated Chronology Based on Official Sources: Summary,* June 16, http://www.google.ca/url?sa=U&start=1&q=http://www.aph.gov.au/library/pubs/chron/2002-03/03chr02.htm&e=7421 (cited January 15, 2004).

D

Defectors

See Cold War

Democratic Republic of Congo

See Zaire/Democratic Republic of Congo and Refugees

Deportation

Deportation is the forcible expulsion of noncitizens from national territory by the state. It is a power that has traditionally been seen to flow from the state's right to control immigration: Just as states are entitled to prevent aliens from entering their territory, so they claim a correlative right to expel aliens who have entered or remain on state territory in breach of immigration laws. In some respects, the right to deport is more revealing of the capacity of states to exercise control over the lives of individuals than almost any other aspect of state power. The deportation of an individual severs permanently and completely the relationship of responsibility between the state and the individual under its authority in a way that only capital punishment surpasses. Furthermore, physically removing noncitizens against their will from communities in which they wish to remain effectively cuts the social, personal, and professional bonds created over the course of residence. Even if one concedes the necessity of deportation, there is no gainsaying the hardships it exacts.

Deportation in Historical Context

The expulsion of aliens by states has a long and inglorious history in the twentieth century. Among other events, the deportation of Jews from Nazi Germany and occupied Europe to concentration camps in the 1930s and 1940s, the expulsion of ethnic Germans from Eastern and Central Europe in the aftermath of the victory of the Allied forces in World War II, and forceful eviction of Ugandan Asians in the early 1970s have made for a powerful association between expulsion and ethnic cleansing, or genocide. Indeed, after World War II, international law turned to the question of expulsions, prohibiting, under Article 49 of the Fourth Geneva Convention, "individual or mass forcible transfers, as well as deportations of protected persons from occupied territory to the territory of the Occupying Power or to that of any other country, occupied or not, . . . regardless of their motive" (United Nations 1949).

These forms of collective deportation on grounds of ethnicity or race are only loosely related to the current operation of deportation power in democratic states. Legitimate deportation power is exercised only against noncitizens, and most contemporary states face tight legal constraints on their ability to strip individuals of citizenship. Moreover, contemporary deportation orders are not a form of collective punishment but are, at least in principle, the result of individual violations of immigration law and established in (quasi-) judicial proceedings. Indeed, deportation power simply flows from the more general sovereign powers of states to control immigration. In the United States, for example, the federal government had no "general deportation statute" throughout most of the nineteenth century. Only in the late 1800s, with "increased federal involvement in the regulation of immigration," did statutes relating to deportation begin to flourish (Aleinikoff and Martin 1985, 348), beginning with an 1882 statute intended to control Chinese immigrants. Later laws made it possible for U.S. officials to deport other groups of undesirable aliens, including those involved with radical political activity, such as Communists.

Jewish civilians: copy of a German photograph taken during the destruction of the Warsaw Ghetto, Poland, 1943. (National Archives)

Deportation in the Contemporary Context

The mechanisms of deportation vary widely between different states. In some, for example, deportation orders are left to subnational rather than national authorities (the German *Länder* (states), for example, have such power); some countries set explicit deportation targets to be fulfilled within a certain time frame (such as the United Kingdom); and in some states, large illegal populations are generally (if unofficially) tolerated (Italy and the United States). In most democratic countries, there are three primary ways in which an individual may become eligible for deportation: (1) by entering the state illegally—for example, by evading port or entrance officials or by using fraudulent documentation; (2) by breaching the specified terms associated with legal entry and residence—for example, by overstaying, working on a tourist visa, or committing a crime; and (3) by gaining entrance or continued residence in the state on the basis of a claim under the 1951 UN Convention Relating to the Status of Refugees that has come, after a process of determination, to be rejected. Many countries do not actually use the term "deportation" to describe their actions in ensuring departure. The term "removal," for example, is the nomenclature of choice in the United Kingdom. In Germany, policy makers avoid the term "deportation" because of its historical connections with the Nazi genocide of the 1930s and 1940s; involuntary return is instead described as *Rückführung* or *Abschiebung* (return) (Gibney and Hansen 2003).

Although contemporary deportation may not be equivalent to the mass expulsions of the past, it is still a controversial activity for democratic states. One reason for this is that it shows, in a clear and unambiguous way, the realities of immigration control and the force that lies behind it. Most citizens appear undisturbed by the practices their state uses to prevent the arrival of unwanted foreigners, such as through the denial of entry visas. Yet they find it harder to ignore television images of distraught families being bundled onto airplanes by officials of their government, even more so when those being removed are their friends, neighbors, or colleagues. Controversy is not dampened by the fact that those being deported are likely to have a very limited range of rights to contest their removal (and, where applicable, their detention). This is so because, as Peter Schuck has noted, in the United States (as in other Western countries) "classical immigration law holds that deportation is a civil, administrative proceeding, not a criminal prosecution" (Schuck 1998, 34–35). Thus the range of constitutional protections available to those subject to deportation, despite the

Indonesian illegal immigrants are removed from a truck to board a naval ship in Pasir Gudang port in Malaysia's southern state of Johore, November 19, 2001. Malaysia carried out its largest ever deportation of illegal immigrants, loading some 2,500 Indonesian workers on two Indonesian naval ships under armed escort. (Reuters/Corbis)

extreme hardships removal may involve, are much more limited than those available to someone who has violated criminal laws.

Yet if deportation represents a potent symbol of both the scope and severity of state power, it is one resorted to relatively infrequently in contemporary democratic states. In recent years, many politicians and government officials across Western countries have referred to what has been called the "deportations gap"—the gap between the number of people eligible for deportation and the actual number of deportations. For example, a recent House of Commons report stated that while around 50,000 rejected asylum seekers were made eligible for deportation in the United Kingdom in 2002, only about 10,000 left the country either voluntarily or involuntarily. Many reasons have been offered to explain gaps of this sort: the interests of governments in having illegal resident populations to service low-wage sectors of the economy (for example, Mexicans in the agricultural and service sectors in the United States); the enormous financial and human resource costs of tracking down individuals who have evaded border controls (for example, the costs associated with detention and chartering flights); and problems with getting states to take back those of their nationals who have been deported (for example, China has proven particularly reluctant to take back citizens from countries such as the United Kingdom and Canada).

Two other factors have also played an important role, especially in democratic states. First, as already suggested, public feelings about deportation are mixed, especially when the individuals at risk of removal have lived in the community for many years. Government policies often mirror this ambivalence: Tough laws are often undermined by inadequate resources for enforcement. Increasingly, also, governments must deal with international law limitations on the removal of foreigners who would face persecution, torture, and cruel and degrading treatment if returned to their country of origin. European states, for example, as well as being bound not to return refugees covered by the 1951 Refugee Convention, are also restricted or forbidden from returning certain categories of individuals under the UN Convention against Torture and Other Cruel and Degrading Treatment (1987) (note the Canadian Supreme Court's decision in the Suresh case of 2001) and the 1950 European Convention on Human Rights (note the decision of the European Court of Human Rights in the Chahal case of 1996) (Lambert 1999). These protections are applicable to only a small number of those eligible for deportation and can slow down the process of removing aliens, adding both expense and complexity. More generally, the deportation practices of states are now increasingly scrutinized by human rights organizations. When Malaysia began to organize the mass deportation of illegal foreign workers after the Asian economic crash of the late 1990s, it found its actions closely monitored by Amnesty International, Human Rights Watch, and the world's media.

The Future of Deportation

Despite these developments, the issue of deportation is likely to remain a potent, if controversial, one in the years ahead. There are two main reasons for this. First, across Western states, a rising number of illegal migrants and asylum seekers has led governments to articulate a need to close the "deportation gap." In recent years, countries such as Canada, Germany, the United Kingdom, and the United States have put more energy and resources into enforcing immigration removals by coordinating information systems and more closely trafficking arrivals and departures (Gibney and Hansen 2003). Many have also signed bilateral agreements with receiving countries to simplify the return of irregular or undocumented migrants. Second, fears of terrorism, especially in the aftermath of September 11, 2001, have created incentives for state officials to create legislation that empowers them to deport larger numbers of people, especially those who are considered suspect, either because they have engaged in terrorist activity or because they are believed to have some connection to it. In democratic countries, both these developments to increase the deportation powers of states have proven politically and legally controversial. The jury is still out on whether they will make deportation a much more common practice in future.

Matthew J. Gibney and Randall Hansen

See also: Asylum Determination; Border Controls; Citizenship; Clandestine Migration; Ethnic Cleansing; Expedited Removal Procedures, U.S.; Migrant Rights; Non-Refoulement; Public Opinion and Immigration; Readmission Agreements; Sovereignty and Migration; UN Convention Relating to the Status of Refugees, 1951

References and further reading:

Aleinikoff, Alex, and David A. Martin. 1985. *Immigration Process and Policy.* St. Paul: West Publishing.

Gibney, Matthew J., and Randall Hansen. 2003. "Deportation and the Liberal State." UNHCR New Issues in Refugee Research Working Paper 77 (February). Geneva: UN High Commissioner for Refugees.

Lambert, Helene. 1999. "Protection against *Refoulement* from Europe: Human Rights Law Comes to the Rescue," *International and Comparative Law Quarterly* 48: 515–544.

Schuck, Peter. 1998. *Citizenship, Strangers, and In-betweens: Essays on Immigration and Citizenship.* Boulder: Westview.

United Nations. 1949. "IV: Relative to the Protection of Civilian Persons in Time of War." *Geneva Conventions on Protection of Victims of War.* August 12, 1949. Geneva: United Nations.

Development-Induced Displacement

Development-induced displacement and resettlement (DIDR) is a type of forced migration that occurs when people have to move to make way for infrastructure development projects. Some 10 million people worldwide are displaced each year (Cernea 2000, 11) in the face of projects such as the construction of dams, irrigation schemes, conservation areas, urban renewal and housing schemes, water or transport supply systems, energy generation projects, and open-cast mining. DIDR has had overwhelmingly negative economic, health, psychological, and social consequences for the vast majority of those displaced; it has evoked widespread resistance; and it has become a highly contentious and politicized issue. The past two decades have seen the development of policy guidelines by international bodies such as the World Bank and the Organisation for Economic Co-operation and Development (OECD), as well as by several countries, resulting in more positive outcomes in some cases. Deep divisions remain as to whether the model of development presupposed by DIDR can be viable, equitable, participatory, or sustainable; whether the (usually involuntary) displacement to which it gives rise constitutes a serious violation of human rights; and whether it can ever be justified.

"Displacement" can mean various things within the context of DIDR. People may simply be ordered or forced to get out of the way and left to fend for themselves elsewhere; they may be ordered to move but given some financial compensation for loss of land, houses, and so on; or they may be moved to a specific new area and provided with land, housing, services, and the like. The first situation seems akin to simple expulsion, whereas the last two constitute instances of resettlement. In considering the resettlement side of the displacement spectrum, it is important to distinguish between development-induced displacement, that is, internal displacement due to economically oriented projects, and politically oriented displacement, that is, internal displacement caused by political conflict. These types of internally displaced persons have different legal standings in national and international immigration law.

It is difficult to obtain accurate statistics about development-induced displacement. The World Commission on Dams (2000, 16) has estimated that "The construction of large dams has led to the displacement of some 40 to 80 million people worldwide." A senior Indian civil servant estimated that some 50 million people have been displaced by development projects of all kinds in India (Roy 1999, 10). Recent figures for China suggest that since the 1950s some 45 million people have been resettled, 52 percent owing to urban development projects (Shi and Chen 2000, 1). Worldwide, urban development has replaced dams as the major cause of displacement.

Resettlement is best seen as a process, unfolding over time, rather than simply as a one-off move. The most influential model of resettlement as a process is that developed by Thayer Scudder based on his observation of schemes judged to be economically and institutionally successful. Scudder (1997) sees such schemes as passing through a series of interrelated stages over a period of at least two generations. The Planning and Recruitment stage relates to events up to just before people actually move, such as consultation between developers or other authorities and the affected people, planning, and site preparation. The Transition or Initial Adaptation stage relates to the actual move and the years immediately thereafter. This is the period of major stress for people, with a rise in morbidity and mortality rates. People usually adopt a conservative, inward-looking, risk-avoidance stance, focusing on immediate relationships, as community leadership often loses legitimacy and as people have to adapt to the new resource situation. As they regain their economic and social feet and their personal confidence, people enter the stage of Economic Development and Community Formation. They shift to a more open-ended, risk-taking stance, diversifying economically and investing in education and consumer goods. Wider, community-oriented relationships reemerge, together with stratification around the new resource dispensation, and community leadership, although often in the hands of a younger generation. The process is rounded off with the Handing Over and Incorporation stage, in which the scheme is handed over to the relocatees, the elder generation hands over production activities to the succeeding generation, and the scheme is incorporated into regional political and economic structures in such a way that it is able to run itself and to compete successfully for resources and services in a sustainable manner. These stages follow each other in a cumulative way, influencing how a resettlement project unfolds through time.

A few resettlement schemes (for example, the resettlement of Egyptian Nubians by the Aswan Dam; see Fernea and Fernea 1991) may be judged as successful in Scudder's terms. However, the socioeconomic consequences of resettlement worldwide have been mainly negative for most of the project-affected people (PAPs). Why should this be the case?

Displacement effects a disruption of spatially based economic, political, and social groupings and patterns of behavior, of what Theodore E. Downing (1996, 36) terms "social geometry" and the "spatial temporal order." Resettlement usually confronts PAPs with an increase of scale. They tend to find themselves in larger, denser, and more heterogeneous settlements, and increasingly incorporated into wider and more centralized administrative structures. Socially disrupted, with kinship and other primary groupings fragmented, and with less autonomy than before, PAPs often find themselves with diminished access to resources and located further away from them. This includes arable land; common property resources; clean water and wood in rural resettlement situations; or jobs, markets, and public transport in urban contexts. Compensation is typically not commensurate with the losses sustained and often late in being awarded. However, where resettlement is properly planned so as to provide new resources, people may find themselves with enhanced access to social services such as education, health, and transport.

Social and political relationships have to be renegotiated within the context of the new resettlement situation, often leading to a realignment in generation-, gender-, and kinship-based relationships, and usually making for greater political say on the part of the younger generation, for more narrowly focused kinship groupings, and for a greater individualism. Such changes in relationships, together with altered access to resources, often result in conflict, at the domestic as well as the community level, and in resistance against wider levels of administration and political power.

Local political processes, which often sideline women, as well as perceptions of gender roles on the part of project planners, tend to work in favor of men's interests. Planners see men, often farmers in these situations, as the "natural" heads of household. Resettlement tends to harden men's control over resources. They are usually the ones consulted during planning, the ones allocated resettlement land (and, critically, title deeds), and the ones granted compensation. They usually control income from cash crops in the new agricultural dispensation. Often less socially mobile than men, women are more severely affected by the fragmentation of social units. They are nonetheless at times more adaptive.

Whereas men may lose their jobs as a result of displacement, women are better able to gain income from informal-sector activities such as brewing beer, making food, doing people's washing, prostitution, and so on—particularly if improved access to resources such as cooking fuel and drinking water gives them more spare time. Though perhaps cut off from their natal kin, women nevertheless have the continuity of ties with their children, as well as the support of other women, and receive recognition from these relationships. These sources of strength may well help them to adapt better than men, although they also often have to contend with domestic violence from maladapted menfolk with reduced incomes and self-esteem. Women may also benefit from the wider social exposure that resettlement brings, with greater opportunities for education, employment, and travel and a wider pool of potential marriage partners. All this said, a woman's well-being after resettlement will be heavily dependent on whether her man, and her domestic group, is economically better or worse off as a result of the move and on the strength of the regional economy (Colson 1999; Koenig 2001; Parasuraman 1999, ch. 10).

Patterns of access to resources reflect prevailing patterns of power and wealth within communities, such as between class, caste, or ethnic groupings. Unless this is consciously planned for and countered, resettlement often exacerbates existing patterns of inequality. The poor, the marginalized, and the vulnerable (such as the very young, the elderly, and the ill) become even more so, while the better-off and more influential benefit from the resource allocation arising out of resettlement. Increased pressure on diminished resources in turn leads to environmental degradation and further impoverishment.

The prevailing approach to resettlement in international funding circles is associated with the World Bank and the guidelines for resettlement that it has drawn up (see World Bank 2002). These guidelines center on Michael Cernea's Risks and Reconstruction model (2000, 23–30), which argues that displacement confronts PAPs with a series of "impoverishment risks," which, if not dealt with, will result in actual impoverishment across a broad range of socioeconomic areas. These risks are : (1) landlessness; (2) joblessness; (3) homelessness; (4) economic, social, and psychological marginalization; (5) food insecurity; (6) increased morbidity and mortality; (7) loss of access to common property resources and social services; and (8) social disarticulation. These risks tend to operate in a cumulative, mutually reinforcing manner. If anticipated and deliberately confronted, and accompanied by proper planning, funding, and administration, these risks can be inverted into opportunities for reconstruction. Resettlement can, and should, become a development opportunity, leaving the resettled people better off. Thus, one overcomes the risk of landlessness, for example, by planning and providing for "land-based resettlement," counters joblessness by providing for "reemployment," and so on (Cernea 2000, 20).

However, the argument goes, this positive approach is often not implemented because World Bank resettlement guidelines are not legally enforceable. Countries implementing infrastructure projects involving displacement usually do not have the appropriate resettlement and legal frameworks in place to protect the rights of the affected people and to ensure that active development programs are set in place and funded. This lack of policy and legal instruments impacts negatively, with predictable results, upon the interrelated elements of baseline surveys, consultation, planning, financing, compensation, implementation, and monitoring. Adequate financial provision is central to successful resettlement projects, with World Bank–funded projects showing a clear correlation between adequate funding and positive outcomes, and vice versa. Why, then, are things not done and funded properly? The World Bank has argued that many governments lack the political will to prioritize resettlement, to push through the necessary laws and development-oriented resettlement policies, and to take on the various interest groups that might stand to lose from such an approach. Borrower countries are seen to hold the key, and "the general risk pattern inherent in displacement *can be controlled through a policy response* that mandates and finances integrated problem resolution" (ibid., 34).

This is essentially an economic and technicist approach, with a distinctly optimistic flavor. It argues that what is needed is the proper inputs: proper policy, planning, provision, and administration. With these inputs, the political and other complexities of the resettlement process can be overcome, and both the national economy, and the PAPs, can be left better off than before.

In contrast to this approach, many scholars and activists argue that DIDR is inherently characterized and constrained by its fundamentally politically and culturally charged nature, which renders the above type of approach highly problematic. Inasmuch as DIDR involves people having to make way (usually involuntarily) for infrastructure, it is essentially about unequal power relations between those who are able to enforce both displacement and their culturally specific vision of what constitutes development, and those upon whom they are imposed.

In this process, the nation-state plays a central role. The state exercises eminent domain over its territory. It has the power to decide what is "in the national interest" and when it is expedient that "a few should suffer for the benefit of the many." Thus, large projects, such as dams (famously described by Jawaharlal Nehru as the "temples of modern

India"), tend to express the state's vision of development and to place the state in an ambiguous position. The state is often the initiator of projects leading to displacement, and its laws are also the last refuge of those obliged to make way for such projects. As such, the state is thus both player and referee (Barutciski 2000, 6). David Turton (2002) sees this as expressing a tension between the two elements of sovereignty and citizenship in the nation-state. Such tensions become even sharper in the case of those rural people (such as "tribals" in India) who do not own any land, who can be denied access to common property resources on which they depend for their livelihood by being turned off what is legally state-owned land, or, in the case of nomads, who are pressured to move into permanent settlements.

Recent years have seen a significant increase in the incidence of resistance to DIDR, in large measure owing to ideological and technological developments at the international level. Ideologically, the past two decades have seen increased interest in three interrelated issues: environmentalism, indigenous cultures, and human rights. Improved communications technology has put people in formerly remote areas in almost instantaneous touch with sympathetic allies and lobby groups worldwide who are opposed to the "Western development ideology." Resistance movements such as Narmada Bachao Andolan (Save the Narmada River movement) in India have an international profile and support network. It has been argued that this international profile was one of the major factors that led to the formation of the World Commission on Dams in 1997 (Oliver-Smith 2001, 101).

Resistance may be seen in terms of a discourse around rights and risks as well as around culturally different views of development: the rights of those who seek infrastructure development versus those who seek to maintain their way of life and sources of livelihood, and what constitute acceptable moral, economic, and cultural risks in the process. Acceptability is culturally conceived, and when PAPs feel that the risks confronting them are unacceptable, or are influenced by outsiders to redefine acceptability, resistance may well result. Particularly unacceptable to locals is the "cost-benefit analysis" approach, which they see as an attempt to reduce cultural valuables to monetary terms for purposes of computing compensation. At stake is political autonomy, cultural integrity, and economic livelihood (Dwivedi 1999).

Relatively few cases of resistance (for example, against the Chico dams in the Philippines and against dams in Brazil; see Gray 1996, 114–115) have been successful in the sense of warding off the intended infrastructure development. Resistance may, however, be successful in other ways, such as in achieving improved terms of resettlement. It may give local people wider contacts and valuable experience in dealing with larger political and administrative structures. At a policy level, resistance has been instrumental in making for improvements in resettlement policy and practice (Oliver-Smith 2001).

After disastrous earlier failures, China has since the 1980s achieved what are widely regarded as some of the most significant resettlement successes in the world. Cases such as the Shuikou and the Xiaolangdi dam resettlement projects have been characterized by a significant degree of settler participation, a substantial increase in household incomes, better housing and services, a high degree of flexibility in actual implementation, and settler satisfaction (Picciotto et al. 2001; Travers and Kimura 1993). These successes are largely due to China's adoption of a new and progressive resettlement policy. The policy includes significant consultation; an effective, decentralized resettlement bureaucratic structure, together with efficient local government structures inherited from the Maoist period; a high financial allocation to resettlement; a strong commitment to income restoration, together with adaptable income strategies; and a sound monitoring and feedback process. China has also pioneered benefit sharing, whereby a percentage of the benefits (such as sale of electricity) is channeled to the resettled people to assist them in the reconstruction and maintenance of livelihoods.

But to what extent are such successes representative? Some accounts of Chinese schemes report that they have run into a range of problems in places where it has not been economically or administratively possible to implement the progressive resettlement policy properly (see, for example, Travers and Kimura 1993). Shuikou and Xiaolangdi were high-profile projects, with Shuikou having had an overall budget of "about $24,000 per family" (Picciotto et al. 2001, 49). Shuikou's success was also strongly facilitated by significant regional economic development "that provided jobs and markets for the displacees" (ibid., 48). Other schemes in less favorable areas, such as at Yantan, have shown a widening negative income gap between resettlers and unaffected people in the area (ibid., 55).

Globalization and the move to a socialist market economy in China means that the government no longer simply underwrites financial shortfalls, guarantees employment, or provides social welfare support in relation to resettlement. Pressures for economic efficiency, the increasing withdrawal of the state, and difficulties in finding replacement land make it increasingly difficult for the progressive resettlement policy to be implemented in practice and for livelihoods to be guaranteed for resettlers (Meikle and Zhu 2000, 127–132). Many other countries implementing DIDR face economic liberalization and global trends from a much less favorable position than China, and one must therefore have reservations about the likelihood of their achieving resettlement with development.

DIDR faces a number of potentially intractable ethical problems, not least because the economic welfare of PAPs seemingly cannot be guaranteed. Is it acceptable to impose a culturally specific view of development and infrastructure upon others? Should some suffer for the sake of the greater good, particularly when it is debatable whether, for example, large dams are economically and environmentally sustainable in the long term? How is one to deal with concerns about political and economic equity and equality when it has almost universally been the case that some have to sacrifice both autonomy and welfare for the benefit of others? How is compensation to be calculated, especially with regard to intangibles such as cultural valuables, disrupted relationships, submerged graves, and the like? Although a cost-benefit approach to these matters is highly unsatisfactory, how else is one to go about computing compensation? It may be argued that the way around these problems is to negotiate and to make the affected people an offer so attractive that they will choose to accept it. But what if agreement cannot be reached? Should a development project requiring resettlement be shelved pending agreement, with prices escalating all the time? If one seeks to overcome this by specifying a time frame for negotiation, will this not make a mockery of negotiation?

In the light of these problems and complexities, how should we go about formulating and implementing sustainable resettlement policies that respect the human rights of all affected parties and leave people economically better off and socially stable? At one level, "inputs" are needed in order to turn the risks identified by Cernea into reconstruction opportunities, and thus to help people progress positively through Scudder's stages. But the cake is more than its ingredients. Policy needs to address the factors that inhibit the cake from rising, such as the fact that many of the problems of DIDR are inherent in the institutional process of resettlement and rehabilitation itself, in what Alan Rew et al. (2000) referred to as "policy practice." Different interests and departments compete and negotiate around the formulation of policy, which is therefore a compromise to start with. Policy is further compromised in the process of implementation as it works its way "down" weak chains of decision making and communication, being further adapted and appropriated by overworked and under-resourced officials who have to implement resettlement at ground level. International and national policies effectively become what officials at the end of the chain seek to, or are able to, make of them.

These factors, together with the politically and culturally charged nature of resettlement, suggest that policy should address *risk* at three interrelated levels: (1) impoverishment risks confronting individuals and households; (2) community-level cultural, political, and social risks; and (3) systemic risks related to the inherent complexity of the resettlement process and to an almost unavoidable top-down, "expertise" element that tends to oversimplify that complexity (de Wet 2001). The challenge to policy makers is to find procedures that enable a more genuinely participatory and open-ended approach to decision making and planning that is better able to accommodate that complexity. This, in turn, may increase the risks for planners, implementers, and funders, all of whom might wish to draw clear boundaries around projects. But the case material repeatedly shows that this is false economy. An unrealistically constrained process generates problems, resistance, and unanticipated outcomes of its own, in a very costly manner. Genuine open-ended participatory planning brings people on board, identifies real problems and practicable solutions, makes for more realistic budgeting and plans, enhances local capacity and leadership, and reduces conflict (Koenig 2001). Proper respect for and management of risk reaps returns. Good policy needs to understand, respect, and manage the complex of risks involved when, in the name of the benefits of a better life for the many, societies ask specific people to put those benefits on the line by moving in order to facilitate infrastructure development.

Chris de Wet

See also: Development-Induced Displacement; Environmental Refugees; Gender and Migration; Internally Displaced Persons; Resettlement; Women, Globalization, and Immigration

References and further reading:

Barutciski, Michael. 2000. "Addressing Legal Constraints and Improving Outcomes in Development-Induced Resettlement Projects." Unpublished Report, Refugee Studies Centre, University of Oxford.

Cernea, Michael. 2000. "Risks, Safeguards and Reconstruction: A Model for Population Displacement and Resettlement." Pp. 11–55 in *Risks and Reconstruction: Experiences of Resettlers and Refugees.* Edited by Michael Cernea and Christopher McDowell. Washington, DC: World Bank.

Colson, Elizabeth.1999. "Gendering Those Uprooted by 'Development.'" Pp. 23–39 in *Engendering Forced Migration: Theory and Practice.* Edited by Doreen Indra. New York: Berghahn.

de Wet, Chris. 2001. "Can Everybody Win? Economic Development and Population Displacement." *Economic and Political Weekly* (Mumbai) 36, no. 50: 4637–4646.

Downing, Theodore E. 1996. "Mitigating Social Impoverishment when People Are Involuntarily Displaced." Pp. 33–48 in *Understanding Impoverishment: The Consequences of Development-Induced Displacement.* Edited by Christopher McDowell. Providence: Berghahn.

Dwivedi, Ranjit. 1999. "Displacement, Risks and Resistance: Local Perceptions and Actions in the Sardar Sarovar." *Development and Change* 30: 43–78.

Fernea, Elizabeth W., and Robert A. Fernea. 1991. *Nubian Ethnographies.* Prospect Heights, IL: Waveland.

Gray, Andrew. 1996. "Indigenous Resistance to Involuntary Relocation." Pp. 99–122 in *Understanding Impoverishment: The Consequences of Development-Induced Displacement.* Edited by Christopher McDowell. Providence: Berghahn.

Koenig, Dolores. 2001. "Toward Local Development and Mitigating Impoverishment in Development-Induced Displacement and Resettlement." Unpublished Report, Refugee Studies Centre, University of Oxford.

Meikle, Sheila, and Youxan Zhu. 2000. "Employment of Displacees in the Socialist Market Economy of China." Pp. 127–143 in *Risks and Reconstruction: Experiences of Resettlers and Refugees.* Edited by Michael Cernea and Christopher McDowell. Washington, DC: World Bank.

Oliver-Smith, Anthony. 2001. "Displacement, Resistance and the Critique of Development: From the Grassroots to the Global." Unpublished Report, Refugee Studies Centre, University of Oxford.

Parasuraman, S. 1999. *The Development Dilemma: Displacement in India.* Basingstoke: Macmillan.

Picciotto, Robert, Warren van Wicklin, and Edward Rice, eds. 2001. *Involuntary Resettlement: Comparative Perspectives.* New Brunswick, NJ: Transaction.

Rew, Alan, Eleanor Fisher, and Balaji Pandey. 2000. "Addressing Policy Constraints and Improving Outcomes in Development-Induced Displacement and Resettlement Projects." Unpublished Report, Refugee Studies Centre, University of Oxford.

Roy, Arundhati. 1999. *The Greater Common Good.* Bombay: India Book Distributors.

Scudder, Thayer. 1997. "Resettlement." Pp. 667–710 in *Water Resources: Environmental Planning, Management and Development.* Edited by Asit K. Biswas. New York: McGraw-Hill.

Shi, Guoqing, and Shaojun Chen. 2000. "Chinese Resettlement Policies and Practices." Unpublished research paper, National Research Center for Resettlement, Nanjing, China.

Travers, L., and Y. Kimura. 1993. "China: Involuntary Resettlement." Report No. 11641-CHA. Washington,DC: World Bank.

Turton, David. 2002. "Forced Displacement and the Nation-State." Pp. 19–75 in *Development and Displacement.* Edited by Jenny Robinson. Oxford: Oxford University Press and The Open University.

World Bank. 2002. "Operational Policy 4.12: Involuntary Resettlement." Washington, DC: World Bank.

World Commission on Dams. 2000. *Dams and Development: A New Framework for Decision-Making.* London: Earthscan.

Diaspora

Diasporas are composed of people whose networks, allegiances, activities, and patterns of life encompass several different locations and whose social, political, and economic relationships span several societies. Though diasporas have a long history, their proliferation has been a significant consequence of the growth of migration in the past three decades. The notion of diaspora has lately gained wide currency among commentators on migration, but like the terms "transnationalism" and "globalization," the concept has been subject to great semantic stretching, leading some to question its usefulness.

The word "diaspora" derives from the Greek "to sow" or "to scatter." It is usually used to denote dispersal from an original homeland, often as a result of catastrophe, to two or more destinations, often far from that homeland: The "classic" or "victim" diasporas, such as those of the Jews, Africans, and Armenians, resemble such a characterization, but so do some other dispersed populations, such as the Palestinians and the Irish. Alternatively, dispersal may be more cumulative, involving the pursuit of employment, trade, or the furtherance of colonial expansion, which leads, respectively, to the formation of labor diasporas, trade diasporas, and imperial auxiliary diasporas. The Indians, Chinese, and Lebanese in various ways feature combinations of these diaspora types (Cohen 1997). Moreover, the dispersal of such people has also involved degrees of force, so that the analytical distinction between the "victim" and other kinds of diaspora participants may not be great. The combination of force and choice in dispersal also applies to more recently formed diasporas, where migration for work, education, or family reunion has mixed with migration resulting from conflict, as with many African populations, the Afghans, the Kurds, the Tamils of Sri Lanka, and other groups, as "diasporization" gathered momentum in the latter quarter of the twentieth century.

As well as dispersal, two other criteria define diasporas. First, their presence abroad is enduring, although exile is not necessarily permanent, and may include movement between the host countries and the homeland. Second, there is some kind of exchange—social, economic, political, or cultural—among the spatially separated populations making up the diaspora. Some commentators maintain that other definitional criteria are needed. William Safran (1991) suggested that, in addition to dispersal from an original center to two or more peripheral regions, these criteria should include retention of collective memory of the homeland; partial alienation from the host society; aspiration to return to an ancestral homeland; commitment to the maintenance or restoration of that homeland; and derivation of collective consciousness and solidarity from a relationship with the homeland.

Types of Diaspora

Following and modifying the typology offered by Robin Cohen (1997), several types of diaspora can be distinguished. Cohen terms *victim diasporas* those precipitated by a catastrophic event or cluster of developments. This category includes some of those thought of as classic diasporas. For the Jews, the cluster of pivotal events was the destruction of Jerusalem, enslavement, and exile to Babylon beginning in the sixth century B.C.E. For Africans, slavery and transshipment across the Atlantic to the Americas for coerced labor was the experience that forged the black diaspora. Massacres, mass displacement, and genocide in the later nineteenth and early twentieth centuries were the disasters that precipitated the dispersal of Armenians to the Middle East, and later to France and the United States. For the Irish, the great famine of the mid-nineteenth century was the traumatic moment prompting mass migration across the Atlantic. The Palestinians began a movement into neighboring parts of the Middle East and beyond following the emergence of the state of Israel in 1948. Subsequent movement of these groups may have been similar to other kinds of dispersal detailed below, but it is the victim origin asserted by the diaspora and often affirmed by outsiders that determines their defining character.

Imperial diasporas form another category. In a way, the archetype for this category is the early Greek diaspora, which spread over Asia Minor and the Mediterranean as a result of conquest, colonization, and settlement. Two millennia later, Spanish, Portuguese, Dutch, French, German, and British colonists established imperial diasporas. Intermarriage with local communities and revolt against the imperial homeland led to the transformation of some of these diasporas. One of the largest and longest lasting of this type was the British diaspora in the empire, and more particularly the dominions—Australia, New Zealand, Canada, and South Africa—a diaspora now fading as links with the "mother country" weaken.

The formation of some *labor diasporas* was linked with imperial expansion. Following the demise of slavery, the deployment of indentured labor, particularly from India and China to work in British, French, and Dutch tropical plantations from the mid-nineteenth until the early twentieth centuries, contributed significantly to the formation of the Indian and Chinese diasporas. A related type, again drawn from southern Asia and China, but also from other places, may be called *imperial auxiliary diasporas* and is made up of those who were recruited by the colonial powers to work as clerks, run the railways, and in other ways service the imperial order. Still another type, *trade diasporas,* composed of groups sometimes known as "middleman minorities," were also associated with imperial expansion, but these groups found or were allowed niches in the colonial order by utilizing their own trading networks. The classic cases are Indian traders in British East African colonies, Chinese traders in the colonies of Southeast Asia, and Lebanese traders in West Africa, the Caribbean, and South America. That Indians and Chinese feature in all three kinds of dispersal, albeit in different proportions, demonstrates the variegated origin of these and other diasporas.

In more recent times, migration for employment, education, or other forms of betterment, or flight to escape conflict or persecution, have supplemented these diaspora groups and helped to create new diasporas. South Europeans who crossed the Atlantic to North and South America, and later to Australia, formed a free labor diaspora that contrasted with the earlier forms of more coerced labor migration. Turks, North Africans, and others entering Europe as migrant workers after World War II were joined by labor recruits from former European colonies, who supplemented diasporas from the Caribbean, Africa, and Asia. From the 1970s, similar movements, particularly from Asian countries, extended the dispersal to the oil-rich states of the Middle East, to the industrializing "tigers" and "dragons" of Southeast and East Asia, and to other destinations. The end of the Cold War, the revolution in global communications, and other features of globalization have given further impetus to the dispersal of migrants, so that they are drawn from more and more countries and spread in ever wider destinations. A vast migration business involving trafficking and smuggling of migrants has emerged to realize this dispersal of people.

Three "New" Diasporas

Migrations of the Afghans, Sri Lankans, and Somalis exemplify some of the main characteristics of diasporas over the past two or three decades because they were forged from a combination of economic factors and induced by conflict.

Afghans

The conflict in Afghanistan since the late 1970s has generated a huge diaspora of Afghan refugees. The largest outflow was during the fighting between the Muslim resistance, or *mujahideen,* and the Soviet-backed Kabul regime, but the exodus continued subsequently as fighting among the *mujahideen* groups ebbed and flowed. At first, movement was largely to the neighboring countries of Pakistan and Iran, the former becoming the center for political and military resistance. Various mujahideen groups took over in Afghanistan after the departure of the Soviet forces in 1989 and the fall of the Soviet-backed regime in 1992. The Taliban regime swept away the fractious mujahideen groups and held sway in Afghanistan from 1996 until late 2001, when it was toppled with the invasion of U.S. forces. From a peak of 6 million refugees in the 1980s, perhaps 4 million returned in the 1990s during lulls in the conflict; but many left again as a result of renewed fighting, so that perhaps 2.5 million Afghans remained in Pakistan and Iran until the overthrow of the Taliban. Early in 2002 another large-scale return got under way, and by the end of the year nearly 2 million refugees had returned.

Afghan refugee camps in Pakistan were the center of the Afghan diaspora throughout the 1980s and early 1990s. They generated economic and political support for those inside Afghanistan and acted as entry points for such support from the wider diaspora in the Gulf region and the West. Although much of the diaspora was located in the countries of first asylum—Pakistan and Iran—other parts of the diaspora accumulated in India, in Central Asian countries that are neighbors of Afghanistan, in Russia (where there are said to be 100,000 Afghans, mainly illegal), and further afield in Europe, North America, and Australia. The Gulf states have also become an important destination for Afghans, especially as labor migration took off as a survival strategy, partly in response to dwindling international assistance to Afghan refugees since the end of the Cold War. Much of this migration is subsumed within the wider flow of Pakistanis to the Middle East. The wider diaspora has played an important part in the formation of the interim administration and the consolidation of a tentative peace since the fall of the Taliban.

Sri Lankans

Sri Lanka has experienced similarly complex forms of migration over the past three decades. At first it was largely economic migration, mainly to the Middle East, and for short-term contracts; by the 1990s, about 200,000 Sri Lankans went each year to work in the Middle East as well in Southeast and East Asia. Out-migration also included a "brain drain" of professionals and of students seeking educational advancement in Western countries, adding to an earlier presence abroad of "imperial auxiliaries," mainly Tamils in Southeast Asia. Since the civil war between the Sri Lankan armed forces and the Liberation Tigers of Tamil Eelam (LTTE) took off in 1983, continuing intermittently ever since, a large-scale outflow of asylum seekers, mainly Tamils, has taken place. Much of this movement was initially to Tamil Nadu in southern India, but many Sri Lankan Tamils have sought asylum further afield, so that a far-flung diaspora has reinvigorated the prior dispersal of Sri Lankan migrants who left for the purposes of education or to take up professional positions abroad. By the 1990s, there were some 100,000 Sri Lankan refugees in southern India, and around 400,000 in Europe and North America, who joined earlier professional migrants. In all, perhaps 600,000 Sri Lankan Tamils live outside the island.

Taking account of the labor migrants, refugees, and others who have settled abroad, there are now large numbers of Sri Lankan households with members outside the country. Those remaining rely on remittances from these migrants for a large part of their livelihoods. Some individuals and households have been displaced many times, and members of a single household are commonly dispersed in several different countries abroad. As with other diasporas, the center of gravity of the Sri Lankan Tamil diaspora has shifted over time. Early on, the LTTE drew its support from refugees in Tamil Nadu, but it has extracted support from a much wider part in the Sri Lankan Tamil diaspora. If the cease-fire signed early in 2002 holds, the diaspora will have an important part to play in the reconstruction of northern Sri Lanka.

Somalis

Somalia has a long-standing tradition of international migration. Early recruitment for the British Merchant Navy created a small but significant expatriate population of Somalis who settled in Britain. In the past thirty-five years, as in the case of Sri Lanka, there have been two much more important forms of movement out of Somalia resulting in a large and influential diaspora. From the early 1970s, many Somalis went as migrant laborers to work in the Gulf states during the oil boom of that time. Perhaps 150,000–200,000 did so annually in the 1970s, and by the end of the 1980s between 200,000 and 375,000 were working in oil-rich Gulf states. Refugee movements have formed the other main kind of flow. In the late 1970s, war in the Ogaden region of Ethiopia led to the flight of ethnic Somalis to refugee camps in Somalia. The outbreak of civil war in Somalia in 1988 and inter-clan fighting after the fall of Siad Barre in 1991 displaced hundreds of thousands of Somalis within the country and drove many others to leave for Ethiopia, Kenya, Djibouti, Yemen, and other neighboring countries, as well as further afield to the United Kingdom, Italy, the Netherlands, Scandinavian countries, Canada, the United States, and other Western states. By 2000 there were thought to be some 300,000 displaced people within Somalia, about 400,000 refugees in other parts of Africa and Yemen, and maybe 100,000 refugees in Western countries. The total number of Somalis living outside Somalia has been estimated at 1 million, a figure that presumably includes those who have naturalized in their countries of residence. As in the other cases, the large Somali diaspora has a potentially important role to play in postwar reconstruction efforts if peace can be built in the Horn of Africa.

The Making and Unmaking of Diasporas

Is the formation of diasporas the inevitable concomitant of the kinds of migration exemplified by these three cases? Not necessarily: Diaspora formation is not necessarily one-way. For if diaspora formation has accelerated in recent times, so, too, has the unmaking of diasporas, seen in the regrouping or "in-gathering" of migrant communities or dispersed ethnic groups (Van Hear 1998). Like the formation of diaspora, these regroupings may involve voluntary or involuntary movements of people back to their place of origin.

This trend toward the in-gathering of some scattered ethnic populations has been seen in the return of ethnic Germans to Germany from the former USSR, Poland, and elsewhere; in the return of Jews from the former USSR and elsewhere to Israel; and in the return of ethnic Greeks to

Greece from various parts of the former USSR. The return of ethnic Germans contributed to much of the newly united Germany's immigration bulge following the revolutions in the Eastern bloc in 1989–1990. The term "return" is somewhat of a misnomer as a description of these and other cases, for many of these populations have not known their "homeland" for generations. It would also be a mistake to see these movements as wholly new phenomena. For example, the in-gathering of ethnic Turks and Hungarians continued for more than a century as the Ottoman and Austro-Hungarian empires intermittently contracted. The new impetus toward such regroupings was predicated on the collapse of the Eastern bloc, and the loosening of rules constraining exit from Eastern bloc countries facilitated the emigration of these populations. Their in-gathering has been made possible by the existence of co-ethnics and territories ready to accept them, namely Germany, Greece, and Israel, all of which have constitutions that include the "right of return" of co-ethnics.

Both the formation of diasporas and their contraction may occur through catastrophe or cumulatively. They may involve forced migration, voluntary migration, or a combination of both. A particular event may spark the dispersal of people, and a particular event may spark their in-gathering to the homeland. Equally, dispersal may be gradual, as through continuous out-migration for employment, trade, education, or other forms of betterment, and the same factors may bring about a gradual return to the homeland. Intermarriage or other forms of assimilation, acculturation, and integration into the host community may also influence both outflows and inflows.

Diasporas for Good and Ill

If the making and unmaking of diasporas ebb and flow, so, too, does their influence. The influence of diasporas in the era of globalization is complex. Diasporas exert influence in several different locations—in the homeland, in the countries hosting the people in diaspora, and in the wider world; at several different levels—national, community, household, and individual; and in several different arenas—political, economic, cultural, and social.

The burgeoning literature on diasporas in recent years has tended to take one of two positions. On the one hand are those studies that stress the positive dimensions of diasporas, pointing to the benefits of remittances, investment, and other flows as well as of cosmopolitan influences that may support or enhance the life chances of those back at home, both individually and collectively. On the other hand are those studies that stress the negative influences of diasporas, particularly in terms of fostering conflict and long-distance nationalism involving the exercise of influence without responsibility. In the aftermath of the events of September 11, 2001, it is the latter view that is in the ascendant.

Political influences on the homeland include diaspora activities directed toward shaping the domestic affairs or the foreign policy of the countries of origin. Such activities have included participation in or support for struggles for independence, postcolonial power struggles, secessionist movements and conflicts, and postconflict reconciliation and reconstruction: Diasporas as diverse as those among the Eritrean, Kurd, Kashmiri, Sri Lankan Tamil, and Somali communities have mobilized in these ways. Activities range from campaigning and voting in home country elections to supporting armed factions.

Diasporas influence host countries on the social, political, and economic level. Countries of origin may intervene in diaspora activities, giving them a transnational character. Transnational influences include mobilization of the diaspora across countries for political purposes linked to the host country or the homeland. Recent examples include the mobilization of the Kurdish diaspora early in 1999 following the arrest and transfer to Turkey of Kurdish nationalist leader Abdullah Ocalan, when simultaneous large protests by Kurds occurred in at least twenty-two major West European cities as well as in Armenia, Russia, and Turkey itself. The mobilization of the Palestinian diaspora in the wake of Israeli military incursions into the West Bank in 2002 was similar in its scale and spread, involving actions in North America, Europe, and Australia in addition to those in the Middle East.

As far as economic influence on the homeland is concerned, three levels may be distinguished. At the national level, diaspora influence is felt on the economy through the contribution of remittances as well as through taxes, levies, and other forms of appropriation from migrants. At the community level, diaspora influence is manifested in hometown associations and similar organizations formed to assist countries of origin by supporting improvements in health care, education, or infrastructure. At the household or individual level, influence is felt through transfers of money for help with education, health care, or migration assistance for family members. Remittances make up a high proportion of household budgets in many parts of the developing world.

Sending money and other gifts or providing access to other resources and assets is arguably the main way that diaspora communities influence conditions in their home countries. Remittances from diasporas have become crucial to the survival of many in developing countries, including those that produce refugees. Estimated at about US$75 billion a year in the early 1990s and US$100 billion in 2000, migrants' remittances represent a large proportion of world financial flows (IMF 2001). The fact that 60 percent of remittances were thought to go to developing countries in

2000 underlines their importance for the developing world. They surpass global official development assistance—in the 1990s, by 20 percent.

Because they move directly from person to person, remittances may have a more direct impact than other resource flows. However, these resources are not evenly distributed: The benefits of remittances are selective. Though not exclusively, they tend to go to the better-off households within the better-off communities in the better-off countries of the developing world, since these households, communities, and countries tend to be the source of migrants. This is crudely reflected in the distribution of remittances by country income level: Of the top ten developing countries receiving remittances in the later 1990s, two were classified by the World Bank as low income (India and Pakistan), six were lower middle income (the Philippines, Turkey, Egypt, Morocco, Thailand, and Jordan), and two were upper middle income (Mexico and Brazil).

There has long been debate about the impact of remittances (Massey et al. 1998; Taylor 1999). The pessimistic view is that they are "wasted" on consumption, luxuries, "rituals," or housing rather than being "usefully" invested in productive enterprises. Such a view may be countered by arguing that investment in housing, health, education, and "social capital" contributes to "development." A more optimistic approach suggests that even if remittances are deployed "unproductively," meeting subsistence needs and satisfying other "nonproductive" demands may reduce risk and possibly free up other surpluses for investment in more directly productive enterprises.

In societies in conflict or emerging from conflict, the picture is even more complex. Remittances from diasporas help families to survive during conflict and to sustain communities in crisis—both in countries of origin and in neighboring countries of first asylum. Many Somali, Afghan, and Sri Lankan Tamil households affected by war in their homeland or living in countries of asylum are sustained by remittances from family members abroad. Following conflict, remittances are potentially a powerful resource for rehabilitation and reconstruction, both of physical infrastructure and the wider society, as the Eritrean case shows. But again, there is selectivity: These transfers do not by any means reach all conflict-affected households. Moreover, remittances and other transfers, as well as international lobbying by diasporas, may help perpetuate the conflicts or crises that beset such families and communities by providing support for armed conflict. Insurgent groups tax diasporas: The LTTE's levies on the several hundred thousand strong Tamil diaspora, for example, have been among the most efficiently—and ruthlessly—organized. For Paul Collier (2000), the existence of a large diaspora is a powerful risk factor predisposing a country to civil war or to its resumption. Mark Duffield (2001) noted that many wars today are sustained by regional and global linkages through which local resources are sold and arms and other essential supplies bought. Diasporas are crucial in providing the flow of money and resources upon which warring parties depend. They also provide markets for commodities extracted from war-torn areas or may indirectly finance such transactions or lubricate the connections needed to effect them.

The Future of Diaspora

The balance between these positive and negative influences of migrants, diasporas, and their transfers varies from case to case. Mindful of such influence, policy makers at national and international levels have been exploring ways to mobilize and utilize transnational activities and resources. Against the background of increased migration to ever more diverse destinations, more and more nation-states have begun to reach out to their nationals abroad to engage them in projects for the benefit of the homeland. There is nothing particularly new about this, but the possibilities are now perhaps greater than ever before because of the communications revolution and the scale of diaspora formation. In some ways, too, this marks a turnaround from earlier periods when migrants were viewed with suspicion, if not hostility, by home governments. Governments of countries as diverse as Haiti, Mali, Eritrea, and India now see their nationals abroad as assets. Such governments have introduced fiscal measures to encourage remittances and investment by nationals abroad, subsidized migrant hometown associations, created channels of communication with nationals abroad and political participation by them, and passed dual citizenship laws to consolidate continuing links with the diaspora.

International organizations, especially development agencies, have also come to recognize the potential of diasporas in recent years. For example, recent discussion within the World Bank and the Development Assistance Committee of the Organisation for Economic Co-operation and Development (OECD) makes reference to encouraging diaspora communities to become engaged in development cooperation in their countries of origin, particularly in the context of conflict (World Bank 2000). The International Organization for Migration (IOM) has also developed modest programs to mobilize diasporas, and the notion of "codevelopment" advocated by the French government sees similar potential in bilateral agreements with migrant-sending countries.

Diasporas predated the nation-state and are well placed to outlive it. Unencumbered by particular attachment to territory and capable of straddling the global and the local, they are able to take advantage of the opportunities globalization offers (Cohen 1997). Peoples in diaspora have found that they can exert a strong influence in the world without a secure homeland to call their own (for example, the Palestinians, the Kurds, and the Tamils). This observation leads to the following paradox: that the diaspora may become more significant and powerful than the homeland, while at the same time it is the notion of the homeland—often portrayed in highly romanticized images—that sustains the diaspora as an enduring entity.

Nicholas Van Hear

See also: Armenian Diaspora; Chinese Diaspora; Economic Determinants of International Migration; Jewish Immigration (UK); Palestinian Refugees; Postnationalism; Refugees; Remittances; Trafficking; Transnationalism; Turkish Diaspora

References and further reading:

Cohen, Robin. 1997. *Global Diasporas: An Introduction.* London: University College London Press.

Collier, Paul. 2000. *Economic Causes of Civil Conflict and Their Implications for Policy.* Washington, DC: World Bank.

Duffield, Mark. 2001. *Global Governance and the New Wars: The Merging of Development and Security.* London: Zed.

Fuglerud, O. 1999. *Life on the Outside: The Tamil Diaspora and Long Distance Nationalism.* London: Pluto.

Griffiths, D. 2002. *Somali and Kurdish Refugees in London: New Identities in the Diaspora.* Aldershot: Ashgate.

International Monetary Fund. 2001. *Balance of Payments Statistics Yearbook.* Washington, DC: IMF.

Massey, Douglas, J. Arango, G. Hugo, A. Kouaouci, A. Pellegrino, and J. Taylor. 1998. *Worlds in Motion: Understanding International Migration at the End of the Millennium.* Oxford: Clarendon.

McDowell, C. 1996. *A Tamil Asylum Diaspora: Sri Lankan Migration, Settlement and Politics in Switzerland.* Oxford: Berghahn.

Rubin, B. 2000. "The Political Economy of War and Peace in Afghanistan." *World Development* 28, no. 10: 1789–1803.

Safran, William. 1991. "Diasporas in Modern Societies: Myths of Homeland and Return." *Diaspora: A Journal of Transnational Studies* 1, no. 1: 83–99.

Taylor, John Edward. 1999. "The New Economics of Labour Migration and the Role of Remittances in the Migration Process." *International Migration* 37, no. 1: 63–86.

Van Hear, Nicholas. 1998. *New Diasporas: The Mass Exodus, Dispersal and Regrouping of Migrant Communities.* London: University College London Press.

World Bank. 2000. *World Development Report 1999–2000.* Oxford: Oxford University Press.

Displaced Persons

The term "displaced person" is most commonly used to refer to those individuals who were displaced by events associated with the closing stages of World War II in Europe. The challenges of dealing with these people during the war and its immediate aftermath spawned a number of different international organizations, including the UN Relief and Rehabilitation Administration (UNRRA) and the International Refugee Organization (IRO). The plight of Europe's displaced persons was to occupy the minds of Western governments until the beginning of the 1960s.

Even excluding the movement of people outside Europe, the volume of people forced from their homes by events associated with World War II was staggering. By 1945, "over 40 million people were estimated to be displaced in Europe" (UNHCR 2000). In the final months of the war, the successful westward march of the Allied forces, and the eastern movement of the Soviets, overwhelmed the Axis forces, liberating millions of Europeans in the process. Liberation was, however, accompanied by unprecedented displacement as large-scale property destruction, the end of Nazi rule, and the desire to flee battle pushed many onto the road.

The term "displaced persons" encompassed a diverse mass of humanity. It included people who fled across Central and Eastern Europe in order to escape the prospect of Soviet rule or punishment as collaborators or suspected collaborators; former forced laborers from Central Europe pressed into service for the Nazi war machine; and some 60,000 "gaunt, starved and half-crazed Jewish survivors" (Loescher 1993, 46) released from concentration camps. More controversially, the displaced included 9.5 million ethnic Germans who, though often unjustly expelled from Central and Eastern European countries as Nazi sympathizers, found few international organizations willing to respond to their desperate humanitarian plight.

Such a huge movement of people could not be ignored by the Allied forces and, led by the United States, the latter quickly established relief and assistance organizations. The UNRRA was set up by the Allied powers in November 1943 with a mandate "to assist in the relief and rehabilitation of devastated areas" (UNHCR 2000, 14). Within six months of starting work, the UNRRA had helped in the repatriation of millions of displaced persons; by the beginning of the year following, "three-quarters of the displaced persons in Europe had already been sent home" (Marrus 2002, 320). For those who remained, most of whom were in Germany, the organization established camps for which it arranged doctors and nurses and other services (ibid.). The UNRRA was eventually replaced in 1947 by the IRO, charged with the task of dealing with those displaced persons who could not be repatriated either because they refused to return to countries now controlled by the Soviets or because, as was the case with Jews, they could not be integrated into the same European countries that had persecuted them. Assisted by a desire for labor migration amongst Western countries, the ILO found resettlement places for just over a million refugees in the United States, Canada, Australia, Israel, and other countries. By the end of the IRO's existence in 1952, only a small number of displaced persons remained.

The issue of the displaced persons remained a nagging problem for Western states throughout the 1950s. A hard core of people, most of whom were undesirable to Western states because they were sick, aged, handicapped, or unemployable (Loescher 1993, 52), remained in camps. Only in 1961 was the issue finally brought to an end. In that year the United Nations launched a new and ultimately successful drive to resettle the last remaining displaced persons (Loescher and Scanlan 1986, 71).

Matthew J. Gibney

See also: Asylum; Displaced Persons Act (1948), U.S.; Ethnic Cleansing: Germans from Central and Eastern Europe; International Refugee Organization; Jewish Diaspora; Refugees; UN Relief and Rehabilitation Administration

References and further reading:

Loescher, Gil. 1993. *Beyond Charity: International Cooperation and the Global Refugee Crisis.* Oxford: Oxford University Press.

Loescher, Gil, and John A. Scanlan. 1986. *Calculated Kindness: Refugees and America's Half-Open Door: 1945 to the Present.* New York: Free Press.

Marrus, Michael R. 2002. *The Unwanted: European Refugees from the First World War through the Cold War.* Philadelphia: Temple University Press.

United Nations High Commissioner for Refugees. 2000. *The State of the World's Refugees 2000.* Oxford: Oxford University Press.

Lithuanian woman with belongings she brought from Europe as she patiently waits for a customs inspector upon her arrival in America as a result of the Displaced Persons Act of 1948 that allowed the resettlement of 200,000 Slavic people who had been imprisoned and persecuted. (Time Life Pictures/Getty Images)

Displaced Persons Act (1948), U.S.

The Displaced Persons Act of 1948 was the first significant refugee law in U.S. history. In 1947, President Harry S. Truman called upon Congress to enact legislation responding to the need for resettlement of "thousands of homeless and suffering refugees" in Europe. At the time of this announcement, more than 1 million persons displaced by World War II or its immediate aftermath were living in camps under Allied control in Germany, Austria, and Italy. The displaced included concentration camp survivors (most of whom were Jewish), forced laborers who had been brought to Germany during the Nazi occupation of Eastern Europe, and those who fled the advance of the Russian Army in the last days of the war or the newly formed Communist regimes established by the Russians in Europe after 1945. Between 1943 and 1946, huge numbers of people displaced during World War II were repatriated to their countries of origin. However, the Allies could not demand the return of concentration camp survivors or of those who had fled infant Communist regimes. Resettlement in a new country was thus the only real option.

Some 40,000 displaced persons (DPs) entered the United States between 1946 and 1948, courtesy of presidential directives. But restrictive U.S. immigration legislation and the manifest need for more resettlement places led the executive branch and pro-refugee lobbyists to call for new legislation. The Displaced Persons Act passed by Congress in 1948 was a restrictive response to this call. Congress, focusing on preserving established restrictive immigration laws and preventing the entrance of "inferior" migrants, savaged the original legislative proposals. The result was legislation that allowed for the entry of only 200,000 displaced persons (as well as 2,000 Czech refugees and 3,000 war orphans). The imprint of Congress was felt not only on the numbers entering, however. Under the act, the places allocated to displaced persons were "mortgaged" against the future immigration quotas of the countries from which the displaced came, thus making the U.S. response compatible with the National Origins Act of 1924. Congress also limited entry to those who had arrived in camps before December 20, 1945. Critics charged that this limitation was designed to prevent Jews from entering under the act, as the bulk of those still in need of resettlement had arrived in the camps after the end of 1945.

The significance of the 1948 act was twofold. First, it made refugees a category of people distinguishable from immigrants in U.S. legislation. Although refugees were not completely removed from the onerous requirements of the National Origins Act, the Displaced Persons Act did establish an important precedent by singling out refugees for special treatment. In the years after the 1948 act was passed, more legislation designed specifically to facilitate the entrance of refugees and further separating refugees from other immigrants was enacted. Moreover, the restrictiveness of the 1948 legislation was soon challenged by an amendment in 1950 that eased the entrance of many of the remaining displaced persons.

Second, the act heralded a period of increasing presidential involvement in entrance decisions as refugee legislation and Cold War foreign policy became intertwined. While the calls for the resettlement of DPs began as a sympathetic response to those who had suffered most at the hands of the Nazis, it soon became a way of rewarding the "heroes of democracy," as Truman called those who had fled Communist regimes in Eastern Europe. The arguments used to support the Displaced Persons Act came to inform legislation and executive actions that led to the entrance of large numbers of refugees from Communist countries, notably Hungary, Cuba, and Vietnam, thus shaping the direction of postwar American refugee policy.

Matthew J. Gibney

See also: Cold War; Displaced Persons; Genocide

References and further reading:

Divine, Robert A. 1957. *American Immigration Policy, 1924–1952.* New Haven, CT: Yale University Press.

Loescher, Gil, and John A. Scanlan. 1986. *Calculated Kindness: Refugees and America's Half-Open Door, 1945 to the Present.* New York: Free Press.

Dominican Republic Diaspora

A large-scale migration of Dominicans that began in the 1960s, mainly to New York City but also to other areas of the United States, as well as to Puerto Rico, Venezuela, the Lesser Antilles, Spain, and Italy, continues to some extent today. Glenn Hendricks's 1974 book, *Dominican Diaspora: From the Dominican Republic to New York City—Villagers in Transition,* drew attention to the Dominican out-migration and probably marked the first use of the term "diaspora" in the Dominican context.

The Dominican Republic has a surface area of 48,380 miles, roughly the size of Denmark, and an estimated population in 2000 of 8.3 million people. The gross domestic product per capita that year was $5,700 (purchasing power parity—that is, reflecting what the currency buys locally rather than the official exchange rate). The main destination of Dominican international migration by far has been New York City and its surrounding areas, including New Jersey, followed by Puerto Rico, Florida, Massachusetts, and Rhode Island.

Dominican emigration has a long history dating to well before the founding of the nation in 1844. Hispaniola for centuries was an impoverished backwater of the Spanish empire in America. During the colonial period, Dominicans emigrated to seek better living conditions, especially to Cuba. After independence, Dominicans frequently sought exile in Cuba and other countries of Latin America.

The contemporary Dominican diaspora began shortly after the end of the dictatorship of General Rafael Leónidas Trujillo (1930–1961). A few Dominicans had migrated to work in the United States much earlier, as far back as the 1920s, but Trujillo tightly controlled emigration during his reign, and it remained at very low levels. The peak emigration decade during the Trujillo era was the 1950s. The U.S. Immigration and Naturalization Service records 9,987 Dominican immigrants admitted between 1951 and 1960. Many of these were political exiles.

Mass migration began in the mid-1960s, when the number of immigrants admitted to the United States increased by a factor of nearly ten, reaching 93,292 in the 1960s. The number of immigrants admitted to the United States from the Dominican Republic has increased every decade since (148,135 in the 1970s; 252,035 in the 1980s; and 335,251 in the 1990s). The Dominican Republic ranked fifth in the world in the number of immigrants admitted to the United States in the 1990s, behind only Mexico, the Soviet Union (Russia), China, and the Philippines. The figure does not include undocumented immigrants. The U.S. Office of Immigration Statistics estimated that in 2000 there were 91,000 unauthorized Dominican immigrants in the United States, the eighth largest total for any country.

Trends in the late 1990s and early 2000s indicate a slowing of Dominican immigration and an increase in expulsions. This trend, which reflects general immigration trends into the United States, has resulted mainly from harsher U.S. immigration policies and procedures instituted since the mid-1990s because of anti-immigration sentiment and security concerns. It is therefore unlikely that the rate of increase of the Dominican population of the United States will be sustained in the decade 2000–2010. But barring a drastic change in U.S. immigration policy, Dominican immigration will continue at relatively high levels and the population will continue to increase at a fairly high pace.

The massive migration of the past three decades has made Dominicans the fourth-largest group of Latinos in the United States after Mexicans, Puerto Ricans, and Cubans. According to the 2000 U.S. Census, there were 764,495 Dominicans in the United States that year. The figure is a significant undercount,

Some of the thirty-seven Dominican refugees taken from a sailboat off the Florida Keys show their exhaustion as they wait on the deck of the U.S. Coast Guard cutter Seahawk *to be interviewed by immigration officials. On a tip-off, forty-two refugees were discovered on the 30-foot sailboat, but five escaped. (Bettmann/Corbis)*

likely resulting from the design of the 2000 census questionnaire. Various researchers have estimated the 2000 Dominican population at slightly over 1 million. Such a number implies a doubling of the population in a single decade (1990–2000), the fastest rate of growth of any Latino group.

The main causes driving Dominican migration are economic, although family reunification and, in the 1960s and 1970s, political persecution played a role. Since the 1960s, the Dominican Republic has experienced substantial economic growth, but this growth has failed to generate nearly the number of jobs necessary to employ the growing labor force. The distribution of income and wealth is highly unequal, and the economy has suffered from external shocks and political and social strife resulting from market-oriented structural adjustments. It is estimated that the poorest half of the population receives less than one-fifth of the national income while the richest 10 percent enjoys about 40 percent of the national income.

Dominican immigrants to the United States range widely in occupation and education, but the data indicate that it is primarily a working-class migration. From 1968 to 1978, for instance, two-thirds of Dominican immigrants to the United States with a declared occupation on admission were laborers, operatives, or service workers. Among the ten leading countries of immigration, only Mexican immigrants were more likely than Dominicans (79 percent) to be in these occupations. At the other end of the spectrum, only 6 percent of immigrants from India were in unskilled occupational fields. Later cohorts of Dominican immigrants included more middle-class and professional immigrants, reflecting rising levels of education in the country and the impact of economic crises on this social class as well as such problems as persistent blackouts and rising crime.

Dominicans in the United States are the second most highly geographically concentrated Latino group (after Cubans). According to data from Current Population Surveys, in the late 1990s two-thirds (67 percent) of U.S. Dominicans resided in the New York–Northern New Jersey–Long Island consolidated metropolitan statistical area (CMSA). The New Jersey cities of Paterson, Passaic, Perth Amboy, and Union

City have substantial Dominican populations. With 7.7 percent of the total, the Miami–Fort Lauderdale CMSA had the second-largest Dominican concentration in the continental United States. Other concentrations are in the cities of Lawrence and Boston, Massachusetts, and in Providence, Rhode Island.

Outside the continental United States there is a major Dominican population on the island of Puerto Rico and a continual inflow of unauthorized immigrants across the narrow but treacherous Mona Channel. Every year, several hundred are intercepted by the U.S. Coast Guard and returned to the Dominican Republic, and dozens more die attempting the crossing.

Although still high, the extreme geographical concentration of the Dominican-origin population of the United States that made "Nueva York" virtually synonymous with "the United States" for many in the Dominican Republic has been declining steadily for two decades. In 1980, New York City alone accounted for nearly three-fourths (73 percent) of all Dominicans in the United States; by 2000, only about half of U.S Dominicans (53 percent) lived in New York City.

The majority of Dominicans in the United States are female and young. In the late 1990s, females outnumbered males by 54 to 46 percent. This gender gap may be due to the structure of employment opportunities and the large role of the garment and service industries in employing Dominican workers. The gap is even wider among Dominican immigrants to other countries, especially Spain, where thousands of Dominican women are employed in domestic service. The gender disparity is diminishing, although not disappearing, in the United States, partly because there is no gender imbalance among U.S.-born Dominicans. Less than 7 percent of the Dominicans in the United States are sixty or older, while 44 percent are under twenty years of age. This is a result of the relatively high birthrate among Dominicans as well as selective migration of young people.

The socioeconomic status of Dominicans looks significantly different from a cross-sectional standpoint than it does from an intergenerational perspective. A static portrait reveals a population with drastically low levels of income and education. Data from the 2000 census indicate that Dominican households receive about half the income per member as the average American household. This gap partly reflects the significantly higher-than-average size of Dominican households, but it also reflects the low levels of education of the first generation. As of the late 1990s, educational attainment of foreign-born Dominicans in the United States was dramatically lower than that for the U.S. population as a whole. It was also below that of Puerto Ricans and Cubans born outside the U.S. mainland, exceeding only that of foreign-born Mexicans. Less than 10 percent of foreign-born Dominicans had graduated from college, and about half failed to graduate from high school. An intergenerational analysis yields a more hopeful picture. Second-generation Dominicans, the U.S-born children of Dominican immigrants, are receiving significantly more schooling than their immigrant parents. In New York City, they are staying in school longer than other minority students. Nearly 20 percent of U.S.-born Dominicans have graduated from college. A similar pattern of upward mobility is observed with respect to income and occupation. For instance, the percentage of second-generation Dominicans in professional and managerial jobs is almost twice that for the immigrant generation.

These data, which suggest good prospects for intergenerational mobility, provide some hope for a community with current low levels of household and per capita income and high levels of poverty, unemployment, and other social problems. U.S.-born Dominicans represent over 43 percent of U.S. Dominicans, but their median age is just under thirteen years. The impact of this generation will be felt for decades to come. However, even second-generation Dominicans have a substantial way to go before achieving the mean level of education, income, and occupational status for the United States population as a whole.

After almost four decades of migration to the United States, Dominicans have created an array of institutions, developed myriad cultural expressions, and begun to make significant inroads in politics and business. Alianza Dominicana, formed in the 1980s and led by Moisés Pérez, stands out as the largest of social service organizations that have sprung up to cater to the needs of the Dominican community in New York City, providing job training, recreation, and other services. The Dominican American National Roundtable (DANR), organized in 1997, a national nonprofit organization with headquarters in Washington, D.C., also serves the Dominican community in the United States, pursuing educational, economic, legal, social, cultural, and political objectives.

In the field of politics, in 1991 Guillermo Linares became the first Dominican to be elected to the New York City Council, and in 1996 Adriano Espaillat became the first to be elected to the New York State Assembly. In 2002, Juan Pichardo became the first Dominican American elected to the Rhode Island State Senate.

Dominicans have also made inroads in academic fields, and in the 1990s the City University of New York established the first Dominican studies program at a U.S. institution of higher learning, the Dominican Studies Institute. The directors of the program have so far included U.S.-based Dominican scholars Silvio Torres-Saillant and Ramona Hernández.

Other outstanding Dominican individuals have also made significant contributions to American society and culture. Designer Oscar de la Renta is not only renowned in the realm of fashion but is also a significant entrepreneur and philanthropist in New York City. The fiction of Julia Alvarez (*How the García Girls Lost Their Accents* and *In the Time of the Butterflies*) has illuminated the Latin American immigrant experience and exposed American readers to Dominican history. Junot Díaz's 1996 collection of short stories (*Drown*) introduced a young Dominican American writer. The narratives in this first book span the gritty streets of the U.S. Northeast and the backwaters of the Dominican Republic and explore themes of generational, gender, and sexual difference within the Dominican experience as much as cultural clashes with the dominant society.

Baseball stars are easily the best-known Dominicans in the United States. Baseball is the national pastime both in the United States and Dominican Republic. There are more players from the Dominican Republic in major league baseball than from any other country in the world. Although most of them are not immigrants, having grown up in the Dominican Republic and often returning there during the off-season and after retirement, they often live a transnational existence during their active careers. Chicago Cubs slugger Sammy Sosa is an icon to fans in the Windy City, to Dominican immigrants in the United States, and to the people back home. President Bill Clinton invited Sosa to sit next to the First Lady during the State of the Union Address to Congress. Shortly thereafter, Hillary Clinton announced her race for a seat in the U.S. Senate from the state of New York, home to more than 600,000 Dominicans and Dominican Americans. Other stars include shortstop Alex Rodriguez and pitcher Pedro Martínez, a certain Hall of Famer, considered by many experts the best player of his generation.

Beyond a large number of bodegas (small grocery stores), beauty shops, restaurants, and travel agencies, Dominicans own many other businesses, including a large chain of supermarkets. Since the 1980s, a significant number of Dominican physicians have migrated to the United States. Although the majority are located in New York City and other major urban medical centers, such as Miami, there are a substantial number who have relocated to nontraditional areas, including several dozen in and around Harlingen, Texas, on the U.S.-Mexico border.

Popular as well as academic analyses of the Dominican diaspora often have stressed the transnational dimension, and media reports describing Dominicans as the most transnational of Latino groups have some basis. Former Dominican president Leonel Fernández (1996–2000) lived and attended school in the United States before returning to the Dominican Republic to attend a university and engage in politics. Remittances represent a major component of Dominican national income. Many small businesses in the Dominican Republic are financed by U.S. earnings and savings. Dominican political parties collect money and campaign extensively in the United States. Conditions in the Dominican Republic affect the volume and composition of the migration flow to the United States and thereby influence the profile of the U.S. Dominican community.

Some scholars claim a distinct diasporic identity for Dominicans in the United States and stress their status as a minority group, their struggle for upward mobility and inclusion, and their resistance against discrimination, racism, and police brutality. Despite enormous challenges, the future looks somewhat brighter than the past for Dominicans in the United States. Dominicans have often felt nearly invisible compared to the three largest Latino groups. But demographic trends indicate that Dominicans probably will become the third-largest Latino group by 2010 or before, and socioeconomic and political trends suggest substantial improvement in the community's social, economic, and political status in the coming decades.

Max Jose Castro

See also: Colombian Diaspora; Class; Gender and Migration; Mexican Immigration; U.S. Immigration; Women, Globalization, and Immigration.

References and further reading:

Atkins, G. Pope, and Larman C. Wilson. 1998. *The Dominican Republic and the United States: From Imperialism to Transnationalism.* Athens: University of Georgia Press.

Black, Jan Knippers. 1986. *The Dominican Republic: Politics and Development in an Unsovereign State.* Boston: Allen and Unwin.

Hendrick, Glenn. 1974. *Dominican Diaspora: From the Dominican Republic to New York City—Villagers in Transition.* New York: Teachers College Press.

Wiarda, Howard J. 1969. *The Dominican Republic: Nation in Transition.* London: Pall Mall.

Dual Nationality

Dual nationality is on the rise in the modern world, a trend increasingly accepted by states but still resisted and criticized in many quarters. The term "nationality," as used here, connotes the legal relationship of membership in a state. Nationals owe the state allegiance and certain concrete duties and are entitled in return to protections from that state. Nationals are distinguished from aliens, persons who lack the state's nationality. In principle, citizens constitute a subset of nationals; citizenship usually entails full political rights in the polity. The distinction between nationals and citizens was more important when colonialism was widespread. Today a great many states consider all or virtually all their nationals as citizens holding full political rights.

Dual nationals possess the legal relationship of nationality with two states. (It is also possible for a person to hold membership in more than two states, but the situation of

Hungarians headed to the polls to vote in an emotionally charged referendum on granting dual citizenship to millions of ethnic Hungarians living abroad. Budapest, December 5, 2004. (Reuters/Corbis)

such plural or multiple nationals is adequately understood by considering dual nationality.) Historically, dual nationality has arisen primarily because of variations among states in their domestic legal provisions for acquiring and losing nationality. Increasing global migration and a growing incidence of marriage involving couples holding different nationalities are expanding the ranks of dual nationals, although no precise statistics exist.

Traditionally regarded as an evil to be reduced or eradicated through diplomacy or strict legal provisions, today dual nationality is increasingly tolerated, or even promoted, by the states involved. In a trend that marked approximately the last quarter of the twentieth century, many countries with large numbers of nationals residing abroad (sending states) eased or repealed rules formerly imposing loss of nationality on those who naturalized in a foreign state. They made these changes primarily in order to promote or sustain ties to their diaspora, often hoping that the continued nationality link might facilitate the flow of remittances or business investment. Some such changes were also motivated by a wish to improve the status and treatment of the emigrants in their states of residence by making sure that they would enjoy the rights of nationals there. Many receiving states have also modified their rules in a direction more receptive to dual nationality, sometimes in response to human rights claims, but in other instances in order to promote the naturalization of long-resident aliens. Such receiving states calculated that resident aliens might have been deterred from naturalizing by the prospect of being required to surrender the former nationality, and they generally hoped that easing the obstacles to naturalization would further the process of assimilation or integration into their societies. But the trend toward greater acceptance of dual nationality is uneven and has met with resistance in some states. Some opponents question whether dual nationality really serves the ends (such as integration) claimed by proponents of dual nationality.

Sources of Dual Nationality

It is considered a hallmark of sovereignty that a state sets its own rules for the acquisition and loss of its nationality. Customary international law sets exceedingly undemanding limits on a state's authority, simply requiring some genuine link before attributed nationality must be recognized by other states. Some states are also parties to treaties, including multilateral agreements regarding statelessness, that set further limits on the state's nationality determinations, but these limits also tend to be quite modest.

Nationality is acquired either at birth or through naturalization. (Acquisition through the cession or conquest of territory is not treated here.)

Acquisition of Nationality at Birth

States follow two basic regimes for the attribution of citizenship at birth. Some ascribe nationality based on birth in the national territory (the *ius soli* principle), while others do so based on descent from persons who are nationals (the *ius sanguinis* principle). States, however, can set their own precise rules and exceptions for applying either. For example, some ius soli states attribute their nationality to virtually all children born on their soil, while others limit attribution to children born there to lawfully domiciled parents or parents domiciled for a stated minimum period. Ius sanguinis states use a variety of mechanisms to curtail transmission of their citizenship to distant generations, primarily minimum periods of residence in national territory by the parent before the birth or by the child before the age of majority. A great many states employ a mix of ius soli and ius sanguinis, and remarkable diversity in details exists among states.

This diversity has historically provided the source of much dual nationality. For example, when a married couple from an ius sanguinis state immigrated to an ius soli state and bore children, the offspring would acquire the nationality of both countries. Some commentators up through the early twentieth century urged that states adopt uniform rules (generally based on ius sanguinis) in order to avoid dual nationality generated in this fashion. But these proposals made little headway, as states remained insistent on nationality provisions that were seen to fit their own national needs and histories.

Cross-national marriages could also result in dual nationality, even if both states concerned followed only ius sanguinis. Until approximately the middle of the twentieth century, however, most states avoided this result by allowing the children in such circumstances to inherit only the nationality of the father. Many such states also required that the wife surrender her former nationality upon marriage and take on the sole nationality of the husband. The women's suffrage movement early targeted such unequal nationality rules, and few survive in twenty-first-century democracies. The modern world's growing insistence on gender equality has contributed significantly to the increase of dual nationality.

One other legal mechanism, often known as election, was meant to reduce the long-term incidence of dual nationality. Some states have required those who obtained dual nationality as minors to choose, or elect, one of the two nationalities upon attaining the age of majority. (Under some of these legal provisions, the only effective way to elect a nationality was to establish or sustain residence in the chosen state.) But this practice was far from uniform, and the modern trend is generally, but unevenly, toward elimination of such a requirement.

Acquisition of Nationality through Naturalization

Until recent decades, naturalization regularly resulted in the loss of previous nationality—and hence in the avoidance of dual nationality. (It still does in many circumstances, but the trend toward preserving the original nationality is described below.) The laws of either the state of origin or the naturalizing state could bring about this result. The former often provided that a national's act of obtaining naturalization elsewhere would result in the automatic loss of the original nationality. Naturalizing states often sought to achieve the same result, conditioning naturalization upon proof of effective surrender of all earlier nationalities, or at least formal renunciation of earlier allegiances as part of the naturalization procedure. But either course might not achieve the result sought by the naturalizing state. The state of original nationality might later find a defect in the attempted surrender, or it might refuse to accept as legally effective mere words of renunciation pronounced as part of another nation's ceremony. It would therefore still regard the individual as a national under its own domestic law. In other instances, the naturalized individual might make use of failures of communication between the two polities or of other loopholes in practice so as to maintain the status of a national in the state of origin. If successful, he or she could continue to make use of rights under both nationalities, such as retaining two passports. And of course, if neither state treats naturalization as an occasion for the loss or surrender of previous nationalities, the person involved can uncontroversially take on a second nationality while retaining the first.

Conflicts over Dual Nationality

Dual nationality can result in competing claims by different states for fulfillment of the duties owed by a national, leading to diplomatic difficulties or even hostilities between nations and to acute dilemmas for the individuals concerned. Historically, clashes over military service—a duty owed to the country of nationality—played an important role in generating a near-consensus, by the early twentieth century, that dual nationality should be suppressed. Further, in many civil law countries (including most states of continental Europe), questions of civil or personal status are resolved by reference to the law of the country of nationality. For example, the laws of one country of nationality may recognize polygamy, the other forbid it. The two states may have quite different standards governing divorce or the disposition of property upon a dual national's death. Dual nationality obviously can give rise to confusion, uncertainty, or conflict in these circumstances. Finally, in some circumstances government officials or other nationals in a state may question the loyalty of dual nationals—particularly if the two countries of nationality are adversaries, either in diplomacy or in military confrontation. And in some renowned wartime cases, dual nationals have been prosecuted for treason in one state of nationality because of support given to the other state of nationality because it was an enemy nation.

A few examples of historical conflicts and the steps taken to avoid or minimize disputes deserve mention. Some early conflicts derived from the adherence by powerful nations, notably Great Britain, to a perpetual allegiance theory: that a sovereign's subjects or nationals remained such forever unless a change were consented to by the sovereign. Under this theory, Britain regarded as its subjects British-born persons who became U.S. citizens after the American Revolution. As the Napoleonic Wars heightened the British need for manpower, this theory took concrete form in the impressment—forcible conscription on the high seas—of seamen from U.S. vessels. The United States resisted because it regarded these individuals as exclusively American citizens whose choice of a new nationality did not depend on another nation's consent. The ongoing controversy became a contributing cause of the War of 1812.

By the latter third of the nineteenth century, the United States was receiving high levels of immigration from many parts of Europe. Several immigrants, upon traveling back to their countries of origin after naturalizing in the United States, encountered difficulties because those countries still considered them nationals. Some German and Scandinavian states, for example, conscripted returning men into their armies. Great Britain applied special punishments normally reserved for British nationals to a group of naturalized Americans who had stirred up opposition to England's dominion over their native Ireland. An aroused U.S. Congress then adopted the Expatriation Act of 1868, declaring that expatriation is "a natural and inherent right of all people, indispensable to the enjoyment of the rights of life, liberty, and the pursuit of happiness," and directing the executive branch to defend the right. Confronted with this response, Britain appointed a commission to study the issue, and in 1870 it decided to recognize an individual right of expatriation in statute and bilateral treaty.

Meantime, many European states entered into treaties with the United States, usually called the Bancroft Treaties after the U.S. diplomat who pressed for their adoption, as well as similar pacts among themselves in order to resolve many of these questions. They provided that the states involved would recognize naturalization by the other country and generally would treat it as an act terminating the original citizenship. Through these measures, potential dual nationality was reduced.

Nineteenth-century conflicts like these gave rise to the growing conviction that dual nationality was an evil that should be suppressed. The motivation was both to avoid diplomatic complication and to protect individuals from unfair burdens. A diplomatic conference was convened in The Hague in 1930 in order to draft a treaty that would bring greater harmony to national laws on nationality. As ultimately adopted, the preamble repeated a widely accepted principle that "every person should have a nationality and should have one nationality only." But for the operative sections of the treaty, agreement proved elusive on concrete steps that might achieve greater uniformity in national practice and thereby significantly reduce the incidence of dual nationality. A rather modest treaty resulted from the deliberations, settling only "certain questions" deriving from the conflict of laws in this realm. The Convention Concerning Certain Questions Relating to the Conflict of Nationality Laws opened for signature on April 12, 1930 (179 L.N.T.S. 89). That the movement to curb the status itself still had momentum several decades later, however, is reflected in the Council of Europe's adoption in 1963 of a more ambitiously named Convention on Reduction of Cases of Multiple Nationality, which entered into force March 28, 1968 (634 U.N.T.S. 221).

But even if the primary treaty adopted at the Hague conference made only limited progress in disciplining domestic laws that resulted in dual nationality, a second treaty agreed upon there was more effective and more widely accepted. It ameliorated one of the major problems that could result even if dual nationality persisted—competing or multiple claims to military service. The Protocol Relating to Military Obligations in Certain Cases of Double Nationality opened for signature on April 12, 1930 (178 L.N.T.S. 227). In essence, the treaty provided that a person would be expected to fulfill military service only in his country of residence. Short of full mobilization, the other country of nationality would consider that such service discharged all further military obligations. Several later treaties at the regional level adopted a similar approach to sort out the military obligations of dual nationals. Other regional and bilateral treaties provided rules that avoided or reduced multiple taxation of persons working outside their country of nationality. Though these were not specifically adopted to assist dual nationals, they did have that effect.

Evolution toward Greater Acceptance of Dual Nationality

By the 1970s, some scholars and government leaders were questioning the traditional stance of hostility to dual nationality. Many states changed their laws, and in some instances judicial decisions limited a government's authority to enforce a policy that its citizens hold only a single nationality.

On the judicial front, decisions by the U.S. Supreme Court played an important role. In 1967, the Court overruled earlier precedents and held that citizenship is an individual right closely protected by the U.S. Constitution. The government therefore lacked power to decree the loss of citizenship upon the commission of certain designated acts, such as naturalizing in a foreign country, unless the person specifically intended to relinquish it. Obviously such a ruling makes it far more likely that a citizen's decision to naturalize elsewhere will result in dual nationality, provided the other country's laws permit the status. Congress changed the expatriation law to conform to the Supreme Court's decisions. It also went beyond what was strictly required by the precedents and provided that those who obtained U.S. citizenship by descent after 1978 (born outside U.S. territory) would no longer have to come to the United States for a stated period of residence before a prescribed age, on pain of losing nationality automatically. Durable dual nationality became a far more likely result for this group as well. U.S. doctrine now wholly accepts dual nationality when it accrues at birth or if it results from a citizen's naturalization in another country. The only formal legal bar to dual nationality occurs upon naturalization, for which U.S. law requires renunciation of other allegiances as part of the ceremonial oath.

The evolution in the thinking of government officials in states that were net receivers of migration was perhaps best reflected in changes in the Council of Europe's treaties. The 1963 convention explicitly meant to reduce dual nationality was followed by the adoption of a protocol in 1993 that was far more accepting of the status. In 1997, the council adopted a wholly new European Convention on Nationality on November 6, 1997 (ETS No. 166, 37 ILM 44). This treaty readily accepts dual nationality, protecting that status for children who acquire multiple nationalities at birth and for spouses who acquire dual nationality automatically as a result of marriage. The convention does allow states to adopt certain specified policies that would seek to minimize the status, however.

Some receiving states, including Australia, modified their laws to permit dual nationality when foreigners naturalized. Others, such as France and the United Kingdom, had long accepted the status. Changes in administrative practices by other receiving states resulted in a de facto relaxation of bars to dual nationality. For example, several states that require proof of termination of another nationality as a condition of naturalization provide exceptions when the other country makes such termination impossible or unreasonable. Many of these, including Germany and the Netherlands, have over the past few decades in practical effect lowered the threshold for finding that the exception applies; those persons granted an exception clearly become dual nationals. Similarly, the United States never required proof of the other nation's recognition of the renunciation oath mandated as part of its naturalization ceremony. But whereas the U.S. State Department was formerly vigilant in identifying and moving against naturalized citizens who acted inconsistently with that part of the oath, it now overtly tolerates continued exercise of the other nationality.

The most visible sign of changing governmental attitudes toward dual nationality in recent decades has been manifested in legal reform by major sending states. Historically, they had tended to follow the rule that one who naturalizes in a foreign state loses the original citizenship. Beginning in the 1970s, however, countries of emigration began to repeal or modify this provision of their laws and to accept dual nationality in some form. Turkey, a major source of emigration to Western Europe, and particularly to Germany, made the change in 1981. In Latin America, only one of the nineteen Spanish- and Portuguese-speaking countries recognized dual nationality before 1972. But Panama changed its rules that year to allow its citizens who naturalized elsewhere to retain nationality. Peru followed suit in 1980, and El Salvador in 1983. Six more made the change in the 1990s, including the hemisphere's two most populous countries, Brazil in 1996 and Mexico in 1998.

Sending states acted for several reasons. Some who advocated the changes reasoned that lack of nationality in the states of residence left their citizens at a disadvantage there. They believed that many of their emigrants were reluctant to naturalize precisely because they would lose the nationality of the original homeland. (Such reluctance was compounded with regard to states of origin where nonnationals could not hold certain types of property, enjoyed only limited inheritance rights, or were subjected to other concrete restrictions.) Further, a strict rule of expatriation upon naturalization could mean that those emigrants who did choose to naturalize were less likely to maintain ties to their country of origin. Such a severance could have a concrete impact in the reduction of remittances, investment, or charitable involvement. A few government officials openly professed the wish that dual nationals under the revised rules would, as voters, help change the policies of the country of residence, typically wealthy or powerful nations—in a direction favorable to the sending state.

The trend toward acceptance of dual nationality has been fueled by the generally positive, or at least neutral, experiences of states that have accepted the status. Most have found that it does not present significant diplomatic or other problems. In part, that experience may reflect the success of international measures seeking to head off specific forms of conflict. These include treaties clarifying the military and tax obligations of dual nationals and the increasing use of a "dominant and effective nationality" test to resolve conflicts over issues of law or to permit diplomatic protection by one state against the other state of nationality.

The Ongoing Controversy

Mexico's amendments in 1998 triggered a modest level of debate in the United States over the desirability of dual nationality. In Germany, during the same period, there was intense controversy over whether to change its rigid anti–dual nationality stance. The government under newly elected Chancellor Gerhard Schroeder proposed to accept dual nationality upon naturalization, and in a wider range of circumstances at birth, in order to promote greater identification with Germany on the part of its large immigrant population. The vast majority of such immigrants, even after long residence, had not naturalized. Therefore their children would also lack German nationality, because Germany did not recognize the ius soli. Germany found itself with a growing population of second- and third-generation "foreigners," though they were persons born on German soil who had never known life elsewhere. The government's proposed legislation met with determined opposition, however, and electoral setbacks led to enactment of a much-reduced measure in 1999. Parliament chose not to accept dual nationality after naturalization (unless, as before, the other country imposes unreasonable conditions impeding relinquishment), but Germany for the first time accepted a form of ius soli. Children born in Germany after January 1, 2000, to parents lawfully resident for eight years will obtain German citizenship automatically at birth. Recognizing that many such children would thereby become dual nationals, the German parliament decided to require that they elect one or the other nationality between the ages of eighteen and twenty-three. Thus Germany's acceptance of dual nationality came with a proviso designed to assure that the status would not be permanent. The full resolution of the question, however, was postponed for two decades—the time when the first elections will be required of the German-born dual nationals. Some observers have questioned whether Germany would by then have the will to enforce such a choice.

The debates in Germany and the United States reflect the wider themes in the ongoing controversy over dual nationality. Proponents argue for acceptance of dual nationality as more reflective of actual loyalties and ties in an era of globalization. The nineteenth-century concern about divided loyalties might have made sense, they acknowledge, in an era when monarchs shifted alliances impulsively and both war and conscription were more common. But multiple allegiance is far less troublesome in today's more peaceful world, inhabited increasingly by states that share both enduring alliances and the same values built around market democracies. Further, a definitive break with the country of origin might have fit a world where cross-border travel was slow and expensive, but modern communications and transportation make it easier to keep up vital links. Therefore it is understandable, proponents argue, that people would be more interested in retaining their former nationality, with the ease of access to the country of origin that its passport provides. Dual nationality, in this view, may also facilitate commerce and can even help promote human rights. Finally, for reluctant countries of immigration that have had limited success in integrating immigrant populations, proponents argue that acceptance of dual nationality would promote naturalization. Naturalization, in turn, would facilitate political involvement and eventually improve the integration of the immigrant population. Lingering controversies over civil status could be resolved by reference to the dominant and effective nationality rule—usually resulting in applying the law of the state of residence.

Opponents of dual nationality question many of the empirical assumptions underlying the proponents' case. Divided loyalties can still be a problem, and war and conscription have not been banished. Some point out the opportunity for manipulative or opportunistic use of dual nationality, including "citizenships of convenience" sometimes sold by tax-haven countries. Opponents worry that dual nationals will exercise their votes in a way that is more favorable to the country of origin than the country of residence. They also question whether naturalization will truly promote integration if dual nationality is accepted; acceptance might instead make it easier for the immigrant group to remain insular. Some argue that having membership rights in two polities, and particularly the possibility of voting in two countries, unfairly privileges dual nationals and departs from the basic norm of equality that citizenship is supposed to embody.

The debate continues in academic journals, popular commentary, and legislatures. States that currently resist acceptance of dual nationality will probably be confronted with the question more insistently as global migration continues to increase.

David A. Martin

See also: Assimilation/Integration; Citizenship; Diaspora; Gender and Migration; Ius Sanguinis; Ius Soli; Naturalization; Remittances; Sovereignty and Migration; Statelessness; Women, Globalization, and Immigration

References and further reading:
Aleinikoff, T. Alexander, and Douglas Klusmeyer, eds. 2000. *From Migrants to Citizens: Membership in a Changing World.* Washington, DC: Carnegie Endowment for International Peace.
———. 2001. *Citizenship Today: Global Perspectives and Practices.* Washington, DC: Carnegie Endowment for International Peace.
Bar-Yaacov, Nissim. 1961. *Dual Nationality.* London: Stevens and Sons.
Bauböck, Rainer. 1994. *Transnational Citizenship: Membership and Rights in International Migration.* Brookfield, VT: E. Elgar.
Brubaker, W. Rogers. 1989. *Immigration and the Politics of Citizenship in Europe and North America.* Lanham, MD: University Press of America.
Hammar, Tomas. 1990. *Democracy and the Nation-State: Aliens, Denizens and Citizens in a World of International Migration.* Brookfield, VT: Gower.
Hansen, Randall, and Patrick Weil, eds. 2001. *Towards a European Nationality: Citizenship, Immigration and Nationality Law in the EU.* Houndsmills, UK: Palgrave.
———. 2002. *Dual Nationality, Social Rights and Federal Citizenship in the U.S. and Europe: The Reinvention of Citizenship.* New York: Berghahn.
Martin, David A. 1999. "New Rules on Dual Nationality for a Democratizing Globe: Between Rejection and Embrace." *Georgetown Immigration Law Journal* 14: 1–34.
Martin, David A., and Kay Hailbronner, eds. 2002. *Rights and Duties of Dual Nationals: Evolution and Prospects.* The Hague: Kluwer Law International.
Pickus, Noah M. J., ed. 1998. *Immigration and Citizenship in the Twenty-First Century.* Lanham, MD: Rowman and Littlefield.
Rubio-Marin, Ruth. 2000. *Immigration as a Democratic Challenge: Citizenship and Inclusion in Germany and the United States.* Cambridge: Cambridge University Press.
Soysal, Yasemin. 1994. *Limits of Citizenship: Migrants and Postnational Membership in Europe.* Chicago: University of Chicago Press.
Spiro, Peter J. 1997. "Dual Nationality and the Meaning of Citizenship." *Emory Law Journal* 46: 1411–1485.
Weis, Paul. 1979. *Nationality and Statelessness in International Law.* 2d ed. Aalphen aan den Rijn, Netherlands: Sijthoff and Noordhoff.

Dublin Convention

The Dublin Convention, signed on June 15, 1990, was a by-product of the European Community's objective of achieving a single market by the end of 1992. The internal market project, which was revitalized by the Single European Act in 1986, planned the abolition of obstacles to the movement of goods, persons, services, and capital among European Union (EU) member states by 1992. The abolition under the Schengen agreement (taking effect in 1995) of border controls among the member states had the effect of permitting all persons, including asylum seekers, to move freely around the Union. Asylum seekers, once admitted into EU territory, would then be permitted to apply concurrently or consecutively for asylum in different member states. The member states also began discussion in 1986 on how to control the movement of third-country nationals (that is, nationals of countries outside the European Union) both into and within the Union.

Methods for controlling the movement of asylum seekers within the territory of the Union as expressed in the Dublin Convention are based on two main principles. The first is that an asylum seeker should have only one occasion upon which to have his or her asylum application considered within the Union, notwithstanding the startling differences in asylum-seeker recognition rates (even when applicants are from the same country) in different member states and the fact that the member states are all parties to the 1951 UN Convention Relating to the Status of Refugees and its 1967 Protocol. According to this principle, the negative decision of one member state regarding an asylum application should be binding on all member states, relieving them of any duty to consider subsequent applications (conversely, when an individual is recognized as a refugee, this is not binding on all member states). The second principle is that member states themselves specify the criteria (for example, family connections) determining how asylum applications are distributed across the Union. The wish of the asylum seeker to have his or her application considered in one state or another, in other words, is not relevant to the allocation of responsibility under the convention.

The Dublin Convention has no formal relationship with European Community treaties but is expressly limited to member states of the EU. It provides that an asylum application will be considered by only one member state but does not require that member state to make a substantive determination of the application. Under the convention, the member state may determine that responsibility for considering the application falls on a third country outside the EU, and may remove the individual to that state. As regards the criteria for determining responsibility for asylum claims, the Dublin Convention sets out a hierarchy of four factors. These include: (1) if the individual has first-degree family members who have already been recognized as refugees in a member state, then that state is responsible for considering the claim; (2) if the individual already has a residence permit or visa granted by a member state, then that state is responsible for the application (a number of qualifications to this rule cover transit visas, multiple visas, and the like); (3) in the absence of a visa or residence permit, the member state that allowed the individual to enter the territory of the EU is responsible; and (4) if it cannot be ascertained which state allowed the individual entry, then the state where the application is made is responsible for its determination.

As the European Commission pointed out in an internal staff working paper regarding the Dublin Convention in 2000, the intention at the time was to place the burden of determining asylum applications and caring for asylum seekers on the member states bordering third states, as these would be the most likely points of entry. Thus there would be a penalty for states which allowed asylum seekers into the territory in that they would be required to take responsibility for those asylum seekers. The Convention contains detailed rules and time limits for requests from one Member State to another to take responsibility for asylum seekers as well as the evidence that may be adduced to substantiate the claim of responsibility of one state as opposed to another. It was assumed that once the Dublin Convention was operational, the majority of asylum applications would be dealt with by states on the borders of the Union.

The Dublin Convention entered into force on September 1, 1997, when it finally achieved ratification by all EU member states. Ironically, this meant that it came into force after political agreement had been reached on the Amsterdam Treaty, which also deals with member state responsibility for the determination of asylum applications. According to information gathered by the European Commission over the first two years of operation of the Dublin Convention, member states actually transferred among themselves 1.7 percent of the asylum seekers who sought asylum in the territory of the Union over that period. In about 4.2 percent of cases, a member state claimed that another state was responsible but the transfer of the individual never took place (European Commission 2001). Thus, the convention is a very minor part of the asylum process in the European Union. Nonetheless, it has been the subject of substantial litigation in the courts in a number of member states and in the European Court of Human Rights. It has also been the subject of substantial criticism by nongovernmental organizations, not least on the ground that it fails to respect the wishes of asylum seekers to seek asylum in one country rather than another. Moreover, critics say that it seeks to impose cross-recognition of negative decisions on asylum without any duty to recognize positive decisions, and that it fails to take account of the fact that there are substantially different recognition rates for asylum seekers from the same countries and with the same types of claims in different member states.

In 1999, a new section on the creation of an area of freedom, security, and justice was introduced into the EC Treaty, bringing the subject matter of the Dublin Convention into the responsibility of the European Community July 26, 2001, the European Commission proposed a regulation establishing the criteria and mechanisms for determining member state responsibility for examining an asylum application lodged in one of the Member States by a third-country national under Article 63(1)(a) EC. The regulation follows very closely the provisions of the Dublin Convention and will give the Convention mechanisms the status (and enforceability) of Community law.

Elspeth Guild

See also: Asylum; Asylum Determination; European Union; UN Convention Relating to the Status of Refugees, 1951

References and further reading:

European Commission. 2001. *Commission Staff Working Paper Evaluation of the Dublin Convention* SEC (2001) 756 Brussels, 13.06.2001.

Guild, E., and C. Harlow. 2001. *Implementing Amsterdam: Immigration and Asylum Law in the EC Treaty.* Oxford, UK: Hart.

Guild, E., and J. Niessen. 1996. *The Developing Immigration and Asylum Policies of the European Union.* The Hague: Kluwer Law International.

Marx, R. 2001. "Adjusting the Dublin Convention: New Approaches to Member State Responsibility for Asylum Applications." *European Journal of Migration and Law* 3, no. 1.

Nicholson, F., and P. Twomey. 1999. *Refugee Rights and Realities: Evolving International Concepts and Regimes.* Cambridge: Cambridge University Press.

Nicol, A., and S. Harrison. 2000. "Lessons of the Dublin Convention." *European Journal of Migration and Law* 2, no. 3 (Winter).

Noll, G. 2000. *Negotiating Asylum: The EU Acquis, Extraterritorial Protection and the Common Market of Deflection.* The Hague: Kluwer Law International.

Vedsted-Hansen, J. 1999. "Non-communitarians: Refugee and Asylum Policies." In *The EU and Human Rights.* Edited by Philip Alston. Oxford: Oxford University Press.

E

East African Asian Expulsions

East African Asians were the descendants of Indian, Pakistani, and Bangladeshi immigrants to East Africa, especially Kenya, Uganda, and Tanzania. Arriving mostly during the colonial period, they were among the first casualties of independence in the 1960s and 1970s: "Africanization" in Kenya and Tanzania impoverished East African Asians and restricted their rights, and Uganda ethnically cleansed the country of them. In all three cases, but most controversially in the Kenyan and Ugandan (the focus of this entry), the Asians sought refuge in the UK.

Asians had lived in Africa for centuries before the European powers divided the continent amongst themselves, but the majority arrived after the British secured hegemony over the area from the mid–nineteenth century. By the 1960s, the largest Asian communities in Africa were in Kenya, with some 200,000 Asians, and Uganda, with 75,000 (Hansen 2000, 158, 197). They arrived as laborers—often indentured workers on the railway—and as traders, but by 1945 they were to be found in all occupations, including business, the police force, the civil service, and the liberal professions.

The commercial skills and administrative competence of the Asians and their descendants contributed to the economic prosperity of East Africa, and, as so often is the case, their success bred suspicion and resentment. The British explorer Sir Richard Burton echoed widely held sentiment when he derided Indian merchants as "local Jews," one sect of which was "unscrupulous and one-idea'd in the pursuit of gain," given to using false weights and measures and receiving stolen goods (quoted in Mangat 1969, 22). The phrase "the Jews of Africa" came to be widely used to describe East African Asians. The term was originally a racist one, à la Burton, but following the expulsions came to be closer to an expression of sympathy, linking the irrational bigotry aimed at a successful (West) European minority with that experienced by Kenyan and Ugandan Asians. Everywhere, Asians encountered resentment because of their economic success and their putative indifference towards independence movements. This hostility eventually became state-sanctioned.

Kenya

When Kenya achieved independence in 1963, the Asians living in the country, like all British colonial citizens between 1948 and 1962, had legal standing as Citizens of the United Kingdom and Colonies (CUKC) (though this status did not give them the right to enter the United Kingdom). At independence, individuals of African descent and those whose families had long been in Kenya acquired Kenyan citizenship automatically. Others, including the majority of Asians, had two years in which to apply for Kenyan citizenship. Most opted to retain their CUKC status, but those who did apply for Kenyan citizenship encountered obstacles and delay. Large numbers of applications were deliberately not processed (Gregory 1993, 99).

Because of the mechanisms determining British immigration control at the time, Kenyan independence unintentionally granted the Asians a right to enter the United Kingdom. Since a CUKC passport was free from immigration control only when issued under the authority of London, the transformation of the office of colonial governor (whose stamp *was* subject to immigration control) into the British high commissioner (the direct representative of London in independent Kenya) at independence released all CUKCs in Kenya from immigration control. This unintended outcome was, however, foreseen and accepted by the Conservative government of the day, and it subsequently pledged to respect the rights engendered by it (Hansen 1999). After 1965, however, Kenyan president Jomo Kenyatta's "Africanization" policies began to squeeze Asians out of the Kenyan economy. They were required to obtain work permits, restricted to

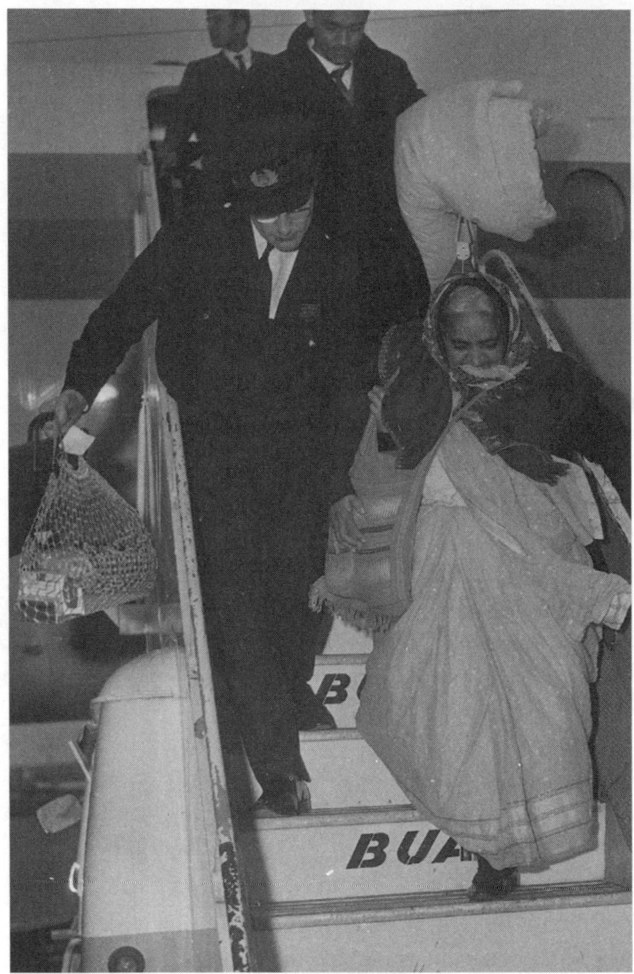

An elderly Asian immigrant from Kenya is helped down the plane steps after arriving at Gatwick Airport. A bill to prevent the entry of Asian immigrants from Kenya to Britain was rushed through Parliament in 1968. The newly arrived Asian immigrants were expelled from Uganda by Idi Amin. (Hulton-Deutsch Collection/Corbis)

certain areas of the country, and sacked from the civil service. Although many, particularly those on the political left, viewed Africanization as a legitimate transfer of economic resources to Africans, they were discriminatory. Without a future in Kenya, and without a right or much inclination to migrate to the subcontinent, Kenyan Asians began moving to the United Kingdom. Although the numbers were in fact trivial—13,600 in 1967—they led to panic in the United Kingdom (Home Office statistics cited in the *Times,* February 16, 1968).

The response of the British government was decisive, callous, and brutal. The new home secretary, James Callaghan, came from the working-class, hard-nosed, antilibertarian wing of the Labour Party. He viewed the permissive society with disdain, homosexuality with disgust, international law with indifference. He was also determined to demonstrate his command of events: In just over a week, he rushed through Parliament a bill that restricted British citizenship to those possessing a "qualifying connection"—a parent or grandparent—in the United Kingdom. The Asians were granted a quota of 1,500 "heads of household" per year. The legislation was the clearest instance of racist immigration legislation in postwar British history: UK citizens were stripped of their right to enter the United Kingdom because of the color of their skin and the bigoted opposition of the British public.

As Richard Crossman, a member of the Labour Cabinet, put it, "[a] few years ago, everyone [in the Cabinet] would have regarded the denial of entry to British nationals with British passports as the most appalling violation of our deepest principles. Now they were quite happily reading aloud their departmental briefs in favour of doing just that" (Crossman 1976, 679). The party that had opposed immigration controls on the Commonwealth as racist, that had loudly proclaimed the virtues of a "multiracial" Commonwealth, and that had adopted the country's first antidiscriminatory laws rammed though Parliament legislation that was racist in intention and effect. It left tens of thousands of Asians stranded in Kenya, devoid of the economic and social rights of citizenship.

Uganda

As bad as the situation was for the Asian community in Kenya, it got much worse for the community in Uganda. In January 1971, Idi Amin executed a coup that removed President Milton Obote from power. In August 1972, Amin announced that there was "no room in Uganda" for the Asians. He accused them of economic sabotage and declared them a British responsibility, giving them three months to leave the country.

The Ugandan constitution at independence in 1962 had given CUKCs without an ethnic lineage in Africa two years to apply for citizenship. Approximately 35,000 Ugandan Asians applied for citizenship by the deadline. Although 23,000 applicants became Ugandan citizens, the other 12,000 applications were not processed, and these applicants remained CUKCs (Patel 1973–1974, 26). Like the Kenyans, the Asians in Uganda found themselves restricted to particular trades in particular parts of the country. Obote, under British pressure, had implemented discriminatory policies slowly, but the Asians' world collapsed when Amin came onto the scene.

The response of the British government—this time a Conservative government under Edward Heath—was decisive and liberal. As Kenya closed its border and India agreed to accept only a limited number of Asians, the United Kingdom spent one week trying to convince Amin to change his mind. The effort was pointless: Amin let it be known that God had presented the plan to him. Then, nine days after

Amin's announcement, the British government accepted full responsibility for the Asians. It appealed to fifty other countries for help (Canada, the United States, West Germany, and Sweden all accepted Asians as refugees); set up a Resettlement Board; and began airlifts by the end of August. By November 8, Amin's deadline, all but 800 stateless Asians, under UN protection, had been evacuated from Uganda.

Amin's "policy" was a clear instance of ethnic cleansing. Asians, many of whom were born to families that had lived in the country for generations, were driven from their homes and forced to abandon their properties or sell them at well below market value (if they got anything for them at all). The government would not allow them to take their savings, and even pocket change and jewelry were wrested from them at the airport. In carrying out its obligation to allow them entry, the Heath government exhibited a generosity and respect for international law that had eluded the supposedly more progressive Labour Party. It has been argued that the Conservatives' liberality was borne of constraint: that it did nothing more than fulfill the United Kingdom's duty under international law. The claim is only partially true, and it trivializes the Heath government's accomplishment. The United Kingdom had an obligation under international law because, under the European Convention on Human Rights, for instance, states may not deny entry to individuals holding citizenship. This is, however, exactly what the Labour government had done to the Kenyan Asians. When the European Commission ruled that the action under Callaghan had contravened the European Convention on Human Rights, the British government ignored the decision. International law, lacking few enforcement mechanisms, seldom drives governments to do that which they are unwilling to do.

The fact that there were fewer Ugandan than Kenyan Asians, and that Amin's policy was more brutal than Kenyatta's, made it more imperative to admit the Ugandan Asians. But it did not make the decision politically easier: If anything, opposition to immigration, in the wake of the articulate anti-immigrant demagoguery of Enoch Powell (a popular Conservative politician), was stronger in 1972 than in 1968. Many thus view the Heath government's decision to admit the Ugandan Asians in the face of this hostility as a decisive moment in British immigration policy..

East Africa Asians in Britain Today

Both the Kenyan and Ugandan Asian communities displayed in the United Kingdom the talents that had served them well in Africa. They quickly integrated economically, and both enjoy educational levels and incomes higher than the UK national average. The only factor differentiating them, and particularly the Ugandan Asians, is political. Whereas the clear majority of ethnic minorities in the United Kingdom supports the Labour Party (comparable to African American support for the Democratic Party in the United States), the Ugandan Asians have rewarded the Conservatives with electoral and financial support. In purely monetary terms, they have done more for the Conservative Party, and for the United Kingdom itself, than any other migrant group in British history.

By contrast, both Kenya and Uganda suffered economically from the departure of the Asians. East Africa's post-Africanization experience is a testament to the self-defeating results of ethnic economic nationalism, parallels to which can be found in the German expulsion and murder of Jews and the Polish, Hungarian, and Czechoslovakian expulsions of Germans.

Randall Hansen

See also: Commonwealth Citizenship and Immigration (UK); Ethnic Cleansing; Populism; United Kingdom

References and further reading:

Crossman, Richard. 1976. *The Diaries of a Cabinet Minister.* London: Hamish Hamilton and Jonathan Cape.

Gregory, R. G. 1993. *Quest for Equality: Asian Politics in East Africa, 1900–1967.* Hyderabad: Orient Longman.

Hansen, Randall. 1999. "The Kenyan Asians, British Politics and the Commonwealth Immigrants Act, 1968." *The Historical Journal* 42, no. 3: 809–834.

———. 2000. *Citizenship and Immigration in Postwar Britain: The Institutional Origins of a Multicultural Nation.* Oxford: Oxford University Press..

London Times. 1968. "Citizens from Kenya." February 16.

Mangat, J. S. 1969. *A History of the Jews in East Africa.* Oxford: Oxford University Press.

Patel, H. H. 1973–1974. "Indians in Uganda and Rhodesia." *Studies in Race and Nations* 5, no.1.

East-West Migration

See Asylum; Berlin Wall; Cold War; Czechoslovakian Refugees; Ethnic Cleansing: Germans from Central and Eastern Europe; Germany; Hungarian Revolution; Polish Diaspora

Economic Determinants of International Migration

Individuals may experience their migration as the outcome of their personal decisions, but the option to migrate is itself socially produced. This fact is easily lost in much immigration analysis because immigration flows tend to share many characteristics—immigrants are mostly, though not exclusively, poor people from less developed countries, with low or medium levels of education, and willing to take undesirable jobs. This has led to the notion that it is poverty and unemployment generally that push migrants to migrate. Yet many countries with great poverty and high unemployment lack any significant emigration history, and in others emigration is a recent event no matter how long-standing the poverty. It takes a number of other conditions to activate poverty into a push factor, and even then, it is likely to be only a small minority of poor and middle-class people who will actually try to emigrate. Emigration is not an undifferentiated escape from poverty and unemployment to prosperity.

Each country is unique, and each migration flow is produced by specific conditions in time and place (see, for example, Castles and Miller 2003; Cohen 1991). But to understand the possible effects of larger conditions, such as economic and cultural globalization, on the formation and reproduction of migration flows, one must abstract from these particularities and examine more general tendencies. For instance, one set of conditions that we now understand is significant is the fact of former colonial bonds. Thus in Europe, a majority of Algerian emigrants are in France, and a majority of emigrants from the Indian subcontinent are in the United Kingdom. More controversial, economic dominance and the formation of transnational spaces for economic activity associated with the presence of US firms overseas are beginning to be recognized as factors explaining some of the migration patterns into the US. Similarly, U.S. direct or indirect overseas military activity—from Vietnam to El Salvador—is clearly a factor conditioning some of the flows of Indo-Chinese and Central Americans into the United States.

Today, the sharp growth in the organized export of workers, both legal and illegal, adds yet another dynamic to the long-standing ones. Organized exports can create entirely new ways of linking emigration and immigration countries, reaching beyond old colonial or new global economic linkages. Yet these new developments are often linked to broader contextual conditions. The formation of global systems has aided the upward scaling of what were often regional networks. It has also induced the formation of new types of trafficking and new flows, often as a response to the devastating effects of the globalization of the economies of poor countries.

Confining the analysis to economic factors that may activate a general condition of poverty and unemployment into a migration push factor we can see several patterns. (See explanations in Massey et al. 1994; Massey et al. 2002; Parnreiter 1995; Papademitriou and Martin 1991). First, most migrations have been *initiated* through direct recruitment by firms, governments, labor contractors, or traffickers. Once an immigrant community exists, the operation of the immigrant network tends to replace outside recruitment, and chain migration tends to set in (Boyd 1989). Second, recruitment by firms and governments typically takes place between countries that already have established linkages—colonial, neocolonial, military, and, increasingly, as part of economic globalization. Third, economic globalization has further strengthened the interdependence among a growing number of countries. It may also have contributed to creating new push factors in countries that already have high levels of government debt by sharpening this debt and its negative impact on overall economic conditions through the imposition of Structural Adjustment Programs. Fourth, there was a significant increase in the organized export of workers during the 1990s. Of particular importance here is the sharp increase in the illegal international trade in people for work and for the sex industry.

Three main themes thus dominate discussions of economic determinants in migration research: (1) the geoeconomics of international migrations which explain the considerable degree of patterning evident in these flows and provide the crucial context within which to understand the dynamic whereby an overall condition of poverty, unemployment or underemployment can become activated into migration push factors; (2) the contemporary formation of mechanisms binding emigration and immigration countries, particularly the impact of various forms of economic globalization; and (3) the organized export, both legal and illegal, of workers.

The Geoeconomics of Migration

Some form of organized recruitment by employers or governments (on behalf of employers) often lies at the heart of immigration flows. This is true both for the 1800s and today. But governmental recruitment tends to be shaped by prior politico-economic bonds, such as colonialism, current foreign investment, or cross-border operations by firms in the context of economic globalization, as well as by the multiplication of global imaginaries. Eventually, most migration flows gain a certain autonomy from the organized recruitment mechanisms.

The large mass migrations of the 1800s emerged as part of the formation of a transatlantic economic system binding several nation-states through economic transactions and wars, particularly war-induced flows of people. The transatlantic economy was at the core of U.S. development. There were massive flows of capital, goods, and workers, and there were specific structures producing the transatlantic system. Before this period, labor movements across the Atlantic had been largely forced, notably in the form of slavery, and mostly from colonized African and Asian territories.

To take another example, the migrations to England in the 1950s originated in what had once been British territories. And the migrations into Western Europe during the

1960s and 1970s occurred in a context of direct recruitment during a period of European regional dominance over both the Mediterranean and some Eastern European countries. In brief, receiving countries have typically been participants in the processes leading to the formation of international migration.

The renewal of mass immigration into the United States in the 1960s, following five decades of little or no immigration, took place at a time of expanded U.S. economic and military activity in Asia and the Caribbean Basin. The United States was, and still is, at the center of an international system of investment and production that binds these various regions. In the 1960s and 1970s, it played a crucial role in the development of a world economic system, passing legislation and promoting international agreements aimed at opening its own and other countries' economies to the flow of capital, goods, services, and information.

This central military, political, and economic role helped to create conditions that mobilized people into migrations, whether local or international, *and* led to the formation of links between the United States and other countries that subsequently were to serve as bridges for international migration. This bridging effect was an unintended consequence of the U.S. role in world affairs. It was probably strengthened by the Cold War context and the active promotion of the advantages of open democratic societies. One controversial observation is that measures commonly thought to deter emigration—foreign investment and the promotion of export-oriented growth in developing countries—seem to have had precisely the opposite effect, at least in the short and middle run (Sassen 1988, 1999). Among the leading senders of immigrants to the United States in the 1970s and 1980s were several of the newly industrialized countries of South and Southeast Asia that had extremely high growth rates generally recognized to be a result of foreign direct investment in export manufacturing. A parallel analysis has now been produced about the "development" effect of the North American Free Trade Agreement on Mexican emigration to the US: ongoing and new emigration and eventual stabilization in thirty years (e.g., Martin 2003).

The forms of internationalization of capital prevalent since the postwar period thus mobilized people into migration streams, building bridges between countries of origin and the United States. Long before the current phase of globalization, the implantation in the 1960s and onward of Western development strategies, from the replacement of smallholder agriculture with export-oriented commercial agriculture to the westernization of educational systems, contributed to mobilize people into migration streams—regional, national, transnational (Portes and Walton 1981; Safa 1995; Bonilla and Campos 1982; Bonilla et al. 1998).

At the same time, the administrative, commercial, and development networks of the former European empires and the newer forms these networks assumed under the Pax Americana, and eventually with the formation of global systems (international direct foreign investment, export processing zones, wars for democracy), not only created bridges for the flow of capital, information, and high-level personnel from the center to the periphery but also for the flow of migrants. Stuart Hall (1991a, 1991b) describes the postwar influx of people from the Commonwealth into Britain and notes that England and "Englishness" were so present in his native Jamaica as to make people feel that London was the capital to which they were all headed sooner or later. This way of narrating the migration events of the postwar era captures the ongoing weight of colonialism and postcolonial forms of empire on major processes of globalization today, and specifically those binding emigration and immigration countries. The major immigration countries are not innocent bystanders; the specific genesis and contents of their responsibility will vary from case to case and period to period.

On a more conceptual level, one could generalize these tendencies and posit that immigration flows take place within systems, and that these systems can be specified in a variety of ways (see, for example, Bustamante and Martinez 1979; Morokvasic 1984; Sassen 1988, 1999; Bonilla et al. 1998). The type of economic specification contained here represents but one of several possibilities. In other cases, the system within which immigration takes place is to be specified in political or ethnic terms. One could ask, for example, if there are systemic linkages underlying the current Central European migrations to Germany and Austria. Thus, before World War II both Berlin and Vienna were major receivers of large migrations from a vast Eastern region (Fassmann and Münz 1994). Furthermore, these practices produced and reproduced migration systems as such. Finally, the aggressive campaign during the Cold War years showing the West as a place where economic well-being is the norm and well-paying jobs as easy to get had an effect in inducing people to migrate westward; a more accurate portrayal of conditions in the West might have deterred potential migrants beyond the absolutely convinced ones who would have come at all costs. These historical and current conditions contain elements for specifying the systems within which the current Eastern European migrations to Germany and Austria are taking place.

The fact that there is a geoeconomics of migration is suggested by major immigration patterns. If immigration were simply a matter of policy and the will to enforce controls, then many of the current unauthorized flows should not exist (Cornelius et al. 1994). In the case of the United States, the major immigration reform passed in 1965 had an immense impact because it happened at a time when the country had a far-flung network of production sites and military operations in several Third World countries. There was not only a pent-up demand for emigration but also a broad network of linkages between those countries and the United States. The new law, based on family reunion, was expected to mainly induce the immigration of relatives of those already in the country, that is, mostly Europeans. Instead, the vast majority of immigrants came from the Caribbean Basin and several Asian countries. The law as such was not enough to bring about the new immigration into the United States. Policy alone cannot engender migrations (Portes and Rumbaut 1996; Briggs 1992).

Sixty percent of the foreign residents in the United Kingdom are from Asian or African countries that were former dominions or colonies; continental European immigration is rather low, and almost three-fourths of these immigrants to Great Britain are from Ireland, also once a colonialized territory. The United Kingdom has few immigrants from such countries as Turkey or Yugoslavia, which provide the largest share to Germany, but is the receiving country for almost all the emigrants from the Indian subcontinent and from the English Caribbean to Europe.

Continuing along these lines, in the first ten years after World War II the majority of "immigrants" to Germany were the 8 million displaced ethnic Germans who resettled there. Another major group consisted of the 3 million who came from the German Democratic Republic before the Berlin Wall was erected in 1961. Almost all ethnic Germans went to Germany, and those who did not went overseas. But 86 percent of the Greek immigrants in Europe also reside in Germany, along with 80 percent of the Turkish immigrants in Europe and 76 percent of the Yugoslav immigrants. More recently, Germany has also expanded its labor recruitment or sourcing area to include Portugal, Algeria, Morocco, and Tunisia, even though the vast majority of immigrants from these countries reside in France. In brief, in the case of Germany a large migration rooted in a long history of domination over the eastern region took place first. This was followed by a migration originating in less developed countries within the context of a by now classic labor-import/labor-export dynamic.

The Netherlands and Belgium both received significant numbers of people from their former colonial empires. They also received foreign workers from labor-exporting countries such as Italy, Morocco, and Turkey. Switzerland similarly receives workers from traditional labor-exporting countries: Italy, Spain, Portugal, Yugoslavia, and Turkey. All three countries organized the recruitment of these workers until a somewhat autonomous set of flows was in place. Sweden receives 93 percent of Finnish immigrants. In Sweden, as in the other countries, there has also been a large expansion of the recruitment area to include workers from the traditional labor-exporting countries on the Mediterranean.

As a given labor migration flow ages, it tends to become more diversified in terms of destination, perhaps because a measure of autonomy from older colonial and neocolonial bonds sets in. Immigrants from Italy, today an older immigration, are now distributed among several countries. Among Italian immigrants in other European countries, one-third reside in Germany, 27 percent in France, 24 percent in Switzerland, and 15 percent in Belgium. On one hand, the fact that the destinations are still somewhat limited could be seen as signaling the presence of migration systems. On the other hand, younger labor migrations reveal very high levels of geographic concentration. The largest single immigrant group in any of Europe's labor-receiving countries today is the Turks, with almost two million in Germany.

Economic Push Factors

The variety of economic conditions that contribute to migration links between sending and receiving countries fall into three major categories: (1) linkages brought about by economic globalization; (2) linkages specifically developed to recruit workers; and (3) the organized export of workers. This section discusses the first two, and the next section discusses the third.

Economic Linkages

Economic internationalization creates a wide range of linkages between nations and regions. The off-shoring of production, the implantation of export-oriented agriculture through foreign investment, and multinational firms all create ties that influence migration. For instance, the development of commercial agriculture and of export-oriented, standardized manufacturing has dislocated traditional economies and eliminated survival opportunities for small producers, who are forced to become wage laborers. These displaced small holders and crafts-based producers in turn become part of labor migration streams, which may initially be internal but eventually can become international. There are multiple examples of this dynamic. Sarah Mahler (1995) found that Salvadoran immigrants to the United States often had prior experience as migrant workers to coffee plantations. Maria Patricia Fernandez-Kelly (1984) found that some of the internal migrants to the Northern Industrialization Zone of Mexico eventually became migrants to the United States. Frank Bonilla and Ricardo Campos (1982) found a similar impact from the U.S.-sponsored "Bootstraps Operation" in Puerto Rico in promoting emigration to the United States.

Another type of economic linkage resulted from the large-scale development of manufacturing operations in low-wage countries by firms from highly developed ones. The aim here was, and continues to be, to lower the costs of production of goods meant for reexport to markets in the firms' home countries. There are two migration-inducing conditions at work here. One is that the better-situated workers may gain access to contacts for migration; the second is that the most disadvantaged workers are often "used up" after a few years and then need to find new ways of surviving and helping their families, which may in turn lead to out-migration. These workers are, partly, in an extended labor market that connects the two countries involved (see Sassen 1988).

The growing use of off-shore production to lower costs also helps to create conditions in the highly developed countries that may lead to recruitment/demand for low-wage immigrant workers, given the growing pressure among firms and countries to lower costs to remain competitive. The internationalization of manufacturing production and of agriculture has weakened unions and led to a search for low-wage workers inside the developed countries themselves.

The case of Japan is of interest here because it captures the intersection of economic internationalization and immigration in a country with a radically different history, culture, and, to a lesser extent, economic organization from those of other advanced economies. Japan's lack of an immigration history in the recent period—it had one in the 1800s—provides us with a clearer picture of these dynamics. Though much later than most advanced economies, Japan now has a growing unauthorized immigrant workforce in low-wage, unskilled jobs in a context where Japanese youth are rejecting such jobs. One cannot help but ask why this has happened now rather than during the period of extremely rapid economic growth in Japan during the 1950s and 1960s, when the country experienced very sharp labor shortages.

In the 1980s, Japan became a major presence in a regional Asian economic system, where it was the leading investor, foreign aid donor, and exporter of consumer goods (including cultural products). Japanese firms began to set up large numbers of manufacturing operations, with a heavy concentration in Asian countries. This created legal and illegal networks between those countries and Japan, and these countries emerged as some of the leading senders of immigrants to Japan (Morita and Sassen 1994). At the peak of its growth, Japan lacked the types of networks and linkages with potential immigrant-sending countries that could have facilitated the formation of international migration flows. As Japan internationalized its economy and became a key investor in South and Southeast Asia, it created—wittingly or not—a transnational space for the circulation of its goods, capital, and culture, which in turn created conditions for the circulation of people. Japan may be in the early stages of formation for an international labor market, a market that both labor contractors and unauthorized immigrants can "step into." Once Asian immigrants became part of the low-wage jobs in many economic sectors, and given ongoing shortages, the Japanese government initiated recruitment of Japanese descendants in Brazil and Peru, adjusting its immigration law to do so. These emergent immigrant communities have now entered the stage of chain migration (Tsuda 1999).

Another type of linkage is shaped by the growing westernization of advanced education systems (Portes and Walton 1981), which facilitates the movement of highly educated workers into developed Western countries. This process, popularly called a "brain drain," has been under way for many decades. Today it assumes specific forms based on the growing interdependence among countries and the formation of global markets and global firms. An increasingly complex and flexible transnational labor market for high-level professionals in advanced corporate services now links a growing number of highly developed and developing countries (Sassen 2001; see also Skeldon 1997). This development is also taking place in the high-tech sector, where computer and software firms of highly developed countries, especially India, have begun to recruit experts. These and similar dynamics can be seen in the strong trend for immigration to be bimodal in terms of educational levels, that is, with two main concentrations of workers: low-wage, poorly educated ones and very highly educated ones.

Recruitment and Ethnic Networks

The second type of linkage includes a variety of mechanisms for the organized or informal recruitment of workers. Recruitment can operate through governments in the framework of a government-supported initiative by employers, through employers directly, through the illegal smuggling of workers, or through kinship and family networks. Some of these mechanisms can also function as more generalized migration channels. Ethnic linkages established between communities of origin and destination, typically via the formation of transnational households or broader kinship structures, emerge as crucial once a flow has been formed and serve to ensure its reproduction over time (see, for example, Levitt 2001; Grasmuck and Pessar 1991; Smith 1997; Basch et al. 1994). These recruitment and ethnic linkages tend to operate within the broader transnational spaces constituted via neocolonial processes and/or economic internationalization.

A key issue facilitating the operation of ethnic networks and recruitment operations is the existence of an effective demand for immigrant workers in the receiving countries. Labor demand, more specifically, the effective labor-market absorption of workers coming from different cultures with mostly lower levels of development, becomes increasingly important in the context of advanced service economies. Immigrants have a long history of getting hired in low-wage jobs requiring little education and often situated in the least advanced sectors.

Much analysis of postindustrial society and advanced economies generally posits a massive growth in the need for highly educated workers and little need for the types of jobs that a majority of immigrants have tended to hold over the past two or three decades. This suggests sharply reduced employment opportunities for workers with low educational levels generally and for immigrants in particular. Yet detailed empirical studies of major cities in highly developed countries show ongoing demand for immigrant workers and a significant supply of old and new jobs requiring little education and paying low wages. One controversial issue is whether this job supply is (a) merely or largely a residual, partly inflated by the large supply of low-wage workers, or (b) mostly part of the reconfiguration of the job supply and employment relations that are in fact a feature of advanced service economies, that is to say, a systemic development that is an integral part of such economies. There are no precise measures, and a focus on the jobs by themselves will hardly illuminate the issue, revealing only that they are low-wage, that they require little education, that they are considered undesirable, that they do not provide advancement opportunities, and, often, that they offer few, if any, fringe benefits. Nevertheless, there are clearly some aspects of the growth dynamics in advanced service economies that are creating at least part of this job supply (Sassen 2001). This supply is a crucial cog in the sets of linkages used and developed by co-ethnics and by recruiters.

One condition in the reproduction of these linkages is that over the past few decades, and, in some cases, over the past century, some countries have become marked as labor-exporting countries. Labor-exporting countries may be put in a subordinate position economically and politically. They are represented in the media and in political discourse as labor-exporting countries, and thus put into a role in which they are expected to supply labor for a given area. This was also the case last century when some labor-sending areas existed in conditions of economic subordination and often also quasi-political subordination. The former Polish territories partitioned off to Germany generated significant migration of "ethnic" Poles to Western Germany and beyond, the Irish exported their labor to England, and Italy reproduced itself as a labor supplier for the rest of Europe.

The history of economic development supports the observation that once an area becomes a significant emigration region, it does not easily catch up in terms of development with those areas that emerge as labor-importing areas. Precisely because the latter have high growth, or at least relatively high growth, a type of cumulative cause-and-effect cycle sets in that amounts to an accumulation of advantage. Whether immigration contributes to this process of cumulative causation is a complex issue, though much scholarship shows that immigration countries have gained multiple benefits from access to immigrant labor in particular periods of high economic growth (Portes and Rumbaut 1996; Castles and Miller 2003). Whether emigration contributes to the negative cumulative causation evident in sending countries is also a complex matter. The evidence shows that individual households and localities may benefit, but not national economies. History suggests that the accumulation of advantage evident in receiving countries has tended to elude labor-sending areas because they either cannot catch up with the receiving nations or are structurally excluded from the actual spatialization of growth, precisely because it is characterized by uneven development. Italy and Ireland were labor exporters for two centuries, and this did not turn out to be a macro-economic advantage. Their current economic dynamism and labor immigration has little to do with their prior history as emigration countries. It results instead from a set of specific economic processes that took hold in each country and rapidly expanded the economy.

In brief, analytically one could argue that as today's labor-receiving countries grew richer and more developed, they kept expanding their zone of recruitment and influence, covering an expanding set of countries and including a variety of emigration-immigration dynamics, some rooted in past imperial conditions, others in the newer development asymmetries that underlie much migration today. There is a dynamic of inequality within which labor migrations are embedded that keeps on marking regions as labor sending and labor receiving, though a given country may switch its category, as is the case with Ireland and Italy today.

The Organized Export of Workers

The 1990s and postmillennium period have seen a sharp growth in the export of workers, both legal and illegal. This growth in exports is not simply the other side, the passive side, of the active recruitment of immigrants; rather, it has its own specific features. The export of workers may be private, profit-making operations, or they may encouraged by governments to enhance revenues. But what are the systemic links, if any, between the growth of organized exports of workers for private profit or for government-revenue enhancement, on the one hand, and economic conditions in developing countries today, on the other? Among these conditions are a growth in unemployment, the closure of a large number of typically small and medium-sized enterprises oriented toward national rather than export markets, and large, often increasing government debt. Although these economies are frequently grouped under the label "developing," they are in some cases struggling or stagnant and even shrinking. (Here "developing" will nevertheless be used as shorthand for this variety of situations.) The evidence for these conditions is incomplete and partial, yet there is a growing consensus among experts that exported labor is expanding and, further, that women often make up a majority of the exported workers, including in situations that used to be mostly male-dominated.

These labor exports have been increasing at a time when the dynamics of economic globalization have been having a significant impact on developing economies. The latter have had to implement a bundle of new policies and accommodate new conditions associated with globalization, including Structural Adjustment Programs, the opening up of these economies to foreign firms, the elimination of multiple state subsidies, and, it would seem almost inevitably, financial crises and the prevailing types of programmatic solutions put forth by the International Monetry Fund (IMF). It is now clear that in most of the countries involved, these conditions have created enormous costs for certain sectors of the economy and population, without fundamentally reducing government debt. Among these costs are, prominently, the growth in unemployment; the closure of a large number of firms in often fairly traditional sectors oriented to the local or national market; the promotion of export-oriented cash crops, which have increasingly replaced survival agriculture and food production for local or national markets; and the ongoing and mostly heavy burden of government debt in most of these economies.

Are there systemic links between these two sets of developments—the growth of organized exports of workers from these developing economies and the rise in unemployment and debt in those same economies? One way of articulating this in substantive terms is to posit (1) the shrinking opportunities for employment in many of these countries; (2) the shrinking opportunities for more traditional forms of profit-making as developing economies increasingly accept foreign firms in a widening range of economic sectors and are pressured to develop export industries; and (3) the fall in revenues for the governments of many of these countries, partly linked to these conditions and to the burden of debt servicing. All of these factors have increased the importance of finding alternative ways of making a living, making a profit, and securing government revenue.

Prostitution and labor migration are ways of making a living; the legal and illegal trafficking in workers, including workers for the sex industry, are growing in importance as ways of making a profit; and the remittances sent by emigrants, as well as the revenues from the organized export of workers, are increasingly important sources of foreign currency for some of these governments. Women are by far the majority group in the illegal trafficking for the sex industry and in the organized government export of workers.

The organized export of workers, whether legal or illegal, is partly facilitated by the organizational and technical infrastructure of the global economy: the formation of global markets, the intensification of transnational and translocal networks, and the development of communication technologies that easily escape conventional surveillance practices. The strengthening and, in some cases, formation of new global networks are embedded or made possible by the existence of a global economic system and its associated development of various institutional supports for cross-border money flows and markets. Once there is an institutional infrastructure for globalization, processes that have basically operated at the national level can scale up to the global level, even when this is not necessary for their operation. This would contrast with processes that are by their very features global, such as the network of financial centers underlying the formation of a global capital market.

Debt and debt-servicing problems have become a systemic feature of the developing world since the 1980s and are contributing to the expanded efforts to export workers, both legally and illegally. There is considerable research showing the detrimental effects of such debt on government programs for women and children, notably education and health care—clearly investments necessary to ensure a better future. Further, the increased unemployment typically associated with the austerity and adjustment programs implemented by international agencies to address government debt has also been found to have adverse effects on broad sectors of the population. Subsistence food production, informal work, emigration, and prostitution have all grown as survival options. Heavy government debt and high unemployment have brought with them the need to search for alternative sources for government revenue, and the shrinking of regular economic opportunities has brought with it a widened use of illegal profit-making schemes by enterprises and organizations.

Generally, most countries that became deeply indebted in the 1980s have not been able to solve this problem. And in the 1990s, a whole new set of countries became deeply indebted. Over these two decades many innovations were launched, most importantly by the IMF and the World Bank through their Structural Adjustment Programs and Structural Adjustment Loans, respectively. The latter were tied to economic policy reform rather than to particular projects. The purpose of such programs is to make states more "competitive," which typically means making sharp cuts in various social programs.

A growing number of countries have been paying a significant share of their total revenues to service their debt.

Thirty-three of the forty-one Highly Indebted Poor Countries (HIPC) paid US$3 in debt service payments to the North for every US$1 in development assistance. Many of these countries pay over 50 percent of their government revenues toward debt service, or 20 to 25 percent of their export earnings; debt-service ratios to gross national product (GNP) in many of the HIPCs exceed sustainable limits (UNCTAD 1999). Today these ratios are far more extreme than what were considered unmanageable levels in the Latin American debt crisis of the 1980s. Debt-to-GNP ratios are especially high in Africa, where they stood at 123 percent, compared with 42 percent in Latin America and 28 percent in Asia. The IMF asks HIPCs to pay 20 to 25 percent of their export earnings toward debt service. In contrast, in 1953 the Allies canceled 80 percent of Germany's war debt and only insisted on 3 to 5 percent of export earnings debt service. These more general terms have also been evident in recent history when Central Europe emerged from under communism.

This debt burden inevitably has large repercussions on state spending composition, and through this, on the population. There is research literature on the devastating impact of government debt, focusing on the implementation of a first generation of Structural Adjustment Programs in several developing countries in the 1980s as well as on a second generation of such programs, one more directly linked to the implementation of the global economy, in the 1990s. This literature has documented the disproportionate burden these programs put on the lower middle classes and the working poor, and most especially, women (for example, Ward 1990; Bose and Acosta-Belen 1995). The conditions push households and individuals into accepting or seeking legal or illegal traffickers to take them to any job, anywhere. Yet even under these extreme conditions, where the traffickers often function as recruiters initiating the process, it is only a minority of people who are emigrating. The participation of traffickers to some extent alters the type of patterning associated with government and firm recruitment, which tend to be embedded in older sets of linkages connecting the countries involved.

Remittances sent by immigrants represent a major source of foreign exchange reserves for governments of many developing countries. Though the flows of remittances may be minor compared to the massive daily capital flows in various financial markets, they are often very significant for developing or struggling economies. In 1998, global remittances sent by immigrants to their home countries reached more than US$70 billion. The true significance of this figure can only be appreciated when the amounts are compared to the GDPs and foreign currency reserves of the specific countries involved, rather than to the global flow of capital. For instance, in the Philippines, a key sender of migrants generally and of women for the entertainment industry in several countries, remittances have represented the third-largest source of foreign exchange over the past several years. In Bangladesh, a country with significant numbers of workers in the Middle East, Japan, and European countries, remittances represent about a third of foreign exchange.

The illegal export of migrants is a profitable business for the traffickers, though it can also add to the flow of legal remittances. According to a United Nations report, criminal organizations in the 1990s generated an estimated $US3.5 billion per year in profits from trafficking male and female migrants for work (IOM 1996). Once this was mostly the trade of petty criminals. Today it is an increasingly organized operation that functions at the global scale. The entry of organized crime is a recent development in the case of migrant trafficking. There are also reports that organized crime groups are creating intercontinental strategic alliances through networks of co-ethnics throughout several countries. Such networks facilitate transport, local contact and distribution, and the provision of false documents.

Although most men and many women are indeed trafficked for work, women are at greater risk of getting diverted to the sex trades. Some women know that they are being trafficked for prostitution when they agree to the recruitment, but for many the conditions of their recruitment and the extent of abuse and bondage only become evident after they arrive in the receiving country. The conditions of confinement are often extreme, akin to slavery, and so are the conditions of abuse, including rape and other forms of sexual violence as well as physical punishments. They are severely underpaid, and wages are often withheld.

Government-Organized Exports

The exportation of workers may be a means by which governments cope with unemployment and foreign debt. There are two ways in which governments have secured benefits through these strategies. One of these is highly formalized, and the other is simply a by-product of the migration process itself. Among the strongest examples of the formalized mode are South Korea and the Philippines (Sassen 1988; Parrenas 2001). In the 1970s, South Korea developed extensive programs to promote the export of workers as an integral part of its growing overseas construction industry, initially to the Organization of Petroleum Exporting Countries (OPEC) in the Middle East and then worldwide. As South Korea entered its own economic boom, exporting workers became a less necessary and attractive option. In contrast, the Philippine government, if anything, expanded and diversified the concept of exporting its citizens as a way of dealing with unemployment and securing needed foreign exchange reserves through remittances.

The Filipino case illuminates a whole series of issues about government exports of workers. The Filipino government has played an important role in the emigration of Filipino women to the United States, the Middle East, and Japan through the Philippines Overseas Employment Administration (POEA). Established in 1982, POEA organized and oversaw the export of nurses and maids to high-demand areas in the world. High foreign debt and high unemployment combined to make this an attractive policy. Filipino overseas workers sent home almost US$1 billion on average a year in the last few years. On the other side, various labor-importing countries welcomed this policy for their own reasons. OPEC countries of the Middle East saw the demand for domestic workers grow sharply after the 1973 oil boom. Confronted with a severe shortage of nurses, a profession that demanded years of training yet garnered rather low wages and little prestige or recognition, the US passed the Immigration Nursing Relief Act of 1989 which allowed for the import of nurses. About 80 percent of the nurses brought in under the new act were from the Philippines. And Japan passed legislation permitting the entry of "entertainment workers" into its booming economy in the 1980s, marked by rising expendable incomes and strong labor shortages.

The Philippine government also passed regulations that permitted mail-order bride agencies to recruit young Filipinas to marry foreign men as a matter of contractual agreement. The rapid increase in this trade was mostly due to an organized effort by the government, and among the major clients were the United States and Japan. Japan's agricultural communities were a key destination for these brides, given enormous shortages of people, and especially young women, in the Japanese countryside when the economy was booming and demand for labor in the large metropolitan areas was extremely high. Municipal governments made it a policy to accept Filipino brides. The Philippine government approved most mail-order bride organizations until 1989. Under the government of Corazon Aquino, the stories of abuse by foreign husbands led to a ban on the mail-order bride business. But it is almost impossible to eliminate these organizations, and they continue to operate in violation of the law.

The largest number of Filipinas going through these government-promoted channels are destined to work overseas as maids, particularly in other Asian countries (Chin 1997; Heyzer 1994; Parrenas 2001). The second-largest group, and the fastest-growing, consists of entertainers, largely migrating to Japan (Sassen 2001, chapter 9). The rapid increase in the number of "entertainers" migrating from the Philippines to Japan is largely due to the more than 500 "entertainment brokers" in the Philippines operating outside the state umbrella—even though the government may still benefit from the remittances of these workers. These brokers work to provide women for the sex industry in Japan, where it is basically supported or controlled by organized gangs rather than going through the government-controlled program for the entry of entertainers. These women are ostensibly recruited for singing and entertaining, but frequently, perhaps mostly, they are forced into prostitution as well. They are recruited and brought in both through formal legal channels and illegally. Either way, they have little power to resist. Even though they are paid below minimum wage, they produce significant profits for the brokers and employers involved, and there has been an enormous increase in so-called entertainment businesses in Japan.

The Philippines, while perhaps the country with the most developed labor-export program, is not the only one to have explored these strategies. Thailand started a campaign in 1998 following a financial crisis in order to promote migration for work and recruitment by firms overseas of Thai workers. The government sought to export workers to the Middle East, the United States, Great Britain, Germany, Australia, and Greece. Sri Lanka's government has tried to export another 200,000 workers, in addition to the 1 million it already has overseas; Sri Lankan women remitted US$880 million in 1998, mostly from their earnings as maids in the Middle East and Far East (*S. Lankan Migrant Workers,* 1999). Bangladesh had already organized extensive labor-export programs to the OPEC countries of the Middle East by the 1970s. This effort has continued, and along with individual migration, both to these countries and to various others, notably the United States and the United Kingdom, it has succeeded in developing a significant source of foreign exchange. Bangladeshi workers remit about $US1.4 billion annually (David 1998).

Trafficking in Women

International trafficking in women for the sex industry grew sharply during the 1990s and into the millennium (see Lin and Marjan 1997; Shannon 1999). The available evidence suggests that the trade is highly profitable for those running it. The United Nations estimates that 4 million people were trafficked in 1998, producing a profit of US$7 billion to criminal groups. These funds include remittances from prostitutes' earnings and payments to organizers and facilitators in these countries.

It is estimated that in recent years several million women and girls have been trafficked within and out of Asia and the former Soviet Union, two major trafficking areas. The growth of trafficking in both these areas can be linked to poverty. Women pushed into poverty, or girls with poor parents, are often sold to brokers, and high unemployment in the former Soviet republics has been one factor promoting growth of criminal gangs in general, including those trafficking in women. For instance, Ukrainian and Russian women, highly prized in the sex market, earn the criminal gangs involved about US$500 to US$1,000 per woman delivered. These women can be expected to service on average fifteen clients a day, and each can be expected to make about US$215,000 per month for the gang (IOM 1996).

Such networks also facilitate the organized circulation of trafficked women among third countries—not only from sending to receiving countries. Traffickers may move women from Burma, Laos, Vietnam, and China to Thailand, while Thai women may have been moved to Japan and the United States. There are various reports on the particular cross-border movements in trafficking. Malay brokers sell Malay women into prostitution in Australia. East European women from Albania and Kosovo have been trafficked by gangs into prostitution in London (Hamzic and Sheehan 1999). European teens from Paris and other cities have been sold to Arab and African customers (Shannon 1999). In the United States, the police broke up an international Asian ring that imported women from China, Thailand, Korea, Malaysia, and Vietnam (Booth 1999). The women were charged between US$30,000 and US$40,000, a debt which they paid through their work in the sex trade or needle trade.

As tourism has grown sharply over the last decade and become a major development strategy for cities, regions and whole countries, the entertainment sector has seen a parallel growth and is seen now as a key development strategy. In many places, the sex trade is part of the entertainment industry and has grown at a similar rate. The sex trade itself can become a development strategy in areas with high unemployment and poverty and for governments desperate for revenue and foreign-exchange reserves. When local manufacturing and agriculture can no longer function as sources of employment, profits, and government revenue, what was once a marginal source of earnings, profits, and revenues may become a far more important one. The increased importance of these sectors in development then generates tie-ins. For instance, when the IMF and the World Bank see tourism as a solution to some of the development impasses in many poor countries and provide loans for its development, they may well be contributing to the development of a broader institutional setting for the expansion of the entertainment industry, and indirectly, of the sex trade. This tie-in with development strategies signals that trafficking in women may well see a sharp expansion in coming years.

The entry of organized crime in the sex trades, the formation of cross-border ethnic networks, and the growing transnationalization in so many aspects of tourism all suggest a thriving global sex industry. This could mean greater attempts to enter into more and more "markets" and a general expansion of the industry in the years ahead. Given a growing number of women with few, if any, employment options, the prospects are grim.

Women in the sex industry become—in certain kinds of economies—a crucial link supporting the expansion of the entertainment industry and through that tourism as a development strategy, which in turn becomes a source of government revenue. These tie-ins are structural, not a function of conspiracies. Their weight in an economy will be increased by the absence or limitations of other sources for securing a livelihood, profits, and revenues for, respectively, workers, enterprises, and governments.

It is clear that international migration flows are conditioned by broader politico-economic dynamics. One of the major implications of this type of analysis is that it is within these broader dynamics that we need to situate the decisions by individual migrants. Three types of economic conditions facilitate and induce individuals to take the decision to migrate. A first set of broad structural conditions has to do with the types of economic linkages brought about by economic internationalization in its many instantiations: old colonial and more recent neo-colonial forms, and particular types of linkages brought about by current forms of economic globalization. A second set of linkages discussed was the direct recruitment of immigrant workers by employers or by governments on behalf of the former, or through the immigrant network. A third and final set of linkages examined was the organized export and trafficking, increasingly illegal, of men, women, and children. These create whole new ways of linking emigration and immigration countries, beyond old colonial or new global economic linkages. It is evident that migration flows cannot be understood simply in terms of such individual decisions. Poverty and unemployment are not by themselves sufficient conditions to understand migration flows.

Saskia Sassen

See also: Clandestine Migration; Cold War; Colonial Immigration; Commonwealth Citizenship and Immigration (UK); Crime and Migration; Economic Effects of Migration; Ethnic Germans; Filipino Diaspora; Gender and Migration; Greek Diaspora; Guestworkers, Europe; Irish Diaspora; Italian Migration Worldwide; Japan: The New Immigration Model; Migration between Northern and Southern Countries; Migration Policy; North American Free Trade Agreement; Polish Diaspora; Primary, Secondary Immigration; Push-Pull Factors; Remittances; Skilled Migration; South Korea; Trafficking; Turkish Diaspora; U.S. Immigration; Women, Globalization, and Immigration

References and further reading:

Basch, Linda, Nina Glick Schiller, and Cristina Szanton Blanc. 1994. *Nations Unbound: Transnational Projects, Postcolonial Predicaments and Deterritorialized Nation-States.* Amsterdam: Gordon and Breach.

Bonilla, Frank, and Ricardo Campos. 1982. "Imperialist Initiatives and the Puerto Rican Worker: From Foraker to Reagan." *Contemporary Marxism* 3: 5–17.

Bonilla, Frank, Edwin Melendez, Rebecca Morales, and Maria De Los Angeles Torres, eds. 1998. *Borderless Borders.* Philadelphia: Temple University Press.

Booth, William. 1999. "Thirteen Charged in Gang Importing Prostitutes." *Washington Post.* August 21.

Bose, Christine E., and Edna Acosta-Belen. 1995. *Women in the Latin American Development Process.* Philadelphia: Temple University Press.

Boyd, Monica. 1989. "Family and Personal Networks in International Migration: Recent Developments and New Agendas." *International Migration Review* 23, no. 3: 638–670.

Briggs, Vernon M. 1992. *Mass Immigration and the National Interest.* Armonk, NY: M. E. Sharpe.

Bustamante, Jorge A., and Geronimo G. Martinez. 1979. "Unauthorized Immigration from Mexico: Beyond Borders but within Systems." *Journal of International Affairs* 33, no. 2 (Fall/Winter): 265–284.

Castles, Stephen, and Mark J. Miller. 2003. *The Age of Migration: International Population Movements in the Modern World.* 3d ed. Basingstoke: Palgrave Macmillan.

Chin, Christine. 1997. "Walls of Silence and Late 20th Century Representations of Foreign Female Domestic Workers: The Case of Filipina and Indonesian Houseservants in Malaysia." *International Migration Review* 31, no. 1: 353–385.

Cohen, Robin. 1991. *Contested Domains: Debates in International Labour Studies.* London: Zed.

Cornelius, Wayne, Philip Martin, and James Hollifield. 1994. *Controlling Immigration: A Global Perspective.* Stanford, CA: Stanford University Press.

David, Natacha. 1998. "Migrants Made the Scapegoats of the Crisis." *ICFTU Online.* January 8. International Confederation of Free Trade Unions, http://www.hartford-hwp.com/archives/50/012.html.

Fassmann, Heinz, and Rainer Munz, eds. 1994. *European Migration in the Late 20th Century: Historical Patterns, Actual Trends and Social Implications.* Aldershot: E. Elgar.

Fernandez-Kelly, Maria Patricia. 1984. "For We Are Sold, I and My People: Women and Industry in Mexico's Frontier." SUNY Series in the Anthropology of Work. Albany: State University of New York Press.

Grasmuck, Sherri, and Patricia Pessar. 1991. *Between Two Islands: Dominican International Migration.* Berkeley: University of California Press.

Hall, Stuart. 1991a. "The Local and the Global: Globalization and Ethnicities." Pp. 19–39 in *Culture, Globalization, and the World System: Contemporary Conditions for the Representation of Identity.* Edited by Anthony King. Basingstoke: Macmillan.

———. 1991b. "Old and New Identities: Old and New Ethnicities." Pp. 41–68 in *Culture, Globalization, and the World System: Contemporary Conditions for the Representation of Identity.* Edited by Anthony King. Basingstoke: Macmillan.

Hamzic, Edin, and Maeve Sheehan. 1999. "Kosovo Sex Slaves Held in Soho Flats." *Sunday Times* (UK), July 4.

Heyzer, Noeleen. 1994. "The Trade in Domestic Workers." London: Zed.

International Organization for Migration. 1996. "Trafficking in Migrants." *Quarterly Bulletin.* Geneva: International Migration Office.

Levitt, Peggy. 2001. *The Transnational Villagers.* Berkeley: University of California Press.

Lin, Lap-Chew, and Wijers Marjan. 1997. *Trafficking in Women, Forced Labour and Slavery-Like Practices in Marriage, Domestic Labour and Prostitution.* Utrecht: Foundation against Trafficking in Women; Bangkok: Global Alliance Against Traffic in Women.

Mahler, Sarah. 1995. *American Dreaming: Immigrant Life on the Margins.* Princeton, NJ: Princeton University Press.

Martin, Susan F. 2003. *Refugee Women.* London: Zed.

Massey, Douglas S., Jorge Durand, and Nolan J. Malone. 2002. *Beyond Smoke and Mirrors: Mexican Immigration in an Age of Economic Integration.* New York: Russell Sage Foundation.

Massey, Douglas S., Luin P. Goldring, and Jorge Durand. 1994. "Continuities in Transnational Migration: An Analysis of Nineteen Mexican Communities." *American Journal of Sociology* 99, no. 6: 1492–1533.

Morita, Kiriro, and Saskia Sassen. 1994. "The New Illegal Immigration in Japan, 1980–1992." *International Migration Review* 28, no. 1 (Spring): 153–163.

Morokvasic, Mirjana, ed. 1984. "Special Issue: Women in Migration." *International Migration Review* 18, no. 4.

Papademitriou, Demetrios G., and Phillip L. Martin, eds. 1991. *The Unsettled Relationship: Labor Migration and Economic Development.* New York: Greenwood.

Parnreiter, Christof. 1995. "Entwurzelung, Globalisierung und Migration." *Journal für Entwicklungpolitik: Schwerpunkt Migration* 3: 245–260.

Parrenas, Rhacel Salazar. 2001. *Servants of Globalization: Women, Migration and Domestic Work.* Stanford, CA: Stanford University Press.

Portes, Alejandro, and Rubén G. Rumbaut. 1996. *Immigrant America: A Portrait.* 2d ed. Los Angeles: University of California Press.

Portes, Alejandro, and John Walton. 1981. *Labor, Class and the International System.* New York: Academic Press.

S. Lankan Migrant Workers Remit Rs. 60 Billion in 1998. 1999. February 12. Woodside, NY: Xinhua News Agency.

Safa, Helen I. 1995. *The Myth of the Male Breadwinner: Women and Industrialization in the Caribbean.* Boulder: Westview.

Sassen, Saskia. 1988. *The Mobility of Labor and Capital: A Study in International Investment and Labor Flow.* New York: Cambridge University Press.

———. 1999. *Guests and Aliens.* New York: The New Press.

———. 2001. *The Global City: New York, London, Tokyo.* 2d ed. Princeton, NJ: Princeton University Press.

Shannon, Susan. 1999. "The Global Sex Trade: Humans as the Ultimate Commodity." *Crime and Justice International* (May): 5–25.

Skeldon, Ronald. 1997. "Hong Kong: Colonial City to Global City to Provincial City?" *Cities* 14, no. 5: 265–271.

Smith, Paul J., ed. 1997. *Human Smuggling: Chinese Migrant Trafficking and the Challenge to America's Immigration Tradition.* Washington, DC: Center for Strategic and International Studies.

Tsuda, Takeyuki. 1999. "Motivation to Migrate: The Ethnic and Socio-cultural Constitution of the Japanese-Brazilian Return-Migration System." *Economic Development and Cultural Change* 48, no. 1: 1–31.

UN Conference on Trade and Development. 1999. *Trade and Development Report 1999.* Geneva: UNCTAD.

Ward, Kathryn. 1990. "Women Workers and Global Restructuring." Cornell International Industrial and Labor Relations Report 17. Ithaca, NY: IRL Press, Cornell University.

Economic Effects of Migration

The economic effects of migration may be classified into several categories. Migration helps bring about "factor price equalization," including a narrowing of wage gaps between the low-wage sending and the higher-wage receiving areas. Migration also affects the level and distribution of income, both among the remaining population in the place of origin and among the original or native population in the place of destination. Moreover, the migration and assimilation process affects the economic well-being of the migrants themselves.

Equalization of Wages

Real wages may differ across countries or regions within countries because of different rates of economic growth or development. This may be due to differences in the exploitation of natural resources or more rapid rates of capital accumulation, including investments in human capital (such as schooling, job training, and health and nutrition). Differences in the rates of adoption of technological change and the stability of political and legal institutions also affect growth rates in wages.

The gap in real wages may provide an incentive for those living in the low-wage region to move to the higher-wage area. The extent to which this movement takes place depends on several factors. These include the size of the wage gap, the duration of the wage gap, the discount rate that individuals use to convert future income into a current value, the costs of migration, and the wealth to finance the costs associated with the migration. There are two types of costs generally associated with migration: out-of-pocket (or direct) expenses and opportunity (foregone or indirect) costs. The direct costs would include, for example, the cost of a steamship or airline ticket; the opportunity cost would include earnings lost during the period of migration. There are costs associated with separating from the place of origin and costs associated with getting established in the place of destination, including those related to finding housing and employment. Leaving family, friends, and a familiar environment for a less familiar location entails numerous other costs as well.

The ability for those in a low-wage area to finance migration is sometimes an important determinant in whether a given wage gap will in fact spur migration. Although movement to a higher-wage area might seem attractive, the very poor may not have the resources to pay for a migration and sustain themselves during the move. Sometimes others finance part or all of the cost of the move, including family members in the place of origin or destination or labor contractors or employers in the place of destination.

Although a larger wage gap will, in general, encourage more migration, sometimes the reverse occurs. People on very low incomes may not be able to finance the migration costs, but if their wages in the country of origin increase, they may then have the resources to finance the migration, even though the wage gap between the countries of origin and destination has narrowed.

The migration of workers from a low-wage area changes the ratio of workers to other productive resources (such as natural resources, farm land, and capital equipment) in both the sending and receiving areas. In the place of origin, labor becomes scarcer and wages tend to increase. In the place of destination, the labor supply is more abundant and wages tend to decline. The relative rise in wages in the low-wage place of origin and the relative decline in wages in the high-wage destination tend to bring about "factor price equalization," or a movement toward a shrinking wage gap.

At times, however, the economic processes become more complex. Although natural resources and farm land are immobile, financial capital that can be used to exploit natural resources and improve farm land, as well as physical capital (for example, machines), is mobile across space. The movement of people sometimes follows the movement of capital. At other times, the movement of capital takes place in response to the movement of people—that is, the capital is taken to a location where greater productivity is expected from its use because of labor availability. Does "capital chase labor" or does "labor chase capital"? This may seem like a chicken-and-egg question. In fact, both occur at different times and places, in different circumstances, and as a result of different migratory flows.

Impact on the Country of Origin and Destination Country Economies

Migration affects the aggregate level and distribution of income in the origin and destination economies in important ways. Although emigration (that is, outward migration) tends to cause wage increases in the place of origin, the returns decrease to complementary factors of production (land and capital). Landlords and owners of capital lose as a consequence, and the total income of the population remaining in the place of origin decreases, unless the losses are offset by remittances sent back by the emigrants. In times past, some governments and property owners have tried, with only limited success, to bar emigration to prevent these losses. In more recent decades, remittances sent by emigrants have been an important source of income and foreign exchange, especially when emigrants from low-wage places of origin, such as Mexico, Africa, and South and East Asia, have moved to relatively high-wage destinations, such as the United States, Europe, and the oil-exporting Persian Gulf States. So, too, have been the investments emigrants have made in housing, farms, and businesses in their countries of origin.

Rin, 4, daughter of a garment worker, stands during a protest against clothing manufacturer Liberty Apparel July 8, 2004, in New York City. Garment workers toiled in one of Liberty's factories in New York City sewing clothing for fourteen hours a day at $3 an hour. After working up to eighty hours a week their wages have been withheld for up to eight months. (Mario Tama/Getty Images)

In the high-wage place of destination, the opposite occurs. The increase in the labor supply, though tending to lower wages, raises the productivity of complementary factors of production (land and capital), thereby tending to raise the aggregate incomes of the native-born population of the place of destination, especially the owners of land and capital, at the expense of native-born workers in the destination area. Thus, historically the owners of natural resources, land, and capital in high-wage countries have tended to favor immigration, while workers already residing in the destination country tend to favor barriers to migration, except perhaps for their own relatives.

The economic impacts of migration have become more complex in the modern world than they were in the past. In earlier eras, workers generally had roughly similar low levels of skill. There is now a much wider variety of skill levels and more complex interrelationships among groups defined by skill. It is useful for expository purposes to think of workers as being either high-skilled or low-skilled. The economic effects of migration differ by the nature of the skills migrants bring with them. Consider two extremes, one where all of the migrants are low-skilled or unskilled production workers, and another where all are high-skilled professionals (for example, doctors, engineers, and computer scientists).

The migration of low-skilled workers increases the low-skilled portion of the labor market and raises the demand for higher-skilled workers and capital. Thus, among the native population in a receiving country the wages of low-skilled workers decline and the wages of high-skilled workers and the returns to the owners of capital increase. The rate of return on investments in skill and capital in the place of destination increases, and income inequality also increases, although the aggregate income of the native population also increases.

If there is an income transfer or welfare system in the place of destination, it may come into play to mitigate the loss in income among the low-skilled native population. In principle, taxes levied against the gain in income among the high-skilled workers and the owners of capital can be collected by the government and transferred to the native low-skilled workers. If this were done, in principle, all of the native population could be "held homeless;" that is, made no worse off as a consequence of the migration.

Alternatively, suppose the migrant workers must be treated by the tax-transfer system in a manner identical to that of the native population. Then they, too, would receive these benefits, and as a result their income level would be no different from that of the native workers. Under such a system, the transfers to the low-skilled workers would exceed the income gains of the high-skilled workers and owners of capital combined. The inclusion in the transfer system of the low-skilled migrants intended to "hold homeless" low-skilled native workers then becomes counterproductive. It is for this reason that countries have adopted a variety of mechanisms to gain the labor of low-skilled foreign workers while excluding them from receiving transfer benefits. These mechanisms include the use of formal "guestworker" or "contract worker" programs, tolerance or encouragement of illegal migration flows of low-skilled workers, and legislation limiting or barring the access of recent migrants to income-transfer programs.

An entirely different outcome results from the migration of high-skilled workers, which tends to lower the wages of high-skilled native workers but raises the productivity of complementary factors of production, such as low-skilled native workers and capital. The differences in wage rates by skill level declines, thereby lowering the rate of return on investment in skill. The inequality in earnings among workers declines. Low-skilled workers make less use of income transfers as their incomes rise, relaxing the pressure on those who pay taxes. Moreover, if the high-skilled workers with science and engineering skills introduce technological changes that expand the productive capacity or competitiveness of the economy, additional gains are to be had. Thus, it is not surprising that most immigrant receiving countries have adopted policies specifically designed to attract high-skilled immigrants, either on a temporary or permanent basis, and that this tendency has increased with the growth of the modern welfare state.

It is often said, however, that advanced industrial economies need low-skilled workers to keep their economies functioning. Who will collect the trash, clean the dishes in restaurants, and mow the lawns? In the absence of low-skilled migrants to do these jobs, wages and working conditions in these occupations would increase, thereby attracting native workers. The higher wages would attract workers from other sectors of the economy and those not employed into the labor market as part-time or full-time employees. Thus, the higher wages in immigrant-intensive, low-skilled occupations would spread throughout the economy, benefiting all low-skilled workers.

Moreover, when there are more native workers in these occupations, but fewer total workers, various forms of substitution result. The higher labor costs would mean a higher cost of producing neatly trimmed lawns, for example, so less frequent mowing would take place. Some would let the grass grow longer; others would replace the grass with ground cover, hedges, or rock gardens. Capital would replace labor: There would be more efficient lawn mowers, slower-growing grass seeds, and fertilizers that promote attractive but slow-growing grass.

Immigrant Adjustment

The economic effects of migration are dependent, in part, on the degree of transferability of skills acquired in the place of origin to the place of destination. Migrants with skills that are highly transferable will have a faster adjustment in the destination labor market and achieve higher earnings that much sooner. Migrants possessing skills that are valuable in the country of origin but have little or no transferability to the country of destination (for example, lawyers, judges, and generals) would initially have low wages, and in fact are seldom found in streams of economic migrants. They are more likely to be found among refugees, that is, among those for whom the usual economic model of migration does not apply.

Whether they are economic migrants or refugees, migrants go through an adjustment process in which previously acquired skills are modified to suit the new economic environment and new skills are acquired. The speed and completeness of adjustment, however, varies by the degree of transferability of the skills and the motivation for migration.

One of the most important skills is proficiency in the dominant language used in the destination labor market. Language proficiency is important in and of itself and in noneconomic interactions, but it is also important for effectively using other skills. There is a complementarity between proficiency in the destination language and other forms of labor-market skills—that is, each enhances the other. The skills of a Russian engineer in the United States are of little value if the engineer does not speak English, and English-language skills are of limited value if the person has no other skills to bring to the labor market.

Barry R. Chiswick

See also: Economic Determinants of International Migration; Guestworkers, Europe; International Labour Organization; Personal Responsibility and Work Opportunity Reconciliation Act, 1966 (U.S.); Push-Pull Factors; Remittances; Skilled Migration; UN Convention on the Rights of Migrant Workers, 1990

References and further reading:

Chiswick, Barry R. 1982. *The Gateway: U.S. Immigration Issues and Policies.* Washington, DC: American Enterprise Institute.

———. 1992. *Immigration, Language and Ethnicity.* Washington, DC: American Enterprise Institute.

Chiswick, Barry R., and Timothy J. Hatton. 2003. "International Migration and the Integration of Labor Markets." In *Globalization in Historical Perspective.* Edited by Michael Bordo, Alan Taylor, and Jeffrey Williamson. Cambridge, MA: National Bureau of Economic Research.

Hatton, Timothy J., and Jeffrey G. Williamson. 1998. *The Age of Mass Migration: Causes and Economic Effects.* New York: Oxford University Press.

Simon, Julian L., and Sanford J. Unger. 1999. *The Economic Consequences of Immigration.* 2d ed. Ann Arbor: University of Michigan.

Ellis Island

Ellis Island, in the upper bay of New York City's harbor, is famous as the gateway to the United States. More than 12 million immigrants passed through Ellis Island between 1892 and 1954. In American iconography, the island is a symbol of the nation's immigrant heritage. This is not surprising. About three-quarters of the immigrants to the United States in the last great wave of immigration, between 1892 and 1924, went through the Ellis Island immigration station. The overwhelming majority of these immigrants were European, and the largest two groups were from Russia and Italy. Today, it is estimated that more than 100 million Americans can trace their ancestry in the United States to a man, woman, or child whose name appears in the record book in the great Registry Room at Ellis Island. In April 2001, when the Ellis Island Foundation digitized its immigration records and debuted its new website, the response was astounding, averaging more than 25,000 hits per second.

Ellis Island officially opened as an immigration station on January 1, 1892. In the peak years between its opening and 1924, Ellis Island received thousands of immigrants a day; it expanded over time to include 27 acres supporting more than thirty buildings. While first- and second-class passengers were inspected on board ship before being transferred to New York, steerage passengers were packed on barges or ferries that took them to Ellis Island. For the vast majority, the processing in Ellis Island's Main Building lasted no more than a day. Immigrants waited in long lines to be observed by medical officers in what became known as the six-second exam, and then in another line for legal inspection. In the latter, they had to confirm, usually in a couple of minutes, the information declared about them on the ship's manifest.

The Federal Immigration Act of 1917 required that every immigrant over the age of fourteen be able to read. Thus, immigrants from that year on were given a simple reading test in the language of their home culture. Perhaps a fifth of the immigrants were detained for further inspection for health and other reasons, but in the end only 2 percent of the immigrants seeking admission to America were turned away. Once cleared through Ellis Island, immigrants went by ferry to Manhattan or took barges to train terminals in New Jersey, where they continued on to destinations throughout the country.

During the massive migration of Europeans to the Americas in the early twentieth century, the largest numbers went to the United States. Immigrants were first received in the Examination Hall of New York Harbor's Ellis Island, shown here in 1904. (Library of Congress)

By the late 1920s, Ellis Island had ceased to become a mass processing station. Restrictive immigration laws had drastically reduced European immigration, and a new provision required the inspection of immigrants at the American consular office in the country of origin rather than after arrival in the United States. Ellis Island became a detention and deportation center for undesirable aliens; it was also used as a hospital for wounded servicemen during both world wars, and part of the island was a U.S. Coast Guard training facility. The government closed the island in 1954, and it was abandoned for more than twenty years.

In 1990, after a six-year, $170 million renovation, the Ellis Island Immigration Museum was opened in the restored Main Building. The museum now receives more than a million visitors a year. Ellis Island is also part of the Statue of Liberty National Monument because of its proximity to Liberty Island and the symbolic importance of the statue to immigrants as they reached the destination of their long voyage. While Ellis Island continues to be associated with New York in the popular imagination, in the late 1990s most of the island officially became part of the state of New Jersey.

Nancy Foner

See also: Border Controls; Deportation; Migration Policy; Public Health; U.S. Immigration; U.S. Immigration Legislation: Post-1945; U.S. Immigration Legislation: Pre-1945

References and further reading:

Pitkin, Thomas M. 1975. *Keepers of the Gate: The History of Ellis Island.* New York: New York University Press.

Yans-McLaughlin, Virginia, and Marjorie Lightman. 1997. *Ellis Island and the Peopling of America: The Official Guide.* New York: The New Press.

Emigration

See Armenian Diaspora; Chinese Diaspora; Colombian Diaspora; Diaspora; Dominican Republic Diaspora; Filipino Diaspora; Greek Diaspora; Indian Diaspora; Iraqi Diaspora; Irish Diaspora; Jewish Diaspora; Korean Diaspora; Polish Diaspora; Russian Diaspora; Sri Lankan Diaspora; Turkish Diaspora

Employer Sanctions

In order to combat the illegal employment of foreign workers, many countries not only prohibit illegal aliens from working but also make employers liable for violations. Employers are thus required to ensure the legality of their workforce. All sanctions relating to employers' noncompliance with this requirement are called "employer sanctions." These sanctions have two major purposes: supporting migration control by discouraging the employment of unauthorized workers, and increasing labor-market control by discouraging off-the-books employment, wages below legal standards, and poor working conditions.

Since 1980, an increasing number of states have introduced or increased employer sanctions. The effects of employer sanctions depend on conditions in the country applying them—namely, the society's general population monitoring, prosecution of tax and labor law violations, enforcement of immigration laws, and antidiscrimination provisions. Once sanctions are put into place, these factors determine whether a country will be more or less effective in deterring illegal employment in the regular and irregular economy. Employer sanctions may also have unintended side-effects because they provide incentives to discriminate against legal residents of immigrant origin and may prevent undocumented immigrants from claiming their basic human and workers' rights.

Types of Employer Sanctions

Employers who hire workers without work and/or residence permits for a regular job may profit from the willingness of the workers to accept long working hours, poor working conditions, and low wages. If the employment is off the books, employers also profit from the avoidance of payroll taxes and the possibility of arbitrary dismissals.

Employer sanctions are designed to curb the profits of illegal employment and thus deter such employment. They may take a number of different forms, including:

- Administrative sanctions for insufficient exercise of verification obligations
- Administrative or criminal sanctions for illegal employment
- Other liabilities and procedural sanctions in connection with illegal employment

In addition, sanctions against other economic actors are often included under employer sanctions if they are designed to curb profits from this type of employment, namely sanctions for final recipients (main contractors, consumers), recruiters, and other people assisting illegal employment.

Administrative Sanctions for Insufficient Exercise of Verification Obligations

If employers are to be held liable for the legality of their workforce, they require some means to determine whether a job applicant is authorized to work (Aleinikoff et al. 1998, 643). Therefore, the introduction of employer sanctions implies the obligation to check identity and work authorization papers. As employers are not documentation experts, they may mistake forged papers for real ones. Additional verification may be introduced in order to enhance reliability. In the United States, for example, there are pilot experiments allowing employers to verify work authorization status against a central database accessible by phone. If employers do not comply with the required hiring procedures, they may face sanctions even if their actions did not lead to unauthorized employment. These types of employer sanctions against "paperwork violations" are designed to prevent employers from hiring unauthorized foreign nationals inadvertently.

In states without a national identity card (such as the United States and the United Kingdom), employers may find it difficult to determine whether someone is a foreign national, because many citizens do not have a handy way of proving citizenship. Introducing employer sanctions may lead to discriminatory hiring or identification practices. Because some ethnic communities have a higher incidence of illegal migration than others, employers may try to avoid employer sanctions by checking people with these backgrounds

President Reagan prepares to sign a landmark immigration reform bill at the White House. The bill gives certain illegal aliens a chance of benefits and citizenship and also includes sanctions against employers who exploit undocumented workers illegally entering the United States. Washington, D.C., 1986. (Bettmann/Corbis)

selectively or avoiding hiring them altogether. If these discriminatory practices are also unlawful, employers face a trade-off between avoiding either employer sanctions or antidiscrimination sanctions. They may often choose to avoid the latter by fulfilling their verification duties loosely. Employers may also verify loosely with the intention to circumvent the law. They pretend to fulfill their obligations while still knowingly hiring unauthorized workers (Calavita 1990). Thus, the effectiveness and the side effects of employer sanctions depend on the existence of a universal identifying document and elaborate antidiscrimination legislation.

Administrative or Criminal Sanctions for Illegal Employment
Administrative sanctions usually consist of fines, but they may also entail exclusion from state contracts, revocation of a necessary license, prevention of recruitment from abroad, and the like. As fines often depend on the number of detected workers and the time period of employment, maximum fines are often substantial. An employer who hires an unauthorized worker unknowingly and inadvertently is usually protected from any severe sanctions as long as he or she has made reasonable efforts to verify the status of the employee concerned. Average sanctions are usually well below maximum limits.

Some states discover illegal employment through data cross-checking. In Germany, for example, every employee has to be registered with the social security administration. The administration checks for false social security numbers and runs quarterly electronic data cross-checks in order to detect foreign workers without work authorization. Therefore, unauthorized workers in regular jobs are discovered relatively quickly unless they used forged passports from other European Union (EU) states or "borrowed" real papers from authorized workers (Vogel 2001, 333). As the scope for unauthorized employment in a regular job is strictly limited when the exchange of information among authorities is high, unauthorized employment is virtually always off the books in such states. In contrast, in states lacking cross-checking mechanisms, the number of regular taxpayers in the undocumented population tends to be high.

Work-site inspections are the most common method of detecting unauthorized workers and employers. Most states expel and/or detain and deport unauthorized workers, but some states also impose fines, especially on individuals with residence status but without work authorization (such as asylum seekers). Administrative structures, cooperation practices, and resources vary widely among states, leading to differing probabilities of detection. In some states (for example, the United States), immigration enforcement is separated from enforcement against other types of activity in the shadow economy, and immigration authorities are solely responsible for detecting unauthorized work by foreign nationals. Other states include the detection of unauthorized workers in a general regime of combating off-the-books employment. In Germany, for example, employment authorities inspect work sites to look for benefit fraud, social security tax evasion, and unauthorized work by nationals simultaneously. In some states, undocumented immigrants can only be detained and deported by general police forces, so that work-site inspectors need the cooperation of police authorities. Other states grant police functions to immigration enforcement units.

Depending on the country, extreme cases of illegal employment can result in criminal sanctions, including imprisonment. Criminal sanctions are, however, usually reserved for situations involving extreme exploitation and the large-scale organization of unauthorized work. The detection of this type of illegal employment usually results from substantial police investigations.

As checking employees at work sites often does not identify employers, more and more states have introduced joint liabilities, that is, sanctions for main contractors or final recipients. Thus, contractors who knowingly profit from illegal employment may be treated as employers or sanctioned in a similar way (see Robin and Barros 2000).

Other Liabilities and Procedural Sanctions

Under some regimes, criminal or administrative sanctions are combined with other measures to increase the probability of proving violations or to siphon off the profits from illegal employment. Most commonly, employers are held responsible for paying for the repatriation of the unauthorized employees. Governments may also seize goods produced with the help of unauthorized work or confiscate equipment to further sanction employers or secure their cooperation. However, such measures are rarely used because they lead to a considerable disruption of production processes that may involve regular employees and compliant companies.

Lack of evidence is a recurring problem with employer sanctions. Unauthorized employees are the best source of information about their work history and often the only ones who can give evidence of the pay, conditions, and duration of illegal work. However, these employees may have no incentive to cooperate with the authorities: Cooperation will not necessarily ensure the return of wages and may result in deportation or prosecution. Although illegal employment usually does not free employers from the obligation to pay wages, unauthorized employees may find these obligations difficult to enforce. Employee organizations (in France) or employment services (in the United States) may be allowed to act on a worker's behalf. In the United States, the Department of Labor has increasingly been focusing on employer compliance activities in low-wage sectors, where both legal and illegal immigrant workers tend to be concentrated. Undocumented workers do not risk exposure to the immigration service when reporting abuses to the Labor Department (Martin and Miller 2000, 35).

On the one hand, noncooperation agreements make it more risky for employers to offer illegal wage and labor conditions, thus reducing the economic incentives for hiring unauthorized workers who are prone to accept such conditions. On the other, cooperation requirements between control agencies (as in Germany) try to reduce illegal employment by increasing the number of public employees who may detect their illegality. In the Netherlands, the burden of proof was shifted to the employer in 2000. The unauthorized employees can claim back wages for six months unless the employer can prove that the employment was shorter or wages have already been paid.

Current Trends

Toward the end of the period of relatively free labor recruitment in the 1970s, major industrial receiving states began to introduce employer sanctions. Some Western European states introduced and refined employer sanctions without much public debate and opposition (for example, France and Germany); others were reluctant to use these means because of fears over ineffectiveness and discrimination (for example, the United States and the United Kingdom). The International Labour Organization accepted employer sanctions as an integral part of effective migration management but also insisted on minimum rights for migrant workers in irregular situations (Martin and Miller 2000).

Especially in the United States, employer sanctions have been a hotly debated issue over the past twenty-five years. The Immigration Reform and Control Act of 1986 introduced employer sanctions along with an amnesty program and other measures. It was thought that the sanctions would provide a counterbalance to the amnesty and prevent future illegal immigration. The concrete legislative design addressed employers' fears of being unduly burdened with bureaucracy, and Hispanic Americans' fears of being discriminated against as suspected undocumented immigrants. Most important, the act simplified the documentation requirements for determining work eligibility. In the absence of a universal identifying document and standardized data cross-checks, employer sanctions turned out to be largely ineffective—a "paper curtain," as a book on the implementation and impact of U.S. sanctions is entitled (Fix 1991). Studies monitoring the results of the sanctions have concluded that they have had little impact. By the end of the 1990s, employer sanctions were still seen by U.S. government authorities as desirable; however, they were no longer a priority (Martin and Miller 2000, 52).

The situation in the United Kingdom is similar. Britain also lacks a handy proof of citizenship for nationals and functioning electronic registers. Only in 1997 were employer sanctions introduced, and then after a long debate. Since the mid-1980s, European states have increasingly exchanged information and coordinated strategies in order to tighten internal and external migration control. As part of these efforts, employer sanctions were introduced in some states and beefed up in others. France and Germany, for example, have continually increased control personnel and maximum fines and broadened registration duties and data-exchange arrangements. In contrast to the United States and the United Kingdom, in much of Western Europe the presence of unauthorized immigrants in regular employment is not an issue of great concern. In some countries, the effective implementation of employer sanctions has played an important part in reducing the possibility that unauthorized workers will be inadvertantly hired. The body of employer sanctions legislation has grown, with recent measures to include main contractors and other beneficiaries and to detect illegal work-sites disguised as places of legal contract labor. This expansive strategy has not proved politically controversial in Western Europe.

It is difficult to determine the overall effectiveness of employer sanctions. Well-designed external monitoring studies attempting to evaluate the impact of sanctions are lacking. Nonetheless, international comparisons show a convergence in their use among Western states (OECD 2000), and employer sanctions are likely to remain in place or increase as governments search for ways to control migration flows and the labor supply.

Dita Vogel

See also: Clandestine Migration; Migration Policy

References and further reading:

Aleinikoff, Thomas Alexander, David A. Martin, and Hiroshi Motomura. 1998. *Immigration and Citizenship: Process and Policy.* 4th ed. St. Paul, MN: West Group.

Calavita, Kitty. 1990. "Employer Sanctions Violations: Toward a Dialectical Model of White Collar Crime." *Law and Society Review* 24: 1046–1055.

Fix, Michael. 1991. *The Paper Curtain: Employer Sanctions' Implementation, Impact, and Reform.* Washington, DC: Urban Institute.

Martin, Philip L., and Mark Miller. 2000. "Employer Sanctions: French, German and US Experiences." In International Migration Papers. Geneva: International Labour Organization.

Organisation for Economic Co-operation and Development, ed. 2000. *Combatting the Illegal Employment of Foreign Workers.* Paris: OECD.

Robin, Sophie, and Lucile Barros. 2000. "Review and Evaluation of the Measures Implemented in OECD Member States." In *Combatting the Illegal Employment of Foreign Workers.* Edited by Organisation for Economic Co-operation and Development. Paris: OECD.

Vogel, Dita. 2001. "Identifying Unauthorized Foreign Workers in the German Labour Market." Pp. 328–344 in *Documenting Individual Identity: The Development of State Practices in the Modern World.* Edited by J. Caplan and J. Torpey. Princeton, NJ: Princeton University Press.

England

See European Union; United Kingdom

Environmental Refugees

The controversial term "environmental refugee" emerged from the 1970s environmentalist literature. The first clear definition of the term was provided by E. El-Hinnawi, who said environmental refugees were "people who have been forced to leave their traditional habitat, temporarily or permanently, because of a marked environmental disruption (natural and/or triggered by people) that has jeopardized their existence and/or seriously compromised the quality of their life" (El-Hinnawi 1985).

Subsequent definitions have varied but have confirmed the term as part of "environmental orthodoxy." For Norman Myers and J. Kent (1995), environmental refugees are "persons who no longer gain a secure livelihood in their traditional homelands because of what are primarily environmental factors of unusual scope," and for Charles Geisler and Ragndra de Sousa (2000), they are "large numbers of the world's least secure people seeking refuge from insecure biophysical environments." However, elsewhere in social science, the concept has been condemned as poorly defined, legally meaningless, and confusing. It is argued that although environmental degradation and catastrophe may be important factors in decisions to migrate, and issues of concern in their own right, their conceptualization as a primary cause of forced displacement may be unhelpful and intellectually unsound, as well as unnecessary in practical terms.

Both the numbers and different types of "environmental refugees" are a matter for some conjecture. Numerous authors have repeated El-Hinnawi's initial estimate of 10 million environmental refugees in the mid-1980s, although it

Raymond Weyiouanna, arguably the world's first refugee from global warming, walks along the front of Shishmaref Island. He stands on the beach where until recently his house used to stand. A violent early winter storm in 1998 took twenty feet off the island, as the storm hit before the sea ice had the chance to form. Global warming not only threatens Shishmaref Island, a low-lying sandbar in the Chukchi Sea, Alaska, but threatens the Inuits' very way of life, as the animals they depend on move further north as the climate warms. (Ashley Cooper/Picimpact/Corbis)

constituted little more than a wild guess. Over a decade later, Myers (2001) put the total number of environmental refugees up to 25 million, on a par with the global total of persons of concern to UN High Commissioner for Refugees (UNHCR). Part of the difficulty in agreeing on the total number of "environmental refugees" is that authors disagree about who should be included. Thus, while those forced to move by sea-level rises caused by climate change appear in most typologies, there is less agreement about those fleeing industrial disasters, those displaced by dam schemes, and those caught up in "environmental conflict."

At first glance, the data available on environmental refugees appear quite impressive. Evidence from around the world of people being forced to abandon their homes and/or countries in the face of environmental collapse is cited. However, despite the breadth of examples provided in the literature, the strength of the academic case put forward is often depressingly weak. For example, Thomas Homer-Dixon (1994) highlighted the case of 12 to 17 million Bangladeshis displaced by environmental factors to Assam in India, yet even in his own article, a number of other explanations for migration vie with that of environmental degradation, including rules on land inheritance, the system of water management in Bangladesh, the standard of living in India, and the encouragement of migration by some Indian politicians eager to gain votes. Moreover, the estimate of migration comes not from any direct measure but from a comparison of the 1951 and 1991 census figures, adjusted for the population growth rate in 1951, which shows a notional excess population. Yet this increase could be accounted for in a number of ways, with likely candidates including a rise in the population growth rate after 1951, undercounting in 1951, or overcounting in 1991.

Such problems strike to the core of the literature on environmental refugees, and nowhere more so than in the generation of statistics on its prevalence. Gathering data on "environmental refugees" might well be seen as an impossible task given the multiple and overlapping causes of most migration streams and the difficulty of agreeing on a definition of the term itself. Insofar as distinctions between causes can be drawn, "environmental migration" may be divided into three different categories; nevertheless, the evidence that has been put forward for the existence of these phenomena is far from convincing.

A "Myth" Extended: Desertification-Induced Displacement?

Desertification-induced migration epitomizes the "threat" posed to industrialized societies by an army of the poor and starving on the move. As Jodi Jacobson put it: "Desertification . . . has irreparably damaged millions of hectares of once productive land and made refugees out of millions of sub-Saharan African farmers. Migration is the signal that land degradation has reached its sorry end" (1988, 6).

Evidence that desertification causes migration in any straightforward way is limited, however. First, recent scientific work has questioned the notion of "desertification" itself, revealing a fluctuation of the "desert margin" in the Sahel from year to year as rainfall changes. Second, even if people did move in poor rainfall years, it is far from clear that this is the main reason for their flight. As evidence for migration as a result of drought and desertification, proponents of the theory generally point to the existence of migration from regions that are prone to such processes. A causal link to drought is seldom established, and in some cases, proponents fail to demonstrate even the existence of "excess migration," ignoring the fact that within the Sahel and other semiarid regions, there is often a tradition of mobility that extends back over decades or centuries. Such migration has long reflected a household strategy to cope with environmental risks, which, although severe, are not necessarily regarded as worsening. Studies have identified how migration plays a cultural role in the transition to manhood. It is also linked to the generation of sufficient revenue to buy livestock. Factors such as the decline of markets for traditional cash crops (which include gum arabic and cotton), the development of Senegal's groundnut basin, and subsequent mechanization of agriculture in the delta provide additional and more recent motivations to move out of the middle and upper parts of the Senegal River Valley.

Refugees from Rising Seas?

There is perhaps more justification of the notion of environmental migrants (if not "refugees") in the case of more dramatic and permanent changes to the environment associated with catastrophic events such as floods, volcanoes, and earthquakes. Sometimes such natural events involve temporary displacement, as in the case of the Kobe earthquake of 1995, where, according to the *Japan Times,* an initial figure of more than 300,000 displaced residents fell to fewer than 50,000 within three months of the tragedy. Similarly, the floods of March 2000 in central and southern Mozambique saw the forced displacement of up to a million people, but a few months on from this tragedy, most had been able to return to their homes.

More significant, however, in terms of arguments for the existence of "environmental refugees," is the predicted effect of human-induced climate change, and the impact this may have on sea-level rise and increased flooding of low-lying coastal areas, as a cause of environmental migration. The Intergovernmental Panel on Climate Change (IPCC) used the forecast of Norman Myers that 150 million environmental refugees could be produced by 2050 in its calculation of the costs of not responding to climate change (Bruce et al. 1996).

Nonetheless, the question of predicting how many people might be forced to leave their homes as a result of shoreline erosion, coastal flooding, and agricultural disruption linked to climate change is far from straightforward. A number of countries, including Bangladesh, Egypt, China, Vietnam, Thailand, Myanmar, Pakistan, Iraq, Mozambique, Nigeria, Gambia, Senegal, Colombia, Venezuela, British Guyana, Brazil, and Argentina, are threatened by "a moderate degree of sea-level rise" (Myers 1993, 194–195) and have seen flood-related deaths, but it is less clear which specific populations have been forced to *relocate* from flood-prone areas in the recent past as a result of sea-level rises that have already occurred. There are many potential responses to increased flooding, of which migration is only one. Some of the rural-urban migration that has occurred in areas prone to flooding has been to cities that are hardly better placed to withstand the effects of sea-level rise.

In general, calculating the population "at risk" from sea-level rise is a long way from predicting mass flight of a "refugee" nature with its attendant need for international protection and assistance. For example, in a study of response to floods in Bangladesh, C. Emhad Haque and M. Q. Zaman (1993) pointed out that local populations resort to a range of adaptive responses, including forecasting, the use of warning systems, flood insurance, and relief and rehabilitation efforts. Interestingly, they noted that "in contrast to the English meaning of 'flood' as a destructive phenomenon, its usage in Bengali refers to it as both a positive and a negative resource" (Haque and Zaman 1993, 102). In Bangladesh, and in many other flood-prone deltas, land is constantly being eroded, but it is also constantly being deposited, often in fertile sediments that are highly attractive to farmers.

Environmental Conflict and Refugee Movements

In addition to the direct links between deteriorating environmental circumstances and induced migration, a further postulated cause of "environmental refugees," and a link back to the literature on "political refugees," is the notion that environmental degradation is increasingly at the root of conflicts that feed back into refugee movements. A review of conflicts that have caused large-scale forced migration during the 1990s, however, provides little evidence for the existence of environmental "hotspots" that have developed into war. Instead, many of the recent wars that have led to forced displacement could be better described as conflicts over abundant resources. Thus, the Gulf War of 1991 occurred as a result of one oil-rich nation seeking to control its oil-rich neighbor, and wars in Sudan, Angola, Liberia, and Sierra Leone are (at least in part) about struggles over oil and diamonds.

Environmental Explanations of Migration: Whose Agenda?

An examination of statistics on "environmental refugees," and of the detailed case studies in which this category of forced migrant is supposed to be prominent, does not produce a persuasive case in favor of "environmental refugees" as a pressing policy problem or new area of academic study. Yet the list of international organizations that have stressed concern about "environmental refugees" remains impressive. Organizations from the International Organization for Migration (IOM) to the United Nations Environment Programme (UNEP) and the Intergovernmental Panel on Climate Change (IPCC) have shown an interest in the concept, sponsoring a wide range of reports and initiatives. Lester Brown and Norman Myers, in particular, have been prominent in popularizing the term amongst dignitaries ranging from former president Bill Clinton to former UN secretary general Boutros Boutros-Ghali (Kibreab 1997; Saunders 2000). As Gaim Kibreab has pointed out, "prominent international personalities are irrelevant in determining the explanatory or predictive value of a term" (1997, 21)—but they are important in allowing it to gain currency.

Why, then, has the term "environmental refugee" been so seductive? For Kibreab, the answer lies in the agenda of policy makers in the North, who wish to further restrict asylum laws and procedures: Thus the term was "invented at least in part to depoliticize the causes of displacement, so enabling states to derogate their obligation to provide asylum." Since current international law does not require states to provide asylum to those displaced by environmental degradation, argued Kibreab, the notion that many or even most migrants leaving Africa for Europe, or leaving Central America for the United States, are forced to move by environmental factors allows governments to exclude a significant number from asylum. Academics, in turn, have been complicit in this process by endorsing the term.

However, the notion that "environmental refugees" have been talked up by northern governments seeking to restrict asylum sits somewhat uneasily with the fact that much of the literature on "environmental refugees" has in practice argued for an *extension* of asylum law and/or humanitarian assistance to cover those forcibly displaced by environmental degradation, rather than endorsing a differentiation between "political" and "environmental" causes as a matter of policy. Even if the practical impact of literature on "environmental refugees" has been to endorse northern states' moves to restrict the definition of asylum still further, this does not appear to have been the conscious intention of many of those writing on the subject.

An alternative view sees the term "environmental refugee" as having its origins primarily in the environmental literature. For example, Norman Myers comes not from a background in migration or refugees or asylum, but from the science of ecology; the principal concern of his writing is not migration, but the imminent threat of environmental catastrophe surrounding climate change, deforestation, and desertification (Myers 1993). More important still in pushing the notion of "environmental refugees" to center stage have been writers in the field of conflict studies. Thus, a major project sponsored by the American Academy of Arts and Sciences and led by Thomas Homer-Dixon has argued both that environmental scarcity causes large population movement, which in turn causes group-identity conflict, and that environmental scarcity causes economic deprivation and disrupts social institutions, leading to "deprivation" conflicts. Such a view has found a ready audience amongst policy makers influenced by writers such as Robert Kaplan, and his notion of a "coming anarchy."

Richard Black

See also: Asylum

References and further reading:

Black, Richard. 1999. *Refugees, Environment and Development.* Harlow, UK: Longman.

Bruce, J. P., H. Lee, and E. F. Haites. 1996. *Climate Change 1995: Economic and Social Dimensions of Climate Change.* Contribution of Working Group III to the Second Assessment Report of the Intergovernmental Panel on Climate Change. Cambridge: Cambridge University Press.

El-Hinnawi, E. 1985. *Environmental Refugees.* Nairobi: UN Environment Programme.

Geisler, Charles, and Ragndra de Sousa. 2000. *From Refuge to Refugee: The African Case.* Working paper 38. Madison: Land Tenure Center, University of Wisconsin at Madison.

Haque, C. Emhad, and M. Q. Zaman. 1993. "Human Response to Riverine Hazards in Bangladesh: A Proposal for Sustainable Floodplain Development." *World Development* 21, no. 1: 93–108.

Homer-Dixon, Thomas. 1994. "Environmental Scarcities and Violent Conflict: Evidence from Cases." *International Security* 19, no. 1: 5–40.

Jacobson, Jodi. 1988. *Environmental Refugees: A Yardstick of Habitability.* World Watch Paper 86. Washington, DC: World Watch Institute.

Kibreab, Gaim. 1997. "Environmental Causes and Impact of Refugee Movements: A Critique of the Current Debate." *Disasters* 21, no. 1: 20–38.

Myers, Norman. 1993. *Ultimate Security: The Environmental Basis of Political Stability.* New York and London: W. W. Norton.

———. 2001. "Environmental Refugees: A Growing Phenomenon of the 21st Century." *Philosophical Transactions of the Royal Society of London B.*

Myers, Norman, and J. Kent. 1995. *Environmental Exodus: An Emergent Crisis in the Global Arena.* Washington, DC: The Climate Institute.

Saunders, Patricia L. 2000. "Environmental Refugees: The Origins of a Construct." Pp. 218–246 in *Political Ecology: Science, Myth and Power.* Edited by Philip Stott and Sian Sullivan. London: Arnold; New York: Oxford University Press.

Eritrea and Refugees

Located on an important sea route between Europe and Asia, Eritrea has often been occupied by foreign invaders. Parts of the Eritrean plateau formed the core of the Axumite civilization. After the decline of Axum, Beja kingdoms emerged and ruled Eritrea until the end of the thirteenth century. The Turks occupied Massawa in 1557 and continued their rule in the coastal area (in the vicinity of Massawa) until 1865, when the Egyptians took over. With British support, Egypt secured transfer of all Turkish possessions in Eritrea through a treaty in 1875 (Habte Selassie 1980). In 1890 all the territories that constitute present-day Eritrea were occupied and placed under Italian colonial rule.

Italy was defeated in the beginning of World War II (1941) by the Allied Forces and was replaced by a British Military Administration that lasted for ten years. When the Four Powers failed to agree on a new status for Eritrea after the war, the case was brought before the United Nations. Contrary to the expressed wishes of the majority of the Eritrean people, the British government proposed to dismember Eritrea and its people along ethno-religious lines (Kibreab 2001). Following protracted negotiations, the foreign ministers of Great Britain and Italy reached an agreement known as the Bevin-Sforza Compromise, which would have divided Eritrea between Ethiopia and Sudan. The former was a trusted ally of Britain and the United States, and the latter was under the Anglo-Egyptian Sudan.

The British proposal was vehemently opposed by the Eritreans, who in a single voice argued that their national identity was territorial rather than ethno-religious. Though the Bevin-Sforza Compromise was rejected owing to the opposition of numerous Eritrean political movements, the Eritreans' demands for independence fell on deaf ears. In 1952, the United Nations established a federal arrangement between Eritrea and Ethiopia under the sovereignty of Emperor Haile Selassie. Eritrea was annexed by the latter in 1962, and herein lay the root cause of the mass production of refugees in the country.

Causes of Refugee Production

In poor countries such as Eritrea, the interplay of political, economic, social, military, and environmental factors produces refugees and internally displaced persons (IDPs). These factors are often so inextricably interwoven that it is difficult to isolate one from the other and to determine the importance of each factor in the process. In an arid or semi-arid environment, population movements have always been part of the majority of the people's way of life. People move from place to place to maximize safety or to take advantage of environmental variations. It has also been common for people to move in pursuit of trade and other economic interests. The multidimensional nature of involuntary displacement has thus been integral to refugee production in Eritrea throughout its history.

Involuntary Displacement under Ethiopian Occupation

Contrary to the assumptions and principles underlying the federal arrangement, Ethiopia from the beginning of the federal arrangement paved the way for annexing Eritrea into its empire by undermining all the structures and institutions representing Eritrean cultural and political identity. As the aims of the Ethiopian government became clear, Eritrean nationalist leaders such as Ibrahim Sultan and Wolde Ab Woldemariam strongly opposed the policies of annexation and called for immediate independence. The Ethiopian government adopted draconian methods to silence the voice of Eritrean nationalism by imprisoning, deporting, and harassing nationalist and trade union leaders (Killion 1997). In 1961, the peaceful resistance culminated in organized armed resistance led by the Eritrean Liberation Front (ELF). In 1962, Ethiopia, through machinations and intimidation of the Eritrean parliament, annexed Eritrea, and the latter became one of its fourteen provinces.

Given their thirst for independence, the Eritrean people quickly embraced the ELF, particularly in the Western Lowlands where the organization was first established. In order to nip the armed struggle in the bud, Ethiopia launched a pacification campaign that in most cases targeted the civilian population in the affected areas. To those Eritreans who were directly or indirectly affected by Ethiopian persecution and campaigns of pacification, flight to safety became the only means of escaping Ethiopian violence. Though mass population displacement began in the second half of the 1960s,

Newly arrived refugees from Eritrea sit together in a tent in Wad Sheriffe refugee camp in Sudan near the border crossing at Laffa. (Peter Turnley/Corbis)

there were many individuals who fled the country from as early as 1953–1954, that is, immediately after the federal arrangement was put in place in 1952. The cause of displacement then was the steady erosion of Eritrea's federal status and violence perpetrated by Ethiopian security forces. For example, in 1963 there were about 3,000 Eritrean nationalists in prison throughout the country, "under suspicion of helping or sympathising with the guerrillas" (Pool 1982, 46).

Even though the period between the birth of the ELF (September 1961) and the country's de facto independence (May 1991) was marked throughout by continuous production of refugees and IDPs, it is possible to identify eight discernible periods in which the largest number of refugees fled the country. It is also possible to trace these movements to triggering events that occurred in different parts of Eritrea.

1. The first large-scale involuntary displacement took place when the Ethiopian army launched its counterinsurgency and pacification campaign in February–March 1967 in the Western Lowlands, resulting in the destruction of lives and property and the flight of nearly 30,000 pastoralists and agro-pastoralists, as well some sedentary farmers.
2. The second major displacement occurred in 1969 when the Eastern Lowlands were subjected to infantry and air raids. Many people died, and villages were burned, causing massive internal displacement. With the escalation of the war, most of the displaced people crossed the Sudanese border in search of international protection (Kibreab 1987).
3. The third large-scale displacement took place in 1970 following the massacre of 460 civilians, including women and children, in the vicinity of Keren in a village called Ouna (Knutsson 1971). Another ten villages were also burned down in the vicinity of Ouna and thousands of people lost their livelihoods (Knutsson 1971). The survivors were left with no alternative but to flee in search of international protection.
4. The fourth and largest involuntary displacement occurred in 1974–1975 when the Provisional Military Council, the Derg, deposed Emperor Haile Selassie. The Derg unleashed an unprecedented degree of violence, and the number of people fleeing the country increased dramatically. In December 1974, dozens of bodies of civilians were found strangled with piano wires in Asmara. At the

beginning of 1975, "over 1,600 people had been killed and thousands more wounded, while Eritrean community and religious leaders continued to accuse government troops of committing acts of atrocity and terror against civilians. Some 16,000 refugees were accommodated in camps set up by church workers" (Keesing 1975). At the end of 1974, a state of emergency was declared covering the capital, Asmara, and its vicinity, and this was extended to the whole country on February 15, 1975 (Kibreab 1987). These acts of terror wreaked havoc, and tens of thousands of Eritreans fled the country to seek asylum, mainly in Sudan.

5. The fifth group fled Eritrea in 1978 when the Eritrean liberation movements suffered a setback as a result of direct military involvement by the Soviet Union. By 1977, the Eritrean People's Liberation Front (EPLF) and the ELF were in control of all Eritrean rural and urban areas save the cities of Asmara, Assab, Barentu, and parts of Massawa. In 1978, the Ethiopian troops, fully backed by Soviet troops, launched a massive counteroffensive, and by July and August, they had recaptured most of the towns under the control of the rebel fronts, with the exception of Nakfa. Widespread repression, arrests, and summary executions followed (Dines 1988). These atrocities and counteroffensives caused the displacement of a large number of people. Some of these fled to Sudan in search of international protection.
6. The sixth wave of displacement occurred as a result of the civil war waged between the EPLF and the ELF in 1981 and the consequent retreat of the latter to Sudan. In the immediate aftermath of the civil war, some of the ELF forces, such as the Sagem, joined ranks with the EPLF, but others regrouped on the Sudanese side of the border. The latter eventually joined the Eritrean refugees in Sudan and elsewhere.
7. The seventh wave of mass displacement occurred in 1983–1985 owing to a combination of famine and war that devastated most of the Eritrean rural and semiurban areas (Duffield and Prendergast 1994). During this period, about 827,000 Eritreans were affected by drought in Ethiopian-controlled areas. In the liberated and semiliberated areas, the total numbers of villages and people affected by drought during 1983–1985 were 1,505 and 1,189,000, respectively (ERA 1983). Drought, in combination with insecurity, looting, and destruction of animals, engendered an acute crisis of livelihood, resulting in massive internal and external displacement.
8. The eighth group was displaced in 1988 when the combined effects of war and drought again forced thousands of people to abandon their homes in search of safe haven and help in Sudan (Bondestam et al. 1988).

Along with these eight major periods of large-scale involuntary displacement, there was also a continuous trickle throughout the entire period of integration with Ethiopia.

Involuntary Displacement in the Postindependence Period

The protracted war came to an end in May 1991 when the Ethiopian forces of occupation suffered a defeat at the hands of the EPLF. It was hoped that the end of the war and the country's independence would bring a permanent end to the factors producing refugees and IDPs in the country. As history is rarely made to order, the Eritrean state, like its predecessors, has not been immune from adopting policies that, on the one hand, produce refugees, and on the other, discourage those in exile from returning.

Following the ELF's military drawback during the internecine war between the two fronts in 1981, most of its fighters and some of its sympathizers felt alienated from the struggle. Most Eritreans hoped that a government of national unity would be formed in the immediate postindependence period. Contrary to expectations, the EPLF opted for a "winner receives all" policy which discouraged many politically motivated exiles from returning. Though about 265,000 Eritrean refugees have returned from Sudan (190,000 self-repatriates and about 52,000 displaced due to a border war against Ethiopia), there are still more than 100,000 Eritrean refugees in Sudan as of 2004. Though their hesitation to repatriate may have been influenced by livelihood considerations, some refugees have no doubt been influenced by opposition groups in exile. The Eritrean government's violations of basic human rights of individuals who try to bring about democratic change has caused generalized fear throughout the country. However, during the three years of fieldwork (1997–2000) in the areas of return, I did not come across any evidence of returnees being detained upon arrival or thereafter. Sometimes perceptions are more important than facts, and the government's failure to observe international human rights standards is one factor that has contributed to the decision of some refugees not to return.

Though the number of Eritreans fleeing persecution perpetrated by the independent state has been insignificant, the government's open-end policy of national service is forcing many to flee the country. Initially, nationals between the ages of eighteen and forty were required to perform eighteen months of national service—six months military training and the rest in civic work. Three years after the program was launched in May 1998, the border war with Ethiopia broke out. Those who had completed their obligation were recalled to fight, and those who joined the program later were not demobilized. More than three years after the two countries signed a peace agreement, there had not been any demobilization in Eritrea. In December 2002, the government announced that it would demobilize women who had completed their obligation (nothing was said about the men in the service). However, even the demobilization of women has not yet been implemented. Some of those in military service have been away from home since 1994, and the burden of their open-ended obligation to the state has led some to flee in order to free themselves or avoid a similar fate. The government's crackdown on reformers and journalists, and its altogether cavalier attitude toward the rule of law and international human rights standards, has also created a generalized sense of insecurity throughout most of the country. Some individuals see flight as the only viable option.

The border war, particularly Ethiopia's temporary occupation of sovereign Eritrean territories, also caused the internal displacement of more than a million Eritreans and more than 50,000 refugees. Most of the IDPs have by now returned to their places of origin, but there are many who are still living in makeshift camps. The large majority of those who fled to Sudan, with the exception of a few thousand, has also returned voluntarily, with assistance from the UN High Commissioner for Refugees.

Gaim Kibreab

See also: Asylum; Civil Wars and Migration; Colonial Immigration; Economic Determinants of International Migration; Internally Displaced Persons; Refugee Camps; Refugees; Return Migration; Sudan and Refugees

References and further reading:

Bondestam, Lars, Lionel Cliffe, and Philip White. 1988. *An Independent Evaluation of the Food Situation in Eritrea Submitted to the Emergency Relief Desk: Eritrea Food and Agricultural Assessment Study.* Final Report. Leeds: University of Leeds, Centre of Development Studies.

Dines, Mary. 1988. "Ethiopian Violations of Human Rights in Eritrea." Pp. 139–162 in *The Long Struggle of Eritrea for Independence and Constructive Peace.* Edited by Lionel Cliffe and Basil Davidson. Nottingham: Spokesman.

Duffield, Mark, and John Prendergast. 1994. *Without Troops and Tanks: Humanitarian Intervention in Ethiopia and Eritrea.* Lawrenceville: The Red Sea Press.

Eritrean Relief Association. 1983. *Eritrea Drought Report.* Eritrea: ERA.

Habte Selassie, Bereket. 1980. "From British Rule to Federation and Annexation." In *Behind the War in Eritrea.* Edited by Basil Davidson, Lionel Cliffe, and Bereket Habte Selassie. Nottingham: Spokesman.

Keesing Contemporary Archives, 27031 (March 24–30, 1975).

Kibreab, Gaim. 1987. *Refugees and Development: The Case of Eritrea.* Trenton, NJ: Red Sea Press.

———. 2001. *British Strategic Interests: The Politics of Ethno-Religion and the Disposal of Eritrea.* Paper prepared for the International Conference on Eritrean Studies, Asmara, July.

Killion, Tom. 1997. "Eritrean Workers' Organisation and Early Nationalist Mobilization." *Eritrean Studies Review* 2, no. 1 (Spring): 1–58.

Knutsson, Karl Eric. 1971. "Problemet Eritrea." *Dagens Nyheter.* Stockholm, February 6.

Pool, David. 1982. "Eritrea: Africa's Longest War." Anti-Slavery Society Human Rights Series Report No. 3 (revised). Bradenton, FL: Anti-Slavery Society.

Public Record Office (PRO) Archives, General Secretaries, Asmara, July 25, 1949, FO 371/73846. London.

Ethnic Cleansing

Ethnic cleansing is the forced migration of an ethnic or racial group with the intent to remove the group in whole or substantial part from a given territory. Often accomplished with significant violence or threat of violence, ethnic cleansing can shade into genocide when the instigators' intent is to destroy, and not just remove, a targeted ethnic or racial group. The hallmarks of ethnic cleansing include door-to-door roundups, forced marches, concentration camps, and terror induced by rape, murder, and other violence. Expulsion is often accompanied by the destruction of cultural monuments and other signs of the cleansed group's former presence. Perpetrators in ethnic cleansing range from armies to paramilitaries to local vigilantes, all usually inspired by orders and/or vitriolic rhetoric from political leaders.

The term "ethnic cleansing" (*etnièko èišœenje* in Serbo-Croatian) dates only to the 1980s, when Serbs chose this formulation to describe perceived persecution at the hands of majority ethnic Albanians in the Yugoslav province of Kosovo. It subsequently reached widespread circulation in 1992 in reference to Serb and Croat efforts to drive Muslims and each other from disputed regions of multiethnic Bosnia-Herzegovina. In spite of the recent coinage, the concept of ethnic cleansing in its modern form dates to the first decades of the twentieth century, when Balkan countries fought to build ethnically pure national states, expelling millions in the process. The term "cleansing" (*Säuberung*) can be found in Nazi rhetoric of the 1930s and 1940s referring both to internal purges of "non-Aryan racial stock" and to the clearing of "living space" (*Lebensraum*) for Germans in the East. In the wake of the Nazi defeat in 1945, Czechs and Poles often referred to their expulsion of millions of ethnic Germans as "cleansing" (*očistění, oczyszczanie*). Though still lacking the "ethnic" adjective, all of these examples involved the forced removal of ethnic or racial groups as such.

Ethnic cleansing can be broken into at least three types of forced migration. The first, often dubbed "population exchange" or "transfer," is the least violent, involving the more or less organized removal of an ethnic or racial group from one country to another. Population exchanges are often internationally sanctioned and supervised. Though inevitably accompanied by hardship, such exchanges generally do not involve murder or extreme violence. The second, more common and more violent form of ethnic cleansing is expulsion, a unilateral effort to remove a group from a region by force and intimidation. Expulsions almost always include massacres and violence intended to inspire or hasten the departure of a targeted group. The third and most extreme type of ethnic cleansing is genocidal cleansing, where tactics typical of cleansing campaigns are used with the aim of exterminating, not simply removing, a target population. It should be noted that most cases of genocide do not fall into this category, but that a few, such as the mass murder of Armenians in 1915, deserve such a hybrid appellation.

History of Ethnic Cleansing

Though some scholars have posited occurrences of ethnic cleansing dating to biblical times, premodern cases involved groups defined by religion or political loyalties, not ethnicity per se. Ethnic cleansing is a modern phenomenon aimed at constructing a nation-state unencumbered by the political and economic aspirations of self-aware minorities. The idea of a state representing a single ethnic group emerged only in the late eighteenth century, with the birth of nationalism at the crux of the Enlightenment and Romanticism. With the spread of modernity across late nineteenth-century Europe—industrialization, mass education, and widespread political participation—many politicians realized the political efficacy of what became known as "integral nationalism," defining linguistic or religious minorities as alien, existing outside of the nation. Often, too, the tools of ethnic cleansing have been modern, including machine guns, railroads, barbed wire, bulldozers, and bureaucracies. Thus the modern state and the modern nation emerged in tandem with modern technology, generating a dangerous brew amidst the ethnic diversity of Europe's great multinational empires: Austria-Hungary, Russia, and Ottoman Turkey. All three of these colossi were in decline in the late nineteenth century, with Ottoman decay the most advanced.

Struggle for the Ottoman Succession

Amidst the death throes of the sultan's empire and the birth pangs of new national states struggling to replace Ottoman sovereignty in Southeast Europe, ethnic cleansing made its first appearance during the Balkan Wars of 1912–1913. Serbian, Bulgarian, and Greek armies fought the Turks and each other, driving hundreds of thousands of Muslim (considered Turkish) refugees out of Europe. These struggles continued into the mid-1920s, during which time close to 2 million Orthodox Greeks and Muslim Turks were forced from their homes in actions calculated to remove the respective minority from conquered territory. In the first major case of negotiated population transfer, the Greek and Turkish governments agreed in the 1923 Treaty of Lausanne to finalize the preceding expulsions and exchange remaining minorities. Brokered and monitored by the League of Nations, the Greco-Turkish exchange became a precedent for subsequent "transfers" of population in the 1930s and 1940s.

In the vast Eastern theater of World War I, refugees numbered in the millions, taking flight from warfare, military evacuations, famine, and marauding soldiers. But the Armenians were refugees of a different kind. In the midst of remaking itself as a Turkish national state, the shrunken Ottoman Empire increasingly viewed its non-Muslim populations as subversive and inimical to the state's survival. Capitalizing in 1915 on reports of Armenian cooperation with enemy Russia, the government began the massive deportation of Armenians across Anatolia to the deserts beyond the Euphrates River. The terror, forced marches, overloaded boxcars, rapes, and murders were hallmarks of ethnic cleansing, but the intent of the Turkish leadership was extermination, not simply removal, of the Armenian population. Though a few hundred thousand Armenians survived the deportations, close to 800,000 died in conditions calculated to kill as many refugees as possible.

World War II and Aftermath

Just under twenty-five years later, as Adolf Hitler prepared to destroy Poland in 1939, he announced to his generals a policy of "physical destruction of the enemy." After all, he mused, who "speaks today about the annihilation of the Armenians?" (quoted in Naimark 2001, 57). Hitler took a number of lessons from the forced migrations of the preceding three decades. First, minorities could and should be moved to create homogeneous nation-states. Second, under the right conditions, such as the cover of war, the international community would summon neither the will nor the means for preventing cleansing and even extermination of minorities. Hitler's war launched a massive ethnic reorganization of Central and Eastern Europe, as the Nazis relocated millions of Poles, Ukrainians, and Jews to the east (and to the *Reich* as slave labor) and moved several hundred thousand ethnic Germans (the *Volksdeutsche*) westward to take their place. Until late 1941, these forced migrations can be classified as ethnic cleansing, though with Hitler's invasion of the Soviet Union in June 1941, special detachments of the Nazi SS, known as the *Einsatzgruppen,* undertook genocidal sweeps in newly captured eastern territories. Over the next twenty-four months, the Einsatzgruppen killed more than 2 million Soviet citizens, most of whom were Jews. By late 1941, the systematic murder of all European Jews was well under way.

Stalin, too, practiced ethnic cleansing during the war. In the 1930s, Stalinist social engineering had led to the deportation of millions of class enemies to Siberia, accompanied by the intentional famine deaths of millions more due to forced collectivization. Until 1937, the deportations had a class more than an ethnic character, though some ethnic groups, such as the Ukrainians, bore a disproportionate amount of the violence. After 1937, Stalin began large-scale deportations of ethnic groups considered unreliable, including Finns, Koreans, Chinese, Poles, and ethnic Germans. In 1944, the Soviet NKVD deported close to 500,000 Chechens and Ingush from the militarily vulnerable Caucasus to more isolated Central Asia. More than 10,000 died in transit via sealed boxcars, but arrival proved even more deadly. Over the next three years, as many as 100,000 of the settlers died in the harsh conditions of Kazakhstan and Kirghizia (Naimark 2001, 97). Only through the generosity of Nikita Khrushchev were the expellees allowed to return home to the Caucasus in 1957, a rare case of reversal in the annals of ethnic cleansing.

As World War II came to a close in early 1945, the advancing Red Army and newly liberated Czechs and Poles turned on ethnic Germans in their reconstituted states. Until the Potsdam Conference settled the fate of East European Germans in August 1945, retributive violence and sporadic expulsions took the lives of tens of thousands and displaced several million Germans. Millions more fled East Prussia as the Red Army approached, often making their escapes in overcrowded boats or across treacherous ice. When the war ended, the Allied powers agreed to move Polish borders from 100 to 150 kilometers to the west, at the expense of occupied Germany. The Soviet Union kept much of East Prussia and Poland's former eastern territories (the *kresy*). The new borders were accompanied by an agreement at Potsdam to "transfer" the remaining German population from Polish territory to occupied Germany. In all, at least 3.5 million Germans fled the Red Army, close to a million were forced across the border of Poland in the months leading up to Potsdam, and 2 million left during the "organized," internationally sanctioned transfer in 1946 and 1947. Tens and perhaps hundreds of thousands of Germans died during flight and expulsion from Poland, though sources differ wildly on the exact number of deaths.

Expulsions followed a similar pattern in Czechoslovakia, with paramilitaries, army detachments, and vigilantes terrorizing Germans and driving close to a million across the border to Germany in the summer of 1945. The Potsdam agreement called for the "organized transfer" of the remaining 2 million Sudeten Germans, who left on regularized transports throughout 1946. A 1996 report by a Czech and German historians' commission estimated the number of deaths at between 18,000 and 30,000.

The expulsions from Czechoslovakia and Poland had profound political, economic, and cultural effects on both those countries and on the destination zones of East and West Germany. The departure countries faced large labor shortages for a number of years following the war, as German farmers, miners, and factory workers vacated vast industrial and agricultural regions. Poland made up some of the labor shortfall, with an influx of close to 2 million ethnic Poles expelled from Lwów/L'viv and other eastern cities recently annexed to the Soviet Union. Both countries found settlers from their interior lands glad to exchange life in war-damaged and overcrowded cities or backwards agricultural regions for the productive soil and empty German homes and businesses in the borderlands. Around 2 million Czechs and Slovaks settled in the Sudetenland, and 3.5 million Poles poured into the formerly German western regions known as the "recovered territories." In both countries, new settlers came from diverse regional, religious, and socioeconomic backgrounds; torn loose from their traditional community networks, settlers were susceptible to organizational efforts of highly focused Communist parties. Moreover, Communists astutely grabbed the ministries responsible for redistributing German property, using this power to reward supporters and cement their popularity in the borderlands. The Communists won close to 60 percent of the vote in the former Sudetenland in Czechoslovak elections in 1946. In Poland, too, Communist organization was strongest in the "recovered territories."

In the longer term, the expulsions poisoned relations with the countries' German neighbors, as well as increased dependency on the Soviet Union, seen as a guarantor of the expulsions and of Poland's new borders. Both German states at first had difficulty digesting the 12 million refugees from Poland, Czechoslovakia, and other Eastern countries. Arriving destitute, speaking strange dialects, and traumatized by their migrations, the expellees were often scorned by native residents and initially lacked work, housing, and dignity. Though West Germany substantially improved expellee living standards by the early 1950s, Sudeten expellees remained a bitter and influential political pressure group into the early twenty-first century, when they tried to block the entry of the post-Communist Czech Republic into the European Union. German expellees from Poland have been more conciliatory, and few have sought compensation or restitution from the Polish government.

Africa and Asia

Though the term "ethnic cleansing" has typically referred to expulsions in Europe, its definition applies equally well to cases of forced migration in Africa and Asia. As in Europe, ethnic cleansing in the developing world has been intimately tied to nation- and state-building efforts. In all the cases examined below, nation-states were either emerging or recently formed, usually in the void left by retreating colonial empires. As in Yugoslavia and Greece/Turkey, religious differences were often the central identifiers of otherness, with elites grafting modern national ideologies onto ancient religious cleavages.

With British imperial rule dissolving in India in the 1930s, Muslims in the majority Hindu Raj increasingly distrusted the leadership of the independence-oriented Congress Party. Led by Muhammed Ali Jinnah, the Muslim League demanded the partition of India into two states, India and Pakistan. In August 1947, Britain granted independence to India and recognized the new state of Pakistan, which comprised the Muslim-dominated regions of eastern and western India. Upon the creation of India and Pakistan, the former colony exploded into violence, with 5 million Muslim refugees flowing to Pakistan and 3.5 million Hindus and Sikhs fleeing to India. Although much of this migration was voluntary, if haphazard, hundreds of thousands of the refugees fled communal violence aimed to provoke flight, thus qualifying as ethnic cleansing. As many as 500,000 Muslims and Hindus died during the violence and exodus of 1947.

British Palestine, too, inched toward independence after World War II, sparking a war between the emerging Jewish state of Israel and its Arab neighbors in 1948. Forged largely of settlers inspired by Theodor Herzl's Zionist dream of a Jewish state in the Holy Land, Israel's partisans used terror and conventional warfare to drive Arabs from the Palestinian Mandate. Jewish paramilitary groups, Irgun and Hagannah, used intimidation, destruction of homes, spreading of rumors of cholera, and murder to encourage Arabs to flee regions around Jaffa, Haifa, and Jerusalem. The most extreme of Irgun's acts of intimidation was the Deir Yassin massacre on April 9, 1948, where a paramilitary force commanded by Menachem Begin murdered 240 civilians. Accompanied by rapes and other public violence, the massacre was explicitly meant as a warning to Arabs around Jerusalem who would not leave Jewish-controlled areas (Bickerton and Klausner 1995, 98). By 1949, more than 700,000 Arabs had fled or been driven out of Israeli-controlled regions of Palestine, creating the refugee problem that still plagues Israeli-Palestinian relations in the twenty-first century.

Other than the return of ethnic cleansing to southeastern Europe in the 1990s, the locus of ethnic cleansing in the second half of the twentieth century moved to Africa, where postcolonial rulers have often exploited ethnic or religious diversity to consolidate their power. Since taking control in a 1989 coup, the Islamic military government of Sudan has undertaken or encouraged the ethnic cleansing of several million non-Muslims (and some non-Arabic Muslims) during that country's ongoing civil war. In the largely Muslim north, the government has bulldozed shantytowns containing several hundred thousand Christians on the outskirts of Khartoum. Sent to euphemistically labeled "peace villages" well away from the capital, refugees faced starvation in these dismal and neglected camps. In central and southern Sudan, the government has encouraged different ethnic and religious groups to turn on each other, thus weakening support for southern separatist groups. Regional paramilitaries terrorize the south, driving members of the Dinka ethnic group from their homes and often preventing the delivery of humanitarian food aid.

Yugoslavia

Among the most recent cases of ethnic cleansing was Yugoslavia, a multinational state that shattered along ethnic lines as Communist authoritarianism lost its hold over the country in the 1990s. Known for its dramatic mountains, sunny Adriatic coastline, and diverse population, Communist Yugoslavia was long a popular vacation destination for Europeans. Sarajevo, a city of mosques and Orthodox and Catholic churches, proudly hosted the 1984 winter Olympics. Eight years later, the Olympic stadium lay in ruins, Sarajevo under siege, as ethnic war ravaged Bosnia-Herzegovina. It was there, in the southeast of Europe, that ethnic cleansing came into the international spotlight.

The Kingdom of Serbs, Croats, and Slovenes (renamed Yugoslavia in 1929) began as a grand experiment in ethnic federalism following World War I. Uniting Orthodox Serbs with Catholic Croats and Slovenes and Muslim Slavs, the new kingdom struggled from the beginning to reconcile the varied interests and expectations of its peoples. Serbs, with a tradition of modern statehood and a plurality of the new state's population, expected to lead Yugoslavia, with some considering the country simply a "greater Serbia" with religious diversity. Croats and Slovenes, however, resented Serb domination of their more developed economies and pluralist political cultures. When the Nazis invaded Yugoslavia in 1941, political conflicts turned violent, with Croatian fascists massacring hundreds of thousands of Serbs and guerrilla bands attacking both Nazis and each other. Led by the half-Slovene, half-Croat Josip Broz Tito, Communist partisans built a multiethnic guerrilla army that plagued the German occupiers and reestablished multinational Yugoslavia in the waning days of the war. Tito quickly assumed dictatorial powers and declared a government of "brotherhood and unity," a sign that ethnic conflict would not be tolerated in Communist Yugoslavia.

Emulating a successful Soviet strategy, Tito instituted a nominal federalism with tightly centralized Communist political control. Croats and Slovenes were given their own national republics, led, however, by a Communist apparatus appointed by Tito from Belgrade. After Tito died in 1981, centralized political control began slowly to unravel. By the late 1980s, communism was in rapid retreat in much of Eastern Europe, and Yugoslavia was no exception. Looking for new sources of legitimacy, the rising Communist star Slobodan Milošević turned to populist Serbian nationalism. Fearing the reimposition of interwar Serbian dominance, Slovenia and Croatia declared independence from Yugoslavia in 1991. In an attempt to prevent secession (and the loss of several hundred thousand ethnic Serbs in Croatia), Milošević went to war against the breakaway republics. The multiethnic republic of Bosnia-Herzegovina declared its own independence in 1992, setting off a three-sided war among the republic's three main ethnic groups, Serbs, Croats, and Bosnian Muslims, with the added participation of soldiers from Croatia and Serb-dominated rump Yugoslavia.

The war in Bosnia became a battle over ethnic territory, with Serbs and Croats driving Muslims out of areas claimed for envisioned greater Serbian and Croatian states. Serb paramilitaries, including those under the notorious "Arkan" (Zeljko Raznatovic), terrorized Muslim noncombatants with systematic rape, torture, and murder, forcing hundreds of thousands to flee their homes. In a calculated strategy of dehumanization, Serb forces raped between 20,000 and 40,000 Muslim women, sometimes expressing a desire to implant Serbs in Muslim wombs. This was an absurd racialization of religious differences, as Orthodox Serbs, Catholic Croatians, and Bosnian Muslims all descended from the same Slavic tribes and spoke the same language. Bosnian Serbs also established Europe's first concentration camps in almost half a century, isolating several thousand Muslim men in makeshift detention centers. Some of these, most notably Omarska, turned into death camps, with starvation, murderous beatings, and systematic executions used to liquidate Muslim inmates. At least some of the cleansing campaigns became genocidal, such as the mass murder of up to 8,000 Muslims at Srebrenica in 1995.

Serbs and Croats not only cleansed regions of Bosnia of Muslim inhabitants; they also tried to cleanse the landscape of Muslim culture, dynamiting mosques, libraries, graveyards, and municipal records and institutions. By trying to erase all record of Muslim existence in Bosnia, Serbs and Croats sought to make return undesirable, if not impossible. Even after the 1995 Dayton Accords ended the conflict in Bosnia and guaranteed safe return to refugees, few expelled Muslims went back to their destroyed homes and towns.

With hopes for a greater Serbia smashed by the internationally enforced peace in Bosnia and Croatia, Slobodan Milošević turned his populist nationalism against a minority within Serbia, the Albanians of the Kosovo autonomous region. Central to Serbian nationalist mythology, Kosovo was nonetheless almost 90 percent ethnic Albanian by the 1980s. Milošević had begun his transformation from Communist to nationalist by decrying Albanian mistreatment of Kosovo's small Serb population in 1987. Milošević had since revoked Kosovo's autonomy within Serbia, provoking first nonviolent, then violent protest among Albanians. Using mounting violent resistance as an excuse in 1998, Milošević sent in troops to repress the uprising and cleanse vast portions of Kosovo of Albanians. Following failed negotiations and mounting atrocities in 1999, the American-led North Atlantic Treaty Organization (NATO) began bombing Serbia, including targets in Kosovo, Belgrade, and other strategic Serbian cities. Defiant, Milošević used the cover of war to accelerate cleansing actions against Albanians, uprooting almost one-half of the region's 1.8 million people. After two months of bombing, Milošević agreed to international oversight of Kosovo, and many of the Albanian refugees returned under NATO protection.

Eagle Glassheim

See also: East African Asian Expulsions; Ethnic Cleansing: Armenia; Ethnic Cleansing: Bosnia-Herzegovina; Ethnic Cleansing: Croatia; Ethnic Cleansing: Germans from Central and Eastern Europe; Ethnic Cleansing: Kosovo; Ethnic Cleansing: Poles from Western Ukraine; Eugenics; Genocide; Indian Partition; Lausanne Convention; Racism and Racially Motivated Attacks

References and further reading:

Bickerton, Ian, and Carla Klausner. 1995. *A Concise History of the Arab-Israeli Conflict.* Englewood Cliffs, NJ: Prentice Hall.

De Zayas, Alfred. 1989 [1977]. *Nemesis at Potsdam: The Expulsion of the Germans from the East.* Lincoln: University of Nebraska Press.

———. 1994. *A Terrible Revenge: The Ethnic Cleansing of the East European Germans, 1944–1950.* New York: St. Martin's Press.

Glassheim, Eagle. 2000. "National Mythologies and Ethnic Cleansing: The Expulsion of Czechoslovak Germans in 1945." *Central European History* 33, no. 4: 463–486.

Gutman, Roy. 1993. *A Witness to Genocide.* New York: Macmillan.

Hayden, Robert. 1996. "Schindler's Fate: Genocide, Ethnic Cleansing, and Population Transfers." *Slavic Review* 55, no. 4: 727–748.

Marrus, Michael. 1985. *The Unwanted: European Refugees in the Twentieth Century.* New York: Oxford University Press.

Mazower, Mark. 1999. *Dark Continent: Europe's Twentieth Century.* New York: Alfred A. Knopf.

Morris, Benny. 1987. *The Birth of the Palestinian Refugee Problem, 1947–49.* Cambridge: Cambridge University Press.

Naimark, Norman M. 2001. *Fires of Hatred: Ethnic Cleansing in Twentieth-Century Europe.* Cambridge: Harvard University Press.

Rieber, Alfred, ed. 2000. *Forced Migration in Central and Eastern Europe.* London: Frank Cass.

Schieder, Theodor. 1960. *The Expulsion of the German Population from Czechoslovakia: A Selection and Translation from Dokumentation der Vertreibung der Deutschen aus Ost-*

Mitteleuropa, Band IV. Bonn: Federal Ministry for Expellees, Refugees and War Victims.

Stiglmayer, Alexandra, ed. 1992. *Mass Rape: The War against Women in Bosnia-Herzegovina.* Lincoln: University of Nebraska Press.

Ther, Philipp, and Ana Siljak, eds. 2001. *Redrawing Nations: Ethnic Cleansing in East-Central Europe, 1944–1948.* Harvard Cold War Studies Series. Lanham, MD: Rowman and Littlefield.

Ethnic Cleansing: Armenia

During World War I, between 800,000 and 1.5 million Armenians were deported and massacred by order of the Ottoman Turkish authorities, an event that has come to be known as the first genocide of the twentieth century. By these acts a people who had lived for millennia in what they considered to be their historic homeland were forced into exile and dispersion.

A Christian people in a Muslim-dominated empire, Armenians had inhabited the mountainous plateau of eastern Anatolia (present-day Turkey) for thousand of years but had fallen under the rule of Ottoman Turkish conquerors in the fifteenth and sixteenth centuries. Peasants and artisans made up the bulk of the population. Often living in separate communities, with their own institutions and leaders, the Armenians maintained their distinct religion and language. Until the nineteenth century, the acknowledged leaders of the community were the clergy and the wealthy. Many townspeople managed to advance into a prosperous middle class, and a fortunate few even became favorites of the Ottoman sultan. From the 1840s a secular intelligentsia emerged from Armenian and European schools, and in time, reformist and, later, revolutionary activists became influential in the community. Known until the late nineteenth century as the "loyal people," the Armenians came into conflict with their overlords as the empire began to decline economically.

Armenians developed a powerful sense of secular nationality in the nineteenth century, reconceiving of themselves as a modern nation instead of a primarily religious community. Over time, their sense of kinship with Christian Europe and their acquired national consciousness alienated them from the Muslim peoples among whom they lived. In the provinces of eastern Anatolia where the bulk of the Armenians lived, an intense four-sided struggle for power, position, and survival pitted the agents of the Ottoman government, the Kurdish nomadic leaders, the semiautonomous Turkish notables of the towns, and the Armenians against one another. Local Turkish officials ran the towns with little regard to central authority, and Kurdish tribal chieftains held much of the countryside under their sway. As the population of Muslims and Christians grew, with new Muslim immigrants from the Caucasus and the Balkans moving into historic Armenia, the competition for the limited agricultural resources of the area intensified. After some decades of social and political reforms, the Ottoman government authorities turned toward an alliance with their fellow Muslims, the Kurds, who were permitted to attack Anatolian Armenians with relative impunity. Armenians could not rely on the Ottoman state to defend them from the more powerful Muslim landlords, and Armenians had to decide either to leave their homes or to protect their endangered position. Small revolutionary parties attempted to mobilize the Armenians, but with very limited success. Resistance and clashes nevertheless led to massive killing of Armenians by Turkish and Kurdish forces in 1894–1896.

For brief periods, the European Great Powers became interested in the fate of the Armenians, but most often they stood by while the Armenians' situation deteriorated. Many Turks looked upon Armenians as an alien element, allied to the Europeans, who wished to dominate the weakened Ottoman Empire. The source of resentment between Armenians and Muslims originated in religious and social distinctions and a growing discomfort with the advancement of Christian peoples. Muslims dominated the empire politically, and Armenians were highly visible in the business world. The largest towns of Anatolia were home to substantial Armenian and Greek populations. According to the Ottoman censuses, which have been subjected to much scrutiny and criticism, at the beginning of the twentieth century non-Muslims made up only about 17 percent of the population of Anatolia, but over 50 percent of Istanbul and over 60 percent of Izmir. Armenians and Greeks owned most printing presses and many large industries. Muslims, particularly the conservative clerics, resented this reversal of the traditional hierarchy in which Muslims were supposed to be superior to Christians.

After the Young Turk Revolution of 1908, non-Muslims anticipated a better future for the Christian minorities of the empire, but the new government turned steadily toward a program of pro-Turkish nationalism and imperialism. The policies of the Young Turks were far more radical than the traditional Ottoman strategy of intermittent movement of populations and occasional massacres to thwart rebellion. The Committee of Union and Progress (CUP), as the principal faction of the Young Turks was officially known, wanted to modernize the empire in order to save it from the territorial ambitions of the Great Powers. Many Turkish nationalists came to believe that the Armenians were a dangerous and subversive internal enemy that had to be eradicated. The goal of a Turkic or Pan-Islamic empire that might include the Turkic-speaking and Muslim peoples of the Caucasus and Central Asia faced a serious obstacle in the Christian Armenians, hundreds of thousands of whom lived in the northeastern regions of the empire. By eliminating the Armenians from the

Armenian refugees on Black Sea beach, gathered around seated person. Novorossiisk, Russia, 1920. (Library of Congress)

four-way power struggle in the region, the CUP could with one blow end Western and Russian interference in Ottoman affairs, achieve the long-desired goal of Turkish nationalists to create a secure homeland for the Turkish people, and even work toward the Pan-Turkish or Pan-Islamic utopia of a Turkish-dominated empire stretching from Istanbul to Central Asia. Genocide, then, had its origins in the aspirations of a small group of Turkish politicians, the CUP, but both the radicalization of their intentions and the final implementation of their plans occurred at a moment of deep social and political crisis and the near defeat of the Ottoman state by external enemies.

While the present-day Turkish government and affiliated historians deny the responsibility of the Ottoman government for the deportations and massacres, the records in European and American archives present an overwhelming case for a systematic effort on the part of officials to carry out forced marches, massacres, and the eventual starvation of the survivors in the Syrian desert. Particularly damning are the archives of Germany, the principal ally of the Ottomans during World War I, but Turkish memoirs, accounts by missionaries and diplomats, and the diary of the American ambassador to Istanbul, Henry Morgenthau, also testify to the actions and motives of the perpetrators.

Just before the outbreak of World War I, the Young Turks formed a secret organization, the Teshkilat-i Mahsusa, that would form paramilitary units aimed at organizing uprisings in Egypt, Caucasia, Iran, and India. As early as August 1914, attacks were launched on Russian troops and Armenian villages in Russian Transcaucasia, looting and destroying them. When the leading Armenian political party in Turkey, the Armenian Revolutionary Federation, met in its Eighth World Congress in the eastern Anatolian town of Erzerum, the Ottomans proposed that in the event of war with Russia, Armenian leaders should foment revolt among Russian Armenians. In exchange, the Turks promised an autonomous state for the Armenians that would include Russian Armenia and several districts in eastern Anatolia. The Armenians rejected his offer and affirmed the party's neutrality as well as Turkish Armenian loyalty to the empire. They encouraged Armenian young men to join the Ottoman army.

As the Ottomans approached war, Muslim religious authorities in Istanbul proclaimed a "holy war" (*jihad*) against the enemies of the empire. The government ordered the removal of a large number of Greeks from the Western coast of Anatolia as a protective measure, but there was no attempt to kill them. On December 18, 1914, Minister of War Enver Pasha launched a massive offensive against the Russians, but

Angered by Armenian defiance, the Ottoman government told the German embassy that it could no longer trust the Armenians. The Van resistance was presented as an uprising by the government and was used as a rationale for further anti-Armenian actions. By the end of April, the government abolished the "millet system," the administrative organization that had permitted autonomy and a limited degree of self-government to the non-Muslim minorities. On April 24, now the traditional date that Armenians around the world commemorate "the Genocide," the Young Turk government arrested several hundred Armenian intellectuals and leaders in Istanbul, beginning with a raid on the offices of an influential newspaper.

Some historians believe that the Young Turk government, which had launched the deportations in March, made a second, more radical decision in April to physically liquidate the Armenians. Whereas the orders for deportation went out from the Ministry of the Interior, the orders for massacre were carried to the provinces by responsible party secretaries and implemented by the paramilitary Teshkilat-i Mahsusa. The army was reluctant in some cases to become involved in the deportations and massacres and often stood aside when local governors organized the caravans of exiles. The Genocide was largely the work of the Ministry of the Interior, the forces of the Teshkilat-i-Mahsusa, and the Young Turk party (the Committee of Union and Progress).

The Turkish forces began evacuations of Armenian villages around Erzerum in the first weeks of May and soon after in Sivas, Harput, Diarbekir, Bitlis, and Trabzon. Usually the Turks rounded up young men and took them outside the town, where they were killed. Then the surviving old men, children, and women were organized in caravans and marched eastward to the desert. In May, the minister of the interior, Talaat Pasha, ordered the governors of Van, Bitlis, and Erzerum to "deport" Armenians to southern Urfa and Mosul *sanjaks* (districts) and to the *vilayet* (province) of Zor. Orders also went out to the governors of Adana, Marash, and Aleppo to deport Armenians from Adana, Mersin, Sis, Jebel-i Bereket, and Marash sanjaks, with the exception of the regional centers, as well as Armenians from Alexandretta, Beylan, Jisr-ash-Shughur, and Antioch *kazas* (subdistricts). They were to be sent to eastern parts of Syria vilayet. In June, deportations were ordered in the vilayets of Trabzon, Sivas, Diarbekir, and Mamuret-ul-Aziz (Harput), and in the sanjak of Janik. The ministry ordered that Armenians were not to exceed 10 percent of the population in the resettlement areas in Syria, that no Armenian village should have more than fifty houses, and that there should be no freedom of movement.

Though the laws seemed to suggest that deportation and resettlement were the extent of Young Turk intentions, massacres continued. Many of the arrested Armenian leaders from Istanbul were killed sometime at the end of May. Massacres became widespread in June. On June 26, the Armenian men of Marsovan were deported. By July 1, rumors were heard that many of them had been killed, and a few days later all Armenians were ordered to leave Marsovan, a town of about 12,000. On July 7, Turkish troops captured the Armenian quarter of Mush, herded Armenian women and children into houses in nearby villages, and burned them alive. The murder of the demobilized Armenian soldiers also occurred in the late spring and early summer. Some estimate that by July almost 200,000 Armenians had been killed.

The process of ethnic cleansing and genocide became more radical as the months passed. Turkish governors who refused to follow the orders to deport were removed; a few were killed, and more militant officials were appointed. Henry Morgenthau, the American ambassador to the Ottoman Empire, tried to intervene with Enver and Talaat to stop the massacres, but to no avail. As more and more evidence came into the American embassy that Armenians were being deported and murdered, Morgenthau requested a meeting with Enver and found the minister of war quite frank about what was happening. According to Morgenthau, Enver said:

> The Armenians had a fair warning . . . of what would happen to them in case they joined our enemies. Three months ago I sent for the Armenian Patriarch and I told him that if the Armenians attempted to start a revolution or to assist the Russians, I would be unable to prevent mischief from happening to them. My warning produced no effect and the Armenians started a revolution and helped the Russians. You know what happened at Van. They obtained control of the city, used bombs against government buildings, and killed a large number of Moslems. We knew that they were planning uprisings in other places. You must understand that we are now fighting for our lives at the Dardanelles and that we are sacrificing thousands of men. While we are engaged in such a struggle as this, we cannot permit people in our own country to attack us in the back. We have got to prevent this no matter what means we have to resort to. It is absolutely true that I am not opposed to the Armenians as a people. I have the greatest admiration for their intelligence and industry, and I would like nothing better than to see them become a real part of our nation. But if they ally themselves with our enemies, as they did in the Van district, they will have to be destroyed.

Enver further told Morganthau that the "Cabinet itself has ordered the deportations. I am convinced that we are completely justified in doing this owing to the hostile attitude of the Armenians toward the Ottoman Government, but we are the real rulers of Turkey, and no underling would dare proceed in a matter of this kind without our orders." Similarly, inept leadership and the poor preparation for the winter campaign led to a disastrous Turkish defeat and massive loss of life at Sarikamish. This seemed to end the Pan-Turkish dreams for a while. Some Armenians from Russia served as volunteers in the Russian army, and it was clear to the Turks that many Armenians preferred the Russians to the Ottomans. Moreover, the Russian tsar and his officials in the Caucasus had called upon Armenians in Turkey to rally to the Christian cause.

Enver's defeat on the Caucasian front was the prelude to the "final solution" of the Armenian Question. The Russians posed a real danger to the Turks, just at the moment that Allied forces were attacking at Gallipoli in the west. In this moment of defeat and desperation, the triumvirate in Istanbul decided to demobilize the Armenian soldiers in the Ottoman army and to deport Armenians from Anatolia. What might have been rationalized as a military necessity, given the imperial ambitions and distorted perceptions of the Ottoman leaders, quickly became a massive attack on their Armenian subjects, a systematic program of murder and pillage. Against a background of long-standing fears and hatred of Armenians, key Turkish leaders turned the moment of defeat into a monstrous opportunity to rid Anatolia once and for all of a people who seemed to present an internal threat as well as an obstacle to the CUP's plans for a Pan-Turkish empire.

Early in 1915, the Ottoman army in the east retreated. Instances of spontaneous violence had already occurred in the fall of 1914 and winter of 1914–1915. At one large Armenian village, Dortyol, near the Syrian coast, the villagers had sheltered two British Armenian spies. Since local Armenians had not responded to the draft, the regional governor sent the military and arrested most of the adult Armenian men, who were then deported into labor battalions. In the middle of February, the influential Young Turk leader Bahaeddin Shakir arrived in Istanbul and reported on the situation in the east to other party leaders, convincing them that the internal enemy was as dangerous as the foreign enemy. Shortly after this, the Teshkilat-i Mahsusa was removed from army control and placed under the direct supervision of the Young Turk party. At the end of February, Enver ordered that the more than 200,000 Armenians in the Ottoman army be disarmed and placed in labor battalions. Some other non-Muslims, such as Jews in Palestine, were subjected to similar orders. Up to this time there probably had been no concrete plans to deal systematically with the Armenians, but about the time of Shakir's report, in late February or early March 1915, the CUP leaders decided in secret to remove the Armenians from eastern Anatolia. The decision was taken by the Central Committee of the Young Turk political party rather than by a governmental agency.

Tensions increased between Armenians and Muslims as more and more exactions were demanded from the Christians. When, at the end of February, about thirty young men from the mountain town of Zeitun attacked Turkish gendarmes whom they believed had raped local girls, their action provided the excuse for the deportation of the Zeituntsis in early April. Reports came in from various districts that Armenian soldiers were being disarmed and forced to serve in special units (worker battalions, sappers' units) as porters or laborers. Later they were shot in groups. In March, the government suspended the Ottoman Parliament, in which Armenian deputies still served, and Armenian political leaders throughout the country were rounded up. Armenian newspapers were banned. A German officer observed that Armenians no longer trusted the government, but they continued to cooperate for fear of reprisals. The first recorded deportations—in Zeitun and Dortyol—began in March and were completed by May 1915.

The Turkish military attacked Zeitun, killing Armenian men. After three days of fighting, local men were deported to Deir el-Zor in the Syrian desert, while the women, old people, and children were sent northwestward to Sultania and Konia. But this was the only deportation to head toward the west. Soon all caravans and death marches moved eastward. The American consul at Aleppo, J. B. Jackson, reported that some 28,000 people had been removed by government orders from the districts of Zeitun and Marash. American missionaries in the region were appalled at the "crushing and deportation of the educated and able Christian population of the Marash field," which they saw as "a direct blow at American missionary interests, menacing the results of more than fifty years of work and many thousands of dollars of expenditure."

The ancient citadel of Van, near the lake of the same name, was a town in which Armenians made up a majority of the population. The local governor, Jevdet Pasha, the brother-in-law of Enver Pasha, was a hard-liner who had replaced a more moderate predecessor. In mid-April, the Turkish authorities killed the prominent revolutionary leaders in Van, Ishkhan and Vramian. A few days later, Turkish soldiers attacked some Armenian villages around Van, massacring Armenians. In the town of Van, the Armenians dug trenches around the Armenian quarter and began a desperate defense of their community. Their hope lay in rescue by the Russian troops, which began an advance across the Turkish border on May 4. On May 16, Jevdet retreated south of Lake Van. When Russian troops briefly took Van, the local Armenians took revenge against local Turks. In mid-July, the Ottomans retook Van and carried out deportations and massacres of the Armenians. By then, however, many Armenians had left with the Russian troops and fled to the Caucasus.

Talaat Pasha admitted, "We have already disposed of three quarters of the Armenians; there are none at all left in Bitlis, Van, and Erzeroum. The hatred between the Turks and the Armenians is now so intense that we have got to finish with them. If we don't, they will plan their revenge."

In the summer of 1915, tens of thousands of Armenians, perhaps as many as 30,000, were deported from Istanbul. Later the Armenians of Baghdad were deported to Mosul. In the fall, Armenians were deported from Mesopotamia and northern Syria. In a few places besides Van, Armenians resisted the fate planned by the Turks. After witnessing columns of exiled Armenians passing, the Armenians of Urfa barricaded themselves in their quarters and resisted deportations for a month, from August 20 to September 20. At a village near the Mediterranean, Musa Dagh, the local Armenians held out against the Turkish army for over a month until rescued by European ships. This act of defiance was later immortalized in 1933 by the Czech-Jewish writer Franz Werfel in his popular novel *The Forty Days of Musa Dagh.*

Europe was already aware of the massacres of Armenians by the spring of 1915, and the Allied powers protested, but to no avail. The governments of Britain, France, and Russia jointly published a declaration deploring "these new crimes of Turkey against humanity and civilization" and holding the Ottoman officials personally responsible for Armenian deaths. In 1916, the British issued a collection of documents demonstrating the crimes of the Ottomans against the Armenians. Published under the name of James Bryce and edited by the young historian Arnold Toynbee, the collection was both effective anti-Turkish propaganda at the time and an appeal for future international prevention of crimes by states against defenseless humans. The Germans, who might have prevailed upon their allies, the Turks, were reluctant to intervene. German ambassador von Wagenheim soon realized that these brutal measures could not be justified by reasons of war, for they were taking place far from the front. The humanitarian Dr. Johannes Lepsius met with Enver in August to express opposition to the treatment of Armenians. That same day, the new German ambassador, Prince Hohenlohe, protested the actions of the Sublime Porte, but the secretary of state to the foreign office, Zimmerman, said that no break with Turkey was possible. The Kaiser himself equivocated and cautioned against affronting the Turks.

By the fall of 1915, the bulk of the deportations and killing had been accomplished, but Armenians continued to die from starvation and occasional brutalities in their places of exile. Mass killings continued in the desert camps. When in 1918 the Turkish army advanced across the Russian border into the South Caucasus, they engaged in further massacres of Armenians in Karabakh, Baku, and elsewhere. Defeated Turkey left the war in the fall of 1918, and briefly the new postwar government investigated the policies of their Young Turk predecessors. A military court indicted some twenty perpetrators, but none were ever tried and found guilty. British efforts to investigate and try Turks for the massacres also ended without result. Later, Armenians would carry out their own retribution against two of the key architects of the Genocide, most notably assassinating Talaat in Berlin and Jemal in Tiflis in the early 1920s. In the postwar years, as the Turkish nationalists under Kemal Pasha gained control of Anatolia and founded the Turkish Republic, they drove Armenians from towns and cities to which they had returned. In 1920, thousands of Armenians were killed in Marash and other towns by advancing nationalist troops.

The costs of the Genocide to Armenians were immeasurable, but they were also enormous, in a quite different way, to the Turks. The deportations and massacres, both in 1915 and in its aftermath, disrupted the economy of Anatolia, and widespread famine and disease resulted, which dealt equally cruelly with Muslims and surviving Christians. Productive farmers, workers, and intellectuals, many of them loyal members of Ottoman society, were eliminated simply because they were Armenian. The Genocide took time and energy from the Turks that compromised their war effort and contributed to Turkey's defeat in World War I. But as a result of the elimination of the Armenians, the Turks eventually controlled a much more ethnically and religiously homogeneous territory than they had held before 1915. The horrors of ethnic cleansing and genocide became the unacknowledged foundational acts of nation-building.

Ronal Grigor Suny

See also: Armenian Diaspora; Ethnic Cleansing; Ethnic Cleansing: Bosnia-Herzegovina; Ethnic Cleansing: Croatia; Ethnic Cleansing: Kosovo; Ethnic Cleansing: Poles from Western Ukraine; Genocide

References and further reading:

Ahmad, Feroz. 1969. *The Young Turks: The Committee of Union and Progress in Turkish Politics, 1908–1914.* Oxford: Clarendon.

Bartov, Omer, and Phyllis Mack, eds. 2001. *In God's Name: Genocide and Religion in the Twentieth Century.* New York and Oxford: Berghahn.

A Crime of Silence: The Armenian Genocide. The Permanent People's Tribunal. 1985. London: Zed.

Dadrian, Vahakn N. 1995. *The History of the Armenian Genocide: Ethnic Conflict from the Balkans to Anatolia to the Caucasus.* Providence, RI: Berghahn.

———. 1996. *German Responsibility in the Armenian Genocide.* Watertown, MA: Blue Crane.

———. 1999. *Warrant for Genocide: Key Elements of Turco-Armenian Conflict.* New Brunswick, NJ: Transaction.

Djemal Pasha. n.d. *Memories of a Turkish Statesman, 1913–1919.* London: Hutchinson.

Hovannisian, Richard G., ed. 1986. *The Armenian Genocide in Perspective.* New Brunswick and Oxford: Transaction.

———. 1992. *The Armenian Genocide: History, Politics, Ethics.* New York: St. Martin's Press.

———, ed. 1999. *Remembrance and Denial: The Case of the Armenian Genocide.* Detroit: Wayne State University Press.

Kaiser, Hilmar, ed. 2001. *Eberhard Count Wolfskeel von Reichenberg, Zeitoun, Mousa Dagh, Ourfa: Letters on the Armenian Genocide.* Princeton, NJ: Gomidas Institute.

Mann, Michael. N.d. *The Dark-Side of Democracy: Explaining Ethnic Cleansing.* Unpublished manuscript.

Melson, Robert F. 1992. *Revolution and Genocide.* Chicago: University of Chicago Press.

Morgenthau, Henry. 2000. *Ambassador Morgenthau's Story.* Ann Arbor, MI: Gomidas Institute.

Naimark, Norman M. 2001. *Fires of Hatred: Ethnic Cleansing in Twentieth-Century Europe.* Cambridge: Harvard University Press.

Suny, Ronald Grigor. 1993. *Looking Toward Ararat: Armenia in Modern History.* Bloomington: Indiana University Press.

Ethnic Cleansing: Bosnia-Herzegovina

The war in Bosnia-Herzegovina lasted from April 1992 to November 1995 and created the largest flow of internally displaced persons and refugees seen in Europe since World War II. In this war, initiated by the actions of the Bosnian Serbs, both they and the Bosnian Croats attempted to carve out ethnically homogeneous para-states within Bosnia-Herzegovina and to attach these to Serbia or Croatia, respectively. This involved the use of ethnic cleansing as a technique of creating ethnically homogeneous territories. The Bosnian Muslims, or Bosniaks, who suffered disproportionately, fought largely to defend themselves and the concept of a multiethnic Bosnian state. However, under severe pressure from Bosnian Serb and Bosnian Croat attacks, a small but significant minority of Bosnian Muslims responded with occasional indiscriminate attacks on the non-Muslim civilian population. At the height of the war, an estimated 2.2 million people, or more than half of Bosnia-Herzegovina's prewar population, had been displaced from their homes. By the end of the war in Bosnia-Herzegovina, the country had effectively been partitioned into three ethnically based entities.

Bosnia-Herzegovina emerged as a major point of contention in the second half of the nineteenth century, as Ottoman rule began to crumble in the Balkans. After the Congress of Berlin in 1878, the Austro-Hungarian Empire occupied the Ottoman province, annexing it in 1908. This led to the migration of large numbers of Bosnian Muslims and Turks from Bosnia-Herzegovina to the remaining portions of the Ottoman Empire. At the same time, the Austro-Hungarian presence only further provoked growing nationalist tensions, particularly between the Roman Catholic Croats and the Orthodox Serbs. The latter group, in particular, grew progressively more radical in its demands for union with the Kingdom of Serbia. In June 1914, a Serb nationalist youth activist assassinated Archduke Franz Ferdinand of Austria-Hungary. This event precipitated the outbreak of World War I.

Bosnia-Herzegovina sustained tremendous losses in World War I. The ethnic Serb population, singled out for retribution by the armies of the Central Powers, suffered disproportionately great losses. When the war ended and Bosnia-Herzegovina was incorporated into the Kingdom of Serbs, Croats, and Slovenes (known as the Kingdom of Yugoslavia after 1929), the Bosnian Serbs perceived themselves as having the right to govern.

In one area in particular, land reform, the 1920s proved turbulent for Bosnia-Herzegovina. Taking advantage of the new political constellation, Bosnian Serbs pressed for a redistribution of the large estates held by Muslim landlords. Rather than relying on institutional and legal reform to effect this change, many Bosnian Serbs forcibly seized land and attacked Muslim landowners. The political representatives of the Bosnian Serbs had a heavy orientation toward Belgrade and claimed not infrequently that both Bosnia-Herzegovina and the Bosnian Muslims were "Serb." This, along with attacks on Islamic cultural objects, poisoned the atmosphere between Muslims and Serbs in Bosnia.

In 1929, King Aleksandar of Yugoslavia divided the territory of Bosnia-Herzegovina among several separate *banovine,* or provinces. This represented a gerrymandering of Bosnia-Herzegovina—and the Yugoslav kingdom as a whole—in favor of the Serbs. Like all other political parties, the Yugoslav Muslim Organization, the main party of the Bosnian Muslims, was banned during the dictatorship of King Aleksandar, which lasted from 1929 to 1934. In addition, the seat of the Bosnian Muslims' spiritual leader, the *reis-ul-ulema,* was also moved from Sarajevo to Belgrade.

Bosnian Croats also perceived themselves to be disadvantaged in interwar Yugoslavia. In response, they aligned themselves with political trends emanating from the main Croat metropolis, Zagreb. By the end of the 1930s, the Croats succeeded in forcing another redistricting of Yugoslavia. In this compromise agreement between the Croats and the Serbs, the Bosnian Muslims' voices were not heard.

World War II witnessed intense fratricidal strife. In Yugoslavia, and particularly in Bosnia-Herzegovina, World War II was at least as much a civil war as an international armed conflict. Most historians agree that the numbers of Yugoslavs killed by other Yugoslavs exceeded the number killed by the occupying armies. Yugoslavia was occupied by Nazi Germany, Italy, and the pro-German Bulgarian and Hungarian states. Bosnia-Herzegovina became the main site of continuous armed conflict between the resistance, led by the Yugoslav Communist partisans, and the occupying forces and their collaborators. Even seen within the full context of World War II, the human losses in Bosnia-Herzegovina were disproportionately heavy.

During World War II, Bosnian Muslims fought on all sides. Fatefully for the Bosnian Muslims, the fact that Mus-

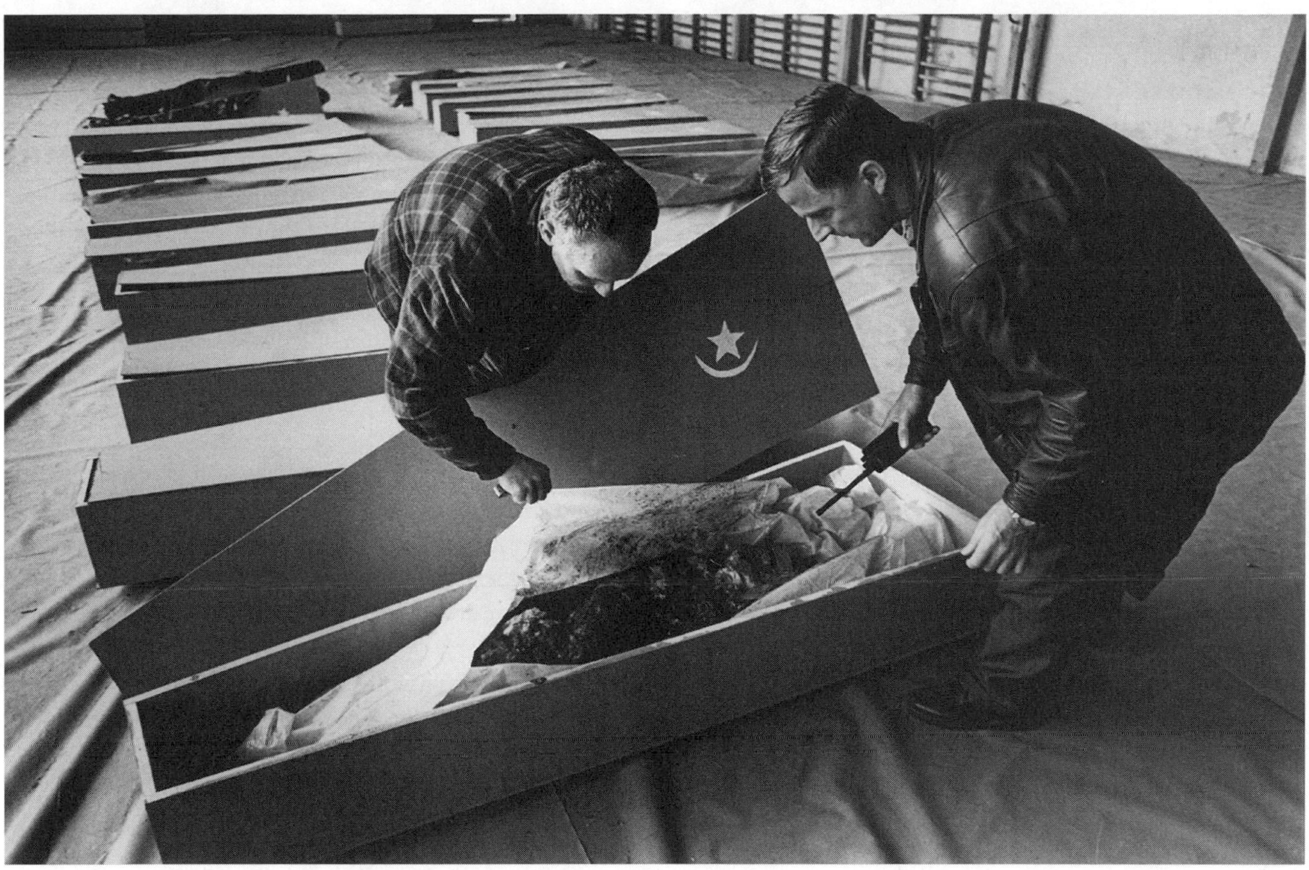

A Bosnian Muslim man, home from refuge in the United Kingdom, views the remains of victims found in the Laniste 1 mass grave in Kljuc, 1996. (Howard Davies/Corbis)

lims had appeared in the ranks of both the Quisling Croat armed forces and the Yugoslav partisans allowed the formation of prejudices and collective memories that would reemerge in the 1990s. No objective discussion of collaboration and resistance during World War II was possible in socialist Yugoslavia.

After the negative experience of interwar Yugoslavia, the Socialist Federative Republic of Yugoslavia proved to be the "golden age" of the Bosnian Muslims and of Bosnia-Herzegovina in general. Although Tito's Yugoslavia repressed any political expressions of Islam, this was part of the general atheistic nature of the Yugoslav socialist state. By the 1960s, the Yugoslav state openly encouraged the formation of a Bosnian Muslim identity, distinct from both Croat and Serb identities. In 1961, Muslims were recognized for the first time as a group in the census, and in 1967 Muslims were recognized as a nation, that is, as an ethnically and not merely religiously defined group. In the late 1960s and 1970s, intermarriage rates among Muslims, Croats, and Serbs increased in Bosnia-Herzegovina.

After the death of Tito in 1980, the political and economic situation in Yugoslavia, and hence in Bosnia-Herzegovina, first drifted into stagnation and then began to deteriorate with increasing speed. During the second half of the 1980s, nationalist movements began to emerge among all three major nations. A return to the nationalist and communal grievances of the past informed a salient portion of these parties' platforms.

The results of the first multiparty elections in November confirmed the new dominance of nationalism as a political force, and the discrediting of socialist rule. In place of the League of Communists, Bosnia-Herzegovina came to be dominated by the (Muslim) Party of Democratic Action (Stranka demokratske akcije, or SDA), the Serb Democratic Party (Srpska demokratska stranka, or SDS), and the Croat Democratic Union (Hrvatska demokratska zajednica, or HDZ).

In the wake of the November 1990 elections, the SDA, SDS, and HDZ agreed to divide all important government portfolios and offices among themselves. This agreement ensured that all important state and economic business found expression in nationalist form and did little to stabilize the situation. The three parties complained ceaselessly of violations of the multiparty agreement.

The situation deteriorated even further after the outbreak of armed conflict in Slovenia and Croatia. Whereas the Bosnian Serbs depicted the war in Croatia as a defensive one aimed at thwarting the establishment of a Croat fascist state, the Bosnian Croats and Muslims believed that the Serbs sought to dominate Yugoslavia. As a result, while the Bosnian Serbs generally responded to calls for military mobilization, the Bosnian Croats and Bosnian Muslims did not. The SDS leadership in particular, led by Radovan Karadžić made frequent threats alluding to the possibility of war if the Serbs' political demands were not met in full. The Bosnian Serb leadership made frequent allusions to past grievances, such as the suffering of the Serb nation during World War II, and accused the Bosnian Muslims of harboring plans to create an Islamic theocracy. In formulating and implementing their political program, the Bosnian Serb leadership received political, moral, and material support from President Slobodan Milošević of Serbia and his associates and supporters.

Complicating matters still further, all three nationalist parties formed paramilitary units that they could rely upon in the event of armed conflict. The Bosnian Serbs and Bosnian Croats pursued this path most actively, with the Bosnian Muslims mostly reacting. By April 1992, these processes had reached a climax. Even as Bosnia-Herzegovina received recognition as an independent state, the Bosnian Serbs launched an attempt to form their own state, the Serb Republic of Bosnia Herzegovina (Republika Srpska). They did so with the overt assistance of the Yugoslav People's Army, which was gradually transformed into a pro-Serb force. By mid-April 1992, Bosnia-Herzegovina had plunged into full-scale war.

From the very outset of the war in Bosnia-Herzegovina, the Bosnian Serbs pursued the creation of an ethnically homogeneous state and its eventual attachment to Serbia. Beginning in early April in eastern Bosnia-Herzegovina, Serb forces adopted a set of tactics that would become known internationally as "ethnic cleansing." This involved using political and physical terror to intimidate the non-Serb population into submission and into "voluntarily" leaving their homes. Throughout the self-proclaimed Republika Srpska, non-Serbs rapidly lost their political and civil rights, and most were forced to leave their jobs. During the crucial phase in which Serb military, police, and paramilitary forces "liberated" areas and established "Serb municipalities," virtually indiscriminate force was deployed against the non-Serb population. This included the calculated use of killings, beatings, torture, and rape. Males of military age presented the main target. They were charged with fabricated crimes, such as membership in Muslim or Croat "fascist" paramilitary organizations. Thousands of non-Serbs were killed or deported to detention centers and concentration camps where they were kept in inhumane conditions. Although the Bosnian Serb security forces primarily targeted males of military age, no non-Serbs were completely immune to human rights abuses.

Ethnic cleansing's status as a military objective in the war in Bosnia-Herzegovina put international organizations intervening in the conflict in a very difficult position. Organizations such as the UN High Commissioner for Refugees (UNHCR) faced an excruciating choice. If they did not evacuate noncombatants from locations under attack or the impending threat of attack, many people risked death or injury. Yet if the organizations evacuated these threatened populations preemptively, they became vulnerable to charges of aiding and abetting ethnic cleansing. In certain areas of Bosnia-Herzegovina, such as Sarajevo, Goražde, and Srebrenica, the Bosnian Serbs proved unable to expel forcibly the non-Serb population. As a result, the Serbs set siege to these enclaves, subjecting them to regular shelling, sniper attacks, and a constant shortage of essential supplies.

The discovery of the detention centers and camps in Bosnia-Herzegovina in the summer of 1992 outraged international public opinion. The most notorious of these camps, Manjača, Keraterm, Omarska, and Trnopolje, were located in the Bosanska Krajina region of northwestern Bosnia-Herzegovina. They had been established and were operated by officials of the Bosnian Serbs' self-proclaimed state. These camps, combined with the large and widespread scale of attacks against noncombatants inherent in ethnic cleansing, led to the establishment of a UN commission of experts to investigate serious violations of international humanitarian law. This commission produced a report that became the basis for the foundation of the International Criminal Tribunal for the Former Yugoslavia (ICTY). Beginning with its inception in 1994, ICTY charged dozens of individuals from Bosnia-Herzegovina for allegedly committing crimes against humanity, including persecutions and killings linked to ethnic cleansing.

At the outset of the war in Bosnia-Herzegovina, the Bosnian Croats and Bosnian Muslims had fought together against the Bosnian Serbs and their Yugoslav and Serb allies. However, in 1993, the fragile coalition between the Bosnian Croats and the Bosnian Muslims fell apart as the Bosnian Croats manifested ambitions for a Great Croat state. With military and financial assistance from Croatia, the Bosnian Croats attempted to carve out ethnically pure territory in Herzegovina. This involved the expulsions of non-Croats from the areas coveted by the Bosnian Croats. In the process, mimicking the Bosnian Serbs, the Bosnian Croats established detention camps in which non-Croats were held and grievously mistreated. Only in the spring of 1994 did the mediation of the United States lead to the reemergence of a nominal Muslim-Croat coalition.

The Bosnian Serb and Bosnian Croat forces were the main protagonists of ethnic cleansing in Bosnia-Herzegovina. However, to a significantly smaller extent, forces under the control of the Muslim-dominated government of Bosnia-Herzegovina also engaged in ethnic cleansing. This included the establishment of detention camps for non-Muslims and the expulsion of non-Muslims from selected areas controlled by the government of Bosnia-Herzegovina. It should be noted that, unlike the expulsions conducted by the para-states of the Bosnian Serbs and Bosnian Croats, the expulsions of Serbs and Croats by Bosnian Muslims never took on the character of official policy. Perversely, the extreme nationalism manifested by many Bosnian Serbs and Croats produced a strong nationalist reaction from a minority of Bosnian Muslims. Serb and Croat nationalism thus succeeded to some extent in accelerating the creation of the very phenomenon they claimed to oppose—Muslim nationalists. The vast majority of Bosnian Muslims, however, rejected nationalism.

In the context of the war in Bosnia-Herzegovina, women proved particularly vulnerable. Paramilitary and regular armed forces perpetrated indiscriminate attacks, often including aggravated sexual assault and rape, against women. In the worst cases, such as in the notorious "rape camps" established by Serb forces in Foèa in southeastern Bosnia-Herzegovina, these attacks assumed a systematic character. This caused the UN Tribunal for the Former Yugoslavia to charge and successfully prosecute rape as a violation of international humanitarian law.

The last year of the war, 1995, was one of the most brutal in terms of ethnic cleansing. In an attempt to secure their grip on eastern Bosnia-Herzegovina, the Bosnian Serbs used the late spring and summer of 1995 to launch a series of assaults on the handful of remaining Bosnian Muslim enclaves in that region. The UN Security Council had designated these pockets as "safe havens" and had threatened the Bosnian Serbs with armed intervention if they were attacked. In the most violent of these attacks, the Bosnian Serb army and combat forces of the Bosnian Serb Ministry of Internal Affairs overran the Srebrenica enclave in mid-July 1995. Within days of the fall of Srebrenica, the Bosnian Serbs had massacred all adolescent and adult males, an estimated 7,000 to 8,000 men. The Dutch UN battalion responsible for maintaining the Srebrenica "safe haven" failed to prevent the fall of the enclave or the ensuing massacre. Younger Muslim boys and women were transferred to territory controlled by the government of Bosnia-Herzegovina.

The Srebrenica massacre helped to galvanize the international community into military intervention. In September 1995, the NATO alliance began to conduct air strikes against Bosnian Serb military positions besieging Sarajevo. Within weeks, these strikes, combined with simultaneous ground-based attacks by Muslim and Croat forces, and by the UN Protection Force, significantly reduced the amount of territory controlled by the Bosnian Serbs. After several weeks, a cease-fire was achieved. In November 1995, the United States convened an international conference designed to end the war. Leading representatives of all the combatants in Bosnia-Herzegovina attended the conference, which was held at a U.S. Air Force base in Dayton, Ohio. The resulting Dayton Accords formally ended the war in Bosnia-Herzegovina.

Seen from the perspective of ethnic cleansing, the Dayton Accords did little to reverse the traumatic expulsions that had taken place from 1992 to 1995. An entire annex (Annex 7) of the Dayton Accords was devoted to the issue of return. However, by confirming the establishment of two ethnically defined entities in Bosnia-Herzegovina—the overwhelmingly Serb Republika Srpska and the barely extant Muslim-Croat federation—the Dayton Accords came close to codifying ethnic segregation. Indeed, in some cases, the drawing of the "Dayton boundaries" encouraged additional postwar ethnic cleansing. For example, Bosnian Serbs largely departed from Sarajevo after several suburbs of Sarajevo shifted to Bosnian government control. Significantly, many Serbs from these suburbs who had contemplated staying reported being coerced by hard-line nationalist Serbs into leaving.

In the years following the end of the war, the rate of return of refugees and displaced persons proceeded extremely slowly. This was especially the case in Republika Srpska. From 1995 to 2000, refugees and displaced persons in general returned only if their former homes were in areas controlled primarily by their own ethnic group. However, since 2000 an increasing number of people have chosen to return even to areas located in an entity controlled by the opposing ethnic group. According to the most reliable estimates, some 900,000 people have returned to their prewar residences. Yet throughout Bosnia-Herzegovina, many nationalist politicians remain in power. They and their supporters use both political and other obstacles to obstruct the undoing of ethnic cleansing.

Christian A. Nielsen

See also: Bosnia-Herzegovina and Refugees; Ethnic Cleansing; Ethnic Cleansing: Armenia; Ethnic Cleansing: Croatia; Ethnic Cleansing: Kosovo; Ethnic Cleansing: Poles from Western Ukraine; Genocide; Indian Partition

References and further reading:

Banac, Ivo. 1983. *The National Question in Yugoslavia.* Ithaca, NY: Cornell University Press.

Bogoeva, Julija, and Caroline Fetscher, eds. 2002. *Srebrenica: Ein Prozess.* Frankfurt: Suhrkamp.

Bringa, Tone. 1995. *Being Muslim the Bosnian Way: Identity and Community in a Central Bosnian Village.* Princeton, NJ: Princeton University Press.

International Crisis Group. 2002. "The Continuing Challenge of Refugee Return in Bosnia and Herzegovina." Sarajevo: International Crisis Group.

Kennedy-Pipe, Caroline, and Penny Stanley. 2001. "Rape in War: Lessons of the Balkan Conflicts in the 1990s." In *The Kosovo Tragedy: The Human Rights Dimensions.* Edited by Ken Booth. London: Frank Cass.

Malcolm, Noel. 1996. *Bosnia: A Short History.* New York: New York University Press.

Pinson, Mark, ed. 1994. *The Muslims of Bosnia-Herzegovina: Their Historical Development from the Middle Ages to the Dissolution of Yugoslavia.* Cambridge: Harvard University Press.

Riedlmayer, András. 1994. *Killing Memory: Bosnia's Cultural Heritage and Its Destruction* (video). Philadelphia: Community of Bosnia.

Sells, Michael A., "Reports on War Crimes in the Former Yugoslavia," http://www.haverford.edu/relg/sells/reports.html.

Silber, Laura, and Alan Little. 1996. *The Death of Yugoslavia.* Rev. ed. London: Penguin.

Simms, Brendan. 2001. *Unfinest Hour: Britain and the Destruction of Bosnia.* London: Penguin.

Ethnic Cleansing: Croatia

Although preceded by a brief period of armed conflict in Slovenia, the war that broke out in Croatia in June 1991 was the first major war to occur as the Socialist Federal Republic of Yugoslavia began to implode. The war in Croatia had its most intense period in the autumn of 1991 but lasted intermittently until August 1995. It was accompanied by the large-scale displacement of persons within Croatia, as well as the creation of a significant number of refugees. Whereas the refugees were predominantly Croats during the early phase of the war, the eventual legacy of the war was the expulsion of approximately three-quarters of Croatia's centuries-old Serb minority. In sum, the war in Croatia marked the debut of a hallmark feature of the conflict in the former Yugoslavia—the deliberate displacement of noncombatants as a military and political goal, and not as a mere side-effect. Both sides in the conflict, Croatia and the Federal Republic of Yugoslavia (Serbia-Montenegro), strove to create ethnically homogeneous states.

The presence of large numbers of ethnic Serbs in Croatia dated to the sixteenth century, when the Hapsburg Empire had stationed ethnic Serbs to protect the military frontier (*vojna krajina*) with the Ottoman Empire. Beginning in the mid–nineteenth century, relations between the Catholic Croats and the Serbian Orthodox Serbs began to deteriorate as nationalism emerged as a major political force. After World War I, many Croats perceived the Kingdom of Serbs, Croats, and Slovenes (known as the Kingdom of Yugoslavia after 1929) as being dominated by Serbs. When Nazi Germany invaded Yugoslavia in April 1941, the Germans permitted the establishment of a Quisling regime known as the Independent State of Croatia. Although it did not include Dalmatia, which came under Italian rule, this Croatian puppet state did include all of Bosnia-Herzegovina and large parts of Syrmium, a part of Vojvodina. From its inception until its collapse in 1945, the Independent State of Croatia pursued a highly discriminatory and often genocidal policy against Serbs, Jews, and Roma. These groups, led by the Serbs, therefore flocked to join the Communist partisan resistance against fascism. The incompetent and corrupt nature of the Independent State of Croatia also caused it to lose legitimacy among the Croats. Consequently, many Croats also joined the partisans.

After World War II, in the Socialist Federal Republic of Yugoslavia, the authorities strove to submerge the Serbo-Croat dispute beneath the official slogan of "brotherhood and unity." Although this campaign experienced considerable success, especially in the 1960s and 1970s, the painful and traumatic episodes of the past received no objective or balanced discussion in Yugoslavia itself. This left the often-nationalist émigré historians as well as internal nationalist dissidents to exploit the history of World War II for their own political ends.

At the beginning of the 1990s, the Serbs in Croatia constituted approximately 12 percent of the population. As multiparty rule emerged in the Socialist Republic of Croatia, this minority quickly became the main object of political debate. At the first pluralist elections, held in the spring of 1990, the nationalist Croat Democratic Union (Hrvatska demokratska zajednica, or HDZ), led by Franjo Tudjman, emerged victorious. To Tudjman and many of his followers, the Serbs of Croatia represented an alien presence and a security threat to the emerging independent Croatian state. The party's rhetoric frequently made use of ethnic stereotypes. According to the HDZ, the Croats had suffered in Yugoslavia under Serb domination.

In the meantime, in Serbia, President Slobodan Milošević presided over an attempt to centralize power firmly in Belgrade. In doing so, he exploited a strong nationalist movement that aimed to keep all Serbs within Yugoslavia. Failing that, Serb nationalists sought to create a "Great Serbian" state for the ethnic Serbs of Yugoslavia. These two contradictory views clashed politically and would eventually lead to armed conflict.

The print and broadcast media and the deliberate misreading played important roles on both the Serb and Croat sides of the dispute. The Tudjman regime appropriated symbols and political rhetoric from the Independent State of Croatia, a puppet state of Nazi Germany during World War II. This alienated and alarmed the Serbs of Croatia. The Serb community in Croatia had preserved a strong collective memory of the genocidal policies pursued against them by

Serbian refugees wait for a train as they flee a Croat offensive in Krajina. After the fall of Communism in 1989–1990, Yugoslavia broke into Croatia, Bosnia, and Serbia, all of which claimed areas within the others, and which led to the war still going on ten years later. By autumn of 1995, the fighting and "ethnic cleansing" had displaced about 3.5 million people. (Peter Turnley/Corbis)

the Independent State of Croatia. The combination of this memory and the political constellation of the early 1990s predisposed the Serbs of Croatia to the political solutions offered by nationalist intellectuals and politicians. It would not be an exaggeration to state that Tudjman and Milošević derived mutual benefit from the propaganda generated by one another's regimes.

On June 25, 1991, Croatia declared independence. The new state had no proper army and therefore had to rely initially on police and paramilitary forces to defend itself. Opposing them was the Yugoslav People's Army (Jugoslovenska narodna armija, or JNA), Yugoslav territorial defense units, and large numbers of Serb paramilitary forces. As combat began, the civilian population started to flee to safer areas of Croatia, to other areas of the former Yugoslavia, or abroad.

Yet to a significant extent, ethnic cleansing preceded the war. As early as the summer of 1990, rebellious Serbs had set up barricades and blocked access to whole sections of Croatia. These regions became known as Serbian Autonomous Regions (Srpske autonomne oblasti, or SAOs). As these self-proclaimed regional governments established themselves, Croats left. Eventually, on July 25, 1990, these regions fused together to form the self-proclaimed Serbian Republic of Krajina (Republika Srpska Krajina, or RSK). Unlike Croatia, which was recognized as an independent state by the United Nations in April 1992, the Serbian Republic of Krajina never gained international legitimacy.

The most intense combat in Croatia took place between July and December 1991. In the course of the war, large portions of Croatia were severely devastated by warfare. The Eastern Slavonian city of Vukovar was perhaps the hardest hit major settlement. When the city capitulated on November 17, 1991, it was almost completely destroyed. However, many other cities, including Dubrovnik, listed as a World Heritage Site by the United Nations Educational, Scientific, and Cultural Organization (UNESCO), withstood major attacks by the Yugoslav, Montenegrin, and Bosnian Serb forces. The minority of non-Serbs who did not take the opportunity to leave areas falling under the occupation of Serb forces faced constant threats to their physical existence. Both the battles for

Vukovar and Dubrovnik eventually resulted in indictments being brought at the International Criminal Tribunal for the Former Yugoslavia (ICTY).

In December 1991, Croatia and the rebellious Serb forces signed a cease-fire agreement. Roughly one-third of Croatia remained under RSK control. A UN "protection force" was inserted to act as a buffer zone between Croat and Serb forces. Although this strategy succeeded in subduing the armed conflict in Croatia, it also had the side-effect of allowing RSK forces to cement their hold on the territory they had occupied.

From this time until 1995, only intermittent skirmishes took place. By May 1995, the Croat government and military gained sufficient confidence to launch a rapid attack ("Operation Flash") against the RSK enclave in Western Slavonia. Only a few months later, on August 4, 1995, the Croatian army conducted a massive offensive ("Operation Storm") against the bulk of the RSK. Only the Serb-administered areas in Eastern Slavonia remained unscathed. The RSK forces offered very little military resistance. It is estimated that between 100,000 and 300,000 Serbs fled to the Federal Republic of Yugoslavia or to Serb-controlled areas of Bosnia-Herzegovina.

In the wake of both of the major Croatian military operations in 1995, major atrocities were committed against the Serbs of Croatia. In several instances, elderly Serbs remaining behind were summarily killed by Croat forces or paramilitaries. Both Serbs from Croatia and Croats were indicted by ICTY on charges of serious violations of international humanitarian law in 1995.

Those Serb refugees arriving in the Federal Republic of Yugoslavia from Croatia did not receive a warm welcome. Although the Milo<shacek>evi<cacute> regime had once encouraged these Serbs to rebel against Croat rule, the same regime now believed that the disgruntled mass of refugees represented a force of political opposition. For this reason, the Serbs of Croatia experienced considerable difficulties and delays in regularizing their legal status and obtaining civil and political rights in the Federal Republic of Yugoslavia.

In 1998, the transfer of Eastern Slavonia to Croatian rule took place. With the exception of the small, contested Prevlaka peninsula near Dubrovnik, which was returned to Croatian jurisdiction in 2002, this marked the end of Serb control of Croatian territory.

The process of undoing ethnic cleansing in Croatia is further complicated by the presence of refugees from Bosnia-Herzegovina. After 1992, Croatia became home to large numbers of Bosnian Croats who had been expelled from areas controlled by the Bosnian Serbs or Bosnian Muslims. Upon arrival in Croatia, the Bosnian Croat refugees often settled in houses from which Serbs had been displaced. The return of large numbers of Serbs would therefore require the relocation of many Bosnian Croat families.

In December 1999, President Franjo Tudjman died. In subsequent and parliamentary elections, the ruling HDZ coalition lost dramatically to a coalition of nonnationalist and moderate nationalist parties. However, initial hopes about the impact of the new government on interethnic relations in Croatia proved overly optimistic. The post-Tudjman coalition proved unwilling to confront the politically explosive issue of refugee returns. At the same time, the government did not seem willing to acknowledge publicly the forcible expulsion of much of Croatia's Serb minority during the 1991–1995 war, officially known in Croatia as the "Homeland War." For this reason, the government procrastinated over the publication of the 2001 census, which revealed a drastic drop in the Serb minority population when compared to the 1991 census. The most recent studies estimate that less than one-third of displaced Serbs have returned to Croatia. Many Serbs who have returned have encountered official and informal hostility, including trials for crimes allegedly committed against the Croatian state. By contrast, few Croats have faced charges related to the persecution of Serbs during the 1991–1995 period.

Christian A. Nielsen

See also: Ethnic Cleansing; Ethnic Cleansing: Armenia; Ethnic Cleansing: Bosnia-Herzegovina; Ethnic Cleansing: Kosovo; Ethnic Cleansing: Poles from Western Ukraine; Genocide; Indian Partition

References and further reading:

Banac, Ivo. 1983. *The National Question in Yugoslavia.* Ithaca, NY: Cornell University Press.

Goldstein, Ivo. 1999. *Croatia: A History.* Montreal: McGill-Queen's University Press.

Human Rights Watch. 1996. "Impunity for Abuses Committed during 'Operation Storm' and the Denial of Rights of Refugees to Return to the Krajina." New York: Human Rights Watch.

———. 2003. "Broken Promises: Impediments to Refugee Return to Croatia." New York: Human Rights Watch.

International Crisis Group. 2002. "A Half-Hearted Welcome: Refugee Returns to Croatia." Brussels: International Crisis Group.

Sells, Michael A., "Reports on War Crimes in the Former Yugoslavia," http://www.haverford.edu/relg/sells/reports.html.

Silber, Laura, and Alan Little. 1996. *The Death of Yugoslavia.* Rev. ed. London: Penguin.

Ethnic Cleansing: Germans from Central and Eastern Europe

From 1944 to 1949, 14 million Germans and ethnic Germans were forcibly moved from Central and Eastern Europe. About 8 million of them arrived in what became West Germany; 4 million ended up in East Germany. It was the largest single case of ethnic cleansing in human history (where ethnic cleansing is understood as including expulsion and death). Some 2 million people died during the transfer through hunger, intemperate weather, or murder at the hands of Soviet troops, mobs of Poles, Czechs, and Slovaks, or other locals, and many others suffered beatings and rape. The figures for both the number of expulsions and the number of deaths remain contested and politically controversial. The Federal Republic of Germany (FRG) defined all individuals forced to leave their traditional homeland (*Siedlungsgebiet*) in Germany's eastern territories, or elsewhere in Central and Eastern Europe, as refugees or expellees. The refugees were those who, from the spring of 1944, fled the advancing Red Army; the expellees were those who remained in their homelands and then fled or were forcibly expelled after the end of the war. So-called "wild" or spontaneous expulsions, without legal basis, occurred in Czechoslovakia and Yugoslavia, and to some degree also in Poland. The majority of expulsions occurred under Article 12 of the Potsdam Agreement of August 1945, which specified that they occur in an "orderly and humane manner."

The expulsions occurred in three broad phases. First, refugees fled East Prussia, Pomerania, Silesia, and eastern Brandenburg as Soviet troops pushed through these territories. This movement, which took place between mid-1944 and the end of the war in May 1945, was spontaneous and lacked international and legal legitimacy. Second, in 1945 and 1946, chaotic, poorly organized, and often citizen-led expulsions drove Germans from east of the Oder and Neisse rivers (in East Prussia, Silesia, and so on), from the Sudetenland in Czechoslovakia, and from Poland, Hungary, and Yugoslavia. Finally, from 1946, the Allies attempted, with limited success, to regulate and humanize the population transfers. These movements followed the July-August 1945 Potsdam Conference. At the conference, the Soviet Union, the United States, and the United Kingdom agreed to allow the Soviet Union to keep the half of Poland that it had annexed under the Ribbentrop-Molotov Pact of 1939, to compensate Poland for this lost territory, and to reverse the 1938 Munich Agreement, which had transferred the Sudetenland from Czechoslovakia to Nazi Germany. As a result, Germany lost all territories east of the Oder-Neisse, including the ancient cities of Königsberg (now Kaliningrad, in Russia) and Breslau (now Wroc(aw, in Poland). These territorial shifts were to be accompanied by the "orderly and humane" transfer of the German inhabitants of these territories. By the early 1950s, the expulsions were complete.

There are a number of perspectives from which one can approach the expulsions. The first is comparative perspective: They might be taken as a case study in expulsion and compared to other major twentieth-century instances of ethnic cleansing, such as the Armenians from Turkey, the Poles from the Western Ukraine, and the Bosnians, Croatians, and Kosovars from the former Yugoslavia. Norman Naimark's (2001) work is in this vein. The second perspective considers the expellees from the standpoint of the nation-building efforts in the states of Central and Eastern Europe—Hungary, the Czech Republic, and Poland. Here, the expulsions are viewed as part of a broader state-sanctioned pursuit of homogeneity as the foundation for ethnically based nationhood. This pursuit of an elusive racial purity had its roots in nineteenth- and twentieth-century state formation, found its most complete expression in National Socialist (Nazi) race policy, and outlived the destruction of Nazism, as illustrated in former Yugoslavia. The third approach is to view the expulsions from the perspective of the expellees: the Germans from Breslau, Königsberg, the Sudetenland, and so on as they fled or were driven out. Alfred de Zayas wrote some of the earliest English-language work in this tradition.

Although the expellees themselves welcomed the work in this third category, seeing it as a serious attempt to draw attention to their plight, others have viewed it as excessively focused on the victims to the neglect of context and as an apology for particularly Sudeten-German sympathy for National Socialist designs on Czechoslovakian sovereignty. The critics also complain that such work is one-sided, sentimental, and romantic in its depiction of the expellees. This entry focuses in particular on the second perspective, but with appropriate balance all three can play a role in placing the expulsions in their twentieth-century historical and ideological context.

The Historical Context of the Expulsions

The twentieth century has been characterized as the "century of refugees" (Schlögel 2003), and expulsions have left their traces throughout the period. They began with the Balkan wars of 1912–1913, and ended—again in the Balkans—with the Kosovo war of 1999. In the intervening years, Europe was transformed through the resettlement, expulsion, and destruction of entire populations. The former ethnic, linguistic, and cultural diversity of massive geopolitical entities—namely, the Ottoman and the Hapsburg empires—disappeared. In their place, states sought to secure a correspondence of nation, state, and ethnicity, or one ethnic group per nation-state. They pursued this aim through assimilation, border changes, resettlement (for instance, population exchanges), expulsion, and, finally, genocide.

It is possible to distinguish three phrases of forced migration in the twentieth century. The first occurred between 1912/1913 and the 1920s in southern Europe, including Bulgaria, Greece, the Ottoman Empire (Turkey), Romania, and Serbia. The second phase of "ethnic unmixing" began in 1938, when Nazi Germany forced through the Munich

Agreement the transfer of the Sudetenland from Czechoslovakia to Germany. The action had two implications: It led to the flight of ethnic Czechs from the Sudetenland to Czechoslovakia, and it was the prelude to the National Socialists' expansionist policy. The latter sought a complete ethno-demographic reorganization of Central and Eastern Europe on the basis of racism and race policy. Briefly, this policy involved, first, the physical destruction of European Jews; second, the resettlement and enslavement of Slavs; and finally, the repatriation of German minority populations out of Central and Eastern Europe. The resettlement of so-called *Volksdeutschen* (from the Balkans, parts of Romania, the north Black Sea region, Slovenia, and part of Tirol) from 1940 mostly affected regions from which the Jewish or Slavic population had been expelled or deported, particularly in occupied Poland (the so-called *Warthegau*).

After the end of World War II, the price of National Socialist policy was horribly paid by those of German lineage who lived as a German minority in Central/Eastern Europe or as German citizens in pre-1945 eastern Germany. They were partly the victims of revenge, but also of the Allies' geostrategic machinations: The decision at the February 1945 Yalta Conference to shift Poland westward was preconditioned on the expulsion of the Germans. The shifting of an entire country inevitably involved the transfer in massive numbers of different populations: Germans, driven from their historical homelands west of the Oder-Neisse into the Allied zones of occupied Germany; Poles from historical eastern Poland into the former German eastern territories; and Russians and Ukrainians, who settled in the eastern areas "cleansed" of Poles.

The flight and expulsions of the Germans from Eastern Europe ended a centuries-long history. The story of the Germans in Central and Eastern Europe began with the eastern colonization in the late Middle Ages and the west-east migration in the early modern period. In the latter, tsarist Russia under Catherine II and Austria-Hungary under Maria Theresia and Joseph II populated their territories with German settlers. These colonizers stemmed in large measure from the south and southwest and former German states.

The Expulsions before 1945

By the summer of 1944, it was obvious that Germany was going to lose the war, and lose it badly. On June 22, the Soviets launched their Great Offensive and pushed into German territory; the Western Allies had already landed at Normandy on June 6. The last hope for the German resistance, the July plot on the 20th, had ended in failure when the bomb placed by Claus von Stauffenberg near Adolf Hitler was moved under a large desk, protecting the dictator from the blast. From the east, the Russians were advancing toward Berlin, and German civilians began taking flight as they approached.

The first Germans to move westward as the Soviets approached were those settled by the Nazi regime after 1939 in territories lost by Germany in the Versailles Treaty—the former German provinces of West Prussia and Posen—as well as in occupied Polish territory and in Germany itself. The German military also began organizing evacuations (de Zayas 1977, 60). On October 16, 1944, the Red Army launched a major offensive into East Prussia; three weeks later, a German counteroffensive pushed them back. In the small village of Nemmersdorf, Wehrmacht and Volkssturm soldiers found women naked and crucified with nails, infants with crushed skulls, and an old woman with an axe through her head (Diestelkamp et al. 1984, eyewitness report No. 5 in Schieder et al. 1984).

Nemmersdorf seemed to confirm German propaganda about Russian barbarity, but the fear of it had already done the job: Before and after the incident, hundreds of thousands fled. As winter came, they pushed their carts through the snow; formed miles-long queues; and tried to keep ahead of the advancing Russians. In East Prussia, they boarded ships in the thousands and attempted to cross the Baltic before the Russians enclosed them. Some made it. Others drowned as their ships were sunk by Soviet torpedoes (the most famous—recently revisited by the Nobel Laureate Günther Grass—was the *Wilhelm Gustloff,* on which more than 9,000 people died), were shot on the ice by low-flying planes, or were mowed down by tanks.

Poland and Czechoslovakia

Germany's treatment of the Poles—surpassed in brutality only by their treatment of the Jews—instilled in some of the occupied people an undying hatred. What's more, the Germans' own expulsion of more than a million Poles from annexed territory tempered reservations about population transfer. Before German territories were formally transferred to Poland, the Soviets gave the Poles permission to move into the German provinces of East Prussia, Pomerania, and Silesia. There were also hundreds of thousands of Germans in territories transferred from Germany to Poland by the Treaty of Versailles. The Poles began driving Germans out of their homes with a brutality that had by then almost become commonplace: People were beaten, shot, and raped. Even Soviet soldiers were taken aback, and some protected the German civilians (Naimark 2001, 119). At the same time, however, there were instances of great kindness: Polish workers, even slave laborers, would disguise Germans as Poles to protect them from vengeful mobs.

In Czechoslovakia, hostility between the Czechs and the Germans dated at least to the nineteenth century, and the Versailles Treaty intensified it. There were more than 3 million Germans in the Sudetenland. The area was incorporated into Czechoslovakia after World War I. The German population resented what they regarded as subjugation; the broader Czechoslovakian government and population viewed them as treacherous. The majority of the Sudeten leadership (there was also a non-Nazi social-democratic faction) looked to Hitler, and when the Munich Agreement, negotiated without Czechoslovakian participation to appease Hitler, transferred the Sudetenland to Nazi Germany, the German population there was overwhelmingly rapturous. Many were equally so when German tanks rolled into Prague in 1939. As soon as the war had ended, but as yet without international legitimacy, the Czechoslovakian population began driving the Germans out. As in Poland, the Germans were given minutes to gather a few belongings and to leave their homes; they were marched out on foot (and later in trains) and ended up in hastily arranged refugee camps in Austria. In most cases, ethnicity rather than actions determined the expulsions: German Jews and anti-Nazis were not immune.

By July 1945, 3.5 million Germans had fled the Soviet offensive; 700,000 to 800,000 Germans had already left or been driven out of the former Sudetenland, and a similar number had fled Poland (Naimark 2001, 111). But the expulsions had only begun.

Potsdam

In July 1945, the big three—Winston Churchill, Joseph Stalin, and Harry S. Truman—met at Potsdam, just outside Berlin. The division and amputation of Germany had been agreed at previous conferences, at Yalta, Teheran, and Malta. The Soviet Union would retain territories it secured through the Ribbentrop-Molotov Pact, including a large slice of Poland, and gain the northern part of east Prussia; Poland would be compensated with German territory; and the Sudetenland would be given back to Czechoslovakia. At Potsdam, the three leaders agreed to the transfer. Article 12 of the Potsdam Protocol stated: "The Three Governments, having considered the question in all its aspects, recognize that the transfer to Germany of German populations, or elements thereof, remaining in Poland, Czechoslovakia and Hungary, will have to be undertaken. They agree that any transfers that take place should be effected in an orderly and humane manner." The last three words have given rise to much ironic comment.

At the time of the Potsdam Agreement, the expulsions were in full swing. Germans were loaded onto trains in Poland, Hungary, and Czechoslovakia and shipped to Germany; long queues of Germans continued to trek slowly across Central Europe; and beatings, rapes, and murders continued to accompany the expulsions. One young woman from Stettin watched Russian soldiers shoot her father and heard them rape her mother and sister as she hid. On a train to Berlin, she was raped by Russian soldiers, then by Polish soldiers, and saw a Polish soldier crush the head of a crying infant against a post while raping its mother (*Daily News* report of October 7, 1945, quoted in de Zayas 1977, 114). She got off comparatively lightly: Some women were raped dozens of times on the journey.

An unknown figure—from 200,000 to 2 million—would die in the flight to Germany. Those who made it, particularly in the early years, found the arrival as bad as the flight. They arrived hungry, cold, and weak in cities that had been flattened by Allied bombing. Particularly during the disastrously cold winter of 1945–1946, trains arrived in Berlin and Munich with the dead and dying in each carriage (other dead had been thrown from the train along the way), and with others ill and weak. Babies had died in their mothers' arms; children left as sons and daughters but arrived as orphans. The stench of rotting clothes, excrement, and death was everywhere.

The Allies, increasingly dismayed by reports of beatings, rapes, and death, attempted to impose order on the expulsions and to improve conditions. It would be a linguistic stretch to describe them as "orderly and humane," but they were better than they had been in 1945: Some expulsions were spaced over a longer period of time, fewer trains were sent in the winter, and the International Red Cross was able to put a stop to the practice of using German civilians from the Svidnik camp in Czechoslovakia to clear mines. These changes saved lives, but they only made the expulsions less horrible, rather than anything approaching humane. Things would continue that way until 1949, when the expulsions ended. Hundreds of thousands of Germans were still left in Eastern Europe; they had managed to hide their nationality (for instance, by adopting Polish names and no longer speaking German), were regarded as too professionally essential by the authorities to expel, or were sheltered by sympathetic locals. Moreover, the Soviet Union did not expel its ethnic German population, which it had deported to Siberia and Kazakhstan in 1941 following the German attack on the Soviet Union.

The Expellees in Postwar Germany

Legally, the expellees and refugees entered and were integrated into Germany under Article 116 (1) of the Basic Law (*Grundgesetz*), the 1952 Equalization of Burdens Law (*Lastenausgleichsgesetz*), and the 1953 Expellees Law (*Bundesvertriebenengesetz*). From 1949 until 1969, there was a federal ministry dealing exclusively with expellee and refugee issues. In the Communist German Democratic Republic (GDR), by contrast, the question of the so-called "resettlement" was, for political and ideological reasons, not dealt with through separate administrative bodies. Given the Soviet Union's central role in the expulsions, it was effectively impossible to discuss them officially (by contrast, the GDR annually marked and politicized the destruction of Dresden by Anglo-American "terror bombing").

The arrival of millions of expellees and refugees in a divided, occupied, impoverished, and thoroughly destroyed country presented seemingly intractable social, political, and economic problems. The social and economic strain on a bankrupt country led the local population to react with skepticism, suspicion, and at times open hostility. Although the financial strain would gradually ease with the 1950s' upswing in the German economy, the housing shortage would last, both in the FRG and the GDR, through the 1960s. The integration of the expellees/refugees was a conflict of scarce resources, one punctuated with envy and competition between both Germans and expellees/refugees and among the expellees/refugees themselves. It was also, ultimately, a success, at least in the FRG. Part of the success reflected the equalization law, which restored part of the expellees' and refugees' lost wealth and property. "Native" West Germans were taxed according to their own income and possession, a sort of state-enforced exercise in national solidarity (repeated again, with mixed results, through the postunification solidarity tax for eastern Germany). It also, however, reflected the expellees' and refugees' early coordination through regional organizations (the East Prussian association, the Silesian association, and so on) and an umbrella organization (the Federal Expellees Association). In the 1950s, there was a distinct right-wing nationalist party, the Federation for Expellees and Deprived Persons, but the Christian Democratic Union (CDU) Chancellor Konrad Adenauer, partly through maintaining official support for territorial revision, and partly because of the party's own internal divisions, managed to integrate it into Germany's established conservative parties.

For several reasons, the flight and the expulsions of Germans was, and remains to this day, a controversial topic. Until 1989, it was often viewed through the lens of the Cold War. The GDR wished to avoid conflict with its socialist neighbors and partners: the Soviets, who had legitimized the expulsions, and the Czechoslovakians and Poles, who implemented them. If the GDR largely ignored the theme, these other countries offered only an official interpretation of the expulsions as a just punishment for Nazi crimes. Only after 1989 was this interpretation questioned. By contrast, in the FRG, despite the opposition of the left, the state supported the expellees' political and cultural development, and the expulsions attracted sustained attention, much of it highly controversial, throughout the postwar period.

Broadly, one can distinguish three phases in its development. First, from the early years until the 1960s, politicians, academics, and commentators treated the expellees as victims of World War II, along with soldiers on the eastern front and civilians in cities bombed by the Allies. This interpretation was challenged in the late 1960s by two developments. First, Ostpolitik, a policy of easing tensions and establishing contacts with eastern Germany and the rest of Communist Eastern Europe, required the acceptance of the territorial status quo and the rejection of the expellees' demands for compensation and (though this was rarer) territorial revision. In a series of treaties, Germany effectively recognized Europe's post-1945 borders. The expellees bitterly opposed the move, and Chancellor Willy Brandt found it difficult to get the treaties through the German Parliament. His eloquently expressed view that "I did not give up anything that was not lost long ago" nonetheless reflected the opinion of the majority of Germans.

As a result of Ostpolitik, debate over the expulsions became politicized, emotional, and polarized along left-right lines. Flight and expulsion became an increasingly conservative topic and was stigmatized by the center and the left as revisionist. At the same time, from the 1960s the West German public increasingly discussed the Holocaust, National Socialism, and German guilt. This new attention raised the question—still unanswered—of how to locate the history of one's own victims in the larger history of a nation of perpetrators: How does one locate German suffering within the broader context of German guilt? Finally, the end of the Cold War ushered in a new, and less politically polarized, interest in the topic. National television stations aired documentaries about it, and the weekly newsmagazine *Der Spiegel* devoted headline articles to it. The expellees themselves changed their focus from their own suffering and demand for compensation to a new demand for historical and media attention to the topic (including a controversial call for a "Center against Expulsions" in Berlin).

The flight and expulsion of the Germans was, like the war and their defeat, a fundamental break, a rupture, in the French sense of the word, in German and European history. A centuries-old German history in Central and Eastern Europe ended. At the same time, the expulsions changed Germany itself: The arrival of millions of refugees and expellees altered the social and religious makeup of the receiving German states, disrupting traditional class and social hierarchies. It also contributed to the process of the ethnic cleansing and homogenization of Eastern Europe (one frozen by the Cold War, then reignited again in post-1989 Yugoslavia), achieving a closer correspondence of nation and state. In a newly enlarged and reunited Europe, the historical and normative issues raised by the expulsions—their legality, morality, and economic and social consequences—will be addressed by observers of what until May 2004 was Eastern and Western Europe.

Randall Hansen and Rainer Ohliger

See also: Ethnic Cleansing; Ethnic Germans; Genocide; Germany

References and further reading:
Beevor, Anthony. 1999. *Stalingrad.* London: Penguin.
De Zayas, Alfred. 1977. *Nemesis at Potsdam.* London: Routledge and Kegan Paul.
Grass, Günter. 2002. *Crabwalk.* New York: Harcourt.
Marrus, Michael. 2002. *The Unwanted.* Philadelphia: Temple University Press.
Naimark, Norman. 2001. *Fires of Hatred: Ethnic Cleansing in Twentieth Century Europe.* Oxford: Oxford University Press.
Schieder, Theodor, et al. 1984. *Dokumentation der Vertreibung der Deutschen aus Ost-Mitteleuropa.* Bonn: Federal Ministry for Expellees.
Schlögel, Karl. 2003. "Ethnic Cleansing as an Invention of the Twentieth Century: An Account of Expulsions in Europe." Pp. 98–111 in *Diasporas and Ethnic Migrants: Germany, Israel and Post-Soviet Successor States in Comparative Perspective.* Edited by Rainer Münz and Rainer Ohliger. London: Frank Cass.

Ethnic Cleansing: Kosovo

In the spring of 1999, the forced expulsion of ethnic Albanians from the province of Kosovo, located in the Federal Republic of Yugoslavia (Serbia-Montenegro), provided the main motivation for a major international military and humanitarian intervention. Beginning on March 24, 1999, the North Atlantic Treaty Organization (NATO) conducted ten weeks of aerial bombardment of targets in the Federal Republic of Yugoslavia in an attempt to force the cessation of a low-intensity conflict in Kosovo. This conflict was accompanied by a deliberate campaign, conducted by the Yugoslav and Serb security forces, aimed at forcibly altering the ethnic landscape of Kosovo. In particular, these forces sought to assert Serb control over Kosovo and increase the proportion of Serbs in the population through expulsions of the Kosovo Albanian population. At the end of the NATO intervention, the Yugoslav and Serb forces were forced to withdraw from Kosovo, which was put under the administration of the United Nations.

Historically, Kosovo featured as a region of contention between the emerging Serb and Albanian nationalisms. In 1389, a battle—later heavily mythologized—took place in Kosovo between Serb and Ottoman forces. This, combined with the presence of a significant number of Serbian Orthodox churches and monasteries, ensured that Kosovo would remain a sacred place for Serb nationalism. Moreover, directly connected to any discussion of migration, the Serbs of Kosovo memorialized a "Great Migration" of Serbs to escape Ottoman repression in 1690.

Although historians debate the character and dimensions of this Great Migration, it cannot be disputed that the event featured prominently in Serb attitudes toward Kosovo. In Serb nationalist historiography, Kosovo has been consistently portrayed as the cradle of Serb civilization and as a center of the nation's suffering. Serb historians claim that Serbs have systematically been expelled and marginalized by a growing, "alien" Albanian presence in Kosovo. This view was most vividly articulated in an unpublished draft memorandum of the Serbian Academy of Sciences and Arts in 1986. The memorandum bluntly accused the Kosovo Albanians of committing cultural and economic genocide against the Serb nation. The drafters of the memorandum also asserted that the high fertility of the Kosovo Albanians formed part of a conscious campaign to "Albanianize" Kosovo.

After several centuries of Ottoman rule, Serbia first asserted full control over Kosovo during the Balkan Wars of 1912–1913. Ethnic cleansing was a major phenomenon of these two wars, as clearly reported by the Carnegie Commission sent to investigate the conflict. As the Ottoman Empire receded, Muslims, including large numbers of Albanians, were forcibly displaced from Serbia and Montenegro. At the same time, in November 1912 an independent Albanian state came into existence. This constellation, with heavily Albanian, but Serbian-ruled, Kosovo bordering the Albanian state, would prove constant for most of the twentieth century.

After World War I, Kosovo existed as a part of Serbia within the Kingdom of Serbs, Croats, and Slovenes. Regarded as part of "Southern" or "Old" Serbia by Serb officials in Belgrade, Kosovo suffered from poverty, misadministration, and widespread corruption. The non-Serb population, of which the largest portion consisted of ethnic Albanians, lived under a repressive and discriminatory regime. In World War II, Kosovo was divided into German, Italian, and Bulgarian sectors. After the war, in socialist Yugoslavia, Kosovo was granted the status of an administrative region within the Socialist Republic of Serbia. Following an initial period under strong (Serbian) centralized rule, more autonomy was granted after 1966. The 1974 constitution in Yugoslavia elevated Kosovo to the status of an autonomous region within Serbia. This reform allowed the first significant emergence of ethnic Albanian administrators and officials in Yugoslavia. However, as macroeconomic problems mounted in Yugoslavia, tensions between ethnic Serbs and Albanians began to reemerge. During the last two decades of Yugoslavia, many Serbs left Kosovo in search of better economic opportunities elsewhere in the country. By 1991, ethnic Albanians constituted nearly 90 percent of the population in Kosovo.

In the second half of the 1980s, Slobodan Milošević a rising socialist apparatchik, inadvertently identified real and perceived Serb grievances in Kosovo as a resource that he could use to mobilize political support. As in many other collapsing socialist states in East Central Europe and the

Victims of ethnic cleansing, thousands upon thousands of Kosovar refugees arrive in Blace at the Macedonian border. (Grazia Neri/R. Arcari/Corbis Sygma)

Balkans, the Serb population latched on to nationalist ideology as a replacement for discredited socialist ideology. Police oppression increased markedly. In 1988, Milošević revoked Kosovo's autonomous status and commenced a crackdown on cultural and other minority rights in Kosovo. Seen from the perspective of Serbia, Milošević's campaign of centralization was compatible with Yugoslavism and simply marked an attempt to strengthen the Yugoslav state. However, non-Serbs in Yugoslavia did not share this viewpoint. The other republics interpreted the rescinding of Kosovo's autonomy as a harbinger of things to come for them. As a result, this decision marked a turning point for Yugoslavia as a whole and led directly to the alienation of Slovenia, Croatia, and Bosnia-Herzegovina from Serbia.

Through the extensive use of repressive mechanisms, the leadership of Serbia prevented the outbreak of armed conflict in Kosovo in the first half of the 1990s, even as war visited Slovenia, Croatia, and Bosnia-Herzegovina. Factors on the ethnic Albanian side also played a role. The Albanian state, mired in post-Communist collapse, and separated from the ethnic Albanians of Kosovo by a decades-long historical divide, did not seek to intervene in Kosovo. Moreover, the leading ethnic Albanian politician in Kosovo, Ibrahim Rugova, strongly preferred nonviolent means of conflict resolution. Rather than fomenting armed rebellion and secession, Rugova and his followers concentrated on the establishment of a virtual parallel state. This included education in the Albanian language, local government, health care, and many other elements. The creation of a parallel Albanian state in Kosovo confirmed an accomplished fact. On almost every issue of significance, the Serbs and Albanians of Kosovo lived in separate realities and held diametrically opposed views.

In December 1995, the Dayton Accords were signed, ending the war in Bosnia-Herzegovina. Ethnic Albanians felt great disappointment that their situation did not find any mention in this agreement. Among a small but radical element in the ethnic Albanian population, the idea took root that guerrilla and terrorist tactics offered the only hope of change. Those pursuing this option correctly assumed that the reaction of the Yugoslav and Serb security forces to such tactics would be disproportionate and violent attacks against the civilian population. These attacks would, in turn, force the international community to take action.

Consequently, in the mid-1990s, the radical group within the majority ethnic Albanian population in Kosovo began to conduct selected attacks on representatives of Serb officialdom and the security forces. This group called itself the Kosovo Liberation Army (Ushtria Çlirimtare e Kosovës, or UÇK). Although initially poorly armed, the UÇK received an enormous windfall of armaments when Albania collapsed into civil unrest in the summer of 1997. During this period, Albanian citizens looted the armories of the Albanian military. A substantial portion of the weapons and ammunition made its way to the Kosovo Albanian rebels. By 1998, the UÇK had succeeded in establishing de facto control of large swaths of territory in Kosovo. The leaders of the UÇK rejected the nonviolent tactics of Rugova in favor of guerrilla warfare.

The UÇK correctly calculated that the Serb security forces would respond with disproportionate force to its presence and attacks. An escalating spiral of violence was the consequence, with an accompanying increase in the civilian death toll. This greatly alarmed the United States and the European Union, both of which feared a repetition of a major armed conflict similar to the preceding wars in Croatia and Bosnia-Herzegovina. International public opinion also played a significant role and was kept alarmed by recurring reports of massacres of ethnic Albanians in Kosovo.

In January 1999, an observer mission from the Organization for Security and Cooperation in Europe (OSCE) uncovered another massacre of ethnic Albanians. This prompted an international conference convened at Rambouillet in France in February and March 1999. However, the Rambouillet conference failed to produce a solution to the continuing crisis in Kosovo when the Yugoslav delegation refused to submit to what it perceived as a military ultimatum. After the collapse of the Rambouillet conference, NATO took rapid steps against the Federal Republic of Yugoslavia. From March 24 until June 10, 1999, NATO planes bombarded targets throughout the country. Although NATO did consider ground operations, ultimately only air strikes took place.

Almost immediately after the commencement of NATO bombing, tens of thousands of Kosovo Albanians were driven out of Kosovo and into neighboring Albania and Macedonia. In a pattern resembling that of the previous conflicts in the former Yugoslavia in the 1990s, armed paramilitary groups worked together with the Yugoslav military and Serb police to attack and terrorize the non-Serb civilian population. According to Human Rights Watch (2001), "The Yugoslav military and Serbian police and paramilitaries expelled 862,979 Albanians from Kosovo." The Serb security forces burned villages and frequently killed any ethnic Albanians who had not taken the opportunity to leave in advance of the arrival of the police or army. Large numbers of rapes and enforced pregnancies were also perpetrated against the ethnic Albanians. The police and military also deliberately damaged or destroyed hundreds of Albanian and Islamic cultural and religious objects in Kosovo. Crucially, however, this marked the acceleration of an established practice. A subsequent independent statistical study by the American Association for the Advancement of Science rejected the hypothesis that NATO bombing had been the causal factor for the forced migration of ethnic Albanians from Kosovo.

NATO and other multilateral international organizations failed to anticipate and prepare for the massive flow of refugees from Kosovo in 1999. The task of the international humanitarian effort in Kosovo was greatly complicated by the fact that many refugees arrived with few, if any, documents attesting to their identity. As part of the process to expel ethnic Albanians from Kosovo, the Yugoslav security forces attempted to confiscate any documents that would allow them to demonstrate their previous places of residence. This policy was designed to frustrate any attempted returns of ethnic Albanians to Kosovo.

Notwithstanding the lack of international foresight, the refugee flow arguably proved fortuitous for the NATO coalition. The publicity devoted to the plight of ethnic Albanians leaving Kosovo galvanized Western public opinion and largely neutralized public opposition against the bombardment campaign. After the end of the war, the Yugoslav government, led by Slobodan Milošević agreed to NATO's demand that all Yugoslav security forces withdraw completely from Kosovo. In their place came a large NATO force known as KFOR (Kosovo Force). Although legally still a part of the Federal Republic of Yugoslavia, Kosovo was administered by the United Nations as a virtual international protectorate. Eventually, as a result of investigations into crimes committed in Kosovo since 1991, the International Criminal Tribunal for the Former Yugoslavia (ICTY) in The Hague indicted Milošević other Yugoslav and Serb leaders, and several ethnic Albanians. The arrest and extradition of Milošević to The Hague in 2001 marked the first time a former head of state had been brought to trial for war crimes.

In the wake of the conflict with Serbs, many ethnic Albanians took the opportunity of their return to Kosovo to seek revenge against Serbs and other non-Albanians. As a result, non-Albanians were physically threatened or harmed, and many found themselves forced to leave Kosovo. In a further reversal of the situation previous to June 1999, Albanian nationalist extremists targeted Serb cultural objects, especially churches and monasteries, for arson attacks. Although attacks and discrimination against such objects and non-Albanians were condemned by both the UN and KFOR, both of these organizations in practice proved unable or unwilling to prevent them from happening. The postconflict situation also had other negative migratory side-effects, as Kosovo became a major transit point for illegal human migrants and international prostitution rings. As of December 2003, more than four years after the commencement of the NATO aerial campaign against the Federal Republic of Yugoslavia, the legal status of Kosovo remained unresolved.

Christian A. Nielsen

See also: Ethnic Cleansing; Ethnic Cleansing: Armenia; Ethnic Cleansing: Bosnia-Herzegovina; Ethnic Cleansing: Croatia; Ethnic Cleansing: Poles from Western Ukraine; Genocide; Indian Partition

References and further reading:

Booth, Ken, ed. 2001. *The Kosovo Tragedy: The Human Rights Dimensions.* London: Frank Cass.

Duijzings, Ger. 2000. *Religion and the Politics of Identity in Kosovo.* New York: Columbia University Press.

Human Rights Watch. 2001. *Under Orders: War Crimes in Kosovo.* New York: Human Rights Watch.

Kennan, George F. 1993. *The Other Balkan Wars: A 1913 Carnegie Endowment Inquiry in Retrospect.* Washington, DC: Carnegie Endowment.

Malcolm, Noel. 1998. *Kosovo: A Short History.* New York: Macmillan.

Mertus, Julie. 1999. *How Lies and Truths Started a War.* Berkeley: University of California Press.

Riedlmayer, András, and Andrew Herscher. 2000. "The Destruction and Reconstruction of Architectural Heritage in Kosovo: A Post-War Report," http://www.bosnia.org.uk/bosrep/report_format.cfm?articleid=703&reportid=146.

Sells, Michael A., "Reports on War Crimes in the Former Yugoslavia," http://www.haverford.edu/relg/sells/reports.html.

Ethnic Cleansing: Poles from Western Ukraine

In 1943–1944, a campaign of murder and mass expulsion was carried out by the radical Organization of Ukrainian Nationalists (OUN) and its military arm, the Ukrainian Insurgent Army (UPA), against Polish settlements in the Western Ukrainian lands of Volhynia and Eastern Galicia. The assault generated a mass exodus of Poles and drastically changed the ethnic composition of these regions.

After World War I, Poland was resurrected as an independent state. The new Polish state incorporated Volhynia and Eastern Galicia, part of the so-called Eastern Borderlands (Kresy Wshodnie), as a result of the Polish-Ukrainian and Polish-Soviet wars in 1918–1920. Ethnic Ukrainians constituted a numerical majority in the Volhynian and East Galician countryside, whereas Polish and Jewish minorities dominated urban areas and local economies. In the city and countryside, ethnic Poles held key positions in the administration, in the police force, and in the school system.

Ukrainian political activists, however, never gave up their aspirations for independence, and in the early 1920s former officers of the Ukrainian national armies organized clandestine groups aimed at establishing Ukrainian statehood. The main Ukrainian underground group, the Ukrainian Military Organization (UVO), carried out an anti-Polish propaganda campaign, acts of sabotage, and the assassinations of Polish officials and Ukrainians suspected of pro-Polish sympathies. In 1929, the UVO and several other nationalist groups fused into the OUN, which continued to conduct terrorist activities. Reprisals by the Polish government, and the socioeconomic depression in Western Ukraine in the 1920s, further exacerbated ethnic animosities, and hundreds of Ukrainians joined the OUN.

The OUN aimed at national and social revolution in Ukraine and displayed visible tendencies toward strong authoritarian rule. It was built on military principles and strict hierarchy, and its symbols emulated those of the fascist movements in Western Europe. Its main goal was to create an independent Ukraine and remove—by force, if necessary—non-Ukrainians from the social and economic spheres of a future Ukrainian state. On the eve of World War II, the OUN had established links with and received assistance from the German, Czechoslovak, and Lithuanian intelligence services and had increased its terrorist activities in Poland. In the wake of the German invasion of Poland in September 1939, OUN units carried out acts of sabotage in the rear of the Polish army.

According to the secret agreements between Nazi Germany and the USSR, Volhynia and Eastern Galicia fell within the Soviet zone of occupation. Using the "class approach" to ethnic policies, Soviet authorities closed Polish cultural institutions and combatant organizations and replaced Polish civil employees with Ukrainians, Belorussians, and Jews. Competition in the socioeconomic sphere further fueled ethnic animosities. In 1940–1941, the Soviet secret police launched large-scale deportations that decimated Polish communities—approximately 210,000 Poles were deported to the remote areas of the USSR.

At the same time, the OUN experienced an internal split. In 1938, a Soviet agent assassinated its leader, Evhen Konovalets'. The younger members of the OUN grouped themselves around Stepan Bandera and formed OUN-B, while the veterans of the wars of 1918–1920, headed by Colonel Andrii Mel'nyk, formed OUN-M. Both groups made necessary adjustments to the new political order in Eastern Europe. In April 1941, the Second Congress of the OUN-B in German-occupied Poland outlined the immediate objectives for the national revolution, which included purging the Ukrainian ethnographic lands of "aliens"—Russians, Poles, and Jews. With the German invasion of the Soviet Union in June 1941, and in coordination with the German military intelligence, OUN units attacked retreating Soviet troops and carried out acts of sabotage on communications facilities. The OUN-B and OUN-M propaganda detachments incited Ukrainians to a national struggle and focused ethnic vitriol against Poles and "Judeo-Bolsheviks." The OUN-organized Ukrainian militia staged anti-Jewish pogroms and assisted the German security police in arrests and executions of the Polish intelligentsia and Jewish civilians.

However, the OUN-B soon found itself in full-blown conflict with the Germans. At the end of June 1941 in L'viv, OUN-B leaders announced the resurrection of Ukrainian statehood. This action infuriated Hitler, who had envisioned the Ukraine merely as a breadbasket and a source of slave labor. The German response was swift, and hundreds of Ukrainian nationalists were arrested or executed. OUN-B militarized formations were disbanded and fused into police battalions sent into the antipartisan struggle in Ukraine and Belorussia. The surviving OUN-B leadership went underground.

By the autumn of 1942, Nazi economic exploitation, forced labor, and frequent requisitions of grain and cattle in Ukraine had generated mass anti-German hostility. In this atmosphere, the OUN-B leadership decided to create a national army that would seize power at the moment Germany and the Soviet Union had exhausted each other in battle. Several OUN-B armed units sprang up in Volhynia, where the marshy and densely forested terrain in the region provided a suitable environment for guerrilla struggle. The nationalists utilized abandoned Soviet military warehouses as their main supply sources and set up NCO and officer training camps. In the spring of 1943, about 6,000 Ukrainian auxiliary policemen deserted to the forests and joined the OUN-B. The OUN-B military formations, now under a new name (the UPA), had already been shaped into a relatively well-armed, disciplined, and mobile force of about 8,000 armed members. During large-scale operations, thousands of local villagers were recruited on a temporary basis into self-defense units.

Simultaneously, steps were undertaken to eliminate "foreign elements" in Ukraine. OUN-B posters and leaflets incited the Ukrainian population to murder Poles and "Judeo-Moscovites." Since the majority of Jews in German-occupied Ukraine had already perished at the hands of the Nazis, the OUN-B concentrated its assault on Poles. In February 1943, taking into account the possibility of Germany's defeat, the Third Conference of the OUN-B finalized its plans. Fearing that the Polish-Ukrainian conflict would compel Poles to gravitate toward an alliance with the Soviets, the nationalist leadership decided to launch a preventive strike to eliminate a potential Soviet power-base in Western Ukraine. The OUN-B leadership also reasoned that the victorious Allies, who would determine the postwar border settlement, would be forced to recognize ethnically homogeneous Ukrainian lands as a fait accompli.

In the late winter and early spring of 1943, the assault on Polish settlements began. Backed by peasant self-defense units, the OUN-B detachments attacked Polish villages at night or in the early morning, butchering all inhabitants regardless of age or sex. Bullets were often spared in favor of axes, knives, and pitchforks. After the killing was completed, Polish houses were looted and set on fire. The inhabitants of most Polish settlements were caught unaware and perished without a struggle. The main Polish underground organization, the AK (the Home Army), was unable to stem the assault owing to a lack of arms and insufficient manpower. Only a few Polish strongholds stood their ground. For example, in the village of Przebraże in the Sarny district, some 1,000 Polish civilians, in cooperation with Soviet partisans, beat off numerous UPA attacks.

The OUN-B/UPA command planned and organized attacks thoroughly. Through rapid concentration and swift convergence upon a targeted location, the nationalists almost always had the element of surprise and superiority in numbers. After a village was overrun, mass murder, pillage, and burning of houses followed in quick succession. All vestiges of Polish existence were eradicated, and by torturing its victims and mutilating bodies, the OUN-B/UPA made deliberate efforts to generate a mass flight of the Poles. Some villages were given short notice to leave the premises. If the evacuation took place, abandoned sites were still burned to the ground. The death toll grew dramatically, and in April–May 1943 in the Rivne province alone, 3,000 Poles lost their lives.

The assault on Polish settlements took the German administration by surprise and greatly affected food deliveries from villages. German garrisons in the cities were increased and put on high alert. The shortage of manpower, however, impeded German efforts to restore order in the countryside, and the nationalist violence rapidly gained momentum. The German administration tried to stem the spread of terror by enlisting Polish refugees into police units, which were dispatched to pacify Ukrainian villages. These expeditions, as well as widespread banditry in the region (often committed by bands with no clear political affiliation), added to the prevailing chaos. The economic situation of the region deteriorated further as the mass flight of Polish refugees led to overcrowding in towns and cities. Hunger and disease spread rapidly, and the Germans used the opportunity to induce large numbers of Poles to join the labor force in the Reich. Facing no alternative, many Poles volunteered to be sent to Germany in labor detachments.

The ethnic cleansing reached its peak in July and August 1943. The prime stimulus for the escalation of terror was the great Soviet offensive at the Kursk salient. A directive issued by a senior UPA commander, Dmytro Kliachkivs'kyi in Volhynia, stipulated the extermination of the entire Polish population of between sixteen and sixty years of age. During the last five days of August, nationalist attacks resulted in the deaths of approximately 15,000 Poles. Eyewitnesses conveyed horrifying pictures of total destruction and catastrophic loss of life. In several districts, the entire Polish population was annihilated.

The OUN-B/UPA efforts to "cleanse" the area seemed to bear fruit as thousands of Polish refugees inundated towns and cities. By the end of August 1943, 10,000 men, women, and children had been crammed into temporary camps around the town of Sarny. Thousands of Poles also crossed over into Eastern Galicia, where Polish relief committees set up camps and kitchens in many localities.

Ukrainians' attitudes about the Volhynia tragedy varied from place to place. The nationalists used various methods to involve the Ukrainian population in ethnic cleansing, and undoubtedly the opportunity to loot served as a powerful incentive. The OUN-B/UPA propagandists skillfully played on long-standing Polish-Ukrainian animosities and collective fears of Polish retaliation. The dominating presence of the brutal OUN-B security service often sufficed to intimidate Ukrainians to enlist into self-defense units. Still, some Ukrainians were reluctant to join the assault, while others provided shelter and help to their Polish neighbors. A number of Polish survivors received warnings of impending attacks from Ukrainian villagers.

Some OUN-B activists argued against the anti-Polish terror, and several Ukrainian political groups also voiced their objections to the mass murder. In August 1943, the main Ukrainian institution in Poland and Western Ukraine, the German-sponsored Ukrainian Central Committee (Ukrains'kyi Tsentrałnyi Komitet), appealed to Ukrainians to stop the massacres. At the same time, the head of the Greek Catholic Church in Eastern Galicia, Andrej Sheptyts'kyi, warned the Ukrainian population against "shedding innocent blood." The Ukrainian bishops of Stanisławów and Przemyśl and a number of Ukrainian organizations and unions issued similar appeals.

In the fall of 1943, the Soviet offensive on the right bank of the Dnieper River introduced new elements into the tragedy unfolding in Western Ukraine. The prospect of an inevitable encounter with the Soviet army forced the OUN leadership to reconsider its ethnic policies. The pace of ethnic cleansing clearly slowed down in November, and OUN-B leaflets promised equality of all citizens in a future Ukrainian state. However, while it is conceivable that more moderate OUN-B leaders tried to mitigate anti-Polish violence, at the time of their issuance these reassuring appeals seemed to be merely a shallow gesture. Mass murder and wanton destruction of property had inflicted an irreparable damage on the Polish community. In addition, at the same time that OUN propaganda was calling for Polish-Ukrainian rapprochement, attacks on Polish settlements continued. In October–November 1943, the UPA units totally wiped out five Polish villages—430 households—in the Ludvipol' district.

Similarly, high-level Polish-Ukrainian contacts failed to bring an end to the massacres. Throughout the war, meetings between Polish and Ukrainian representatives revealed irreconcilable differences in their approaches to the question of the Eastern Borderlands. While each side solemnly promised equality and justice for ethnic minorities after the war, both passionately claimed Western Ukraine as a crucial component of their respective national states. For the Poles, Eastern Galicia and Volhynia represented a historical bastion of Polish civilization in the East. For Ukrainians, they were inseparable parts of ethnic Ukraine. On one hand, the credibility of Polish promises was also seriously undermined by the fact that Poland had violated an international agreement of 1923 that had guaranteed autonomous status to Eastern Galicia. On the other hand, Polish nationalist circles considered the resettlement of Ukrainians (possibly to Polish western territories) as the only viable ethnic solution in the Eastern Borderlands. Mutual intransigence, therefore, rendered Polish-Ukrainian talks useless and had no impact on the situation in Western Ukraine.

The autumn of 1943 witnessed the escalation of anti-Polish violence in Eastern Galicia, which until then had remained relatively quiet. The quick pace of the Soviet offense was mirrored by the OUN-UPA drive to "cleanse" the area before the arrival of the Soviet army, and Polish villages in Tarnopol province sustained heavy casualties. The attacks followed similar patterns to that established in Volhynia. The OUN-UPA units surrounded Polish villages, murdered all the residents, and pillaged and burned houses and barns. Corpses were often mutilated and defiled. The Polish population in some localities was given forty-eight hours to leave the premises, and the nationalist agitators called for a mass extermination of all Poles to achieve Ukrainian national liberation.

In Eastern Galicia, however, the Polish underground was better armed and organized. More important, the Germans were determined to preserve stability in this important strategic oil-producing region. In addition, excepting the districts adjacent to the Carpathian mountains, a flat terrain rendered guerrilla warfare much more difficult than in Volhynia. German propaganda called for united Polish-Ukrainian-German efforts to stem the Soviet offensive, and in December 1943 the Galician governor, Otto Wächter, warned Ukrainians against any actions that could disrupt the functioning of the district.

Eventually, however, German efforts to keep Galicia quiet failed. The shortage of manpower—all available German reserves were siphoned off by the Eastern Front—allowed the

OUN-UPA to attack remote Polish settlements at will. In January and February 1944, UPA units, augmented by self-defense detachments, annihilated several Polish villages in Tarnopol province, murdering more than 600 men, women, and children. The Polish underground retaliated by burning Ukrainian villages and killing their residents. The situation in the region began to deteriorate rapidly as the German police and gendarmerie entered the fray on one side or the other depending on the local situation. In some instances, German units randomly executed Ukrainian or Polish villagers and burned their homes. The approach of the Soviet army and the German retreat generated several waves of Polish refugees. In May and June alone, up to 100,000 Poles fled Eastern Galicia for central Poland.

Having lived through the OUN-UPA terror, the majority of Poles enthusiastically welcomed Soviet troops. A number of Poles enlisted in anti-insurgent battalions set up by the Soviets to fight the Ukrainian underground and took positions in civil offices. The Soviet military administration and police initially encouraged Polish participation in local administration, and soldiers of Polish background harassed Ukrainians and forcibly requisitioned food and cattle in Ukrainian villages. Instances of Polish-Soviet collaboration prompted a renewal of OUN-UPA attacks, and in winter and spring of 1944, UPA units attacked several Polish villages in Eastern Galicia, killing off all the inhabitants.

The last stage of ethnic cleansing in Western Ukraine was completed by the Soviet-Polish agreement signed on September 9, 1944, which stipulated a "voluntary" population exchange between Ukraine and the newly established Polish republic. In the same month, Polish government units in Lublin and Rzeszów provinces were deployed to speed up the resettlement of Ukrainians. The repatriation of ethnic Poles from Eastern Galicia and Volhynia also grew in numbers, and by early 1945 reached about 117,000.

The Polish-Ukrainian conflict continued in Poland after World War II. In southeastern Polish provinces, the army and security police waged an antiguerrilla campaign until the autumn of 1947. Brutalities were common on both sides, and memories of the massacres in Western Ukraine often turned antiguerrilla actions into punitive expeditions as Polish units burned Ukrainian villages to the ground and shot the villagers on the spot. Hard-pressed by Polish troops and deprived of their bases and supplies by the mass resettlement of the Ukrainian population, the remnants of the OUN-UPA dispersed through the mountains to Slovakia and then to Austria. Some cut their way through to the forests of Western Ukraine.

Mass murder and the flight of Polish refugees irreversibly changed the ethnic composition in Volhynia and Eastern Galicia in favor of ethnic Ukrainians. The OUN-UPA killing campaign in Western Ukraine brought the death toll to 50,000 spread across more than 900 localities. The numbers of Poles who fled the massacres can be estimated at between 350,000 and 400,000. Volhynia alone lost more than half of its prewar Polish population of 340,000.

In the end, the ethnic cleansing in Volhynia and Eastern Galicia proved to be a Pyrrhic victory for the OUN-B/UPA. Although the nationalist terror drastically reduced the number of Poles in these regions, it was the Soviet government that reaped the benefits when it integrated Volhynia and Eastern Galicia into the USSR as "primordial Ukrainian lands."

Alexander V. Prusin

See also: Civil Wars and Migration; Ethnic Cleansing; Genocide; Polish Diaspora; Racism and Racially Motivated Attacks

References and further reading:

Armstrong, John A. 2000. *Ukrainian Nationalism.* Englewood, CO: Ukrainian Academic Press.

Motyl, Alexander. 1980. *The Turn to the Right: The Ideological Origins and Development of Ukrainian Nationalism.* New York: Columbia University Press.

———. 1985. "Ukrainian Nationalist Political Violence in Inter-War Poland, 1921–1939." *East European Quarterly* 19: 45–55.

Piotrkowski, Tadeusz. 1998. *Poland's Holocaust: Ethnic Strife, Collaboration with Occupying Forces and Genocide in the Second Republic, 1918–1947.* Jefferson, NC: McFarland.

Polishchuk, Wiktor. 1997. *Legal and Political Assessment of the OUN and UPA.* Toronto: Viktor Poliszczuk.

Prusin, Alexander V. 2002. "Revolution and Ethnic Cleansing in Western Ukraine: The OUN-UPA Assault against Polish Settlements in Volynia and East Galicia, 1943–1944." Pp. 517–535 in *Ethnic Cleansing in Twentieth-Century Europe.* Edited by Hunt Tooley and Steven B. Vardy. New York: Columbia University Press.

Snyder, Timothy. 1999. "'To Resolve the Ukrainian Problem Once and for All': The Ethnic Cleansing of Ukrainians in Poland, 1943–1947." *Journal of Cold War Studies* 1, no. 2: 86–120.

Terleś, Mikołaj. 1993. *Ethnic Cleansing of Poles in Volhynia and Eastern Galicia, 1942–1946.* Toronto: Alliance of the Polish Eastern Provinces.

Torzecki, Ryszard. 1993. *Polacy i Ukraińcy: spawa ukraińska w czasie II wojny œwiatowej na terenie II Rzeczy Pospolitej.* Warsaw: Wydawnictwo Naukowe PWN.

Ethnic Germans

The German term *Aussiedler,* literally "out-settlers" or "emigrants," refers to ethnic Germans from eastern and southeastern Europe who migrated to the Federal Republic of Germany (FRG) and Germany between 1950 and 1992. Their status is similar to that of ethnic Germans expelled from these same areas in the immediate postwar years (*Vertriebene*) and Germans who came from the German Democratic Republic (GDR) to the FRG during the Cold War, but it differs markedly from that of other immigrant groups in Germany.

Ethnic Germans newly arrived from Russia attend a German "civilization" class at a holding center. Around 2.5 million Russian-Germans have "come home" from the former Soviet Union, the vast majority since the early 1990s, according to officials. Pietz, Germany. September 4, 2003. (AFP/Getty Images)

This difference stems from the special legal status that was assigned to all Germans living east of the Oder-Neisse border through FRG citizenship laws, Article 116 of the German Basic Law, and the 1953 Expellees Law. These laws guaranteed ethnic Germans access to FRG territory and citizenship and put into place special integrative measures, such as access to the welfare and pensions system, housing benefits, language courses, and compensation for property left behind. Since the late 1980s, this privileged status has been subject to a series of restrictions; in 1992, it was supplanted by the new *Spätaussiedler* (late out-settler, late emigrant) status. The main countries of origin have been the former Soviet Union and then Russia, Poland, and Romania. From 1950 to 2000, approximately 4 million ethnic Germans were granted Aussiedler and Spätaussiedler status. The Aussiedler constitute the second-largest immigrant group in Germany after the guestworkers, and Aussiedler migration represents one of the largest migratory movements in Europe since 1950.

Aussiedler Immigration during the Cold War

Until German reunification, the FRG government pursued a policy of actively encouraging Aussiedler immigration, through such measures as per capita payments for Aussiedler from Romania or an exchange for financial loans to Poland. The FRG interpreted ethnic Germans' decisions to migrate to its territory as a choice for a superior political system, and the migration rate was thought to enhance West Germany's standing vis-à-vis the GDR by showing that the FRG was the sole legitimate state for the German people. Due to solid German-language skills, the integrative measures, and a generally favorable public opinion toward Aussiedler immigration, the integration of Aussiedler into West German society was largely unproblematic. Up to the late 1980s, the numbers of Aussiedler were not overwhelmingly large (approximately 38,000 per year [Münz and Ohliger 1998]). After the collapse of the Soviet Union, however, the numbers increased dramatically.

From Aussiedler to Spätaussiedler Status

With an easing of exit requirements in the Eastern bloc from the late 1980s onward, Aussiedler numbers reached unprecedented heights (in 1990 almost 400,000 [Münz and Ohliger 1998, 160]). This increase was compounded by the migrants' poor grasp of German and a parallel increased influx of asylum seekers, and the movement and its regulation became increasingly subject to public debate. In the 1990s, most Aussiedler came from the former Soviet Union. Their German-language competence was mostly poor, integration proved problematic, and these Aussiedler were perceived as Russian Germans or even Russians instead of fellow Germans. Moreover, the gap in status between Aussiedler and resident foreigners came into question. The latter, in contrast to the Aussiedler, had only limited access to citizenship (until 1999/2000) and were unable to keep their original citizenship when naturalizing.

In the early 1990s, the German government therefore adopted a more restrictive policy that made immigration less attractive to potential Aussiedler. It reduced the benefits, instituted an application procedure in the country of origin, and required German-language proficiency as a condition for immigration. The 1992 Act Dealing with the Consequences of the War replaced the Aussiedler with the Spätaussiedler status. Besides fixing a yearly quota for Spätaussiedler immigration (since 1993, 220,000 per year; and since 2000, 100,000 per year), the law presumed there was no longer a general need to emigrate except from the successor states of the Soviet Union. All others in Eastern Europe would have to establish proof of discrimination on ethnic grounds by state authorities after 1992, which proves to be essentially impossible. In addition, the status is being phased out, as all those born after 1992 are barred from applying. Due to a backlog of undecided cases, unused entry permits, and the possibility of family reunification, it is assumed that Aussiedler migration will continue at least until 2010 (Bade and Oltmer 1999, 29–30). Despite an alleged cultural affinity, the problems of Aussiedler integration into German society in the 1990s had made it abundantly clear, however, that their movement was immigration in a traditional sense, presenting all the possibilities and problems associated with it. The Aussiedlers' cool reception also suggests that language, as much as culture or ethnicity, define Germans' current sense of themselves.

Stefan Ihrig

See also: Basic Law (Germany); Citizenship; Cold War; Dual Nationality; Ethnic Cleansing: Germans from Central and Eastern Europe

References and further reading:

Bade, Klaus J., and Jochen Oltmer. 1999. "Einführung: Aussiedlerzuwanderung und Aussiedlerintegration. Historische Entwicklung und aktuelle Probleme." Pp. 9–39 in *Aussiedler: deutsche Einwanderer aus Osteuropa.* Edited by Klaus J. Bade and Jochen Oltmer. Osnabrück: Universitätsverlag Rasch.

Groenendijk, Kees. 1997. "Regulating Ethnic Immigration: The Case of the Aussiedler." *New Community* 23, no. 4: 461–482.

Münz, Rainer, and Rainer Ohliger. 1998. "Long-Distance Citizens, Ethnic Germans and Their Immigration to Germany." Pp. 155–201 in *Paths to Inclusion.* Edited by Peter H. Schuck and Rainer Münz. New York: Berghahn.

Spevack, Edmund. 1996. "Ethnic Germans from the East: Aussiedler in Germany, 1970–1994." *German Politics and Society* 14, no. 1: 71–91.

Eugenics

Eugenics was defined by its founder, the Victorian scientist Francis Galton, as the science of improving the human gene pool by granting "the more suitable races or strains of blood a better chance of prevailing speedily over the less suitable" (quoted in Kevles 1995, xiii). Although there were scientific and policy differences among eugenicists (for example, over the factors and mechanisms determining heredity), they were united by several key beliefs. The first was that heredity was the most important factor explaining mental illnesses. Following an early form of statistical analysis, Galton—inspired by his cousin, Charles Darwin—argued that certain character traits showed a constancy across the generations (Kevles 1995, 18). He developed this argument in *Natural Inheritance* (1889), which noted through biographical searches that the eminent descended in disproportionate numbers from the eminent. Casually rejecting environmentalist arguments, Galton concluded that intelligence and the other qualities necessary for success were inherited.

Karl Pearson, in collaboration with Walter Weldon, expanded upon Galton's ideas while the two were at University College, London. Using statistical analysis, Pearson correlated the intelligence of schoolchildren—as measured by their teachers—and concluded that "the physical and psychical characters of man are inherited within broad lines in the same manner and with the same intensity" (Kevles 1995, 32). This hereditarianism was of an increasingly uncompromising sort. Largely because of the work of the German biologist August Weissmann on germ plasma, the environmentalist theories of Jean-Baptiste Lamarck—the French theorist holding that acquired characteristics could be inherited—were taken less and less seriously in the German and Anglo-American scientific communities (Proctor 1988, 50–55; Weiss 1990).

Hereditarian arguments were confirmed by a series of family histories published in North America, all of which are now recognized to be flawed. The most influential, written by Richard Dugdale, was *The Jukes,* an 1877 study that traced seven generations of prostitutes, criminals, and social misfits to a single family in upstate New York. Although offering an environmentalist explanation of this misery, the hereditarian *Zeitgeist* twisted the conclusion and implications (Kevles 1995, 71; Carlson 2001, 170–172), and the

Great Britain's Francis Galton was a nineteenth-century scientist and anthropologist whose achievements spanned an incredible variety of fields and disciplines. He is best known as the inventor of the science of eugenics. (Library of Congress)

Jukes were reinterpreted as a gloomy story of biological determinism. The study inspired many more, including an influential one called *The Kallikak Family: A Study in the Heredity of Feeblemindedness* in 1912. The author was Henry H. Goddard, physician at the Vineland Training School. Goddard invented the term "moron" and brought (flawed) IQ tests to the United States. Comparing two familial lines (one august, the other abysmal) descending from a single revolutionary soldier, he argued the Kallikak family history proved that feeblemindedness was a dominant hereditary trait, and further, that the feebleminded were highly fertile (Dowbiggin 1997, 101).

Although scholars once believed that eugenicists were conservative and reactionary, recent scholarship has made abundantly clear that it was a diverse, complex, and not always coherent movement (Paul 1998; Searle 1976). It comprised conservatives and social democrats; doctors, psychiatrists, and social workers; policy makers and activists. These professions had complex and varied relationships to different strands of eugenics, and eugenics itself (to the degree that it was a unified ideology at all) had complicated links with broader nineteenth- and twentieth-century intellectual movements: social Darwinism, neo-Malthusianism, degeneration, and national efficiency. It is impossible to do justice to this intricate web, but it is worth mentioning some of the key figures in the various national eugenic movements (though Galton and Pearson often viewed them with suspicion).

In the United Kingdom, eugenicists grouped in the Education Eugenics Society (later the Eugenics Society), which published the *Eugenics Review.* Its first president was Montague Crackanthorpe, a prominent barrister, and Major Leonard Darwin (the son of Charles Darwin) led it from 1911 until 1928. Subsequent presidents included C. P. Blacker and Julian Huxley, the first director general of the UN Educational, Scientific, and Cultural Organization (UNESCO). In the United States, the most prominent member of the American Eugenics Society was the Yale economist Irving Fisher (who wrote the definitive early piece on deflation), but the most active eugenicists worked outside the universities. The most notable were Charles Davenport, founder and first director of the Eugenics Record Office (ERO) at Cold Spring Harbor, and Harry H. Laughlin, superintendent at the ERO. The ERO's yearly budget in 1906 was $21,000 (twice that of Pearson's at University College, London), and its expanded size and resources in 1910 made it the key foundation for research on eugenics in the United States, and perhaps in the world. Davenport's papers (held at the American Philosophical Society, Philadelphia) attest to his prolific research on a range of scientific and sociological questions: heredity, agriculture, race, physical anthropology, feeblemindedness, and alcoholism. The ERO served as a repository of information on family histories, numbered in the tens of thousands; established an "analytical" index of some 250,000 cards containing information on families and family traits; and trained several hundred field workers in the methods of data collection on families. Laughlin was handpicked by Davenport, and he made the issue of sterilization his own. For the next thirty years, until the Carnegie Foundation, increasingly embarrassed by Laughlin's obsession with race, drove him out, he was a tireless worker for and zealot of eugenics.

In the early years of the twentieth century, all these organizations and individuals were united in a basic hereditarian belief. The argument that intelligence, and thus "feeblemindedness," was inherited would in itself have only served to validate the existing class structure; if not ordained by God, then it was ordained by nature. People have long sought (and continue to seek) theories that provide justification for social and economic inequalities. The hereditarian argument, however, intersected with two other early twentieth-century concerns: a *declining* overall birthrate and a perceived *increasing* birthrate among the working class and/or genetically unfit. From the 1870s until the 1950s, European demographers, politicians, and eugenicists feared that a below-replacement birthrate would mean inexorable decline. The fear manifested itself differently in different countries—in Britain it was bound up with fear of American and German industrial supremacy, in France it was compounded by an earlier start to decline and a lower birthrate than Germany—but was shared across Europe. At precisely the moment of Europe's overall declining rate, social and physical scientists detected a differential birthrate: The upper classes were having fewer children, while the working classes, the indigent, and the "feebleminded" were having more (Schneider 1990; Soloway 1995; Weingart 1989).

As this early twentieth-century fear of upper/lower class differentials faded with the downward convergence of the two groups' fertility rates, the focus shifted in the late 1920s and 1930s to what in Britain was called "the social problem group": chronic paupers putatively given to unrestrained breeding and producing large numbers of mentally, morally, and physically defective children. In both cases, demographic trends were thus fundamentally "dysgenic." Internationally, this pessimistic conclusion was confirmed by broader developments: The Boer War highlighted British military and bodily weakness (officers were appalled by the poor condition of the conscripts) (Barker 1989; Dowbiggin 1997, 100–102), and World War I led to the slaughter of millions of healthy German, French, and British youth (Kühl 2001; Stoddard 1920, 190–191; Johnson and Popenoe 1918, 202). Domestically, it was confirmed by social policy: Early nineteenth-century optimism about the capacity of institutions to combat mental illness evaporated as their numbers swelled, and their curative function evolved into an increasingly custodial one (Grob 1994; Dowbiggin 1997).

A scientific confidence in the (non-Lamarckian) hereditarian basis of intelligence, a growing institutional pessimism in the field of mental health, and a differential fertility rate collectively demanded a policy response. Two types of policy proposals emerged: first, those encouraging breeding among the genetically fit, and second, those discouraging it among the unfit. The former are grouped together under the term "positive eugenics," the latter under "negative eugenics." Positive eugenics required pronatalist policies (only pursued with any consistency by France, Finland, and Nazi Germany); negative eugenics required marriage restrictions, segregation and sterilization, and finally, immigration control.

Eugenics and immigration were linked, among other ways, through race. Eugenicists had different views on the concept. The division was not one between good Britons and bad Germans; rather, the movement divided in the two countries between those who thought that eugenics, or "race hygiene," as the movement was known in Germany, was about improving the lot of all races, and those who thought that it was about privileging and perfecting the superior races. It should be borne in mind that the idea that some races are superior over others, today regarded as racist, was widely held in the pre-1945 period, including among people otherwise viewed as moderate or liberal in their time. Unsurprisingly, the U.S. eugenicists most in favor of nationality-based immigration legislation saw innate and incontrovertible differences between races. Until recently, most people took this for granted, but scholars now agree that what used to be viewed as racial differences are "socially constructed," that is, they acquire meaning only through their use in society. Put another way, although there might be physiological differences between, say, Africans and Europeans, there are also physiological differences between the French and the Germans, Swedes and Italians, people with black hair and those with blond, people with blue eyes and those with brown. Instead, society ignores these differences and attaches meaning to skin color and to putative physiological differences between Africans and Europeans. One could imagine a world in which what mattered to people was not whether one is black or white, but blue- or brown-eyed.

For the eugenicists, of course, the existence of distinct races was obvious. Working in an age when the world was divided into empires, they found the related claim that there was a hierarchy of races equally unproblematic. For Davenport, race was much more than "black," "white," and "yellow." He spoke of Celtic, Teutonic, English, Indian, Latin, and so on as if these were important racial categories. The eugenicists' work on race attempted at times to approach scientific standards, but it all too often collapsed into an unreflective willingness to recycle prejudiced clichés. In a series of essays on race, Charles Davenport casually said whites were "dominant" and Indians/"Negroes" "inferior"; that blacks were less intelligent but more musical and possessed of better rhythm than whites; that Jews had crooked noses; and that mixing any of the above would lead to predictable (and predictably substandard) genetic results (Davenport 1924, 1928). However absurd this seems now, Davenport represented a strain of American thought, shared by large numbers of his country's intellectual elite, that saw racial differences in intelligence that could not be overcome. He wrote:

> In their mental traits . . . different peoples are unlike. It has been formerly maintained that the obvious mental differences in race are due to differences of education and training merely, but the experience with native tribes in Australia and in Africa has shown that the children of these peoples do not respond in the same way as the white children to the same sort of education. . . . [T]he army intelligence test . . . showed that there is a marked difference in average mental capacity between the major races of mankind, and even between the peoples of different parts of Europe. . . . In fact, it seems probable that in the same country we have, living side by side, persons of advanced mentality, persons who have

> inherited the mentality of their ancestors of the early Stone Age, and persons of intermediate evolutionary stages. (Davenport, n.d.)

He went on to link these "obvious" mental differences with temperament. The result, had it not been so harmful, might be amusing: "The different races of man are unlike in temperament also. Some of them, like the Scotch, are prevailing profound, thorough, somewhat somber; others like the Mediterranean peoples are prevailingly mercurial and light hearted; The trait of reserve has been developed to a high degree among the North American Indians; that of fidelity to a superior race among the Bantu Negroes; that of industry and dependability in the Chinese; and so on" (Davenport, n.d.).

Among the eugenicists' many fears was the phenomenon, which has long titillated, fascinated, and repelled Europeans, of miscegenation. Evidence from Jamaica was meant to establish that while "Whites" scored higher on mental tests than "Blacks," "Browns" scored lower than both. Just as mixing racehorses and workhorses leads to animals "too torpid to win races and too light for heavy work," the reasoning went, so the "crossing of distinct races is not good for the community in which the hybrids dwell" (Davenport, n.d.).

One should leave the final word on the eugenicists' method to the (hard) scientists, but much of the research on race did not even meet the most minimal standards of sociological inquiry. In one 1921 study Davenport and a colleague, L. C. Crayter (n.d.), undertook a study of just over one hundred schoolchildren divided into the following nationalities: English (5), Germans (10), Irish (9), Italians (22), Austrians (31), Russians (30) and Jews (61—the Austrians and Russians together). Even the most rudimentary statistical analysis today shows that a sample size of less than 1,000 cannot be viewed as large enough to form the basis of any scientific conclusions. Absurdly, the authors expressed their joy in the text at having "doubled" their sample size from a "confessedly fragmentary" study of fifty-one children. The school itself was chosen because it was available, not because it had any claim to being representative. After drawing up their charts, the authors then provided a shopping list of conclusions: German children, they said, are frank and possessed of humor and leadership qualities; Irish possess the full two characteristics along with loyalty; Italians are humorless and incapable of leadership; and Jewish are frank, suspicious, and pernicious but also display leadership and humor. Today, this sort of work would not be taken at all seriously, but at the turn of the century it was.

Second, the intellectual peak in the eugenics movement—from, broadly, 1900 until 1920—coincided with a period of intense racist and xenophobic anti-immigration sentiment, above all in North America. As the traditional source countries of the United Kingdom, Germany, and Ireland (migrants from the last of which were viewed with suspicion and loathing in their day, leading to the formation of the anti-migrant American Party, which flourished in the 1850s) gave way to Southern and Eastern Europe, China and Japan, anti-immigrant sentiment lobbying increased, reaching near-hysterical levels in the 1910s. In 1875, the United States barred convicts and prostitutes. Legislation of 1882 prohibited the entry of "mental defectives" and paupers. In the 1860s, California imposed a "head tax" of $2.50 per month on Chinese migrants. Canada followed with a similar tax of C$50.00 per person in the 1880s. In 1907, the United States negotiated the "Gentleman's Agreement" with Japan to limit Japanese migration (the Japanese government stopped issuing passports to laborers). Eugenics fed both off and into this anti-immigrant hostility, and the categories of "immigrant" and "feebleminded" began to blur.

The key intellectual (if that is not too generous a term) figure was Harry Laughlin. Albert Johnson, a Republican congressman of the hard-line and hard-drinking variety, appointed Laughlin as expert witness to the House of Representatives Committee on Immigration, which Johnson chaired. Johnson saw immigration as not merely an economic but a biological question. Backed by congressional resources, Laughlin undertook a survey of 445 state institutions for the "socially inadequate": the mentally ill (the "insane") and the cognitively impaired (the "feebleminded") (Laughlin 1922, 10). It worked out a quota for comparing the number of inmates from each nationality relative to the population as a whole (based on the 1910 census). Thus, as Germans made up 2.71 percent of the U.S. population, Laughlin expected 2,288 Germans in state institutions (a 100 percent quota fulfillment) (ibid., 14). Laughlin applied this quota to ten categories of "defects": feeblemindedness, insanity, criminality, epilepsy, inebriety, disease (tuberculosis and leprosy), blindness, deafness, physical deformity, and dependency (ibid., 11). He included both first- and second-generation migrants in his study.

Focusing on the category of greatest concern to eugenicists, he concluded, "For feeblemindedness the foreign born as a whole fulfilled their quota only about one-third, which shows that the immigration laws are fairly effective in the most degenerate cases of feeblemindedness; but the striking thing comes in relation to another group, namely, the native born with both parents foreign born. This group fulfilled their quota 165%, while the native born, one parent foreign and one parent native, fulfilled their quota 190%, thus showing that the immigration sieve works well on individuals, but in relation to family stock it is worse than a failure" (Laughlin 1922, 11–12). The percentages were lower for all other defects. Laughlin also noted that certain nations, such as Serbia, showed a "very high quota fulfillment for all types of defect," suggesting that the "nation is either an inferior race or has sent its inferior stock to America" (ibid., 12). In either case, policy makers had to reflect on the consequences.

The argument about the second generation was important, as it fed into a particular eugenic concern: that the genetic (or, as they would have then said, "racial") composition of an immigrant stream was such that otherwise healthy-looking immigrants could infect the national "racial stock." In doing so, they would create a trend toward degeneration: Migrants would arrive and give birth in disproportionate numbers to the feebleminded, and the pattern would continue. Immigration was thus "dysgenic." Laughlin's arguments informed the committee's conclusions, which advocated race-based immigration quotas. In 1924, an immigration act (the Johnson-Reed Act) set the total annual quota for immigration at 150,000 (plus dependents), and it limited immigration from any one country to the percentage of that country's migrants in the United States in 1920 (King 1999, ch. 4). So if those of a particular nationality made up 3 percent of thc 1920 U.S. population, for example, they would receive 3 percent of the 150,000 quota, or 4,500 places per year. The legislation succeeded in its goal of locking in the white and northern European character of immigration patterns: Over 80 percent of the quota went to northern and western Europe. The quota was only changed in 1965, when legislation abolished it and gave preference to family and skilled migration. The Immigration Act of 1965 created the conditions for what is now almost forty years of non-European immigration to the United States. Although anti-migrant sentiment drew on multiple sources and in part preceded eugenic thought, eugenics nonetheless cast a long shadow over U.S. immigration policy.

Randall Hansen

See also: Canada; Ethnic Cleansing; Genocide; Racism and Racially Motivated Attacks; U.S. Multiculturalism; U.S. Nativism; White Australia Policy

References and further reading:

Barker, David. 1989. "The Biology of Stupidity: Genetics, Eugenics and Mental Deficiency in the Inter-War Years." *British Journal of the History of Science* 22: 347–375.

Carlson, Elof A. 2001. *The Unfit: A History of a Bad Idea.* Cold Spring Harbor, NY: Cold Spring Harbor Laboratory Press.

Davenport, Charles. N.d. "Is the Crossing of Races Useful?" American Philosophical Society Archives, Philadelphia. File BD 27 CD.

———. 1924. "Body Build: Its Development and Inheritance." American Philosophical Society Archives, Philadelphia. File BD 27 CD.

———. 1928. "Race Crossing in Jamaica." American Philosophical Society Archives, Philadelphia. File BD 27 CD.

Davenport, Charles, and L. C. Crayter. N.d. "Comparative Social Traits of the Various Races." American Philosophical Society Archives, Philadelphia. File BD 27 CD.

Dowbiggin, Ian R. 1997. *Keeping America Sane. Psychiatry and Eugenics in the United States and Canada, 1880–1940.* Ithaca, NY: Cornell University Press.

Grob, Gerald N. 1994. *The Mad among Us: A History of the Care of America's Mentally Ill.* Cambridge: Harvard University Press.

Kevles, Daniel J. 1995. *In the Name of Genetics: Genetics and the Uses of Human Heredity.* Cambridge: Harvard University Press.

King, Desmond. 1999. *In the Name of Illiberalism: Illiberal Social Policy in the USA and Britain.* Oxford: Oxford University Press.

Kühl, Stefan. 2001. "The Relationship between Eugenics and the So-Called 'Euthanasia Action' in Nazi Germany." In *Science in the Third Reich.* Edited by Margit Szöllisi-Janze. Oxford: Berghahn.

Laughlin, Harry H. 1922. "The Measure of Specific Degeneracies in Immigration and Native Populative Groups of the United States." Submission to *Proceedings, Conference on Human Migration.* Arranged by the Committee on the Scientific Problem of Immigration. National Research Council, Washington DC. Series 3, Box 58, Folder 629. Tarrytown, NY: Rockefeller Foundation Archives.

Paul, Diane B. 1998. "Eugenics and the Left." Pp. 11–35 in *Politics of Heredity. Essays on Eugenics, Biometrics, and the Nature-Nature Debate.* Edited by Diane Paul. Albany: State University of New York Press.

Popenoe, Paul, and H. Roswell Johnson. 1918. *Applied Eugenics.* New York: Macmillan.

Proctor, Robert. 1988. *Racial Hygiene: Medicine under the Nazis.* Cambridge: Harvard University Press.

Schneider, William H. 1990. *Quality and Quantity: The Biological Request for Regeneration in 20th Century France.* Cambridge: Cambridge University Press.

Searle, Geoffrey R. 1976. *Eugenics and Politics in Britain.* Leiden: Noordhof.

Soloway, Richard A. 1995. *Demography and Degeneration: Eugenics and the Declining Birthrate in Twentieth Century Britain.* Chapel Hill: University of North Carolina Press.

Stoddard, Lothrop. 1920. *The Rising Tide of Color against White World-Supremacy.* New York: Scribner.

Weingart, Peter. 1989. "German Eugenics between Science and Politics." *OSIRIS* 2: 260–282.

Weiss, Sheila F. 1990. *The Wellborn Science: Eugenics in Germany, France, Brazil, and Russia.* Edited by M. B. Adams. New York: Oxford University Press.

European Citizenship

"European citizenship" is an unprecedented and novel form of supranational citizenship created by the European Union (EU) to give the citizens of its member states a set of political rights vis-à-vis the Union as a whole. It was formalized in the Treaty on European Union (1992) and amended and clarified in the Treaty of Amsterdam (1997). Its greatest impact will be on those who make use of the right to freedom of movement for employment and residence purposes that it guarantees.

The desire to create an EU level of citizenship was stimulated by a greater interest in freedom of movement that emerged following the Treaty of Rome. There was a desire to

European Commission president Romano Prodi (L) and Irish prime minister Bertie Ahern (R) present a model of the new social security card for European citizens during the final news conference of a European Union summit in Brussels March 26, 2004. (Yves Herman/Reuters/Corbis)

create a European identity that would extend the European integration project beyond the elites, and beyond the economic centrality of the Economic and Monetary Union, to include a larger proportion of the citizenry of member states. However, most commentators describe the form of citizenship included in the Treaty on European Union as "empty," and it actually affects only a small proportion of the citizens of EU states. In the late 1990s, only 5.5 million of the more than 350 million citizens of EU member states (automatic European citizens) were taking advantage of the right to reside, work, and study outside of their own state in other EU nations.

Eligibility for European Citizenship

Article 17 (ex Article 8) of the Consolidated Version of the Treaty Establishing the European Community (1992) states, "Every person holding the nationality of a Member State shall be a citizen of the Union. Citizenship of the Union shall complement and not replace national citizenship." Immigrants to EU member states from outside the Union can only become European citizens by naturalizing in one of the member states.

Voting

Article 19 (ex Article 8b) of the Consolidated Version states, "Every citizen of the Union residing in a Member State of which he or she is not a national shall have the right to vote and to stand as a candidate at municipal elections in the Member State in which he or she resides, under the same conditions as nationals of that State." Furthermore, European citizens have "the right to vote and to stand as a candidate in elections to the European Parliament in the Member State in which he resides, under the same conditions as nationals of that State." European citizens may not vote in national elections in the state in which they reside but of which they are not national citizens, nor are they permitted to vote in the European Parliament elections in more than one state at one time.

Consular Protection

Article 20 (ex Article 8c) of the Consolidated Version states that every EU citizen will be "entitled to protection by the diplomatic or consular authorities of any Member State" if he or she is "in the territory of a third country in which the Member State of which he is a national is not represented." That protection will be similar to that of nationals of the state providing it.

Other Rights

European citizens also have the right to petition the European Parliament and the European Ombudsman. They may write in any of the twelve European Union languages and receive a response in the same language.

Joanne van Selm

See also: Citizenship; European Union; Postnationalism

References and further reading:
Cesarani, David, and Mary Fulbrook, eds. 1996. *Citizenship, Nationality and Migration in Europe.* London: Routledge.
Hansen, Randall. 1998. "A European Citizenship or a Europe of Citizens? Third Country Nationals in the EU." *Journal of Ethnic and Migration Studies* 24, no. 4: 639–656.
Kostakopoulou, Theodora. 1998. "European Citizenship and Immigration after Amsterdam: Openings, Silences and Paradoxes." *Journal of Ethnic and Migration Studies* 24, no. 4: 639–656.

European Court of Human Rights

The European Court of Human Rights (ECHR) in Strasbourg has mainly affected state discretion with regard to the expulsion of foreigners either because their family ties were in the receiving country or they could suffer inhuman treatment if sent back. This human rights court—the first in history that can make decisions binding on signatory states—started functioning in 1953 in order to review cases that violate the 1950 European Convention on Human Rights adopted within the framework of the Council of Europe (CE), which comprises forty-one member states. The first cases involving alien immigrants date from the mid-1980s, and their numbers have greatly increased since then, reflecting in part the restrictive migration and asylum policies of many contracting parties in a region in which an estimated 20 million foreigners reside. There remains significant cross-national variations in the incorporation of ECHR jurisprudence in domestic law and jurisprudence, as well as in the number of individual appeals by country.

Most plaintiffs whose cases were examined by the ECHR after they had exhausted all domestic means of redress appealed expulsion decisions or administrative refusals of entry and residence permits. They generally purported that, in the handling of their cases, public authorities had violated rights guaranteed under Article 3 (protection against torture or inhuman treatment) and/or Article 8 (right to lead a normal family life) of the convention.

In the first case involving a foreigner where the court ruled that the right to family and private life as enshrined in Article 8 had been violated (the 1986 *Berrehab v. Netherlands* decision), the judges found that a divorced foreign father of a Dutch girl could not be denied entry into or residence within the Netherlands so as to see his daughter. Yet the court made clear that this decision did not imply a right to family reunification in the receiving country and did not extend an obligation on the part of a contracting state to accept nonnational spouses for settlement in that country. In fact, subsequent cases did not regard entry but exit. They involved expulsion cases in which the court weighed the right of the individual against the interests of the state according to the principle of proportionality. In some cases involving foreigners who had lived in the host country since childhood and had tenuous ties to their country of origin, the ECHR has considered that their expulsion from the receiving country could not be tolerated even if they had an important criminal record. The court's case-by-case approach has meant that other rulings have gone in another direction. Judges have not established a general rule whereby all second-generation migrants should not be expelled.

Article 3 is invoked by foreigners who fear inhuman or degrading treatment if they are sent back to their country of origin. In the case of asylum seekers whose demand for refugee status has been rejected, it complements the principle of *non-refoulement* of the 1951 UN Convention Relating to the Status of Refugees. In a 1996 ruling (*Chahal v. UK*), the court stated that the absolute character of the provision means that protection cannot be ruled out by considerations relating to the public security of the state. In this and another two cases, the court found that Article 3 would be violated if the applicants were to be deported or extradited. Although the court recognizes different kinds of inhuman treatment, the applicants must show that they face a real risk if they are sent back, and the court's standard when it comes to the burden of proof is very high.

Other convention provisions may be relevant to foreigners' rights. Article 14 of the convention bans discrimination on many grounds, including race, color, language, religion, and national origin. Although it has been invoked by litigating parties in many cases involving aliens, only in one 1996 case (*Gaygusuz v. Austria*) did the court consider that refusing a Turk emergency assistance in Austria was a breach of Article 14 on the basis of national origin. As in many national legal systems, proving discrimination is often difficult. Beforehand, in 1985, there had been a famous immigration case (*Abdulaziz, Cabales, and Balkandali v. UK*) in which the court found the United Kingdom in violation of Article 14 because of gender discrimination: It was easier for foreign wives to join their husbands in the United Kingdom than it was for foreign husbands to join their wives. There is no case before the court involving dispositions written into additional protocols to the convention that specifically protect foreigners against expulsion (Article 1, 7th Protocol) and collective expulsion (Article 4, 4th Protocol), many countries having yet to ratify these protocols.

Another body of ECHR jurisprudence that could affect the lives of migrants regards freedom of religious expression as protected by Article 9 of the convention. Up until now, the European Commission on Human Rights, which decides whether cases are admissible and should be examined by the

File photo dated January 23, 1995 of a partial view of the European Court for Human Rights in Strasbourg. (AFP/Getty Images)

court, has only admitted four cases in which plaintiffs—none of whom were foreign—invoked Article 9. In cases such as the one involving a Muslim teacher who did not want to work on Friday afternoons, or that of another Muslim man who wanted to marry a girl under sixteen in the United Kingdom, the commission prudently restricted its own ability to interpret the article by relying on other parts of the convention that, in its view, could not accommodate religiously based claims for exemption from general laws. The commission has also referred to limitations to religious freedom deemed legitimate in a democratic society, such as for reasons involving health and security: In this fashion, a Buddhist prisoner could not grow a beard that would prevent his guards from identifying him, nor could a Sikh motorcyclist refuse to wear a crash helmet to keep his turban on. The cases reveal the complex range of issues that arise in a multicultural society. After years of unsuccessful applications to Strasbourg in cases involving religious or cultural minorities, calls for a new, optional protocol guaranteeing the rights of minorities have been heeded in order to circumvent the caution of the Commission of Human Rights. In any case, it seems that national courts in countries such as France and Germany have gone further than the ECHR in protecting the freedom of religious expression of migrant populations.

The ECHR's jurisprudence has been circumscribed to very specific areas of rights with respect to the protection of aliens. This has to do with the logic of increasing returns of litigation whereby one success in court based on a particular provision leads lawyers to multiply cases based on those grounds. In addition, a focus on specific areas can be explained by the preexistence of national jurisprudence in these areas. The ECHR has thus clarified the pertinence of preexisting legal principles and tried to harmonize practices rather than impose new ones. It is not fortuitous that the main jurisprudence on aliens centers around Article 8 on family life. The constitutions of many European countries include clauses resembling Article 8 on the right to lead a normal family life. Furthermore, the high courts of immigration countries had already issued important rulings based on domestic provisions before the ECHR did (for example, the French Council of State in 1978 and the German Constitutional Court in 1983). Compatible national legal norms have thus been the pillar on which international ones have been elaborated. In contrast to the bolder European Court of Justice, the Court of Human Rights' strategy to establish its legitimacy has been incrementalism and prudence.

There remains cross-national variation in the number of appeals to the ECHR. In particular, very few cases have been brought against Germany in spite of a significant number of expulsion orders against criminal foreigners. This can be explained by the strong human rights guarantees offered by the German Basic Law and the elaborate system of appeals that protects foreigners from arbitrary expulsions. German nongovernmental organizations (NGOs) seem less inclined to put forth test cases in Strasbourg than their French, Dutch, or British counterparts. Perhaps they do not need to and concur with legal scholars who prefer domestic legal guarantees to international law. In France, NGOs have used the ECHR to fill gaps in the system of legal protection such as the lack of suspensive effect of administrative appeals and the use of exceptional powers in national legislation. Many cases involve the United Kingdom, which can be attributed both to the lack of a written constitution and the activism of legal aid groups.

Although the impact of ECHR jurisprudence on domestic law and the incorporation of convention provisions by national courts both vary from country to country, some converging trends can be observed. National courts have been slow in making reference to the convention or citing ECHR jurisprudence, though, by the 1990s, most had. In many countries, including those with a high number of foreigners, such as Austria, Belgium, Germany, France, and the Netherlands, the ECHR's interpretation of Article 8 is explicitly mentioned in laws, regulations, and instructions to immigration authorities. In the United Kingdom, there is a standard paragraph that refers to Article 8 in immigration decisions, yet it does not seem to be genuinely taken into account. The ECHR has also indirectly inspired domestic reforms, such as the 1998 introduction of a special residence title called "private and family life" in French law. The ECHR has supported domestic developments toward the granting of a secure residence status to long-term foreign residents and the decoupling of rights and legal protection from nationality.

Virginie Guiraudon

See also: Assimilation/Integration; Asylum; Basic Law (Germany); Border Controls; Deportation; European Court of Justice; European Union; Family Reunification; Gender and Migration; Migrant Rights; Migration Policy; Multiculturalism; Non-Refoulement; Refugees; UN Convention Relating to the Status of Refugees, 1951; Women, Globalization, and Immigration

References and further reading:

Groenendijk, Kees. 2001. "Long-Term Immigrants and the Council of Europe." In *Security of Residence and Expulsion: Protection of Aliens in Europe.* Edited by Elspeth Guild and Paul Minderhoud. London: Kluwer.

Guiraudon, Virginie. 2000. "European Courts and Foreigners' Rights: A Comparative Study of Norms Diffusion." *International Migration Review* 34, no. 4: 1088–1125.

Harvey, Colin. 2001. "Promoting Insecurity: Public Order, Expulsion and the European Convention on Human Rights." In *Security of Residence and Expulsion: Protection of Aliens in Europe.* Edited by Elspeth Guild and Paul Minderhoud. London: Kluwer.

Stavros, Stephanos. 1997. "Freedom of Religion and Claims for Exemption from Generally Applicable, Neutral Laws: Lessons from across the Pond?" *European Human Rights Law Review* 6: 607–625.

Van Dijk, Pieter. 1999. "Protection of 'Integrated' Aliens against Expulsion under the European Convention on Human Rights." *European Journal of Migration and Law* 1: 293–312.

European Court of Justice

The European Court of Justice (ECJ) in Luxembourg, which comprises judges from each European Union (EU) member state, has played an important role in guaranteeing the right of free movement of European Union nationals and their families. It has also developed a body of jurisprudence regarding the rights of nationals of states that signed association agreements with the European Community (EC) and of employees of EU firms that deliver services in other member states. Since May 1999, it has had jurisdiction over common measures adopted as part of the emerging EU migration and asylum policies.

The main responsibility of the ECJ is to interpret the provisions of EU law and ensure that it is uniformly and consistently applied by ruling on cases that are referred to it. This institution has been key in both strengthening the status of EU law and extending EU policy competence. Cases related to immigration were generally brought before the court using the preliminary ruling procedure whereby a national court asks the ECJ to help it interpret EU law.

The ECJ, unlike the European Court of Human Rights in Strasbourg, does not base its jurisprudence regarding the rights of foreigners on human rights considerations. Although the court has reiterated that it must ensure observance of fundamental rights in EU law, it does so in a self-limiting way. The court has had to strike a balance between expanding EC competence in an area not covered by the treaties and remaining within the legitimate bounds of its sphere of duty, which concerns economic rights rather than human rights and EU citizens rather than non-EU citizens.

The legal status of third-country nationals has been affected by the jurisprudence of the ECJ in three major types of cases. First, according to the ECJ, the individual family members of an EU national who exercises his or her freedom of movement in another member state are entitled to the same residence, work, and welfare rights as member-state nationals even if they are not EU citizens, and they may only be required to obtain an entry visa. Family members do not have rights of their own but derive them from the EU worker moving to another member state.

Second, the ECJ has ruled on cases involving non-EU workers employed by EC firms performing services in another member state. In the Rush Portuguesa decision of March 27, 1990, the ECJ stated that a company could move with its own staff in line with the provisions for the suppression of restrictions to the freedom of establishment and the freedom to deliver services. If some of the company employees are third-country nationals, member states cannot refuse them entry to protect their own labor market on the grounds that immigration from non-EU states is a national prerogative. It is deemed a discrimination against the company (not the employees); yet, by the same token, non-EU nationals benefit from a derived right of employment in these cases for as long as they work for the company. The implications of the ECJ ruling have been wide ranging, especially in sectors such as the construction industry. In Germany, where many Portuguese or English companies received building contracts and paid their workers much lower wages and social security and fiscal contributions than the German ones, the debate raged in the 1990s between trade unions, employers, and the government, since the former considered that "posted workers," as they are called, contributed to "social dumping." The ECJ ruling also highlighted the consequences of incomplete

European integration, whereby the liberalization of services has been supranationalized, yet tax and welfare policy remain a matter of national sovereignty. The European Commission only partly solved the problem by proposing a directive setting minimum standards for posted workers.

Third, the ECJ has interpreted the 1964 EC/Turkey Association Treaty and subsequent decisions of the council set up to implement it (the Council of Ministers of Associations of the EC-Turkey Association Agreement), as well as the cooperation agreements with North African countries that the European Economic Community (EEC) entered into under Article 238 of the Treaty of Rome. Given the high numbers of Turkish and North African workers in European countries, any provision on freedom of movement for the nationals of the signatory countries could affect the status of a large number of foreign residents. Yet, in a few decisions in the late 1980s, the ECJ ruled that nationals of the association contracting states had directly enforceable rights in a way that made them part of the *acquis communautaire,* and that these rights had to be upheld by national courts. In this respect, the court went against the interests of major European receiving states. In the 1987 *Demirel* case (*Meryem Demirel v. Stadt Schwäbisch Gmünd,* ECR [1987] 3719), the ECJ first established EC competence with respect to the entry and stay of the nationals of EC-associated states. In the 1990 *Sevince* case (*S. Z. Sevince v. Staatsecretaris van Justitie,* Decision of September 20, 1990), the court ruled that a right of residence could be implied from the Association Council decisions. The judges pointed out that the right to employment that they contained would be useless without a right of residence. In the 1991 *Kziber* case (*National Employment Office v. B. Kziber,* Judgment of January 31, 1991), the ECJ interpreted an equal treatment clause in the Cooperation Agreement with Morocco according to the same line of reasoning, vindicating a Moroccan living in Belgium who had applied for special unemployment benefits, one of the social benefits covered by Article 2 of regulation 1612/68 applicable to EC migrant workers. In effect, the court neglected the difference between an EC national and a non-EC national covered by a Cooperation Agreement and ignored the international legal principle of reciprocity, since there are no such benefits in Morocco.

Member-state governments were furious at the ECJ decisions. This was especially the reaction of Germany after it lost in *Karim Kus v. Landeshauptstadt Wiesbaden.* In fact, German high courts did not deem that Turkish citizens could invoke Association Council decisions as law. Yet national courts and later executives have abided by the ECJ jurisprudence to a large extent. The ECJ ruling thus created a category of third-country nationals whose rights are better protected than others, fragmenting further the status of nonnationals. Still, the ECJ judges, realizing that they had spent their legitimacy capital in their path-breaking decisions and in later rulings in the mid-1990s, softened their stance. For their part, member states tried to preempt future developments in the impact of association treaties. When these treaties were renegotiated and new ones signed, member states wished to exclude freedom-of-movement clauses. The "Europe agreements" signed with former Soviet bloc countries do not contain rights for the free movement of workers but only a circumscribed right of establishment for the self-employed.

Furthermore, member states have circumscribed the role of the ECJ when initiating intergovernmental cooperation on immigration and asylum. The ECJ had no review powers over the 1990 Schengen Agreement, or measures adopted under the "third pillar" framework set up after 1993. Since May 1, 1999, when the Treaty of Amsterdam came into force, the ECJ can be asked for a ruling on the interpretation of the new Title IV ("visa, asylum, immigration and other policies related to free movement of persons"). Nonetheless, member states, mainly under French pressure, have limited the role of the court. Notably, the application of preliminary rulings in areas covered by Title IV is restricted to courts of last instance, thus depriving the court of a major source of case referrals. Moreover, the ECJ has no jurisdiction with regard to national measures adopted to regulate border crossings in order to maintain law and order and safeguard internal security. Finally, the court rulings do not apply retroactively to preexisting national judgments.

In spite of these restrictions, the ECJ is bound to play a crucial role in immigration law. First, the court has a tendency to increase its own competence by interpreting its mandate in an expansive manner. Second, the need for a supranational court able to harmonize national practices has become pressing, as demonstrated by the implementation of the Schengen Agreement. One example regards the denial of a visa to a third-country national who has been registered in the Schengen Information System (SIS). In June 1999, the French Council of State had to examine the case of a woman denied a visa to France because the Germans had registered her in the SIS. They had done so because her asylum request had been denied in Germany. The French Council of State did not deem this a valid reason for a SIS inscription, yet it nevertheless felt uneasy judging on a foreign decision. It is thus likely that national courts will embrace the new competence of the ECJ.

Virginie Guiraudon

See also: Employer Sanctions; European Citizenship; European Court of Human Rights; European Union; European Union Accession Countries; Family Reunification; Guestworkers, Europe; Migrant Rights; Migration Policy; Schengen Agreement; Skilled Migration; Sovereignty and Migration; UN Convention on the Rights of Migrant Workers, 1990; Visas

References and further reading:
Guild, Elspeth. 1999. "Adjudicating Schengen: National Judicial Control in France." *European Journal of Migration and Law* 1: 419–439.
———. 2000. *European Community Law from a Migrant's Perspective.* London: Kluwer.
Guild, Elspeth, and Paul Minderhoud. 2001. *Security of Residence and Expulsion: Protection of Aliens in Europe.* London: Kluwer.
Guiraudon, Virginie. 1998. "Third Country Nationals and European Law: Obstacles to Rights Expansion." *Journal of Ethnic and Migration Studies* 24, no. 4: 657–674.
Harlow, Carol, and Elspeth Guild. 2001. *Implementing Amsterdam.* Oxford: Hart.
Peers, Steve. 1996. "Towards Equality: Actual and Potential Rights of Third-Country Nationals in the European Union." *Common Market Law Review* 33: 7–50.
Staples, Helen. 1999. *The Legal Status of Third Country Nationals in the European Union.* London: Kluwer.

European Union

In a June 2000 speech, a European Union (EU) commissioner spoke of the need for what he called "more Europe" in immigration and asylum matters. By this he meant deeper integration with common policies as well as more responsibilities for the European Commission and other EU institutions. During the 1990s, immigration and asylum became core EU issues. This does not mean that common policies are inevitable. It does, however, show how far the EU has come that issues so closely linked to nation-states and their sovereignty are discussed as candidates for common policies. In addition to these two issues, EU migration policy deals with free movement for nationals of member states (classed since the Maastricht Treaty came into force in 1993 as EU citizens) and free movement of workers within the European Union. Taken together, all three elements constitute the migration policy framework.

Understanding this framework requires delving into the origins of the EU and its founding treaty, the Treaty of Rome (1957), which provided for free movement of workers within a common market in which barriers to trade between participating states would be removed. In the 1980s, the idea of a European single market, defined by the Single European Act (SEA, 1986) as an area without internal frontiers within which people, goods, services, and capital would be able to move freely, came into its own.

Single-market integration changes the nature of borders and border regimes within the EU but does not necessarily imply movement toward common immigration and asylum policies. It is too simplistic to assume that integration in one area necessarily draws other associated areas into a web of interdependence, with the effect that they, too, become the subject of common policies. Rather, immigration and asylum became important aspects of expanded EU competencies in the 1990s following the Maastricht Treaty (1992), the Amsterdam Treaty (1997), and the Treaty of Nice (2000). In EU jargon, the Maastricht Treaty "formalized" while the Amsterdam Treaty "communitarized" aspects of immigration and asylum policy. The Amsterdam Treaty also announced that the EU would be "an area of freedom, security and justice": "Freedom" for EU citizens to move between member states would be accompanied by "compensating" immigration and asylum measures that would regulate entry by non-EU nationals.

Because they seek to promote freer movement for EU citizens, EU migration policy competencies have important effects on the twenty-five member states to regulate access to their territory. Analysis of policy development in these areas needs to be located in relation to the EU's supranationalism, a feature that distinguishes it from other international organizations. EU institutions—mainly based in Brussels—possess the capacity to make laws that bind the member states. The resistance from some member states, such as the United Kingdom and Denmark, to supranationalization of immigration and asylum has been an important aspect of debates about closer European integration in these areas.

The functional right of free movement for workers—a right linked to the performance of an economic function—was guaranteed by two directives issued in 1968. This right has subsequently been extended to cover other categories of movers, such as students and retired people. A substantial body of European law, backed by European institutions such as the European Court of Justice, has developed over the years in support of this right. This supranationalization of free movement did not necessarily bring with it common immigration and asylum policies because these remained the preserve of member states' governments.

It was, however, difficult to maintain a strict distinction between the right of free movement for nationals of member states and immigration and asylum policies covering third-country nationals. One explanation for this is that migration pressures in the late 1980s and early 1990s on EU member states prompted a search for collective solutions to the regulation of international migration. Interdependencies had also become more apparent as a result of single-market integration.

EU immigration and asylum cooperation as it developed from the mid-1980s could thus be seen as an attempt to institute a system of international regulation in an area where the policy context had been altered by single-market integration. In short, a distinction developed between free movement for EU citizens and the regulation of movement by people who were not citizens of a member state. Free movement for EU citizens tied in with the market-building imperative that has underpinned the EU since its inception in the 1950s. Immigration and asylum were different matters because policies since the early 1970s had centered on the restriction of labor migration and attempts to curtail subsequent forms of migration, such as family migration and asylum-seeking.

By this reasoning, migration pressures and single-market integration raised collective action problems that were best resolved through EU cooperation aimed at the regulation of migration from outside the EU. This explanation also suggests that European cooperation and integration in these areas can strengthen rather than weaken state sovereignty, in the sense that European cooperation can help states achieve their policy objectives without constituting a "loss" or even "surrender" of their national sovereignty. At the same time, it should not be assumed that immigration and asylum were drawn into the realm of European integration as a result of single-market integration. It could also be argued that there was an awareness in national interior ministries about legal and political constraints on immigration controls and that the EU could provide a new "venue" where these constraints were much less evident.

From the mid-1980s, "informal cooperation" on immigration and asylum developed between member states. In 1986, the Ad Hoc Working Group on Immigration (AHWGI) was established as a forum for cooperation between member states. These arrangements were outside of the treaty framework, and institutions such as the European Commission and the European Court of Justice were specifically excluded. In 1988, the AHWGI established a Group of Co-ordinators, which in turn produced a report (the Palma Report, 1988) that outlined a series of immigration and asylum measures to accompany single-market integration. These included measures on asylum and external frontiers.

The main problem with this form of cooperation was that it lacked the institutional capacity to turn these intentions into anything more substantive. There was an agreement to cooperate that included more pro-integration states such as France, Germany, the Netherlands, and Belgium and more skeptical states such as Denmark and the United Kingdom. There was, however, no agreement that this should extend to the creation of European capacity in politically sensitive issue areas that could override member states' own policies. This institutional deficit is illustrated by the two main outputs of this period of informal cooperation. First, the 1990 Dublin Convention on asylum sought a "one-stop" asylum procedure so that asylum seekers could not make claims in more than one member state (that is, engage in "asylum shopping"). If a claim was made and rejected in one member state, then this refusal applied to all member states. This rule was accompanied by measures agreed upon in London in December 1992 that covered countries deemed "safe" (that is, from which asylum applications would not be considered because human rights abuses are presumed not to occur there) and other measures regarding applications deemed to be "manifestly unfounded," because of forged documents, for instance. The Dublin Convention was, however, an agreement in international law and thus separate from the supranational legal structures of the EU. As such, it needed to be ratified in all member states. This took seven years. This was as nothing compared with the travails of the External Frontiers Convention, which tried to put in place some common rules on the crossing of the external frontiers of member states. This was held up by a dispute between Britain and Spain that dated back to the Treaty of Utrecht of 1713. The sticking point was whether Gibraltar, which Britain had acquired in the 1713 treaty, should be included within the EU's external frontier borders. As a result, not all EU member states signed the External Frontiers Convention.

At the same time, another development was occurring outside of the treaty framework. The Schengen Agreement, signed by six member states (Belgium, France, Germany, Italy, Luxembourg, and the Netherlands) in the eponymous Luxembourg town in 1984, built on the free movement arrangements that had already been put in place by the Benelux countries and the Franco-German Saarbrucken Agreement, which sought to ease frontier crossing problems that were holding up truck drivers at national borders.

Schengen focused on putting in place provisions for free movement and the removal of frontiers between participating states with "compensating" immigration, asylum, and internal security measures. It thus allowed more pro-integration states to move toward their goals without the foot-dragging presence of more reluctant member states. It also served as a laboratory for the kinds of measures that needed to be put in place if free movement and the necessary compensating measures were to be realized for all member states.

In terms of policy content, both Schengen and the informal cooperation established following the Single European Act had a restrictive focus. In such terms, EU cooperation reflected national policy preferences for tight immigration controls. Moreover, the form of policy facilitated the attainment of these objectives because the actors who participated in these European forums were ministers and officials from the executive branches of national governments. They were to encounter few judicial or parliamentary constraints as they developed a European frame for policy cooperation on free movement, immigration, and asylum. This migration policy frame—the patterns of factual and normative understanding that influence the understanding of a policy question—was heavily influenced by concerns about security and insecurity linked to unwanted immigration and fears about large-scale migration either from the east or the south. It also reflected a changed post–Cold War understanding of security in Western Europe, with new issues entering the security agenda, as well as new ideas about societal security with a stronger focus on population control.

Changed ideas about security and insecurity were particularly apparent during the relatively rapid policy developments of the 1990s. The first major event was the (Maastricht) Treaty on European Union. In the negotiations that led up to this treaty, the member states once again had to seek a compromise between those member states favoring more rapid integration and those more reluctant states, such as the United Kingdom and Denmark, that wished to retain national decision-making in these areas. The member states faced the dilemma of establishing procedures that were more efficient while also attempting to address some of the concerns about accountability and scrutiny. As with all EU negotiations, the Maastricht Treaty was essentially a compromise. It brought immigration and asylum into the structures of the European Union, but did so within an intergovernmental Justice and Home Affairs (JHA) pillar that was separate from European Community (EC) decision-making procedures.

In this JHA pillar, unanimity would be the basis for decision making. The roles of the European Commission, European Court of Justice, and European Parliament were minimized. This allowed the member states to keep a tight grip on policy and reduce the scope for unexpected outcomes. Declarations attached to the treaty made it clear that immigration policies and nationality were national prerogatives.

Article K1-6 of the JHA pillar dealing with what were called JHA issues stated that the following were matters of "common interest" (note that they were not defined as the subject for "common policies," which would have been altogether more ambitious):

- Asylum policy
- Rules governing external border crossings of the member states
- Immigration policy and policy regarding third-country nationals (that is, people who were not nationals of a member state or covered by an agreement between the EU and a third country)
- Conditions of entry to and movement within the territory of member states
- Conditions of residence on the territory of member states, including family reunion and access to employment
- Policies combating unauthorized immigration, residence, and work on the territory of member states.

The only concessions to the supranational method of decision making were provisions on a common visa list, which was placed in the main EC "pillar."

Within the JHA pillar, the member states were able to maintain a tight grip on policy. The emphasis was squarely on the restriction of unwanted immigration at a time during the early 1990s when there had been a large increase in various forms of immigration, particularly asylum-seeking. Supranational institutions were largely excluded, although the commission did secure a seat at the intergovernmental table so that it could at least try to contribute to debates, even though its formal powers in these areas were extremely limited.

The Maastricht method of cooperation soon displayed its limitations. Any hopes that it might lead to more scrutiny and accountability were confounded by the development of secretive structures. Any optimism that the Maastricht structures might lead to more effective decision-making was also soon dashed. The intergovernmental pillar did not provide the member states with the capacity to enact binding laws. Instead the output consisted of a series of nonbinding "decisions," "recommendations," and "conclusions" that covered many aspects of policy but were of dubious legal status and very difficult to implement.

In parallel with this, there was continued development of the Schengen Agreement. By the end of the 1990s, only the United Kingdom and Ireland remained outside of the Schengen group, which had implemented the measures necessary for free movement within the Schengen space. Schengen put in place those "compensating" immigration, asylum, and internal security measures that were seen as necessary if frontiers between participating states were to be removed.

Schengen's status as a "laboratory" within which preparation for free movement with compensating immigration and asylum measures would occur was demonstrated by the Amsterdam Treaty, which brought Schengen into the European Union. The Amsterdam Treaty was a particularly important development because it added a new title (Title IV) covering free movement, immigration, and asylum. Moreover, a phrase was added to the treaty's preamble to declare that the EU would be "an area of freedom, security and justice." Title IV, Article 61, specified that the Council of the European Union should adopt with five years of treaty ratification measures to ensure the free movement of persons and "directly related flanking measures" regarding external frontier controls, asylum, and immigration. Article 62 deals with the removal of external frontier controls, and Article 63 covers asylum and brings in the key elements of the Dublin Convention (one-stop asylum procedures). Articles 64–68 lay out institutional provisions, such as a five-year transitional period, emphasizing unanimity until at least 2004. At the end of the five-year period the member states could agree to move to qualified majority voting (71 percent of a weighted vote in the Council of Ministers).

Amsterdam made explicit the connections that had previously been implicit between free movement, immigration, and asylum. Rather than being separated—with free movement in the EC pillar and immigration and asylum residing in the intergovernmental JHA pillar—they were to be dealt with together. That said, there were to be some constraints because the issues were "communitarized" but not "supranationalized."

The distinction might sound insignificant and replete with the kinds of jargon that riddle discussion of the EU, but it is important nevertheless. The issues were communitarized in the sense that immigration and asylum were brought from the JHA pillar into the EC pillar and linked with free movement. They were not supranationalized, because there were still substantial constraints on the role of supranational institutions. The commission, for instance, shared its power of proposal with the member states. Unanimity was also to be the decisional modus operandi for at least five years following treaty ratification (thus at least until May 2004). The ECJ's role was also constrained through, for instance, measures that allowed cases to be dealt with at the European level only when avenues for redress at the national level had been exhausted. This appeared to minimize the scope for ECJ preliminary rulings to shape national law and contribute to EU "competence creep" as a result of legal processes. It is, though, possible to detect a policy trajectory in the sense that immigration and asylum have moved into the EC method of decision making, but at the same time, the member states have maintained a tight grip on this politically sensitive policy area.

There are some relatively fine points associated with the Amsterdam Treaty that need to be emphasized because they relate very directly to the type of migration policy that is developing within the EU. First, Schengen was brought into the EU, but whether the precise elements of the Schengen Agreement were to be placed in the community pillar (in the new Title IV), or in a recast intergovernmental pillar dealing with Judicial and Police Co-operation (JPC), was a matter for the member states. Second, the wholesale importation of the Schengen Agreement meant that decisions made by ministers and officials in the secretive intergovernmental forums of the Schengen group were to be placed within the EU without any proper parliamentary or judicial oversight. Third, the Amsterdam Treaty brought an element of flexibility to the way in which free movement, immigration, and asylum would be dealt with. As already mentioned, the United Kingdom and Ireland were not Schengen states. The United Kingdom refused to relinquish its external frontier controls, and Ireland was tied to the United Kingdom by the Common Travel Area that existed between the two countries. The United Kingdom and Ireland also opted out of Title IV of the Amsterdam Treaty, which appeared to presage the kind of frontier-free Europe that would force the United Kingdom to abolish external frontier controls applying to intra-EU travel. Given that this method of control had been relatively effective and that the new European method of integration was untested, there were good grounds for UK governmental skepticism. The United Kingdom could opt back in to those measures that it liked. Indeed, this has been the case, because the more general security-related orientation of policy has connected with UK governmental preferences. Another opt-out applied to Denmark. Even though Denmark was a Schengen state, its government opted out of Schengen measures that were placed in the new Title IV and where EU institutions would have a greater policy role and thus potentially override national decisions.

The Amsterdam Treaty provided a foothold for the commission and the European Court of Justice, although it did little to boost the role of the European Parliament. The member states asked the commission to draw up an action plan for implementation of Title IV measures. This was presented to the December 1998 meeting held in Vienna of the European Council (heads of government). The political priority of immigration and asylum was emphasized by a special meeting of heads of state held in Tampere in October 1999 calling for common asylum and migration policies. The Tampere summit also called for a common EU migration policy and provided political impetus from the highest governmental level. The common policy was to be based on:

- Partnership with countries of origin. The post-Amsterdam role of the High Level Working Group on Immigration and Asylum has been crucial here, not only because it illustrates the links between internal security concerns and foreign policy, but also because it has been seen as displaying the EU's intention to try to keep migrants closer to their countries of origin. There had been an air of artificiality about the division between internal security (JHA) and external security (the Common Foreign and Security Policy [CFSP]). EU responses to international migration since the 1990s highlight the blurring of this distinction and the tendencies toward what is known as "cross-pillarization," with functional linkages made between the concerns dealt with by the CFSP and JHA pillars (and thus between the concerns of foreign and interior ministries).
- Asylum measures. These were specified to include a workable determination of the state responsible for the examination of an asylum application, common

standards on processing applications, common minimum conditions of reception of asylum seekers, and the approximation of rules on the recognition and content of the refugee status. This would be accompanied by measures on temporary protection for displaced people (based on solidarity between member states). In the longer term, the member states proposed that EC rules should lead to a common asylum procedure and a uniform status for those granted asylum valid throughout the Union. The commission was asked to prepare within one year a communication on this matter. The Council of Ministers was also urged to finalize its work on the system for the identification of asylum seekers (Eurodac).

- Fair treatment for third-country nationals (TCNs) who reside legally on the territory of a member state. The member states talked about "more vigorous" policies aimed at granting TCNs rights and obligations comparable to those of EU citizens with measures to enforce the principle of equal treatment in economic, social, and cultural life. There was also a call for measures to combat racism and xenophobia.
- The management of migration flows based on cooperation with countries of origin and transit, information campaigns on the actual possibilities for legal immigration, and the prevention of trafficking in human beings. The heads of government also called for common policies on visas and false documents, including closer cooperation between EU consulates in third countries and, where necessary, the establishment of common EU visa-issuing offices. The member states also reaffirmed their determination to tackle illegal immigration, traffick in human beings, and economic exploitation of migrants. There was renewed commitment to closer cooperation and mutual technical assistance between member states on border controls and technology transfer, especially on maritime borders, and for the rapid inclusion of the applicant states in this cooperation. It was stated that applicant countries must accept the Schengen *acquis* (the total body of accumulated EU law) in full. Finally, the Amsterdam Treaty conferred powers on the EC for readmission. The council was mandated to conclude readmission agreements or to include standard clauses in other agreements between the EC and relevant third countries or groups of countries.

In November 2000, the commission published a "communication" outlining a number of options for immigration and asylum policy. By the end of the 1990s it had become apparent that demographic and labor-market changes in member states were creating new demands for migrant labor, and the commission sought to balance the existing strong focus on security with openings to new migration. Another commission communication in July 2001 outlined measures for the coordination of national migration policies putting the commission in a key role as the identifier of "European solutions to common problems."

So far, the discussion has concentrated on the member states and on institutional dynamics at the EU level. It is, however, important to bear in mind that the effects of EU migration policy are not only felt by the member states. The EU migration framework has an impact on surrounding states and regions. States in Central and Eastern Europe that are seeking to join the EU must adopt the EU's immigration and asylum *acquis* (body of law) as a condition for membership. Their domestic structures and international relations are affected as they develop a migration policy infrastructure that fits with the "Schengenland" model. Thus, adaptation is a prerequisite for membership.

Explanations of EU migration policy must take the timing, content, form, and effects of that policy into account. Cooperation and integration since the mid-1980s have allowed member states to avoid domestic legal and political constraints and have empowered ministers and officials from the executive branches of national governments. The member states have managed to keep a relatively tight grip on policy development to minimize the role of EC institutions and reduce the scope for unexpected policy outcomes. Yet immigration and asylum—classic issues of high politics that are closely linked to national sovereignty—have moved closer to the EC method of decision making and seem likely to become the subject for common policies covering EU member states (or most of them, if the EU develops in a "flexible" way). Thus, free movement, immigration, and asylum have been the subjects of intensified interstate cooperation in a unique form of supranational organization. Moreover, these patterns of cooperation have important effects on EU member states and on surrounding states and regions. Indeed, it seems likely that the international migration relations of the EU will be a major feature of its developing role in the years to come.

Andrew Geddes

See also: European Citizenship; European Court of Human Rights; European Court of Justice; European Union Accession Countries

References and further reading:

Geddes, Andrew. 2000. *Immigration and European Integration: Towards Fortress Europe.* Manchester: Manchester University Press.

Lavenex, Sandra, and Emek Uçarer. 2002. *Externalities of Integration: The Wider Impact of the EU's Developing Asylum and Immigration Policy.* Lanham, MD: Lexington.

Waever, Ole, Barry Buzan, Morten Kelstrup, and Pierre Lemaitre. 1993. *Identity, Migration and the New Security Agenda in Europe*. London: Pinter.

European Union Accession Countries

European Union (EU) accession—the process by which new members join the EU—is nothing less than the expansion of Europe. It provides new members with the entitlements and obligations, including free movement, associated with membership of the world's most developed regional organization. Cyprus, the Czech Republic, Estonia, Hungary, Latvia, Lithuania, Malta, Poland, the Slovak Republic, and Slovenia were admitted in May 2004, and two additional countries, Bulgaria and Romania, are currently pursuing accession negotiations with the EU. For Turkey, a specific Accession Partnership has been drafted, and Croatia and the former Yugoslav Republic of Macedonia have applied for membership. To join the EU, applicants must adapt their immigration provisions to the EU *acquis* (body of law). This includes the introduction of new legislation on visa policy, admission of third-country nationals, asylum, and border management as well as free-movement provisions.

Given their geographical location, accession countries risk becoming Europe's buffer zone, and the immigration flows indicate potential future migration to Europe. Although the majority of immigrants originate from neighboring countries, however, newer trends suggest a diversification of migration flows. These flows include documented and undocumented migrants, asylum seekers, permanent immigrants, and an important number of short-term, "pendular" migrations for trade purposes. The main factors accounting for these developments are strong economic inequalities in the region and legislative changes introduced in the 1990s, in particular, modification of nationality laws, the introduction of short- and long-term resident permits for foreigners, the (provisional) abolition of visa requirements, and the ratification of the 1951 UN Convention Relating to the Status of Refugees. It is also relevant that more

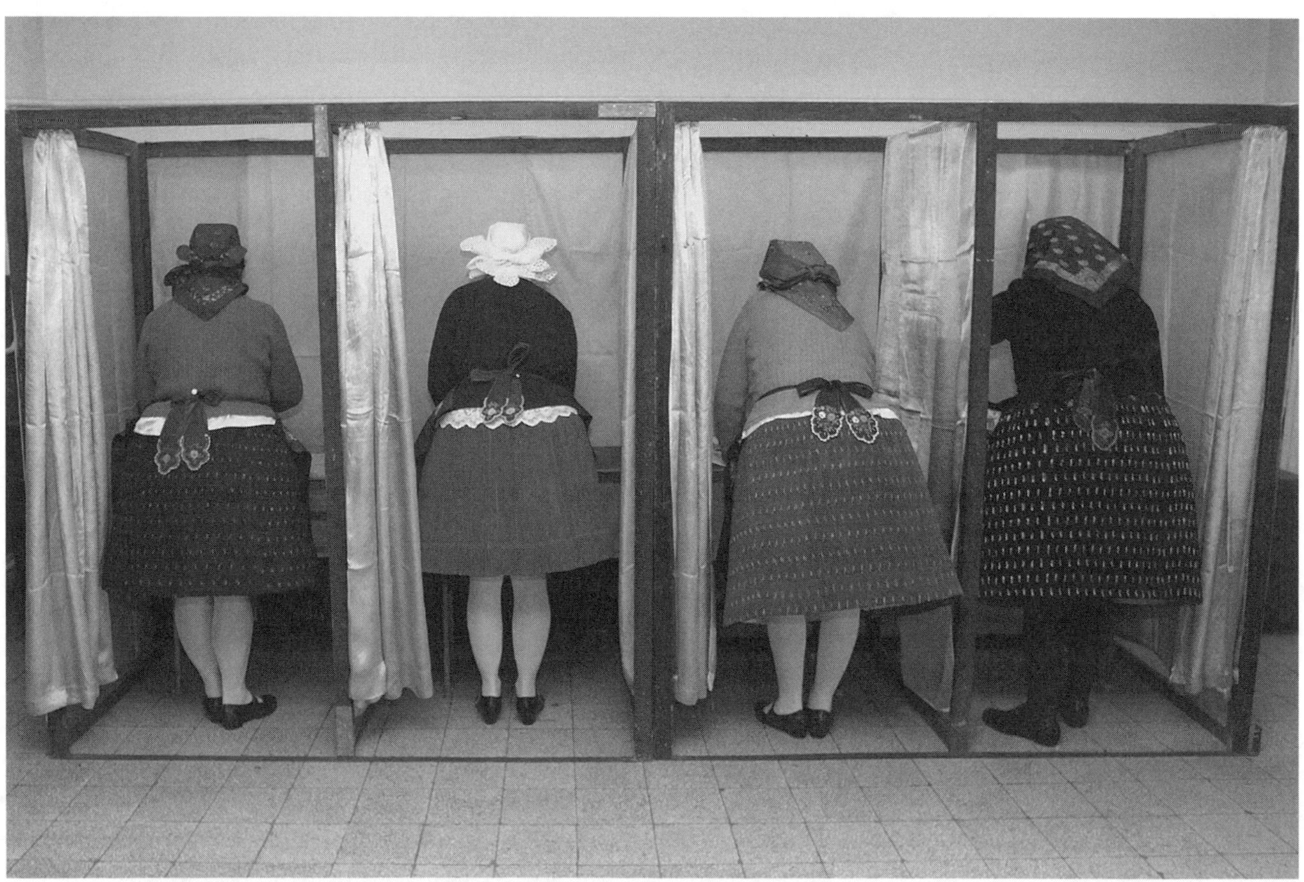

Hungarian women vote during a referendum on European Union membership in Veresegyhaza, thirty kilometers east of Budapest, April 12, 2003. Hungary was the third candidate to hold a referendum among the ten states invited to join the European Union in May 2004—Slovenia and Malta have already approved membership—but the first major post-Communist country to cast ballots on accession. (Reuters/Corbis)

and more transit migrants heading toward Western Europe actually remain in the Central Eastern European Countries (CEECs) because of enhanced controls at the EU's external borders.

Free Movement

Free movement between the accession countries and EU member states is regulated by the Association and Europe Agreements concluded with the European Community (EC) as well as by a number of bilateral treaties with individual member states. The most generous provisions regarding the movement of persons are included in the EC Association Agreement with Turkey concluded in 1963. Turkey, however, remains exceptional, as some member states, Germany in particular, worry that their large Turkish populations will lead to sharply increased Turkish migration. The Europe Agreements concluded with the CEECs between 1991 and 1996 include provisions on the movement of workers, the establishment of businesses, and the provision of services. However, no reference is made to the Treaty of Rome's provisions on the free movement of persons, nor is an automatic right of access to the labor market or freedom to reside in EU member states recognized. Upon accession, the original EU member states negotiated a maximal transition period of seven years before full free-movement rights are realized. With the exception of the United Kingdom and Ireland, all EU member states have announced that they will make use of these transitional provisions at least for an initial period of time.

Asylum and immigration policies have become a central element in the EU's enlargement strategy vis-à-vis the accession countries, as they have been gradually "communitarised" (included under the European Commission and European Court of Justice's influence). In order to join the Union, candidate countries are required to respect the acquis communautaire and the Schengen acquis in full, that is, the totality of legislation and instruments that have been adopted in these fields. In practice, the candidate countries' adaptation to the EU acquis is promoted at different levels: through unilateral measures of EU member states, through bilateral cooperation between individual countries, through multilateral intergovernmental cooperation outside the EU framework, and through the EU's official accession partnerships.

Visa Policies

All accession countries have introduced changes to their visa regulations as part of their national preparation for EU membership. The adaptation to the EU's strict visa requirements has important implications for the former countries of the Warsaw Pact, as it affects these countries' economic and cultural relations with their eastern and southern neighbors, including the ethnic minorities spread over different countries. Bulgaria and Romania, whose citizens until recently required a visa to travel to the EU, have significantly tightened their own visa requirements in their effort to be taken from the EU visa list.

Admission

In spite of the absence of a common immigration policy in the EU, accession countries are gradually aligning their provisions on the entry and stay of foreign nationals to policy principles in EU member states. This includes admission for the purpose of study, employment, self-employed activities, and family reunification as well as regulations against illegal employment and trafficking in human beings.

Border Management

The accession partnerships with the EU put particular emphasis on securing future EU external borders. This includes the implementation of the Schengen acquis, in particular the strengthening of national borders through technological innovation, the training of border guards, the introduction of information and communication systems, and changes to criminal law, for example, the effective punishment of trafficking in human beings or the forging of documents.

Asylum

With transition to democracy, all CEECs have implemented the 1951 Refugee Convention, with the three Baltic states being the last ones to join the international refugee regime in 1997. Turkey applies a geographical limitation to the 1951 Refugee Convention: asylum claims by non-European countries are processed by UNHCR. In all accession countries, preparation for EU membership has a mixed impact on asylum provisions. While stressing the need to comply with fundamental principles of human rights and refugee law, the emphasis on tight border controls in the EU migration acquis, and the export of policies geared at fighting illegal immigration and unfounded asylum claims, impose limits to the implementation of liberal asylum regimes. Tighter border controls and stricter asylum policies in the West have also led to a considerable increase in the number of asylum seekers in certain CEECs, notably those sharing a border with an EU member state.

Sandra Lavenex

See also: Asylum; Border Controls; Carrier Sanctions; Citizenship; Employer Sanctions; European Citizenship; European Union; Family Reunification; Foreign Students; Germany; Migration Policy; Open Borders; Passports; Refugees; Schengen Agreement; Sovereignty and Migration; Trafficking; Turkish Diaspora; UN Convention Relating to the Status of Refugees, 1951; Visas

References and further reading:
Lavenex, Sandra. 1999. *Safe Third Countries. Extending the EU Asylum and Immigration Policies to Central and Eastern Europe.* Budapest and New York: Central European University Press.
Lavenex, Sandra, and Emek M. Uçarer, eds. 2002. *Migration and the Externalities of European Integration.* Lanham, MD: Lexington.
Morawska, Ewa. 2000. "Transnational Migrations in the Enlarged European Union: A Perspective from East Central Europe." Working Paper of the Robert Schuman Centre, Florence, 19.
Organization for Economic Co-operation and Development. 2001. *Migration Policies and EU Enlargement. The Case of Central and Eastern Europe.* Paris: OECD.
Wallace, Claire, and Dariusz Stola, eds. 2000. *Patterns of Migration in Central Europe.* London: Palgrave.

Exile

See Asylum; Displaced Persons; Internally Displaced Persons; Refugees

Expedited Removal Procedures, U.S.

In 1996, the United States enacted legislation creating an "expedited removal" program for certain noncitizens who present themselves at U.S. ports of entry—land borders, airports, and seaports. When it applies, expedited removal is an exception to the fuller, usual procedure for the admission of noncitizens into the territory of the United States. Like its European counterparts, the U.S. program has been highly controversial. Amid mounting concerns over both high levels of illegal immigration and large numbers of asylum applicants, Western nations are increasingly prone to prescribe various summary procedures for the admission and exclusion of noncitizens. The new procedures are designed to deter fraudulent entries, reduce the number of asylum applications, and dispose cheaply and speedily of those asylum applications that are filed.

The Regular Admission Procedure

To understand expedited removal, it is necessary to understand the regular procedure to which it is an exception. Ordinarily, when a noncitizen wishes to enter the United States, either for permanent residence or for a temporary purpose, he or she must first obtain a visa from a U.S. consulate overseas. Upon arrival at the port of entry, the person is inspected by an official of the U.S. Department of Homeland Security (DHS). The purpose of the inspection is to assure that the person is not within any of the statutory grounds that render noncitizens inadmissible, such as criminal convictions, inadequate funds, and the like. If the DHS inspector is confident that the person is admissible, he or she is admitted. If the DHS inspector has doubts on that score, the person is referred to an administrative official whose title is "immigration judge" for a "removal" hearing to be held at some future date. The hearing is a quasi-formal event at which two opposing parties—the DHS and the noncitizen—present evidence. At the conclusion of the hearing, the immigration judge decides whether to admit or remove. The losing party—either the noncitizen or the DHS—has the right to appeal the immigration judge's decision to an administrative tribunal called the Board of Immigration Appeals (BIA). Both the corps of immigration judges and the BIA are under the organizational auspices of an agency called the Executive Office for Immigration Review (EOIR), which is part of the U.S. Department of Justice. Normally, if the BIA orders the noncitizen removed, he or she has a further right of review before a three-judge panel of the U.S. Court of Appeals. With some exceptions, the noncitizen is detained throughout this multistep process until he or she is either removed from the United States or ordered admitted.

In these removal proceedings, there are typically two kinds of issues to be resolved. One is whether the noncitizen does indeed fall within one of the statutory grounds of inadmissibility. If so, then the other issue is whether the noncitizen qualifies nonetheless for some form of discretionary relief from removal. Some forms of relief require a specified combination of unusual hardship and U.S. family ties. Others are for certain noncitizens who fear persecution. The remedy that U.S. law calls "asylum" requires that the person be a "refugee," a term defined to require either past persecution or a well-founded fear of future persecution because of race, religion, nationality, membership in a particular social group, or political opinion. Upon finding the person to be a refugee, the immigration judge has the discretion to grant asylum, which permits the person to remain in the United States (usually permanently). A related remedy, known as "withholding of removal" (or "non-refoulement," in international parlance), requires showing that the person's life or freedom would be threatened because of his or her race, religion, nationality, membership in a social group, or political opinion. Upon such a showing, the person may not be sent to the country of persecution, though he or she may be sent to a safe third country if asylum is not granted. Any of these determinations might entail either findings of fact or interpretations of law, and some might also entail the exercise of administrative discretion.

The Adoption of Expedited Removal

In the 1980s and 1990s, two things happened: First, with heightened attention to the problem of illegal immigration, the Immigration and Naturalization Service (INS, the predecessor to DHS) apprehended increasing numbers of undocumented immigrants. As a result, there were suddenly far more removal hearings, which were then called either exclusion or deportation hearings, depending on whether the person was arriving at a port of entry or apprehended in the interior. Second, there were far more asylum applications. Many members of Congress and executive branch officials believed that the vast majority of the latter were unfounded and being filed solely to prolong the applicant's stay in the United States for the often lengthy time that it took to reach a final decision. Many others, in contrast, believed that a high proportion of the applicants were genuine refugees or people who at least had reasonable claims to refugee status.

In 1996, Congress enacted a package of harsh measures concerned with both legal and illegal immigration. One of these measures was the expedited removal procedure. It applies whenever a DHS immigration inspector at a port of entry "determines" that an arriving noncitizen is inadmissible on one of two grounds—that he or she lacks proper documentation, or that he or she is engaged in the commission of a fraud. In such a case, the regular procedure described above is inapplicable. Instead, the immigration officer must order the noncitizen removed from the United States without any further hearing or review.

There are some important exceptions. Not subject to expedited removal are noncitizens who claim under oath that they have previously been admitted to the United States as permanent residents or refugees or granted asylum. Cuban nationals who arrive in the United States by air are also immune from expedited removal.

But the most important exception is for potential refugees. If a noncitizen who would otherwise be subject to expedited removal indicates an intention to apply for asylum or a fear of persecution, the immigration inspector is required to refer him or her to a DHS asylum officer for an interview. At that interview, the noncitizen must introduce enough evidence to make a full asylum determination worthwhile. For this purpose, the law requires a showing of a "credible fear" of persecution. The law defines "credible fear" as "a significant possibility, taking into account the credibility of the statements made by the alien in support of the alien's claim and such other facts as are known to the officer, that the alien could establish eligibility for asylum."

If the person establishes a credible fear, the regular removal process described earlier is reinstated. In that event, the immigration judge holds a full evidentiary hearing and decides whether to grant asylum. The immigration judge's decision is subject to appeal to the BIA and possibly judicial review in the usual way. If, instead, the asylum officer determines that the applicant did not establish a credible fear, the officer orders the applicant removed from the United States. The officer then writes up a report summarizing the facts and the reasons for the finding. Upon the applicant's request, an immigration judge will "promptly" review the finding, either in person or by telephone or video, within twenty-four hours, if practicable, and in any case within seven days. There is no other administrative review unless the applicant swears under oath that he or she has already been admitted to the United States as a permanent resident or a refugee or has already received asylum. Nor, with very limited exceptions, is there any judicial review.

Actual Experience with Expedited Removal

Information on the actual experience with expedited removal has proved difficult to obtain. The leading study is the Expedited Removal Study, a project based at the University of California at Hastings and led by Professor Karen Musalo. For several years, the INS, citing concerns of personal privacy, declined to release statistical data or files or to permit observation of the process by either the Expedited Removal Study or other nongovernmental organizations (NGOs). In 2000, however, as a result of negotiations conducted during litigation over the study's Freedom of Information Act request, the INS released much of the requested data, though not all. The data summarized in the next two paragraphs come from the May 2000 report of the Expedited Removal Study.

The data covered the years 1997 through 1999. Perhaps the most significant revelation was that approximately 99 percent of the persons whom immigration inspectors found inadmissible for either documentary or fraud reasons (and thus subject to expedited removal) were removed on the spot. Only the remaining 1 percent were referred to asylum officers for credible-fear interviews. Among the latter, however, 88 percent succeeded in demonstrating credible fear of persecution and thus were granted a full hearing on their asylum claims. The INS data also showed that expedited removal now accounts for approximately one-half of all removals of noncitizens from the United States. During the 1997–1999 study period, some 91 percent of all expedited removals were Mexicans. Next came natives of Jamaica, the Dominican Republic, Canada, and Ecuador. Approximately 44 percent of all the expedited removals took place at San Ysidro, California, a land border port of entry. Of the ten leading expedited removal ports of entry, all but one (New York, which was eighth) were land borders.

In each of the three years studied, between 80 and 89 percent of all the expedited removals were on grounds of suspected fraud rather than on grounds of invalid documentation. This last fact is extremely important, because U.S. immigration laws render inadmissible for life any person removed on grounds of fraud; those removed only because of invalid documentation become inadmissible only for five years. A common ground for a finding of fraud is that the person states an intention to return home upon the expiration of his or her temporary visa and the DHS inspector believes the true intention is to remain permanently. In other cases, it is clear that the person has misstated a fact, but there is uncertainty whether the misstatement was deliberate or inadvertent. Both a determination that a fact has been misstated and the determination that the misstatement was intentional require judgment.

Because the consequences of removal—both the five-year or lifetime ban on readmission and the possibility of erroneous return to persecution—are so serious, and because refugee advocates have expressed a range of concerns about the process and its implementation, Congress requested the General Accounting Office (GAO) to study four specific questions of particular concern. The GAO found itself unable to answer the questions directly, citing a lack of expertise in legal matters, inadequate resources, and the lack of an acceptable methodology. It did, however, compile some additional data and study the INS management controls.

The first area of concern was whether INS inspectors were inappropriately encouraging people to withdraw their applications for admission rather than face expedited removal (with its consequent bar on future admission). An INS fact sheet released in 1998 revealed that approximately half of the 160,000 noncitizens who were found to be subject to expedited removal were permitted to withdraw their applications and thus avoid formal removals. In cases in which there is little chance of admission, withdrawal is generally a sensible option, but the concern is whether significant numbers of people who might otherwise have been admitted felt pressured to withdraw. The GAO, examining INS statistics and randomly selected files compiled by immigration inspectors in cases in which withdrawal was permitted, found that INS inspectors were complying with agency procedures in 74–95 percent of the cases. In particular, in somewhere between 2 percent and 21 percent of all the withdrawal cases, the INS inspectors had failed to ask mandatory questions about the applicant's fear of harm. The Expedited Removal Study criticized the GAO methodology, however, for relying solely on INS self-reporting and failing to include any on-site observation, thus possibly understating the degree of INS noncompliance.

The second area of congressional concern related to noncitizens who did not voluntarily withdraw their applications. The question was whether INS inspectors were wrongly failing to refer people for credible-fear interviews. Although, again, the GAO relied on INS self-reporting rather than on-site observation, it found that in 2 percent of the expedited removal cases, the person expressed a fear of persecution but was not referred for a credible-fear interview. The GAO also found significant noncompliance with various official procedures that had been adopted to ensure accuracy. The Expedited Removal Study suggested that even a rate of 2 percent would be a significant problem in absolute terms, but that, in any event, in the face of significant noncompliance with relevant quality-control mechanisms, the GAO methodology made it impossible to know whether the actual percentage of incorrect nonreferrals was much higher.

A third area of congressional concern was a general one that subsumed the first two. Congress wanted to know whether, ultimately, INS inspectors were incorrectly removing asylum seekers to countries in which they faced risks of persecution. The GAO did not attempt to answer this question, but it did find that the asylum officers who conducted the credible-fear interviews generally documented that they had complied with the proper management procedures. As the Expedited Removal Study observed, however, the GAO did not attempt to review the substantive outcomes of the credible-fear determinations for factual or legal correctness or otherwise try to track the postremoval experiences of selected noncitizens in their countries of origin.

The fourth congressional concern was detention. From the time a noncitizen subject to expedited removal arrives at a U.S. port of entry until the time he or she is physically removed, the statute requires detention. As an exception, the DHS has the discretion to release a person, pending completion of the case, once it has found that that person has a credible fear of persecution. The DHS official policy is to exercise that discretion favorably in cases in which the person is likely to appear for his or her scheduled hearing and does not represent a danger to the community. In 1999, the INS reported that it released 78 percent of the people who had successfully demonstrated a credible fear. The GAO found, however, that the various INS geographic districts had dramatically different policies governing release and that the actual release percentages also varied greatly by district. Because many of the released persons failed to appear for their hearings (probably about 25 percent, once necessary adjustments to the data are made), and because 43 percent of the people who had successfully demonstrated credible fear did not follow through with formal asylum applications within the one-year legal window, the GAO concluded that many individuals might be using the credible-fear process as a means to remain in the United States illegally. The policy implication is that perhaps too many people subject to expedited removal, but demonstrating a credible fear of persecution, were improperly released. As the Expedited Removal Study pointed out, however, some 44 percent of the persons counted as no-shows were Sri Lankans, and Sri Lankans frequently transit to Canada. The study also noted that the GAO had not examined the converse question—whether substantial numbers of those who were found to possess credible fears of persecution were improperly detained.

The Present Status of Expedited Removal

In light of all these considerations, there remains considerable difference of opinion concerning the benefits and dangers of expedited removal and concerning possible improvements. Many observers continue to feel that expedited removal serves the beneficial functions of discouraging illegal immigration, disposing quickly and cheaply of those cases that present no substantial factual or legal issues, and saving administrative resources for the cases in which significant risks of persecution are truly presented. Other observers concede the legitimacy of those goals but contend that expedited removal—because of either the law itself or DHS implementation—sacrifices accuracy and procedural fairness to an unacceptable degree. Substantial anecdotal evidence supplied by noncitizens subjected to expedited removal and their attorneys, and reported in the Expedited Removal Study, lends credence to that view. In the absence of reliable empirical data, the verdict is still out.

Stephen H. Legomsky

See also: Asylum; Asylum Determination; Border Controls; Deportation; Mexican Immigration; Migrant Rights; Non-Refoulement; Refugees; Safe Country, Safe Third Country; U.S. Immigration Legislation: Post-1945

References and further reading:

Cooper, Bo. 1997. "Procedures for Expedited Removal and Asylum Screening under the Illegal Immigration Reform and Immigrant Responsibility Act of 1996." *Connecticut Law Review* 29: 1501–1524.

Martin, David A. 2000. "Two Cheers for Expedited Removal in the New Immigration Laws." *Virginia Journal of International Law* 40: 673–704.

Musalo, Karen, Lauren Gibson, Stephen Knight, and J. Edward Taylor. 2000. "Evaluation of the General Accounting Office's Second Report on Expedited Removal." The Expedited Removal Study, University of California, Hastings College of Law.

———. 2001. "Report on the First Three Years of Implementation of Expedited Removal. May 2000." The Expedited Removal Study, University of California, Hastings College of Law. *Notre Dame Journal of Law, Ethics and Public Policy* 15 (Special Issue 2001).

Osuna, Juan P., and Patricia Mariani. 1997. "Expedited Removal: Authorities, Implementation, and Ongoing Policy and Practice Issues." *Immigration Briefings,* November.

U.S. Commission on Immigration Reform. 1997. *Report to Congress, U.S. Refugee Policy: Taking Leadership.* June.

U.S. General Accounting Office. 2000. *Illegal Aliens: Opportunities to Improve the Expedited Removal Process.* September.

Expulsions

See Deportation; East African Asian Expulsions; Ethnic Cleansing: Germans from Central and Eastern Europe

Extreme Right Parties

See Far-Right Parties

F

Family Reunification

The need for family reunification through migration arises following family separation, whether such separation is lengthy or short-lived, voluntary or involuntary, and it is promoted by family solidarity and constrained by the cost of relocation. In the context of international migration, family reunification is not only a social and economic matter but also a political issue. In particular, a state's obligation to uphold the integrity of the family, and to respect the family and family life in accordance with international conventions on human rights, may conflict with its right to defend perceived national interests by controlling immigration and determining who enters its territory.

A distinction is frequently drawn between countries of permanent immigration, such as the United States, which is often described as a "nation of immigrants," and countries where immigration is supposedly temporary. This distinction has important implications for family reunification. Where immigration is seen as permanent, family reunification is more likely to be thought essential to integrating immigrants into the receiving society, with all the benefits that are believed to follow. Indeed, it has been argued that immigrants sponsoring the entry of their relatives are the best "agents of integration." If immigration is regarded as temporary, perhaps because the need for immigrants will disappear after a brief time, or because individual migrants are expected to stay in the receiving society for a limited time for some other reason, then family reunification will be discouraged or precluded. In this case, it is sometimes argued that family integrity is best achieved when temporary migrants return to their country of origin.

Family reunification first became an important issue in the United States following the imposition of immigration restrictions in the 1920s. In Western Europe, the other great destination for immigrants in the twentieth century, family reunification became a pressing issue only when labor-receiving countries began to halt primary immigration.

Some 11 million immigrants arrived in the United States in the 1990s, of whom 3 million were unauthorized. By the end of the decade approximately 10 percent of U.S. residents were foreign born. Yet immigration to the United States has been restricted since the 1920s. Legislation was introduced in 1921 requiring that aliens seeking to join family members must be admitted according to national quotas, though there were special preferences for close family of U.S. citizens and aliens who had applied for U.S. citizenship. Further legislation in 1924 permitted wives and children of U.S. citizens to be admitted regardless of whether particular national quotas were filled. Subsequently, the 1952 Immigration and Naturalization Act extended this entitlement to relatives of aliens holding permanent resident status.

In 1965, the United States changed its immigration policy. Instead of prioritizing immigrants by nationality and favoring those from northern and western Europe, the new system was based on a universal quota and a standard figure for each country. Within this system priority was given to two categories of foreigners: those with sought-after skills, and those with U.S. relatives. The effect was to shift the source of immigration flows away from developed Western countries to developing countries. Family reunification has since become by far the main means of entry to the United States for legal immigrants. In 1996 and 1997, for example, approximately two-thirds of immigrants to the United States were granted entry for this reason.

Debate has focused on two principal questions: (1) What is the appropriate balance between quotas for immediate relatives of legal immigrants and those for more distant relatives of U.S. citizens? (2) What is the appropriate balance between immigrants sponsored by U.S. employers and those sponsored by U.S. relatives? (Martin and Midgley 1999).

Daili Martinez, left, hugs Margarita Martinez as they are overcome with emotion after being reunited August 9, 2001, in Miami, Florida. Margarita survived an ill-fated apparent immigrant smuggling trip by boat from Cuba to Key West, Florida. Six people on board the board perished when it capsized 20 miles off the coast of Key West on August 1, 2001. (Joe Raedle/Getty Images)

Though spouses and children of U.S. citizens may enter the United States without waiting, families of legal immigrants, as well as married children and siblings of U.S. citizens, must wait for a visa, and waiting times are often lengthy. In 1995, about 1.1 million spouses and children were in the queue, and in 1999 legal Mexican immigrants in the United States had to wait five years for immigrant visas for their spouses and children (ibid.).

In the Federal Republic of Germany (FRG) during the 1960s and early 1970s, immigration was characterized as a "mobile labor potential." Individual immigrants were described as guestworkers (*Gastarbeiter*) who could be "rotated"; that is, they could depart when labor shortages abated. The arrival of dependent family members was deemed unnecessary, and little thought was devoted to family reunification. Nevertheless, some employers believed that foreigners made better workers when joined by their families, arguing that single adult migrants spent their leisure time drinking and getting into trouble with police, whereas married migrant workers would simply return home after work (Sen 1987). But a study of Turkish workers revealed sharply contrasting attitudes to family life: One-third of men saw family structure in the Federal Republic in extremely negative terms, whereas women welcomed the equality of status between husband and wife possible in Germany (Granjeat 1966, 65).

In practice, the difference between "temporary" and "permanent" immigration is not as great as might appear. In part, this is because of the extent to which supposedly temporary immigration turns out to be self-perpetuating. Even in the late 1980s, despite the appearance of second-generation immigrants, it was still maintained in official circles that Germany was not a country of immigration. Typically, migrants who came for the short-term underwent a comprehensive secondary socialization. They acquired the desire for consumer goods prevailing in West German society, and it proved more difficult than anticipated to save enough to resettle in their country of origin. The subjective intentions of migrants in Germany did little to predict their behavior. As Stephen Castles and others, writing on ethnic minorities in Europe, have observed: "As the hope of return receded into an uncertain future, many workers found it intolerable to spend the best years of their lives alone and isolated. So the wife or husband came too, and the children followed. . . . The realization that migration is irreversible comes—if at all—when parents find their children speaking German better than Greek or Spanish or Turkish. Then they realize that their children will stay, and that if they themselves return, the family will be irrevocably broken" (Castles et al. 1984, 124).

Many postwar immigrants to the United Kingdom had also apparently viewed their stay as temporary, sustained by what Muhammed Anwar called *The Myth of Return* in his 1979 book title. But their intentions to return to their country of origin—even if sincere—were often postponed or abandoned (Glover et al. 2001). There were structural factors, too. It is well established that from the late 1940s, immigrants had arrived in the United Kingdom to fill labor shortages in a range of occupations where remuneration was low and conditions poor. It is less well appreciated that this further lowered the status of such occupations. As a result, recruitment remained difficult in many sectors, and immigrants continued to be a key source of new labor. Commonwealth citizens had had privileged access as British subjects, and family reunification had not been an issue. With the 1962 Commonwealth Immigrants Act, the character of the immigrant population changed fundamentally as the prospect of immigration control persuaded Commonwealth immigrants to bring in their families before it was too late. The question of how much family reunification to accept dominated discussions of immigration until 1971 (Hansen 2000, ch. 5).

Certain underlying connections between immigration and family reunification are evident in Wolf Ruediger Böhning's analysis of postwar immigration to Western Europe (written after the economic downturn following the oil crisis of 1973):

> No country in Europe . . . purposely desires to be a country of immigration *in the traditional sense of the word,* and given the disaffection of indigenous workers from socially undesirable jobs, the resulting immigration policies of Western European countries all center around the composite problem of how (i) to fill existing labor market gaps so that both micro-economic and macro-economic profitability remain assured without (ii) detriment to a strained social situation and (iii) without infringing basic human rights. Put another way, immigration policies define immigrants economically as a stop-gap, socially as a liability and personally as a nuisance. In the final analysis all countries define future immigration in terms of temporary labor immigration." (Böhning 1974, 157–158; italics added)

Strict curbs on primary immigration were introduced in a number of Western European countries in the early 1970s in response to changing economic conditions, though growing popular concern about immigration was also a factor, as it had been in the United Kingdom in the 1960s. These curbs lasted thirty years, and they reinforced the presumption that though demand for foreign workers had drastically reduced, migrants from less-developed countries were as anxious as ever to gain entry. Migration was viewed as an inevitable consequence of the perceived gulf between economic opportunities in receiving societies and the scale of poverty in less-developed countries—especially the latter—and of the ease of travel and communication between rich and poor countries. But too great an emphasis on economic considerations helped obscure the extent to which, as Douglas Massey et al. (1993) have suggested, "chain migration" has to do with ethnic and family links instead of demand for migrant labor per se. This concept of a "chain" highlights a process in which a first generation of migrant workers is followed by other migrants from the same family, ethnic group, or migrant-exporting locality and then by spouses and children.

The presumption that migrants from poor countries are desperate to enter has aroused suspicions that claims of eligibility for family reunification are often bogus. Sometimes the suspicion is that children carry false documentation attesting to their relationship with an existing migrant or misrepresenting their true age. But most attention has been given to fraudulent marriage. In the 1970s, such suspicions prompted UK immigration authorities to perform "virginity tests" on brides arriving from the Indian subcontinent, a practice eventually discontinued as degrading. Later, the "Primary Purpose Rule" was introduced in the United Kingdom to refuse entry to those judged by officials to be marrying merely to gain entry. This rule was rescinded in 1997. In a number of countries, notably the United States, the authorities stipulate that if the married couple no longer cohabit for a specified period, such as one year, the "reunified" spouse will be deported. In some cases, this policy may place the spouse in virtual captivity, possibly enduring domestic violence as the price of remaining in the country.

At the turn of the twenty-first century, according to the European Commission (2000b), legal immigration into the EU was divisible into three categories—humanitarian, labor market, and family reunification. The commission therefore sought to develop policy on three fronts: management of migration flows, a common asylum system, and fair treatment of those born outside the European Union (EU)—designated "third-country nationals"—which included their right to family reunification. None of this would be easy to achieve. For one thing, rules on the admission of third-country nationals to reside and work in the EU were complicated and varied from one member state to another, presenting a significant obstacle for both third-country nationals seeking work in the EU and employers wishing to recruit them. But by the late 1990s, it had become widely recognized that the "zero" immigration policies pursued in many EU countries since the 1970s were inappropriate. It was, above all, the aging of national populations and the consequent diminishment of the proportion of the population that was economically active that prompted this reappraisal. Yet securing rights for third-country nationals comparable to those of EU citizens seemed a remote prospect, even if tackled incrementally.

There were, nevertheless, several factors favoring family reunification. Various international conventions and instruments contain rules and principles on family reunification that might influence national legislation. Family reunification draws on two areas of international law: the free movement of people, and the place of the family in human society. According to the European Commission (2000a), the right to family reunification "must be adopted in conformity with the obligation to protect the family and respect family life which is laid down in a number of international legal instruments, including the European Convention on Human Rights and Fundamental Freedoms . . . [which the] . . . Union respects by virtue of Article 62(2) of the treaty on European Union."

The idea that the family, in the words of the International Covenant on Civil and Political Rights (1966), is "the natural and fundamental group unit in society and is entitled to protection by society and the state" is present in several international treaties and declarations: the Universal Declaration of Human Rights (1948, Article 16, paragraph 3); the International Covenant on Economic, Social and Cultural Rights (1966, Articles 10, 17, and 23); the European Social Charter (1965, Article 16); and the European Convention on Human Rights (1950, Article 8). The International Convention on the Rights of the Child (1989, Article 10:1) states that applications for a child or parent to enter (or leave) a state for the purpose of family should be treated positively, expeditiously, and humanely, but it is uncertain what legal force this carries. None of these treaties appears to establish a *right* to family reunification. The chief impediment to such a right is state sovereignty: A state exercises discretion about who is eligible for family reunification and uses immigration laws and controls to restrict entry in the interests of security or public welfare. In these circumstances, exhortations to migrant-receiving countries to facilitate family reunification for noncitizen migrant workers offer only moderate hope of success.

Even as legal economic migration was being discouraged, however, family reunification provided a legitimate means of entry to the EU, becoming one of the main vectors of immigration. Subsequently, the realization grew that in an increasingly global labor market, the need to attract third-country workers might depend on offering them improved rights. Moreover, family reunification began to be seen as vital to integrating those already admitted to the EU, in keeping with the EU's commitments to respect ethnic, cultural, and religious diversity and foster social inclusion. Thus, in its proposal on family reunification, the European Commission (2000a) argued that reunification, by making family life possible, helped create stable sociocultural conditions. This would facilitate integration of third-country nationals and promote social and economic cohesion; a fundamental objective specified in Articles 2 and 3 of the EC (European Community) Treaty. Family reunification could therefore be said to offer advantages to migrant and receiving society alike.

The European Commission (2000a) has defined family reunification as "the entry into and residence in a Member state by family members of a citizen of the Union or a third-country national residing lawfully in that Member state in order to form or preserve the family unit, whether the family relationship arose before or after the resident's entry." The commission's proposal was that third-country nationals might qualify for family reunification if they were legally resident in a member state *and* possessed a resident permit of at least one year. Those eligible for family reunification would be spouses and minor children (including adopted children); children of full age; and relatives in the ascending line (where objective reasons existed as to why they could not live apart from a third-country national legally resident in an EU state). It was also proposed that an unmarried partner living in a durable relationship should be admitted into a member state if that state treated unmarried and married couples identically. In its approach, the commission therefore extended the definition of "family" beyond the nuclear family, but others argued that differences in definitions must be taken into account. For example, the European Council on Refugees and Exiles contended that in certain cases de facto or extended family members should be included.

The commission suggested that when an application for family reunification is lodged, applicants should satisfy the authorities that their accommodation meets prevailing health and safety standards and that they have resources above the level at which social assistance is granted. Thus, an applicant for family reunification should be able to satisfy family needs without recourse to public funds. Similarly, in the United States assurance is sought that reunified family members will not depend on social assistance, and residents who wish to sponsor family members for immigration must prove that their incomes—taking account of the new arrivals—are in excess of 125 percent of the poverty line. Thus a family of four wishing to sponsor two immigrants would need to show an income of 125 percent of the poverty line for *six* people. This kind of requirement is designed to protect the interests of the receiving society, but it is also arguable that it is against the interests of reunified family members to live in conditions of poverty.

The European Commission also recommended that, in order to aid the integration of individuals admitted to an EU state under family reunification provisions, after a qualifying period their status should be independent of the third-country national they had joined and they should be given independent access to education, vocational training, and employment. This recommendation was also designed to improve the chances that reunified family members could contribute to a receiving society's labor market.

A significant proportion of cases of family reunification concerns refugees. The legal status of refugees is defined in the Geneva Convention (1949), the UN Convention Relating to the Status of Refugees (1951), and the UN Protocol Relating to the Status of Refugees (1967)—though these contain no specific right to refugee family reunification. The Conference of Plenipotentiaries on the Status of Refugees and Stateless Persons (1951) saw it as self-evident that refugees' families be accorded identical protection to refugees themselves. Though not legally binding, this principle might influence the way states treat refugee family reunification. The assumption was that reunification of refugee families promotes rapid integration of refugees, and to this end assistance with housing difficulties might be justifiable. But the primary rationale was humanitarian: Persecution prevents the family from reuniting in their country of origin, and the presence of family helps refugees overcome traumatic experiences.

Two developments have affected official attitudes toward refugees. One is the considerable growth in the numbers of refugees, particularly in the 1990s. The other is the belief that economic migrants attempt to enter as refugees when channels of labor migration are closed. These developments have led to efforts to prevent the influx of "bogus refugees" and to variously restrict those who have entered from claiming asylum. Inevitably, this undermines the presumption that absence of documentary proof of the validity of a marriage or the filiation of children should not, per se, impede the right to refugee family reunification.

Peter Braham

See also: Citizenship; European Union; Guestworkers, Europe; Migration Policy; Push-Pull Factors; UN Convention Relating to the Status of Refugees, 1951; U.S. Immigration Legislation: Post-1945

References and further reading:

Anwar, Muhammed. 1979. *The Myth of Return.* London: Heinemann.

Böhning, Wolf Ruediger. 1974. "Immigration Policies of Western European Countries." *International Migration Review* 8, no. 2: 155–163.

Castles, Stephen, Heather Booth, and Tina Wallace. 1984. *Here for Good: Western Europe's New Ethnic Minorities.* London: Pluto.

Commission of the European Communities. 2000a. "Amended Proposal on the Right to Family Reunification." Brussels: Com 624.

———. 2000b. "Communication to the Council and the European Parliament on a Community Immigration Policy." Brussels: Com 757.

Glover, Stephen, Ceri Gott, Anais Loizillon, Jonathan Portes, Richard Price, Sarah Spencer, Vasanthi Srinivisan, and Carole Willis. 2001. *Migration: An Economic Analysis.* Occasional Paper 67. London: Research Development and Statistics Office.

Granjeat, Pierre. 1966. *Les Migrations de Travailleurs en Europe.* Paris: Cahiers de L'Institut International des Etudes Sociales.

Hansen, Randall. 2000. *Citizenship and Immigration in Postwar Britain: The Institutional Origins of a Multicultural Nation.* Oxford: Oxford University Press.

Martin, Philip, and Elizabeth Midgley. 1999. "Immigration to the United States: Journey to an Unfinished Nation." *Population Bulletin* 54, no.2 (June). Washington, DC: Population Reference Bureau.

Massey, Douglas, Juaquis Arango, Graeme Hugo, Ali Kouaouci, Adelfa Pellegrino, and J. Edward Taylor. 1993. "Theories of International Migration: A Review and Appraisal." *Population and Development Review* 19, no.3 (September): 4311–4466.

———. 1998. *Worlds in Motion: Understanding International Migration at the End of the Millennium.* Oxford: Oxford University Press.

Sen, Faruk. 1987. "Turks in the Federal Republic of Germany: Achievements, Problems, Expectations." Essen, Germany: Zentrum für Turkeistudien.

Famine

See Irish Diaspora

Far-Right Parties

Far-right parties encompass a variety of political organizations that pursue policies and public discourse inspired by extreme nationalist, xenophobic, and chauvinistic ideas. Although afflicting Australia, New Zealand, the United States, and other advanced industrial societies to various degrees, far-right groups and parties are especially prominent within contemporary Western Europe, including Austria, Belgium, Denmark, France, Germany, the Netherlands, Sweden,

Switzerland, and the United Kingdom. Alternatively referred to as the "new right," "extreme right," or "radical, populist right," far-right political parties, whatever their differences, are generally motivated by two common goals: halting all new immigration and resisting the trend toward a multicultural society that is an inevitable byproduct of mass immigration.

Origins and Shared Characteristics

Few phenomena affecting the advanced industrial democracies during the past three decades have precipitated greater political convulsions than the surge of popular and electoral support for far-right political groups and parties. These actors have come to the fore wherever immigration-related issues have surfaced as salient political cleavages. Diffuse xenophobic sentiments among so-called native citizens are exploited by far-right groups that articulate, validate, and aggregate these sentiments. These groups are especially skillful at painting immigrants as subverting the dominant cultural environment and values of the advanced industrial societies and threatening the livelihoods of native workers who are mired at the bottom of the socioeconomic ladder.

Post–World War II mass immigration did not, however, cause most far-right groups to coalesce. The origins of some groups predate World War II; others, such as the French National Front (Front National, FN), emerged more recently, but before immigration-related issues became politically salient among the mass public. Whatever their origins, there is little doubt that the successive waves of post–World War II immigration have fertilized the political soil in which far-right groups grow. Virtually all of the far-right groups that have politically prospered since the mid-1970s share two characteristics. First, as indicated by a wealth of cross-national opinion and election exit poll data, these groups owe much of their modest political success to the social tensions that have accompanied the settlement of post–World War II immigrants. Second, to varying degrees, these groups have actively cultivated a climate of public hostility toward immigrants and refugees that in turn has fostered a more favorable political environment for themselves.

Crowds during a speech given by right-wing French politician Jean-Marie Le Pen of the National Front, during presidential elections on May, Workers' Day. (Owen Franken/Corbis)

The Proliferation of Far-Right Parties

Unlike its British namesake, which was founded in 1967 and came to prominence a decade later, the National Front in France emerged as a significant political actor only in 1984, when its list of candidates in the elections for the European Parliament, headed by Jean-Marie Le Pen, attracted almost 10 percent of the vote. Retaining this implicit constituency in the national parliamentary elections held in 1986, the FN won 35 seats on 9.6 percent of the vote (Simmons 1996, 267).

Two years later, in April 1988, Le Pen shook the foundations of established French political conservatism by garnering 14.4 percent of the vote in the first round of the presidential elections. In the city of Marseilles, the National Front's standard-bearer emerged as the most popular presidential candidate, with 28.3 percent of the vote. Although the FN ceded all but one of its 35 seats in the National Assembly, the lower legislative body, in the June 1988 elections, this political setback did not signal that its electoral appeal had significantly eroded. Rather, the FN received 9.6 percent of the vote, the same support that it had received two years earlier, and it was the French government's decision to return to a less proportional electoral system that resulted in the FN's parliamentary losses (ibid.).

The FN's march through the mainstream representative institutions of French politics continued throughout the 1990s. Its performance at all electoral levels either nearly equaled or exceeded its results from the previous decade, peaking at 15.5 percent in the regional elections of 1998. More disturbing than these gains is the fact that the National Front's electorate over time became increasingly disposed to perceive the FN as a conduit for implementing meaningful policy change. Fully 86 percent of those who cast their ballots for Le Pen in the first round of the presidential elections in 1995 were primarily inspired by his political program (ibid., 182).

In Germany, the modest growth of far-right groups during the 1980s and early 1990s occurred concurrently, and not coincidentally, with an increase in the number of racial attacks on Turkish and other ethnic minority immigrants. These far-right groups are currently splintered into several dozen separate organizations with approximately 51,000 members or supporters (Bundesamt für Verfassungsschutz 2000).

The most popular group, with approximately 17,000 members, is the German People's Union (Deutsche Volksunion, DVU). Founded during the early 1970s, the DVU is organizationally linked to several neo-fascist organizations that emerged in the early post–World War II period during West Germany's managed transition to liberal democracy. Until very recently, the DVU was electorally quiescent. Only on one occasion, when the party garnered 12.9 percent of the vote in the Saxony-Anhalt state elections in April 1998, has the DVU gained representation in a state legislature. However, this promising result was followed by a dismal performance in the 1998 national parliamentary elections, when the DVU garnered but 1.2 percent of the vote (Mudde 2000, 63–64).

Also operating on the political far right in Germany, with a reported 14,000 members, is the Republican Party (Die Republikaner, REP). The Republican Party's first modest electoral breakthroughs occurred in 1989 in the Berlin municipal elections, when it garnered 7.5 percent of the vote, and in the elections to the European Parliament, when it obtained 7.1 percent. Although the party's performance in subnational elections occasionally has been spectacular since 1989, most notably in the 1992 elections to the Baden-Württemberg state parliament (10.9 percent), it has failed to translate these regional results into national gains. In the federal elections in 1998, the REP garnered only 1.8 percent of the vote, or slightly less than the support it received in the federal elections of 1994 (ibid., 37).

In contrast to the sclerotic advance of its German counterparts, the rise of the xenophobic Freedom Party (Freiheitliche Partei Österreichs, FPÖ) to national prominence in Austria during the past decade and a half has been nothing less than meteoric. Propelled by its charismatic leader, Jörg Haider, the Freedom Party has transformed itself from a moderate conservative party on the fringe of the Austrian party system during the 1950s, 1960s, and 1970s into a dynamic force on the political far right during the 1980s, 1990s, and beyond.

Founded in 1955, the Freedom Party was very much a mainstream party until 1986 when, under Haider's leadership, it adopted a platform of animosity toward immigrants and asylum seekers. Primarily on the basis of its embrace of this and other nationalist and populist positions, the Freedom Party improved its vote in the elections for the national lower legislative assembly, the Nationalrat, from 5 percent in 1983 to 9.7 percent in 1986. The Freedom Party further expanded its share of the national vote to 16.6 percent in 1990, thus netting 33 of 183 legislative seats. Additional and often spectacular gains in regional elections followed during the early 1990s as the FPÖ routinely gained between 16 and 33 percent of the vote. In the elections of December 1995, the Freedom Party garnered 40 seats in the Nationalrat on the basis of 21.9 percent of the national vote. The FPÖ further solidified its status as the most popular, anti-immigrant voice in Western Europe when it won 27.5 percent of the vote in elections for the European Parliament in October 1996 (Sully 1997, 189).

The Freedom Party's greatest electoral and political breakthrough occurred in October 1999, when its candidates finished second in the balloting for the Nationalrat, earning the party 53 legislative seats and four cabinet posts in Austria's national government. Particularly disturbing to the mainstream political parties and a potential harbinger of future political complications for them were the sources of the Freedom Party's electoral support. One election exit poll indicated that no other political party, including the Social Democrats, had more working-class voters as a percentage of its supporters than the Freedom Party. The FPÖ was also the leading party among male voters in 1999 (Stas 2001).

In Denmark, where the far right was slow to organize, the populist, anti-tax Progress Party (Fremskridtspartiet, FrP) stepped forward to capitalize politically upon anti-immigrant popular sentiment during the 1980s. After conducting an electoral campaign against foreigners, and particularly Iranian and Lebanese refugees, the party increased its representation in the national parliament from 4 to 9 in September 1987. The national parliamentary delegation of the party expanded further to 16 after the May 1988 general election, as its national vote virtually doubled within eight months—from 4.8 percent in 1987 to 9 percent in 1988. During the 1990s, however, support for the Progress Party precipitously declined. The party's performance in the national parliamentary elections in 1998 (2.4 percent and 4 seats) represented a dramatic decline from its electoral showing in both 1990 (6.4 percent and 11 seats) and 1994 (6.4 percent and 12 seats).

The case of the Flemish Block (Vlaams Blok, VB) in Belgium is an example of how a surge in popular xenophobia can accelerate the electoral progress of political parties that have been historically organized around deep-seated, traditional ethnic cleavages. Founded in 1979, the Flemish Block has married, only since the 1990s, the plank of repatriating immigrants to its core demand that the region of Flanders be granted political independence by Belgium's central government. On the basis of these twin planks, the Flemish Block increased its representation in the National Assembly from 2 to 12 seats after the 1991 general election, a rise of 400 percent in its electoral support. Two-thirds of those who voted for the VB cited immigration as their primary motivation (Betz 1994, 65). The Flemish Block has historically polled well in major cities where immigrants from North Africa have settled within predominantly Flemish communities.

The VB maintained this level of support four years later, when it garnered 7.8 percent of the vote in the May 1995 elections for both the Kamer, the lower national legislative assembly, and the Senaat, the upper chamber. The xenophobic party further improved upon these results in June 1999, when it won 14 seats in the Kamer on 9.9 percent of the vote and 4 seats in the Senaat on 9.4 percent of the vote (Mudde 2000, 92).

American Exceptionalism

In contrast to Western Europe, far-right parties in the United States have historically enjoyed little political success. Although American society has spawned its share of extreme right groups, including the Ku Klux Klan, the John Birch Society, the American Nazi Party, Posse Comitatus, and a plethora of smaller and less well known racist, anti-Semitic, and xenophobic groups, none of these have metamorphosed into a significant vote-attracting, national political party. Why, despite its deep-seated racial problems and its large and ever growing immigrant population, is the United States different from Western Europe?

Although definitive answers are elusive, several factors are likely responsible for American exceptionalism. First, unlike many European countries, the United States has always been a country of immigration. Although nativist movements have periodically surfaced in the United States, the message of these movements has eventually, and perhaps predictably, failed to appeal to a population largely descended from recent immigrants. Second, the plurality, single-member district system that elects members of Congress severely handicaps all but the Democratic and Republican parties. Denied access to the House of Representatives and the Senate, the best that far-right groups can hope for is to gain seats in a handful of state legislatures. Third, in contrast to Germany and several other European countries, the United States has never suffered the kind of national economic or political humiliation that facilitates a surge in far-right political recruitment and popular support. Victorious in two world wars and, with the exception of the Great Depression years, economically self-confident and affluent, the United States has never suffered the worst of economic or political crisis. Finally, whenever politically expressed racism, nativism, or xenophobia have threatened to gain ground, each has been coopted eventually into mainstream political channels. Specifically, the uncanny abilities of the Democratic and Republican parties to absorb and domesticate illiberal political and social currents in American society has circumscribed the popular appeal of extreme right groups.

Classifying Far-Right Parties

As prominent political actors opposed to new immigration and multiculturalism, far-right groups, movements, and political parties can be divided into at least five broad categories: generic groups; neo-fascist groups; ostensibly traditional political parties that fit into the class of the "opportunistic right"; new, radical right parties; and the ethnonational right. Although several parties can be subsumed under more than one label—the German Republican Party, for example, evinces some of the characteristics of a neo-fascist group as well as most of the major features of a new, radical right party—in order to appreciate the diverse nature of these groups and their respective roles in the politics of the immigration-receiving countries it is useful to delimit the boundaries of each of the five categories.

Generic Groups

"Pure" or generic groups, such as Keep Sweden Swedish (Bevara Sverige Svenskt) or the Movement against Insecurity and Immigration Abuses in Belgium (Mouvement contre l'insécurité et l'immigration abusive, MIIA), share several characteristics that distinguish them from all other far-right political actors. First, and most important, these groups are exclusively defined by their opposition toward new immigration and a multicultural society. As a rule, generic groups do not promote grand ideas or political ideologies. They do not adopt detailed economic or other policies that are not directly linked to their core obsession with government immigrant and immigration policy. If post–World War II immigrants and refugees had never migrated to and eventually settled within the advanced industrial countries, these groups would have had no founding purpose and, hence, no reason for existence. Their activities and political strategies are thus negatively and narrowly inspired. They are geared toward impeding all new immigration and coercing settled immigrants either to return to their country of origin or to adopt, as a condition of their permanent settlement, the dominant social mores, language, and religious traditions of the host society.

A second distinguishing feature of generic groups is their lack of formal organizational structure. Generic groups do not have regular members. Because they exist to achieve predominantly negative purposes, they tend to assume the shape of ephemeral political movements.

Neo-Fascist Groups

Unlike generic groups, neo-fascist groups are inspired by an overarching ideology, a set of ideas similar to those which motivated the pre–World War II authoritarian fascist parties of Austria, Italy, and Germany, parties that were slavishly devoted to the values of social and political order and the primacy of the state over the individual. The antagonism of neo-fascist groups toward immigrants springs from their convictions about the naturalness of racial hierarchy and the inevitability of inter-ethnic and racial conflict and competition whenever incompatible groups mix in the domestic and international arenas. Most neo-fascist groups are careful to distance themselves, however, from their infamous forerunners. Few attempt to subvert the democratic process through violence or extra-legal activities.

Unlike their generic counterparts, neo-fascist groups are not obsessed with questions of race relations or ethnic conflict. They are less focused on altering the immediate course of public policy, including immigration policy, than generic groups are. Since their long-term goal is to govern nationally and reconfigure domestic politics, neo-fascist groups maintain long-lived organizations, typically participating in local, regional, and national elections.

An important difference between neo-fascist groups and mainstream conservative political parties is that few of the former are fit to join electoral or parliamentary coalitions. Their lack of fitness stems from the reluctance of mainstream parties to ally with them as well as their own ideological aversion to democratic political compromise and parliamentary bargaining. As political pariahs, neo-fascist groups rarely exercise formal political power.

Opportunistic Right

Perhaps the most distinctive feature of the opportunistic right, of which the Freedom Party in Austria and the People's Party in Switzerland are prominent examples, is that its resistance to immigration and multiculturalism is primarily driven by a calculated strategy to win votes. The opportunistic right is not primarily motivated by a race-based ideology. Rather, its hostility to government immigrant and immigration policy is folded into a broader, populist political appeal, an appeal that pragmatically weaves immigration-related issues into a larger critique of the existing political and economic order. In contrast to neo-fascist groups, the opportunistic right will trim its illiberal views on immigration-related issues if they do not attract significant voter support, but accentuate such issues if and when, in so doing, it appeals to a critical mass of voters.

A second important feature that distinguishes the opportunistic right from neo-fascist groups is the pliableness of its ideological commitments. Opportunistic right parties will, at various points in their history, waver between the extreme and the more moderate political right. Where such parties are situated on the ideological spectrum at any given moment in time depends upon a confluence of political variables, including the personal, ideological disposition of its leaders. Although the opportunistic right and neo-fascist groups sometimes share a similar ideological heritage, the former is not unduly or forever burdened by this heritage.

The opportunistic right can also be distinguished from neo-fascist groups with regard to its relations with the mainstream parties of government. Unlike neo-fascist groups, the opportunistic right is not permanently constrained either by its ideology or by its policies from allying itself with or being embraced by mainstream parties. As a consequence, the opportunistic right is a potential player in the formation of governments and parliamentary coalitions.

New Radical Right

Out of all the far-right actors, it is perhaps the "new radical right" (NRR) that has had the most immediate influence on immigration-related public discourse. Although scholars dissent about which parties can be appropriately subsumed under this category, at least three, the French National Front and the Progress parties of Denmark and Norway, represent important examples of this genre.

Like the previously cited categories, new radical right parties are inspired by a right-wing authoritarianism that situates them at the forefront of the domestic political opposition to new immigration and the permanent settlement of immigrants. As with the opportunistic right, many of the electoral appeals of the new radical right have a populist foundation. What makes the new radical right very different from other far-right actors, however, is the unique manner in which it combines a commitment to capitalism and individual economic freedom with an illiberalism toward immigrants, immigration, and materialism.

For the new radical right, the social conflict engendered by immigration serves as a political catalyst. It provides an opportunity to mobilize citizens who, in the first instance, are deeply disillusioned with the broader political and economic order. The new radical right should not be subsumed under the umbrella of the opportunistic right, however, because its hostility toward immigration and multiculturalism, while subordinate to its larger commitment to pro-market and authoritarian positions, is not politically disposable. Unlike the opportunistic right, the new radical right does not propagate anti-immigrant views in a cynical attempt to win votes. On the contrary, its xenophobia is deeply embedded in its authoritarian ideological orientation.

To date, both its virulent racism and its xenophobia have made the new radical right unfit to join the mainstream political parties in electoral pacts or governing coalitions. Unlike the opportunistic right, the NRR parties cannot trim their illiberal positions in order to accommodate or placate potential mainstream conservative political allies. Mainstream conservative parties, in turn, cannot safely embrace new radical right parties without alienating their core, predominantly politically moderate, supporters.

Ethnonational Right

In many respects, the ethnonational right overlaps with the opportunistic right. Like the latter, it co-opts anti-immigrant and anti-immigration policies in a calculated effort to attract votes. It, too, enjoys the political luxury of accentuating or submerging immigration-related issues as short-term electoral circumstances dictate. Moreover, the ethnonational right is formally organized, it regularly contests elections, and it focuses on achieving political power through conventional political and electoral means.

In contrast to the opportunistic right and every other far-right party, bar generic groups, however, ethnonational parties are primarily single-issue oriented. The single issue that energizes them is ethnonationalism, a nationalist sentiment inspired by a form of group solidarity founded upon ethnicity rather than territory. Ethnonational groups are adept at politically exploiting the subjective attachments that demarcate one particular group from others within the national population. Without ethnonationalism, the ethnonational right could not long survive politically.

The fact that the ethnonational right is primarily organized around ethnonationalism not only relegates its anti-immigration posture to a secondary status but, more important, prevents it from becoming too prominent in its rhetoric or electoral appeals. Just as the new radical right cannot easily jettison its pro-market policies, so, too, the ethnonational right is similarly constrained with respect to ethnonationalism. Like the new radical right, the ethnonational right cannot fully exploit anti-immigration sentiment within the electorate without compromising its core mission, the advancement of an ethnonationalist agenda. Anti-immigration appeals merely complement and reinforce the traditional agenda of the ethnonational right by explicitly linking the economic, cultural, and political "exploitation" of the traditional regions or national homelands by central government with its simultaneous human "invasion" by unwanted immigrants.

Although its racial illiberalism and xenophobia are sufficient reasons for traditional political parties to shun it, it is, in fact, the ethnonationalist agenda of the ethnonational right that ultimately makes it an unattractive, although not entirely unfit, partner in national governmental coalitions. Its demand of regional autonomy or sovereignty cannot be easily accommodated within the framework of prevailing domestic constitutional arrangements. Although many ethnonational groups currently operate across contemporary Western Europe, only the Italian Northern League (Lega Nord) and the Belgian Flemish Block properly belong to the ethnonational right. They alone marry traditional ethnonational appeals with a publicly articulated animosity toward immigration and settled immigrants and refugees.

The Significance of Far-Right Parties

Despite their proliferation in recent years, the political influence and the future electoral prospects of far-right parties should not be overestimated. Nowhere can these groups induce radical change in government immigration or immigrant settlement policy. None but the Austrian Freedom

Party has achieved a major electoral or political breakthrough. Nevertheless, it is evident that since the early 1970s the political environment within the immigration-receiving societies has become much more favorable than previously for these illiberal actors.

Given their ubiquity and their organizational and ideational diversity, it is also obvious that far-right groups occupy a very important niche in the immigration-receiving societies. Anti-immigrant groups, it seems, are vital, if disruptive, participants in the ongoing struggle within the immigrant-receiving societies to come to grips with the political and social fallout from the successive waves of post–World War II immigration. Indeed, wherever generic groups are not prominent or, for reasons unrelated to the conflict over post–World War II immigration, fail to emerge, alternative groups or previously established political parties have co-opted immigration-related issues. In Austria and Norway, for example, where generic groups did not become firmly rooted, either the new radical right or the opportunistic right seized political center stage. Similarly, in Italy, where existing neo-fascist groups were sluggish to exploit anti-immigration public sentiment, the ethnonationalist Northern League aggressively stepped forward.

The Role of Mainstream Political Parties

Whether more or less politically peripheral, far-right groups carve out, secure, and/or advance their position in domestic politics by publicly opposing both new immigration and the presence of settled immigrants. In staking out this illiberal political ground, anti-immigrant groups often fill the lacuna created when more mainstream political actors and parties do not address the anxieties of a critical mass of so-called native citizens.

Although there appears to be no single best strategy the mainstream parties can pursue to undercut the support of far-right parties, they can affect the latter's political trajectory in one or both of two ways. First, mainstream political parties can articulate and aggregate anti-immigrant public sentiment in a more responsible manner, thus stealing political support from far-right groups. This political strategy was effected with considerable success by the Conservative Party in Britain during the 1980s. Second, through their enlightened policies and/or political rhetoric, the established parties can indirectly affect the long-term political fortunes of far-right groups by allaying, at least to some degree, the feelings of anxiety and threat that are pervasive within the native population.

Anthony M. Messina

See also: Multiculturalism; Public Opinion and Immigration; Racism and Racially Motivated Attacks; Repatriation

References and further reading:

Betz, Hans-Georg. 1994. *Radical Right-Wing Populism in Western Europe.* New York: St. Martin's Press.

Betz, Hans-Georg, and Stephan Immerfall, eds. 1998. *The New Politics of the Right: Neo-Populist Parties and Movements in Established Democracies.* New York: St. Martin's Press.

Braun, Aurel, and Stephen Scheinberg, eds. 1997. *The Extreme Right: Freedom and Security at Risk.* Boulder: Westview.

Bundesamt für Verfassungsschutz. "The State of Right-Wing Extremism in Germany: A Situation Based on the Annual Report 1999," http://verfassungsschutz.de/publikationen/gesamt/page5.html (cited May 2000).

DeClair, Edward G. 1999. *Politics on the Fringe: The People, Policies and Organization of the French National Front.* Durham: Duke University Press.

Fetzer, Joel S. 2000. *Public Attitudes toward Immigration in the United States, France, and Germany.* New York: Cambridge University Press.

Hainsworth, Paul, ed. 2000. *The Politics of the Extreme Right: From the Margins to the Mainstream.* London: Pinter.

Kitschelt, Herbert. 1995. *The Radical Right in Western Europe: A Comparative Analysis.* Ann Arbor: University of Michigan Press.

Marcus, Jonathan. 1995. *The National Front and French Politics: The Resistible Rise of Jean-Marie Le Pen.* London: Macmillan.

Merkl, Peter H., and Leonard Weinberg, eds. 1997. *The Revival of Right-Wing Extremism in the Nineties.* London: Frank Cass.

Mudde, Cas. 2000. *The Ideology of the Extreme Right.* New York: Manchester University Press.

Simmons, Harvey G. 1996. *The French National Front: The Extremist Challenge to Democracy.* Boulder: Westview.

Stas, Karl. "Austria," http://users.belga.com.net/gc192975/austria.htm (cited November 2001).

Stöss, Richard. 1991. *Politics against Democracy: Right-Wing Extremism in West Germany.* New York: Berg.

Sully, Melanie A. 1997. *The Haider Phenomenon.* New York: Columbia University Press.

Filipino Diaspora

The history of the Philippines chronicles a history of migration. Through the years, the Philippines has developed a culture of emigration born out of a long history of out-migration that fosters, if not highly values, working and living abroad. The various phases of the country's international diaspora experience documents the peripatetic nature of its people. In 2001, the Commission on Filipinos Overseas estimated the migrant stock at 7.4 million Filipinos scattered in about 200 countries around the world. Of these, 42 percent were temporary labor migrants, 37 percent were permanent migrants, and 21 percent were irregular migrants.

Migration Patterns and Trends

Early Beginnings to the 1950s

During the Spanish colonial period (sixteenth to nineteenth centuries), the overseas Filipino migrants consisted of young

Ten thousand immigrants, many holding umbrellas in their left hands as they take thieir American citizenship oath, are sworn in as United States citizens in a mass ceremony at the Los Angeles Memorial Coliseum. Immigrants from 73 nations took part in the ceremony, the largest group being more than 1,600 from the Philippines. (Bettmann/Corbis)

men who went to Spain, either as students or refugees escaping persecution, and revolutionaries exiled to the Marianas. The earliest Filipino immigrants to the United States were Filipino sailors, then known as "Manilamen," who deserted the Spanish ships of the Manila-Acapulco galleon trade to escape oppressive conditions and in 1763 settled in the marshlands of Louisiana. In the late nineteenth century, European and American companies employed Manilamen as seafarers; consequently, Filipino seamen were found in many ports around the world. In the late nineteenth and early twentieth centuries, Manilamen found their way to Australia, where, together with other immigrants, they were hired as divers and crew in Australia's pearl industry.

There were two distinct waves of migration from the Philippines to the United States and its protectorates between 1898 and 1944. The first started in 1903 and consisted of *pensionados*, or Filipino scholars. The second occurred in the 1920s and 1930s and entailed large-scale recruitment of Filipino workers for the pineapple plantations of Hawaii as well as the apple, orange, and grape farms of California. Labor migration from the Philippines after World War II shifted to the rehabilitation and reconstruction of U.S. strongholds in the Pacific.

The 1960s

In the 1960s, permanent and temporary (contract labor) migration became more distinct categories. Professionals and technical workers, mostly medical personnel, moved to the United States as permanent immigrants, while skilled workers and craftsmen found temporary contractual employment with U.S. construction companies in Guam and Indochina.

Other skilled workers found contractual jobs with Filipino and U.S. logging companies operating in Borneo, Indonesia, and Malaysia during the same period. Jazz performers and other Filipino artists obtained employment contracts in Japan and Hong Kong, and their artistic talent earned them the distinction of being the "Entertainers of Asia."

The 1970s and Early 1980s

The 1970s marked the beginning of the most dramatic period of international contract labor migration from the

Philippines. The construction boom in the Middle East, spurred on by a sharp increase in oil prices and deteriorating economic conditions in the Philippines, gave impetus to this phenomenon. The term "Middle East fever" may rightfully describe international labor migration from the Philippines at this time.

Labor migration streams from the country consisted largely of married, able-bodied young men with fairly high levels of education compared to the rest of the Filipino population. The Middle East, particularly Saudi Arabia, was the number one work destination for Filipino workers.

The Mid-1980s to the 1990s

International migration from the Philippines in the mid-1980s and 1990s followed specific patterns involving increases in (1) the primacy of temporary labor migration over permanent migration; (2) the prominence of Asia as a work destination and the decline in importance of the Middle East as a job site; (3) the feminization of labor migration; and (4) the increasing proportion of service workers, particularly domestic helpers, in the occupational distribution. Since the mid-1970s, and especially since the 1980s, temporary migration from the Philippines has increased dramatically relative to permanent migration. In 1974, the Philippine government instituted an overseas employment program. In the program's first five years, 31 percent of the Filipinos who left the country were emigrants; in 1995–1999, only 6 percent of Filipinos emigrated permanently.

Although the Middle East remains the primary destination of Filipino workers, its importance has waned since the mid-1980s. Meanwhile, Asia has become more prominent as a destination for Filipino workers, especially women, becoming nearly equal in importance to the Middle East. Out of every 100 Filipinos leaving the country to work abroad in 1995–1999, 42 went to other Asian countries, while 44 went to countries in the Middle East, particularly Saudi Arabia. In Asia, the bulk of the Filipino workers have found employment in Hong Kong, Taiwan, Japan, and Singapore.

The shift in the international demand for labor in the 1980s resulted in an increasing feminization of Filipino contract-labor migration. There was a decline in the relative share of production workers in the labor out-migration stream, and a corresponding increase in the international demand for service workers, particularly domestic helpers and, to a lesser degree, entertainers. Although the service sector covers a wide range of occupations, the largest subcategory is that of domestic helpers, who are mostly female. Entertainers are also overwhelmingly female, and a substantial proportion of other professionals, particularly nurses, are women.

The proportion of women among first-time migrant workers from the Philippines has been steadily increasing. In 1992, half of the newly hired Filipino workers around the world were women. By 1995, 58 percent of the neophyte Filipino workers around the world were women, and this figure rose to 61 percent in 1998 and 72 percent in 2001. The predominance of Filipino women in vulnerable occupations—such as domestic helpers in Hong Kong, Italy, and Saudi Arabia and entertainers in Japan—has been cause for much concern. Because of the nature of their employment, these women have become easy prey to exploitation and abuse. Although this abuse is widely known, and many Filipino women are aware as they make their decision to work abroad that they may gain very little from the experience personally, they opt to work abroad anyway, primarily for the good of their families.

The migration of Filipinos as overseas contract workers in fact does have significant implications for family dynamics. Because they migrate on their own and their stay is considered only "temporary" in nature, contract-labor migrants must leave their families behind. For married women, this often means leaving young children in the care of relatives and making arrangements for someone else to perform their normal household duties while they are away.

The Importance of Foreign Remittances

The fact that remittances make a significant contribution to the Philippine economy has been widely documented; however, the exact amount of the remittances from overseas Filipino workers to their relatives cannot be determined with any certainty. The formal banking system is able to capture only a fraction of the total amount sent. The rest of the remittances travels via an informal system of couriers, money-changers, friends, and relatives who hand-carry the money to its end recipients. In 2003, the Central Bank of the Philippines estimated that more than US$5 billion in remittances from overseas Filipino workers passed through these informal channels.

Despite this limitation, the contribution of remittances to the foreign exchange earnings of the country has been considerable. Remittances have made up for the shortfall in the foreign direct investments, the portfolio investments, and even exports. By providing a steady supply of dollars in the market, they have helped to stabilize the peso and to boost the economy through consumption and investments. From 1990 to 2002 alone, the workers remitted a total of US$67,019.7 billion—or an average of US$5 billion every year—through the formal banking system. Of the total amount, the land-based workers contributed 86.5 percent. Between 1993 and 2002, these remittances contributed an average of 19.4 percent to the export earnings of the country and 6.6 percent to the gross national product (GNP). Because of the role that they play in propping up the economy through the money they send home, the millions of migrant Filipino workers abroad have been dubbed "modern-day heroes."

Motivations for Labor Migration

Many different factors come into play for migrant workers from the Philippines who make the decision to work abroad. These factors may be personal, economic, or both. A concern for the family and its economic welfare is usually central. Moreover, the lives of the overseas workers are intricately linked with the families they left behind: Globalization and international labor migration have led to the development of the Filipino family as a transnational family. Although overseas workers are separated by distance and time from their families in the Philippines, their principal commitments and obligations are to their Filipino families and households. This affects a significant percentage of Filipino families. Census data for 2000 revealed that 5.24 percent of all Filipino households, or 800,051 households, had overseas workers. Migration is a survival strategy through which the Filipino family strives to achieve a better fit between resources, consumption, and various options to generate monetary and nonmonetary income and goods. By doing so, the family attempts to escape possible threats to its existence and to improve its quality of life.

Personal, noneconomic reasons have also prodded migrants to work abroad. Among these are the lure of travel to a foreign land, the desire for change or to see the world, and wanting to have different experiences (Go 1994; Tacoli 1996). Female migrants may work abroad because they want to become independent. For older single women, migration offers an escape from sibling control (Tacoli 1996), and for the married woman, it may provide an escape from an unhappy marriage (Battistella and Conaco 1996).

Consequences of Labor Migration

Economic Gains

Without a doubt, the economic gains are the most tangible positive effect of labor migration for both the family and Philippine society (Go and Postrado 1986; Tacoli 1996; Go 1994; Asis 1995). In the face of the economic difficulties confronting the society today, labor migration provides an attractive avenue for social mobility and an improved quality of life for the Filipino family. Within a short period of time, families and households have been able to buy appliances, improve their houses or buy new ones, finance the education of their children or siblings, and for some, start a small business. Although the sustainability and long-term economic gains of labor migration for the Filipino family have been questioned, many husbands and fathers, wives and mothers, and sons and daughters continue to work overseas.

For the migrant worker, the economic returns vary considerably across skills levels and by country destination (Tan 2001). Professionals receive higher wages than domestic helpers, and wages vary significantly by destination country within each skill category (ibid.). For instance, in 1998, domestic helpers in Europe received higher wages than those in the Middle East, while within Asia, Hong Kong paid higher wages than Singapore and Malaysia. Computer programmers were paid five times more in the United States than in Saudi Arabia, while accountants in Singapore were paid three times more than those in American Samoa. The economic gains are also influenced by the duration of overseas employment: The longer the stay, the larger the total monetary benefit. At the societal level, the remittances of overseas Filipino workers have played a significant role in boosting the Philippine economy over the past thirty years.

Social Costs

The social costs of migration, especially the migration of women, and its effects on the Filipino family as an institution have been a continuing concern. There is a prevailing perception, fueled by anecdotal accounts in the print and broadcast media, that the institutions of marriage and the family are slowly being eroded by international labor migration. Moreover, the absence of the mother is perceived to have more negative effects on the family, especially young children, than the absence of the father. Because of the difficulty of quantifying the social costs of migration, studies on the issue have been few and the results mixed and inconclusive. Those studies that have been conducted indicate that the negative effects of labor migration on the family are not as widespread or as damaging as is commonly believed (Battistella and Conaco 1996; Asis 1995; Arcinas, 1991; Go and Postrado 1986).

The studies revealed that marital infidelity and marital dissolution are not common in sending communities. Nor was juvenile delinquency, in the form of drug abuse, drinking, and street-corner gangs among children from sending communities, attributable to international labor migration. Studies have also shown that migrant workers may go abroad to escape from difficult marriages and intolerable family situations (Tacoli 1996; Battistella and Conaco 1996). Consequently, family problems might be the cause rather than the effect of emigration.

It is nonetheless undeniable that, for both the migrating spouse and the spouse left behind, labor migration results in psychological stress. The sources of the stress include homesickness, loneliness, and anxiety over family-related concerns, such as the possibility of spouses' marital infidelity and the care and discipline of the children while a parent is away (Go and Postrado 1986).

There is some inconclusive evidence that a mother's absence may have a greater negative impact on younger children than on older children, specifically in the area of school performance and social adjustment (Battistella and Conaco 1996). This evidence, however, is contradicted by (limited) research suggesting that the absence of one or both parents has not been very disruptive for children (Battistella and Conaco 1996; Asis 1995; Go and Postrado 1986).

Another issue of great concern is the protection and welfare of Filipino workers abroad. What's more, the feminization of labor migration from the Philippines has added a gender dimension to the phenomenon that brings with it special problems. The many problems and difficulties faced by Filipino migrant women have been documented in the literature (see, for example, Abrera-Mangahas 1998; Lim and Oishi 1996; Osteria 1994). They suffer from various forms of exploitation, including physical abuse (for example, long work hours, physical violence); economic exploitation (exorbitant recruitment fees, low wages); sexual exploitation and abuse (trafficking, sexual harassment); curtailment of human rights (prohibition against forming unions or associations championing their cause, mandatory HIV/AIDS testing; mandatory pregnancy tests); and cultural discrimination (restricted opportunities to practice cultural traditions).

Illegal migration aggravates the welfare and human rights issues for both male and female migrant workers because their status affords them little or no protection under the law. Illegal migrants are more vulnerable to exploitation and abuse than legal migrants, and employers are under no obligation to grant them the benefits that legal foreign workers are entitled to under the law.

Migration Policy

Filipino labor migration policies can best be described as reactive rather than proactive, ambivalent rather than decisive. They were formulated in response to the difficulties that surfaced as the overseas employment program accelerated and evolved over time to address emerging issues such as illegal recruitment; the welfare and protection of workers and their families; the plight of undocumented workers; the exploitation and abuse of migrant women; the use of remittances; the rights of migrant workers; and the economic and social reintegration of returning migrant workers.

From 1974 to 1994, Philippine migration policy focused on encouraging the export of labor. Despite pronouncements to the contrary in policy statements, there was little attention paid to creating safety nets to ensure the protection and welfare of workers. Instead, the government heavily promoted the concept of labor migration to advance economic interests. In 1995, however, a Filipino domestic helper in Singapore was found guilty of murder, sentenced, and subsequently hanged. The case, which drew the collective outrage of the Filipino people and brought into sharp focus the human rights and welfare issues of international labor migration, was a catalyst for a major policy shift.

The Republic Act 8042, or the Migrant Workers and Overseas Filipino Act, of 1995 became the overarching legislation governing and mandating all government efforts at protecting the rights and welfare of overseas Filipinos. Whereas previously authorities had seen the government's role as one of promoting the export of labor, they now saw it as one of managing the export of labor—regulating the labor outflow and ensuring respect for the migrants' security and human rights. In 2001, this policy was expanded. Since then, the government has explicitly recognized overseas employment as a legitimate option for the country's workforce. It provides for the protection and welfare needs of those who choose to work abroad while actively exploring and developing better employment opportunities and modes of engagement in overseas labor markets consistent with its regional and international commitments and agreements. Rather than simply managing the flow, government now seeks to actively promote international labor migration, especially of highly skilled, knowledge-based workers, as a growth strategy while attempting to ensure that checks are in place to avoid, or at least limit, abuses that were once common.

Stella P. Go

See also: Gender and Migration; Remittances; Skilled Migration; Women, Globalization, and Immigration

References and further reading:

Abrera-Mangahas, Ma. Alcestis. 1998. "Violence against Women Migrant Workers: The Philippine Experience." Pp. 45–80 in *Filipino Workers on the Move: Trends, Dilemmas and Policy Options.* Edited by Benjamin Carino. Philippines: Philippine Migration Research Network and the Philippine Social Science Council.

Arcinas, Fe. R. 1991. "Asian Migration to the Gulf Region: The Philippine Case." Pp. 103–149 in *Migration in the Arab World: Experiences of Returning Migrants.* Edited by Godfrey Gunatilleke. Tokyo: United Nations University Press.

Asis, Maruja M. B. 1995. "Overseas Employment and Social Transformation in Source Communities: Findings from the Philippines." *Asian and Pacific Migration Journal* 4, nos. 2–3: 327–346.

Battistella, Graziano, and Ma. Cecilia G. Conaco. 1996. "Impact of Migration on Children Left Behind." *Asian Migrant* 9, no. 3: 86–91.

Go, Stella P. 1994. "Working in Japan: The Experience of Filipino Overseas Contract Workers." In *Kyoto Conference on Japanese Studies.* Vol. 4. Kyoto: International Center for Japanese Studies and the Japan Foundation.

Go, Stella P., and Leticia T. Postrado. 1986. "Filipino Overseas Contract Workers: Their Families and Communities." Pp. 125–144 in *Asian Labor Migration: Pipeline to the Middle East.* Edited by Fred Arnold and Nasra Shah. Boulder: Westview.

Lim, Lin Lean, and Nana Oishi. 1996. "International Labor Migration of Asian Women: Distinctive Characteristics and Policy Concerns." *Asian and Pacific Migration Journal* 5, no. 1: 85–116.

Osteria, Trinidad S. 1994. *Filipino Labor Migration to Japan: Economic Causes and Consequences.* Manila: De La Salle University Press.

Tacoli, Cecilia. 1996. "Migrating 'for the Sake of the Family'? Gender, Life Course and Intra-Household Relations among Filipino Migrants in Rome." *Philippine Sociological Review* 44, nos. 1–4: 12–32.

Tan, Edita A. 2001. "Labor Market Adjustments to Large Scale Emigration: The Philippine Case." *Asian and Pacific Migration Journal* 2, no. 3: 379–340.

Forced Migration

See Asylum; Displaced Persons; Internally Displaced Persons; Refugees

Foreign Students

Foreign students are persons who are granted admission to enroll in and pursue a course of study in another country. They may be enrolled in an academic, vocational, or language institution. Enrollment may lead to a degree or certification, although many foreign students are enrolled in shorter courses of study, particularly those who pursue exchange or "study abroad" programs. The duration of stay is generally determined by the period required to complete the proposed course of study. Hence, some foreign students are admitted for a period of weeks, particularly those studying foreign languages, whereas others are allowed to remain in the country for a period of years until they obtain an academic degree.

According to the Organisation for Economic Co-operation and Development (OECD), 1.6 million foreign students were enrolled in tertiary-level (that is, higher educational) institutions in 2000. Of these, 1.5 million were studying in OECD countries. The total number and proportion of foreign students in destination countries vary considerably. OECD statistics indicate that five countries account for more than 70 percent of all foreign students in the highly developed countries. The United States attracts about 30 percent, followed by the United Kingdom (14 percent) and Germany (12 percent). English-speaking countries account for over 50 percent of the OECD total (OECD 2002).

The United States has more than 500,000 foreign students at its colleges, universities, and other educational institutions in any given year (Institute for International Education 2002). Yet, because of the large number of students overall in U.S. education, foreign nationals represent a small proportion (less than 4 percent) of the total student population. By contrast, foreign students represent more than 10 percent of the student bodies in several other countries (OECD). Switzerland, Australia, Austria, and the United Kingdom, among OECD members, have the highest proportion of foreign students in tertiary education. Foreign students represent more than 10 percent of their student enrollment. Foreign students represent less than 1 percent of Japan's and Korea's tertiary enrollment (OECD 2002).

Foreign-student enrollment also varies by region and country of origin, with Asia dominating today. According to the OECD (2002), China represents the largest number of foreign students in OECD countries, with about 7 percent of the total foreign-student population. Japan, Korea, and India produce sizable foreign-student enrollments, with 4.6, 3.9, and 3.4 percent, respectively. Significant numbers also come from several European countries, including Greece (3.6 percent), Germany (3.5 percent), France (3.4 percent), and Italy (2.7 percent).

Enrollment of foreign students varies by field of study and academic degree. According to the *Open Doors* survey conducted by the Institute for International Education each year, about 28 percent of foreign students in the United States were enrolled in engineering, mathematics, and computer science programs during the 2001/2002 term. Another 20 percent of foreign students were enrolled in business administration programs. By contrast, the humanities attracted only 3 percent of the foreign students. Foreign students particularly dominate graduate education in science and engineering (S&E) at U.S. universities. According to the National Science Foundation (NSF), "With the decline in the U.S. college-age population from 1980 to 1997 and subsequent falloff in degrees in many S&E fields, U.S. universities began to rely on foreign students to fill graduate S&E programs, particularly in the physical sciences, engineering, and computer sciences" (NSF 2002). Between 1986 and 1999, foreign students earned 120,000 doctoral degrees in S&E fields, with China as the top country of origin (ibid.).

In a trend seen in other countries, an increasing proportion of foreign students have planned to stay in the United States after graduation. According to the National Science Foundation, by 1999 "more than 72 percent of foreign students who earned S&E doctoral degrees at universities in the United States reported that they planned to stay in the United States after graduation, and 50 percent accepted firm offers to do so" (ibid.). The propensity to return varied by the professional and economic opportunities offered in the home country relative to the United States.

Foreign students represent a financial benefit to recipient countries, although the extent of this benefit is debated. *Open Doors 2002* reported that foreign students contribute nearly $12 billion to the U.S. economy in money spent on tuition, living expenses, and related costs. The *Open Doors* survey in-

Foreign students gather in front of the Chinese language learning center at Beijing University, September 29, 2004. China was expecting 86,000 foreign students, a record number, to enroll in its universities that year as foreigners sought to cash in on the country's booming economy by becoming proficient in Mandarin. (AFP/Getty Images)

dicates that almost 75 percent of all funding for foreign students comes from personal and family sources or other sources outside of the United States. Economist George Borjas questioned the calculation, however, arguing that taxpayers subsidize higher education in the United States even when students pay what is determined to be full tuition. There is broader agreement, however, that foreign graduate students provide important human capital for universities and the broader economies of recipient countries, particularly through the research that they undertake during and after their studies.

The issue of "brain drain" remains a major concern, though, when large numbers of foreign students from developing countries remain in countries with more advanced economies. As noted above, the 1990s saw growth in the number of foreign S&E graduate students staying in the United States (as well as other highly developed countries) after graduation. The reversal of this trend in certain countries that had improved their own capacity to utilize postgraduate scientists and engineers (such as South Korea) suggests that brain drain is not inevitable. In fact, some policy makers and scholars promote greater "brain circulation" as a way to help ensure that all parties—source and destination countries as well as the foreign students themselves—benefit from international education programs. Accomplishing brain circulation requires financial and professional incentives for foreign students to return to their home countries for at least temporary stays as well as changes in immigration policies to permit foreign nationals with residency permits to reenter after such stays.

Foreign students have received particular scrutiny in the period since the September 11, 2001, terrorist attacks on New York and Washington, D.C. Several of the alleged hijackers had obtained or requested student visas, including visas to study aviation in U.S. flight schools. Because the foreign student programs had already been abused by persons who posed security risks, the U.S. Congress had passed legislation in 1996 requiring the development of a foreign-student tracking system. Little progress had been made on the computer system by the time of the terrorist attacks. Efforts to develop the system gained new urgency, however, and the Student and Exchange Visitor Information System (SEVIS) became operational in February 2003. SEVIS collects information on the name, place and date of birth, country of citizenship, U.S. address, status (full-time, part-time), date of commencement of studies, degree program and field of study, termination date and known reasons, and number of credits completed per year.

In addition to the tracking system, the United States, along with other countries, has heightened the scrutiny given to foreign-student applicants for visas as well as to the educational institutions that sponsor the applicants. Policy makers are also looking to ensure that foreign students from countries supporting terrorism or trying to develop weapons of mass destruction not be permitted to follow courses of study, such as nuclear physics, that would contribute knowledge that would threaten international peace and security. Officials also recognize the value of international education, however, particularly in exposing future leaders of other countries to the tenets of liberal democracies. With appropriate use of technology and intelligence to separate security threats from bona fide foreign students, it should be possible to maintain foreign-student programs without risking undue security threats.

Susan F. Martin

References and further reading:

Borjas, George. 2002. "Rethinking Foreign Students: A Question of the National Interest." *National Review,* http://www.nationalreview.com/issue/borjas061702.asp (cited November 17, 2003).

Institute of International Education. 2002. *Open Doors: 2002.* Washington, DC: Institute of International Education.

National Science Foundation. 2002. *Science and Engineering Indicators 2002.* Washington, DC: National Science Foundation.

Organisation for Economic Co-operation and Development. 2002. *Education at a Glance—OECD Indicators.* Paris: OECD.

France

From the mid–nineteenth century to the present, France has had a more sustained history of inward migration than any other country of Western Europe. The primary factors contributing to this migration have been France's relatively low birthrate and associated labor shortages, heavy population losses in military conflicts (especially World War I), a tradition of offering asylum rooted in the republican values of the French Revolution, and, in more recent decades, the legacy of overseas colonization.

During the interwar period, France's foreign population was, as a proportion of the national population, greater than that of the United States. Until the second half of the twentieth century, the overwhelming majority of immigrants were of European origin. With the advent of decolonization, which reached its climax with the independence of Algeria in 1962, former French colonies in Africa, Asia, and the Caribbean became increasingly important sources of migratory inflows. Today, France has both the largest Arab population and the largest Jewish population in Western Europe. The nation's republican traditions at home and the colonial experience overseas have been important factors in shaping "integration" policies and popular attitudes toward immigrant minorities. The dominant norms have traditionally been represented as assimilationist in character, but exclusionary tendencies have also been present, especially toward postcolonial migrants, and more generally during periods of economic insecurity.

Regions of Origin

Until as recently as 1968, the majority of the foreign population in France came from neighboring countries. Prior to the 1920s, Belgium and Italy alone accounted for over half of all foreign residents. Belgians, attracted by job opportunities in the coal, steel, and textile industries just over the border in northeastern France, outnumbered Italians until the beginning of the twentieth century. Italians, who were traditionally concentrated in unskilled jobs in southeastern France, then took over as the largest single national group, which they remained until being outnumbered by Spaniards in 1968. Spanish immigrants were particularly numerous in southwestern France, where many worked as agricultural laborers.

Between the wars, large numbers of Poles migrated to France. Most Polish immigrants took jobs on the land or in the mines. They quickly became the largest expatriate community originating in a country without a shared border with France, second only in size to that of the Italians. By 1931, they accounted for half of all foreign workers in the mining industry. The economic depression of the 1930s hit this sector particularly hard, forcing tens of thousands of Poles to return home. Up to 100,000 more followed them immediately after World War II. When the Iron Curtain sealed Poland's borders shortly afterward, the remaining community in France stagnated and then declined rapidly in importance.

Until the middle of the twentieth century, these four states—Belgium, Italy, Spain, and Poland—dominated migratory inflows to France. Although economic motives were generally to the fore, political factors also played a significant role for two of these countries. Throughout the nineteenth

An Italian, employed as a steel worker in the French town of Joeuf, repairs the handle of a bag as he sits on the doorstep of his home with his wife and son. (Hulton-Deutsch Collection/Corbis)

century, political exiles from Italy had found a refuge in France, and their numbers were swollen following Benito Mussolini's accession to power in 1922. Political refugees began leaving Spain almost as soon as the Spanish Civil War began in 1936. When it ended three years later with the defeat of the Republicans, almost half a million Spaniards crossed into France; though many later returned home, at least half of them stayed.

A number of smaller immigrant communities were formed mainly as a result of political persecution. Armenians, for example, regrouped in France during the 1920s after fleeing a campaign of genocide instigated by Turkey. At about the same time, more than 100,000 Russians hostile to the Bolshevik Revolution settled in France, mainly in the Paris area. Before World War I, about 40,000 Jews had fled to France from the Russian Empire, where they were threatened by widespread pogroms. With the rise of fascism during the 1930s, well over 100,000 Jews from Germany and Eastern Europe sought refuge in France. During World War II, foreigners—particularly those who had come to France because of political persecution—played a vigorous role in the Resistance, thereby contributing to the liberation from Nazi occupation.

In recent decades, most asylum seekers entering France have come from the Third World, that is, former European colonies in Africa, Asia, and other regions. At the same time, the distinction between economic and political factors in motivating migration has often become blurred. The largest group to whom refugee status has been granted during this period consists of exiles from former French territories in Southeast Asia. The formal decolonization of French Indochina, which began with the termination of French protectorates over Laos and Cambodia, was completed in 1954 following the military defeat inflicted that year on France by Vietnamese nationalists at Dien Bien Phu. Following the French withdrawal, the Vietnam War between the Communist North and a U.S.-backed regime in the South ended with a Communist victory in 1975, prompting an exodus of asylum seekers known as "boat people" because of the small craft in which many of them fled. Vietnamese exiles, often middle-class people fearing poorer economic opportunities and/or political persecution under Communist rule, were soon joined by Cambodians fleeing the authoritarian regime of Pol Pot and by Laotians who feared for their safety because they had assisted the United States during the Vietnam War. Most went to the United States, but about 100,000—divided more or less evenly between Vietnamese, Cambodians, and Laotians—entered France; several thousand Chinese nationals, who had a long history of commercial activity in the region, came with them.

Decolonization had also prompted major population movements from North Africa for a similar mixture of economic and political reasons. Temporary labor migration from Algeria, France's principal North African colony, had begun in the early years of the twentieth century, but it was not until the 1960s that significant numbers of migrants originating in Algeria and the former French protectorates of Morocco and Tunisia began to settle permanently in France. Among them, four main groups may be distinguished. The first of these—now constituting the largest single group of non-European migrants in France—consisted of economic migrants originating in North Africa's predominantly Muslim population. In 1982, this sector numbered more than 800,000, making it the largest national group among the foreign population. Their migration to France had been favored by a 1947 statute granting them freedom of movement, which was reaffirmed under the terms of the agreements that granted Algeria independence in 1962. A second group of Algerian Muslims, known as *harkis*—auxiliary soldiers who fought with the French against Algerian nationalists during the war of independence—came to France as political exiles, fearing reprisals in their home country. Unlike the economic migrants from Algeria, who became citizens of the new Algerian state when French rule ended in 1962, the harkis retained French citizenship and were not therefore officially classified as Algerians, though the majority ethnic population often failed to distinguish between the two groups. Popular prejudices against non-Europeans, widespread during the colonial period, were sharpened, in the case of Algerians, by the bitterness of the war of independence, which has continued to weigh on ethnic relations in France until the present day.

The two other groups fled North Africa en masse at the time of independence and settled mainly in France: about a million European settlers, popularly known as *pieds-noirs,* and more than 100,000 Sephardic Jews. Smoldering resentment among the pieds-noirs toward Algerian Muslims was to be a significant source of support for the extreme right in France during the 1980s and 1990s, when hostility toward immigration from Third World countries became highly politicized. The Jewish population in France underwent major changes with the inflow of Sephardic Jews, who now outnumber Ashkenazi Jews. Although French is their main language in dealings with non-Jews, there are internal speech differences separating Ashkenazis, who brought Yiddish with them from Eastern Europe, from Sephardic Jews, among whom a number of Arabic dialects are spoken. There are also growing differences between secular or nonpracticing Jews and those who favor the more orthodox observance of religious practices. In addition, there are many political divergences, especially concerning Israel and its relations with Palestinians and the wider Arab world.

Colonization and its aftermath have been significant factors in the movements of three other groups of migrants: those originating in Portugal, sub-Saharan Africa, and France's remaining Départements d'Outre-Mer and Territoires d'Outre-Mer (DOM-TOM, Overseas Departments and Overseas Territories). There were few Portuguese migrants in France until the 1960s and early 1970s, when their numbers rose rapidly in the face of wars in Portugal's overseas empire against nationalist groups seeking independence. To avoid the military draft, many young Portuguese men headed for France, where the authorities unofficially waived normal entry regulations. By 1975, there were more than 750,000 Portuguese expatriates in France, making them the largest national group in the foreign population at that time. Like Algerians, migrants from sub-Saharan Africa gravitated to France in the wake of former colonial links. But migratory flows from Central and West Africa generally came later than those from North Africa, against the tide of tight immigration controls imposed by France on non-European economic migrants from 1974 onward. For this and other reasons, sub-Saharan Africans became prominent among flows of asylum seekers (who were not subject to the same immigration controls as economic migrants) and among undocumented migrants, who in the 1990s became widely known as *sans-papiers.*

Migrants from the DOM-TOM, remnants of the colonial empire still administered by France, are not affected by migratory controls of that kind. Because the Départements d'Outre-Mer—the Caribbean islands and Martinique and Guadeloupe, the nearby South American territory of French Guyana, and the Indian Ocean island of Réunion—are officially classified as integral parts of France, their inhabitants are entitled to move freely in and out of metropolitan France. Relatively low living standards in the overseas départements, marked by the legacy of slavery, have generated significant migratory flows. In all, about a third of a million migrants from the DOM-TOM now live in France, including a quarter of the entire population born in Martinique and Guadeloupe.

Immigration Controls and the Myth of Assimilation

It is often said that France's republican traditions and population shortages have encouraged the public authorities to pursue assimilationist policies in relation to immigrant minorities. There is considerable truth in this, but it is something of an oversimplification for at least two main reasons. First, the authorities have always reserved the right to halt or even reverse migratory inflows, by the same token cutting across assimilationist objectives. Until World War I, France exercised relatively weak immigration controls, effectively leaving most population movements to the free play of market forces. During the interwar period, the powers of the state were used initially to stimulate immigration in response to chronic labor shortages, but when reconstruction gave way to the slump of the 1930s, this policy was thrown into reverse, with the forced repatriation of Poles and other economic migrants. Second, some ethnic groups have been made more or less welcome than others. During the Nazi occupation of France, the collaborationist Vichy regime pursued a vigorous policy of anti-Semitism, handing tens of thousands of mainly foreign-born Jews to the Nazis for deportation to their death camps. Though these openly racist measures were the work of a militantly antirepublican regime that is generally regarded as an aberration in the course of modern French history, milder forms of ethnic differentiation have informed public policy throughout the postwar period.

Immediately after World War II, a serious debate took place within the provisional government over whether to impose ethnic quotas in regulating the migratory inflows that all agreed were necessary to assist in reconstruction work and to compensate for France's weak demographic growth. Although there was general agreement that Africans and Asians were less desirable than Europeans, those in the policy-making community who were primarily concerned to relieve immediate labor shortages were less keen on formal ethnic quotas than those who saw immigration as vital to the nation's long-term demographic future. A compromise eventually emerged through a government ordinance issued in 1945. No ethnic quotas were laid down in the ordinance, but successive governments operating within the constitutional framework of restored republican governance sought as far as possible to encourage European rather than African or Asian immigrants.

Thus the Office National d'Immigration (ONI, National Immigration Office), a state-run agency established under the 1945 ordinance with the task of regulating migratory inflows, immediately opened recruitment offices in Italy while leaving other countries untouched. Unlike Italians and other Europeans, Algerians who used their de facto right of entry to France before and immediately after independence in 1962 were not encouraged to bring in their families. When, in response to fears of economic recession after the oil crisis of 1973, the center-right government of the day attempted to protect the national labor market by halting further inward migration in 1974, citizens of European Community member states were exempted from the ban, the main weight of which consequently fell on would-be migrants from Third World countries. During the next few years, amid a backdrop of rising unemployment, the authorities made determined though largely unsuccessful attempts to block immigration by family members of Third World migrants already resident in France and seriously considered the more or less forced repatriation of Algerians, the nation's largest Third World minority.

None of these measures is consonant with the idea that republican governance in France goes unequivocally hand in hand with a policy of assimilation. Far from encouraging Algerians to assimilate, successive governments from the beginning of the twentieth century until the 1980s favored only temporary labor migration, discouraged family settlement, and during times of economic recession did everything in their power to promote repatriation to Algeria. Even when the left came to power in 1981 and halted many of the repressive measures enacted by the previous administration, it was still far from clear that the nation was set on a course of assimilation. For a time, the left flirted with ideas of multiculturalism while the rise of the extreme right-wing Front National (FN) led the center-right parties to borrow some of its anti-immigrant clothes in the hoping of countering the FN's electoral appeal. With unemployment rising relentlessly until the late 1990s, immigration became one of the most contentious issues in French politics. Emblematic of this was the debate over French nationality laws, which had until then epitomized the assimilationist dimension of French policy toward immigrant minorities.

Nationality, Citizenship, and Ethnicity

In contrast to countries such as Germany, where access to nationality and citizenship was largely restricted to people of German ancestry, France has traditionally complemented a system of *ius sanguinis* with liberal doses of *ius soli*, granting citizenship to large numbers of people born on French soil regardless of their parental or ancestral origins. In this way, they are officially assimilated into the French nation as defined by the boundaries of formal citizenship. Once incorporated into the French nation, immigrants and their descendants are expected to throw off any affiliations linked to their ethnic origins, which are rigorously excluded from any form of public recognition in France. Typical of this is the way in which census and other official data have generally eschewed the use of any type of ethnic criteria, with the sole exception of nationality. It is only very recently that official agencies have begun to publish significant but still limited data sets based on place of birth or, more exceptionally still, other indicators of ethnic origin. To do otherwise, it was argued, would run counter to the assimilationist spirit of France's republican principles and risk stimulating ethnic factionalism, labeled by its enemies as *communautarisme.* Officials were also haunted by memories of the Vichy period, when the compilation by the state of centralized records identifying the Jewish population had been a vital tool in the persecution, deportation, and extermination of Jews. Fears of centralized ethnic data being misused for sinister purposes remain today a powerful factor in the widespread rejection in France of the types of ethnic monitoring undertaken by states such as Britain and the United States in the detection of racial disadvantage and/or discrimination.

In the mid-1980s, worried by the electoral appeal of FN proposals to radically reduce the access of Third World immigrants to citizenship, and even to strip citizenship from those who had become French nationals, the center-right parties began campaigning for a more modest but highly charged reform of French nationality laws, which they eventually enacted in 1993. This had the effect of forcing the children of immigrants to request French citizenship instead of receiving it automatically on reaching the age of majority. Among the anti-immigrant lobby it was widely expected, or hoped, that many of those forced to choose in this way would opt against French citizenship, thereby rendering themselves liable to expulsion from France in the event of the passage of other repressive measures. In practice, the vast majority opted for French citizenship.

On returning to office in 1997, the left reversed the reform, reinstating the traditional system of ius soli. Simultaneously, for the first time in almost a quarter of a century unemployment began to fall and internecine strife within the extreme right blunted its electoral appeal. Although similar divisions on the left enabled the FN's leader, Jean-Marie Le Pen, to achieve a shock result in the first round of the 2002 presidential election, coming in second to the center-right incumbent,

Jacques Chirac, Le Pen was heavily defeated in the run-off, and the center-right parties later appeared increasingly committed to a policy of "integration," which did not necessarily mean outright assimilation.

Assimilation, Integration, and Insertion

"Integration" had first become a buzzword in policy-making circles amid the political uproar provoked by the Islamic headscarf affair. This had erupted initially in 1989, when three Muslim schoolgirls were barred from their public school for refusing to remove their Islamic headscarves, which the head teacher regarded as a symbol of communautarisme incompatible with the French laws of *laïcité*, designed to separate the state and spaces under its control (such as the educational system) from any form of religious influence. When French courts were asked to rule on the matter, they found consistently that although it would be unlawful for Muslims or anyone else to proselytize in public spaces, it was perfectly lawful for students to wear headscarves or other religious clothing, such as yarmulkas, if they wished. Freedom of religious belief and expression was enshrined in the French Constitution and, indeed, in the 1789 Declaration of the Rights of Man, the founding document of French republicanism. By the same token, France was committed to a greater degree of cultural diversity than many thought or wished. This was often lost sight of in the heated debates surrounding Muslim immigrant minorities in the 1980s and 1990s. In the face of huge public opposition to the wearing of Islamic headscarves, which were widely perceived as a threat to French norms and proof that Muslims could not be assimilated into French society, the Socialist-led government of Michel Rocard attempted to forge a new political consensus around the idea of "integration."

In the lexicon of French public policy, "integration" has come to occupy a now dominant position midway between "assimilation" and "insertion." Though many, especially on the right of the political spectrum, have always favored assimilation, the word itself has been used relatively little in recent decades, probably in part because of its colonial connotations. Overseas colonization had often been justified by the so-called civilizing mission, according to which France would eventually assimilate "inferior" colonized peoples into her own "superior" civilization. The bloody debacles in which the overseas empire foundered led many to wish that the entire colonial enterprise could be forgotten, hence the avoidance of colonially tainted terms such as "assimilation." Similarly, "Nord-Africain" (North African) has now been largely supplanted by "Maghrébin" (Maghrebi).

These changes of nomenclature did little, if anything, to attenuate distrust of Muslim immigrant minorities, whom a large part of the majority ethnic population feared were inassimilable. In seeking to assuage these fears, Rocard argued that with a cross-party consensus around the idea of "integration," those minorities could be successfully incorporated into French society. Though the term was not without ambiguity—many on the right saw it as a code for assimilation, while some on the left saw it as a new version of "insertion," which the Socialists had championed during the early 1980s as a mild form of multiculturalism—"integration" became a watchword for all the main political parties except the extreme right. Its key components include a commitment to combating the social and economic marginalization of immigrant minorities while dissuading them from engaging in ethnic factionalism, at the same time recognizing their right to maintain cultural differences in the private (as distinct from the public) sphere. Antidiscrimination measures, essential to overcome deep-seated prejudices slowing the incorporation of postcolonial minorities—especially those of Muslim heritage—in many areas of French society, have developed relatively slowly and remain hampered by the refusal to engage in ethnic monitoring.

Alec G. Hargreaves

See also: Citizenship; Colonial Immigration; Far-Right Parties; France d'Outre-Mer; Genocide; Germany

References and further reading:

Bleich, Erik. 2003. *Race Politics in Britain and France: Ideas and Policymaking since the 1960s.* Cambridge: Cambridge University Press.

Brubaker, Rogers. 1992. *Citizenship and Nationhood in France and Germany.* Cambridge: Harvard University Press.

"Migration and Migrants in France." 1991. Special issue. *Ethnic and Racial Studies* 14, no. 3.

Favell, Adrian. 2001. *Philosophies of Integration: Immigration and the Idea of Citizenship in France and Britain.* 2d ed. Houndmills: Palgrave.

Freeman, Gary P. 1979. *Immigrant Labor and Racial Conflict in Industrial Societies: The French and British Experience, 1945–1975.* Princeton, NJ: Princeton University Press.

Fysh, Peter, and Jim Wolfreys. 1998. *The Politics of Racism in France.* Houndmills: Macmillan.

Hargreaves, Alec G. 1995. *Immigration, "Race" and Ethnicity in Contemporary France.* London and New York: Routledge.

Hollifield, James F. 1992. *Immigrants, Markets and States.* Cambridge: Harvard University Press.

Horowitz, Donald L., and Gérard Noiriel, eds. 1992. *Immigrants in Two Democracies: French and American Experience.* New York: New York University Press.

Ireland, Patrick. *The Policy Challenge of Ethnic Diversity: Immigrant Politics in France and Switzerland.* Cambridge: Harvard University Press.

Lloyd, Catherine. 1998. *Discourses of Antiracism in France.* Aldershot: Ashgate.

MacMaster, Neil. 1997. *Colonial Migrants and Racism: Algerians in France, 1900–62.* Houndmills: Macmillan; New York: St. Martin's Press.

Miller, Mark. 1981. *Foreign Workers in Western Europe: An Emerging Political Force?* New York: Praeger.

Noiriel, Gérard. 1996. *The French Melting Pot: Immigration, Citizenship and National Identity.* Minneapolis: University of Minnesota Press.

Ogden, Philip E., and Paul E. White, eds. 1989. *Migrants in Modern France.* London: Unwin Hyman.

Schapper, Dominique. 1998. *Community of Citizens: On the Modern Idea of Nationality.* New Brunswick, NJ, and London: Transaction.

Silverman, Maxim. 1992. *Deconstructing the Nation: Immigration, Racism and Citizenship in Modern France.* London: Routledge.

Weil, Patrick. 2001. "The History of French Nationality: A Lesson for Europe." Pp. 52–68 in *Towards a European Nationality: Citizenship, Immigration and Nationality Law in the EU.* Edited by Randall Hansen and Patrick Weil. Houndmills: Palgrave.

Weil, Patrick, and John Crowley. 1994. "Integration in Theory and Practice: A Comparison of France and Britain." *West European Politics* 17, no. 2: 110–126.

France d'Outre-Mer

The France d'Outre-Mer (Overseas France) is the remnant of the French colonial empire, or French territories outside of Europe that did not gain independence in the 1950s and 1960s. An important source of migration to mainland France in recent decades, it now includes four Départements d'Outre-Mer (DOMs, Overseas Departments); four Territoires d'Outre-Mer (TOMs, Overseas Territories); and two Collectivités Territoriales (Territorial Communities). The DOMs are Guadeloupe and Martinique in the Caribbean, French Guiana in South America, and Réunion, an island in the Indian Ocean; the TOMs are French Polynesia, New Caledonia, the Pacific islands Wallis and Futuna, and Antarctic territories; and the Territorial Communities are Saint-Pierre and Miquelon, off the eastern coast of Canada, and Mayotte in the Indian Ocean. All the populations of these territories have full French citizenship.

The four DOMs are home to more than three-quarters of the total Outre-Mer population, approximately 1.5 million people out of a total of about 1.8 million (Ziller 1991, 19). These populations are in majority made up of black and mixed-race descendants of African slaves, particularly in the Caribbean. The Caribbean DOMs have distinct *créole* languages and cultures that are reflected in a rich literary tradition that produced the concepts of *négritude* and *créolité.* They are thus uniquely Caribbean, in many ways closer to their Anglophone neighbors, such as Jamaica or Barbados, than to Metropolitan France. But they also identify closely with the French republic and more generally with French culture and political values. This identification is due to a large extent to the fact that the second French republic enfranchised the slave population of these islands in 1848, making them full French citizens and enabling them to vote in all French elections since then. The institutional attachment of these territories to France has also been strong since 1946, when they were granted their present-day DOM status, which means they are regular territorial suddivisions of the French state. Since then they have benefited from the legal regime of the mainland.

The TOMs and Territorial Communities are less populated than the DOMs and may be either socially or politically closer to the mainland. The small population of Saint-Pierre and Miquelon, for example, is ethnically French. Some TOMs and Territorial Communities, however, such as French Polynesia, are more prone to harbor independentist tendencies. Others are actively engaged in pursuing a self-determination process. New Caledonia since 1988 is an example of the latter.

The DOMs have seen large percentages of their populations migrate to mainland France because of overpopulation, crises in their traditional plantation economies since the 1950s and 1960s, and cultural attachments to French institutions and values. In total, 192,000 migrants from the French West Indies moved to mainland France during the main migration wave of 1961–1982. Of these, 108,000 migrated spontaneously, attracted by the prospect of economic and social mobility in the "motherland," and 84,000 were encouraged to migrate by the state agency Bureau pour le Développement des Migrations des Départements d'Outre-Mer (BUMIDOM) (Anselin 1995, 114). BUMIDOM was created in 1961 by French planners who saw in the West Indian immigration to France a way to solve in one stroke overpopulation in the islands and shortage of the workforce on the mainland. The agency provided migrants with low-ranking jobs in various administrations, concentrating them in the Paris area. Immigration from Réunion took place in the 1970s and 1980s on a smaller scale.

The French authorities have presented these migrations as internal population movements rather than as an international migration flow. But these populations, which now total around 700,000, taking into account the second generation (Ziller 1991, 19), have also suffered from the typical ailments of extra-European migrant workers in Europe, such as racial discrimination on the job and in the housing market and cultural alienation. They can also be described as members of a wider West Indian diaspora in Europe that includes communities from Surinam (former Dutch Guiana) in Amsterdam and Jamaicans in British cities.

In the early years of the twenty-first century, these territories and their populations are experiencing more than ever the weight of their colonial heritage, caught up between extra-European identity and persistent political and economic links with the French state, which is increasingly tightly integrated in the European Union.

Romain Garbaye

See also: Colonial Immigration; European Citizenship; France; Schengen Agreement

References and further reading:

Anselin, Alain. 1995. "West Indians in France." Pp. 112–119 in *French and West-Indian: Martinica, Guadeloupe and French Guiana Today.* Edited by Richard Burton and Fred Reno. London: Macmillan.

Domenach, Hervé, and Michel Picouet, eds. 1992. *La Dimension Migratoire des Antilles.* Paris: Economica.

Matthieu, Jean-Luc. 1988. *Les DOM-TOM.* Paris: Presses Universitaires de France.

Rallu, Jean-Louis. 1997. "La Population des Départements d'Outre-Mer: Evolution Récente, Migration et Activité." *Population* 3: 699–728.

Ziller, Jacques. 1991. *Les DOM-TOM.* Paris: LGDJ.

G

Gender and Migration

One of the most significant trends in immigration has been the feminization of migration streams that had heretofore been primarily male. About half the migrants in the world today are women. Although most accompany or join family members, increasing numbers of female migrants migrate on their own. They are the principal wage earners for themselves and their families. The feminization of migration affects the roles of both female and male migrants as well as immigration and refugee policies that address such issues as family reunification and formation, labor migration, trafficking and smuggling, and forced migration.

Gender Distribution of Migrants

The gender distribution of migrants varies substantially by country (see Table G-1). The proportion of legal immigrants who are women is particularly high in the traditional immigration countries (United States, Canada, and Australia). In 1998, for example, 54 percent of legal immigrants to the United States were women (INS 1998). By contrast, migration to the Gulf states traditionally has been temporary, with men dominating, and this pattern continues (IOM 2000). Differences can also be seen among different emigration countries. Although the Philippines has a considerably higher proportion of female migrants living abroad (about 60 percent in data collected during the 1990s), Mexico has many more male migrants (69 percent in a census conducted in 1995) (ILO 1999).

The gender distribution also tends to vary by type of migration. Women migrants, as with all international migrants, belong to two broad groups: voluntary migrants and forced migrants. Women move voluntarily for purposes of employment, study, family reunification, or other personal factors. Women have also been forced to leave their countries to escape persecution, conflict, repression, natural and human-made disasters, and ecological degradation or other situations that endanger their lives, freedom, or livelihood. Among them are women raped and sexually attacked by government and rebel troops or other authorities, often in the process referred to as ethnic cleansing.

Distinguishing between voluntary and forced migrants can be difficult. Voluntary migrants may feel compelled to seek new homes because of pressing problems at home; forced migrants may choose a particular refuge because of family and community ties or economic opportunities. Moreover, one form of migration often leads to another. Forced migrants who settle in a new country may then bring family members to join them. Voluntary migrants may find that the situation changes in their home countries, preventing their repatriation and making them into forced migrants.

Women can be found among all types of migrants, but they tend to dominate in two categories: family reunification/formation and forced migration. Not surprisingly, though, as women gain greater autonomy through education and work, they are also migrating as principal applicants for work visas.

Family-Based Migration

Family reunification and formation are principal avenues for the immigration of women. Governments often admit close family members of migrants, although this policy is found more frequently in the traditional immigration countries than in those authorizing contract laborers only. The anchor relative in the host country may have been married and had children at the time of arrival but left his family members behind. Having determined to remain in the host country, he petitions for family reunification. Alternately, a citizen or international migrant already living in the host country marries a foreign national and seeks her admission.

Table G-1: Percentage of Female Migrants among the Total Number of International Migrants, by Major Area, 1960–2000

Major area	1960	1970	1980	1990	2000
World	46.6	47.2	47.4	47.9	48.8
More developed regions	47.9	48.2	49.4	50.8	50.9
Less developed regions	45.7	46.3	45.5	44.7	45.7
Europe	48.5	48.0	48.5	51.7	52.4
North America	49.8	51.1	52.6	51.0	51.0
Oceania	44.4	46.5	47.9	49.1	50.5
Northern Africa	49.5	47.7	45.8	44.9	42.8
Sub-Saharan Africa	40.6	42.1	43.8	46.0	47.2
Southern Asia	46.3	46.9	45.9	44.4	44.4
Eastern and Southeastern Asia	46.1	47.6	47.0	48.5	50.1
Western Asia	45.2	46.6	47.2	47.9	48.3
Caribbean	45.3	46.1	46.5	47.7	48.9
Latin America	44.7	46.9	48.4	50.2	50.5

Source: Hania Zlotnik, "The Global Dimensions of Female Migration," in the Migration Information Source, http://www.migrationinformation.org/feature/display.cfm?ID=109, March 1, 2003.

The willingness of states to authorize family reunification is supported by international human rights law. Article 16(3) of the Universal Declaration of Human Rights of 1948 states clearly that "the family is the natural and fundamental group unit of society and is entitled to protection by the society and the state." Splitting families apart deprives each member of the fundamental right to respect of family life. Since the family unit is often the principal support to its members, separating families also undermines other rights. Children and women, in particular, become vulnerable to exploitation when they are separated from their relatives.

Migrating spouses are more likely to be women than men. In the United States, for example, almost twice as many women than men immigrated as the spouses of U.S. citizens and permanent residents. These figures are not surprising because family reunification often follows male-dominated labor migration. For example, in the years after guestworker programs ended in Europe, most officially sanctioned international migration consisted of family reunion as former guestworkers brought their spouses and children to join them. Although a distinct minority of guestworkers was female, the majority comprised men who then sought the admission of their female spouses and children. Similarly, the wives and dependent children of the mostly male, unauthorized migrants who gained legal status through the Immigration Reform and Control Act of 1986 constitute a substantial share of the migration into the United States in the past decade.

Family reunification and formation programs can invite various abuses unless managed well. If marriage to a citizen or permanent resident is the only or principal route to admission, marriage fraud may result. Companies recruiting mail-order brides tend to be highly successful in countries with poor economies and few economic opportunities for women. Although many companies have a legitimate interest in matching spouses, some of these businesses use the lure of immigration as a pretext for trafficking the women into prostitution. To combat the potential for fraud, the United States offers conditional status to the immigrating spouse in recent marriages and reviews the cases after one year to make sure that the marriage is valid before granting permanent status.

Forced Migrants

By most estimates, 75 to 80 percent of the world's refugee population is composed of women and their dependent children (Martin 2003). Children account for about half of all refugees, with adult women often outnumbering adult men. This picture varies, however, by countries of origin and refuge. It is particularly true when refugees flee conflict in one developing country and take refuge in another, usually neighboring country. This distribution does not generally hold for asylum seekers who seek admission to more developed countries in North America, Europe, and Oceania. A higher proportion of male applicants can be found making their way to these more distant places.

Women who are forced migrants present many challenges to the international community. Foremost are their special needs for legal and physical protection. Gender is not included in the international definition of a refugee as a person with a well-founded fear of persecution on the basis of race, religion, nationality, political opinion, or membership in a social group. Yet, women asylum-seekers may be fleeing such gender-based persecution as rape, widow burnings, honor killings, domestic violence, forced marriages, and female genital mutilation from which their home country governments are unwilling or unable to protect them. Such countries as the United States, Canada, and the United Kingdom recognize these women as members of a "particular social group," but others, such as Germany and France, do not grant asylum if the persecution is at the hands of nonstate actors instead of directly by governments.

The protection of refugee women closer to conflict situations is even more problematic. Civilians are increasingly the targets of attacks in civil conflicts, with rape and sexual violence now a recognized war crime. Rape and sexual assault also occur during flight at the hands of border guards, government and rebel military units, bandits, and others. Women refugees' safety may be no more ensured once they are in refugee camps. For example, refugee women have faced serious threat of rape when they pick firewood, often the only source of heating and cooking fuel. Refugee women have been forced to provide sexual favors in exchange for obtaining food rations for themselves and their families. In some cases, only male heads of household receive documentation of their status, leaving their spouses vulnerable to harassment each time they leave their homes. Such problems do not necessarily stop when the women return home. The conflict may still be continuing, and even if a peace agreement has been signed, political instability, the continued presence of land mines, and the destruction of the economy and infrastructure make conditions dangerous for women and their families.

Labor Migrants

Several distinct categories of women migrate for work purposes, differentiated by their skills, the permanence of their residence in the host country, and their legal status. At the lower end of the skills spectrum, women migrants pick fruits and vegetables, manufacture garments and other items, process meat and poultry, work as nursing home and hospital aides, clean restaurants and hotels, and provide myriad other services. Overseas domestic service is a common occupation for migrant women. Women migrants from a wide range of countries provide domestic services in a wide range of receiving countries in almost all parts of the globe. They may migrate through official contract-labor programs that match workers and employers, or they may obtain such employment after migrating, often through informal networks.

At the higher end of the skills spectrum, women migrants engage in equally diverse activities. They fill jobs requiring specialized skills, run multinational corporations, teach in universities, provide research and development expertise to industry and academia, and design, build, and program computers, to name only a few activities. Sizable numbers of migrant women are in the health professions, particularly nursing and physical therapy. Again, they can be found undertaking such assignments throughout the world.

Although many women migrate through legal work programs, female unauthorized workers can be found in almost as diverse a range of jobs and industries as authorized workers, with agricultural and food-processing jobs, light manufacturing, and service jobs being the most common types of employment. Unauthorized women migrants also are smuggled into countries by professional traffickers. Though some migrant women know and accept the expectations of the traffickers, many others have been recruited to work in legitimate occupations and then find themselves trapped into forced prostitution, marriages, domestic work, sweatshops, and other forms of exploitation.

Rights of Migrant Women

Not surprisingly, given the types of migration discussed above, some migrant women are especially vulnerable to deprivation, hardship, discrimination, and abuse. Their status as migrants and their status as women both put them at risk. They have limited access to employment and generally earn less than men and native-born women. Legally, many migrant women are vulnerable if their residence is dependent upon a relationship with a citizen or "primary migrant." Migrant women, particularly forced migrants, face real risks of physical and sexual abuse during travel and in the country of destination. In short, the rights of migrant women are violated frequently, drastically, and all too often with impunity.

The rights of migrant workers have been specifically enumerated in various international instruments. In 1990, the General Assembly of the United Nations adopted the International Convention on the Protection of the Rights of All Migrant Workers and Members of Their Families. The convention reaffirms basic human rights norms and embodies them in an instrument applicable to migrant workers and their families. It was recognized that this group of people is often in a vulnerable and unprotected position, especially given the added problems encountered from clandestine movements and trafficking in workers. The underlying goal of the convention, therefore, is to guarantee minimum protection for migrant workers and members of their families who are in

Traditional Sunday meeting of Filipino maids, 1996.(Setboun Michel/Corbis Sygma)

either a legal or an undocumented/irregular situation. Its implementation could significantly encourage basic humane treatment of all migrant workers. However, the number of states ratifying the convention is still disappointingly small.

Although there is an increasing focus on women's rights and the special needs of migrant women in the international community today, this knowledge has rarely been translated into effective policies. To move forward, there must be greater awareness and understanding of the conditions and needs specific to migrant women. Countries may need to take steps to ensure that migrant women have equal access to projects and services so that they can fully participate in and benefit from them. In some cases, there is need to design and implement migrant women–specific projects and services because mainstream programs are inappropriate to the needs of this population.

One area that has received attention and support from governments is education to combat trafficking in women (IOM 2000). Accurate, timely information about migration and trafficking that is disseminated to would-be migrants gives them the means to make an informed choice about migrating. Information is thus an important empowerment tool, diminishing the possibility of traffickers being able to exploit a lack of knowledge in potential migrants.

The education campaigns are aimed at preventing the victimization of migrants, but once they do try to enter, governments also grapple with defining the standards governing the treatment accorded to them. Three issues serve as examples. First are the rights of migrants attempting illegal entry to be protected from physical abuse at the hands of smugglers, other predators, and immigration officials. Second are witness-protection and other programs for those who testify against smugglers. Often, successful prosecution of traffickers requires the cooperation of those who have been smuggled into the country. Third are programs for the safe and orderly return of smuggled women to their home countries. Smuggled aliens who are stranded or apprehended often do not have the resources to return home. Abused migrants may need special help to return home.

Impact of Migration on Gender Relations

International migration profoundly affects gender relations, particularly the role of women in households and communities. The impacts are complex. In many respects, migration enhances the autonomy and power of women. When women from traditional societies migrate to advanced industrial societies, they become familiar with new norms regarding women's rights and opportunities. If they take outside employment, they may have access to financial resources for the first time. Even if their pay is pooled with other family members, this new wage-earning capacity often gives women greater ability to direct household priorities.

Women who are left at home as their husbands migrate also experience changes in their role. The stay-at-home spouses may now have greater household and economic responsibilities. Although they may be financially dependent on remittances from their overseas relatives, the women may have substantial autonomy over decisions about how the funds will be used. Should their husbands not return home, or stop sending remittances, the women may have to assume even greater responsibility for themselves and their children.

In other respects, migration can serve to reinforce traditional gender roles. This is particularly the case when women are expected to preserve cultural and religious norms that appear to be under attack. This process could be seen, for example, in Afghan refugee camps in Pakistan, where *purdah*, the separation of men and women, was practiced more rigidly than in Afghanistan itself. Upon return to Afghanistan, the Taliban leaders carried the intensified practice back, imposing it on the whole country.

International migration can lead to generational tensions, particularly when children adapt more quickly than their parents to a new language and social system. Seeing their children adopt unfamiliar practices may prompt some immigrant women to recommit themselves and their families to more traditional, often patriarchal mores.

Immigration rules can also reinforce traditional roles. Because many migrant women obtain legal residency status through family reunification or formation, their ability to exercise rights may be limited by their spouses' willingness to support their immigration claims. Migrant women who are victims of spousal abuse, for example, may be unwilling to leave the abuser if he controls access to legal status. In recognition that immigration laws can make women and their children vulnerable, the United States passed legislation permitting abused women to petition on their own for permanent residence.

It is not only the role of women that may change dramatically through international migration. Men's roles change as well. They must often adjust to their wives' and daughters' new participation in the labor market with the greater economic autonomy that accompanies wage earning. The adjustment may be particularly difficult in forced-migration situations. Women in refugee camps generally continue to be productive members of their families, responsible for such domestic activities as food, water, and firewood collection, preparation of meals, and other household chores. By contrast, men often find that they cannot fulfill their traditional productive role in agricultural or other employment. Adolescent boys may have no economic alternatives other than joining military forces. The frustrations experienced by men can result in increased family tensions, domestic violence, depression, and/or alcoholism.

Policy Impacts

Just as migration can affect gender roles, changing gender roles can influence immigration policies. The growing participation of native-born women in the labor force has helped precipitate programs for admission of foreign workers to undertake child care, elder care, housekeeping, and other services. For example, the United States and Canada have explicit programs for admission of "au pairs" and "live-in caregivers," respectively, who provide such services. Lagging behind but also under consideration are programs that give work permits to the spouses of executives, managers, and professionals, in recognition that many of these highly sought migrants will not move if their spouses arc unlikely to carry on their own professions. In announcing a pilot program for spousal work authorization, the Canadian government acknowledged the "modern two-career family" and stated there was a need for "labour market and immigration policy to reflect this reality" (Citizenship and Immigration Canada 1998).

Discriminatory immigration and citizenship policies are also under review. As discussed above, some countries have instituted special measures to protect the immigration rights of victims of domestic violence. Citizenship laws with gender discriminatory provisions have also been changed in some countries. For example, until 1977 a child born abroad only had a claim to Canadian citizenship if the father was Canadian or if the child was born to an unmarried Canadian mother. The Citizenship Act of 1977 allowed children born abroad to a married Canadian mother to apply for Canadian citizenship. By contrast, the U.S. Supreme Court upheld significantly more stringent requirements for citizenship for children born outside the United States to an out-of-wedlock father. The children born out of wedlock to U.S. citizen fathers cannot obtain citizenship unless paternity is established before the child is eighteen years of age and, if the child is still a minor, the father agrees to provide financial support until the child is eighteen years of age. There are no time limitations or strict financial requirements if the mother is the U.S. citizen.

Susan F. Martin

See also: Asylum; Citizenship; Clandestine Migration; Economic Determinants of International Migration; Economic Effects of

Migration; Ethnic Cleansing; Family Reunification; Filipino Diaspora; Guestworkers, Europe; Migrant Rights; Migration Policy; Naturalization; Refugees; Remittances; Skilled Migration; Trafficking; UN Convention on the Rights of Migrant Workers, 1990; UN Convention Relating to the Status of Refugees, 1951; Women, Globalization, and Immigration

References and further reading:

Boyd, Monica. 1999. "Gender, Refugee Status and Permanent Settlement." *Gender Issues* 17 (Winter): 5–25.

Chant, Sylvia. 1992. *Gender and Migration in Developing Countries.* London and New York: Belhaven.

Citizenship and Immigration Canada. 1998. *Pilot Project to Help Canadian Employers Attract Highly Skilled Temporary Workers,* http://www.cic.gc.ca/english/press/98/9853-pre.html.

Immigration and Naturalization Service. 1998. *Statistical Yearbook.* Washington, DC: U.S. Government Printing Office.

International Labour Organization. 1999. *International Labour Migration Database.* Geneva: ILO.

International Organization for Migration. 2000. *World Migration Report: 2000.* Geneva: UN Publications.

Kelson, Gregory A., and Debra L. DeLaet, eds. 1999. *Gender and Immigration.* New York: New York University Press.

Kofman, Eleonore, Annie Phizacklea, Parvati Raghuram, and Rosemary Sales. 2000. *Gender and International Migration in Europe.* London and New York: Routledge.

Martin, Susan Forbes. 2003. *Refugee Women.* Lanham, MD: Lexington.

Momsen, Janet Hensall. 1999. *Gender, Migration and Domestic Service.* London and New York: Routledge.

Morokvasic, Mirjana. 1984. "Birds of Passage Are Also Women." *International Migration Review* 18, no. 4: 886–907.

Pessar, Patricia. 1999. "Engendering Migration Studies: The Case of New Immigrants in the United States." *American Behavioral Scientist* 42, no. 2: 577–600.

Turner, Simon. 1999. "Angry Young Men in Camps: International Assistance and Changing Hierarchies of Authority amongst Burundian Refugees in Tanzania." UNHCR Working Paper 9. Geneva: UN High Commissioner for Refugees.

UN Population Division. 2003. *Trends in Total Migrant Stock, 1960–2000: 2003 Revision.* New York: United Nations.

Willis, Katie, and Brenda Yeoh. 2000. *Gender and Migration.* Cheltenham, UK, and Northampton, MA: Edward Elgar.

Zlotnik, Hania. 2003. "The Global Dimensions of Female Migration." Migration Information Source, http://www.migrationinformation.org/Feature/display.cfm?ID=109 (cited March 1, 2003).

Geneva Convention

See UN Convention Relating to the Status of Refugees, 1951

Genocide

Genocidal policies have generated a substantial portion of the forced migrations of the twentieth century, a period described by Holocaust survivor Hugo Gryn as "the century of the refugee." Certainly some of the largest refugee movements—such as Armenians during and after World War I; Jews and others during the Nazi era; and Kurds, Bangladeshis, former Yugoslavs, Burundians, and Rwandans from 1945 to the present—have been directly connected to attempts at genocide (defined here as the physical or cultural destruction of groups, or part of groups, usually minorities, perceived by perpetrators as dangerously different). It is no accident that the two key pieces of United Nations international legislation in this respect—the 1948 Convention on the Prevention and Punishment of the Crime of Genocide and the 1951 Convention Relating to the Status of Refugees (Geneva Convention)—have similar origins. Both largely relate to developments during the Nazi era, and especially World War II. It is important to note that the reference point of these conventions was mainly European and their context time-specific, leading to increasing problems of implementation as the problems they refer to have evolved and become truly global.

The study of genocide is still in its infancy. Academic research on refugees, whether at a level of detailed case studies or more theoretically, is also relatively undeveloped, even within the growing area of migration studies. It is not surprising that the connection between genocide and refugees remains almost totally unexplored. International developments in the first half of the twentieth century, culminating in the 1951 Geneva Convention, provide the background for this area of study today.

The Impact of World War I and the League of Nations

Before the twentieth century, few Western nations had either the state apparatus or the legislation to stop the free movement of people. In addition, countries such as Britain, France, and the United States had, as part of their national mythologies, a commitment to granting asylum to those fleeing persecution outside their borders. By the turn of the twentieth century, however, growing nationalism and racialism, as well as the attempt to define citizenship within the nation-state, led to the first major immigration controls. Even so, in the case of Britain, the Aliens Act (1905) exempted those immigrants seeking entry "solely to avoid persecution or punishment on religious or political grounds." World War I intensified the insular tendencies of the pre-1914 period, and most, if not all, Western nations implemented racially exclusive immigration controls after 1918. A classic example was the "quota laws" imposed in the United States in 1921 and 1924, which discriminated against immigrants from eastern and southern Europe and worked in favor of "Nordics" or "Anglo-Saxons" from the west and the north. With such legislation came increasing documentation, such as passports and visas, the requirements for which increased the misery and uncertainty of those seeking flight.

World War I had important implications for migration both inside and outside of Europe. For the first time, the scale and nature of refugee movements were so problematic that they became the focus of international politics. By the mid-1920s, for example, there were still close to 10 million European refugees displaced either directly or indirectly as a result of the war. These desperate people had no protection in international law. As Michael Marrus has stated, "Before the establishment of the League of Nations High Commission for Refugees in 1921, private agencies not only shouldered the principal burden of refugee aid but coordinated international efforts as well" (Marrus 1985, 82).

Among these refugees were the survivors of the Turkish genocide of Armenians in which perhaps half of the communal Armenian population of an estimated 1.5 million had died. But this was only the most egregious World War I example of, in modern terminology, "ethnic cleansing." The redrawing of the map of Eastern Europe, and the effects of civil war, anti-Semitism, and revolution in this vast region, were initially the prime focus of the League of Nations High Commissioner for Refugees (LNHCR). Two million displaced Russians and Ukrainians alone were destitute. Under the inspired leadership of the Norwegian Fridtjof Nansen, the scope of the LNHCR expanded beyond Eastern European refugees, in spite of the indifference and antipathy of many of the member states and those who were outside the region, such as the United States. Nansen attempted to address the problem of documentation, or its absence, through the creation of "passports" for the stateless, such as Armenians. "Nansen" passports, although limited in scope, at least gave refugees some status in a Western world increasingly driven by bureaucracy.

Of equal or even greater importance was the role of the International Labour Organization (ILO), which helped to integrate refugees by easing their employment in various European countries. Most receptive was France, which actively recruited immigrants from across Europe. Some one-third of its 1.5 million foreign workers were refugees—including Russians, Armenians, Greeks, and Italians. The successful integration of large numbers of refugees in France illustrates that such influxes were not always perceived by contemporaries as a "problem." Indeed, France rightly saw them as the solution to its loss of workers and overall population loss during the war. Not all were welcomed—those from its colonies, for example, were seen as racially undesirable—but generally France replaced the United States as the main destination of European refugees in the 1920s. With its desire for mass immigration, its commitment to the concept of asylum remained powerful. This commitment was rapidly reversed in the late 1930s, however, as more xenophobic and intolerant tendencies increased, paving the way for the Vichy regime. The welcome extended to immigrants was fragile without international legal or institutional backing.

The 1930s and the Evian Conference

By the later 1920s, through the efforts of the LNHCR and the ILO, and with the relative stabilization of Europe, the number of stateless refugees decreased markedly from its postwar peak. Nevertheless, the fragility and powerlessness of the international bodies was exposed in the 1930s as yet another refugee crisis emerged from within Europe. Most famous of the refugees were the Jews escaping the ever-increasing boundaries of the Third Reich. Alongside them, however, were 400,000 refugees from the Spanish Civil War (1936–1939), many of whom fled the border to France and were treated with increasing animosity; Italian refugees from fascist Italy; and smaller numbers of Ethiopians, victims of the brutal colonial policies of Benito Mussolini.

It was Jewish refugees, however, who were at the center of international discussions about refugees during the 1930s, although there was a constant desire not to emphasize that fact. It is often assumed that the large Jewish refugee movements in the modern era were confined to the late tsarist period and to the years of the Third Reich. In fact, there was much more continuity throughout the period as a whole. Indeed, it was the post-1918 period, with civil war, intense nationalism, and famine in Eastern Europe, that led to much more extensive violence against Jews (including pogroms that have been described as genocidal) than had occurred at the turn of the century and, as a result, to a desperate search for refuge. State anti-Semitism in Poland, Hungary, and Romania, which together were home to nearly 5 million Jews, intensified the Jewish desire to leave. Countries such as Britain and the United States, which had previously been major destinations for Eastern European Jews, were now determined to keep out those considered racially and politically undesirable. The newly expanded state structures dealing with aliens were particularly concerned about the potential numbers involved. The bureaucratic, political, and cultural animosity in Western nations toward Eastern European Jews, which extended as far as South Africa and Australia, was to continue throughout and beyond the Nazi era.

The Nazi persecution of the Jews was incremental and immensely complex in its development. It is unfair, for example, to criticize contemporaries before World War II for not anticipating the horrors of the "Final Solution," that is, the total physical extermination of the Jews. Nevertheless, by 1939 it was clear that there was no place for the Jews in "Greater Germany"—Germany, Austria, and annexed Czechoslovakia. By then the Jews in the Third Reich had been outlawed, stripped of all rights, their wealth and property confiscated, and subject to increasing physical violence—the "Kristallnacht" pogrom of November 1938 had left more than 100 dead, much to the shock of the outside world.

Jewish emigration from the Third Reich in its early years corresponded to the level of persecution. Some 60,000 refugees had left Germany by the end of 1933, most of them Jews. France, again, played the leading role, with just less than half of the refugees finding refuge there. In contrast, by April 1934 the United States had only taken in 2,500 German refugees. Thereafter, France's role diminished, and the increasingly desperate search for asylum led the refugees from Germany to a wide range of other countries. Britain, which had been given the Mandate to Palestine in 1920 by the League of Nations, allowed in 25,000 German Jewish refugees by 1935 but thereafter attempted to limit the number to appease Arab unrest.

In July 1935, James McDonald, the new League of Nations high commissioner, highlighted the work that had been done in helping to resettle so many German refugees, stating that "nearly the whole credit is due to private organizations and individuals, Jewish and non-Jewish" (McDonald 1935, 5–6). Later that year, with Nazism's legal anti-Semitism intensifying, and the potential number of refugees increasing, McDonald, a true humanitarian successor to Nansen, resigned his post. He again praised the private organizations, but he made clear that their task would be impossible if the League of Nations was unable "to remove or mitigate the causes which create German refugees" (McDonald 1936, 6). McDonald's warnings to address the problem at its source were not heeded, and in March 1938, with the *Anschluss,* the German annexation of Austria, an even greater refugee crisis was created. Some 200,000 Jews living in Austria were subject to intensive anti-Semitism in the weeks following the Nazi takeover.

Out of a mixture of genuine sympathy and a desire to control the scope of American responsibility, President Franklin D. Roosevelt called an international conference on refugees, which was held at Evian in July 1938. The Evian Conference has been subject to much criticism. Many see it as an exercise in cynicism where sympathy was demonstrated but no meaningful action was taken. It is certainly the case that few of the thirty-two countries attending pledged to open up their doors of entry. The reasons given were largely economic relating to the global depression. Unemployment was high in most Western countries. Others were more concerned about anti-Semitism being "imported" into their countries if sizable numbers of Jews were allowed entry. The fear of anti-Semitism reflected the earlier and ongoing concern about Eastern European Jews—it was assumed that Jews, as undesirable aliens, brought anti-Semitism with them. It was for this reason that the focus of the Evian Conference on *Jewish* refugees was never recognized officially.

The most prominent result of the Evian Conference was the creation of a new international body, the Intergovernmental Committee on Refugees (IGC). Its aims were, first, to "to improve the present conditions of exodus and to replace them by conditions of orderly emigration," and second, to encourage receiving countries to develop "opportunities for permanent settlement." It certainly failed on the first count—Jewish emigration was officially encouraged by the Third Reich until 1941, and the removal of the Jews was done in the most humiliating and unsystematic way possible. This humiliation was an integral part of the expulsion process: By degrading Jews, the Nazis encouraged Germans to view them as objects of loathing; by stripping Jews of their possessions, the Nazis made them less "desirable" to possible places of refuge. On the second count, some limited progress was made. Britain, particularly, relaxed some of its immigration control procedures, and 40,000–50,000 refugees were allowed in, largely on temporary transit visas, between the Anschluss and the outbreak of war. Although some, especially the elderly and infirm, found the prospect of emigrating too daunting to attempt, by 1939 all Jews under Nazi rule realized that only further persecution awaited them if they remained. Other, more unusual places of entry were found, such as Shanghai, which allowed in roughly 20,000 Jews, as did Bolivia. All in all, fewer than 400,000 Jews, well less than half the Jewish population of Germany, Austria, and Czechoslovakia in 1933, escaped before the outbreak of war.

It is difficult to generalize about the responses of governments, state structures, and publics to this movement. Anti-Semitism played its role, leading, in the case of Canada, to the infamous comment of one Canadian official that "none is too many." Humanitarianism and genuine shock at Nazi anti-Semitism was also present, even among some who held personal antipathy against the Jews, such as British Prime Minister Neville Chamberlain. Indeed, the majority of reactions and responses were ambivalent and led to policies that were neither totally positive nor negative. A good example of this was the open-ended Kindertransport scheme in Britain, which enabled 10,000 children to escape yet denied entry to most of their parents. Although the number of Jewish refugees who reached Britain has recently been revised upward to 80,000, it has been pointed out that over half a million people applied for entry. British officials tried to restrict entry to what one called "the right kind of refugee," that is, those who were skilled and westernized, not Eastern European Jews, who were seen as coming from inferior or dangerous stock.

Much of the literature on the responses to the Jewish refugee crisis has focused on the state. What has not been sufficiently acknowledged is the role of many thousands of ordinary people who campaigned on behalf of the persecuted and in many cases offered their homes and support. In comparison to pro-fascist and anti-Semitic organizations, grassroots, pro-refugee organizations have been unfairly neglected. But, as James McDonald was aware, their role was essential.

World War II and Genocide

By World War II, the ambivalence that the liberal democracies had illustrated during the 1930s had been replaced by more negative responses to Jewish refugees. France interned many of its refugees at the outbreak of war; French xenophobic and anti-Semitic tendencies reached their climax later in the war when Vichy officials, rather than the Nazi regime, began to deport foreign Jews "eastward." Some 70,000 Jews from France were murdered in Auschwitz, and over two-thirds of these had been refugees. Britain, in the crisis period of 1940 when invasion seemed inevitable, interned 27,000 "enemy aliens," mainly Jews who had fled from Nazism. It also canceled all visas for entry granted before the war and made it extremely difficult for Jews to enter. Although some Jewish refugees entered the United States in the first years of the conflict, the U.S. government continued its discriminatory quota policies. Meanwhile, Nazi expansion across Europe drastically increased the number of Jews under Nazi control. Some 400,000 managed to escape from Poland to the Soviet Union. Though treated harshly—many were sent to labor camps in Siberia—these refugees, numbering over a quarter of a million, constituted the largest group of Jews on the continent to survive the war.

The vastness and comprehensiveness of the forced population movements and genocidal policies imposed by the Nazi state are still being assimilated by historians and others. It is widely known that the victims of genocide included 6 million Jews and anywhere between half a million and 2.5 million Gypsies, but many other ethnic and religious minorities and national groups also suffered severe losses. At least 30 million Europeans were displaced during the war, many through the Nazis' attempts to reorder the "racial" map of Europe. Late in 1943, the United Nations Relief and Rehabilitation Administration (UNRRA) was created. It was overwhelmed in 1945 when confronted with the scale of displacement. Before then, Western efforts to help the victims of Nazism had been limited.

Due to public pressure from pro-Jewish campaigners in Britain and America, a conference on refugees was held in Bermuda in April 1943. The Anglo-American Refugee Conference has been regarded, like the Evian Conference five years earlier, as a sham exercise. Held behind closed doors, it followed a carefully controlled agenda. And like Evian, although the major internal focus of the conference was *Jewish* refugees, the official proclamations did not accept that particularity. Officials and politicians were driven by two contradictory considerations—first, that "rescue" of Jews was impossible, and second, that the Nazis might "flood" the Western Allies with Jewish refugees, causing economic havoc and stimulating anti-Semitism. A year after the conference, when the million Jews in Hungary were under Nazi control, and with the gas chambers of Auschwitz working at full capacity, the British home secretary wrote that it was "essential that we should do nothing at all which involves the risk that the further reception of refugees here might be the ultimate outcome" (Herbert Morrison, July 1, 1944, in National Archives, FO 371/42807 WR170, quoted in Bauer 1994, 188).

The most tangible result of the Bermuda conference was the revival of the Intergovernmental Committee on Refugees. Understaffed and underfunded, its impact was minimal, although it did relax visa restrictions in minor ways that aided the movement of refugees into neutral countries. Much more impressive was the War Refugee Board (WRB), set up in January 1944 by President Roosevelt owing to pressure from those within the U.S. Treasury Department who believed their colleagues in the State Department had deliberately suppressed information about the Nazi extermination program. With official backing, but supported financially largely by American Jewry, the WRB claimed at the end of the war to have helped save the lives of 200,000 people through rescue and relief.

There is still much controversy about Western Allied responses to the Holocaust and especially policies toward Jewish refugees. Although the issues involved are highly emotional, context and balance are critical. Many Jews were beyond reach once Nazi control of Eastern Europe was established. Nevertheless, tens of thousands of Jews did escape, and many schemes to help Jews, either by offering relief or documentation, were turned down by the British and U.S. governments regardless of their feasibility. Until autumn 1941, emigration was still the Nazi "solution" to what they perceived as the Jewish problem. At this stage, the Jews were not beyond rescue, but the Western democracies were nevertheless being highly selective in the refugees they allowed entry. The anti-refugee/anti-Semitic tendencies of the 1930s came to a head during World War II. The Holocaust, though ultimately a result of the determination of the Nazi elite to destroy the "Jewish peril," was also enabled by many local initiatives in both Western and Eastern Europe.

Post-1945: The Geneva Convention and UNHCR

The refugee crisis after 1945 outweighed the one that had followed World War I. The role of UNRRA, largely under U.S. control, was circumscribed, and the Soviet Union was wary of its existence. UNRRA followed a policy, wherever possible, of repatriation, often leading to brutal population movements, especially for those forced to go back to the Soviet Union. After much debate in 1945 and 1946 in a growing Cold War context, the United Nations member states eventually agreed to create the International Refugee Organization (IRO) to deal with the remaining refugees in Europe, hundreds of thousands of whom still languished in displaced persons camps. Most were integrated into Western Europe, and only a minority were sent back "east." Like the ILO before it, the IRO had its greatest success in helping to ensure the economic integration of the refugees. In this, the United States played a leading role alongside Britain and other Western European countries. Jewish displaced persons faced greater difficulties than their non-Jewish counterparts. Prewar animosity to those from Eastern Europe continued—Jewish displaced persons were seen as poor workers, communistic, of inferior stock, and too exclusive. In addition to state discrimination in Britain and the United States, the doors of entry to Palestine were still largely closed, leading to increasing British-Jewish tension.

The IRO was not seen as a permanent body, and in 1949 the United Nations High Commissioner for Refugees (UNHCR) was established. A compromise between those who saw it as having a temporary, limited function and those who believed it should have a global, ongoing role, initially UNHCR had a limited budget and influence. It was shaped by the experience of World War II and the Cold War, and much of its expertise was focused on Europe. Nevertheless, within it the seeds of its later international role (as well as its continuing underfunding) were there from the start. The universal and particular focuses were present in the 1951 Geneva Convention.

The Geneva Convention defined refugees as "any person who owing to a well founded fear of being persecuted for reasons of race, religion, nationality, membership of a particular social group or political opinion, is outside the country of his nationality and is unable, or owing to such a fear, is unwilling to avail himself of the protection of that country; or who, not having a nationality and being outside the country of his former habitual residence, is unable, or owing to such a fear, is unwilling to return to it." It established the principle of "non-refoulement," that is, the prohibition on returning an asylum seeker to a country in which they might be persecuted. The convention has survived for half a century because of the universal aspirations that it reflects. Its particularity to time and place, however, have created problems. For example, the types of persecution listed do not confront the problem of war, especially civil war, or the problems of the internally displaced. In the early twenty-first century, many Western leaders have criticized the Geneva Convention for being too open-ended. Those from developing regions see its definitions as restricting and its terminology often irrelevant to contemporary problems.

Rwanda

The problems and complexities of genocide come to the fore in a more recent example—that of Rwanda in 1994. It would be impossible here to do justice to the causes and outcomes of this conflict, a genocide in which a now estimated 800,000 Rwandans—mostly Tutsi—were murdered in a matter of weeks. It is important in this context to highlight the scale of refugee movements in the critical period from 1990 to 1994, which provided the immediate backdrop to the genocide.

The country's civil war, precipitated by the invasion of the Tutsi-dominated Rwandanese Patriotic Front (RPF) from Uganda in 1990, led to the internal displacement of at least 1 million people in the north of the country, mostly from the majority Hutu population. Many of the participants of this invasion were themselves children of an earlier wave of Rwandan refugees from the 1960s and 1970s. With further ethnic polarization, many Tutsi fled to other countries. The continuing war and political unrest reached a breaking point when President Juvenal Habyarimana's plane was brought down on April 6, 1994, on his way back from having signed an international peace accord with the RPF at Arusha, Tanzania. An extremist group of Hutus seized power and proceeded to launch a systematic, countrywide extermination of Tutsi (as well as moderate Hutu). The majority of Tutsi who survived did so by fleeing Rwanda to neighboring countries. With the victory of the RPF in the civil war, however, an even greater flow, this time of Hutu refugees, occurred. Numbering at least 2 million, they fled mostly to the already destabilized eastern Zaire (now the Democratic Republic of Congo). Ironically, many of these people had participated in or supported the genocide, but remained protected by the Geneva Convention.

Rwanda showed yet again the intimate and frightening relationship between genocide and refugees. It also emphasized their vital connection to civil war and the problem of internal displacement, neither of which are adequately addressed in the 1951 convention. Finally, the Rwandan genocide showed that global responsibility for refugees is hopelessly out of balance with wealth and power. For all the anxieties of the prosperous West about the "threat" posed by asylum seekers and refugees, the vast majority of these people are located in the poorest countries on earth.

Tony Kushner

See also: Armenian Diaspora; Ethnic Cleansing; Ethnic Cleansing: Armenia; Ethnic Cleansing: Bosnia-Herzegovina; Ethnic Cleansing: Croatia; Ethnic Cleansing: Germans from Central and Eastern Europe; Ethnic Cleansing: Kosovo; Ethnic Cleansing: Poles from Western Ukraine; Eugenics; Internally Displaced Persons; League of Nations; Nansen and Nansen Passport; Passports; Rwanda and Refugees; UN Convention Relating to the Status of Refugees, 1951; UN High Commissioner for Refugees; Visas

[The author is grateful to Mark Levene for his assistance with the Rwanda section of this contribution.]

References and further reading:
Ager, Alastair, ed. 1999. *Refugees: Perspectives on the Experience of Forced Migration.* London: Continuum.
Bauer, Yehuda. 1994. *Jews for Sale? Nazi-Jewish Negotiations, 1933–1945.* New Haven, CT: Yale University Press.
Bramwell, Anna, ed. 1988. *Refugees in an Age of Total War.* London: Unwin Hyman.
Kuper, Leo. 1981. *Genocide.* New Haven, CT: Yale University Press.
Kushner, Tony, and Katharine Knox. 1999. *Refugees in an Age of Genocide: Global, National and Local Perspectives during the Twentieth Century.* London: Frank Cass.
London, Louise. 2000. *Whitehall and the Jews, 1933–1948.* Cambridge: Cambridge University Press.
McDonald, James. 1935. *Report of the Fourth Meeting of the Governing Body of the High Commission for Refugees.* London: High Commission for Refugees.
———. 1936. "Letter of Resignation." In *The German Refugee and the League of Nations.* London: Friends of Europe Publications.
Marrus, Michael. 1985. *The Unwanted: European Refugees in the Twentieth Century.* Oxford: Oxford University Press.
Noiriel, Gerard. 1991. *La Tyrannie du National: Le droit d'aile en Europe, 1793–1993.* Paris: Calmann-Levy.
Proudfoot, Malcolm. 1957. *European Refugees, 1939–52. A Study in Forced Population Movement.* London: Faber and Faber.
Prunier, Gerald. 1995. *The Rwanda Crisis, 1959–1994: History of a Genocide.* London: Hurst and Company.
Richmond, Anthony. 1994. *Global Apartheid: Refugees, Racism and the New World Order.* Toronto: Oxford University Press.
Simpson, John Hope. 1939. *The Refugee Problem: Report of a Survey.* London: Oxford University Press.
Sjoberg, Tommie. 1991. *The Powers and the Persecuted: The Refugee Problem and the Intergovernmental Committee on Refugees.* Lund: Lund University Press.
Skran, Claudena. 1995. *Refugees in Inter-War Europe: The Emergence of a Regime.* Oxford: Clarendon.
Tuitt, Patricia. 1996. *False Images: The Law's Construction of the Refugee.* London: Pluto.
Vernant, Jacques. 1953. *The Refugee in the Post-War World.* London: George Allen and Unwin.
Zolberg, Aristide. 1989. *Escape from Violence: Conflict and the Refugee Crisis in the Developing World.* New York: Oxford University Press.

German Constitution

See Basic Law (Germany); Germany

German Expulsions

See Ethnic Cleansing: Germans from Central and Eastern Europe; Germany

Germany

Since 1945, Germany has been by far the most popular destination for immigration in the European Union (EU), and it has witnessed net immigration for all but ten years between 1955 and 2002. Between 1945 and 2002, more than 30 million persons arrived in the country, around half of whom were of German or ethnic German origin. The other 15 million were mainly labor migrants until 1973, then dependents and asylum seekers from 1973 onward (Münz and Ulrich 1999). Yet until a change in government took place in 1998, Germany refused to consider itself as a country of immigration. As a result, its policy structures have been among the most restrictive in the EU. For instance, because of Germany's comparatively narrow interpretation of citizenship, relatively few of its immigrants have managed to obtain German nationality. In consequence, there were more than 7.3 million nonnational residents living in the country at the end of 2002, representing 8.9 percent of the population, one of the highest proportions in the EU. The total included almost 2 million Turkish citizens, 1.9 million citizens from other EU member states, and almost 1 million nationals from the former Yugoslavia. Since 1998, however, some tentative steps toward liberalization have been taken, and Germany is set to develop more active labor migration policies once again to meet skills and demographic shortages.

Sources of Immigration

In common with other European countries, Germany's status as a country of immigration stands largely in contrast with its pre-1945 history. During the preceding centuries, large-scale emigration had taken place, first to Eastern Europe, especially Romania and Russia, and later to the New World, and in particular to the United States. Immigration, too, mainly from the east in the form of Polish laborers, was taking place, and in 1913 imperial Germany had more than 1 million foreign residents. Emigration continued during the Nazi era, and during World War II millions of people, mainly from Eastern Europe, were forced to work in German factories. But Germany's history as a country of immigration really begins after 1945. Since then, there have been five main categories of immigrant groups, first to West Germany, and then, from October 1990, to united Germany: World War II refugees, labor migrants, family reunification migrants, asylum seekers, and ethnic Germans. There were also two smaller groups: refugees from Eastern Europe in the 1990s and Jewish immigrants.

German War Refugees and East German Citizens

Between 1945 and 1949, around 12 million Germans were expelled from the formerly German territories of East Prussia, Pomerania, and Silesia as well as from the Czechoslovakian Sudetenland. Two-thirds of these arrived in the Federal Republic of Germany (FRG, West Germany), and the remaining 4 million found new homes in the German

Immigrant children eat a meal at a refugee center in West Berlin. They receive room and board while they await the government's decision to accept them as political refugees or send them back to the last country they came from. (David Turnley/Corbis)

Democratic Republic (GDR, East Germany). Their integration has been largely successful, no doubt aided by their high degree of political organization in the early 1950s, which encouraged the West German government of Chancellor Konrad Adenauer to provide generous financial assistance for the reconstruction of their livelihood. During the 1950s, increasing numbers of GDR citizens also fled their country to settle in West Germany. Between 1949 and 1961, when the Berlin Wall was constructed, around 3 million persons arrived via this route. These, too, were successfully integrated into West German society.

Labor Migration

A key role in West Germany's ability to integrate these millions of war refugees and GDR citizens was played by the country's "economic miracle." West Germany's economy grew by up to 10 percent annually throughout the 1950s. In fact, growth was so strong that even with the additional labor provided by war refugees and GDR citizens, shortages were looming by the mid-1950s. In consequence, the federal government began to sign recruitment treaties with a series of Mediterranean countries to pursue recruitment of temporary workers (so-called *Gastarbeiter,* or guestworkers), especially for the nation's industrial sector. The first such treaty was signed with Italy in 1955, followed by further treaties with Spain and Greece (1960), Turkey (1961), Morocco (1963), Portugal (1964), Tunisia (1965), and Yugoslavia (1968).

The scheme was massively successful, and although estimates vary as to how many young, mainly male workers were actually recruited, the number of resident nonnationals in West Germany rose steadily during the 1960s to reach 4 million in 1973, when Gastarbeiter recruitment was ended in anticipation of the first oil shock. By then, most held permanent positions and long-term work permits; they thereby constituted the core of the country's large nonethnic German immigrant population. Consequently, it is among these nationalities that the highest residence periods can be found: in 2000, 43 percent of Turkish, 53 percent of Italian, and 68 percent of Spanish nationals living in Germany had residence periods of twenty years or longer (all nationalities: 33 percent). The GDR operated a similar program in the 1980s, but on a much smaller scale, and mainly from other socialist countries, such as Vietnam and Mozambique.

Dependent Migration

Following the end of recruitment in 1973, a new source of immigration developed as the former guestworkers began to bring their wives and children to West Germany. As a result of this new development, and contrary to political expectations, the end of recruitment did not signal a gradual reduction in the number of nonnational residents. In fact, the number of nonnational residents increased from 4 million in 1973 to 4.5 million in 1980. Descendants of this first generation have continued to seek partners in their parents' countries of origin. Thus, dependent migration has continued through the 1980s and 1990s and remains a major source of new arrivals in the new millennium.

Asylum Seekers

From the late 1970s onward, West Germany began to emerge as the principal European destination for asylum seekers. Already in 1980, more than 100,000 asylum applications were lodged, and although numbers fell in the early 1980s, the approaching end of the Cold War pushed applications to a new record. Between 1990 and 1993, Germany received more than 1.2 million asylum applications, surpassing 438,000 in 1992 alone. Following a 1993 change in immigration law, applications dropped dramatically, to below 100,000, by 1998 (see Figure G-1). The majority of applications have come from European countries, especially Turkey and Yugoslavia, but other countries, such as Afghanistan, Sri Lanka, Iran, and Iraq, have also featured prominently. Germany remains a major destination for asylum seekers, although since numbers have dropped in the late 1990s, other EU countries, such as the Netherlands, Belgium, and Sweden, have overtaken it in terms of applications on a per capita basis.

Ethnic Germans

Along with Israel, Germany was unique in providing a right of return for members of its ethnic group. In 1953, a law extended West Germany's obligation to provide a home to war

Figure G-1: Annual Asylum and Ethnic German Immigration to Germany, 1978–2002

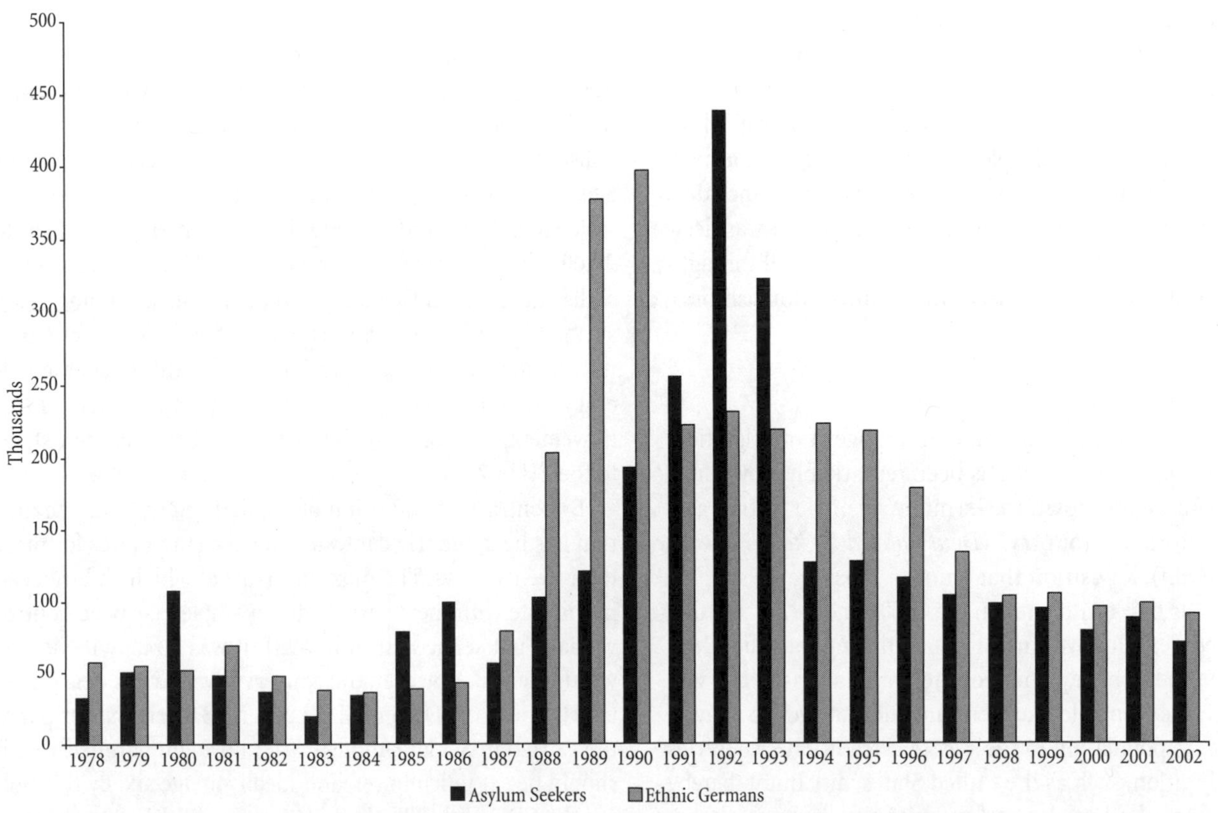

Source: Bundesamt für die Anerkennung ausländischer Flüchtlinge; Bundesverwaltungsamt. Cited in Simon Green, *The Politics of Exclusion: Institutions and Immigration Policy in Contemporary Germany* (Manchester: Manchester University Press, 2004).

refugees to anyone who had suffered persecution as a result of their ethnic German (*Aussiedler*) origin. This included not only those ethnic Germans who remained in Poland after 1945, but also those whose ancestors had emigrated centuries earlier to countries such as Romania or the former Soviet Union. Even though the ability of ethnic Germans to take up this right of return was severely circumscribed during the Cold War, there was nonetheless a steady stream of immigrants numbering around 30,000–40,000 annually. However, by the late 1980s, like asylum seekers, numbers of ethnic Germans had shot up, peaking at 400,000 in 1990 alone. Following the establishment of procedural restrictions and an immigration quota of 225,000 in 1993, numbers have dropped, but, as shown by Figure G-1, they still remain at around 90,000 per annum. No one born after 1993 is granted this right. Between 1950 and 2002, 4.3 million ethnic Germans arrived in Germany. In contrast to nonethnic immigrants, they and their dependents are granted citizenship by right and have access to comprehensive welfare support, including language tuition.

Other Migration

Finally, two other forms of immigration must be mentioned. First, Germany provided sanctuary to around 400,000 temporary war refugees from Bosnia-Herzegovina and Kosovo in the mid-1990s, although by 2000, all but 40,000 of the Bosnian refugees had returned voluntarily. Second, between 1990 and 2001, more than 150,000 Jewish immigrants from the former Soviet Union arrived in Germany. Germany's Jewish community has quadrupled in size, making it the fastest-growing community anywhere in the world, Israel included. As a result, Germany's Jewish population, which was decimated under the Third Reich and remained small throughout the Cold War, has since 1990 begun to flourish once again.

Policy Responses

Despite experiencing such a scale and range of immigration, Germany's policy response has been remarkably slow. Much of this can be put down to Germany's self-definition as a "nonimmigration country" (*Deutschland ist kein Einwanderungsland*), a position that enjoyed cross-party support when it was first formulated in the 1960s and 1970s and that remained default government policy throughout the 1980s and 1990s. In theory, this counter-factual assertion was based on the principle that Germany did not seek to actively increase its population in the way that traditional countries of immigration, such as the United States, did. But it thereby also precluded a broader and more comprehensive discussion about immigration management, citizenship, and integration. The result was a patchwork of uncoordinated policies that developed over a period of some forty years. What is more, Germany's highly gradualist policy-making framework has meant that where policy change has taken place, it has invariably been nothing more than incremental (Green 2004).

At the same time, immigration policy in Germany cannot be detached from the country's Nazi past and its impact on right-wing extremism. Although such parties have never gained a firm foothold in either the West German or united Germany's party system, their occasional successes at regional elections can be put down, albeit not exclusively, to successful politicization of the immigration issue. During the 1990s, the focus has been more on neo-Nazi violence, most notably in anti-immigrant riots in eastern Germany in 1991 and 1992, as well as in fatal arson attacks against Turkish families in western Germany in 1992 and 1993. In response, the federal government attempted to ban one of the main extremist parties in a law overturned by the country's Constitutional Court in 2002.

Despite the slow, nonsystematic nature of German policy responses to issues in immigration management, five main types of policies can be discerned: general policies involving labor migration and family reunification; asylum policies; policies specifically affecting ethnic Germans; residence policies; and citizenship and naturalization policies.

Immigration Policy

Basically, no new labor migration has been permitted since the 1973 recruitment ban, which formally remains in force. However, more recently, some exceptions have been made: Seasonal migration, for instance in agriculture, has been possible since 1990, and in 2000 the government offered up to 20,000 five-year work permits to non-EU nationals to meet skills shortages in Germany's information technology (IT) sector. All parties in Germany remain firmly opposed to permitting low-skilled immigration, and on this basis the federal government secured a seven-year postponement of free movement of labor following the accession of ten new states to the EU in 2004.

By contrast, the question of regulating dependent migration has been bitterly contested in German politics for more than twenty years. The maximum age at which children can immigrate with their parents, for example, has been controversial. First set at sixteen in 1981, it was already the lowest within the EU. However, the conservative parties (the Christian Democratic Union [CDU] and its Bavarian sister party, the Christian Social Union [CSU]) have long argued that it should be set much lower, and ideally at age six. By this policy, the CDU and CSU aimed to maximize the time spent by immigrant children in the German school system, thereby, as they argued, increasing their chances in later life. However, this idea has been rejected by the other main parties ever since the 1980s, and the level in 2002 remained set at sixteen.

Asylum Policy

Asylum policy has always been an emotive issue in Germany. In 1949, asylum was given an unlimited constitutional status by West Germany's Basic Law as a direct response to the persecution of the Nazi era. Germany is also a signatory to both the 1951 Convention Relating to the Status of Refugees and its 1967 Protocol. As long as applications remained low, asylum had little political relevance, but as numbers increased rapidly in the late 1980s, calls from the CDU/CSU to amend the Basic Law became louder. Initially, the political left, represented by the Social Democratic Party (SPD) and the environmentalist Greens, for whom this unique provision has always been of great symbolic significance, refused to provide the necessary parliamentary support. Only in late 1992, in a climate of rising public concern over levels of new applications and amid anti-immigrant riots and sporadic success for extremist parties in regional elections, did the SPD relent and agree to a comprehensive asylum reform. The result was a white list of safe countries of origin as well as the "safe third country" rule. Simultaneously, Germany made far-reaching cuts in asylum seekers' access to welfare in an attempt both to cut costs and to dissuade economic refugees. Introduced in 1993, the new rules had an almost immediate effect in reducing asylum applications.

Germany has been heavily criticized by international refugee organizations, including the United Nations High Commissioner for Refugees (UNHCR), for its narrow interpretation of standards of recognition. It recognizes neither nonstate agents of persecution nor gender-specific persecution, and as a result it has had some of the lowest recognition rates in the EU: Of the 2.6 million applications made between 1985 and 2001, just 8.3 percent were initially recognized by the authorities.

Ethnic German Policy

Like asylum, the right of return for ethnic Germans was more or less unlimited prior to the late 1980s. And their arrival, like that of asylum seekers, caused few political problems as long as their numbers remained low. But in response to the dramatic increase in arrivals in 1989 and especially 1990, the federal government first introduced procedural restrictions in 1990 and in 1992 limited the right to immigrate altogether, declaring that only those born before 1993 would continue to have the right to immigrate solely on the basis of their ethnic German status. Since 1997, ethnic Germans also have had to pass a language test in order to immigrate. As a result, their numbers have dropped, although the highly gradualist solution introduced in 1992 means that ethnic German immigration will continue for some decades to come. What is more, there are generous provisions for dependents: Already in 2001, only 25 percent of arrivals were actually ethnic Germans. The remaining 75 percent, who are not required to pass the language test, were dependents.

Residence Policy

Along with citizenship, Germany's residence policy has been defined more than most areas by the policy maxim of being a nonimmigration country. Because Germany's labor migrants were considered only temporary residents (as the term *Gastarbeiter* implied), permanent residence permits were only issued exceptionally during the 1960s and 1970s. This practice was changed in favor of legal entitlements following a landmark ruling by the country's Constitutional Court in 1978, which was later formalized in a legal reform in 1990. The relatively high requirements for such a permit mean that it is still surprisingly common for nonnationals to reside in the country for many years on nothing more than temporary permits. In part, at least, this is due to the large numbers of asylum seekers who are either still being processed or have been rejected but are unable to leave for humanitarian reasons. In 2001, more than 400,000 people fell into these two categories.

Citizenship and Naturalization

German citizenship policy has traditionally been highly focused on ethnicity. In contrast to France and the United Kingdom, Germany before 2000 never employed *ius soli* in its citizenship laws, instead relying solely on *ius sanguinis.* The epitome of Germany's ethnic and cultural conception of nationality was the 1913 citizenship law, which not only survived World War I, the Weimar Republic, and Nazi Germany but was retained as the basis for citizenship after 1945. In combination with Article 116 of the Basic Law, it extended German citizenship to all GDR nationals, thereby serving the West German government's purpose of undermining the GDR's legitimacy. The very existence of the GDR also ruled out, at least politically, the amendment of the 1913 law to make naturalization easier for Germany's burgeoning nonnational population.

But Germany's citizenship policy has also been decisively influenced by its self-definition as a nonimmigration country. This assumption implied that naturalization could only be an exceptional act, subject to a high standard of proof of integration by the applicant, including high fees and the rejection of dual citizenship. This was the framework laid down in the government's 1977 Guidelines on Naturalization. But when combined with the exclusive reliance on ius sanguinis, under which none of the 2.2 million children born to nonnational parents in Germany between 1974 and 1999 gained

Figure G-2: Annual Naturalizations and Naturalization Rate in Germany, 1978–2002

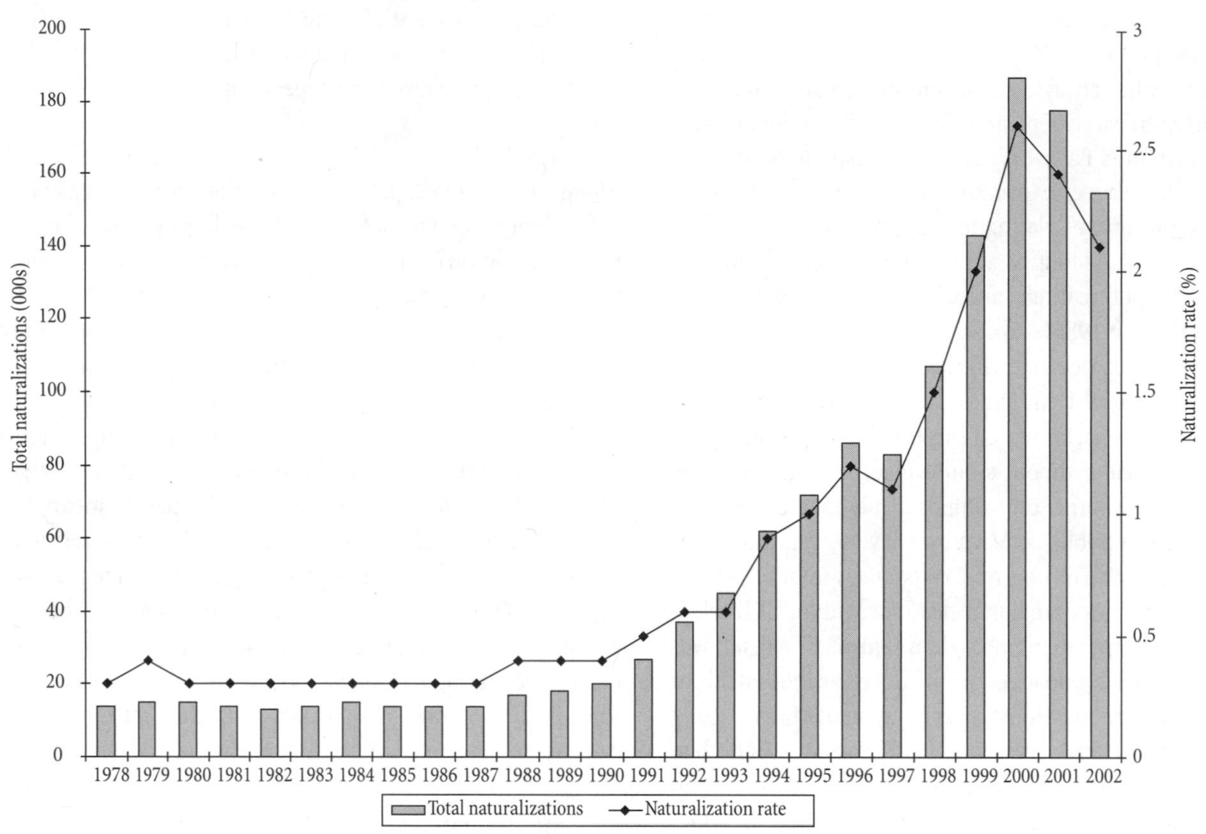

Figures exclude naturalizations of ethnic Germans.

Source: Beauftragte der Bundesregierung, 2002; Statistisches Bundesamt. Cited in Simon Green, *The Politics of Exclusion: Institutions and Immigration Policy in Contemporary Germany* (Manchester: Manchester University Press, 2004).

German citizenship at birth, it meant that few nonnationals were naturalized, despite very long periods of residence. Indeed, during the 1970s and 1980s, the annual naturalization rate of Germany's nonnational population failed to rise above an insignificant 0.4 percent (see Figure G-2).

During the 1980s, the liberalization of citizenship became a major policy goal for the SPD and the Greens, who saw this as a crucial step toward improving the integration of Germany's ever more settled nonnational population. Indeed, the CDU/CSU government acknowledged in 1984 that naturalization levels would have to rise to prevent the permanent exclusion from the political process of a significant section of the population. However, even after unification removed the rationale for retaining the 1913 law, the CDU/CSU remained wedded to its traditional conceptions of citizenship, arguing that naturalization could only take place once integration had been completed, and that successful integration ruled out a nonnational's attachment to another country via dual citizenship. For the same reason, the party also rejected ius soli.

Despite some modest liberalizations in 1990 and 1993, which did produce an increase in naturalizations, the dispute continued through the 1990s. When the SPD and the Greens won the 1998 federal election, a full citizenship reform was at the top of their agenda. A new law came into force in 2000, but only after the CDU/CSU had used a contentious petition campaign to force the government to drop its plans for the introduction of dual citizenship. The law did almost halve waiting times for citizenship to eight years, as well as introduce ius soli for the first time in German history. However, this in fact only applies to about 40–50 percent of all children born to nonnational parents in the country. It also limits the dual citizenship thereby created by requiring beneficiaries to opt out of their parents' nationality by age twenty-three or else lose their German citizenship. Although the naturalization rate rose sharply in 2000, it has since fallen back to only just above pre-reform levels (see Figure G-2), and remains far below that of other European countries with a similar immigration history.

New Policy Challenges

Since the election of the SPD-Green federal government under Chancellor Gerhard Schröder in 1998, much has changed in the debate over immigration in Germany. The self-denial of the reality that Germany is an immigration country has ended, although the new government has found it difficult to depart from established policy norms, such as the rejection of dual citizenship. In consequence, where policy changes have taken place, their impact has been relatively incremental. But immigration remains firmly on the agenda, and a number of different policy challenges can be identified for the coming years. Specifically, labor immigration policy, integration policy, and Europeanization are likely to garner attention in coming years.

An Active Immigration Policy

With skills shortages in key sectors of the economy emerging in 2000, the government has already been under increasing pressure from business interests to permit new labor migration. In addition, its initiative to permit high-skilled migration in the IT sector symbolized its determination to leave the notion of Germany as a nonimmigration country behind. Demographic developments have given this agenda added urgency. Germany's population is predicted to shrink from its current 82 million to around 60–70 million by 2050. Moreover, this smaller population is set to be older as life expectancy continues to rise. As several studies have shown, without new immigration, Germany's social welfare systems, in particular its pension system, will be close to collapse within a generation.

In response, the new SPD-Green government attempted in 2002 to introduce a radical new immigration law that would have introduced points-based high-skilled labor migration, albeit on a strictly limited scale. However, the CDU/CSU opposition firmly opposed such proposals, pointing to Germany's high unemployment rates, and its control of the upper chamber of parliament meant that the bill was ultimately rejected. Although the government has reintroduced the law following the 2002 election, the outcome of its passage through parliament remained open in summer 2003.

Integration Policy

A second policy challenge is the formalized promotion of integration. By 2000, nonnational residents in Germany were displaying severe structural deficits in their socioeconomic situation, most obviously in their much higher unemployment rate, but also in their lower educational attainments (Deutsches Pisa-Konsortium 2001). In its 2002 immigration bill, the government also planned to introduce formalized integration courses drawing on the Dutch model of language and citizenship courses. However, with the bill's rejection, this, too, has been postponed.

Meanwhile, the question of immigrants' legal integration has not been resolved. The immigration bill contained proposals to radically simplify Germany's labyrinthine residence legislation, which would have brought major benefits for all nonnational residents. Once again, the bill's rejection in 2002 means that such improvements have been delayed. In addition, by 2003, Germany had not yet fulfilled its obligation to implement two EU directives on antidiscrimination policy. Finally, the 2000 citizenship reform has so far failed to make much impression on the total numbers of nonnationals, which, once net migration, births, deaths, and even ius soli are taken into account, has effectively remained constant since 1998 at 7.3 million. Without higher naturalization rates, the political exclusion of these residents, over half of whom had residence periods of ten years or longer in 2001, will just be accentuated. This is of particular salience for Germany's 5.4 million third-country nationals, who account for almost half of all third-country nationals resident in the EU.

Europeanization

A third policy challenge is the harmonization of asylum and immigration policies across the EU. As one of the original signatories of the Schengen Agreement of 1985, Germany has warmly supported this development, especially in the area of asylum policy, in which it initially hoped for a full cross-EU system of burden-sharing. However, since the asylum reform in 1992, its enthusiasm has waned as other member states have pressed for standards to be set more liberally than Germany's, especially in the areas of family reunification and asylum policy. Germany is therefore likely to continue to negotiate hard for its interests and standards to be reflected in future compromises at the EU level.

Simon Green

See also: Asylum Determination; Basic Law (Germany); Citizenship; Dual Nationality; Ethnic Germans; European Union; Family Reunification; Israel; Ius Sanguinis; Ius Soli; Law of Return; Safe Country, Safe Third Country; Turkish Diaspora

References and further reading:

Beauftragte der Bundesregierung für Ausländerfragen. 2002. *Bericht der Beauftragten der Bundesregierung für Ausländerfragen über die Lage der Ausländer in der Bundesrepublik Deutschland,* http://www.integrationsbeauftragte.de (cited August 13, 2003).

Brubaker, Rogers. 1992. *Citizenship and Nationhood in France and Germany.* Cambridge: Harvard University Press.

Bundesamt für die Anerkennung ausländischer Flüchtlinge, http://www.bafl.de (cited August 15, 2003).

Deutsches Pisa-Konsortium, eds. 2001. *PISA 2000: Basiskompetenzen von Schülerinnen und Schülern im internationalen Vergleich.* Opladen: Leske and Budrich.

Green, Simon. 2000. "Beyond Ethnoculturalism? German Citizenship in the New Millennium." *German Politics* 9, no. 3: 105–124.

———. 2004. *The Politics of Exclusion: Institutions and Immigration Policy in Contemporary Germany.* Manchester: Manchester University Press.

Herbert, Ulrich. 2001. *Geschichte der Ausländerpolitik in Deutschland.* München: C. H. Beck.

Joppke, Christian. 1999. *Immigration and the Nation-State: The United States, Germany and Great Britain.* Oxford: Oxford University Press.

Layton-Henry, Zig, and Czarina Wilpert, eds. 2003. *Challenging Racism in Britain and Germany.* London: Palgrave.

Münz, Rainer, and Ralf Ulrich. 1999. "Immigration and Citizenship in Germany." *German Politics and Society* 17, no. 4: 1–33.

O'Brien, Peter. 1996. *Beyond the Swastika.* London: Routledge.

Rock, David, and Stefan Wolff, eds. 2002. *Coming Home to Germany? The Integration of Ethnic Germans from Central and Eastern Europe in the Federal Republic since 1945.* Oxford: Berghahn.

Rubio-Marin, Ruth. 2000. *Immigration as a Democratic Challenge: Citizenship and Inclusion in Germany and the United States.* Cambridge: Cambridge University Press.

Statistisches Bundesamt, http://www.destatis.de, various pages (cited August 14, 2003).

Globalization

See Economic Determinants of International Migration; Women, Globalization, and Immigration

Great Britain

See Commonwealth Citizenship and Immigration (UK); European Union; United Kingdom

Greek Diaspora

The Greek diaspora developed along with Greek state-building during the nineteenth and twentieth centuries through massive waves of emigration driven by the political and economic instability of southeastern Europe and the eastern Mediterranean. Its major structuring element was the Greek Orthodox Church under the leadership of the Ecumenical Patriarch of Constantinople. The Greeks in the diaspora number about half as many as those in Greece, and the main diaspora communities are in the United States, Australia, and Germany. Together with new opportunities related to globalization, the Greek diaspora today faces major challenges, some of which originate in the Greek state and its efforts to turn the diaspora into an instrument of its foreign policy. Others relate to centrifugal tendencies.

Along with the Jewish and the Armenian diasporas, the Greek diaspora is usually considered one of the few historical Mediterranean diasporas. Although there can be no doubt about the existence of a Greek diaspora during the past two centuries, historians debate whether older diasporic phenomena, like the prosperous Orthodox merchant communities of southeastern Europe during the eighteenth century, can really be considered "Greek." It is therefore preferable to begin the history of the Greek diaspora with the emergence of a modern Greek national identity at the end of the eighteenth century. The Greek diaspora has undoubtedly inherited a series of cultural, economic, and institutional elements that explain its successful adaptation to a changing international environment. Their roots go as far as the colonizing traditions of the ancient Greek city-states. However, establishing a linear connection between the ancient Greek networks and today's Greek diaspora, in order to give it a historical depth similar to that of the Jewish diaspora, is a dangerous oversimplification.

And yet it would be too restrictive to exclude from the nineteenth-century Greek diaspora the urban populations that lived outside the Greek state but assumed a modern Greek identity, even though their presence there was not the result of a migration out of a Greek "homeland." At that time, a series of Greek urban communities in the Ottoman Empire had developed links with similar communities in France, Austria-Hungary, Russia, and so on, creating a transnational network that played an important role in the commerce between East and West. The Greeks competed with the Jews and the Armenians and contributed to the multicultural atmosphere of cities such as Alexandria (Egypt), Smyrna (Izmir), Salonica, or Constantinople (Istanbul), characterized both by friction and cooperation between structured diaspora communities.

This urban Mediterranean world of diaspora networks was to be short-lived. Under the competition of the French and the British, and as a result of the growth of nationalism, Greeks abandoned their cosmopolitan cities either to find refuge in the homeland or to establish new diaspora communities in Western Europe and the Americas. At the same time, poor Greeks from rural areas sought security and a better fortune in the West.

Thus, from the end of the nineteenth century onward, a new global Greek diaspora came into being while the traditional Balkan, Black Sea, and Mediterranean diaspora gradually disappeared (with the exception of the Greek Russian community). The decline of the old diaspora, the growth of the new one, and the territorial expansion of the Greek state in a context of generalized "ethnic cleansing" in the Balkans and in Asia Minor created a complex pattern of migrations. This pattern is reflected today in the heterogeneity of many important Greek diaspora communities. Thus, the Greek French community is made up of numerous separate groups, including the descendants of immigrants brought to France

Greek immigrants embarking in a small boat bound for America. Patras, Greece, July 11, 1910. (Library of Congress)

during World War I to work in French industry, refugees from Asia Minor, Greeks from Egypt expelled by Egyptian president Gamal Abdel Nasser, political refugees from Greece, and other groups. By contrast, Greeks in Germany mostly came voluntarily after 1945 as workers.

Among the major currents of Greek diaspora formation since the nineteenth century are the following:

1. The rural proletarian emigration from mainland Greece toward the United States during the last decades of the nineteenth century and the first decades of the twentieth (which created the foundations of the Greek American community).
2. The migratory currents related to the Balkan Wars, World War I, the Russian Revolution, the Greek defeat in Asia Minor (1922), and the forced migrations of the Stalin era. Although the majority of the victims of ethnic cleansing sought refuge in Greece, a significant number went to Western Europe or the Americas (such as Aristotle Onasis, the well-known Greek tycoon). The forced migrations of the Pontic Greeks (indigenous communities around the Black Sea) created a Greek Soviet diaspora, largely ignored until the end of the Cold War (a large part of which "returned" to Greece after 1990).
3. The political emigration following the Civil War (1944–1949) and the dictatorship (1967–1974), which created new Greek communities inside the Communist bloc (as far as Central Asia, such as the Tashkent Greek Communist community of the 1950s) and politicized existing Greek communities in Western Europe, the United States, and Canada.
4. The new proletarian emigration of the 1950s and the 1960s, caused by unemployment in Greece and encouraged by the Greek governments. The main destinations were Germany and Australia, although Canada, Belgium, and Sweden also attracted Greek *Gastarbeiter* (guestworkers).
5. Emigration from Cyprus—related to the colonial situation and the tension between the Christian and Muslim communities—created a Greek Cypriot diaspora. Most of its members live in the United Kingdom.
6. Emigration for business has also created or reinforced Greek diaspora communities. In London, there is a large and influential Greek shipping community. The Greek South African business community is also very prosperous.

These and other currents make for a complex map of the Greek diaspora. Population estimates for the most important community, the Greek American, vary from 1 million to 2.5 million. The other communities at the top of the list number as follows: Australia, 500,000; the former Soviet Union, 300,000; South Africa, 100,000; and Argentina, 20,000–40,000. Smaller numbers of Greek immigrants live in Germany, Canada, the United Kingdom (mostly Cypriot), Belgium, Brazil, France, Italy, Sweden, Switzerland, Romania, Austria, Egypt, Holland, New Zealand, Zaire, and Zimbabwe.

Estimates of the total population of the Greek diaspora vary from 4 million to 7 million. Different sources use often contradictory criteria in defining the members and scope of the diaspora. Many sources compare the number of those living in diaspora with the number of Greeks living in Greece (around 10 million), often pointing out that the number of the latter, *Helladic* Greeks, is only approximately twice as large as the diaspora, making the Greek nation highly diasporic. This perspective, however, is usually forgotten in studies of Greece focusing on other matters, and thus the influence of the diaspora on Greek destinies is usually ignored.

The characteristics of the various Greek communities differ widely. Comparisons between the left-wing Greek German proletarian community and the wealthy Greek community of London are difficult. The latter counts among its members the Greek king in exile. It is also difficult to find similarities between the less sophisticated Greek Australians and the Greek intelligentsia communities of Paris or Boston. To the geographical and economic contrasts, generational differences are added: The descendants of the first Greek Americans, who struggled for survival while building the

Panama Canal, are prominent American personalities in politics and academia.

The question of unity is therefore fundamental. The traditional unifying factor for the Greek diaspora was the Greek Orthodox Church. Without exception, when Greeks found themselves together abroad, they founded local church communities that became the focus of their communal life. Those church communities played a fundamental role in reproducing a religious, linguistic, and national identity. They also promoted philanthropic activities that contributed to creating solidarity inside the community and in facilitating the immigration of new members.

The church communities of the Greek diaspora have belonged to the jurisdiction of the Greek Ecumenical Patriarchate of Constantinople. This institution, the most prestigious in the Orthodox world, and which is antinationalist in essence, has seen its influence shrinking during the nineteenth and twentieth centuries with the growth of national churches and the collapse of the Ottoman Empire. The Greek diaspora has gradually become its major field of responsibility. The premodern traditions of the patriarchate explain its success in unifying a diaspora now growing in a postmodern environment. Thus, the Greek diaspora has become a network of local church communities coordinated by the patriarchate.

This global network is structured along wide geographical lines and exercises important local influences. The Greek Orthodox archbishops have a large degree of autonomy and often play a major social and political role in the host countries. In such countries as the United States and Australia, the Greek archbishop can be an influential political personality, especially before important elections.

Until the 1980s, the activity of the church in diaspora found no resistance from the Greek state. The prominent view in Greece was that the Greek diaspora constituted a historical anomaly to disappear sooner or later, either by the "return" of its members to the home country (for which a specific term has been coined: *palinostisis*) or by their assimilation to the culture of the host country. Even the Greek term for "diaspora" was banished from the official vocabulary, which used instead a term meaning "Greeks abroad." In fact, the state was interested in one and only one aspect of the Greek international presence, its influence in covering part of the chronic trade deficit. The remittances of the Greek expatriates represented one of the three contributors to the balance of payments.

Things changed after the Cyprus crisis of 1974. The Greek American community managed to mobilize to defend Greek interests against what it perceived as a pro-Turkish bias in U.S. foreign policy. This movement was extremely effective and gave rise to the influential "Greek American lobby." The politicization of the Greek American diaspora highlighted the role of those in diaspora as central actors in international politics. From that time onward, the Greek state perceived the Greek diaspora as an instrument for its foreign policy; at the same time, the state vied the church as a potential obstacle to it.

The competition between the state and the church became obvious only after 1981, when the Socialist Party of Andreas Papandreou (Panellinio Sosialistiko Kinima, PASOK) came into power. The ideological opposition of the Socialist Party to the influence of the church reinforced the conflict between the two centers (Athens and Istanbul). During the 1980s, the struggle took place on a local basis in the form of competition between church communities and ethnonational associations (which already existed or were created ad hoc). In 1995, an important new step was taken. On the initiative of the Greek government, a Council of Greeks Abroad (Symboulion Apodimou Ellinismou, SAE) was established. The role of this council is to coordinate and organize the Greek diaspora by creating a new network of communities and associations, either religious or ethnonational. Although the official discourse favors the autonomy of the diaspora (the term of "self-organization" of the diaspora is often used), the council is financially and politically dependent on the Greek state, and only the fact that its president is a Greek American differentiates it from a state institution.

The competitive nature of the relationship between the SAE and the Ecumenical Patriarchate was more than obvious. The patriarchate did not support and was even hostile toward creation of the council. Today, however, it is clear that the SAE does not present any real threat to the Ecumenical Patriarchate in its leadership of the Greek diaspora. The state culture makes the SAE unable to cope with the chaotic and heterogeneous character of the diaspora networks, whereas the Greek church can mobilize the community out of its centuries-long experience in network management and coordination.

Along with church and state organizations, numerous institutions structuring the Greek diaspora have arisen in response to the needs of those living in the host countries. Thus, the Greek Americans created the American Hellenic Educational Progressive Association (AHEPA) in 1922 in order "to protect Hellenes from the evils of bigotry and to help assimilate them into American society" (www.ahepa.org). An association of immigrants fighting for recognition in their new environment, the AHEPA has grown into an influential and conservative American institution with chapters in Canada and Australia.

Associations founded on the basis of common geographical origins constitute another important set of institutions. In the Balkans and in the eastern Mediterranean, local and regional identities from the past can be much more deeply rooted than modern national identities. In addition, migration patterns often follow the paths of local networks. For this reason, many of the members of specific diaspora communities have the same geographical origin (Greek villages, cities, or regions). In this way, the Greek diaspora can be perceived as a sum of local and regional diasporas. Among these, the Cypriot diaspora is most easily distinguishable. However, there are also many other regional associations that very often take an institutional form. Thus, the Cretan diaspora is structured around confederations of Cretan associations.

Globalization has offered to the Greek diaspora new opportunities and a visibility that did not exist in the past, when "Greeks abroad" were considered as marginal elements of Hellenism. At the same time, new challenges have appeared, such as the danger of becoming simple instruments of the Greek state. Until now, it has been a challenge that the diaspora has successfully resisted. A new challenge, which is now appearing, is the demand of autonomy from the patriarchate in order to create local Orthodox churches. Thus, in France there is a movement in favor of a French-speaking Orthodox church that could unite Greek French, Lebanese French, Russian French, Serbian French, and pure French Orthodox populations. Similar proposals are emerging in the United States, although the demand for autonomy from Istanbul often takes anti-Turkish tones.

The Greek diaspora is a dynamic phenomenon founded on a Mediterranean diasporic tradition, on a strong national mythology, and on a variety of institutional links, the strongest of which is undoubtedly the church. In a changing world, it is faced with the dilemma of choice between continuity and adaptation. Although its components will certainly survive and prosper, its limits, its structures, and its personality may have to evolve.

Georges Prevelakis

See also: Armenian Diaspora; Colonial Immigration; Ethnic Cleansing; Jewish Diaspora; Remittances; Transnationalism; World War I

References and further reading:

Chimbos, Peter. 1980. *The Canadian Odyssey: The Greek Experience in Canada.* Toronto: MacClelland and Steward.

Clogg, Richard, ed. 1999. *The Greek Diaspora in the Twentieth Century.* Basingstoke: Macmillan; New York: St. Martin's.

Constantinides, Stephanos. 1983. *Les Grecs du Québec: Analyse historique et sociologique.* Montreal: Editions le Meteque.

———. 1991. *The Greeks in Canada: Studies and Documents.* Montreal: Editions le Méteque.

Constas, Dimitri, and Athanassios Platias, eds. 1993. *Diasporas in World Politics: The Greeks in Comparative Perspective.* Basingstoke: Macmillan.

Fossey, John M. 1991. *Proceedings of the First International Congress on the Hellenic Diaspora: From Antiquity to Modern Times.* Vol. 1: *From Antiquity to 1453.* Vol. 2: *From 1453 to Modern Times.* Amsterdam: J. C. Gieben.

Hasiotis, I. K. 1993. *Episkopisi tis Historias tis Neohellinikis Diasporas.* Athens: Vanias.

Hellenic Studies Forum. 1993. *Greeks in English Speaking Countries: Proceedings of the First International Seminar.* Melbourne: Hellenic Studies Forum.

Kitroeff, Alexander. 1989. *The Greeks in Egypt, 1919–1937. Ethnicity and Class.* Oxford: Ithaca.

Moscos, Charles C., Jr. 1989. *Greek Americans: Struggle and Success.* 2d ed. Englewood Cliffs, NJ: Prentice Hall.

Prevelakis, George, ed. 1996. *The Networks of Diasporas/Les réseaux des diasporas.* Paris: L'Harmattan; Nicosia: KYKEM.

Psomiades, Harry, Alice J. Scourby, and John G. Zenelis. 1982. *The Greek American Community in Transition.* New York: Pella.

Saloutos, Theodore. 1964. *The Greeks in the United States.* Cambridge: Harvard University Press.

Guantanamo Bay

Although Guantanamo Bay in Cuba has recently achieved international prominence as a holding place for prisoners captured in the U.S. war in Afghanistan of 2001, the base has a longer history as a short-term camp for people wishing to claim asylum in the United States. Haitian and Cuban asylum seekers were held at the base throughout much of the 1990s before being repatriated, granted asylum in a third country, or gaining entrance to the United States as refugees.

U.S. involvement at Guantanamo Bay, one of Cuba's finest natural harbors, dates back to 1898. In that year, during the Spanish-American War, U.S. Marines landed. In 1903, U.S. officials signed a treaty with Cuba allowing the United States to lease the area surrounding the bay for the purpose of establishing a military base. In return, the United States agreed to pay the Cuban government 2,000 gold coins annually. Between the early 1900s and 1958, the base was used as a staging point for a number of U.S. interventions in Cuba—notably in 1906, when U.S. forces helped to extinguish a revolution. Prefiguring its later use, the base was used as a haven for conservative Cubans escaping further revolutions in 1917 and 1930. It was, however, with the emergence of socialist leader Fidel Castro to power as Cuban president in 1959, resulting in a complete breakdown in U.S.-Cuban relations, that the U.S. presence on the island became most contentious. Despite President Dwight Eisenhower's declaration in January 1961 that the hostility between the new socialist regime in Cuba and the United States had "no effect" on the U.S. use of the base, Castro refused (as he does to this day) to cash checks from the United States as payment for lease of the territory, and he remains implacably opposed to the American presence.

The base first became an extended arm of U.S. immigration and refugee policy in November 1991. The administration of George H. W. Bush decided that, in order to prevent the

A U.S. Army Special Forces soldier speaks to a family of recently arrived Cuban refugees at the Guantanamo Bay refugee camp in Cuba, 1994. (Leif Skoogfors/Corbis)

arrival of Haitian boat people fleeing the aftermath of a military coup in Haiti reaching U.S. territory, coast guards would be ordered to interdict asylum seekers at sea and take them to Guantanamo, where their refugee status could be determined and a decision made on their future. The conditions Haitians faced at Guantanamo were bleak: Most were held in disused cruise ships, and all were deprived of many of the protections they would have had if they had been applying for asylum on U.S. territory; riots subsequently ensued. Although some Haitians received refugee status and were admitted to the United States, U.S. officials searched, largely unsuccessfully, for countries in the region to accept others. The vast bulk of Haitians were eventually repatriated to Haiti following U.S. intervention to restore the democratically elected leader of the country, Jean-Bertrand Aristide, in 1994. By the end of January 1995, there were only a few hundred Haitians left at the camp.

By 1994, Haitians at the base had been joined by Cubans. Most of these people had made their way to Guantanamo, with Castro's permission, following a series of antigovernment riots in Havana in the hope of eventually being resettled in the United States. By November there were some 30,000 Cubans in addition to 20,000 Haitians being held at the base, at an estimated cost of $1 million per day. U.S. policy toward the Cubans was initially that they would have to return to their homes in order to apply for admittance to the United States. Nevertheless, on May 2, 1995, the William Clinton administration announced that the 21,000 Cubans still at Guantanamo would be allowed entry to the United States. Although the Clinton administration later flirted with the idea of using the base to house refugees from the conflict in Kosovo in 1999, the base has not since been used for asylum seekers or refugees since the last Cubans left on January 31, 1996.

The appeal of Guantanamo Bay to U.S. authorities as an offshore holding place for asylum seekers has stemmed primarily from two main factors. First, the base enabled the United States to hold asylum seekers without concern that they would "disappear" into the American community and thus add to the number of clandestine immigrants in the country. Second, the power of the U.S. government over the asylum seekers was not constrained by protections of domestic constitutional law; for example, children born on the island could not claim U.S. citizenship, and their access to lawyers and the courts was either extremely limited or nonexistent.

Just these features of the base made Guantanamo a lightning rod for controversy. The U.S. government was taken to the courts many times during the 1990s over the status of children and juveniles held on the base and over claims of poor general conditions. Despite some victories, the courts were resistant to seeing the base as a place where the full panoply of U.S. law applied. In 1994, the Eleventh Circuit Court of Appeals determined that aliens held at Guantanamo "had no legal rights under the domestic law of the US or under international law." These rights, the court found, were available only to persons on U.S. territory. The court accepted the government's argument that Guantanamo Bay, while under U.S. "jurisidiction and control," was not U.S. sovereign territory (Jones 1995, 498–505).

The implicit lesson of this ruling—that states can liberate themselves from the constraints of domestic law by leasing foreign territory—has been well learnt. Despite incurring international condemnation, the United States has held prisoners of war (or, in the George W. Bush administration's casuistical parlance, "enemy combatants") captured in Afghanistan at the base since 2001. Albeit with less publicity, the lessons of Guantanamo are also on display on the other side of the world: Since 2001, the Australian government has held asylum seekers arriving by boat on its northern shore in camps on territory leased from the impoverished island nation of Nauru.

Matthew J. Gibney

See also: Asylum; Asylum Determination; Border Controls; Cold War; Cuban Migration; Haiti and Refugees; Migrant Rights; Public Opinion and Immigration; U.S. Immigration; Visitors, Immigrants, and U.S. Border Security after September 11, 2001

References and further reading:

Jones, Thomas D. 1995. "A Human Rights Tragedy: The Cuban and Haitian Refugee Crises Revisited." *Georgetown Immigration Law Journal* 9, no. 3: 479–523.

Perusse, Roland I. 1995. *Haitian Democracy Restored: 1991–1995.* Lanham, MD: University Press of America.

Ricardo, Roger. 1994. *Guantanamo: The Bay of Discord.* New York: Ocean Press.

Steyne, Lord. 2003. "Guantanamo Bay: The Legal Black Hole." Twenty-Seventh F. A. Mann Lecture, November 25. Cambridge: Cambridge University.

Guestworkers, Europe

"Guestworkers" are migrants who arrive in a host country on temporary work visas with the expectation that they will return to their country of origin when their labor is no longer needed. It is one of the four archetypal examples of immigration, along with permanent labor migration, family migration, and colonial migration. Guestworker policies have been implemented in the United States, Canada, Japan, South Korea, and the Middle East. The most famous experiment in guestworker policies, however, occurred in Europe, and above all in West Germany from the 1950s to the 1990s. Nonetheless, France, Austria, Switzerland, and the United Kingdom have implemented similar programs. Guestworker policies were of crucial importance for the postwar European economic boom and, over the medium term, for the transformation of Germany, Austria, and Switzerland into multicultural countries.

By the early 1950s, the once-devastated European economy was thriving. Despite having to integrate between 10 million and 12 million ethnic Germans who had been expelled from former German territories and elsewhere in Eastern Europe, Germany faced labor shortages. In the absence of any colonies (which were lost after World War I), Germany looked to establish temporary labor schemes for foreign workers. Guestworker schemes were negotiated with Italy in 1955 (originally for farm workers), and with Greece and Spain in 1961. When these labor sources proved insufficient, new schemes were established with Turkey in 1961, Morocco in 1963, Portugal in 1964, Tunisia in 1965, and Yugoslavia in 1968.

Under these agreements, companies interested in foreign workers would apply to the Bundesanstalt für Arbeit (BFI, Federal Bureau for Labor), which would authorize the recruitment. Companies would send a request for workers to the BFI, it would make a cursory search for local workers, and then it would send the request to its office in Istanbul, where workers would be selected and put on trains or planes for Germany (Martin 2002, 9). Most workers were recruited anonymously, but companies could request workers by name; soon, migrants learned to jump the queue by asking friends working in Germany to request them (ibid.). Although some 20–30 percent of guestworkers came as tourists and then applied for jobs (ibid.), Germany's guestworker system was relatively centralized: Most migrants' applications were made by companies in Germany, and they were approved by the BFI before the migrant left his home country. By 1964, Germany had its millionth guestworker, Armando Rodriquez, whose status was recognized through the gift of a motorcycle and his picture on the front cover of Germany's famous weekly magazine, *Der Spiegel.* Germany's first postwar recession, in 1967, was followed by a noticeable return of guestworkers, encouraging the impression that the rotation policy would work.

As elsewhere in Europe, Germany's guestworker policy ended in the early 1970s in response to wildcat strikes involving guestworkers and a slowdown in the overall European

Turkish guestworker picking grapes during vine harvest, Hunsruck area, Germany. (Albrecht G. Schaefer/Corbis)

economy (almost overnight, growth rates halved, from approximately 5 percent to 2.5 percent annually). At the time of the migration stop, there were 2.6 million guestworkers in the country and 4 million foreigners overall (Wilson 2001, 1). The former figure has been interpreted as evidence of the "failure" of Germany's guestworker policy. In fact, as Philip Martin has pointed out, the majority of guestworkers did leave: Of the 30 million foreigners who stayed in Germany for more than ninety days (that is, those who were more than tourists), 21 million, or 70 percent, left the county (Martin 2000, 9). The problem was that this movement still left 2.6 million.

Germany, along with Switzerland and Austria, was the ideal-type guestworker migration. Britain, which attempted to attract guestworkers but quickly found itself unable to compete with France and Germany, was an ideal-type of colonial migration. France represents a hybrid of the two types. After the war, France looked to a dirigiste economic policy to foster growth. The National Planning Commission adopted a five-year plan after the war (which, though it sounds vaguely Stalinist now, was considered highly forward-looking then) and created a National Office of Immigration (Office National d'Immigration, ONI) to recruit immigrants. By 1953, the French economy, though inflation-prone, was prospering, and the country needed workers. During this period, there was an impassioned debate within the French state about which sort of migrants to attract. Demographers argued for ethnic migration, particularly of Italian Catholics, who could be easily integrated, while the economics ministry, backed by Charles de Gaulle, wanted a race-blind immigration policy. To complicate the debate further, the Communist General Confederation of Workers (Confédération générale du travail) wanted to screen Italian workers for their political sympathies. French policy began by informally following the demographers' dictates, then followed those of the market. When the ONI set up offices for recruiting labor, it limited them to southern Europe in an obvious attempt to privilege European migrants.

Soon, however, these offices were unable to meet the demand in France, or to compete with offers from Switzerland and Germany, and France's guestworker scheme evolved into a colonial migration scheme. From the late 1950s, immigration to France came to be increasingly dominated by North Africans, and especially Algerians (who were free from immigration control, as the country was then part of France). From 1954 until 1962, France's Algerian community increased in size from 7,000 to some 300,000 (Hargreaves 1998, 37). These migrants were taking advantage of better economic opportunities in mainland France, fleeing instability created by the post-1958 Algerian war of independence, and, after independence, taking advantage of temporary free-movement provisions. This development meant that the ONI soon lost control of France's immigration policy. Whereas in Germany some 70 percent of guestworker applications were approved before the workers entered the country, the majority of French guestworkers traveled to France without permission and then regularized their status once they were there. By 1960, it was estimated that only 10–30 percent of immigrants to France were legal (Lynch and Simon 2003, 148).

The claim that guestworker policies were a "failure" is untenable. If nothing else, the workers solved the labor shortages and helped France, Germany, and the rest of Europe (the United Kingdom excepted) to enjoy low-inflation growth throughout 1950s (Germany) and the 1960s (France and Germany). Guestworkers were an essential part of Germany's economic miracle (*das deutsche Wirtschaftswunder*) and France's "thirty glorious years" (*les Trentes glorieuses*). Anyone nostalgic for these years (and most citizens of contemporary France and Germany are) must recognize that immigration played an essential role in them. That said, guestworker programs led to a series of unfulfilled expectations, both for guestworkers and for the countries that invited them.

The guestworkers, and especially the Turks, overestimated how much they would earn in Germany: They believed that they would earn Frankfurt wages and pay Istanbul prices. The relatively high cost of living in Germany forced them, in order to save enough money, to stay on longer than they intended and to bring their families with them (some of whom were welcomed by companies as extra workers) (Martin 2002, 10). Many migrants, as sociological studies have made clear, maintained the myth of return for years and even decades (though this is arguably a common experience among many immigrants, and not simply guestworkers). For France and especially Germany, complete "rotation" clearly did not work, and millions of guestworkers stayed on. At the same time, changes in the European economy meant that the industrial jobs for which they came eventually no longer existed. Some guestworkers, if they were young and had a good grasp of German, were able to find other jobs, but many went from work to permanent unemployment. In Germany, joblessness is particularly high among foreign workers over fifty years of age, that is, among first-generation guestworkers.

In response to high unemployment and anti-immigrant sentiment (and, according to some, following the logic of the original guestworker scheme), both France and Germany offered financial packages for guestworkers who wished to return home; in France, this offer extended to other migrants as well. These policies largely failed. They only had a temporary effect on the number of foreigners in these countries, and the migrants who did depart were (a) the ones most likely to leave anyway, and (b) at least in France's case, precisely the migrants that the country wanted least to lose (Italian, Spanish, and Portuguese citizens). Both countries also attempted to limit family immigration, but the courts largely blocked this effort (though waiting periods were ruled constitutionally acceptable). In the end, both countries had to accept that their guests would stay, and integration became a major issue.

In France, because the country had a long tradition of immigration and a sense of itself as a country of immigration, there was an integrationist philosophy and structure in place. Migrants were expected to abandon, at least in the public sphere, their religious, ethnic, and national peculiarities; to assume French republic values; and to immerse themselves in the French language and culture. At the same time, a cornerstone of France's citizenship law has long been "double ius soli": Children born in France of a parent born in France are French at birth. France's assimilationist framework has not been trouble-free. The republic's commitment to secularism (*laïcité*) has twice led to passionate debates concerning Muslims' right to wear headscarves in schools and other public institutions: in the late 1980s, and in the new millennium (Pfaff 2004). In the former case, the debate led to a national commission on citizenship and informed a 1993 decision (subsequently largely reversed) to restrict access to French citizenship; in the latter, it led to a controversial decision to ban overt religious dress (including headscarves) in schools. But at the very least, France had an assimilationist framework. Germany, by contrast, was divided between a belief that assimilation required efforts on the migrants' part and that the grant of citizenship could only be a culmination of and not a contribution to this process, on the one hand, and an almost postmodern opposition to assimilation as a new version of National Socialist *Zwangsgermanisierung* (forced Germanization), on the other. A moderate, pro-integrationist position did emerge, but the vagaries of Germany's policy-making process meant that a new citizenship law did not take effect until January 2000 (Green 2004).

In Germany and elsewhere, debates about the legacies of guestworker policies are arguments about whether the glass is half empty or half full. Optimists point to better educational attainment, language acquisition, and intermarriage among the second and third generations; pessimists point to continued high unemployment levels for ethnic minorities (approximately twice the national average in Germany), patterns of ghettoization in the large cities, and, since September 11, 2001, Islamic extremism (Martin 2002). The debate cannot be easily resolved, but what is clear is that the guestworker experience has implications for current immigration policy in Europe, especially as demographic pressures make expanded immigration to Europe inevitable.

Above all, policy makers should abandon the myth that there can be large-scale, temporary migration. If migrants are to make a significant contribution to an economy, they will have to integrate into it for a period of years; as they do so, they acquire equities that give them an interest in remaining and a desire to do so. Temporary policies are no more likely to work in the future than they have in the past. At the same time, there is an international competition for high-skilled workers (the only workers any developed country wants), and they are going to compare national benefit packages, of which rights to both family reunification and permanent residence will form an important part. Countries interested in attracting skilled workers would be wise to offer them access to permanent immigration channels, and to expect that the migrants are likely to remain. Unfortunately, Germany's recent "green card" program, and U.S. president George W. Bush's 2004 legalization proposal, respectively, repeated and threatened to repeat the mistakes of the guestworker experience.

Looking at it from another perspective, states welcoming migrants most likely do not have to fear a repeat of the guestworker experience of mass immigration followed by mass unemployment. The boom of the 1950s and 1960s created a very particular demand, no longer found in the West, for unskilled industrial labor; unsurprisingly, it attracted unskilled, poorly educated, and socially immobile workers. The sort of migrants that Europe now seeks will be skilled, flexible, and educated. Policy makers might emulate Canada, which pioneered skills-based immigration and now rewards education and training rather than experience in a particular profession. In short, Europe's experience suggests that immigration policy should seek to attract immigrants rather than paid tourists. To paraphrase the Swiss author Max Frisch, when we ask for hands, we get people.

Randall Hansen

See also: Assimilation/Integration; France; Germany; Skilled Migration

References and further reading:

Green, Simon. 2004. *The Politics of Exclusion: Institutions and Immigration Policy in Contemporary Germany.* Manchester: Manchester University Press.

Hargreaves, Alec. 1998. "Algerians in Contemporary France: Incorporation or Exclusion?" *The Journal of Algerian Studies* 3: 31–47.

Lynch, J. P., and Rita J. Simon. 2003. *Immigration the World Over: Statutes, Policies, and Practices.* Oxford: Rowman and Littlefield.

Pfaff, William. 2004. "Why France Still Insists on Cultural Assimilation." *International Herald Tribune.* July 17.

Wilson, Tom. 2001. "Postwar International Migration: Trends to, from and within Western Europe," 222.socstats.soton.ac.uk/courses/st218318/02_Post-war_intl_migr_in_W_Eup_handout.PDF (cited January 12, 2004).

Guestworkers, Middle East

See Middle East Guestworkers

Gypsies

See Roma

H

Haiti and Refugees

The arrival of boatloads of desperate Haitians on Florida's tourist beaches, especially from the 1970s onward, raised in dramatic fashion some of the core issues of global migration: how to manage relationships between the poorest and wealthiest nations; whether one can distinguish between "economic" and "political" refugees; and how to fashion equitable immigration policies. Haitians have been fleeing political repression and dire poverty since the 1960s. U.S. responses to Haitian boat people have been mixed. They range from forced repatriation or detention to recognition of Haitians as refugees. Haitian immigrants have faced discrimination and challenges of culture and identity as they enter into American society.

Historical and Political Background

Haiti broke from France as an independent nation in 1804 following the only fully successful slave rebellion in the Americas. The Haitian Revolution destroyed the brutal slave system that had created enormous wealth for French planters from the production of sugar. Haiti developed into a peasant-based society as the former slaves established farms throughout the country. The agricultural economy produced food for local consumption and coffee for export. The Haitian state continued the colonial model of extracting wealth from the agricultural producers, principally through taxes on imports and the export of coffee. Members of the upper class depended on the state revenues to fund their lifestyle.

In 1825, Haiti signed a disastrous treaty with France in which the latter agreed to recognize Haitian sovereignty in return for an enormous sum of money (150 million francs to be paid within five years—reduced in 1838 to 60 million francs). Haiti immediately assumed an international debt from which it never recovered. France remained the dominant political and cultural force in Haiti throughout the nineteenth century. The United States maintained trade but not diplomatic relations until the 1860s, in part because it did not want to acknowledge blacks as diplomatic equals.

Haiti's debt ultimately became the cause of the country's loss of sovereignty when, in 1915, the U.S. Marines invaded Haiti, in part to recover its loans. The first occupation lasted nineteen years and placed the United States at the center of Haitian economic and political affairs. The 1934–1957 period was marked by a succession of presidents—heavily dependent upon the military, or Garde d'Haïti. Elections were held after the revolution ousting president Elie Lescot in 1946, after the coup that deposed Dumarsais Estimé in 1950, and once again in 1957, when the corrupt former junta leader Paul E. Magloire was replaced as president by François Duvalier.

For almost thirty years (1957–1986), the Duvalier family maintained tight control over Haiti, largely through the use of terror. The Duvalier government was notorious for its abuse of human rights, and Haiti fell into deep poverty under its stewardship. From the 1970s, the Duvalier government was more open to international investment and occasionally lessened its political repression in response to international pressure. U.S. administrations disdained the Duvalier government but supported it because it maintained order, posed as a bulwark against Cuban communism, and provided a source of cheap labor for offshore American businesses. In 1986, Jean-Claude Duvalier was escorted to exile by the United States and France following a popular uprising.

Jean-Claude Duvalier was succeeded by a series of generals and puppet presidents until 1991, when Jean-Bertrand Aristide, a popular Catholic priest, was elected president by two-thirds of the electorate. Aristide's election raised hope in the Haitian populace but was regarded as a threat by business leaders and the military, who ousted him after nine

"Boat people"—Haitian refugees from economic and political oppression—sail on a rickety boat into Biscayne Bay as they seek asylum in the United States. The boat is followed closely by members of the sheriff's department. When they land in Key Biscayne, the refugees are taken into custody to await processing by the U.S. Immigration and Naturalization Service. 1981. (Nathan Benn/Corbis)

months. The military ruled brutally for three years, killing an estimated 3,000 citizens. The Organization of American States (OAS) placed an economic embargo on Haiti.

In 1994, the United States invaded Haiti and restored Aristide to the presidency. The U.S. decision to restore Aristide to power was motivated in part by the desire to stem the tide of Haitian boat people. The administration of U.S. president Bill Clinton was ambivalent about President Aristide's populist program, and elements in the U.S. government continued to support his Duvalierist opponents.

From the 1990s the Haitian economy faltered. Haiti progressively became involved in the transshipment of illegal drugs, especially cocaine, to the United States. Urban crime increased greatly, with both wealthy and poor Haitians concerned for their safety. Even after President Aristide returned to power, political impasses led to blockages in international aid. Promises for basic government reforms, improvements in human rights, and economic revival went unmet. The World Bank estimate of per capita income in Haiti in 2001 was US$480.

Haitian Emigration

Significant Haitian emigration to the United States began in the late 1950s, when largely upper- and middle-class Haitians began to flee the terror of the early Duvalier period. These people typically settled in New York, where there was already a small Haitian American community. Emigrants traveled to the United States by airplane, which required the cost of a ticket and at least a tourist visa. By the late 1960s, they were joined by poorer Haitians, and more Haitians overstayed their visas or arrived with no documents at all.

The first known Haitian boat people to head toward the United States arrived in Florida in 1972. Previously Haitian boat people had settled in the Bahamas. In 1978, the Bahamas declared illegal Haitians unwelcome, which led to an exodus of Haitians west to Florida, where they were joined by other boat people coming directly from Haiti. In 1978, the Immigration and Naturalization Service (INS) apprehended nearly 4,000 Haitians. The figure peaked in 1980, with 25,000 apprehensions. The INS estimated that they picked up about half of the boat people arriving from Haiti.

U.S. Responses to Haitian Boat People

The U.S. response to Haitian immigration is best understood in the context of U.S. relations with Haiti, U.S. policy toward Cuban refugees, and what U.S. courts have repeatedly denounced as official racism. Cubans have generally been embraced as refugees from a Communist dictatorship, in contrast to Haitians, who have been seen as illegal aliens fleeing poverty and a "friendly" government. Cubans were often portrayed as ideal immigrants, bringing their skills and love of freedom, whereas Haitians were seen as uneducated, a drain on resources, and black. Cubans were seen as political refugees, Haitians as economic refugees, a dichotomy that oversimplifies the circumstances of both sets of migrants.

The contradictions in U.S. attitudes toward Cuban and Haitian boat people became apparent during the Mariel boat lift of 1980. Americans welcomed 125,000 Cubans to south Florida but disregarded the 25,000 Haitian boat people arriving the same year. Criticized for its policy toward Haitians, the Jimmy Carter administration created a vague category, "Cuban/Haitian entrant (status pending)," to permit these undocumented immigrants to stay in the United States. Haitians were given some but not all of the benefits available to refugees. Later, the Immigration Reform and Control Act of 1986 resolved the legal status of Cuban/Haitian entrants and other undocumented Haitians who arrived before 1982.

In 1981, the Ronald Reagan administration changed course by stopping the resettlement of Haitian boat people and initiating the policy of "interdiction." With the assent of the Duvalier government, the U.S. Coast Guard patrolled the seas around Haiti to stop boats that were attempting to leave with passengers aboard. The passengers were interviewed to see if any qualified to apply for political asylum, and those not qualified were returned to Haiti. In the ten years (1981–1991) of the interdiction policy, only 28 out of 22,000 Haitians intercepted were given political asylum. These policies greatly decreased the number of Haitians attempting to leave by boat.

The military coup d'état against President Aristide in 1991 forced a change in U.S. policy toward Haitian boat people. The administration of George H. W. Bush reacted by discontinuing the interviews of Haitians who had been intercepted on the seas; they were simply repatriated by force. Soon there was a political uproar about this practice because of increasingly flagrant human rights abuses by the coup leaders in Haiti. The U.S. government stopped repatriations and instead incarcerated the Haitian boat people at the U.S. military base in Guantanamo, Cuba. During the seven months after the coup, about 34,000 Haitians were intercepted by the U.S. Coast Guard, by far the largest wave of people fleeing Haiti since 1980. More than 10,000 of the boat people were allowed to apply for political asylum.

After President Aristide was returned to Haiti, the Clinton administration resumed the policy of interdiction and forced repatriation. Haitians who were allowed to apply for asylum were released pending their hearing, like asylum seekers from other countries. Haitian refugees received additional relief when the U.S. Congress passed the Haitian Refugee Immigration Fairness Act (HRIFA) of 1998. This act enabled Haitians who had lived in the United States since 1995 to become permanent residents without having to prove a case for asylum. Legislation directed toward Nicaraguan and other Central American refugees passed previously had pointedly ignored Haitians.

In late 2001, however, the administration of George W. Bush began to detain newly arrived Haitians who were seeking asylum, in contrast to its policy for every other country. The INS stated that the purpose of the policy was to deter other Haitians from seeking asylum. Furthermore, the Haitians were put on a fast track for asylum hearings with little legal representation. Nine out of ten cases were rejected. Criticized for anti-Haitian bias, the INS changed the wording of its policy to eliminate mention of "Haitians," but its effect was unchanged. Groups such as the National Coalition for Haitian Rights continued to press for equal treatment of Haitians.

Integration into U.S. Society

The U.S. 2000 Census counted 419,000 residents born in Haiti and 453,000 who spoke French Creole, the language of Haiti. These figures should be regarded as approximations of the Haitian population in the United States. New York City is home to the oldest Haitian American community, but Boston and Chicago also have large numbers of Haitian immigrants. Before the 1980s, Miami had a relatively small Haitian population, but since then it has become the site of one of the most important, though relatively poor, Haitian communities. Not all the Haitian boat people settled in urban areas, however. A large number entered the agricultural sector, initially settling in Belle Glade, Florida, a center of sugar production.

Haitians have encountered discrimination in the United States, especially racism. Although there are color and class distinctions in Haiti, racism is not part of Haitian immigrants' previous experience. Haitians have also been discriminated against specifically for being Haitian. For example, in 1982 the U.S. Centers for Disease Control falsely identified Haiti as a source of Acquired Immune Deficiency Syndrome (AIDS). This position was retracted in 1985, but in the meantime numerous Haitians lost jobs or were not hired because of fears that they were carriers of human immunodeficiency virus (HIV). (It is most likely that HIV was brought to Haiti by North American tourists.)

A tragic example of discrimination against Haitians in the United States occurred in 1997, with the brutal sexual attack by New York City police officers on a male Haitian immigrant, Abner Louima. This incident galvanized the Haitian community and its supporters. One of the police officers was eventually convicted, but the community was not satisfied because other convictions were overturned on appeal.

Cultural and ethnic identity are evolving issues for Haitian immigrants and their children. Adult Haitian immigrants often identify themselves as Haitian rather than African American. Their children's identity is less sharply defined. The children often grow up in wider African American communities and identify less with Haitian culture and politics than their parents do. Young Haitians face prejudice in school, often from African American students, and they tend to abandon Haitian cultural models in favor of African American styles. Young people sometimes try to hide or deny their Haitian identity. Like the children of other immigrants, they lead bicultural lives, trying to meet parental expectations at home and those of their peers outside.

Haitians who have left their homeland for the United States, Canada, France, and other countries are seen as part of a "diaspora" that links them to each other and to their fellows in Haiti. President Aristide embraced the Haitian diaspora, calling it the "Tenth Department," since Haiti consists of nine geographical departments. He reflected the continuing interest of Haitian Americans in political and cultural events in Haiti. Not only do Creole language radio programs broadcast news of Haiti to the major immigrant communities, but Haitian periodicals published in the United States have a ready audience in both countries. Hundreds of thousands of families in even the remotest parts of Haiti depend on relatives abroad for support. The Haitian diaspora has formed many organizations to help alleviate poverty and enhance development in Haiti.

Frederick J. Conway

See also: Assimilation/Integration; Asylum; Asylum Determination; Clandestine Migration; Cuban Migration; Guantanamo Bay; Mariel Boatlift; Racism and Racially Motivated Attacks; Transnationalism; U.S. Immigration Legislation, Post-1945; U.S. Immigration Legislation, Pre-1945

References and further reading:

Bellegarde-Smith, Patrick. 1990. *Haiti: The Breached Citadel.* Boulder: Westview.

Catanese, Anthony V. 1999. *Haitians: Migration and Diaspora.* Boulder: Westview.

Conway, Frederick J., and Susan Buchanan Stafford. 1996. "Haitians." Pp. 170–190 in *Refugees in America in the 1990s: A Reference Handbook.* Edited by David W. Haines. Westport, CT: Greenwood.

Danticat, Edwidge. 2001. *The Butterfly's Way: Voices from the Haitian Dyaspora.* New York: Soho Press.

Laguerre, Michel. S. 1998. *Diasporic Citizenship: Haitian Americans in Transnational America.* New York: St. Martin's Press.

Martinez, Samuel. 1999. "Migration from the Caribbean: Economic and Political Factors versus Legal and Illegal Status." Pp. 273–292 in *Illegal Immigration in America: A Reference Handbook.* Edited by David W. Haines and Karen Rosenblum. Westport, CT: Greenwood.

Pamphile, Leon D. 2001. *Haitians and African-Americans: A Heritage of Tragedy and Hope.* Gainesville: University of Florida Press.

Stepick, Alex. 1998. *Pride against Prejudice: Haitians in the United States.* Boston: Allyn and Bacon.

Trouillot, Michel Rolph.1990. *Haiti, Nation against State: The Origins and Legacy of Duvalierism.* New York: Monthly Review Press.

Zephir, Flore. 1996. *Haitian Immigrants in Black America: A Sociological and Sociolingiustic Portrait.* Westport, CT: Bergin and Garvey.

———. 2001. *Trends in Ethnic Identification among Second-Generation Haitian Immigrants in New York City.* Westport, CT: Bergin and Garvey.

Harmonization

See Dublin Convention; European Citizenship; European Union; European Union Accession Countries; Schengen Agreement

Human Rights

See Asylum; Asylum Determination; European Court of Human Rights; European Court of Justice; Migrant Rights; Open Borders; Refugees; UN Convention on the Rights of Migrant Workers, 1990

Humanitarian Intervention

"Humanitarian intervention," in its classical sense, is the coercive use of armed force by one or more states in another state without the consent of its authorities, and with the purpose of preventing widespread suffering or death among the inhabitants (Abiew 1999, 18). It is a contested concept that has for centuries been used in international public debate as a description and justification of certain military interventions. The term has sometimes been used, especially in some relief agencies, with a much broader and less precise meaning: major humanitarian action in an emergency situation, not necessarily involving use of armed force, and not necessarily against the will of the government. The following discussion sticks to the classical meaning of the term.

This entry concentrates on the last thirty years of the twentieth century, when more interventions were justified in humanitarian terms than in earlier periods. It considers whether humanitarian intervention is a distinct category;

points to the significant role of refugee issues; briefly surveys the causation and course of certain interventions; and discusses the question of authorization, particularly by the United Nations (UN) Security Council. Finally, it summarizes the ongoing debate about whether, in international law, states can be said to have a general "right" to intervene in extreme cases of repression or failure of government, and suggests that it may be a mistake to frame the issue in terms of a "right."

Refugee Issues in Interventions

Many military interventions that have been defended at least partly on humanitarian grounds were influenced by concerns about refugees and internally displaced persons (IDPs). Actual and feared refugee flows from countries in crisis, coupled with the unwillingness of other countries to accept refugees on a permanent basis, powerfully influenced opinion in many countries, especially owing to the development of the media. In many cases, military action was seen as a means of changing a situation that had caused an IDP and refugee crisis, and enabling those who had fled to return home.

Is It a Category?

The UN Security Council, or states acting independently, have only very rarely cited humanitarian considerations alone as a basis for intervention. They have almost always referred to other considerations as well, including those relating to peace and security. In a few instances, intervention has additionally been justified in terms of support of a self-determination struggle: This is a problem, because while humanitarian issues are widely viewed as "nonpolitical," and not directed at achieving a specific permanent change in the status of a territory, self-determination in the form of sovereign statehood is a political goal. This is one of many ways in which humanitarian and other issues coexist awkwardly. Although doubts persist about whether "humanitarian intervention" is an entirely separate legal or conceptual category, experience since 1945 confirms that the issue of whether intervention can be justified on humanitarian grounds does repeatedly crop up.

The following short illustrative survey of interventions omits many cases. It most notably omits Vietnam's intervention in Cambodia in December 1978 and Tanzania's intervention in Uganda in January 1979, in which the justifications offered did not rely heavily on humanitarian issues despite the record of criminal violence of the rulers of the invaded states, who were, in each case, dethroned. The nine cases surveyed below are among those in which humanitarian justifications were a significant and plausible part of the rationale for intervention given at the time. As will be seen, in three of these cases the military actions taken did not meet all the usual criteria for "humanitarian intervention" indicated at the beginning of this entry, though they did come close.

East Pakistan, 1971

The Indian decision to intervene by force in East Pakistan followed mass killings perpetrated by Pakistani government forces there—a situation that had resulted in 10 million refugees fleeing to India. In a short campaign that began on December 3, 1971, the Indian armed forces and the local resistance movement (Mukti Bahini) that they supported were completely victorious, removing the Pakistan government presence from the territory, which quickly emerged as a new state, Bangladesh. Indian justifications during the crisis have often been described as relying principally on arguments of self-defense (Gray 2000, 26). However, they were also phrased in humanitarian terms.

On December 4, 1971, in a discussion in the UN Security Council on the Indian military action, the Indian representative said: "We have on this particular occasion nothing but the purest of motives and the purest of intentions: to rescue the people of East Bengal from what they are suffering." The U.S. representative strongly opposed the Indian action: "The time is past when any of us could justifiably resort to war to bring about change in a neighboring country that might better suit our national interests as we see them" (UN 1971, 14–18). In a further Security Council meeting, held on December 13, the Soviet representative strongly supported India, particularly on the grounds that a situation producing 10 million refugees demanded action, and that this was a case in which the principle of self-determination should be applied; the Indian foreign minister emphasized Pakistan's human rights violations in East Bengal, stating specifically that the massive violation of human rights was a direct threat to the security of nations. At these meetings, three resolutions, which India strongly opposed, calling for a withdrawal of forces and a cease-fire, were defeated owing to the Soviet veto.

Grenada, 1983

The United States led an intervention on Grenada following a violent and extreme Marxist coup d'état on the Caribbean island in October 1983, rescuing U.S. citizens there and ushering in a change of regime. U.S. troops withdrew in December. In the decision-making process that preceded the intervention, actual or possible refugee flows do not appear to have been a major consideration. The military action was justified by U.S. spokesmen on the basis of an invitation from the governor-general, the need to rescue U.S. citizens, a claim to protect citizens of Grenada from human rights violations by the government, and general considerations of peace and security.

The Organization of Eastern Caribbean States, in a controversial plea for outside military action that helped to legitimize

CARE relief workers distribute the first military convoy of humanitarian aid in Mogadishu. In December 1992 the U.S.Army launched Operation Restore Hope, under the cover of the United Nations Operation in Somalia (UNOSOM), dubbed a humanitarian mission to feed starving people following a prolonged drought. U.S. Marines were sent to protect relief workers, whose job was becoming increasingly difficult due to clan violence in the city. (Patrick Robert/Sygma/Corbis)

the U.S. operation, referred to "the serious violations of human rights and bloodshed that have occurred and the consequent unprecedented threat to the peace and security of the region" (O'Shaughnessy 1984, 243). A draft resolution in the UN Security Council deploring the armed intervention in Grenada was vetoed by the United States. However, on November 2 the UN General Assembly, in a resolution that was a typical product of the collaboration between the Soviet bloc and nonaligned states in that period, deplored the U.S.-led military intervention as "a flagrant violation of international law." Despite this, there was little evidence of strong or continuing objection by states to this intervention.

Northern Iraq, 1991

Following a failed uprising within Iraq and a huge refugee exodus of Kurds and others to neighboring countries, UN Security Council Resolution 688 of April 5, 1991, required that "Iraq allow immediate access by international humanitarian organizations to all those in need of assistance in all parts of Iraq" and stated that Iraqi government actions causing the refugee flows threatened "international peace and security in the region." The resolution, while less than a formal authorization of intervention, was of considerable help to the United States and its coalition partners when the U.S.-led military operation to create a "safe haven" in northern Iraq began on April 17, 1991. This operation enabled refugees to return from Turkey, where they had been kept in the area adjoining the Iraqi border. Iraq subsequently consented to the presence of a UN Guards Contingent in Iraq, which took over some functions of the departing U.S.-led force. Like many interventions with a humanitarian purpose, the action in northern Iraq rescued many people in danger but did not provide a political context for their long-term safety (Wheeler 2000, 170).

Somalia, 1992

This intervention followed a period of lawlessness and famine in Somalia in which a small peacekeeping force, UN Operation in Somalia (UNOSOM), had lacked the mandate and resources to tackle widespread violence, including that against aid workers and convoys. The U.S.-led invasion of December 9, 1992, was authorized by UN Security Council Resolution 794 of December 3, which referred to "the urgent calls from Somalia for the international community to take measures to ensure the delivery of humanitarian assistance" and expressed alarm at "continuing reports of widespread violations of international humanitarian law." Although refugee flows were not the main issue, concern about possible refugee problems did reinforce the willingness of neighboring African states to support this intervention.

Four months after the intervention, Security Council Resolution 814 of March 26, 1993, authorized the establishment of an expanded UN peacekeeping force with considerable powers, UNOSOM II. However, the U.S.-led forces retained a role in Somalia. A number of fatal incidents, mainly in Mogadishu in 1993 and 1994, raised questions about the command structure of these forces, their failures to observe fundamental humanitarian norms, and their continuing utility or lack thereof. Both the U.S. and UN forces left Somalia by March 1995. The record of the international forces in Somalia has been harshly criticized: "It would require quite remarkable ignorance to consider all this a UN success" (Mayall 1996, 124).

Rwanda, 1994

The main issue raised by the genocide in Rwanda in April-July 1994 is the humanitarian intervention that did not happen: the failure of states and the UN to intervene promptly and decisively in the period up to May when faced with evidence of genocide, massive internal displacement, and refugee flows. A small UN peacekeeping force, the UN Assistance Mission for Rwanda (UNAMIR), was already present in the country in connection with the war between the government and the Rwandese Patriotic Front (RPF). However, with a limited mandate and force structure, it could do little to stop the government-backed killings of Tutsis.

When the UN Security Council did belatedly begin to call for forceful action in response to the crisis, it stressed the importance of humanitarian issues as a reason. Security Council Resolution 918 of May 17, 1994, expressed concern over "a humanitarian crisis of enormous proportions" and decided on an expansion of UNAMIR's mandate. A further resolution of June 8 referred to "reports indicating that acts of genocide have occurred in Rwanda" and underscored that "the internal displacement of some 1.5 million Rwandans facing starvation and disease and the massive exodus of refugees to neighboring countries constitute a humanitarian crisis of enormous proportions." Difficulties arose in obtaining forces to carry out the mandate: This was partly because the experiences of outside forces in Somalia in 1993–1994 induced caution about involvement in Rwanda.

In Resolution 929 of June 22, 1994, the Security Council accepted an offer from France and other member states to establish a temporary operation in Rwanda under French command and control. The council authorized France to use "all necessary means to achieve the humanitarian objectives." The government of Rwanda (at that time a member of the UN Security Council) voted in favor of this resolution; thus, the ensuing French-led Opération Turquoise in western Rwanda in summer 1994 was not a typical case of "humanitarian intervention" within the definition offered here. After the RPF capture of the capital, Kigali, on July 4, 1994, and the advent to power of a new regime, the French-led intervention in western Rwanda continued. Its role throughout was controversial. A UN-commissioned survey of the 1994 genocide was critical of the failure both of the UN and its member states to intervene more promptly. (UN 1999, 30).

Haiti, 1994

Following a coup d'état in Haiti in September 1991, the UN Security Council eventually passed Resolution 940 of July 31, 1994, stating that it was "gravely concerned by the significant further deterioration of the humanitarian situation in Haiti, in particular the continuing escalation by the illegal de facto regime of systematic violations of civil liberties, the desperate plight of Haitian refugees and the recent expulsion of the International Civilian Mission." The resolution went on to authorize the use of "all necessary means to facilitate the departure from Haiti of the military leadership . . . and to establish and maintain a secure and stable environment." This resolution is remarkable for its unequivocal call for action to topple an existing regime and restore a democratically elected one. The U.S.-led invasion followed in September 1994. At the last minute, with the invading forces already in the air, the military regime gave its consent to the presence of the Multinational Force (MNF) in Haiti. There was a prompt change of government and elections, and the refugee crisis eased. In 1995, the UN Mission in Haiti, a peacekeeping force, took over from the MNF, inheriting some of its powers. Although the intervention had achieved some results, Haiti remained a fractured society (Malone 1998, 184).

Kosovo, 1999

From February 1998 onward there were hostilities and atrocities in Kosovo, a province of Serbia, the latter being the principal component part of the Federal Republic of Yugoslavia. Government troops and police were increasingly involved, not just in combating incipient insurgency, but in repression of the population of the province, which is predominantly ethnic Albanian. The situation worsened over the summer, and a huge proportion of the Albanian population became IDPs or refugees. A critically important presentation made by a representative of the UN High Commissioner for Refugees (UNHCR) to the UN Security Council on September 10, 1998, led to a hardening of the council's position on Kosovo. In Resolution 1199 of September 23, 1998, the council demanded that the parties take certain concrete steps, including a cease-fire and acceptance of an effective international monitoring force in the province. The resolution also demanded that Yugoslavia facilitate "the safe return of refugees and displaced persons to their homes and allow free and unimpeded access for humanitarian organizations and supplies to Kosovo."

The subsequent major resolution on Kosovo, endorsing agreements concluded in Belgrade on October 15–16, made similar references to humanitarian issues as a basis for action. The Security Council did not explicitly authorize the use of force, but it did spell out a number of demands, some of which were on humanitarian issues. When Yugoslavia failed to comply, these resolutions were then cited as evidence that the military action being taken, even though not endorsed by the Security Council, was in pursuit of goals that the council had proclaimed. The ensuing war between states of the North Atlantic Treaty Organization (NATO) and Yugoslavia in March-June 1999 was exceptional in many respects, not least for NATO's reliance on bombing as a means to attain humanitarian (as well as other) objectives. Partly because of the humanitarian issues involved, NATO placed much emphasis on minimizing civilian casualties (Clark 2001, 438–440). At the end of the war, the Security Council passed Resolution 1244 of June 10, 1999, deciding to deploy an international civil and security presence in Kosovo, the latter with substantial NATO participation and with extensive powers. Its assigned tasks included establishing "a secure environment in which refugees and displaced persons can return home in safety, the international civil presence can operate, a transitional administration can be established, and humanitarian aid can be delivered."

Albania, 1997/East Timor, 1999

There have been many other military actions in which humanitarian issues were a major consideration. Like the operation in Rwanda, some bear many similarities to, but do not fully qualify as, "humanitarian intervention" in its classical definition because they were with the advance consent of the government of the host state. Examples include the Italian-led operation in Albania in 1997, following chaos and breakdown of government; and the Australian-led operation in East Timor in 1999, following killings by pro-Indonesian forces seeking to stop the territory's moves toward independence. In the case of East Timor, the consent of Indonesia to an international military presence was obtained only after heavy international pressure was exerted on its government. In both cases, the external intervention had the explicit approval of the UN Security Council. In both, refugee flows were a major factor in leading to decisions to intervene, and afterward conditions were created in which many refugees were able to return home.

Questions of UN Authorization and Host-State Consent

Of the nine cases surveyed above, in five (Somalia, Rwanda, Haiti, Albania, and East Timor) there was explicit UN Security Council authorization of military action. In two of these five, Somalia and Haiti, host-state consent was not obtained in advance of the military action. However, even in these cases the right of the Security Council to take decisions to intervene was not seriously contested. In Somalia in 1992 there had been no government to give or refuse consent. Although the Somalia action was to be heavily criticized, this was because of particular actions taken by international forces in Somalia, not because of any claim that the original decision to authorize intervention was illegal.

In the remaining four cases surveyed (East Pakistan, Grenada, northern Iraq, and Kosovo) there was no UN Security Council authorization before military action was undertaken, and there was no advance host-state consent. In northern Iraq and Kosovo, the intervening states claimed to be acting in support of policies supported by the UN Security Council even if they did not have its specific authorization to use force, and in these two cases the presence of foreign contingents was eventually regularized by the UN and the host state. In all these cases, the intervening states or coalitions cited a range of reasons for their interventions, not confined to humanitarian issues. Despite this, each of these four cases provoked particularly intense discussion of a possible "right" of humanitarian intervention.

Is There a "Right" of Humanitarian Intervention?

The question of whether states or groups of states, when operating without specific UN Security Council authorization, have a "right" in international law to engage in humanitarian intervention remains contentious. In none of the nine cases did an intervening state explicitly justify its action on the basis of the purported existence of a general right of humanitarian intervention. The rule against forcible intervention within sovereign states, reflected in Article 2(4) of the UN Charter, has long been an important underlying norm in international relations and a principal reason why many international lawyers have taken a hostile view of any doctrine or practice of humanitarian intervention (Brownlie 1963, 338–342; Chesterman 2001, 234–236).

Against this view, and drawing on those provisions of the UN Charter that establish human rights as key purposes and principles, some lawyers and international relations scholars have taken a broadly favorable view of a right of humanitarian intervention (Tesón 1997, 150–151; Wheeler 2000, 307–310). An important basis for justifying military action on behalf of people (including refugees) who are threatened in their own country has been the development, especially marked in the years since 1945, of international human rights law, and also the law of war (often called "international humanitarian law applicable in armed conflict"). This development has reinforced the sense that there is an international right or even duty of states to protect vulnerable individuals.

The result of legal development in the post-1945 period is a clash of two impressive bodies of international law. On the one hand there is a body of law restricting the right of states to use force, and on the other hand a body of human rights and humanitarian law. Because of the parallel development of these bodies of law, it is inherently no less difficult than in earlier times to resolve the clash that occasionally arises between the principles of nonintervention and humanitarian intervention. In particular, it is difficult to arrive at a general answer regarding the legality of interventions on humanitarian grounds that are not based on UN Security Council authorization.

There is no serious sign of states agreeing to a doctrine of humanitarian intervention. It may be more useful to think of humanitarian intervention not as a general right or even a duty, but rather as an occasional and exceptional necessity that is the outcome of a situation in which legal requirements clash. One could sum up a complex situation in international law by saying that humanitarian intervention is not absolutely excluded. It is wrong in principle to expect international law to provide anything even approaching generic approval in advance for a type of action resulting from unique situations in which powerful considerations, both legal and moral, have to be balanced against each other (Roberts 2001, 42–49).

Despite continuing problems with many aspects of the concept and practice, humanitarian intervention is a response to serious situations, including massive refugee flows, that are not likely to disappear. The emerging pattern comprises some interventions authorized by the UN Security Council, and others that, lacking such authorization, are opposed by some states and tacitly tolerated by others. A common thread linking most cases is the difficulty of turning an initial rescue into a long-term remedy of the situation that led to crisis.

Adam Roberts

See also: Civil Wars and Migration; Displaced Persons; Ethnic Cleansing: Kosovo; Haiti and Refugees; Kurdish Refugees; Mass Influx; Pakistan and Refugees; Refugees; Rwanda and Refugees; Somalia and Refugees; Sovereignty and Migration; UN High Commissioner for Refugees

References and further reading:

Abiew, Francis Kofi. 1999. *The Evolution of the Doctrine and Practice of Humanitarian Intervention.* The Hague: Kluwer Law International.

Brownlie, Ian. 1963. *International Law and the Use of Force by States.* Oxford: Clarendon.

Chesterman, Simon. 2001. *Just War or Just Peace? Humanitarian Intervention and International Law.* Oxford: Oxford University Press.

Clark, Wesley K. 2001. *Waging Modern War: Bosnia, Kosovo and the Future of Conflict.* Oxford: Public Affairs.

Gray, Christine. 2000. *International Law and the Use of Force.* Oxford: Oxford University Press.

Malone, David. 1998. *Decision-Making in the UN Security Council: The Case of Haiti.* Oxford: Oxford University Press.

Mayall, James, ed. 1996. *The New Interventionism, 1991–1994: United Nations Experience in Cambodia, former Yugoslavia and Somalia.* Cambridge: Cambridge University Press.

O'Shaughnessy, Hugh. 1984. *Grenada: Revolution, Invasion and Aftermath.* London: Sphere Books.

Roberts, Adam. 2001. "The So-Called 'Right' of Humanitarian Intervention." *Yearbook of International Humanitarian Law: 2000,* 3: 1–49. The Hague: T. M. C. Asser.

Tesón, Fernando R. 1997. *Humanitarian Intervention: An Inquiry into Law and Morality.* 2d ed. Dobbs Ferry, NY: Transnational.

United Nations. 1971. *Security Council Official Records (SCOR).* 26th year, 1606th meeting, December 4, 1971. New York: UN.

———. 1999. *Report of the Independent Inquiry into the Actions of the United Nations during the 1994 Genocide in Rwanda,* attached to UN doc. S/1999/1257 of December 16, 1999. New York: UN.

Wheeler, Nicholas J., 2000. *Saving Strangers: Humanitarian Intervention in International Society.* Oxford: Oxford University Press.

Hungarian Revolution

The refugee crisis generated by the Hungarian revolt of 1956 was the first major refugee movement associated with the Cold War. Although the number of refugees involved was relatively small by twentieth-century standards, the event was a defining moment in the development of responses to refugees, confirming the importance of the United Nations High Commissioner for Refugees (UNHCR) and demonstrating the willingness of Western states to assist refugees from Communist countries.

The refugee crisis in Hungary had it origins in Communist control of the Eastern European state, which dated back to the immediate aftermath of World War II. In 1947–1948, a Communist regime took power in the country and brought it in line with the Soviet Union through the regular purging of opponents of Communist rule. The death of Stalin in 1953, however, and the process of de-Stalinization launched afterward by the new Soviet premier, Nikita Khrushchev, offered hope of increasing liberalization and autonomy to Hungary and other satellite countries in Eastern and Central Europe, including Poland. Although these hopes bore some fruit in Poland, developments took a far more sinister turn in Hungary. In the mid-1950s, a movement for liberalizing reform developed, resulting in popular demonstrations and the emergence of a government, led by Imre Nagy, that removed Communist hard-liners from the cabinet and promised free elections and the demise of one-party rule. Fatefully, the government also pledged itself from removing Hungary from the Warsaw Pact, the Soviet bloc's answer to the North Atlantic Treaty Organization (NATO).

In response to this move, a Soviet army of more than 200,000 troops attacked Budapest, the Hungarian capital, on November 4, 1956, crushing opposition to the Soviet regime. This led to more than 300 deaths, mass deportations, and the execution of Nagy. The severity of the Soviet attempt to reinstall a hard-line regime also resulted in a mass exodus from the country. In the period between October 23, 1956, and the end of the year, about 155,000 people crossed the border into Austria and Yugoslavia (Branyan and Larsen 1971, 1968).

Faced with large numbers of refugees and limited resources in the aftermath of the devastating effects of World War II, the Austrian government called upon the fledgling UNHCR for financial assistance and help with resettlement. Soon afterward, the newly appointed High Commissioner,

Hungarian citizens flee in response to the Soviet intervention of 1956. (Hulton-Deutsch Collection/Corbis)

Auguste Lindt, traveled to Vienna, the Austrian capital, to assess the needs of the refugees (UNHCR 2000, 29). UNHCR thereupon embarked upon a large-scale and highly successful resettlement program and, with the help of the International Committee of the Red Cross, relief efforts. By mid-1958, the results of the program were impressive: The United States had resettled some 38,000 refugees; Canada, 35,000; the United Kingdom, 16,000; the Federal Republic of Germany, 15,000; and Australia, 13,000. France and Switzerland and a range of other countries also accepted refugees (UNHCR 2000, 32).

The nature of the response to Hungarian refugees was key to the success in these resettlement programs, as exemplified by the case of the United States. The Dwight D. Eisenhower administration's success in speedily resettling the refugees can be attributed largely to the popularity of the refugees themselves. Their plight was extensively and sympathetically documented by American television networks. Forces in Congress usually hostile to immigration also faced real problems opposing the entry of refugees whose plight the United States had had a hand in creating (Gibney 2004), for the United States in its radio networks in Europe before the Soviet attack had encouraged Hungarians to rise up against the Communist government. Hungary was thus the first real example of refugee admission to the United States based on what Gil Loescher and J. A. Scanlan have described as "the politics of failed revolution" (1986, 50). The Hungary crisis set in train a period, lasting at least until the end of the Cold War, during which the United States would use refugee admission largely as a reward for those who shared its foreign policy goals and battled unsuccessfully against Communist regimes.

By April 1961, after the resettlement of almost 200,000 refugees had been achieved, UNHCR announced that it was no longer necessary to treat Hungarian refugees as a special group (UNHCR 2000, 34). It was fitting that UNHCR would be the body that announced the end of the refugee crisis. For the refugee exodus from Hungary had both consolidated the fledgling organization and signaled the important role it was to play in the post–World War II world.

Matthew J. Gibney

See also: Asylum; Burden Sharing; Civil Wars and Migration; Cold War; Deportation; Refugees; Resettlement; UN High Commissioner for Refugees

References and further reading:

Binsten, M. A. 1958. *Escape from Fear.* New York: Syracuse University Press.

Branyan, R. L., and L. H. Larsen. 1971. *The Eisenhower Administration, 1953–1961.* Vol. 1: *A Documentary History.* New York: Random House.

Gibney, Matthew J. 2004. *Ethics and Politics of Asylum: Liberal Democracy and the Response to Refugees.* Cambridge: Cambridge University Press.

Loescher, Gil, and J. A. Scanlan. 1986. *Calculated Kindness: Refugees and America's Half-Open Door, 1945 to the Present.* New York: Free Press.

United Nations High Commissioner for Refugees. 2000. *The State of the World's Refugees 2000: Fifty Years of Humanitarian Action.* Oxford: Oxford University Press.

I

Illegal Immigration

See Clandestine Migration

Indentured Migration

See Indian Diaspora

Indian Diaspora

With some 20 million people of Indian origin living outside India, Indians are one of the world's largest and most widely spread diasporas (see Figure I-1). The Indian diaspora includes persons who themselves, or whose ancestors, emigrated from British India before 1947 or the Republic of India after 1947. Indians have settled abroad in considerable numbers since the 19th century as a result of indentured and free migration. Various types of postcolonial migrations have led to a sharp increase in the number of overseas Indians from some 5 million in the early 1960s to four times that number in the early twenty-first century (Kotkin 1993, 204). India had never before experienced such a large outflow of people. Moreover, the Indian diaspora remains very much a work in progress as the factors propelling migration continue to evolve.

The fact that descendants of some of the nineteenth-century migrants have undertaken a second or third migration makes the Indian diaspora a highly diverse one. In addition, India, with a geographical, historical, and cultural diversity matched by few other countries, has produced not one diaspora but many. Numerous religious, cultural, linguistic, and regional communities exist under its umbrella. All communities of Indian origin, however, share some features, such as certain cultural traits, and are subject to certain regulations of the Indian government owing to its recent efforts to foster relations between India and its diaspora population (see Figure I-1).

Indian Culture and Migration

Although the number of overseas Indians is substantial, it is tiny compared to the 1 billion Indians in India. About half of the 20 million overseas Indians emigrated from India; the other half were born abroad to immigrant parents. Emigrants make up just 1 percent of India's population (Voigt-Graf 2002, 62). The low levels of emigration through much of India's history, especially compared to levels experienced in other developing countries, are partly due to specific teachings of the Hindu religion.

In colonial times, a taboo on crossing the *kala pani* ("the black water," that is, any stretch of ocean) became ingrained in folk Hinduism (Gillion 1962). Hinduism is inextricably linked to the social system and the land of India. For most Hindus, India is a sacred space abounding in sacred places, from the local shrines and holy rivers to the sites described in the Hindu epics (Vertovec 2000a, 1–4). Moreover, Indians, regardless of their religion, are deeply tied to their particular caste community, each one with its specific mores and cultural practices. Even today, the caste system, the joint family system, regional particularities in culture and language, low levels of knowledge of the outside world in many rural areas, as well as inadequate means of transportation and communications contribute to a comparatively low level of migration. In addition, emigration became stigmatized because the majority of Indian migrants in colonial times belonged to underprivileged parts of society.

In postcolonial times, Indians have started to regard emigration in more positive terms. Most migrants to Western countries come from the privileged middle classes, which supply the role models for India's poor masses. Nevertheless,

Figure I-1: Number of Indians in the diaspora

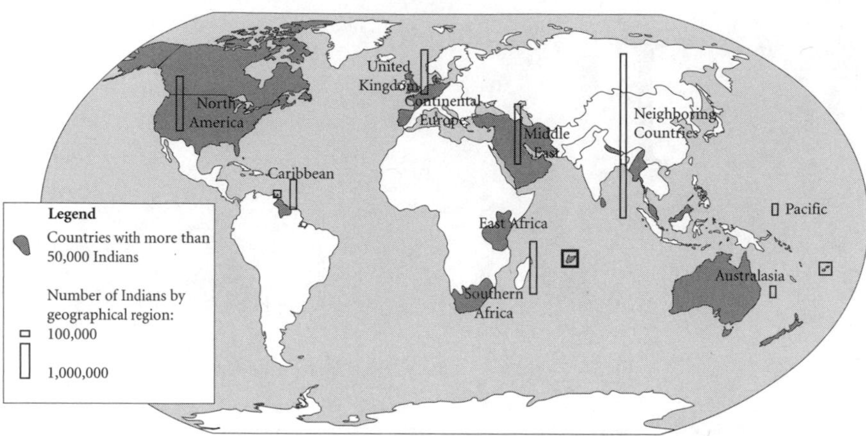

the Indian population has been one of the least mobile in the world in terms of international migration. There is one major exception to this rule—the region of Punjab. Some 2 million Punjabis, or 8 percent of the Punjabi population, live abroad (Voigt-Graf 2002, 101). The history of the region and its location on the invasion route into India, as well as the Sikh religion, which, in contrast to Hinduism, regards mobility as a virtue, have been the main contributing factors.

Migration in Colonial Times

Indian traders have ventured out by sea for over two millennia. It was not until the colonial era, however, that Indians permanently settled abroad in significant numbers (see Table I-1). Population movements during the colonial period can be traced back to the economic situation resulting from India's integration into the imperial world economy. India became a major outlet for British investment capital, which had devastating effects on India's handicraft and manufacturing industries (Jain 1989, 159–160). Meanwhile, new land policies and an increase in prices for agricultural commodities became very burdensome to the peasantry, and the frequency of famines increased, during the nineteenth century. The huge mass of unemployed and underemployed people had nothing to lose by seeking better fortunes abroad, despite prejudices in Hindu society against emigration. At the same time, demand for labor was growing in British plantation colonies, especially after the abolition of slavery in 1834. As a consequence, the United Kingdom introduced a system of international contract labor migration between India and these colonies.

Between 1834 and 1917, some 1.5 million Indians went abroad as indentured laborers, mostly to work on plantations in Guyana, Trinidad, Suriname, Mauritius, Fiji, South Africa, and some other British, French, and Dutch colonies (Tinker 1974). Under the indenture system, migrants were recruited in India with the help of government supervision and given a free passage to the colonies. Most came from Bihar, eastern Uttar Pradesh, Bengal, and some South Indian areas (see Figure I-2). In the colonies, they served as indentured agricultural laborers for a specific period of time, with penal sanctions to enforce the contract. Details of the contract varied over time and from colony to colony. In spite of the dire conditions on the plantations, about two-thirds opted to stay in the colonies after the expiry of their contracts.

Other systems of labor migration included the "maistry system," under which Indians were recruited for work in Burma, and the "kangani system," applied in Ceylon (today's Sri Lanka) and Malaya. These systems differed from the indenture system in that the recruitment was for a shorter period of time and the workers were legally free. At a rough estimate, some 10 million Indians, mainly from the poverty-stricken South Indian districts, moved back and forth between their home region and Burma, Ceylon, and Malaya from the early nineteenth century until 1938 (Jain 1989, 162). Most of these emigrants finally returned to India.

Indians also migrated to colonies within the British Empire as free migrants. Most of these were Gujaratis, who worked as merchants and provided clerical and technical services to colonial governments. Smaller numbers came from Punjab, often to work as policemen, guards, and farmers. Free migration usually involved some chain migration as people from the same family, village, or caste joined their brethren abroad.

Some migrants made their way to metropolitan areas in other countries, in particular in the United Kingdom, the United States, Canada, and Australia. Migration from Punjab to North America started in the late nineteenth century. Many migrants worked in railway construction, in the lumber industry, and in agriculture. By the 1920s, many owned farms, and their descendants today live in British Columbia and California. Overall, however, this type of migration was modest in scale, as immigration barriers were almost insurmountable for Indians.

Migration in Postcolonial Times

The first stream of postcolonial Indian migrants consisted of unskilled male workers to the United Kingdom, where there was a demand in factories. Their families later joined them. Since the 1960s, professionally and technically skilled people have migrated to industrialized countries. Indian migration

Table I-1: Major Types of Migration from India

Type	*Period*	*Major Source Areas*	*Major Destination Countries*	*Estimated Numbers Involved*
PRECOLONIAL				
1. Trade migration	Since 0 A.D.	Tamil Nadu, Gujarat	Southeast Asia, Indian Ocean region	Unknown
COLONIAL				
2. Labor migration				
a) Indentured migration	1834–1920	Uttar Pradesh, Bihar, Tamil Nadu	Mauritius, Trinidad, Guyana, Suriname, Fiji, South Africa	1,500,000
b) Kangani/maistry migration	1820–1938	Tamil Nadu	Burma, Malaysia, Sri Lanka	10,000,000
3. Free migration to colonies	1790s–1947	Gujarat, Punjab	East Africa, other British colonies	100,000
4. Free migration to metropolitan countries	1790s–1947	All over India	United Kingdom, other metropolitan countries	20,000
POSTCOLONIAL				
5. Labor migration (including subsequent family reunion)	1950s	All over India	United Kingdom	800,000
6. Professional migration (increasingly temporary since 1980)	1960–	All over India	United States, Canada, Australia, United Kingdom, New Zealand	1,000,000
a) IT professional migration (often temporary)	1990–	Bangalore, Hyderabad, Chennai	United States, Canada, Australia	200,000
7. Refugee migration	Since 1947, increased in 1980s	Punjab, Kashmir	United States, Canada, Australia, United Kingdom, Europe	Unknown
8. Labor contract migration (temporary)	1973–	Kerala, South India	Saudi Arabia, United Arab Emirates, Oman, Kuwait, Qatar, Bahrain	10,000,000
9. Secondary/multiple migration	1960s–	East Africa, Fiji, West Indies	United Kingdom, United States, Canada, Australia	500,000

Source: Carmen Voigt-Graf, *The Construction of Transnational Spaces: Travelling between India, Fiji and Australia*. Ph.D. dissertation, University of Sydney, 2002, p. 64.

to the United Kingdom slowed in the 1970s and stabilized at a low level in the 1980s. In contrast, migration from India to North America gained momentum in the mid-1960s, coinciding with the implementation of nonracist immigration legislation. Receiving an average of 30,000–40,000 new migrants from India per year, the United States is currently the most popular destination country for permanent migrants from India. With the end of the "White Australia Policy" in the early 1970s, Australia also became increasingly popular. It currently receives some 5,000 permanent Indian migrants per year (Voigt-Graf 2002, 66–68, 79). Since the late 1980s, an increasing number of migrants have been software developers and IT specialists whose skills are in demand globally. A growing proportion of the professional migration flow is temporary in nature. Professional migrants are drawn from many regions in India. South India has emerged as an increasingly important source area, in line with the fact that India's IT industry is centered in the southern cities of Bangalore, Hyderabad, and Chennai.

Another postcolonial migration flow consists of Indian migrants and their descendants who make a secondary migration, traveling from various former colonies to Western countries. In the 1960s, Indian "twice migrants" (Bhachu 1985) first emerged on the world stage following political independence in East Africa, and in particular the expulsion of Indians from Uganda in 1972. Most were eventually resettled in the United Kingdom, though a substantial number made their way to Canada. Another example is Indo-Fijians, who left Fiji in considerable numbers owing to political and economic discrimination. Most have resettled in Australia, making up some 20 percent of Australia's Indian population (Voigt-Graf 2003a).

In comparison to professional migrants, whose skills are in demand globally, unskilled Indians wishing to work abroad have limited opportunities. Many accept temporary labor contracts in the oil-rich Middle East. Some 2 million Indians worked in the Gulf countries at the turn of the millennium (Jain 2000). About half of them originated from Kerala (see Figure I-2), and many are Christians and Muslims. Some 70 percent are unskilled or semiskilled workers, though the proportion of professionals and entrepreneurs is growing (Jain 2000). This temporary migration is prompted by wage differentials, and most migrants stay between two and eight years. Working and living conditions are extremely difficult for Indians in the Middle East, as there is no freedom of political expression, no occupational choice, and no trade unions to protect the workers' rights. Indian migrants are socially and residentially segregated from the Arab population, and their cultural and religious activities are restricted, especially in the case of non-Muslims. Since many of their families remain in India, Indians in the Gulf are the most reliable senders of remittances among all overseas Indians.

The Indian Diaspora Today

Any attempt to generalize about the Indian diaspora obscures as much as it reveals and does little justice to the diversity of overseas Indians. The situation in the various diasporic nodes is dependent on a variety of factors, such as the time and type of migration, the structure of society, the number of Indians compared to the total population, the social distance felt towards the non-Indian population, and economic circumstances.

Postcolonial societies present extremely different challenges and opportunities for Indian migrants. In Mauritius, for example, Indians make up two-thirds of the population and are a dominant political force, whereas in Fiji, Indians face significant discrimination. Two military coups in 1987 removed an Indo-Fijian-friendly government, and a civilian coup in 2000 forcefully removed Fiji's first Indo-Fijian prime minister. Indo-Fijians are also discriminated against in the economic sphere as a result of affirmative action measures in favor of ethnic Fijians. Indo-Fijians are by and large excluded from landownership, despite forming the backbone of Fiji's sugarcane industry. Consequently, some 150,000 Indo-Fijians have left Fiji since political independence in 1970, shifting the population balance in the Pacific nation slightly in favor of ethnic Fijians (Voigt-Graf 2003a).

In addition to enormous differences by country, there are considerable differences between the descendants of indentured laborers and the descendants of free migrants. Free migrants have often kept their personal links to India through communication in writing and in person. They have preserved much of their ancestral culture by importing spouses from their home villages. Indian laborers lacked the financial means and often the inclination to stay in touch with their families in India and to visit the subcontinent and therefore lost their personal links to India. In other ways, all Indians abroad have been affected by the experience of migration similarly. New working and living conditions have had an irreversible impact on various aspects of their social and cultural lives. In most colonies, the caste system was lost, religious practices underwent enormous changes, and new lingua francas emerged out of the Indian languages they had brought with them.

In many industrialized countries, the diversity of the Indian population, in terms of country of birth, religion, and language, is enormous. In Australia, for instance, where the Indian immigrant population numbers an estimated 230,000, some 110,000 were born in India, some 60,000 are second-generation Indians, some 45,000 Indo-Fijians, and 15,000 are Indians born in other countries, such as Malaysia,

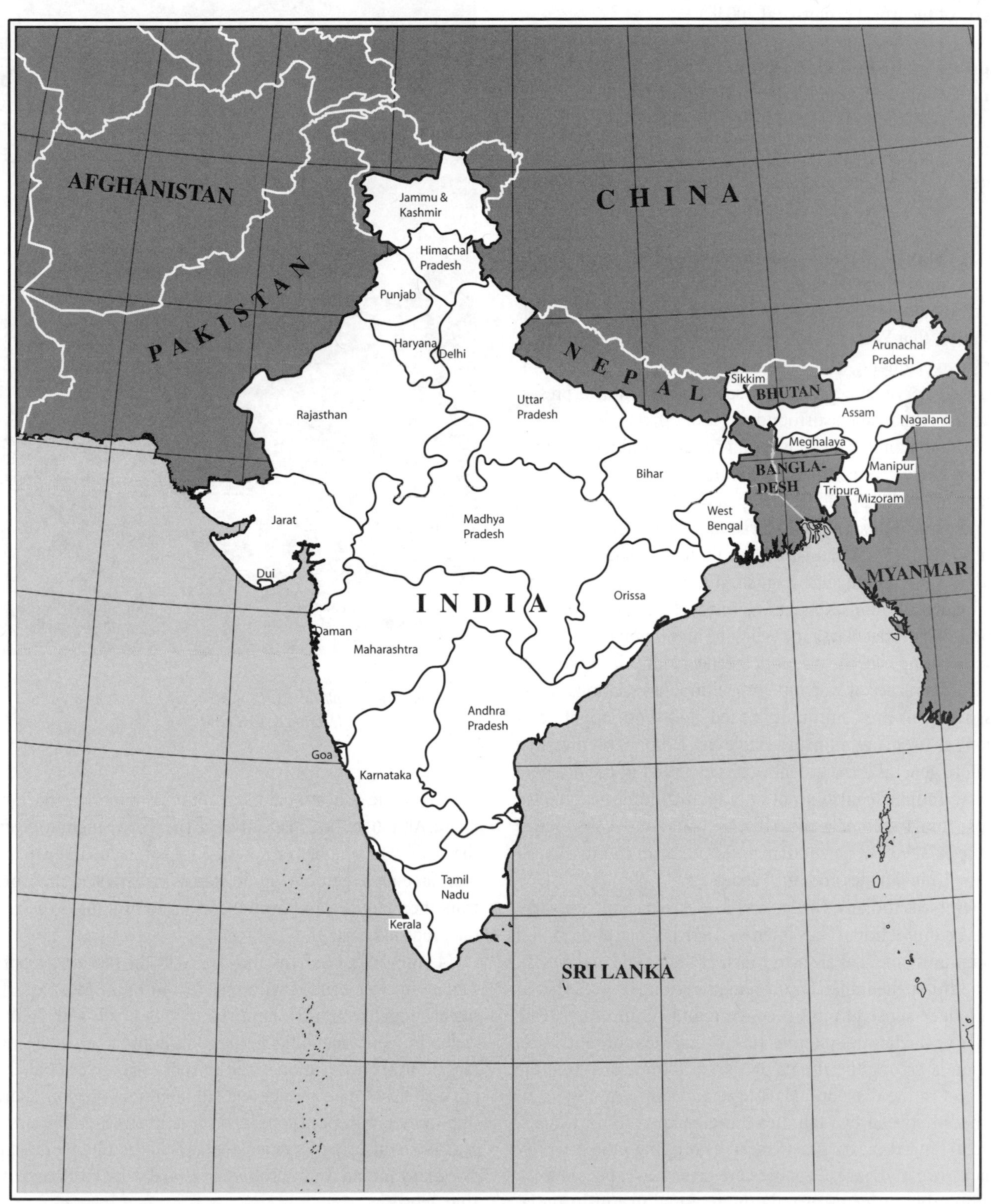
AFGHANISTAN
CHINA
Jammu & Kashmir
Himachal Pradesh
PAKISTAN
Punjab
Haryana
Delhi
NEPAL
Sikkim
BHUTAN
Arunachal Pradesh
Assam
Nagaland
Meghalaya
Manipur
BANGLA-DESH
Tripura
Mizoram
Rajasthan
Uttar Pradesh
Bihar
Jarat
Madhya Pradesh
West Bengal
Dui
MYANMAR
INDIA
Orissa
Daman
Maharashtra
Andhra Pradesh
Goa
Karnataka
Tamil Nadu
Kerala
SRI LANKA

Singapore, New Zealand, South Africa, and the United Kingdom. A new trend adding to this complexity is the sharp rise in the number of temporary migrants from India to other parts of the world (Voigt-Graf 2003b).

Culture in the Indian Diaspora

One distinctive feature of diasporic Indians is that they ostensibly adhere to their culture. Overseas Indians, especially the recent migrants, are haunted by a feeling of guilt at having left India, a nation with ancient cultural traditions that they perceive as richer than any of the New World cultures. Particularly when children have to be brought up in the diaspora, the issue of cultural and religious preservation comes to the foreground. Indians see their own traditions threatened by the individualism in Western societies and the attraction that Western culture might have for their children. Pride in belonging to an ancient culture is one reason for cultural conservatism; the sense of security that cultural preservation offers in alien surroundings is another.

In India and in the diaspora, primary loyalties generally follow narrower lines than an overarching Indian identity. Indians belong to a variety of religious backgrounds, including Hinduism, Sikhism, Islam, Christianity, Jainism, Buddhism, Baha'i, and Zoroastrianism. Their mother tongues are similarly diverse and include English, Hindi, Urdu, Punjabi, Bengali, Gujarati, Tamil, Konkani, Kannada, Malayalam, and several other vernaculars. The religious and linguistic diversity in many nodes of the diaspora is reflected in a large number of Indian places of worship and cultural associations. Many associations are community based, and there might be as many as twenty or more in a single city. Despite this diversity, a more general Indian identity has emerged in the diaspora where Indians confront not only their differences but also those things that make them distinctly Indians. A sign of this is the existence of pan-Indian associations in countries such as the United States and Australia.

Overseas Indians, particularly in Western countries, share some cultural traits. They often lead a rich social and cultural community life that absorbs much of their time and energy. In addition, the Indian family remains strong overseas based on a deep sense of mutual concern and commitment. One pillar of the family system is the arrangement of marriages, which is among the rituals that seem to have survived the longest in the diaspora. Marriages are considered to be alliances between two families rather than two individuals, and arranged marriages are seen as offering more security than "love marriages." Spouses are generally expected to be compatible in terms of religion, regional origin in India, mother language, education, and sometimes caste, and to match one another's life circumstances. The previously strict rule of caste endogamy has been gradually relaxed, and today

Indian merchants display a colorful array of vegetables at an open air market in Fiji, 1971. (Morton Beebe/Corbis)

a comparable educational background is a more important factor. Although the prospective partners are generally given the last say in whether or not they are willing to agree to the marriage arrangement, some young Indians feel pressure from their families and from the wider community to accept the proposed partner.

Many overseas Indians and especially the recent migrants remain in close contact with their kin in India. Most are affluent enough to afford long-distance phone calls and regular visits. Transnational links to their kin in India greatly facilitate cultural preservation in the diaspora as overseas Indians are kept up-to-date about events in their home region, share important family occasions, and sometimes send their overseas-born offspring for extensive stays to their home region. The many Indian communities are globally linked along kinship networks.

Facilitated by their close-knit family networks and the arrangement of marriages, Indians have successfully recreated their culture in diverse locations. Religion is particularly important for the constitution of diasporas. Hindu temples, Sikh *gurdwaras,* Muslim mosques, and Christian churches serve as cultural and social centers in the diaspora over and above their religious functions. Most Hindus and Sikhs in the diaspora participate at least occasionally in temple activities, the frequency often depending on the distance between their homes and the nearest temple. In addition, most Hindu homes have a mini-altar to perform *puja,* a form of worship honoring specific gods or goddesses whose presence is believed to protect the family and to engender good fortune. In some settings, such as the United Kingdom and East Africa, caste, sectarian, regional, and community traditions within Hinduism have remained largely intact through ongoing contacts with India. In other places, Hindutva Hinduism, which favors a singular definition of Hinduism, is predominant. In others, a form of ecumenical Hinduism has emerged that recognizes a variety of Hindu practices (Vertovec 2000a).

Religion's main rival in terms of constituting a cultural link to India is Mumbai's film industry, "Bollywood." Regardless of age, gender, religion, and duration of settlement abroad, nearly all Indian migrants share an interest in Hindi movies. Many overseas Indians watch several movies a week, the two main genres being love stories and religious films. The latter often recount the great Hindu epics and thereby are of significant educational value for the overseas-born second generation. In many countries, Hindi video libraries are numerous, and some cities have cinemas showing exclusively Hindi movies. In addition to Hindi movies, an Indian overseas entertainment industry is booming. Classical and popular performers from India regularly tour various diaspora settlements. Overseas Indians have thus re-created their ethnic identity partly through their consumption of Bollywood movies, other forms of Indian entertainment, and Indian food.

Despite these and other forms of cultural preservation, Indian cultures have undergone considerable changes in the diaspora, the caste system being one example. In India, the caste system means a hierarchical rank, and ideas of possible pollution caused by relations with members of other castes govern endogamy, hereditary occupation, and ritual duties. In some diaspora settlements, caste has been entirely lost, whereas in others caste identities have been preserved but the associated patterns of behavior have been lost.

Indian migrants constantly discuss the virtues of staying abroad or returning to India. Those who emigrate do so primarily for economic reasons and not out of any disregard for the culture and values of India. This love of their home country underlies the cultural conservatism of Indians, which is as much a feature of the community as are economic achievements.

Economy in the Indian Diaspora

Indians are among the most economically successful migrant groups in Western countries, particularly as highly skilled professionals. In the United States, the success of Indians is documented across various economic sectors—for example, as farmers running successful family-owned farms, as small business owners of ventures such as motels, and as professionals working in a gamut of other realms, including medicine, academia, engineering, and information technology (IT). Many Indian immigrants in the United States are extremely prosperous entrepreneurs and employees in the IT industry.

Skilled labor, in particular in the IT field, has become the most sought-after resource in industrialized countries at the turn of the millennium. In 2000, the United States itself was facing a shortage of some 1.6 million IT workers. Therefore, the previous annual cap of 65,000 temporary H-1B visas, which allow migrants with technical skills and a job offer from a U.S.-based company to work in the country for three to six years, was raised to 115,000 in 1998. As many as 45 percent of all H-1B visas are allocated to Indians. It is estimated that some 100,000 IT workers leave India for the United States each year (Iredale 2001, 14) and that 80 to 90 percent of India's brain drain is bound for the United States.

The global slowdown of the IT industry in 2001 affected the demand for Indian workers, particularly in the United States, where Indian IT workers were fired en masse. It remains to be seen how the industry's downturn will affect migration patterns in the long run.

Scholars theorize that the roots of Indian economic success overseas lie within a strong family system, maintenance of traditional values and linkages, an emphasis on education, and a fairly widespread preparedness to eschew immediate pleasure for long-term gain (Kotkin 1993, 102). Indians enter the global labor market with the advantage of speaking English and having a Western-style education. Overseas Indians place enormous emphasis on education. This attitude is very instrumental in terms of gaining entry into moneymaking professions.

The importance of cultural values and family resources should not obscure the fact that Indians' economic success is to a large extent a function of the opportunity structure present in the labor market. At the same time, in lauding the success of overseas Indians one may overlook the fact that not all Indians are uniformly privileged. In all Western countries, a substantial number of Indians work as security guards, taxi drivers, and in other unskilled occupations. Though not as conspicuous as the highly successful professionals and entrepreneurs, they nevertheless make up a significant portion of the Indian diaspora.

Redefining the Relationship between the Diaspora and India

The relationship between India and its diaspora is presently being redefined. The Indian government has started to perceive its diaspora as a source of investment and entrepreneurial activities—and as a market. It is looking for strategies to foster this relationship by translating cultural ties into ongoing and reliable economic links.

Given the cultural identification of overseas Indians with their homeland and the maintenance of personal ties to their kin in India, the Indian government could never be totally indifferent toward its diaspora even when its attitude bordered on ambivalence. Nevertheless, for almost fifty years after the beginning of indentured migration in 1834, neither the Indian government nor the general population was particularly concerned about the maltreatment of Indian workers abroad. It was only with Mohandas K. Gandhi's agitation that recruitment stopped in 1917. In 1920, the government of India asked all colonies to terminate the indenture system. Once indenture was abolished, mainstream Indian politics again lost interest in the Indian diaspora.

Migration issues entered the political agenda again in the 1970s, when Indian families received vast amounts of remittances from labor migrants to the Gulf region. In the early 1970s, the Indian government laid claim on overseas Indians by introducing the term "Non-Resident Indian" (NRI). "Non Resident (External) Accounts," that is, tax-free accounts, were introduced so that this remittance money could enter the Indian economic system without constraints. Since embarking on economic reform in the early 1990s, the Indian government has introduced several measures aimed at increasing cooperation with its diaspora. Specifically, NRIs are encouraged to open a variety of different types of bank accounts offering numerous investment options in Indian companies and properties. In 1999, the Indian government introduced "Person of Indian Origin" (PIO) cards intended to guarantee equal treatment for Indians in the diaspora regardless of their citizenship status. In 2002, dual citizenship was introduced for persons of Indian origin who are citizens of certain other countries.

From cooperating with NRIs, India expects to receive not only monetary remittances and portfolio investments but also technological resource flows and skill transfers through exchange visits and remigration (Khadria 1999). The success of the initiatives has varied. In 1999, India was the largest single receiver of remittances, receiving some $9 billion out of an estimated worldwide total of more than $61 billion a year (Vertovec 2000b). In the mid-1990s, some 30 percent of Indian remittances came from North America, 10 percent from Europe, 12 percent from the United Kingdom and Australia, 41 percent from the Middle East, and 7 percent from other developing countries (Khadria 1999, 143).

A major shortcoming of the initiatives is that NRIs invest largely in the safe sectors of India's economy, such as government bonds and securities, while industrial investments have remained below expectations. In the instance of an economic downturn in India, NRI money is quickly withdrawn. It has been noted that the Indian diaspora is behind the Chinese in terms of investments in their homeland. Despite the tendency of many authors (and the Indian government) to compare the Indian with the Chinese diaspora, the backgrounds of the two diasporas are too different to allow useful comparisons. Most overseas Chinese are members of an entrepreneurial class, whereas most Indians, particularly in Western countries, are professionals. It is only recently that prosperous NRIs, particularly in the United States, have returned to India to start companies, invest their capital, and indulge in philanthropy. From the point of view of overseas Indians, many of whom retain a deep emotional attachment to India, investing in India provides an excuse to visit regularly and maybe even to return permanently. The equation, however, is not as simple as it seems. Many overseas Indians are not as patriotic as the Indian government would like them to be. Acting out of economic rationalism rather than Indian patriotism, they invest in India only if returns there are better than from overseas investments.

Carmen Voigt-Graf

See also: Bangladesh and India; Chinese Diaspora; Colonial Immigration; Diaspora; East African Asian Expulsions; Indian Partition; Remittances; Transnationalism

References and further reading:

Ballard, Roger, ed. 1994. *Desh Pardesh: The South Asian Presence in Britain.* London: Hurst and Company.

Bhachu, Parminder. 1985. *Twice Migrants: East African Sikh Settlers in Britain.* London: Tavistock.

Bilimoria, Purushottama. 1996. *The Hindus and Sikhs in Australia.* Canberra: Australian Government Publishing Service.

Clarke, Colin, Ceri Peach, and Steven Vertovec, eds. 1990. *South Asians Overseas: Migration and Ethnicity.* Cambridge: Cambridge University Press.

Gillion, K. L. 1962. *Fiji's Indian Migrants: A History to the End of Indenture in 1920.* Melbourne: Oxford University Press.

Iredale, Robyn. 2001. "The Migration of Professionals: Theories and Typologies." *International Migration* 39, no. 5: 7–26.

Jain, Prakash. 1989. "Emigration and Settlement of Indians Abroad." *Sociological Bulletin* 38, no. 1: 155–168.

———. 2000. "Culture and Economy in an Incipient Diaspora: Indians in the Persian Gulf Region." Conference paper presented at "Culture and Economy in the Indian Diaspora," India International Centre, New Delhi, April 8–10.

Khadria, Binod. 1999. *The Migration of Knowledge Workers: Second-Generation Effects of India's Brain Drain.* New Delhi: Sage.

Kotkin, Joel. 1993. *Tribes: How Race, Religion and Identity Determine Success in the New Global Economy.* New York: Random House.

Lessinger, Johanna. 1995. *From the Ganges to the Hudson.* Needham Heights, MA: Allyn and Bacon.

Tinker, Hugh. 1974. *A New System of Slavery: The Export of Indian Labour Overseas, 1830–1920.* London: Oxford University Press.

Vertovec, Steven, ed. 1991. *Aspects of the South Asian Diaspora.* New Delhi: Oxford University Press.

———. 2000a. *The Hindu Diaspora: Comparative Patterns.* London: Routledge.

———. 2000b. "Rethinking Remittances." Plenary Lecture presented at Fifth International Metropolis Conference, Vancouver, November 13–17.

Voigt-Graf, Carmen. 1998. *Asian Communities in Tanzania: A Journey through Past and Present Times.* Hamburg: Institute of African Affairs.

———. 2002. *The Construction of Transnational Spaces: Travelling between India, Fiji and Australia.* Ph.D. dissertation, University of Sydney.

———. 2003a. "The Emergence of an Indo-Fijian Transnational Community." Pp. 367–387 in *Migration in the Asia Pacific: Population, Settlement and Citizenship Issues.* Edited by Robyn Iredale, Charles Hawksley, and Stephen Castles. Cheltenham, UK, and Northampton, MA: Edward Elgar.

———. 2003b. "Indians at Home in the Antipodes: Migrating with Ph.D.s, Bytes and Kava in Their Bags." Pp. 142–164 in *Culture and Economy in the Indian Diaspora.* Edited by Bhikhu Parekh, Gurharpal Singh, and Steven Vertovec. London and New York: Routledge.

Indian Partition

The partition of British India in August 1947 occasioned one of the largest forced movements of persons in contemporary history. On this date the British colonial administration relinquished political control to the successor states of India and Pakistan, which had been divided on the basis of religion. The violence and turmoil that surrounded the partition were unprecedented. Escaping religious persecution and generalized violence, approximately 7 million Muslims crossed the border from independent India to the newly created state of Pakistan, while an estimated 8 million Hindus and Sikhs fled in the opposite direction. The flow of refugees took place in two major arenas: between West Pakistan and the Indian Punjab in the west of the Indian subcontinent, and between East Pakistan and Indian West Bengal in the east. In the former arena, the flow of refugees had largely eased by 1949, while in the latter it continued until 1953 at the earliest.

Despite the partition of the subcontinent on communal lines, the governments of India and Pakistan were not looking to organize an orderly population exchange along those same lines. However, violence against the minority community on both sides of the border increased to unmanageable proportions, and this, coupled with the near collapse of the local state infrastructure, forced both states at various times to organize the emergency evacuation of their coreligionists. Both states also established an impressive array of institutional and legal mechanisms for the relief and long-term rehabilitation of this vast population movement. This was accomplished in the near absence of international aid, despite Indian and Pakistani appeals for material assistance from the United Nations. Unlike the Korean and Palestinian refugees, the partition refugees were not viewed by the United States and other Western countries as geopolitically important. Indeed, the debate surrounding the creation of the postwar international refugee regime, which took place between 1949 and 1951 and was centered on the office of the United Nations High Commissioner for Refugees (UNHCR), explicitly excluded consideration of the partition refugees.

Partition of the Indian Subcontinent

Partition was the result of a complex of factors. Scholars differ as to the relative weight of each factor but agree that the most important were imperial design, internal socioeconomic and class-based factors, and the role of prominent individuals such as Mohammed Ali Jinnah, Jawaharlal Nehru, and Lord Mountbatten. By the end of World War II, it was evident that Britain was going to relinquish its political control over the country. In 1942, the Cripps mission had offered full Dominion status to India after the war and had included the crucial proviso that no part of British India would be forced to join the new state. By 1946, as the politics of the Muslim community, spearheaded by the Muslim League, became increasingly homogenized, and the largely Hindu Indian National Congress party sought to consolidate its mass support base, a division of British India on communal lines looked inevitable.

On August 16, 1946, during the "Great Calcutta Killing," 4,000 Hindus and Muslims were killed and more than 10,000 forced from their homes as a result of religious violence in the provincial capital of Bengal. By September 1946, rioting had broken out in other parts of the subcontinent, and the possibility of mass population movements was starting to become a grim reality. Estimates for the numbers of forcibly displaced persons in the period immediately prior to independence range from 20,000 to 60,000. On August 14 and 15, respectively, Pakistan and India celebrated their independence from British rule.

Classification of Partition Refugees

There is some debate about the status of the displaced persons who crossed the newly created international borders at the time of partition. This debate focuses on the question of whether the partition displacement constituted an orderly "exchange of population" agreed to by India and Pakistan, or whether these were people forced to flee their place of origin under duress. The vast numbers of people uprooted from their homes did not, as is expected of persons in refugee situations, lose their citizenship of a state. Rather, they expected that their coreligionists in India and Pakistan would grant them both a nationality and succor. Western observers argued at the time, in the United Nations, among other forums, that this was an exchange of population rather than a refugee exodus, and that these persons continued to enjoy the protection of the country of their nationality. However, other scholars have argued that those displaced at partition had lost the *effective* protection of a state and would certainly have been able to prove "a well-founded fear of persecution" as their reason for seeking admission into another country. This was not a sanitized exchange of population. Many of the refugees fleeing across the border to the safety of their coreligionists did not intend to leave their homes forever.

Neither India nor Pakistan anticipated vast population movements in the immediate aftermath of independence and, despite the religious antagonism surrounding partition, did not intend to create communally homogeneous postcolonial states. Although they envisaged a division and rearrangement of the armed forces and civil administration, there was little preparation for the accompanying refugee crisis. Both new states tried initially to stem this vast movement of persons. In the course of the 1948 Inter-Dominion Conference, the two governments signed an agreement that was designed to discourage mass migration by reassuring minorities in the east that they would be protected by the state in which they were resident.

Those persons forced to leave their homes at partition were fleeing persecution, had crossed international borders in their flight, were unable to return to their homes, and the states in which they sought refuge, though not unwilling to host them, believed that the vast majority would return to their places of origin. During the first chaotic months of the refugee exodus, it is questionable whether the mechanisms to provide effective state protection to the displaced even existed.

Infrastructure of Relief and Rehabilitation in the West

The August 1947 agreement establishing the new boundaries of India and Pakistan (the Radcliffe Award) had left 27 percent of the Punjab region's Muslims on Indian territory, and 32.5 percent of Punjabi Hindus and Sikhs on Pakistani territory. On September 3, 1947, following a meeting between Indian prime minister Jawaharlal Nehru and Pakistani prime minister Liaquat Ali Khan, the Military Evacuation Organization (MEO) was created to organize secure refugee movements to either country. In the West, refugees traveled out of their countries of origin in three ways: by train, by motorized transport, or on foot. Each of these options was fraught with danger.

Transport by Train

An estimated 4.5 million Hindus and Sikhs moved into East Punjab at partition, while around 5.5 million Muslims traveled in the opposite direction. The bulk of this migration took place between August and November 1947. Both trains and railway stations became "veritable death traps" in the turbulent months that followed partition as people attempted to flee the growing disorder. Trains would frequently arrive at their destinations carrying only corpses. In early September 1947, Prime Minister Nehru formed a special ministry to deal with the problem of refugee evacuation and relief. On September 6, K. C. Neogy was sworn in as minister for relief and rehabilitation. By mid-September, the government of Pakistan had similarly appointed Mian Iftikhar-ud-Din as the first minister for refugees and rehabilitation. The two governments were able to provide a remarkable degree of security to train evacuations, such that attacks on trains had almost died down by the middle of October. About sixty trains were organized to ferry refugees in November, and by the first week of December mass evacuation by rail from West Punjab had been completed and a normal train service largely restored.

Motorized Transport

In the immediate aftermath of independence, there was an urgent need to reach isolated pockets of rural minorities in each country and evacuate them to safety. These refugees were then escorted to transit camps; from there, they would be moved by motorized transport to evacuation points. However, the security of these transit camps themselves was of some concern, as they were located in "enemy" territory. In an attempt to address this concern, the Joint Defense Council of India and Pakistan decided that refugees would be protected by troops of their own community while in camps and en route to their destination. The governments of East and West Punjab also agreed to take effective measures to protect and feed refugees of all communities in camps on their territory. By November 15, 313,400 non-Muslims and 209,440 Muslims in the Punjab had been moved by motorized transport.

Foot Convoys

The most evocative image of the partition refugee movements is that of the enormous foot convoys snaking their way across hundreds of kilometers in search of safety. Typically such convoys were composed of up to 50,000 refugees, although the largest, organized from Lyallpur in West Punjab to India on September 11,1947, ultimately comprised 400,000 people and took eight days to pass any given point on its route. The two governments had to organize halting points for rest, food, and medical aid. Schedules had to be

Lord Louis Mountbatten, British viceroy of India (fifth from right), hands over power to Quaid-i-Azam Mahomed Ali Jinnah on August 14, 1947, when the state of Pakistan came into being. (Library of Congress)

drawn up to avoid clashes between convoys of the other community moving in the opposite direction. In addition, armed protection had to be provided for such movements, as they were easy targets, laden as the refugees were with cattle, household equipment, and the elderly and the ill. On October 20, 1947, the MEO established a Joint Evacuation Movement Plan, which laid down the routes to be followed by foot convoys moving in either direction. It also organized constant patrols of armored cars and instituted night curfews on areas through which these foot convoys passed. By the end of October, the movement of large foot convoys of non-Muslims from West Punjab had been completed, although smaller columns continued to arrive until February 1948. In the other direction, major movements of Muslims from East Punjab and adjoining areas continued until December 1947.

Both governments also airlifted a smaller number of refugees to safety. However, for the most part, only refugees with private means were able to afford to fly out of insecure areas. In addition to the evacuation of refugees from the Punjab, the government of India organized the removal of refugees from the North West Frontier Province and the Pakistani provinces of Baluchistan and Sind. A small number of Muslim refugees was also evacuated by ship and train by the government of Pakistan from Rajasthan and the United Provinces in India to Sind.

Refugees would at times pay the price for the hostile state of relations between the two newly independent countries. At other times, the highly communalized nature of the armed and police forces created delays in refugee movements as neutral troops (such as the Gurkha or Madras regiments) had to be transported to the Punjab to accompany evacuees. Yet, despite the magnitude of the task with which they were confronted, the disinterest shown by the international community, and the fact that these states were simultaneously engaged in the complex business of nation building, India and Pakistan were able by the end of 1948 to move almost 10 million refugees to safety in the Punjab.

Relief and Rehabilitation in Western India

Prior to August 1947, the vast majority of refugees in India and Pakistan had been accommodated through private channels, either with friends and relatives or by charitable organizations. However, once the trickle of refugees became a flood, the governments of both countries were called upon to provide interim relief. Refugees were initially brought to transit camps, most of which were administered by the central or provincial governments. They were then transported to more permanent camps either in the Punjab or further afield. Typically these were hastily commandeered public buildings such as schools or army barracks.

By the end of March 1948, approximately 670,000 partition refugees were accommodated in official camps in East Punjab. Responsibility for running these camps was awarded to the local East Punjab government because matters pertaining to local law and order came under the purview of provincial governments. In addition, local authorities could draw on their administrative and police services for personnel to manage the camps. The central government oversaw this administration and bore the vast majority of expenses.

In June 1948, the Ministry for Relief and Rehabilitation was renamed the Ministry of Rehabilitation. In order to prepare refugees for resettlement in newly constructed townships, the government instituted vocational and technical training in the camps. In an effort to wean refugees off the cash doles that had been provided in the first months of the refugee crisis, the government provided "remunerative employment" for the refugees in such work centers. However, providing employment to all refugees within the camps proved impossible. Therefore, dispersing refugees from camps around the country quickly became a priority of both central and provincial governments. Government cash doles to refugees were stopped on October 31, 1949, in a bid to motivate refugees to seek employment.

Relief and Rehabilitation in West Pakistan

The vast influx of Muslim refugees into West Punjab constituted a real challenge for the inexperienced Pakistani administration. Unlike India, which had inherited both the colonial state's central apparatus in Delhi and the Bengal provincial secretariat in Calcutta, Pakistan had to improvise a state infrastructure in Karachi and Dhaka. In late September 1947, the government began to formulate a coherent policy toward refugees settled in refugee camps in West Punjab and surrounding areas. An Emergency Committee of the Cabinet was created. The Joint Refugee Council, which had been created in August 1947, supplemented its work. In much the same manner as the relief effort organized in India, food and medical aid were provided free to refugees situated in camps, and vocational training centers were set up. By January 1948 there were some 900,000 refugees in camps in West Punjab, of which nearly 250,000 were without proper shelter. On August 27, 1948, the central government declared a state of emergency, which gave it the authority to resettle refugees in other provinces apart from the severely overcrowded West Punjab. Some 200,000 refugees were subsequently sent to the province of Sind, and by the end of October 1948 the Punjabi camps had been cleared of refugees from East Punjab.

The Pakistan Refugee Rehabilitation Finance Corporation was created in April 1948 to provide loans and grants to refugee traders and craftsmen. The central government also arranged schemes whereby refugee students were provided with scholarships and loans for higher education. In November 1949, the central government created a committee tasked with the responsibility of providing incoming refugees with as much land as they had left behind in India. Tractors and other agricultural implements were also hired out to refugee agriculturalists. The urgent nature of the task of refugee rehabilitation in Pakistan can be gleaned from the fact that one in every ten people in that country was enumerated as of refugee origin in the 1951 census.

Infrastructure of Relief and Rehabilitation in the East

Once the initial violence of the Great Calcutta Killing had died down, Bengal returned to an uneasy calm. The geographic distribution of religious communities played some part in making wholesale population movements like those witnessed in the west unfeasible. Almost 42 percent of the Hindu population of undivided Bengal lived, after partition, in Pakistani territory. In some areas of East Pakistan, such as the Chittagong Hill Tracts, non-Muslims constituted over 90 percent of the population. In addition, notwithstanding the communal rioting in mid-1946 and during the transfer of British power, a common feeling of "Bengali nationhood" crosscut the religious identity of Bengali Muslims and Hindus, thereby reducing the risk of generalized mass violence.

In the first two years following partition, Bengali Muslims and Hindus did move toward their coreligionists, but these were in the main either voluntary or relatively minor movements. The Inter-Dominion Conference of April 1948 decided that the responsibility for the protection of minorities would rest exclusively with the country in which the minorities resided. However, this relatively manageable movement was disrupted in late 1949 by the outbreak of communal rioting in Khulna and Barisal in East Pakistan and the consequent mass exodus of refugees. In 1950, the number of refugees entering India from East Pakistan nearly equaled the number that had entered during the previous three years.

In an effort to regulate or solve the refugee problem in the east, Prime Ministers Nehru and Liaquat Ali Khan signed an agreement in April 1950 that guaranteed equality of citizenship to minorities in the two countries. In addition, freedom of movement was guaranteed, including the right to move personal property across the border. Immediately after this pact was signed, there was a drop in refugee numbers, and both governments carried out small but well-publicized repatriation movements. In 1951–1952, however, threatened by unrest in East Pakistan over the issue of Kashmir, an estimated 340,000 refugees fled to West Bengal. Over the next six years, the flow of Muslim refugees from West Bengal and adjoining states slowed to a trickle, but the migration of non-Muslims from East Pakistan took place in a more or less continuous stream. Events such as the proposed adoption of Urdu as Pakistan's national language in 1955, and of an Islamic constitution in 1956, triggered increased refugee movements out of East Pakistan.

Relief and Rehabilitation in Eastern India

Refugee movements between East Pakistan and India were not expected to be permanent. This belief was based on a lack of generalized violence and persecution of minorities in the region as well as on a notion that communal relations in this part of the Indian subcontinent were more harmonious than in the west. In contrast to its policy in the Punjab, the government aimed to prevent any outward movement of non-Muslims by negotiating secure conditions for minorities with the East Pakistani authorities. By 1950, however, as the influx of non-Muslims into West Bengal reached its peak, Indian authorities were forced to augment private relief and rehabilitation efforts. A Branch Secretariat of the Ministry of Rehabilitation was set up in Calcutta in early 1950. In March 1950 alone, an estimated 75,000 refugees were admitted to camps in West Bengal. The camps in the east were set up along the same lines as those in the west of the country, providing temporary relief facilities to thousands of incoming refugees. They were then dispersed to refugee camps, most of which were located in West Bengal, but which were also increasingly situated in the northeastern states of Assam and Tripura.

Refugees arriving in West Bengal during and subsequent to 1950 were overwhelmingly rural. Under government policy, refugee agriculturalists were allotted land on government schemes or granted loans with which to purchase land. Extreme pressure on agricultural land in West Bengal, coupled with the fact that evacuee land was scarce because comparatively fewer Muslims had left for East Pakistan, meant that attempts were made to disperse refugees to other areas of the country. However, patterns of cultivation, as well as cultural sensibilities, made many loath to leave the region, and the majority of refugees eventually settled in West Bengal.

Due largely to the different circumstances in which the two migrations took place, it was more difficult to put a full stop to the refugee crisis from East Pakistan than had been the case in the west. Where the refugee exodus in the west had been a short, concentrated migration in response to partition, the movement from East Pakistan included also elements of established seasonal migration, gradually worsening relations between the two new states, and increasing demographic pressures. The initial target date for camp closure in West Bengal set by the government of India was April 30, 1950. Yet, as refugees continued to enter the state, the government of West Bengal was forced to reopen camps in 1951. A conference of central and West Bengal government ministers took place in Calcutta in the first week of July 1958, where a decision was taken that all refugee camps would be closed by the end of July 1959.

Relief and Rehabilitation in East Pakistan

In East Pakistan, the refugees from West Bengal were perceived in a different light from Punjabi Muslim refugees. This was exacerbated by the growing divide between the two wings of the country, which would lead eventually to the secession of East Pakistan from West Pakistan in 1971. The vast majority of Muslim refugees who crossed into East Bengal were relatively poor agricultural laborers. Here, as was the case in West Bengal, the pressure on agricultural land was very great, thus complicating the task of refugee rehabilitation. Prior to the end of 1949, only a few thousand Muslims had sought refuge in East Pakistan.

As was the case across the border, the government of Pakistan nurtured the belief that no great exodus would occur. Following serious communal riots, however, more than 1 million refugees fled eastern India in February 1950. On March 5, 1950, the government of East Pakistan appointed a refugee relief commissioner to take charge of the 4,000 refugees in camps in the capital city of Dhaka, as well as the millions spread around the country. Over the next month the government arranged for the evacuation of Muslim refugees in West Bengal by steamer yet continued officially to discourage any population movement across the border.

With the conclusion of the Nehru-Liaquat Pact in April 1950, the government publicly stated its intent to reverse this refugee influx. During the next few months, refugee traffic into East Pakistan began to decline, although the daily average influx continued at 8,000 until mid-1950. By 1953, the central government reported that 2.5 million refugees had entered the province; 1.3 million of these were Muslims from West Bengal and Assam, and the rest were Hindus who had returned to East Pakistan after the 1950 pact. By 1952, the Pakistan–East Bengal Refugee Council had been set up along the lines of the Joint Refugee Councils operating in other Pakistani provinces. Schemes for the short-term relief of Muslim refugees were instituted. In addition, houses were constructed for urban refugees, and rural refugees were provided with loans for the purchase of agricultural implements. By the mid-1950s, the flow of refugees into East Pakistan had largely abated.

Legislative Structure

The extraordinary movement of refugees at partition necessitated the formulation of extensive legislation in order to facilitate their rehabilitation. Laws relating to compensation, claim-realization, and settlement were enacted by both the central and provincial governments of the two new states, creating a body of legislation that is still largely in operation. Such legislation includes the Displaced Persons (Legal Proceedings) Act (1949) in India and the Displaced Persons (Compensation and Rehabilitation) Act (1958) in Pakistan. Within the terms of this legislation, the governments of India and Pakistan formulated a particular definition of what constituted a "refugee" in the eyes of the state. Although this was not a universal definition, restricted as it was to partition refugees, both countries expanded the refugee definition contained within the 1951 UN Convention Relating to the Status of Refugees to also include persons fleeing "civil disturbances or the fear of disturbances."

In the special circumstances of the partition refugee crisis, the conceptual end point of refugee existence was the attainment of citizenship in the host country. India and Pakistan accordingly formulated citizenship legislation that specifically addressed the particular needs of their refugee populations. On a practical level, this included the removal of administrative hurdles for refugees seeking citizenship, but it also included a guarantee of their right to remain within their country of refuge.

Pia Oberoi

See also: Assimilation/Integration; Ethnic Cleansing; Indian Diaspora; Mass Influx; Muslim Immigration; Pakistan and Refugees; Refugee Camps; Refugees; Resettlement

References and further reading:

Aiyar, Swarna. 1995. "August Anarchy: The Partition Massacres in Punjab, 1947." *South Asia* 18, special issue: 13–36.

Ansari, Sarah. 1995. "Partition, Migration and Refugees: Responses to the Arrival of *Muhajirs* in Sind during 1947–48." *South Asia* 18, special issue: 95–108.

Bhalla, Alok, ed. 1994. *Stories about the Partition of India.* 3 vols. New Delhi: HarperCollins.

Butalia, Urvashi. 2000. *The Other Side of Silence.* London: C. Hurst.

Khosla, G. D. 1948. *Stern Reckoning, A Survey of the Events Leading Up To and Following the Partition of India.* Delhi: Oxford University Press.

Moon, Penderel. 1998. *Divide and Quit: An Eyewitness Account of the Partition of India.* Delhi: Oxford University Press.

Naqvi, Mushtaq. 1995. *Partition: The Real Story.* Delhi: Renaissance.

Rao, U. Bhaskar. 1965. *The Story of Rehabilitation.* Delhi: Department of Rehabilitation, Ministry of Labour.

Schechtman, Joseph. 1949. *Population Transfers in Asia.* New York: Hallsby.

Singh, Kirpal, ed. 1991. *Select Documents on Partition of the Punjab—1947.* Delhi: National Bookshop.

Talbot, Ian. 1995. "Literature and the Human Drama of the 1947 Partition." *South Asia* 18, special issue: 37–56.

Vernant, Jacques. 1953. *The Refugee in the Post-War World.* New Haven, CT: Yale University Press.

Integration

See Assimilation/Integration

Internally Displaced Persons

The United Nations and most nongovernmental agencies currently define internally displaced persons (IDPs) as individuals or groups "who have been forced or obliged to flee or to leave their homes or places of habitual residence, in particular as a result of or in order to avoid the effects of armed conflict, situations of generalized violence, violations of human rights or natural or human-made disasters, and who have not crossed an internationally recognized State border" (UNOCHA 1998). These "internal refugees" face material, physical, and psychological deprivation, are often invisible to international eyes, and usually lack the benefits and protections associated with sanctuary in a neighboring country.

Allowing for uncertainties over estimates and definition, there may be as many as 23 million to 26 million IDPs in the world today. By contrast, recent estimates by the United Nations High Commissioner for Refugees (UNHCR) show official refugees to run at half this number. Though IDPs are not unique to our times, their numbers are on the rise. In part, this increase is due to a corresponding increase in internal (or civil) wars since the end of the Cold War. Between 1989 and 1994, a period in which there was a dramatic growth in IDP numbers, there were ninety-four conflicts in sixty-four locations across the world, yet only four of these were traditional interstate wars.

The international system set up after World War II took almost no account of the problem of internal displacement, despite the fact that the war created numerous pockets of internally displaced persons. In keeping with traditional notions of sovereignty, those forcibly displaced within their own countries—albeit for much the same reasons as refugees—were excluded from the organized systems of international protection and assistance established for refugees. The Geneva Conventions, which gave the International Committee of the Red Cross (ICRC) a mandate to help protect victims of armed conflict, were an exception. However, the limited

Kabul, March 1, 2002. Afghan women who are internally displaced persons (IDPs) wait to register their names with the UNHCR for help with transportation home. Tens of thousands of IDPs across Afghanistan hope to return to their homes following the fall of the Taliban. Many IDPs have spent five years living in near destitution in Kabul after their homes and farms were destroyed. (Reuters/Corbis)

scope of the conventions has come to be most keenly felt in cases of displacement caused by natural disasters and low-intensity conflicts.

Counting IDPs

The limitations of the international regime were not really challenged until the early 1990s, when the number of internally displaced persons swelled dramatically. By 2001, the largest (approximate) number of war-induced IDPs were found in Sudan (4 million), Angola (3.7 million), Colombia (2 million), Indonesia (530,000), the Russian Federation (510,000), Afghanistan (400,000), and Burundi (325,000). Although there is little doubt that the number of IDPs has risen in recent years, unlike registered refugees, IDPs are notoriously difficult to count. In several countries where significant IDP numbers are known to exist (for example, Algeria, Myanmar, and Turkey), lack of international access makes accurate estimates very difficult to determine.

Although the working definition of IDPs highlights war-induced displacement, there remains a question of whether those displaced by development projects should constitute a distinct subcategory. Where large numbers of people are moved against their will as a result of, for example, a dam project, the lack of protection and adequate compensation by the government concerned might demand international attention. In spite of guidelines issued by the World Bank and Asian Development Bank, for example, there are many hundreds of thousands of people in China, India, and Nigeria who fall into this category. Another gray area exists in situations where governments move people en masse "for their own protection" against insurgency. Such forced relocation has occurred in Burundi, Rwanda, and Uganda in recent years, ostensibly as a security measure. Obliged to live in "protected villages" with only rudimentary services, these people are recipients of a protracted relief operation by international aid agencies and increasingly reluctant donors.

"Internalizing Refugees"

One reason for the growing numbers of IDPs has been increasingly restrictive asylum policies in both the North and the South since the late 1980s and a desire on the part of Western states to keep refugees contained within their region of origin. Because of these developments, forced movements of people are increasingly internalized. People who would otherwise flee across an international border for protection are now forced to seek sanctuary in putatively safer parts of their own country. Internal movement is, in many cases, however, a poor substitute for asylum in another country. The internally displaced often fall into a vacuum where state responsibility for their welfare is derogated owing to the loss of control of vast areas of a country. Worse still, an almost total disintegration of statehood in countries such as Angola and Afghanistan has left the fate of thousands in the hands of various rebel groups or warlords. IDPs have no dedicated United Nations agency to which to turn, and there is no specific set of ratified legal norms in their favor.

Some human rights advocates feel uneasy about the containment of refugee flows in the country of origin. They fear that pragmatic solutions will be promoted above the fundamental right to seek asylum. Implicitly, the term "internally displaced persons" recognizes borders and upholds the responsibility of governments to protect all people within those borders. In reality, the most common cause of internal displacement is precisely the opposite: People are forcibly uprooted (often by the very government charged with their protection), move, or are moved en masse to and fro between borders; become a "shield" for insurgent activities; and are subject to harassment and human rights abuses. Finding the appropriate balance between protecting human rights and upholding state responsibilities goes to the very core of current debates concerning IDPs.

Appointment of a Representative

The growing interest in IDP assistance and protection has been matched by significant institutional changes at the international level. In 1992, the UN Commission for Human Rights requested the UN secretary general to appoint a representative to examine the legal, operational, and institutional issues surrounding internal displacement. The representative, Francis Deng, with a team of lawyers, academics, and aid personnel, compiled a set of legal norms that apply to IDPs; formulated and published *Guiding Principles on Internal Displacement,* which forms the core principles for governments and for international aid bodies; and visited and reported to the UN General Assembly on IDP issues in countries throughout the world.

Published in 1998, *Guiding Principles on Internal Displacement* has been translated and disseminated worldwide. It provides an international standard that identifies the rights and guarantees relevant to the protection and assistance of IDPs in all phases of displacement. It includes principles of protection from displacement, protection during displacement, and protection upon return, resettlement, and reintegration. The publication also outlines basic principles of humanitarian assistance and reflects and is consistent with international human rights and humanitarian law and analogous refugee law.

Further Institutional Changes

One of the most important recent developments is the placement of human rights concerns explicitly within the portfolio of the UN's humanitarian coordinating agency, the Inter-Agency Standing Committee (IASC). In 1997, protection and assistance concerns for IDPs became part of the IASC's mandate. In 2000, a UN special coordinator on internal displacement was appointed to work within the Office for the Coordination of Humanitarian Affairs (OCHA). The coordinator's role is to carry out reviews of selected countries and to make proposals for an improved interagency response to IDP needs. In 2001, this role was strengthened by the formation of a small dedicated IDP Bureau based within OCHA.

Though somewhat reluctant to acknowledge IDPs as a distinct category, the three agencies with the most consistent and visible involvement with IDPs, and mandates that most effectively address their protection needs, are the ICRC, the UNHCR, and the United Nations Children's Fund (UNICEF). Each is familiar with the task of combining their protection function with the implementation of large-scale assistance programs. However, historically each agency has also developed its own legal framework under which "protection" is used in a qualified fashion. The ICRC views the provisions for war-related needs articulated in the Geneva Conventions as complementary to the protections provided by human rights law. UNICEF defines protection as "ensuring respect for the rights expressed in the Convention on the Rights of the Child" (*Humanitarian Principles* 1998).

UNHCR

For UNHCR, "international protection" covers the whole range of activities under which refugees' (and, where applicable, IDPs') rights are secured. UNHCR has been the lead agency for IDP assistance and protection in, for example, Bosnia and Kosovo. The organization already assists some 5 million IDPs around the world. Given its preeminent capacity, protection mandate, and prior experience, UNHCR in 1999 clarified its policy by stipulating five conditions for its involvement in an operation for IDPs:

- A specific request or authorization from the UN secretary general or other competent principle organ of the UN (except when the work would be part of mandated activities, such as assisting IDPs in a returnee reintegration program);
- Consent of the state concerned and, where relevant, other entities in a conflict;
- Access to the affected population and adequate security for UNHCR and partners;
- Clear lines of responsibility and accountability;
- Adequate resources and capacity to conduct the activities.

The future of international community responses to IDPs appears to be anything but clear. As simmering conflicts and restrictive asylum policies cause their numbers to grow, even more attention is likely to be focused on their plight. However, in many ways the institutional, normative, and practical challenges associated with assisting and protecting IDPs appear even more daunting than those involving refugees.

Jon Bennett

See also: Asylum; Development-Induced Displacement

References and further reading:

Cohen, Roberta, and Francis Deng. 1998a. *Masses in Flight: The Global Crisis of Internal Displacement.* Washington, DC: Brookings Institution.

———. 1998b. *The Forsaken People: Case Studies of the Internally Displaced.* Washington, DC: Brookings Institution.

Humanitarian Principles Training: A Child Rights Approach to Complex Emergencies. New York: UNICEF, 1998.

Korn, David A. 1999. *Exodus within Borders: An Introduction to the Crisis of Internal Displacement.* Washington, DC: Brookings Institution.

Norwegian Refugee Council. 1998. *Rights Have No Borders: Worldwide Internal Displacement.* Geneva: NRC/Global IDP Survey.
United Nations Office for the Coordination of Humanitarian Affairs. 1998. *Guiding Principles on Internal Displacement.* New York: OCHA.

International Labour Organization

The International Labour Organization (ILO) is a specialized agency of the United Nations created in 1919 to improve labor conditions and living standards throughout the world. The ILO became the UN's first affiliated specialized agency in 1946, and it was awarded the Nobel Prize for Peace in 1969. The ILO is unique among intergovernmental organizations because its 175 member states are represented by government, employer, and worker-union delegates at the annual International Labour Conference, which elects a fifty-six-member governing body.

The ILO develops and promotes international labor standards in the form of conventions and recommendations that establish basic labor rights: freedom of association, the right to organize, collective bargaining, abolition of forced labor, and equality of opportunity and treatment. In addition, the ILO provides technical assistance in social policy and administration, fosters cooperative organizations and rural industries, and conducts research on unemployment and underemployment.

The ILO has three major divisions: Standards and Fundamental Principles and Rights at Work; Employment; and Social Protection. The International Migration Branch is part of the Social Protection division. The ILO has adopted 180 conventions, which are international treaties subject to ratification by member states, and 185 recommendations, nonbinding instruments that often deal with the same subjects as conventions and establish guidelines for national policy. Eight of the conventions, dealing with freedom of association (nos. 87 and 98), the abolition of forced labor (nos. 29 and 105), equality (nos. 100 and 111), and the elimination of child labor (nos. 138 and 182), are considered "fundamental" to the rights of human beings at work.

The ILO has adopted two major conventions and two major recommendations on migrant workers aiming to regulate labor migration and protect migrant workers by organizing labor migration to meet the needs of the countries of employment, providing information that allows migrants to make informed decisions about migrating abroad for employment, and ensuring equality of treatment to protect migrant workers as well as national workers. The Migration for Employment Convention of 1949 (no. 97) outlines conditions for recruiting, transporting, and employing migrants, stressing the need for equality of treatment for migrant workers. This is supplemented by Recommendation no. 86. The Migrant Workers Convention of 1975 (no. 143) outlines steps for countries to take to protect the basic human rights of migrants and guarantee equality for migrants in social security and to prevent illegal migration and employment. Recommendation no. 151 supplements this convention. Once conventions are ratified, countries are to report periodically on what they have done to implement them.

Key aims of the International Migration Branch of the ILO are to protect migrant workers and promote their integration in countries of destination and countries of origin, to help develop an international consensus on how to manage migration, and to improve information on migration patterns. In addition, the branch:

- Provides advice to governments on migration policies, helps to ensure awareness and enforcement of ILO conventions and recommendations on migrant workers, and campaigns against trafficking and discrimination
- Convenes meetings to improve understanding of and forge consensus on migration management
- Conducts research and collects data on migration

Examples of ILO migrant activities include providing assistance to governments to detect and prevent discrimination against migrants; undertaking studies of legal and irregular migration for employment in particular countries; conducting studies of emigration pressures in particular countries; and developing guidance manuals, especially for middle-income developing countries allowing the employment of migrants and for countries supplying workers for jobs abroad. For example, the ILO's 1996 manual for labor-importing countries recommends that the labor ministry in the destination country should determine whether and how many migrant workers are needed and ensure that employers abide by the terms of migrant workers' contracts. It suggests that migrant-labor policies be flexible, since they must constantly "balance nationals' legitimate expectation of some preferential treatment against human, economic and social rights that foreigners can justifiably claim to be theirs" (Böhning 1996, 87).

Countries that export labor can have policies that range from laissez-faire (the United States and the United Kingdom) to a state monopoly on going abroad for employment (China). Most labor exporters are between these extremes, with systems to regulate the recruitment of workers for overseas jobs. The 1997 manual recommends that the labor ministry be the lead agency in organizing the recruitment and deployment of migrants. There are often far more workers wanting to go abroad than there are jobs, and regulating, for example, the fees that migrants pay, or the contracts they sign, is difficult. Government agencies must therefore weigh trade-offs between competing goods, such as protecting women going abroad to work from abuse and permitting them to increase their earnings. Without the proper balance, policies meant to channel migrants through official channels may have the unintended consequence of pushing more migrants into unofficial channels (Abella 1997).

The ILO has been especially active in advocating better treatment of migrants in the Middle East, who make up 50 to 90 percent of private-sector workers in the region. In many labor-importing countries, migrants are vulnerable to exploitation because they need a local sponsor to enter and remain in the country. Moreover, many migrants are women who live with their employers. The ILO played a major role in compensating migrants who lost their jobs, and often their savings, when Iraq invaded Kuwait in 1991.

Middle-income developing countries, such as Thailand and Malaysia, Poland and Hungary, Ivory Coast and South Africa, and Argentina and Costa Rica, are confronting the issue of managing migration for employment, and realizing that the experiences of the industrial democracies may not be applicable. For example, Thailand officially prohibits the entry of unskilled foreign workers, but there are 600,000 to 800,000 such workers in the country. The ILO is helping the Thai government to evolve from an ad hoc policy of registering some of these migrants and deferring their removal for six months to a policy of anticipating a medium-term demand for migrants and developing an appropriate policy to deal with that demand.

On the first UN International Migrants Day, December 18, 2001, the ILO director general Juan Somavia said, "Migrant workers are an asset to every country where they bring their labor . . . [but] the fate of these immigrants runs contrary to the ILO goal of promoting decent work for all." The ILO statement asked countries to give migrants "the dignity they deserve as human beings and the respect they deserve as workers."

Philip Martin

See also: Guestworkers; Middle East Guestworkers; Migrant Rights; Migration Policy; UN Convention on the Rights of Migrant Workers, 1990

References and further reading:

Abella, Manolo I. 1997. *Sending Workers Abroad.* Geneva: International Labour Office.

Böhning, W. R. 1996. *Employing Foreign Workers. A Manual on Policies and Procedures of Special Interest to Middle- and Low-Income Countries.* Geneva: International Labour Office.

Galenson, Walter. 1981. *The International Labor Organization: An American View.* Madison: University of Wisconsin Press.

International Labour Organization website, http://www.ilo.org/.

National Industrial Conference. 1983. *The Work of the International Labor Organization.* New York: William S. Hein.

International Refugee Organization

The International Refugee Organization (IRO), formed to maintain, register, repatriate, and resettle European refugees in the aftermath of World War II, was in many respects the predecessor of the current United Nations High Commissioner for Refugees (UNHCR). A nonpermanent specialized agency of the United Nations, the IRO provided care and assistance to more than 1 million refugees and displaced persons during its period of operation from July 1, 1947, to January 31, 1952.

The roots of the IRO's establishment lay in attempts by the United States to find an alternative to the repatriation of European refugees displaced by the war and its aftermath, most of whom were located in camps in countries under Allied occupation. The United States believed that these individuals should not be forcefully repatriated back to Communist countries, where they would almost certainly face collective punishment or persecution. The Russians, by contrast, believed that "the refugee problem was non-existent" and generally saw the displaced persons in camps across Europe who refused to return as "quislings, traitors and war criminals" keen, with the help of the Americans, to mobilize anti-Soviet sentiment (Marrus 2002, 340–341). Debates over formation of the IRO both exemplified and reinforced the emerging East/West tensions that would come to characterize the Cold War. Although some concessions to Soviet concerns were made, the IRO was established with a constitution that declared that "no refugees or displaced persons [with valid objections] shall be compelled to return to their country of origin" (UNHCR 2000, 16). By 1948, the organization's program had "expanded beyond displaced persons from World War II to include escapees from East European communist regimes" (Loescher 1993, 51).

The IRO's success in facilitating resettlement and in resolving the plight of refugees was impressive. Within the first year of its existence, the organization had resettled the majority of the refugees it had inherited from its wartime predecessor, the United Nations Relief and Rehabilitation Administration (ibid., 52). Its success was partly due to the need for unskilled and semiskilled labor across Western European countries and beyond during the period of postwar reconstruction and economic expansion of the 1940s and early 1950s. During this period, "single men, childless couples and manual labourers" were particularly welcome as immigrants in capitalist states (ibid.). In charge of a fleet of some forty ships, the IRO could take refugees to countries of resettle-

Simon Stanevicius, a 76-year-old displaced person from Munich, Germany, gazes at the New York skyline through a porthole of the U.S. transport General W. G. Hann, *as he arrives from Europe. Resettled by the International Refugee Organization, Stanevicius is going to live in Rochester, New York. (Bettmann/Corbis)*

ment around the world (Marrus 2002, 343). By the end of the IRO's period of operation, "the United States [had] received 31.7 percent of the refugees resettled; Australia, 17.5; Israel, 12.7; Canada, 11.9; Britain, 8.3; Western Europe, 6.8; and the countries of Latin America, 6.5" (Loescher 1993, 52).

Despite the IRO's successes, a "hard core" of refugees, either undesirable as labor or not fitting under the IRO's mandate, remained in camps in Europe at the end of the organization's tenure. Yet there could be no denying the fact that the IRO had made an important difference to international responses to refugees. In total, it had resettled 1,039,150 persons in the four years of its operation (Marrus 2002, 344); by contrast, only 73,000 persons had been repatriated. Moreover, its mandate, by defining refugees in terms of their experience, rather than their country of origin, presaged the universal definition of a refugee that would become an influential part of international law both through the statute of the UNHCR in 1950 and through the Convention Relating to the Status of Refugees in 1951.

Matthew J. Gibney

See also: Cold War; Displaced Persons; Refugee Camps; Refugees; Repatriation; Resettlement; Skilled Migration; Soviet Repatriation after World War II; UN Convention Relating to the Status of Refugees, 1951; UN High Commissioner for Refugees; UN Relief and Rehabilitation Administration

References and further reading:

Holborn, Louise W. 1956. *The International Refugee Organization.* Oxford: Oxford University Press.

Loescher, Gil. 1993. *Beyond Charity: International Cooperation and the Global Refugee Crisis.* Oxford: Oxford University Press.

Marrus, Michael R. 2002. *The Unwanted: European Refugees from the First World War through the Cold War.* Philadelphia: Temple University Press.

Skran, Claudena. 1995. *Refugees in Inter-War Europe: The Emergence of a Regime.* Oxford: Clarendon.

United Nations High Commissioner for Refugees. 2000. *The State of the World's Refugees 2000.* Oxford: Oxford University Press.

Iran and Refugees

At the end of the twentieth century the Islamic Republic of Iran hosted the largest refugee population in the world. In 1999, Iranian officials reported that there were more than 1.8 million refugees in the country. Afghans constituted the largest group, numbering 1.3 million, and there were more than 500,000 mainly Kurdish Iraqis. It was also estimated that Iran hosted 30,000 asylum seekers of other nationalities, mainly from Pakistan, Bangladesh, and Sri Lanka (USCR 2000).

Iran first started to recognize refugees in 1963 under an ordinance designed specifically for this purpose. In 1976, the Iranian government ratified the 1951 United Nations Convention Relating to the Status of Refugees and its 1967 Protocol, making reservations to Articles 17 (wage-earning employment), 23 (public relief), 24 (labor legislation and social security), and 26 (freedom of movement). The provisions of the 1951 convention, the 1967 Protocol, and the ordinance of 1963 all have force of law in Iran. In addition, Article 155 of the 1979 Iranian constitution stipulates that asylum is to be granted to those who claim it unless they have been deemed traitors or criminals under Iranian law (USCR 2000). Apart from international and national policies regarding refugees, Iran has opened its borders to asylum seekers based on Islamic solidarity with those who are oppressed (Amiri 2000). Even before ratifying the 1951 convention, Iran was accepting refugees fleeing northern Iraq.

Refugees from Iraq

Iraqi Kurds began to arrive in Iran in 1975 as a consequence of the Algiers Agreement between Mohammad Reza, the shah of Iran, and Saddam Hussein of Iraq. According to this agreement, the shah withdrew his support of the Kurdish rebellion in northern Iraq in exchange for settlement of a border dispute with Iraq. Nevertheless, many Kurds fled into neighboring Iran seeking refuge.

During the Iran-Iraq war of the 1980s, approximately 350,000 additional Iraqi Kurds fled northern Iraq because of persecution due to their alleged Iranian ancestry. In 1988, the use of chemical weapons by Saddam Hussein's army also prompted the flight of Iraqi Kurds to Iran. The majority were Feilli Kurds, a Shia minority, many of whom have been denied both Iraqi and Iranian citizenship (UNHCR 2000; USCR 1999a, 2000).

More than 1.5 million Iraqis fled to Iran during the 1991 Gulf War to escape the bombardments of northern Iraq as well as Saddam Hussein's retaliation against Arabs in the southern marshlands for staging a rebellion. However, almost all of these refugees returned to Iraq shortly after their arrival in Iran. Nevertheless, an estimated 70,000 Shia Arabs from the southern Iraqi marshlands have sought asylum over the years in Iran's southern province of Khuzestan. In 1996, another major influx of Iraqi refugees (between 65,000 and 85,000 Kurds) arrived in Iran from interfactional fighting around Suleymania and Erbil. In 1999, the Iraqi government decreed that Iraqis who had left the country illegally would not be prosecuted if they returned so long as their reason for flight was not based on "political/expulsion." The Iraqi government also said it would issue passports to those in Iran, excluding the Iraqi Kurds expelled in the 1980s. By the end of the year, more than 2,500 Iraqis returned despite the caution expressed by the UN High Commissioner for Refugees (UNHCR) (UNHCR 1999, 2000; USCR 1999a, 2000).

An estimated 18,000 Kurds also returned home in 1999. These migrants voluntarily returned to northern Iraq but did not comply with a 1998 Iraqi provision requiring all Iraqi refugees repatriating from Iran to go through Iraqi government controls (USCR 2000).

Nearly all Iraqi refugees in Iran have settled near the Iran-Iraq border. The Iraqi Kurds live in the northwestern provinces of Kermanshah, West Azerbaijan, and Kurdistan, and the Shia Arabs in the southwestern province of Khuzestan (USCR 2000). Because of the freedom of movement that refugees enjoy in Iran, less than 5 percent of the total refugee population lives in camps (UNHCR 2000). As Iran ratified the Refugee Convention with reservations on Article 26, the fact that refugees largely enjoy freedom of movement may be interpreted as "benign neglect" of the rules.

Refugees from Afghanistan

The majority of Afghans who have sought asylum are concentrated in two eastern provinces bordering Afghanistan—Khorasan, with 390,000 refugees, and Sistan-Baluchistan, with 400,000 (USCR 2000). There are significant numbers of asylum seekers (approximately 300,000–400,000) who have settled in and near the capital Tehran (Amiri 2000).

The first exodus of Afghan asylum seekers to Iran began in 1979 with the Soviet invasion of Afghanistan. During the Soviet occupation (1979–1989) up to the end of the pro-Soviet government in 1992, some 3 million Afghans sought refuge in Iran. Although many Afghans returned after the liberation of their country from the Soviet Union and the fall of the pro-Soviet government in 1993, subsequent wars between the different *mujahideen* factions during the 1990s and the rise of the Taliban (1996–2001) caused many of the same Afghans to again seek refuge in Iran (Amiri 2000).

Zarean, a refugee camp outside of Khoy, Iran, holds over 50,000 Kurdish refugees from Iraq. This camp has been in existence since the late 1970s to take care of the constant influx of Kurdish refugees fleeing the oppression of Iraqi president Saddam Hussein's regime. (Ed Kashi/Corbis)

With the rise of the Taliban, many Pashtoons, who at the time made up the largest ethnic group in Iran, returned to Afghanistan. Hazaras, a Shia Afghan minority from Hazarajat province and other parts of central and western Afghanistan, fled their country to escape religious persecution, and in 1999 Hazaras replaced Pashtoons as the largest refugee group in Iran. Other major ethnic refugee groups are the Baluchis, Tajiks, and Uzbeks (USCR 2000).

Iranian Refugee Policies

The Iranian Ministry of Interior's Bureau for Aliens and Foreign Immigrant Affairs (BAFIA) is responsible for refugee documentation, including temporary residence cards, repatriation, deportation, and other refugee issues.

The first Afghans to flee to Iran during the Soviet occupation were issued "blue cards" by the Iranian government identifying them as involuntary migrants, not refugees, with temporary legal status. These cards did not have an expiration date but could be revoked at any time. When blue cards were first issued in the 1980s, Afghans were entitled to subsidized health care, free primary and secondary education, and other social services (USCR 1999b, 2000). However, the Iranian government stopped issuing these cards in 1992 and since then has confiscated some of them, leaving many Afghans without legal status (Amiri 2000). In addition, the government withdrew food subsidies for those still holding these cards in 1995. Eligibility for repatriation assistance was, however, retained (USCR 2000).

Afghans who arrived after 1992 were issued temporary residency cards. Approximately 550,000 Afghans entered Iran after this date and were also issued registration cards for repatriation purposes. In 1996, these cards expired. Iranian authorities now consider those who still hold them to be illegal aliens subject to deportation. Nevertheless, they are still offered a repatriation assistance package if they are willing to voluntarily return (Amiri 2000; USCR 1999b).

The number of Afghans holding employment identity cards issued by the Iranian Ministry of Labor is relatively small, and such cards have not been issued in recent years. In the first nine months of 1998 only 7, 885 such cards were printed, and Afghans only received 4.2 percent of them (USCR 1999b). Though Afghans holding employment cards are allowed to work, Iranian law limits this employment to only sixteen specific jobs, mainly manual labor (UNHCR 2000).

The withdrawal and confiscation of various identity cards, and the limits put on them, have led to a significant increase in undocumented refugees in Iran. Undocumented refugees are considered illegal aliens or economic migrants by Iranian authorities. They do not have legal rights and lack access to the health-care, employment, or educational benefits granted documented refugees.

Although living conditions for refugees in Iran have declined significantly since the 1980s, new arrivals, particularly from the Hazarajat province in northern Afghanistan as well as from the adjacent provinces of Nimruz, Farah, and Helmand, continued throughout 1999 (USCR 2000). How many arrived is unclear, since the Iranian government refuses to register them. In the same year, however, the U.S. Committee for Refugees, after visiting the Médecins Sans Frontières (MSF) clinic in Mashhad, reported that over 50 percent of its caseloads were new arrivals (USCR 1999b).

Most of the 500,000-plus Iraqi refugees hold "green cards," which are comparable to the blue cards issued to Afghan refugees. Those Iraqis who arrived in Iran during the prerevolutionary period were issued "white cards," which provide more rights and benefits than the green cards, including the right to work, the right to obtain Convention Travel Documents (CTDs), and exemption from taxes. Unlike those who hold green cards, white-card holders are required to renew their status every three months and must report their movement and place of residence to the authorities. The government has continued to issue white cards, but usually only to highly educated individuals and established professionals, and to more Iraqis than Afghans (USCR 2000).

Unlike Afghan refugees, who are mostly illiterate, unskilled laborers, many Iraqi refugees are educated people who achieved economic self-sufficiency in Iran, and there are discrepancies in Iran's treatment of the two groups. Afghan refugees have frequently been subject to forced repatriation, but Iraqis have not. In July 1999, a London-based Iraqi human rights organization reported the first forced returns of Iraqis, with an estimated 300 to 500 returned to their home country. In comparison, some 100,000 Afghans were forcibly returned to Afghanistan during the same year (USCR 2000).

Changing Attitudes toward Refugees

The Iranian crackdown on both undocumented and documented refugees in the 1990s was said to be a result of Iran's deteriorating economic conditions caused by high inflation and widespread unemployment (UNHCR 1999). After the Gulf War, Iran hosted more than 4 million asylum seekers, although this number significantly dropped, to 2 million refugees, by 1997 (UNESCO 2000). The refugees' alleged negative impact on the economy led the authorities to all but shut the door to further immigration. It is claimed that refugees take jobs and services from nationals. In 1999, the official unemployment rate was 15 percent, and it was claimed that refugees were occupying more than 800,000 jobs. In the past, Iranian authorities ignored businesses that violated labor laws in order to employ cheap foreign labor because such practices helped Iran's economy, but in 1999 they began penalizing firms for hiring undocumented foreigners (USCR 2000).

Some officials also blame refugees for the rising crime rate. The Iranian government has cited reports that Afghan nationals alone make up the largest group of drug smugglers convicted in Iran (DFID 2000). Many think that in order to solve this and other domestic problems, the government will have to crack down further on refugees; others fear that their departure would hurt the economy (Amiri 2000). In response to these concerns, the Iranian government is relocating more refugees to camps in an effort to reduce the number of foreigners in the general population (USCR 1999b).

At the end of the twentieth century, there were an estimated 48,000 Iraqis registered in twenty-three camps; in addition, 36,000 Afghans were registered in seven camps (UNHCR 2000). This represented only 5 percent of the total refugee population. Iranian officials planned to greatly increase this percentage, however, claiming that moving more asylum seekers into camps would benefit both Iranians and refugees. It was hoped that this strategy of dealing with refugees would open more jobs up for Iranian citizens, reduce crime, and make it easier for government officials to repatriate and deport undocumented migrants. Iranian officials also asserted that putting refugees in camps would allow more asylum seekers to benefit from health services and security provisions and that the refugees would be better able to maintain their culture in the camps (USCR 1999b).

Refugee Assistance

The most destitute refugees have settled in camps that are spread across Iran. One of the reasons refugees in Iran have done so well in the past, however, is that the government allowed them to live outside the camps and benefit from living, working, and going to school among the national population (DFID 2000). This policy helped the majority of the migrants to become relatively self-sufficient. Refugees living in camps, in contrast, are isolated and become dependent on the aid provided by UNHCR, the World Food Programme (WFP), and the Iranian government. Even though the majority of refugees live outside of camps, UNHCR has only recently begun to focus on this group, increasing its allocated funds for non-camp refugees from 20 percent in 1998 to 40 percent in 1999 (UNHCR 1999, 2000). In response to Iran's plans to round up refugees and relocate them to camps, a UNHCR official warned that this would undermine the self-reliance these refugees had developed and tip the balance from reasonable self-sufficiency to dependence. He suggested that it would also create new tensions and costs that non-governmental organizations (NGOs) would not be willing to support (USCR 1999b).

UNHCR has worked with the Iranian government on refugee projects since 1983, when it set up an office in Tehran. Although the two have not seen eye to eye on many issues concerning refugees, they have continued to try to work together to implement policies beneficial to the refugee population. Many intergovernmental organizations, such as the United Nations Population Fund (UNFPA), the United Nations Children's Fund (UNICEF), and the United Nations Educational, Scientific and Cultural Organization (UNESCO), have also introduced projects for refugees. The International Consortium for Refugees in Iran (ICRI) was established in 1992, with support from UNHCR and the Iranian government, to act as an umbrella organization for international NGOs working in Iran and to attract new NGOs. However, foreign NGOs had many Iranian legal obstacles to overcome before they could operate in the country. In fact, there is still no provision for the registration of foreign NGOs, although over the past six years procedural agreements have been worked out permitting them to work directly with refugees and to establish project offices for short periods. The Iranian government insists that UNHCR use local instead of foreign NGOs as their partners, but UNHCR has resisted making local NGOs their "implementing partners" (Harrell-Bond 2001; UNHCR 2001). This has allegedly resulted in UNHCR curtailing spending on projects, sending millions of dollars "back to Geneva" rather than employ local NGOs (personal communication with a government official).

Compared to other countries with fewer refugees, Iran receives significantly less funding from international sources to address its needs as host of the largest national refugee population, a matter of great contention within government and accounting for its increasing resistance to accepting refugees. Iran received about US$20 million in assistance annually from international donors during the 1990s, with the main share of these funds going toward refugee camp costs. Pakistan, in contrast, received approximately US$500 million annually during the same period (Iran NGO Initiative, 2000). This lack of funding has not only limited the effectiveness of NGOs in Iran but has also helped fuel Iran's repatriation and deportation policy.

Refugee Women and Children

Refugee women looking after children on their own in Iran face many of the same difficulties as men, such as concerns over legal rights and access to education, health care, and employment. They also face special problems, however, and relatively few resources have been directed toward meeting these needs. A study conducted in 1999 showed that 45 percent of the refugees in Iran were women or children, and that 52 percent of the children were under the age of fifteen (Amiri 2000).

The financial burdens on households headed by women are great. Many rely on their children to work because jobs for women are scarce and pay very little. The types of work available for Afghan women are menial: shelling pistachios, cleaning wool, straightening used nails, and engaging in weaving and handicraft work. Able-bodied working men also find it necessary for their wives and children to work in order to help support the family (Amiri 2000).

Education

Although many Afghan women and their daughters are in favor of obtaining an education, particularly the literacy and skills training necessary to improve their own lives, economic and cultural obstacles prevent many from doing so, and among some tribes, particularly the Pashtoons, there is resistance toward female education. The World Food Programme has set up a program to encourage these families to send their daughters to school. Since its establishment, some areas have doubled their enrollment, but many girls still drop out even when their families can support their education. A number of girls say the subject matter is irrelevant and opt to work in a menial job so they can contribute to their families' economic well-being. Despite the high dropout rate, a number of girls have continued their studies, and some are now working as schoolteachers, helping others to succeed. International and local NGOs, such as UNHCR and the Iranian Literacy Movement Organization (LMO), are also helping Afghan and Iraqi girls to obtain an education (Amiri 2000).

UNHCR has supported the Iranian Ministry of Education in its goal of ensuring that children of documented refugees are able to attend school. In 1999, UNHCR enabled approximately 170,000 Afghan and Iraqi children to attend Iranian schools (UNHCR 1999). The many undocumented children do not receive support from UNHCR, however, and the burden of educating these children has fallen upon the shoulders of their own people. Afghans, for example, have started two schools in Mashhad, mainly for undocumented Hazaras, and there are many other self-help schools in Tehran, some of which have been accredited by the Ministry of Education (Harrell Bond 2001; USCR 1999c). These schools do not have adequate facilities and supplies; most hold classes in shifts divided by grade, and only the teachers have textbooks (*Los Angeles Times* 2001). The literacy rate among Afghans nevertheless rose from 19 percent in 1979 to 42 percent in 1992 (Salam Iran 1995).

Educational opportunities for Iraqis are better than those available to Afghans. About 75 percent of Iraqi boys and 60 percent of girls are literate, and more than three-fourths of around 20,000 Iraqi children in refugee camps attend primary and secondary schools (ibid.). Iraqi children taught an Iranian curriculum often have a difficult time because of the language barrier, however (USCR 1999a). Some Iraqi children are taught an Arabic curriculum by educators from their own community (AMAR, 2003).

Afghan Legal Committees

In response to the many disputes arising between Iranians and Afghans, and because many Afghans felt they would be treated unfairly by the Iranian legal system, in 1992 UNHCR undertook a unique initiative in Iran to establish "legal committees." Legal support for this alternative legal system, which was based on the Afghan tribal structure, was provided by the International Law Office. The first Special Legal Committees for the Settlement of Afghan Disputes were formally established in 1993 with the approval of the Iranian government. These committees provide Afghans with a familiar method for handling legal issues and free legal advice to help insure their protection and safeguard their legal rights (Keyhanlou et al. 2003).

When the committees were first set up in Mashhad, the caseload exceeded the program's capacity to help, and Afghans with legal or counseling skills were brought into the program to assist. They dealt with the majority of the cases, while Iranian lawyers provided support to the committees. In 1994, following the success of the special committee set up in Khorasan province, another committee was set up in the Afghan Embassy in Tehran. Two months later, another committee was established in Tehran, in the office of Unity Party, to represent the Shiite Afghan population. Most of the cases brought before these special committees deal with financial and family disagreements. Crimes, disciplinary problems, and problems with the government are also heard. The committees were first made up of men. In 1996, after it was realized that women were reluctant to go before the committees to raise personal or family issues, women were also appointed to the committees to help handle family issues (ibid.).

Iran and Its Refugees in the Twenty-First Century

In 1999, the government of Iran met with UNHCR to work out a "screening" program for Afghan refugees and a voluntary repatriation program. They did not extend the programs to Iraqi refugees. The joint program, which was concluded the following year, improved the rate of recognition of Afghans as refugees, allowing a number to gain the official documentation required to regularize their status. However, also in the year 2000, as part of its third five-year development plan, the Iranian parliament approved Article 48, which implied that all foreigners without a work permit would have to leave the country by March 2001 unless they faced danger to their lives upon return (UNHCR 2000). This new legislation is another sign that Iran is becoming increasingly intolerant of its refugee population.

Other events of the first few years of the twenty-first century have added to Iran's desire to eliminate its refugee population. In October 2001, in response to the terrorist attacks of September 11, 2001, the United States invaded Afghanistan to rid it of terrorist camps and topple the Taliban regime. During the attack hundreds of thousands of refugees fled toward the Iranian border. The Red Cross set up camps to receive these new arrivals *inside* the Afghan border, hoping to help them there rather than making it necessary for them to cross into Iran to receive aid. Many refugees entered Iran anyway, and even though tens of thousands have returned to their own country since the end of the Afghan conflict, many have stayed in Iran. Iran's intolerance of its refugee population, however, is forcing many Afghans to return home. The Iranian government, citing the fact that there is no longer a threat from the Taliban regime, has stated that there is no reason to seek asylum in Iran. In May 2003, Iranian officials announced that all Afghans would have to leave the country by the end of 2004 (ODVV 2003).

When, in March 2003, the United States attacked Iraq in order to oust Saddam Hussein and rid Iraq of its purported weapons of mass destruction, Iran and UNHCR were expecting a flood of refugees to enter Iran's borders, echoing the events of the U.S.-backed war in Afghanistan two years earlier. However, no great migration occurred. Iraqis who did flee are preparing to return as soon as possible.

It seems that Iran will soon see its wish to be rid of its burdensome refugee population fulfilled. However, many issues regarding the preparation of refugees for their return still need to be addressed in order for their repatriation to be successful.

Barbara Harrell-Bond, Randy Crisler, and Hani Mansourian

References and further reading:

Aftab-e-yazd. 2001. "Carol Foyer: Iran the World's Largest Haven for Refugees." January 27, http://www.netiran.com/?fn=artd(806).

Amiri, S. 2000. "Afghan Gender Equity Programme (AGEP): A Concept Paper, Islamic Republic of Iran." Unpublished paper.

Department for International Development. 2000. "Exclusive Summary Report." London: DFID.

Harrell-Bond, Barbara. 2001. "Report to FRMS on Iran Trip." Forced Migration and Refugee Studies, American University of Cairo. Unpublished paper.

Iran NGO Initiative. 2000. "Iranian NGOs: Situation Analysis." Online report prepared by M. Baquer Namazi, http://www.iranngos.org/.

Keyhanlou, Fatemeh, Hani Mansourian, and Negar Azimi. 2003. "Settling Refugee Disputes in Iran." *Forced Migration Review,* no. 18 (September): 43–44.

Los Angeles Times. 2001. "Afghan Refugees in Iran Learn to Keep School a Secret." December 25.

Organization for Defending Victims of Violence. 2003. "All Afghans to Return Home by 2004." *Organization for Defending Victims of Violence (ODVV) Newsletter* 144, May 29.

Salam Iran. 1995. "Effect of Imposed War on Women," Embassy of the Islamic Republic of Iran, Ottawa, Canada, http://www.salamiran.org/Women/NROW/1995/ImposedWar.html.

United Nations Educational, Scientific and Cultural Organization. 2000. "The EFA 2000 Assessment: Country Reports, Iran," http://www2.unesco.org/wef/countryreports/iran/rapport_2_1.html.

United Nations High Commissioner for Refugees. 1999. "Global Report: Islamic Republic of Iran," http://www.unhcr.ch/cgi-bin/texis/vtx/publ/.

———. 2000. "Islamic Republic of Iran: Annual Protection Report (January–December 2000)."

———. 2001. "Mid-Year Progress Report: Islamic Republic of Iran," http://www.unhcr.ch/pubs/fdrs/my2001/irn.pdf.

———. 2002. "Crisis in Afghanistan." United Nations Research, January 21.

United Nations Office for the Coordination of Humanitarian Affairs. 2002. "Iran: NGO Renews Calls for Assistance for Iraqi Refugees," September 23. Integrated Regional Information Network (IRIN), http://www.irinnews.org/report.asp?ReportID=30018&SelectRegion=Central_Asia&SelectCountry=IRAN.

U.S. Committee for Refugees. 1999a. "Iraqi Refugees in Iran." *Refugee Reports* 20, no. 6 (June): 10–11, http://www.refugees.org/world/articles/iran3_rr99_6.htm.

———. 1999b. "Refugees in Iran: Who Should Go? Who Should Stay?" *Refugee Reports* 20, no. 6 (June): 1–4, 6–9, http://www.refugees.org/world/articles/iran_rr99_6.htm.

———. 1999c. "Afghan Schools Struggle in Iran." *Refugee Reports* 20, no. 6 (June): 5, http://www.refugees.org/world/articles/iran2_rr99_6.htm.

———. 2000. "Country Report: Iran," http://www.refugees.org/mideast.aspx.

Iraqi Diaspora

Throughout the twentieth century, Iraq has been a paradox. Rather than generating a stable economy and employment opportunities for the population, the flow of oil wealth was accompanied by successive waves of migration resulting in the establishment of an Iraqi diaspora in the Middle East, Europe, North America, and Australia. The ethnic and religious diversity of the country, coupled with political turmoil, led to the flight of substantial sections of the population.

Estimating the size of the Iraqi diaspora remains problematic at present. Reliable statistics on Iraqi migration are simply not available. International sources tend to document the number of refugees and asylum seekers, who constitute only one category of migrants. Anecdotal evidence suggests between 2 million and 4 million Iraqis living abroad. A more accurate assessment of the size of the Iraqi diaspora requires the amalgamation of national censuses in more than seventy-five countries. According to the United Nations High Commissioner on Refugees (UNHCR), Iraqi refugee status applications increased dramatically after the Gulf War of 1990–1991, reaching an unprecedented high level of 52,301 applications in 1998, with UNHCR branches in Jordan, Turkey, Germany, and the Netherlands receiving more than 5,000 applications each.

In the first half of the twentieth century, migrants were drawn predominantly from religious minorities (for example, Chaldeans, Armenians, and Assyrians) and ethnic groups (such as Kurds and Turkomans). The establishment of an Iraqi state under British mandate in 1921 was followed by the departure of substantial non-Muslim and non-Arab groups, who joined already established minorities in the United States, Europe, and Australia. As the Arab character of the newly created Iraqi state became increasingly prominent, religious and ethnic minorities feared discrimination; some migrated in search of religious freedom and new economic opportunities. Iraqi Christian enclaves began to be consolidated in Detroit, Chicago, and Sydney.

In the post–World War II period, while the migration of ethnic and religious minorities continued, new migrants belonged to mainstream Iraqi Arab society. During this period, three waves of migration are discerned. The first wave of migration followed the overthrow of the Iraqi monarchy in 1958. Elite urban families, part of the deposed ruling group, fled the country and established Iraqi enclaves in the United Kingdom, mainly in London. Other members of this group established small niches in Lebanon, Syria, Egypt, and the Arab Gulf. As the newly created republic pursued a fierce campaign against dissidents and opposition groups, members of the intelligentsia and professional classes were driven into exile in neighboring Arab countries and Europe. A subcategory during this period was Iraqi Jews, who began to leave Iraq after the establishment of the state of Israel in 1948. Iraqi Jewish minorities began to appear in New York, London, and Israel. The migration of Iraqi Jews, the majority of whom lived in Baghdad, continued until the early 1970s.

The second wave of migration coincided with the Iran-Iraq War of the 1980s. The loyalty of some Iraqi Shia was doubted by the Baathist Arab regime, which deported Shia clergy and families believed to have "Iranian" ancestry. They were accused of divided loyalties at a time when Iraq was at war with neighboring Iran, a predominantly Shia country. Iraqi Shia arrived as refugees in Iran and Arab Gulf countries, with substantial Shia minorities of their own. It was estimated that more than 30,000 Iraqi Shia were deported to Iran. Later some refugees moved to Europe in search of asylum. Others left Iraq voluntarily as a result of

A member of Sydney's Iraqi community joins family and friends in Sydney's Hyde Park April 12, 2003, as Iraqis across Australia celebrate the fall of Saddam Hussein's regime. (Reuters/Corbis)

the deterioration of the Iraqi economy under the pressure of war and forced military service.

The third wave of migration followed Saddam Hussein's invasion of Kuwait in 1990. The collapse of the Iraqi economy under international sanctions, which gradually destroyed the country's infrastructure and local resources, led to widespread migration from all sections of Iraqi society. These latecomers joined the already established Iraqi diaspora in the Arab world, with neighboring Jordan serving as a first transient station. Some migrants and refugees found their way to Europe and North America. Today the largest concentration of Iraqis is believed to be in the United Kingdom, where more than 300,000 Iraqis live.

The Iraqi diaspora consists of religious and ethnic minorities in addition to members of the mainstream Iraqi Arab society. Given the historical context in which this migration has taken place over the past century, the Iraqi diaspora does not fall within clear-cut categories of forced versus voluntary migration or economic versus political migration. Genuine refugees, exiles, and asylum seekers intermingle with discontented Iraqis and those seeking economic opportunities abroad. Thus, like other diasporas, Iraqis abroad do not represent an undifferentiated mass. However, more than in other diasporas, schisms within Iraqi migrant communities are exaggerated because of class, ethnic, and religious divisions predominant in Iraq. The context of migration itself has tended to increase these schisms.

Early migrants in the late 1950s belonged to the wealthy elite, members of which were drawn from established families. These included members of the royal family, diplomats, politicians, and army generals. Some fled Iraq with substantial resources, making their adaptation abroad a smooth process. They established flourishing trade networks between Beirut, London, and New York. In the 1960s, these were followed by middle-class professionals, including writers, artists, political activists, journalists, lawyers, and scientists. Some members of this group experienced downward socioeconomic mobility in the host country because of the untransferable nature of their skills. With time, some were able to acquire new training and engage in entrepreneurial activities and small businesses abroad. In the 1980s, more lower-class Iraqis originating in the urban and rural areas of Iraq fled the country. They sought employment in Arab economic niches established in European, American, and Australian cities.

In addition to economic differences rooted in the Iraqi class system, the diaspora is divided by ethnicity. Iraqi minorities, for example Kurds and Turkomans, establish ethnic enclaves abroad on the basis of perceived shared ethnic origin, language, and culture. Although the majority of Kurds in Iraqi Kurdistan are Sunni Muslims, there are groups who are Shia, known as Faylis, often found in low-income neighborhoods in Baghdad and other Iraqi cities. Migration is often accompanied by a reassertion of ethnic identity and subnational culture. Such ethnic groups build bridges with coethnics whose origins lie in other Middle Eastern countries. They share elements of their ethnic culture with other similar ethnic groups from the Middle East at the expense of links with members of the large Iraqi diaspora.

Further divisions revolve around religion and sectarian identity. Within the Iraqi Christian diaspora, Assyrians, Chaldeans, and Armenians are set apart from each other and from mainstream Iraqis by virtue of belonging to national churches, reflecting diverse denominations within the Christian communities in Iraq itself. Such divisions tend to be reproduced in areas where there are substantial immigrant communities. Within the Arab Iraqi diaspora, sectarian divisions between the Sunnis and Shi'is are also reproduced, with the latter setting themselves apart through belonging to predominantly Shia places of worship and sectarian political parties in the diaspora. Though there tends to be intermingling across the Iraqi ethnic and religious divide, it is often among the educated secular professional elite, both Sunni and Shia, Arab and Kurd. The religious and ethnic identity of members of this group is often overlooked in the pursuit of professional networks and regrouping in the context of the diaspora.

These divisions have led to the fragmentation of the Iraqi diaspora to the extent that it may be inappropriate to invoke the term "Iraqi" in describing it. This is perhaps attributed to the failure of the national project in Iraq itself, a project associated with political turmoil, exclusion of substantial sections of society from the political process, marginalization of minority groups and sects, and promotion of an uncompromising Arab nationalist ideology adopted by a dominant Sunni minority. The exclusion of ethnic and religious minorities in Iraq is also accompanied by systematic co-optation of members of these groups. This makes Iraqi ethnic and religious groups difficult to categorize generally as communities subjected to discrimination or exclusion throughout the second half of the twentieth century.

Notwithstanding this fragmentation, since the 1990s the diaspora has been engaged in transnational political activism, encouraged by outside sponsorship, for example Western and Arab governments, in addition to regional powers, for example Turkey, Syria, Iran, and, since the 1990s, Saudi Arabia. Political activism is not only a reflection of the specific nature of Iraqi migration and the life histories of the actors involved, but also a venue for the promotion of personal political and economic careers. The political economy of this diaspora is one characterized by interconnections between subjective narratives of displacement, political ideology, and economic hardship resulting from dislocation of individuals whose past histories do not lend themselves to easy and quick adaptation in host societies unaware of the complexities of the Iraqi home scene. This has made the Iraqi diaspora an extremely politicized community exhibiting a high level of political activism. So far the main center of activism is London, Iran, and Washington, where opposition political parties establish headquarters in exile. Abroad, around Iraqi research institutes, Iraqi art exhibitions, political party headquarters, welfare and refugee centers, immigrant community clubs, and mosques, a small number of the diaspora find employment as opposition leaders, human right activists, publicists for ethnic and religious identities, artists, writers, and publishers who create a vibrant intellectual life away from home. Literary and artistic creations, political party leaflets, and policy research on political and social issues in the home country proliferate around the globe, particularly in cities where Iraqis have a strong presence. At times, such activities celebrate particularistic identities rooted in ethnic and religious belonging; at other times an all-encompassing Iraqi identity is promoted. Political and intellectual productions shape consciousness of the particular, while at the same time they raise awareness of the common geographical origin among this dispersed and divided diaspora.

In the twenty-first century, it seems that this diaspora is destined to grow in the wake of the U.S.-led military conflict with the Iraqi regime. The toppling of Saddam Hussein's regime in April 2003 was followed by a new wave of migration. This time, the diaspora was drawn from the wide circle of Saddam Hussein's regime supporters, whose destiny was tied with that of his ruling group. As U.S. president George W. Bush declared an end to combat on May 1, 2003, male relatives of Saddam, together with middle-ranking Baath bureaucrats, fled to Jordan, the United Arab Emirates, and other neighboring Arab countries. Established diasporas in the West will not return to Iraq as long as the political and economic future of the country, together with the enforcement of law and order, is yet to be established on solid and stable grounds. Some of the politicized exiled elite began to return immediately after the coalition forces declared the cessation of military activities—in the hope of a share in the new political configuration envisaged after the demise of Saddam's regime. It is doubtful, however, whether established immigrants with economic interests abroad will rush back.

Six months after the occupation of Iraq by coalition forces, security seems to have dramatically deteriorated. The rebuilding of the country's political, social, and economic infrastructure will take a very long time. Several decades of devastation through a succession of military adventures, international sanctions, and plundering and theft following the fall of the regime in April 2003 have taken a heavy toll. This situation is likely to discourage would-be return migrants. Furthermore, Saddam and Baathist loyalists do not seem to have been rooted out of Iraq. This situation will no doubt deter return migration on a massive scale. Moreover, when members of the diaspora do return, their political agenda may collide with those visions locally produced under several years of suppression.

Madawi Al-Rasheed

See also: Diaspora; Middle East Guestworkers; Transnationalism

References and further reading:

Abraham, Sameer, and Nabeel Abraham, eds. 1983. *Arabs in the New World: Studies on Arab-American Communities.* Detroit: Wayne State University.

Aghajani, Valentine. 1989. "The Assyrian Church History and Identity in Australia." In *Religion and Ethnic Identity: An Australian Case.* Vol. 2. Edited by Abe Ata. Richmond, Victoria: Spectrum/Victracc.

Fattah, Halah. 2001. "Negotiating Nationhood on the Net: The Case of the Turkomans and Assyrians of Iraq." In *Going Native on the Net: Indigenous Cyberactivism and Virtual Diasporas over the World Wide Web.* Edited by K. Landzelius. London: Routledge.

International Crisis Group. 2002. *Iraqi Backgrounder: What Lies Beneath.* ICG Middle East Report 6. Amman/Brussels: International Crisis Group.

McDowall, David. 1991. *The Kurds.* London: Minority Rights Groups.

Al-Rasheed, Madawi. 1992. "Political Migration and Downward Socio-Economic Mobility: The Iraqi Community in London." *New Community* 18, no. 4: 537–549.

———. 1994. "The Myth of Return: Iraqi Arab and Assyrian Refugees in London." *Journal of Refugee Studies* 7, nos. 2–3: 199–219.

———. 1998. *Iraqi Assyrian Christians in London: The Construction of Ethnicity.* New York: Edwin Mellen Press.

Yacoub, Joseph. 1994. "La diaspora assyro-chaldeenne." *L'espace geographique,* no. 1: 29–36.

Irish Diaspora

The scattering of population from Ireland has been on a large scale for many centuries, reaching a peak in the years of the Great Famine of 1845–1850 and its aftermath. It is estimated that about 10 million people have left the island of Ireland since 1700, a very large number relative to its population size, which shrank from a maximum of over 8 million in 1841 to a low point of 4 million in 1961. The long period of outward movement means that the global population who recognize themselves to be of Irish descent is now numbered at more than 70 million (Akenson 1996,15). This constitutes the contemporary Irish diaspora, which can be defined as all those living outside Ireland, south and north, who claim some form of Irish identity.

Employing the term "diaspora" to describe this population is relatively recent, one of the earliest uses being by Lawrence McCaffrey (1984 [1976]) in his book *The Irish Diaspora in America.* The subsequent broadening of the concept to the global scale follows theoretical expansion of the term to include displaced populations with themes of a long history of dispersal, alienation in the host country, a desire for eventual return, ongoing support for the homeland, and a collective memory importantly defined by this relationship. For many scholars these themes encapsulate key characteristics of the Irish experience.

The term was given an added boost by Mary Robinson, president of Ireland from 1990 to 1997. She made "Cherishing the Diaspora" a keynote of her presidency, stressing the notion's inclusiveness of different traditions within the island of Ireland, particularly Catholic and Protestant, as well as recognizing claims to an Irish identity amongst those who had emigrated and their descendants (Gray 2004). Her visits to Irish communities abroad placed a new emphasis on the welfare of disadvantaged Irish migrants. This outlook was enshrined in the Irish constitution following the Belfast Agreements in 1998, when Article 2 was amended to include the statement that "the Irish nation cherishes its special affinity with people of Irish ancestry living abroad who share its cultural identity and heritage."

Integration of the diaspora into understandings of Irish society was further signaled by the establishment of the Task Force on Policy Regarding Emigrants in 2001. This represented a radical departure from previous responses to emigration in which it had been constructed as "a silent hemorrhage, treated by denial, and about which only the historians had much to say" (Mac Éinrí, 2000). The task force was charged with identifying problems for Irish emigrants and recommending ways in which a greater input of resources by the Irish government could ameliorate some of them. Clearly the primary purpose of the report was to identify exclusions, whereas the totality of migrant experience is much more varied. As yet very few of the recommendations have been met.

The size, historical longevity, and global spread of the Irish diaspora give it a complex and distinctive character. Five main themes are important in tracing its development: historical patterns; geographic patterns; ongoing connections between the diaspora community and the "homeland"; the social positioning of people of Irish descent within the societies in which they have settled; and key features at the beginning of the twenty-first century.

Historical Patterns

Very broad chronological bands can be used to trace the growth of the Irish diaspora. Its different characteristics at particular times help to account for very varied consequences in specific locations. The earliest period, before 1700, was characterized by a range of small-scale movements, including those to continental Europe by two groups of migrants. Monks from Ireland settled in monasteries at Louvain, Douai, and Paris. Men romantically called "Wild Geese" also left, to serve as mercenaries in European armies, especially following defeats by the English—for example, after the failure of the Gunpowder Plot in 1605. As a result of such migrations, Irish quarters were established in many European cities, notably Bruges, Brussels, and Paris.

Poorer classes also emigrated at this time, including a continuous movement of the "wandering poor" to Britain. Other migration flows extended much further afield, for example to the Caribbean. Catholics were banished to Barbados after the Cromwellian campaigns of the 1640s, where the poor white "Redlegs" are believed to be their present-day descendants. Others were sent as indentured servants, often seized against their will from southern coastal areas. Major areas of settlement were the Leeward Islands, including Montserrat and Antigua, and Jamaica. These migrants account for the Irish surnames still common in Caribbean families.

Emigrants leaving Queenstown for New York. (Library of Congress)

The second phase, lasting throughout the "long" eighteenth century, was especially marked by the movement of Ulster Protestants to North America. As in the earlier period, a substantial proportion were migrants with financial resources migrating primarily for economic advancement, but also seeking greater religious freedom. In many ways this represented a further stage of migration for families descended from Scottish "planters," whose religious practices were seriously restricted by the Penal Laws of the 1690s through the 1780s. Between 1720 and 1760, about 600,000 Irish-born people emigrated to North America, of whom about 100,000 were Catholics. Many Presbyterians became Baptists and Methodists in the New World, and Catholics also changed religion because there was no effective Catholic church structure. This early period of settlement explains why the majority of people of Irish descent in the United States today classify themselves as Protestant.

It has been the third phase of the Irish diaspora, however, which has attracted the most attention and is seen as iconic. This was the huge outpouring that accompanied the disastrous famines of the first half of the nineteenth century and the agricultural restructuring that followed in the second half. Even before the Great Famine of 1845–1850, the number of emigrants had been at a high level. Well over a million left between 1815 and 1845, followed by a further 2.5 million in the decade 1846–1855 alone (Fitzpatrick 1984, 3). The vast majority were Catholics from rural western areas and increasingly included young single people as well as families. Later in the century the proportions of women outnumbered men as the stem family system passed farm holdings intact from father to son, replacing the subdivision between siblings of the pre-famine era. This movement of young, single women as labor migrants, although they usually traveled within networks of family and friends, was a distinctive feature of the Irish diaspora. Women constituted a far smaller proportion of other European migration flows. The availability of working-age migrants from Ireland coincided with a huge demand for manual labor in the rapidly industrializing U.S. economy. In total, more than 8 million Irish people settled in the United States during the nineteenth century (ibid., 1).

A fourth period of the Irish diaspora can be dated from the establishment of the Irish Free State in 1922. The achievement of independence for the twenty-six counties was closely followed by an international economic downturn, which led to the depression of the late 1920s and early 1930s. Immigration to the United States was severely curtailed, and emigration dwindled. When it was reestablished in the late 1930s, the major destination was Britain, though numbers were officially restricted during World War II. In the 1950s, however, there was a massive rise, forming what has been described as the "second wave," the first being that of the famine period. Over 500,000 people left Ireland between 1946 and 1971 as economic stagnation in the 1950s was matched by a postwar surge in demand for manual labor to reconstruct Britain both physically (housing and road building) and socially (education, health, and personal services).

The second wave came to an end in the 1970s when return migration to Ireland exceeded emigration losses for the first time, reflecting the temporary success of the foreign investment packages devised by the Irish government after 1958 and the benefits of joining the European Economic Community in 1972. The "branch factory" economy, however, was superseded by cheaper locations of production in eastern Asia. Coupled with the explosion of birthrates in Ireland, this led to large increases in unemployment and a "third wave" of emigration in the late 1980s on a scale similar to that of the 1950s. In this case, however, the outflow included large numbers of highly qualified young people, many of them college graduates.

Until the 1990s, therefore, the Irish diaspora was continuously replenished by new Irish-born migrants, giving it an unusual degree of continuity over a very long time period. Unlike other large migration flows within the Western industrialized world, such as European migrations to North America, which had already peaked by the early twentieth century (for example, those from Germany and Sweden), or migration streams from Britain's ex-colonies, which were sharply restricted by immigration legislation, the Irish have remained a very flexible source of labor. The poor performance of the Irish economy for most of the twentieth century has failed to provide employment for the economically active labor force, which has therefore been available for recruitment by economies with labor shortages.

The latest—fifth—phase of the Irish diaspora marks a distinctive break with this pattern. The growth of the so-called Celtic Tiger economy from the mid-1990s has created a labor shortage in Ireland that has been met, in part, by return migration. These returns are estimated to make up a quarter of the total in-migration (Walter et al. 2002). Emigration continues, but at a much reduced rate, and has been exceeded by immigration to Ireland since 1996 from a wide range of sources. Instead of scattering its own population, the Republic of Ireland has been attracting immigrants from a very diverse range of origins. As yet, however, parallels between Irish people's own experiences of diaspora and those of new arrivals in Ireland have not been widely recognized at a popular or academic level in Ireland. Indeed, Breda Gray (2004) has argued that invocation of the "Irish diaspora" emphasizes national specificity rather than highlighting shared diasporic locations that might be used to challenge racist exclusions.

Geographical Patterns

To a large extent the spread of the Irish-born population mirrors patterns of British colonization, though it also extends well beyond them. The intertwining of British and Irish histories over many centuries helps to account for this linkage, which has taken a great variety of forms. Irish people have been part of the armies and administration of empire, but above all they have provided "the massive number of everyday settlers" (Akenson 1996, 148). Colonization thus helps to explain the worldwide distribution of Irish people, but it is not the only explanation. The Catholic Church also added to the diaspora's global reach. Irish connections with Spain underlay routes established to Latin America, and the proselytizing imperative of the Catholic Church sent missionaries to destinations throughout Africa and Asia.

The longest-standing connection has been between Ireland and Britain itself. In addition to merchants and paupers, there is also a long tradition of Irish seasonal labor movement to agricultural regions in Scotland and England. The proportion of the "famine" Irish who settled in Britain cannot be known precisely. Census figures indicate that it was about 10 percent of the total emigrants, but it is estimated that about a million Irish people were missed, making the true figure nearer to 25 percent. In the twentieth century the proportion rose dramatically, and from 1930 to 1990 about 80 percent of migrants moved to Britain. Whereas in the nineteenth century the major centers were Strathclyde and Lancashire, in the post–World War II period, London, southeastern England, and the West Midlands became the prime centers of Irish settlement. The Irish diaspora in Britain has been clustered in urban centers to a much greater degree than the British population as a whole. The extended period of immigration and settlement means that a substantial proportion of the population of Britain has Irish ancestry, especially in the longest-settled areas. A Mori poll for the Greater London Authority in 2004 found that 11 percent of the London population had parents from Ireland, or who would describe themselves as Irish, and 19 percent had at least one Irish grandparent.

In the popular imagination, however, the greatest flowering of the Irish diaspora has taken place in the United States. Attention has largely focused around the nineteenth-century immigration of Irish Catholics. Statistical evidence suggests that 60 percent of Irish migrants in the period 1800–1921 settled in the United States, constituting 10 percent of the total immigrant flow over the period. In 1841–1850, the Irish constituted 45.6 percent of all immigrants, the proportion falling to10.5 percent in 1891–1900 and 3.9 percent in 1901–1911, then dropping steadily to 1.1 percent in 1961–1970. The present flow cannot be calculated because of the high proportion of illegal immigrants. In the nineteenth century, the largest Irish American populations were located in the major cities of New York, Boston, Philadelphia, and Chicago, but the Irish also spread to smaller towns and westward to California. In 1990, one-sixth of the U.S. population included Irish as part of their national background, second only to the number claiming German ancestry.

Despite the proximity of Canada to the United States, its continued British ties have provided a very different context for Irish settlement. The relative size of the Irish-born population has been much lower than in the United States, as many Irish immigrants into Canada later moved south. The greatest difference has been the attraction of a much higher proportion of Protestants to settle in Canada. It has been argued that this has discouraged Catholics in Canada from expressing their cultural difference.

Although the absolute numbers were considerably lower, the relative proportion of people with an Irish Catholic background in Australia is much greater. Over 25 percent of all migrants to Australia in the nineteenth century were Irish. Unlike in the United States, where the English and Irish populations continue to be counted separately, in Australia they have been officially linked as the "Anglo-Celtic" majority. It is only recently that scholars have begun disentangling the "British Isles" populations to assess the distinctive positioning of the Irish within Australian society. As in Canada, the proportion of Northern Irish Protestants in New Zealand is a distinctive feature of the Irish diaspora there. This proportion was increased in the 1970s when a significant number of families fled from the "Troubles" to settle in New Zealand.

Other parts of the English-speaking British Empire that have received distinctive groups of Irish settlers include South Africa, where the major groups involved were white-collar workers and policemen. But the Irish were also recruited in some numbers to non-English-speaking countries, including the Latin American republics. For example, Irish people were recruited to work on cattle ranches in Argentina in the mid-nineteenth century. More recently, increasing numbers have moved to other European Union countries, which account for about 20 percent of emigrants from Ireland, the most important destinations being France, Germany, Belgium, and Spain (Walter et al. 2002).

Connections with Ireland

The concept of diaspora highlights the ongoing importance of the "homeland" in the lives and experiences of migrants and their descendants. Emigration suggests a one-way outward movement and is often related implicitly to assumptions about "assimilation" into the society at destination. Diaspora challenges this linear view of movement, replacing it with a dual sense of belonging simultaneously to two societies to a greater or lesser extent.

Ties between Ireland and settlements overseas have been maintained in a myriad of ways at both individual and collective levels. Personal links have been maintained through letters and, more recently, through telephone calls and e-mails (Fitzpatrick 1994). Remittances to Ireland have been on a substantial scale. Cheaper transport, especially in the recent period, has provided the possibility of more frequent visits to Ireland. Indeed, the well-educated migrants of the late 1980s were named the "Ryanair generation" (Gray 2004, 159).

Permanent return movement has taken place, though on a smaller scale than for many other migration streams, especially those from continental Europe to the United States. The "America wakes" of the nineteenth and early twentieth centuries registered the finality of the loss of family members, and "returned Yanks" were seen as failures in Ireland. For some women, however, migration to the United States was part of a strategy to save up for a dowry in order to return to marry a farmer. In the twentieth century, larger-scale return movements from Britain took place in the 1970s and again from the mid-1990s to the present, in both cases reflecting a marked upturn in the Irish economy, which offered well-paid jobs to returners.

At a collective level, Irish people have retained, or built, wide-ranging links with Ireland. Particularly notable has been political involvement with movements in Ireland, usually connected with the ongoing question of national self-determination. In the mid–nineteenth century, Irish political activists in the United States were prominent in the Fenian movement, which also had substantial support in Britain. Irish American nationalism provided political and financial support for the Home Rule campaign in the 1880s, and in the early twentieth century the United Irish League and Sinn Fein looked for support in large diasporic communities, especially in the United States and Britain. More recently, fundraising through Noraid provided support to the Irish Republican Army (IRA) in Northern Ireland after 1968, and U.S. participation in the peace process played a key role in the signing of the Belfast Agreement in 1998.

Connections with Ireland were passed to the second and subsequent generations. In the United States this link is recognized in the widespread adoption of the term "Irish American." In Britain, there has been far more opportunity for the children of Irish migrants to experience their Irish background at first hand. Many have been taken to Ireland for the school holidays to stay with grandparents, uncles, and aunts and have often continued the close family ties into adulthood. Despite the development of a strong sense of Irishness, however, the adoption of a hyphenated identity has been much more problematic for the second-generation Irish in Britain. The Irish-born have frequently denied the authenticity of their Irish identity, using the derogatory term "Plastic Paddy," and the English regard them as "assimilated" and simply "English." This helps to explain the very low take-up of the option to tick the "Irish" box in the 2001 British Census Ethnic Question, which offered a new opportunity for those with an Irish cultural background to identify themselves as "Irish." Only about 10 percent of those with Irish parentage opted to do so.

Ongoing Differentiation of the Irish

Measures of socioeconomic location can also be used to explore the extent to which an Irish element continues to be distinguishable within societies of settlement. Although at different historical periods and in different geographical locations the balance of the more and less prosperous has varied, in all locations the stereotype of the "low-skilled" manual worker—the domestic servant and the construction worker—has been the most prevalent. The extent to which the Irish have retained distinctive social positioning, particularly at the bottom of the social scale, provides a measure of the impact of the political, economic, and social environments in which they settled as well as their place relative to other diasporic groupings.

In the United States it has been argued that the Irish were upwardly mobile in the second half of the nineteenth century and achieved parity with the white mainstream population by about 1910. Thereafter, as a group they have had an above-average occupational profile. This placing of the Irish, however, overlooks ongoing disadvantage amongst "poor whites" of Irish background. Direct links between poverty and discrimination in Irish neighborhoods can be identified in the powerful evocations of South Boston in the 1980s in Michael Patrick MacDonald's (1999) *All Souls: A Family Story from Southie.* As he points out, the issue of busing in the 1970s, which appeared to place the Irish at the defensive frontline of the black/white divide, hid from view the shared positionings and long-standing alliances between African Americans and Irish Americans in Boston.

By contrast, in Britain the Irish-born population continued to show a distinct clustering in the lower socioeconomic groupings throughout the twentieth century. In 1991, for example, Irish-born women and men were overrepresented in the lowest of the Registrar General's groupings, Social Class V (women, 14.1 percent, compared with English-born women, 7.5 percent; men, 12 percent, compared with 5.4 percent of English-born men). But, particularly for women, there is a bimodal structure, so that 32.9 percent were located in Social Classes I and II, compared with only 26.1 percent of English-born women (Hickman and Walter 1997, 250). This reflects the number of Irish-born women in lower professional occupations, particularly nursing. Evidence for the second generation is mixed. Some analyses point to above average rates of upward mobility (Hornsby-Smith and Dale 1988); others suggest an intermediate position between the English- and Irish-born populations (NESC 1991).

Recognition of continuing cultural and socioeconomic difference is blurred by classification of the Irish as "white," with the assumption that they are simply part of the "mainstream" of the societies in which they have settled. Recent scholarship has traced the particular trajectories by which Irish populations have "become white" during the past two centuries (Roediger 1991; Walter 2001). These routes and timings have differed in the United States and Britain. Moreover, Irish "whiteness" may take a distinctive form. By retaining its ethnic rather than simply "mainstream white" character, it can occupy a place between the negative positions of white supremacy and stigmatized "race." Diane Negra (2001, 229) has argued that Irish American ethnicity stands in for "white, normal national culture."

The persistence of a significant religious difference, especially between Catholic members of the Irish diaspora and Protestant mainstream societies, varies sharply between locations. In the nineteenth and early twentieth centuries, it was a major source of difference and discrimination, particularly in Britain, the United States, and Canada. Today it is most acute in Scotland, where the long-standing rivalry between Celtic (Irish Catholic) and Rangers (Scottish Protestant) football teams gives expression to deeper cultural divisions (Bradley 1995).

The Contemporary Irish Diaspora

At the beginning of the twenty-first century, the Irish diaspora presents a very complex picture. The Task Force on Policy Regarding Emigrants (Task Force Report 2002) identified areas in need of more substantial welfare support by the Irish government, especially for particular groups. These included the elderly Irish in Britain, a substantial population stemming from those who arrived in the 1950s and took low-paying jobs. Many retained a distinctive Catholic culture and took the brunt of anti-Irish discrimination, which was heightened during the IRA bombing campaigns of the 1970s and 1980s. In the United States, young illegal migrants were also identified as being at risk of exploitation (Corcoran 1993).

People of Irish descent are found at all levels of the societies in which their ancestors settled. Awareness of Irish origins and opportunities to express them publicly vary over time and are not simply subject to a steady "ethnic fade." Recently there has been a remarkable revaluation of Irish culture, accompanying the prosperity of the Celtic Tiger economy. This is illustrated by the worldwide success of Riverdance and the global spread of the "Irish pub" phenomenon. The numbers of St. Patrick's Day parades in cities outside Ireland have mushroomed over the past ten years. Moves toward establishing a lasting peace in Northern Ireland have contributed to this positive image.

The diaspora continues to receive a smaller trickle of new members, many of whom may be temporary sojourners. Although there was a net inward movement of population to Ireland of 30,000 in 2002–2003, about 20,000 people a year continue to leave. The destinations were varied: 29 percent to the United Kingdom; 22 percent to the rest of Europe; 9 percent to the United States; and 40 percent to the rest of the world, including Australia (Central Statistics Office 2003). The pull of long-established family ties remains salient, but patterns over time and space continue to shift as new economic opportunities arise.

Bronwen Walter

See also: Assimilation/Integration; Clandestine Migration; Class; Colonial Immigration; Diaspora; Economic Determinants of International Migration; Gender and Migration; Remittances; Return Migration; Skilled Migration; United Kingdom; U.S. Immigration; U.S. Multiculturalism; Women, Globalization, and Immigration

References and further reading:

Akenson, Donald. 1996. *The Irish Diaspora: A Primer.* Toronto: P. D. Meany.

Bradley, Joseph M. 1995. *Ethnic and Religious Identity in Modern Scotland: Culture, Politics and Football.* Aldershot: Avebury.

Central Statistics Office, Dublin. 2003. http://www.cso.ie/publications/demog/popmig.pdf (cited June 25, 2004).

Corcoran, Mary P. 1993. *Irish Illegals: Transients between Two Societies.* Westport, CT: Greenwood.

Fitzpatrick, David. 1984. *Irish Emigration, 1801–1921.* Dundalk, Ireland: Dunalgan.

———. 1994. *Oceans of Consolation. Personal Accounts of Irish Migration to Australia.* Cork: Cork University Press.

Gray, Breda. 2004. *Women and the Irish Diaspora.* London: Routledge.

Hickman, Mary J., and Bronwen Walter. 1997. *Discrimination and the Irish Community in Britain.* London: Commission for Racial Equality.

Hornsby-Smith, Michael, and Angela Dale. 1988. "The Assimilation of Irish Immigrants in Britain." *British Journal of Sociology* 36: 519–543.

Mac Éinrí, Piaras. 2000. "Introduction." Pp. 1–15 in *The Irish Diaspora.* Edited by Andy Bielenberg. Harlow, Ireland: Pearson Education.

McAuley, James W. 1996. "Under an Orange Banner: Reflections on the Northern Protestant Experiences of Emigration." Pp. 43–69 in *The Irish World Wide: History, Heritage, Identity.* Vol. 5: *Religion and Identity.* Edited by Patrick O'Sullivan. Leicester: Leicester University Press.

McCaffrey, Lawrence. 1984 [1976]. *The Irish Diaspora in America.* 2d ed. Washington, DC: Catholic University of America Press.

MacDonald, Michael Patrick.1999. *All Souls: A Family Story from Southie.* Boston: Beacon Press.

Miller, Kerby. 1985. *Emigrants and Exiles: Ireland and the Irish Exodus to North America.* Oxford: Oxford University Press.

National Economic and Social Council. 1991. *The Economic and Social Implications of Emigration.* Dublin: NESC.

Negra, Diane. 2001. "The New Primitives: Irishness in Recent US Television." *Irish Studies Review* 9: 229–239.

O'Sullivan, Patrick. 1992. *The Irish World Wide: History, Heritage, Identity.* Vol. 1: *Patterns of Migration.* Leicester: Leicester University Press.

Roediger, David. 1991. *The Wages of Whiteness: Race and the Making of the American Working Class.* London: Verso.

Task Force Report. 2002. *Ireland and the Irish Abroad. Report of the Task Force regarding Emigrants to the Minister for Foreign Affairs Mr Brian Cowen,* http://foreignaffairs.gov.ie/policy/emigrant_taskforce.asp (cited June 25, 2004).

Walter, Bronwen. 2001. *Outsiders Inside: Whiteness, Place and Irish Women.* London: Routledge.

Walter, Bronwen, with Breda Gray, Linda Almeida Dowling, and Sarah Morgan. 2002. *A Study of Existing Sources of Information and Analysis about Irish Emigrants and Irish Communities Abroad. Research Study for the Task Force on Policy Regarding Emigrants to the Minister for Foreign Affairs, Mr Brian Cowen,* http://foreignaffairs.gov.ie/policy/taskforcestudy.pdf (cited June 25, 2004).

Irregular Migration

See Clandestine Migration

Israel

The State of Israel, which gained independence in 1948, can be historically characterized as a country of immigration. The importance of Jewish immigration was central to the ideology of the Zionist movement from its inception in 1897. Israel represents an interesting case in migration from a global perspective because the return of diaspora Jews began before the establishment of an independent state able to regulate immigration on the basis of its own laws. Jewish immigration was historically a political act of ideological commitment and continues to be mythologized in this way today despite the diversity of actual reasons for which Jews have left their countries of origin and come to Israel over the course of the twentieth century. Nevertheless, since the early days of the Zionist movement, immigration of Jews to Palestine—later Israel—was conceived of in the ideological terms of *aliya,* "going up." The use of this value-laden term replaces discussion of *hagira* (migration) in the Israeli context. The latter term has rarely been

Commencing a Jewish settlement in Jerusalem, ca.1920–1930. (Library of Congress)

used in recent years except with reference to non-Jewish incomers (Shuval 1998).

By 1922, early ideological immigration by mainly European "pioneers" accounted for the presence of 83,704 Jews in British-mandated Palestine, which, at the time, was populated by almost 700,000 Palestinian Arabs, according to the first official census. The census taken on March 31, 1947, a year before the creation of the Jewish state, showed that Jews had gone from making up 11.1 percent of the population in 1922 to 31.1 percent, or 649,500 of the overall 1.95 million inhabitants. According to official Israeli historiography (Cohen 2002), this situation had been brought about by five successive waves of Jewish immigration between 1882 and 1939. Until 1932, these immigrants consisted mainly of ideological Zionists originating in Eastern Europe, in particular Russia, Romania, and Poland. These early waves of immigration were accompanied by a settling of the land by means of the *moshava,* the *kibbutz,* and the *moshav,* forms of collective agricultural settlement. Those who arrived following 1932 focused on building the country's urban centers. By the end of the British mandate (the period during which Palestine was entrusted to the British by the League of Nations following World War I), Jewish settlers lived in 6 cities, 22 smaller urban settlements, and 302 agricultural settlements, with 80 percent concentrated in the three largest cities of Tel Aviv, Jerusalem, and Haifa (Neuman and Ziderman 2001).

The period of 1933 to 1939 brought about a sizable inflow from the Jewish populations of Central Europe and Germany, who were fleeing Nazi persecution. After 1933 this immigration was officially constrained under the British mandate. Clandestine immigration, however, took place, especially after 1936, as a result of Zionist activity to bring German Jews to Palestine. An underground military organization, the Haganah (1920–1948), and the Af-al-pi (Despite) project operated in spite of British restrictions and official opposition to clandestine immigration under the Jewish Agency (the prestate Jewish leadership). The Jewish Agency itself refused to violate British mandate regulations regarding visas and certificates for entry into Palestine out of fear of jeopardizing official channels. Its control over entry into Palestine was opposed by a number of sources, including Irgun Zva'i Le'umi (National Military Organization) leader Ze'ev Jabotinsky, who advocated illegal entry in the aim of what he called "free immigration."

The period of immigration between 1939 and 1948, known as Aliya Bet (Immigration B), was characterized by illegal immigration organized covertly by activists in Palestine, mainly those in the *Yishuv* (settlement), together with partisans and Zionist youth groups in Europe and the Middle East. A small number of visas were also issued under the 1939 British White Paper quota. From 1945 to 1948, the British quotas were extremely restrictive, and many boats carrying Jewish immigrants were sent back and their passengers interned in Cyprus. Idith Zertal (1998) has argued that the 80,000 Holocaust survivors who immigrated illegally to Palestine in 1945–1948 were tools of the Zionist leadership in its political struggle against the British.

Following the founding of the state of Israel, a period of mass migration took place between 1948 and 1951. The arrival of nearly 700,000 Jews during this time doubled the total Jewish population in the nascent state, bringing it to 1.4 million. As Yinon Cohen (2002) has pointed out, the demographic impact of this influx is often analyzed without reference to the concurrent Palestinian emigration. The latter, brought about by the expulsion of some 760,000 Palestinian Arabs, most of whom became refugees in neighboring Arab countries, and the destruction of many of their villages, lasted almost two years and took place in two waves, from December 1947 to March 1948 and from April to June 1948 (Morris 1987). In essence, the two movements meant that a new Jewish population replaced much of the Palestinian Arab population, reversing the demographic balance between Arabs and Jews. This shift forged a radical geographical transformation of the mixed Arab-Jewish towns, where, until mid-1949, 124,000 Jews were housed in vacant Arab homes, officially declared abandoned property, as well as across the countryside, where "144 new Jewish communities were established, many of them on or near destroyed Arab villages" (Cohen 2002, 37).

The period 1948–1951 was also characterized by a shift in the demography of the Jewish population. Until 1948, 90 percent of the Jewish immigrants to Palestine originated in Europe. Although many of those immigrating after May 15, 1948, were European Holocaust survivors, by 1951 the percentage of Mizrahim (Oriental) Jews from Asia and Africa had increased from 12 percent to 33 percent, some 300,000 individuals (Cohen 2002; Dominitz 1999). The very mission of the new state was based on the principle of Jewish immigration, or what was referred to as the "ingathering of exiles." The fact that many new arrivals at this time came without capital or property adds to the ideological nature of immigration as conceived by the state's founders. The processes of aliya and *klita* (absorption) were largely funded by international Jewish organizations and the U.S. and German governments as well as by the Israeli state. "Absorption" is a key Zionist concept, and a Ministry for Absorption aimed to provide Jewish immigrants with housing, Hebrew language training, and a basket of financial measures to ease their integration.

The principle of free Jewish immigration at the core of Zionist ideology was institutionalized by the 1950 Law of Return. The law states that "every Jew has the right to come to this country as an *oleh*" (immigrant; "one who goes up") and that all Jews have an automatic right to citizenship of the state of Israel. Jews are classified according to the Orthodox rabbinical definition, which states that those born to a Jewish mother or who have converted to Orthodox Judaism are Jewish. Therefore, Israeli citizenship is founded on the principle of *ius sanguinis,* or "an ascriptive, ethnic-religious criterion based on identification which includes Jews, children and grandchildren of Jews and their nuclear families, even if the latter are not Jewish" (Shuval 1998, 4).

The Law of Return continues to be a source of contention to the present day. It has come under attack mainly from those arguing for a Palestinian right of return that would recognize the dispossession of the Palestinian people following 1948 and accord the same right to Palestinians as that currently held only by Jews to return to their land. It has also been critiqued in recent times by those arguing for a multicultural Israeli state no longer exclusively based on Jewish citizenship. A repeal of the Law of Return under this vision would recognize the fact that "worldwide Jewry is no longer subject to the anti-Semitic attacks that plagued them during the previous centuries" (Altschul 2002, 1346).

Following the foundational period of Israeli nation-building (1948–1951) and the institutionalization of the Law of Return as the basis for Israeli citizenship, immigration to the state was characterized by several distinct periods. The first of these stretched from 1952 to 1966. During this time, immigration declined. The annual growth rate of the Jewish population went from 23.7 percent in 1948–1951 to 3.5 percent in 1952–1966. A sizable number of Jews—155,000—out-migrated (Neuman and Ziderman 2001), though large numbers also entered Israel during this period, notably from Romania and Morocco. The period was characterized by significant demographic changes brought about by the arrival of North African Jews, mainly Moroccans, who, in Cohen's terms, "accentuated the ethnic transformation of the Jewish state, and helped maintain the Jewish majority in the face of the higher fertility rate of the Arab minority" (Cohen 2002, 39).

The immigration of the Mizrahim has proved to be the most problematic in Israel's history hitherto because it sharply highlighted the extent to which the state's public political culture was defined by an elite Ashkenazi (European

Jewish) vision (Kimmerling 2001). The mainly Moroccan-born arrivals added to the Jewish populations originating from Yemen, Bulgaria, and Iraq that had come to Israel during the previous period of mass immigration (Cohen 2002). The 1950s and 1960s saw rising numbers of Mizrahim, with a younger population and a higher birthrate, and the proportion of Mizrahim equaled that of Ashkenazim by the early 1970s. Mizrahi Jews, however, and in particular the North Africans, were stigmatized in Israeli society. Housed in transit camps upon their arrival, they were subsequently sent to so-called development towns often far from the urban centers on confiscated Palestinian lands. Here they generally worked in unskilled labor for low pay and at constant risk of unemployment (Kapeliouk 1997). Culturally, they were seen as inferior by the Ashkenazi elite, and attempts were made to strip them of their Arabic heritage and impose upon them a European vision of modernized Israeli Jewry (Massad 1996). Both the geographical separation of Mizrahim in the frontier regions and their subordination in ethnic and class terms contributed to a strong segregationist element in Jewish Israeli society, thus challenging the success of integration claimed by Israeli leaders and their supporters in the diaspora.

It was in relation to Mizrahim that the sentiment was publicly expressed in Israel for the second time that immigration may not always constitute a good in itself. Previously these beliefs had been expressed in relation to Holocaust survivors, described by some Zionist emissaries to the displaced persons camps as "human dust" and as "unfit human material" for immigration (Grodzinsky 1998). Foreign Minister Moshe Sharet in 1948 said, "There are countries—and I was referring to North Africa—from which not all the Jews need to emigrate. It is not a question of quantity but of quality" (quoted in Massad 1996, 58). Mizrahim reactions to this subjugation began with uprisings against unequal housing conditions in Wadi Salib, a formerly Arab district of Haifa that had become an overpopulated slum inhabited mainly by Moroccans. By the end of the 1960s, Mizrahi discontent was solidified in an outgrowth of the Black Panther organization, the so-called Black Jews, who spoke out against Ashkenazi domination and the idea, expressed, for example, by Israel's first prime minister, David Ben-Gurion, that non-European Jews were devoid of culture and education (Massad 1996).

After 1967, the character of immigration changed once more. Economic development made Israel much less a haven for Jews fleeing persecution and more "an attractive destination country for immigrants seeking to improve their economic situation" (Cohen 2002, 41). Furthermore, following Israel's victory in the 1967 war, some 200,000 Jews from North America, South Africa, Australia, Latin America, and Western Europe were ideologically motivated to immigrate to the country. The occupation of the West Bank and Gaza Strip and the annexation of the Golan Heights in 1967 created more Palestinian refugees, and the ideological immigrants, many of whom held right-wing religious beliefs, established settlements there. It was only in later years, as these expanded, that the occupied territories came to be populated also by groups that were not ideologically motivated but instead encouraged mainly by cheap housing and other subsidies. The individuals who made up this wave of immigrants often left property and family in their countries of origin, preferring to come to Israel on tourist visas or as temporary residents with a view to returning should their aliya fail. As a result, 50 percent of those arriving in the period between June 1969 and October 1970 returned to their countries of origin, according to Ministry for Absorption statistics (Neuman and Ziderman 2001). Thus, a gradual "normalization" of immigration occurred in the Israeli context as unemployment or housing concerns began to figure more prominently in immigration decisions. Such factors were nonetheless denied in official discourse, which continued to emphasize the aliya ethos.

The ideological commitment to immigration was once again fulfilled by the arrival of Soviet Jews in the 1970s. Eighteen Soviet Jewish families, fueled by a commitment to Jewish identity and Zionist principles following the events of 1967, submitted an appeal to the United Nations Committee on Human Rights in November 1969 to assert their right to emigrate. As a result, the Soviet Union permitted 150,000 Jews to leave for Israel. The Soviet Jews arriving in the early 1970s were met with great enthusiasm, not least by Prime Minister Golda Meir, who proclaimed, "You are the real Jews. We have been waiting for you for twenty-five years" (quoted in Massad 1996, 61). The post-1967 Ashkenazi immigration instigated a trend, lasting until the present day, in which the number of first- and second-generation Mizrahis declined and the number of their Ashkenazi counterparts stabilized. Furthermore, 16 percent of the population was defined as of "Israeli origin," that is, born to Israeli-born fathers, by 1983. The choice of these terms of definition of origin and the decision to trace nationality back only one generation must be seen within the context of the Israeli nation-building project and the construction of the figure of the Israeli. They are choices, according to Cohen, that result "in the elimination of ancestry and ethnicity from official statistics within two generations, or about fifty years" (Cohen 2002, 42).

Another minority in Jewish immigration to Israel in the post-1967 period is made up of Ethiopian Jews, who arrived in two airlift operations in 1984 and 1991. Numbering approximately 80,000, Ethiopian Jews were mainly housed in absorption centers in development towns upon their arrival. Several thousand now live in settlement towns in the occupied territories. Their integration into Israeli society continues to be a difficult process. The community faces racism and discrimination, including crippling rates of unemployment.

The most well-known and numerically significant of the recent immigration waves to Israel is that of the Jews of the former Soviet Union. Between 1990 and 1998, 879,486 immigrants, many of them from the former Soviet Union, entered the country, representing an Israeli population growth rate of 19.3 percent (Neuman and Ziderman 2001). The majority of these arrived before 1993, making a significant impact on the Israeli society and economy. The Israeli approach toward this new immigration differed significantly from that adopted in the past. The state implemented a policy of "direct absorption" that eliminated state intervention in housing, education, and employment matters (Razin and Scheinberg 2001). This mass immigration triggered economic growth, especially, for example, in the construction industry, pulling the country out of recession. Although unemployment decreased by 1996, immigrants were not always employed according to their qualifications. Soviet immigrants were generally highly educated, many of them holding professional qualifications, and the demand for their skills was not high. Nevertheless, in general Soviet immigrants were equipped to adapt to a fast-changing modern economy and contributed significantly to its growth during the 1990s (Kapeliouk 1997; Razin and Scheinberg 2001).

The Soviet *olim* (immigrants) of the 1990s, unlike their predecessors who emigrated from the USSR in the 1970s, were not, for the most part, motivated by ideology, but rather by the promise of a better standard of living. Moreover, a significant proportion were not Jewish themselves but admitted under the Law of Return because they had Jewish relatives. This has led to a significant backlash against them, in particular by the religious right wing, elements of which even call for their repatriation. In reaction, many Soviet immigrants have not wholeheartedly adopted an Israeli identity but have retained their own customs and, most important, continue to speak Russian. Russian has thus unofficially become the country's third language after Hebrew and Arabic. The immigrants of the former Soviet Union are also very well organized politically. The most important of the political parties that represent them is the right-wing Yisrael b'Aliyah (Israel in Immigration), headed by the former dissident Nathan Scharansky. Another side of the story of Soviet immigration is represented by organizations such as the Russian Panthers, echoing the 1970s Israeli Black Panther movement, which campaigns against the racism endured by Russian immigrants in Israeli society, which includes incidences of significant violence.

Soviet immigration was accompanied by one other development in the history of Israeli immigration: the arrival of foreign migrant workers from the early 1990s (Rosenhek 2002). Migrants from Thailand, the Philippines, Romania, China, and Bulgaria, among others, started to arrive following Israel's decision to seal the border with the West Bank and Gaza Strip occupied territories in 1993. Once this was done, Palestinian blue-collar workers were no longer able to freely access their workplaces in Israel. Although it was hoped for a time that Soviet immigrants would fill the place of Palestinian workers, it soon became apparent that the mostly overqualified Russians had no intention of doing so-called "Arab work" (Bartram 1998). Recent figures show there are an estimated 300,000 migrant workers in Israel, representing 13 percent of the workforce (Ellman and Laacher 2003). Of these, at least two-thirds (Africans and Latin Americans, in particular) are illegally residing in Israel, having entered the country as tourists, or have expired work permits.

Migrant workers are generally recruited in their country of origin by recruitment agencies on behalf of Israeli employers for fixed-term contracts in a variety of sectors, especially construction, agriculture, and domestic services. Once in Israel, they come under the control of their employers, who generally confiscate their passports, which, since Israeli law requires foreign nationals to carry their passports at all times, forces the contract laborer to break the documentation laws. As soon as the contract comes to an end, whether at the end of the designated term or before it, due to extenuating circumstances, the worker must officially return to his or her country or risk becoming an illegal alien. This risk is taken by the great majority. The presence of undocumented workers in the Israeli economy has led to a campaign to deport them from the country. Despite political commitments to end migration, however, the continuing labor shortages brought about by the ongoing Israeli-Palestinian conflict ensures that the Israeli employers' lobby succeeds in bypassing restrictions. Deported migrants are replaced by new recruits from the sending countries, and the parallel black economy and sex trade, fueled by the ready source of undocumented labor in the country, continues to grow.

Non-Jewish migrants in Israeli society are also beginning to demonstrate an increasing political presence (Kemp et al. 2000). They are testimony to the fact that Israel participates in the global migration regime as a primary destination for the increasingly precarious globalized migrant labor force. Migrant workers in Israel, albeit having no rights of citizenship, account for 8 percent of the population and will continue to be a reality of Israel's social formation in the future. There is also a growing, if still small, number of asylum seekers in the country, particularly Africans, despite the fact that Israel does not recognize political refugees. These developments, in addition to the transformation in the nature of aliya brought about by the Soviet immigration of the 1990s, support Judith T. Shuval's (1998, 18) assertion that "the mythology of Israel's 'uniqueness' in the field of migration no longer seems appropriate." Although Israel officially only accepts Jewish immigrants, the reality posed by migrants and asylum seekers, in addition to the significance of the Palestinian presence within the "Green Line" (borders of Israel proper), may no longer support the future existence of a uniquely Jewish state.

Alana Lentin

See also: Citizenship; Jewish Diaspora; Jewish Immigration (UK); Law of Return; Palestinian Refugees

References and further reading:

Altschul, Mark J. 2002. "Israel's Law of Return and the Debate of Altering, Repealing, or Maintaining Its Present Language." *University of Illinois Law Review,* no. 5: 1345–1372.

Bartram, David V. 1998. "Foreign Workers in Israel: History and Theory." *International Migration Review* 32, no. 2: 303–325.

Cohen, Yinon. 2002. "From Haven to Hell: Changing Patterns of Immigration to Israel."" Pp. 36–53 in *Challenging Ethnic Citizenship: German and Israeli Perspectives on Immigration.* Edited by Daniel Levy and Yfaat Weiss. Oxford and New York: Berghahn.

Dominitz, Yehuda. 1999. "Immigration and Absorption of Jews from Arab Countries." Pp. 155–184 in *The Forgotten Millions: The Modern Jewish Exodus from Arab Lands.* Edited by Malka H. Shulewitz. London and New York: Continuum.

Ellman, Michael, and Smain Laacher. 2003. *Migrant Workers in Israel: A Contemporary Form of Slavery.* Copenhagen and Paris: Euro-Mediterranean Human Rights Network, International Federation for Human Rights.

Grodzinsky, Yosef. 1998. *Khomer Enoshi Tov (Good Human Material).* Or Yehuda: Hed Artzi.

Kapeliouk, Amnon. 1997. "The Changing Pattern of Israeli Immigration." *Le Monde Diplomatique,* November, http://mondediplo.com/1997/11/israel.

Kemp, Adriana, Rebeca Raijman, Julia Resnik, and Silvina Schammah Gesser. 2000. "Contesting the Limits of Political Participation: Latinos and Black African Migrant Workers in Israel." *Ethnic and Racial Studies* 23, no. 1: 94–119.

Kimmerling, Baruch. 2001. *The Invention and Decline of Israeliness: State, Society, and the Military.* Berkeley and Los Angeles: University of California Press.

Massad, Joseph. 1996. "Zionism's Internal Others: Israel and the Oriental Jews." *Journal of Palestine Studies* 25, no. 4: 53–68.

Morris, Benny. 1987. *The Birth of the Palestinian Refugee Problem, 1947–1949.* Cambridge: Cambridge University Press.

Neuman, Shoshana, and Adrian Ziderman. 2001. *Can Vocational Education Improve the Wages of Minorities and Disadvantaged Groups? The Case of Israel.* IZA Discussion Series, Discussion Paper no. 348. Bonn: Institute for the Study of Labor (IZA).

Razin, Eran, and Dan Scheinberg. 2001. "Immigrant Entrepreneurs from the Former USSR in Israel: Not the Traditional Enclave Economy." *Journal of Ethnic and Migration Studies* 27: 259–276.

Rosenhek, Zeev. 2002. "Migration Regimes and Social Rights: Migrant Workers in the Israeli Welfare System." Pp. 137–153 in *Challenging Ethnic Citizenship: German and Israeli Perspectives on Immigration.* Edited by Daniel Levy and Yfaat Weiss. Oxford and New York: Berghahn.

Shuval, Judith T. 1998. "Migration to Israel: The Mythology of 'Uniqueness.'" *International Migration* 36, no. 1: 3–26.

Zertal, Idith. 1998. *From Catastrophe to Power: Holocaust Survivors and the Emergence of Israel.* Berkeley and Los Angeles: University of California Press.

Italian Migration Worldwide

In 1900, Italy was one of the most important exporters of workers worldwide, but by the century's end it had itself begun to import labor. Migrations from Europe to America, including those from Italy, reached their historical peak just prior to World War I. Although emigration from Italy declined thereafter, it nevertheless long remained a far more important influence on national life than was the case in many other European nations. After World War I, the imposition of sharp migration restrictions in the United States and Italy diminished and began to reorient migrations from Italy across the Alps to northern Europe.

For the next two decades, the many Italians living abroad participated in sharp clashes between fascists and anti-fascists worldwide. Emigration then revived in the second postwar era as democratic governments at home and abroad saw new possibilities for economic growth in the recruitment of foreign workers. By the mid-1950s, Italy's migratory "guestworkers" quietly contributed to the beginning of Europe's economic integration. That integration also helped Italy to experience its own "economic miracle," transforming it into one of the wealthiest nations in the world. The result was that Italy quickly became an attractive destination for immigrants from Africa, the Middle East, the Philippines, and Central and Eastern Europe. Nearing the century's end, 5 million Italians still lived abroad, a small part of the more than 60 million people of recent Italian descent living in multiethnic nations as diverse as France and the United States, Canada and Argentina, and Brazil and Germany (Gabaccia 2000, 177).

Italy's Migrants in an Industrial Era of Globalization

Economic historians describe the years between 1870 and 1914 as a dress rehearsal for the globalization of our own times. From 1800 to 1870, the abolition of slavery and the recruitment of settlers for newly independent nations in North and South America had already initiated the largest migrations of recent human history. After 1870, the expansion of Europe's empires into Africa and Asia and the rapid industrialization of cities scattered through northern and western Europe and in North and South America significantly raised demand for labor to build and then to work in mines, cities, railroads, and factories. Labor recruiters, steamship companies, and frustrated peasants and artisans in rural areas throughout the world quickly created a labor market that was truly global in its dimensions. In the century between 1820 and 1920, as many as 150 million Asians and Europeans, mainly from rural areas, left their home villages and native countries in search of work abroad (ibid., 60). Countries that lost citizens to the global labor market worried over the impact of demographic loss on national strength, while countries attracting workers also worried about the impact of cultural diversity on national unity. Still, few countries tried seriously to reduce international mobility before the 1880s.

Among the throngs of international migrants was a surprisingly large migration from the small Mediterranean peninsula of Italy. By 1920, 9 million persons born in Italy lived in North and South America, Europe, Australia, and Africa. They were the residue of a mass emigration that had grown rapidly between 1876 and 1914, as over 14 million Italian citizens announced their intention to leave home (see Table I-2). Together with their foreign-born children (who, under Italy's nationality law of 1912, could easily reclaim Italian citizenship if they returned), these *italiani all'estero* (Italians abroad) formed an impressive group, almost half the size of Italy's resident population. In Argentina, immigrants from Italy constituted almost half the population of the country's rapidly growing cities; Italians were the largest group of immigrants entering the United States between 1899 and 1924 and the first- or second-largest group of foreigners in Brazil, Switzerland, and France. The same persons Italy labeled "emigrants" or "Italians abroad" were "immigrants" in France and the United States and "foreign workers" in Germany.

Table I-2 describes the 14 million persons who applied for permission to leave Italy in the years prior to World War I. Most were peasants and artisans from rural regions of the country. Contrary to popular belief, almost two-thirds were from the north and central regions of Italy and only a third from the south. As Table I-2 indicates, large numbers traveled to Europe as well as to North and South America, while a few went also to Africa and Australia. A very high proportion of the migrants were men. This was a sign that most migrants intended their migrations to be short term or even seasonal "campaigns." In thousands of transnational family economies, the wages men earned abroad shored up a threatened yet familiar way of life in rural villages in Italy. Contemporaries in Italy distinguished sharply between emigrants and temporary "sojourners" but erred in believing that those headed for America deserted their homeland while sojourners to Europe contributed to national development. In fact, rates of return from Europe surpassed three-quarters, but over half of the migrants who ventured to North and South America also returned (ibid., 7).

Table I-2: Regional Origins, Destinations, and Gender and Numbers of Italy's Migrants, 1867–1976

	1876–1915	1916–1945	1946–1976
Regional origins (%):			
North	45	49	28
Center	20	19	19
South	35	32	52
Destinations (%):			
Africa		3	
Australia		1	5
Europe	44	52	68
North America	31	25	13
South America	24	19	13
Gender (%):			
Male	81	67	71
Female	19	33	29
Number (in millions)	14.037	4.482	7.335

Note: Figures are rounded.
Source: Donna Gabaccia, *Italy's Many Diasporas* (London: University College of London Press, 2000).

Although the earliest Italian men had left home under the direction of labor recruiters—the infamous *padrone,* who were stigmatized as merchants of flesh—by the twentieth century most could depend on friends and relatives to help them find work and residences in France or Germany, the United States, Argentina, or Brazil. Nephews followed uncles, wives followed husbands or fiancés, and children followed fathers in "chain migrations" linking small villages in Piedmont or Sicily to specific foreign neighborhoods—La Boca in Buenos Aires or "Brookalino" in New York. High rates of emigration and of return helped to sustain transnational networks of marriage, kinship, and friendship between a village and its *paesani* (fellow villagers) living on several continents. While men sought wages abroad, their wives, sisters, and mothers toiled at home to feed themselves and younger children. Gossip as well as cash circulated freely and internationally through these village-based "diasporas," and residents of Italy who had never left home were often quite knowledgeable about the language, customs, wages, and consumption options of America and Europe.

Italian observers called settlements of Italians abroad "colonies"; some imagined migration establishing a worldwide demographic empire for Italy. In Argentina and Brazil, where significant numbers of Italians settled the Pampas or worked on coffee plantations, this association of emigration with empire-building made some sense. In parts of Europe, Argentina, Canada, and the United States, a settlement of Italians was more often portrayed as an urban "Little Italy." Little Italy provided a temporary home base for the many male laborers who traveled seasonally into the countryside to labor on railroad, road, and water system projects or to harvest sugar, coffee, or wheat. More important, it became home to men who, having gained more stable employment constructing urban streets, buildings, and subways, working in factories or mines, or running small businesses, could consider establishing more permanent homes and reunifying families separated by migration.

Immigrant families in Little Italy lived crowded together in small apartments where women sewed or cooked and laundered for boarders, assisted by their younger children. Sons and daughters of Italian immigrants most often began working for wages around the age of fourteen, usually (in the United States) in factories or (in Argentina) in smaller-scale industrial shops. As a family-based community, Little Italy created a lively demand for a wide variety of Italian-owned and managed businesses—groceries, restaurants, cafés, funeral parlors—and professional services, from doctors to music teachers. Wherever they settled, immigrants established a predictable array of institutions, including Roman Catholic churches founded by missionary orders based in Italy, a surprising variety of ephemeral and more stable but competing newspapers published by middle-class Italian nationalists and radicals of anarchist, syndicalist, and socialist convictions, and scores of small mutual-aid societies that provided health, death, and/or burial services. Over time, the mutual-aid societies federated, becoming, in the United States, for example, the Sons of Italy. Organization on national or ethnic lines facilitated both cultural preservation and incorporation, and sometimes even political activism, in the host society.

Nevertheless, the tendency of Italian immigrants to cluster residentially and occupationally led to charges by nativists in both Argentina and the United States that Italian immigrants resisted adopting the national values of and loyalty to their adopted home. So long as they expected to return to Italy, few Italian men changed their citizenship. By 1900, nativist demands for the exclusion of contract laborers, radical anarchists, or Asians had escalated in Canada, Argentina, and the United States into campaigns to exclude all newcomers from Italy and other parts of southern and eastern Europe.

Fascism, War, and Transitions in International Migration

From 1915 to 1945, international wars and the Great Depression raised nationalist hostility toward migration in both sending and receiving countries, leading to a sharp, if temporary, decline in emigration from Italy. In 1921 and 1924, the United States moved to close its door to new immigrants, allowing only 3,000 Italian newcomers to enter the country each year. Argentine nationalists decried Italian radicals and worried over the "italianization" of Buenos Aires but restricted immigration only after the onset of the depression. In Europe, the Swiss feared *überfremdung* (over-alienization) and imposed harsh restrictions on residence permits for Italians. In Italy, too, Benito Mussolini—who came to power in 1922—was openly and virulently hostile to emigration as a drain on national strength.

As Table I-2 shows, more than 4 million new emigrants nevertheless managed to leave Italy before fascism collapsed in 1943. The number of emigrating Italians dropped rather slowly in the face of restriction. Emigration remained significant throughout the 1920s, ranging from a high of 614,611 in 1920 to a low of 141,000 in 1928 (Gabaccia 2000, 134). Fascist-era emigrants differed but little from those of the prewar mass migrations. Most were underemployed agricultural workers and manual laborers from the north and center. Most of Italy's emigrants still returned, even to a fascist Italy. Women migrants were slightly more common than in the past, as families separated by emigration, yet facing restrictive immigration laws, relocated permanently to the Americas. Internationally, France replaced the United States as the single most popular destination for Italy's laborers in the 1920s and 1930s.

By the end of the 1920s, fascist hostility to emigration sharpened. Abolishing a Commission on Emigration established in 1902, Mussolini replaced it with a Commission on Italians Abroad. His government made passports extremely difficult to obtain and attempted to direct potential emigrants to rural "colonization" projects (meant to help the country become self-sufficient in food production) or to Italy's African colonies. Repatriation was rewarded. The fascist government even attempted to prevent underemployed rural Italians from moving to northern Italian cities. Critics claimed that Mussolini's population policies placed all Italian citizens under house arrest. But it was the collapse of the global economy and rising unemployment abroad, even more than restrictive policies, that caused emigrations from Italy to plummet during the 1930s. Fascist efforts to transfer underemployed Italians to its colonies, including Ethiopia after 1935, failed totally. By 1940, after years of propaganda, only 305,000 Italians lived in Italy's African colonies—far fewer than those living in New York City or Buenos Aires.

Mussolini's dictatorship also sparked a considerable, if clandestine, emigration of political dissidents. These *fuoriusciti* (exiles) included Communist, Socialist, anarchist, republican, and Catholic opponents of the fascist regime. Although most fled to France and other European countries, small numbers also migrated to the United States, Argentina, Brazil, and even the USSR. The exiles challenged Mussolini's efforts to find support among Italians living abroad. Conflicts between fascists and antifascists intensified in the 1930s as Italy invaded Ethiopia, as civil war broke out in Spain, and as Europe again moved toward war.

Abroad, sharp conflicts between antifascists and fascists emerged wherever large numbers of immigrants from Italy had settled. Beginning already in 1923, the Fascist Party encouraged the organization of branches abroad, but facing protests from the U.S. government, immigrant fascist supporters regrouped in several hundred autonomous organizations. While fascist consuls appealed to Italians abroad to join Italian cultural activities and to raise funds for Italy's imperialist ventures in Africa, Catholic clerics, pleased by the reconciliation of church and state in the Lateran Treaties, may have been more influential in encouraging tacit support for fascism in Italy. Unlike the consuls, they met regularly and counseled hundreds of thousands of Italian worshippers in their parishes and children in their parish schools.

Immigrants' attitudes toward fascism differed considerably from country to country and may have been most influenced by prevailing attitudes in the labor movements of their adopted countries. Fascism was particularly popular among immigrants in the United States, where hostility to Bolshevism had made Mussolini an attractive figure and where immigrants' sensitivity to immigration restrictions and anti-Italian prejudices caused them especially to welcome signs of Italy's emerging greatness. In 1935, Italian Americans collected half a million dollars to support Italy's invasion of Ethiopia. In France and Belgium, by contrast, antifascists' close ties to vigorously antifascist labor movements may have helped to isolate Mussolini's supporters. In Argentina and Brazil, antifascists identified with the popular Italian nationalist and republican hero Giuseppe Garibaldi, who had contributed to nation-building in Argentina; they may have found the populist yet authoritarian nationalist movements of Argentina more appealing than Mussolini's fascism.

The onset of World War II quickly resolved conflicts between fascist and antifascists in most immigrant Italian communities. Even in the United States, support for fascism disappeared almost overnight as Italians sought to prove their loyalty and to avoid internment. Ultimately, too, it was World War II and the political crisis of fascism's demise in Italy, rather than fascist policy, that finally terminated migration from Italy. In 1941 and 1942, only a few more than 16,000 Italians escaped their war-torn land; between 1943 and 1945, none at all left home. A victim of nationalism, depression, and war, international migration from Italy had collapsed, along with the global economy and international labor market that had supported it.

Guestworkers and Europe's Economic Miracle

Despite two decades of fascist rule and wartime devastation, Italy at the war's end was by no means one of poorest nations of the world. In fact, its industrial power had advanced relative to traditional Latin American receiving nations such as Argentina or Brazil. Like the other new democracies of Europe, Italy's economic recovery benefited from Marshall Aid from the United States. Although its Communist Party became one of the largest and most influential in Europe, the country also remained firmly in the NATO alliance, led by the United States, throughout the Cold War. However, neither the Marshall Plan nor NATO succeeded in reviving completely the lively Atlantic labor market—or Atlantic labor migrations—of the early twentieth century. The collapse of fascism ended Mussolini's emigration restrictions, but immigration restriction remained the rule in many traditional receiving countries, most notably in the United States. There, Cold War fears kept in place a restrictive immigration policy based on "national origins quotas" and family reunification until 1965. Unlike the United States, however, countries such as Australia, Canada, Switzerland, France, and—somewhat later—Germany saw the recruitment of immigrants and temporary foreign workers as holding the promise of economic recovery. Within two decades, northern Europe was experiencing an "economic miracle," and migration from Italy revived to levels not seen since the early years of the century.

In the first decade after World War II, Italy's new republican government faced many all-too-familiar challenges, notably high rates of underemployment and unemployment in the country's rural regions. Land reform alone could not provide work for a population that continued to grow at a rapid pace. Italy's Christian Democratic rulers believed that migration was most likely to benefit both the migrants and the nation if it was carefully regulated and controlled rather than prohibited. Beginning in 1946, Italy signed a series of bilateral treaties with Belgium, France, Sweden, the Netherlands, Great Britain, Argentina, Brazil, and Uruguay to recruit, select, and transport negotiated numbers of workers from Italy in exchange for trade and other privileges. The governments of receiving countries, in return, stipulated wages, provided housing, or guaranteed social services for the workers recruited in Italy. A particularly large and important agreement followed with Germany in 1955 and with Switzerland in the following decade. In Europe, such programs were soon called "guestworker programs" (from the German term *Gastarbeiter*). What the padrone had provided a half-century early—connections to employers and landlords—was now handled by government bureaucrats. Neither Italy nor its European negotiating partners—notably Germany and Switzerland—envisioned the "guestworkers" remaining, settling, or becoming "immigrants" as they did in the Americas. But many guestworkers did, in fact, settle. Overall, these programs built strong foundations for the regional economy that would ultimately generate the European Union.

Migration patterns also changed significantly with the rise of Europe, as Table I-2 suggests. The proportions of men among Italy's migrants rose again: Only a few nations recruited Italian women as independent workers, and then mainly as domestic servants. The representation of southerners among Italy's migrants also increased notably, and for the first time Calabrians and Sicilians (who had once overwhelmingly preferred migration to the Americas) now headed as guestworkers to Europe. Migrations to both Canada and Australia increased many times over as a result of bilateral negotiations and relaxation of restrictive policies. In fact, migrants leaving Italy to settle in Canada actually outnumbered those going to the United States in the 1950s and 1960s. Still other familiar patterns of the past held firm. Rates of return remained high in the postwar era—a sign that many guestworkers themselves, not just the receiving countries, anticipated and preferred temporary sojourns abroad. Guestworkers returned to Italy to vote, marry, and vacation. Most of those leaving Italy were still workers and peasants from rural regions who found work in most of the same sectors—notably mining and construction—that had offered them employment in the global labor market of the early twentieth century.

Australia and Canada—and, to a lesser extent, Argentina and the United States—saw a new Little Italy grow in almost every major city. Unlike in Europe, where men predominated, a Little Italy in each country was usually a community of working-class families. Representing new chain migrations and often rooted in different regions and villages in Italy, the newcomers did not integrate immediately into the organizational community life established by early migrants. Although they might attend the same parish churches, they typically formed their own fraternal societies and even established new newspapers.

In Europe, too, it soon became obvious that many guestworkers would not return permanently to Italy. Countries that had long accepted immigrants as potential citizens—notably France and Belgium—permitted Italian guestworkers to invite fiancés and wives to join them once they had fixed employment and residence abroad. Less sympathetic to the permanent settlement of guestworkers and to their political incorporation or citizenship, Switzerland and Germany were shocked to discover that the temporary collapse of their economic miracles in the early 1970s did not result in the immediate repatriation of hundreds of thousands of guestworkers. By then, however, Italy had begun to experience its own economic miracle, and other groups (particularly from Turkey and Yugoslavia) had begun to replace Italians as guestworkers.

Italy Imports Labor, 1970–2000

Even as international emigration had boomed in the 1950s, Italians at home saw some surprising signs of economic transformation and growth. Between 1955 and 1981, almost 9 million persons from the rural districts of impoverished southern Italy moved to older and newly emerging centers of large- and medium-scale industry in Italy's center and north. Even larger numbers moved shorter distances. Together with the international migrants, Italy's internal migrants numbered almost 45 million—an impressive figure in a country of 50 million citizens (Gabaccia 2000, 161–162). By 1960, Italians were speaking of their own "economic miracle." As Italy's industrial strength grew and as the countries of northern Europe experienced the recession of the early 1970s, international migrations from Italy dwindled and then almost ceased. Those going abroad, furthermore, were no longer unskilled and semiskilled laborers in search of work in agriculture, mining, construction, or factories. They were students, tourists, businessmen, professionals, and white-collar workers.

As emigration declined and Italians returned from northern Europe and from Latin America, the numbers of foreigners seeking work in Italy also began to rise. By the mid-1980s, this traditional nation of emigration faced the same troubling issues of nativism and social discrimination against foreigners that Italians as foreigners had confronted in the United States and Argentina at the turn of the century. Though many of the foreigners living in Italy in the past two decades of the century were temporary visitors, expatriates, or foreign students, the numbers of workers from the Third World attracted the most negative attention. Domestic servants from the Philippines found work in middle-class homes; ambulatory vendors from Africa sold goods on the beaches of Sicily as well as on the streets of Florence; Chinese restaurants appeared in most major Italian cities; Egyptians found work in Italy's steel industry. Among the newcomers, too, were the children and sometimes even grandchildren of Italy's earlier generations of labor migrants to Latin America; discouraged by poor economic prospects and political violence in Argentina (and unlike immigrants from other backgrounds), they found it relatively easy to acquire citizenship. But it was not easy for them to feel immediately at home in a country that had changed so significantly, both culturally and politically, in recent years.

Although mass emigration had ended, 5 million Italian citizens still lived abroad in the 1990s. Even more than the emigrants of the past, they seemed determined to preserve and even to extend their claim to the rights of Italian citizenship. Many, for example, demanded, and eventually gained, the right to vote while living abroad. In fact, Italy's new government in the 1990s was more interested than any other Italian government since the fascist era in the Italians abroad. But while granting political representation to them, the Italian state was also careful to limit representation to those who registered their intention to remain citizens, thus distinguishing them from the more than 60 million persons of recent Italian descent who also still lived scattered through the world.

Among that very large group, identities had diverged sharply in the intervening years. In Canada, Australia, and the United States, many persons of Italian descent participated in ethnic revivals that occurred almost simultaneously as all three nations began to explore the possibilities of multicultural national solidarity. In sharp contrast to the hyphenated "Italian-American," "Italo-Canadian," and "Italo-Australian" identities common in the English-speaking world, the children and grandchildren of Italian immigrants in France, Argentina, and Brazil—while aware of their cultural origins—did not make ethnicity a central component of their identities. They thought of themselves simply as French, Argentine, or Brazilian nationals or citizens. In Europe, the children of guestworkers faced some of the hardest choices in forging identities. In Germany and Switzerland, for example, they did not automatically acquire access to citizenship by birth. Although many enjoyed close familial and linguistic ties to their Italian homeland, others did not. Rather than feeling the absence of a firm national identity as a loss, others identified with their homeland regions, where governments mounted special problems to assure continued contact with their emigrants.

The formation of the European Union, which opened opportunities for Italians and other national groups to work and to migrate freely anywhere within Europe, offered still other solutions for forming complex identities in a mobile world. Unsurprisingly, Italians—at home and abroad—were among the strongest supporters of the European Union, providing some of the continent's most outspoken Europeanists.

Donna R. Gabaccia

See also: Assimilation/Integration; Citizenship; Class; Family Reunification; Gender and Migration; Guestworkers; Italy; Migration between Northern and Southern Countries; Remittances; Return Migration; Transnationalism; U.S. Nativism

References and further reading:

Baily, Samuel. 1999. *Immigrants in the Lands of Promise: Italians in Buenos Aires and New York City, 1870–1914.* Ithaca, NY: Cornell University Press.

Baldassare, Loretta. 2001. *Visits Home: Migration Experiences between Italy and Australia.* Melbourne: Melbourne University Press.

Briggs, John. 1978. *An Italian Passage: Immigrants to Three American Cities, 1890–1930.* New Haven, CT: Yale University Press.

Cannistraro, Philip V. 1999. *Blackshirts in Little Italy: Italian Americans and Fascism, 1921–1929.* Lafayette, IN: Bordighera.

Cohen, Miriam. 1993. *Workshop to Office: Two Generations of Italian Women in New York City, 1900–1950.* Ithaca, NY: Cornell University Press.

Foerster, Robert. 1969 [1919]. *The Italian Emigration of Our Times.* New York: Arno.

Gabaccia, Donna. 2000. *Italy's Many Diasporas.* London: University College of London Press.

Gabaccia, Donna, and Franca Iacovetta. 2002. *Women, Gender, and Transnational Lives: Italian Workers of the World.* Toronto: University of Toronto Press.

Gabaccia, Donna, and Fraser Ottanelli. 2001. *Italian Workers of the World: Labor Migration and the Making of Multi-ethnic States.* Urbana: University of Illinois Press.

Guglielmo, Jennifer, and Salvatore Salerno, eds. 2003. *Are Italians White? How Race Is Made in America.* London: Routledge.

Herbert, Ulrich. 1984. *A History of Foreign Labor in Germany.* Ann Arbor: University of Michigan Press.

Horowitz, Donald L., and Gerard Noiriel, eds. 1992. *Immigrants in Two Democracies: French and American Experience.* New York: New York University Press.

Iacovetta, Franca. 1993. *Such Hardworking People: Italian Immigrants in Postwar Toronto.* Montreal: McGill-Queen's University Press.

Mangione, Jerre, and Ben Morreale. 1992. *La Storia: Five Centuries of the Italian American Experience.* New York: HarperCollins.

Pozzetta, George, and Bruno Ramirez, eds. 1992. *The Italian Diaspora: Migration across the Globe.* Toronto: Multicultural History Society of Ontario.

Ramirez, Bruno. 1991. *On the Move: French-Canadian and Italian Migrants in the North Atlantic Economy, 1860–1914.* Toronto: McClelland and Stewart.

Vecoli, Rudolph J. 1963. "*Contadini* in Chicago: A Critique of the Uprooted." *Journal of American History* 51: 404–417.

Yans Mclaughlin, Virginia. 1977. *Family and Community: Italian Immigrants in Buffalo, 1880–1930.* Ithaca, NY: Cornell University Press.

Italy

Italy has gone from being a country of substantial emigration to a country of net immigration in the past two decades. Millions of Italians left their homeland beginning in the late 1800s, seeking out economic opportunities around the world. Seven million emigrated in the three decades following World War II, most to jobs in northern Europe, where they formed a critical ingredient of the industrial labor force in the postwar economic boom (Istat 1980). In the early 1980s, the migrant stream began to reverse course, and Italy

A young immigrant from Africa with a sticker that reads "Never more racism" taped over his mouth protests the Italian government's plans to crack down on immigration, Rome, January 19, 2002. On this day, 100,000 people—including many immigrants—calling for a world without borders, took to the streets of Rome. (Reuters NewMedia Inc./Corbis)

is now one of the major immigrant destinations of Europe. Just as Italians supplied a cheap labor force to northern Europe several decades ago, immigrants from the so-called Third World now fill gaps in the Italian labor market and do jobs that locals increasingly shun.

Italy has one of the world's lowest birthrates. A recent United Nations report (United Nations Population Division 2000) found that, with a birthrate of less than 1.2 per couple, it also has the most rapidly aging population and would have to admit over 2.2 million immigrants annually for the next thirty years in order to fill labor demand and stave off a crisis in its pension system. Assuming gradual increases in immigration, the *Annuario Statistico Italiano* (Istat 2002) projects a decline in the Italian population from more than 58 million in 2010 to 52 million by the year 2050. With pensioners already outnumbering active workers, it is not hard to understand the concern of the president of the Banca d'Italia and his blunt warning, "Italy needs immigrants" (quoted in *La Repubblica* 1999, 23).

According to the minister of the interior, there were about 1.4 million legal foreign residents in Italy at the beginning of 2001 (Minister of the Interior 2001; see Table I-3). By 2003, the Catholic charity Caritas estimated that the total number of legal immigrants, plus those who had applied for legalization, had reached 2,395,000 (Caritas 2003, 7). This constitutes almost a tripling of immigrants in little more than a decade. Close to half of Italy's immigrants live in just two regions—Lombardy (the northern region, anchored by Milan) and Lazio (the central region around Rome)—with over 90 percent residing in the north and center of the country. Most gravitate to major cities, but some of the highest per capita concentrations are found in the small towns and villages of northeastern Italy. The size and distribution of the undocumented population in Italy is more difficult to gauge. Recent estimates range from 250,000 (suggested by the minister of the interior) to 300,000 (Caritas) to 340,000 (the Organisation for Economic Co-operation and Development).

The majority of immigrants come from outside the European Union, with Africa the largest source region for non-EU immigrants, followed by Eastern and Central Europe. Morocco is the single largest source country, providing approximately 10 percent of the total. The share of non-EU residents has steadily increased since 1994, including a dramatic increase in immigration from Eastern and Central Europe, and

Table I-3: Legal Foreign Residents in Italy, by Region (January 1, 2001)

Region	Legal Foreign Residents
North	761,298
Valle d'Aosta	2,494
Piedmont	83,811
Lombardy	308,408
Liguria	38,784
Trentino-Alto Aldige	31,799
Veneto	139,522
Friuli	43,432
Emilia-Romagna	113,048
Center	422,483
Tuscany	114,972
Umbria	26,068
Marche	35,777
Lazio	245,666
South	143,121
Abruzzo	18,933
Campania	68,159
Molise	2,039
Basilicata	3,110
Puglia	35,565
Calabria	15,315
Islands	61,251
Sicily	49,808
Sardinia	11,443
Total	1,388,153

Source: Minister of the Interior, *Rapporto del Ministro dell'Interno sullo Stato della Sicurezza in Italia* (Bologna: Il Mulino, 2001).

smaller but significant increases in the proportion of immigrants from African and Asian countries.

Women constitute about 45 percent of the legal immigrant population (Anthias and Lazaridis 2000, 7), but the gender ratio varies considerably by nationality. While 72 percent of foreign residents from Morocco are male, females account for over 66 percent of immigrants from the Philippines, 70 percent of Polish immigrants, and 68 percent of immigrants from Peru; the large population of immigrants from the Cape Verde Islands is almost entirely women (Gruppo Abele 2001, 573; Minister of the Interior 2001, 278). Filipinos were among the first immigrants to arrive in Italy in large numbers in the early 1970s, and although they were originally concentrated in the domestic sector, with family reunification and the passage of time they have become among the most established of immigrant groups (Chell-Robinson 2000).

Immigrants in Italy are somewhat less integrated into the host society than those in countries of long-term immigration, where many foreign residents settled decades ago and have developed deep roots. Fewer than one-quarter of foreign residents have lived in Italy for at least five years, and only about 15 percent have lived there for a decade or more, although these figures are on the rise (Caritas 2000, 170). One important indicator of the degree of integration is the rate of naturalization. The acquisition of Italian citizenship is difficult for those not born with at least one Italian parent. Because Italy is essentially a country of *ius sanguinis* ("the law of blood," a legal concept according to which the acquisition of citizenship is based on paternal or maternal descent), there are only two routes available to foreigners to obtain Italian citizenship—marrying an Italian citizen, or living in Italy as a legal resident for at least ten consecutive years. In 1998, approximately 12,000 foreign citizens were granted Italian citizenship. In 1999, fewer than 11,300 achieved that status, with 85 percent of these based on marriage to an Italian and only 15 percent the result of long-term residency (ibid., 175).

More than 300,000 residence permits were issued to non-EU immigrants for purposes of family unity in 2000. Although the number of immigrant children in Italy is still relatively small, it is increasing rapidly. In January 2000, there were 229,851 immigrant children present, representing a 26.6 percent increase over the previous year (Istat 2000). The number of immigrant children in primary and secondary schools increased from just over 6,000 in the academic year 1983/1984 to more than 85,522 in 1998/1999 (Caritas 2000, 225).

There is increasing recognition on the part of policy makers and employers that immigrants are critical to the survival and competitive edge of the Italian economy, and the vast majority of residence permits are issued for the purpose of work. The economic location of immigrant workers varies by region of the country, sector, and immigrant nationality and gender, but certain patterns and trends are constant. For example, they are found in virtually every sector—immigrants are street vendors, domestic workers, nannies, nurses, factory workers, farm workers, gas station attendants, construction workers, foundry workers, and office "errand boys"—but they tend to be clustered in manufacturing (in the north), agriculture (especially in the south), domestic service

Table I-4: Non-EU Legal Foreign Workers in Italy, by Economic Sector and Geographic Area, 1999 (%)

	Agriculture	Manufacturing	Construction	Domestic	Services
Northwest	9.2	26.3	11.7	30.7	22.2
Northeast	22.0	39.7	7.9	8.5	21.8
Center	15.4	33.0	9.0	22.2	20.5
South	38.3	7.6	2.8	39.7	11.6
Lombardy*	5.7	31.8	5.9	31.0	25.6
Lazio*	7.3	3.1	3.0	71.6	15.0

* Lombardy and Lazio are the regions where Milan and Rome, respectively, are located.

Note: Figures are rounded.
Source: Giovanna Zincone, *Secondo Rapporto sull'integrazione degli Immigrati in Italia* (Bologna: Il Mulino, 2001), 354.

(in major urban areas), and a variety of other services (see Table I-4)

In each sector, they generally do the most arduous, undesirable work for the lowest pay, and they are disproportionately located in Italy's extensive underground and informal economies. While an estimated 15 percent of Italians work in the "submerged" economy, 30 percent of non-EU immigrants work there, and an estimated 62 percent of immigrants find their first job there (Eurispes 2001, 359; Cariplo-ISMU and Caritas, cited in *La Gazzetta del Mezzogiorno* 2002, 5). Underscoring the importance of this "off-the-books" workforce, one study concluded that Italian employers save at least US$13 billion annually on taxes and social security payments by using immigrant workers in "irregular" employment (Osservatorio Ares 2001).

Besides their concentration in the underground economy, immigrants provide an eminently flexible, "contingent" workforce, thereby offsetting the effects of government regulations and union rules in this heavily regulated economy. About 13 percent of non-EU immigrants in Italy work in day labor, 15 percent are part-time, and another 10 percent are seasonal (Cariplo-ISMU and Caritas, cited in *La Gazzetta del Mezzogiorno* 2002, 5). In some regions and sectors—agriculture in the south is a conspicuous example—virtually all immigrant workers are seasonal day laborers. But even in the industrial heartland of the northeast, they are far more likely than locals to be employed on a contingent basis (Ambrosini 1999, 2001).

One of Italy's most respected immigration experts has argued that since the early 1990s immigrants in Italy have undergone a significant "process of stabilization" (Pugliese 2000, 65). By this he meant that immigrants are an increasingly important part of the economy and are more and more likely to be legal residents and have "regular" jobs. Indeed, one out of every four new hires is now a non-EU immigrant. And, they are joining unions in record numbers, even though overall union membership is in decline. According to records of the largest Italian labor confederation—the Confederazione Generale Italiana del Lavoro (CGIL)—immigrant membership increased 22 percent between 1998 and 2000 (Mottura 2000, 123–124; Watts 2000, 21–22). Immigrants working in factories in Italy's southern regions are more likely to be unionized (45 percent) than in the post-Fordist, small enterprises of the north (30 percent). In some southern areas, union membership among factory workers is higher for immigrants than for local workers. But immigrant "stabilization" should not be exaggerated, as evidenced by their continued concentration in the underground economy, their disproportionately contingent and temporary work status, and their low wages.

Immigrant unemployment in Italy is among the lowest of any Western capitalist country (Boeri, Hanson, and McCormick 2002, 27), and with Italy's low birthrates and declining populations, immigrants fill critical labor gaps. Most scholars conclude that immigrants do not usually take jobs away from Italians; rather, their employment tends to have either no effect or a complementary, positive effect on employment opportunities for locals (Gavosto, Venturini, and Villosio 1999). Sociologist Maurizio Ambrosini cautions, however, that the availability of immigrant workers may allow employers to eschew strategies that would bring broad benefits to local workers. For example, the presence of immigrants in the industrial north means that firms do not have to move jobs to southern Italy, where local workers might be more readily available, nor do they have to raise wages or improve working conditions to attract unemployed Italians to areas of high employment (Ambrosini 2001, 61–62).

Italy passed its first comprehensive immigration law in 1986. This law was in part the product of pressure from unions and left opposition parties that contested what members saw as abuse of the rapidly growing number of illegal immigrants. However, it was also the result of substantial pressure from the European Community to close the back door to Europe now that Europe's internal borders were being dismantled. The law consisted of three primary components—foreign workers' rights, rules on the employment of foreigners, and a legalization program—and included an employer sanctions provision that, although rarely used, was to fine employers for the use of unauthorized workers.

The Martelli Law was passed in 1990, named after its primary author and sponsor, then Deputy Prime Minister Claudio Martelli. Among the most important provisions of the Martelli Law was a blueprint for a quota worker system. Annual quotas for specific categories of foreign workers were to be arrived at in consultation with unions, employers, and other interested groups. In addition, the law included a relatively generous legalization program. In contrast to previous legalization programs, under the Martelli Law the process was to be initiated by the immigrants themselves rather than their employers, and employers did not have to pay back contributions to social security for their legalized workers. Residence permits were to be valid for two years, renewable for four years if the immigrant could demonstrate that he or she was continuing to work and had a sufficient income. Approximately 234,000 immigrants applied for legalization under the Martelli Law, but many have since fallen back into illegal status.

The Martelli Law, as with its predecessor, was characterized by a discrepancy between the "law on the books" and the "law in action." Employer sanctions continued to be applied only rarely, and legalization programs regularized some immigrants, but usually only temporarily, and in any case could not be accessed by immigrants in the underground economy. It may be that those characteristics that make Third World immigrants attractive to certain sectors—their invisibility, marginality, and vulnerability—are the same qualities that make it difficult to control their employment (through employer sanctions) or legalize them (through legalization programs). Both employer sanctions and legalization may be destined to fail in a context where immigrants' employment is partly contingent on their marginality.

By the late 1990s, immigrants were increasingly critical to Italian manufacturing and other important sectors of the formal economy, no longer simply filling gaps in the underground and in the service sector. A comprehensive 1998 law, the Turco-Napolitano Law, named for its sponsors in the center-left coalition government, was the first Italian law to recognize the critical importance of Third World immigrants in the economy, and it seemed for the first time to concede the nontransitory nature of many immigrants' sojourns in Italy.

The Turco-Napolitano Law set up a more precise mechanism for determining the annual quota of foreign workers and mandated that the consultation process include consideration of the number of foreign workers already on government hiring lists, employers' labor needs, and unemployment rates. Employers could request specific workers already in Italy, but those requested had to return to their country of origin and reenter with the requisite paperwork. In most cases, residence permits were issued for two years and renewed if the original conditions (usually work in the formal economy) continued to be met. For the first time with this law, immigrant workers who lost their jobs did not lose their residence permits but instead were given one year to find new employment.

The law also established a sponsor system whereby any public entity could sponsor immigrants to come to Italy to look for work, as long as the sponsor could guarantee a source of livelihood and the sponsored immigrants were within the annual quota. Besides employers' associations, labor unions, immigrant advocacy groups, and other nongovernmental organizations (NGOs) were eligible to sponsor immigrants. The Turco-Napolitano Law also provided for family unification, again within the quota, and extended-family members could automatically get work permits.

Turco-Napolitano also expanded the rights of foreigners in Italy. Among its major provisions were the right to equal treatment in the workplace; access to the public health care system; and, for the undocumented, the right to urgent care and the right to attend public school. In addition, it set out an ambitious plan for a network of "reception centers" throughout Italy to provide legal and illegal immigrants with emergency food and shelter as well as language instruction and a wide range of other cultural and social services. Finally, it provided for a residence card that for the first time created a category of permanent legal residents. After five years of continuous legal status, if immigrants had a legitimate job and sufficient income to support themselves and their families, they and their spouses and minor children were eligible for this *carta di soggiorno,* which, unlike all previous residence permits, was open-ended in duration.

More than with any previous Italian policy, the focus in this 1998 law was on the importance of immigrant integration, as exemplified by the establishment of the permanent resident status and the delineation of extensive immigrant rights and access to social services. Executive regulations for the Turco-Napolitano Law called for an annual report to be issued by a commission of experts to evaluate the progress toward these integration goals.

In the spring of 2001, media tycoon Silvio Berlusconi and his coalition of rightist parties replaced the center-left coalition government that had shepherded Turco-Napolitano through the Italian legislature. Prime Minister Berlusconi soon moved to accommodate his coalition partners, the anti-immigrant Northern League (Lega Nord) and the neo-fascist National Alliance Party (Alleanza nazionale), and put immigration reform at the top of his political agenda. A national emergency was declared when a boatload of 928 Iraqi Kurds landed in Sicily in March 2002, among other things allowing police to expedite deportation hearings and to destroy smugglers' boats (*Migration News* 2002, 27; Tagliabue 2002, A18).

Four months later, Italy passed a new immigration law. Named for its anti-immigrant sponsors, Reform Minister Umberto Bossi of the Northern League and Deputy Prime Minister Gianfranco Fini from the National Alliance Party, the Bossi-Fini Law modified many of the liberal provisions of Turco-Napolitano, more closely linked legal residence with work contracts, and added symbolically potent security and police measures. For example, it did away with the sponsorship system that had allowed immigrants to enter Italy without a prearranged job. Under the new law, only those who have a work contract in hand can enter legally, and only within the annual quotas. Further, if immigrants lose their job, they lose their residence permit and automatically fall into illegality if they do not get another work contract within six months.

Residence permits are for a maximum of two years, and renewals must be requested three months before expiration (instead of the thirty days in Turco-Napolitano). The *carta di soggiorno* that provides for the possibility of permanent residence survived the retrenchments, but the number of years of legal residence required to secure it was extended from five to six. Finally, the right of legal immigrant workers to bring family members with them is limited in this law, applying only to spouses and minor children, not the extended family as in the past.

Besides this tightening of the connection between work and legal status, Bossi-Fini heightened the police function of immigration policy. Although the Northern League's proposal that illegal residence itself should be considered a felony and carry a prison sentence was overruled as impractical, the law did criminalize reentry after deportation. The aspect of Bossi-Fini that received the most publicity and provoked the most debate was the mandate that all non-EU immigrants be fingerprinted when they apply for or renew their residence permits.

A legalization program was established for maids and caregivers. Employers were given sixty days from the law's effective date in September 2002 to request legalization for their domestic helpers (limited to one per family for maids, with no limit on caregivers of the elderly and/or disabled). Another legalization plan was launched for immigrants in the underground economy. Just over 700,000 applications were received for these two legalization programs; even considering that some of these were duplicate applications for the same person, the turnout far exceeded initial predictions. Despite the more punitive mentality of the Bossi-Fini Law, it continues to make a nod to the need for immigrant integration, as indicated in part by these legalization programs. The Berlusconi government continues to contract with the local regions to implement integration programs, the scope and expense of which suggest that the government's concern over immigrant incorporation is not just political rhetoric.

Several themes are apparent in this evolution of Italian immigration policy. First, there are continuous starts, shifts, impasses, and changes of course. In less than two decades, there were four major pieces of legislation (1986, 1990, 1998, 2002), with dozens of additional policies established by administrative decrees and government "circulars." In the same period, there were at least six different legalization programs, always accompanied by statements underscoring the extraordinary circumstances justifying this now-standard component of Italian immigration policy. Second, there is often a glaring gap between the stated purpose of these laws and their effects. For example, employer sanctions are rarely invoked, the quota worker system is regularly plagued by controversy and paralysis, relatively few permanent residency cards have been issued, immigrant integration remains an elusive goal, and control efforts even under the restrictive Berlusconi government appear to have little effect on immigration flows. As in many countries of immigration, such gaps between intent and outcome may in fact be consistent with the ambiguous status of immigrants as "wanted but not welcome" (Zolberg 1987).

Public attitudes toward immigrants in Italy run the gamut. On one hand, anti-immigrant right-wing parties such as the Northern League and the National Alliance Party have won regional elections over the past decade in part on their anti-immigrant platforms. Although the Northern League's share of the national electorate has declined to an estimated 4 percent, it constitutes an important component of Berlusconi's coalition government (Agnew 2002). In the wake of the September 11, 2001, terrorist attacks in the United States, the increasing Islamic population in Italy has come under renewed attack, reinvigorating anti-immigrant sentiment in some quarters.

On the other hand, a wide range of immigrant associations, employers' groups, religious organizations, NGOs, and union confederations advocate on behalf of immigrants and lobby for their access to services and an end to discrimination (*Los Angeles Times* 2002). Unions in Italy are a major immigrant support group, with all three major labor confederations operating immigrant service divisions in every major city to help immigrants gain access to jobs, health care, housing, and coveted residence permits.

As immigrants increasingly enter the mainstream economy in Italy, one might expect concern on the part of unions that they represent a competitive challenge to unionized workers. Instead, unions advocate on behalf of laws that make it possible for immigrants to legalize and facilitate their entry into the formal economy where they might be more easily organized. As Julie R. Watts (2000) has pointed out, union officials are aware that immigration flows are difficult to control, and unlikely to disappear, and they have opted to welcome the new workers. At a time when unions are losing ground in all advanced capitalist countries, Italian unions see in these immigrants a vital source of their future strength.

A number of studies have found that, while a significant minority of Italians appear to be xenophobic, on the whole they express less anti-immigrant sentiment than other Euopeans. In a 2001 survey, 15 percent of Italian respondents considered themselves "actively tolerant" toward immigrants and diverse cultures, 45 percent were "passively tolerant," 21 percent ambivalent, and 11 percent rated themselves "intolerant" (compared to an average 14 percent for other countries in the study) (European Study of Racism and Xenophobia, cited in *Il Manifesto* 2001, 6). In another study of xenophobic attitudes, Italian respondents scored lowest of all nationalities on the two central questions of whether "immigrants threaten our culture and identity," and whether they "are a threat to job security." They also were the most "trusting" of "people from the third-world." And, a higher percentage of Italians (72.5 percent) thought legal immigrants should have the right to vote in local elections. At the same time, however, Italians are prone to see immigrants as potential criminals, consistently reporting in surveys that "Immigrants are a threat to public safety and personal security" (Diamanti and Bordignon 2002, 13–15; Melossi 2001).

Right-wing political parties continue to capitalize on and fuel anti-immigrant attitudes in Italy. The Northern League, the National Alliance, and Berlusconi's own Forza Italia (Italian Power) have all made anti-immigrant rhetoric a central plank of their political platforms. Although a long tradition of Catholic charity, Communist Party influence, and union support shores up an important pro-immigrant lobby, a hot streak of populist antagonism toward immigrants is nonetheless readily available for political exploitation.

Kitty Calavita

See also: Assimilation/Integration; Clandestine Migration; Economic Effects of Migration; Gender and Migration; Guestworkers, Europe; Italian Migration Worldwide; Migration Policy; Public Opinion and Immigration; Racism and Racially Motivated Attacks

References and further reading:

Agnew, John A. 2002. *Place and Politics in Modern Italy.* Chicago: University of Chicago Press.

Ambrosini, Maurizio. 1999. *Utili Invasori: L'inserimento degli Immigrati nel Mercato del Lavoro.* Milan: FrancoAngeli.

———. 2001. *La Fatica di Integrarsi: Immigrati e Lavoro in Italia.* Bologna: Il Mulino.

Anthias, Floya, and Gabriella Lazaridis. 2000. "Introduction." Pp. 1–13 in *Gender and Migration in Southern Europe: Women on the Move.* Edited by Floya Anthias and Gabriella Lazaridis. Oxford: Berg.

Boeri, Tito, Gordon Hanson, and Barry McCormick, eds. 2002. *Immigration Policy and the Welfare System.* Oxford: Oxford University Press.

Caritas. 2000. *Immigrazione: Dossier Statistico 2000.* Rome: Caritas.

———. 2003. "Anticipazioni del 'Dossier Statistico Italiano.'" Preliminary report released at press conference, Rome, March 10: 7.

Chell-Robinson, Victoria. 2000. "Female Migrants in Italy: Coping in a Country of New Immigration." Pp. 103–123 in *Gender and Migration in Southern Europe: Women on the Move.* Edited by Floya Anthias and Gabriella Lazaridis. Oxford: Berg.

Diamanti, Ilvo, and Fabio Bordignon. 2002. "Immigrazione e Cittadinanza in Europa." *Quaderni FNN, Collana Osservatorio* 5: 12–13.

Eurispes. 2001. *Rapporto Italia.* Rome: Ufficio Stampa Eurispes.

Gavosto, Andrea, Alessandra Venturini, and Claudia Villosio. 1999. "Do Immigrants Compete with Natives?" *Labour* 13: 603–622.

Gruppo Abele. 2001. *Annuario Sociale 2001.* Milan: Feltrinelli.

Il Manifesto. 2001. "Europa (In)Tollerante." March 21, 6.

Istat (Istituto Nazionale di Statistica). 1980. *Annuario Statistico Italiano.* Rome: Istituto Poligrafico dello Stato.

———. 2000. *Annuario Statistico Italiano.* Rome: Istituto Poligrafico dello Stato.

———. 2001. *Annuario Statistico Italiano.* Rome: Istituto Poligrafico dello Stato.

———. 2002. *Annuario Statistico Italiano.* Rome: Istituto Poligrafico dello Stato.

La Gazzetta del Mezzogiorno. 2002. "Marocchino, Lavora a Tempo Pieno e Manda a Casa 613 Euro Ogni Anno." June 5, 5.

La Repubblica. 1999. "Fazio: 'Saranno gli Immigrati a Salvare le Pensioni Italiane.'" July 31, 23.

Los Angeles Times. 2002. "Rome March Supports Immigration." January 20, A4.

Melossi, Dario. 2001. "The Other in the New Europe: Migrations, Deviance, Social Control." Pp. 151–166 in *Criminal Policy in Transition.* Edited by Penny Green and Andrew Rutherford. Oxford: Hart.

Migration News. 2002. "Southern Europe. Italy." Vol. 9, no. 4 (April): 27.

Minister of the Interior. 2001. *Rapporto del Ministro dell'Interno sullo Stato della Sicurezza in Italia.* Bologna: Il Mulino.

Mottura, Giovanni. 2000. "Immigrati e Sindacato." Pp. 113–134 in *Rapporto Immigrazione: Lavoro, Sindacato, Societa'.* Edited by Enrico Pugliese. Rome: Ediesse.

Organisation for Economic Co-operation and Development (OECD), http://www.oecd.org/home/.

Osservatorio Ares. 2001. "I Dati dell'Osservatorio Ares 2000." Conference paper presented at "Flussi Migratori e Politiche per la Salute," Sicily, March 26.

Pugliese, Enrico. 2000. "Gli Immigrati nel Mercato del Lavoro e nella Struttura dell'Occupazione." Pp. 65–87 in *Rapporto Immigrazione: Lavoro, Sindacato, Societa'.* Edited by Enrcio Pugliese. Rome: Ediesse.

Tagliabue, John. 2002. "Italy Issues Decree to Destroy Ships Used in Refugee Transport." *San Diego Union-Tribune.* March 29, A18.

United Nations Population Division. 2000. *Replacement Migration: Is It a Solution to Declining and Ageing Populations?* New York: United Nations Secretariat.

Watts, Julie R. 2000. *An Unconventional Brotherhood: Union Support for Liberalized Immigration in Europe.* Monograph Series 1. La

Jolla, CA: Center for Comparative Immigration Studies, University of California, San Diego.

Zincone, Giovanna. 2000. "A Model of Reasonable Integration: Summary of the First Report on the Integration of Immigrants in Italy." *International Migration Review* 34: 956–968.

———. 2001. *Secondo Rapporto sull'integrazione degli Immigrati in Italia.* Bologna: Il Mulino.

Zolberg, Aristide. 1987. "Wanted but Not Welcome: Alien Labor in Western Development." Pp. 261–297 in *Population in an Interacting World.* Edited by William A. Alonso. Cambridge: Harvard University Press.

Ius Sanguinis

Ius sanguinis has a Latin derivation and means, literally, "the law of blood." It is a legal concept according to which the acquisition of citizenship is based on paternal or maternal descent, that is, on birth by parents who "own" the inherited citizenship. It stands in contrast to *ius soli,* "law of the soil," which links the acquisition of citizenship to birth on the territory of a state. *Ius domicili,* "the law of residence," is distinguished from both ius sanguinis and ius soli in that it binds the acquisition of citizenship to permanent residence on a state territory, usually by way of naturalization. Ius domicili as well as naturalization by way of marriage amends pure ius sanguinis.

Ius soli and ius sanguinis are decisive legal provisions that determine (and limit) the access to citizenship and political participation in modern states. In its pure form, ius sanguinis (or rather, citizenship based on ius sanguinis) constitutes the body of citizens as a community of descent. Thus, it denies children of immigrants born in their parents' country of immigration the right to acquire automatically the citizenship of their country of birth.

Historical Development

The principle of ius sanguinis dates to Roman law and was rediscovered during the era of European humanism from the late fourteenth century on. It defined the membership and political position of free citizens of Rome within the urban community. Ius sanguinis (and ius soli), however, only developed decisive political importance with the genesis of modern statehood in Europe and the emergence of nations, nation-states, and the freedom of movement for all classes.

The transition from the medieval concept of statehood based on socially bound communities (*Personenverbandsstaat*) to the territorial state of early modern and modern times was a precondition for ius sanguinis's centrality in defining political membership. So was the rise of citizenship as a mechanism of inclusion and exclusion.

Medieval, feudal, and pre-nation-state systems of rule were predominantly characterized by personal loyalty, which included descent-based and territorial components. In this era, membership and loyalty did not depend on citizenship (as the very concept of citizen was unknown), but on the rule of superiors over subjects. The mass of the (largely peasant) population in Europe during early modern times lived in an inherited state of dependency (*Erbuntertänigkeit*). This state was based on birth. Loyalty was owed to property-owning noblemen or the church. At the same time, and more important, this status was based on the obligation to reside on the territory of the property-owning lord (*Schollenpflichtigkeit*). As such, elements of ius sanguinis and ius soli were operative even in premodern times. However, the very terms only became widely used in modern times, namely in the legal system of nineteenth-century Europe.

When the traditional forms of feudal dependency and loyalty were dissolved, citizenship gained crucial importance as a criterion for membership in states as well as for legitimizing power and rule over individuals. It coincided with the evolutionary and revolutionary processes unleashed during early modern times, in particular with the transition to modern statehood and the emergence of societies of citizens. These societies were based on popular sovereignty. Moreover, immigration and emigration, as well as challenges posed by colonialism, made the legal definition of citizenship and the citizenry vital political questions. The emergence of modern citizenship and statehood can be seen as processes of modernization that were directed against the traditional old order of territorially defined dependencies in Europe. Thus, ius sanguinis seemed to be congenial to overcoming this old order.

In continental Europe, the introduction of ius sanguinis as a membership-defining category resulted from reform-oriented bureaucracies during the era of enlightenment and its aftermath. Since the end of the *ancien régime,* the principle of ius sanguinis was generally considered to be more modern and progressive because it was opposed to premodern territorial forms of belonging. In particular, it was in line with the interests of the rising territorial rulers (*Landesherren*) in overcoming the small-scale territorial rule of the local nobility. Ending competing territorial rules allowed the membership of subjects to be more easily defined and power more efficiently exercised. Moreover, the principle of descent made control of immigration, naturalization, and access to social benefits (via poor laws) easier. The preference for descent-based principles of membership was also influenced by concerns that immigrants would not integrate. On the one hand, the ius sanguinis principle excluded immigrants from citizenship status and thus prevented states from having to deal with formal questions of integration. On the other, it made it more complicated to release subjects who emigrated from their citizenship. This turned out to be a problem for those states that wanted to rid themselves of obligations to emigrants who could become social and economic burdens if they returned as impoverished return migrants.

In broad terms, then, two opposing concepts of citizenship emerged when modern states and modern statehood came into being in early modern Europe: One was based on ius sanguinis, the other on ius soli. However, looking at real types, mixed forms as well as shifts from one to the other can be discovered. When states and state elites defined citizenship, questions of national belonging, immigration and emigration, and the very concept of nation and nationhood were crucial parameters that intervened. Historical cases provide ample evidence for this. For instance, postrevolutionary France, the archetype of a modern, Western state, introduced a citizenship law based on ius sanguinis when the Code Napoléon was implemented in 1803. Countries of immigration, however, such as the United States, Australia, or New Zealand, that came to be nation-states opted usually for citizenship based on ius soli. This made full citizens out of children of immigrants, which was in accordance with the raison d'état of these states and reflected a long-standing element of British Common Law tradition, which was transplanted to the New World. The historical case of France shows that the decision to base citizenship law on ius sanguinis or ius soli could change as a consequence of demographic shifts and a resulting change of raison d'état. In 1889, France switched from ius sanguinis to ius soli. The combination of a declining population, the military's steep manpower demands, and large-scale immigration prompted France's shift to ius soli, so that children of immigrants could easily be made into good Frenchmen, thus compensating for low French birthrates. In this age of nationalism and Great Power competition, population size was seen as a prime asset in struggles with rivals such as Germany.

Ius Sanguinis and the Sense of Nationhood

From about the turn of the twentieth century onward, two distinctive patterns emerged to characterize the interrelation of citizenship and nationhood, for which France and Germany became representative examples. On the one hand, in the German case, citizenship based on ius sanguinis happened to go together with a sense of nationhood that was strongly based on ethnocultural (later also on racialized) idioms of belonging. On the other hand, in the French case, a citizenship law based on ius soli emerged alongside a politically and institutionally determined sense of nationhood. In the former case, "the nationalisation of citizens by way of . . . pre-state and pre-political concepts of nationhood found its legitimation in ius sanguinis" (Gosewinkel 2001, 286). In Europe this was also true for most Central and Eastern European states, which followed an ethnocultural mode of nationhood in an effort to ethnically homogenize the population. The acquisition of citizenship based on ius sanguinis was thus turned into a national-political instrument to secure the homogeneity of the nation. In those cases where ius soli prevailed, the concept of nationhood was based instead on voluntaristic principles, that is, common values and political principles. Mixed forms including both ius sanguinis and ius soli emerged mostly in European countries with colonies outside Europe or in a demographic regime that was shaped by immigration comparatively earlier.

Looking at real types, dividing lines were often not as strict, and shifts from one type to the other occurred. In the academic literature, the German and French cases are often cast as diametrically opposed models (Brubaker 1992). This view, however, has given way to more nuanced interpretations (Gosewinkel 2001; Weil 2002). Historically, that is, from 1803 to 1889, it was namely France that epitomized the classical country of ius sanguinis. However, as noted above, the country reacted to social, political, and demographic challenges of the nineteenth and twentieth centuries and shifted from ius sanguinis to ius soli. To a certain degree this is also true for contemporary Germany, as it introduced elements of ius soli into its citizenship law in the year 2000, thus politically acknowledging prior mass immigration and the need to naturalize children of immigrants. Switzerland and (contemporary) Russia, two multiethnic states, demonstrate that a concept of nationhood that is not based on ethnocultural idioms can go in line with citizenship based on ius sanguinis. By contrast, Israel provides the example of a country of immigration (for Jews) that follows an ethnocultural or ethnoreligious concept of nationhood and a citizenship law that is based on ius sanguinis. Contrasting ius sanguinis and ius soli as ideal types is thus an intellectually useful exercise. Reality, however, is much more complex and diverse.

Cultural and Historical Preconditions for Ius Sanguinis

The emergence of citizenship laws based on ius sanguinis (or ius soli) usually mirrors deeply rooted cultural and historical patterns of nation-states as well as images of the self and the other. Of crucial importance is thus the genesis of the nation, nationhood, and the nation-state. Ius sanguinis can only be understood and explained within specific historical contexts and constellations.

The timing of state formation and nation-building is decisive for the different paths that states followed when crafting citizenship along ius sanguinis or ius soli dimensions. Where state formation preceded nation-building, the nation could unfold within the realm of the state. As such, it was unlikely that nationhood would be based on an ethnocultural understanding and citizenship on ius sanguinis. In such cases, state institutions and political values provided the framework for political and politico-cultural commonalties. However, if nation-building preceded state formation, opting for ius sanguinis was more likely, since nationhood emerged along ethnic and cultural lines in these cases. The possibility of relying on political values and traditions was missing in these entities or was only weakly present.

Ius Sanguinis, Migration, and Naturalization

State boundaries are formed through state territory, state power, and the people who owe the state citizenship. Membership in the community of citizens can be attributed or denied according to various criteria of inclusion and exclusion. General and common civil rights are attributed in democracies today without regard to gender, class, or religion. Equal rights, however, are not guaranteed for immigrants. For societies of immigration the question of inclusion and exclusion of migrants and their children arises, namely the inclusion into the full rights of citizenship.

Whether citizenship is gained via ius sanguinis or ius soli is of prime importance for societies of immigration. Ius soli leads to automatic acquisition of citizenship upon birth for children and grandchildren of immigrants. Thus, all civic and political rights are enjoyed by these second and third generations, while the first generation of immigrants can only gain these rights by way of naturalization. Ius sanguinis, however, denies children of immigrants the ability to become citizens automatically upon birth. Thus, they are not part of the citizenry, might only enjoy a proscribed right of residence, and are excluded from political representation and participation—that is, the exercise of political power. In contrast to ius soli, ius sanguinis does not give equal rights to those born on the territory of the state, but makes such rights dependent upon descent. The status of full citizens is only passed on from one generation to the next according to criteria of blood or descent.

The other side of excluding migrants' descendants by way of citizenship based on ius sanguinis is the privileging of coethnic minorities living outside the state territory and giving them possibilities to immigrate and be naturalized. States with citizenship based on ius sanguinis and coethnic minorities in other states often provide special rights of access for these coethnic minorities and offer fast or immediate naturalization. Even if the naturalization of coethnic immigrants is not necessarily linked with an ius sanguinis–based citizenship law, it is typically derived from the same principle: membership in the nation by way of descent.

A breach of the pure ius sanguinis principle and descent criteria could be seen in the naturalization of (noncoethnic) immigrants and their children by way of offering citizenship to them after a certain period of residence has passed. If such a possibility exists in a country that follows ius sanguinis principles, even naturalized citizens will pass on their new citizenship to their future children.

Ius Sanguinis: Two Case Studies

Two prominent examples for the effect that principles of descent have on ethnic migration—that is, ius sanguinis in combination with special gates of entry for coethnic minorities—are Israel since 1948 and (West) Germany since 1949. Both countries implemented citizenship laws based on ius sanguinis, and both opened special gates of entry for coethnic immigrants (Jews in the one case, ethnic Germans in the other). With the 1950 Law of Return, Israel granted all Jews the possibility of immigrating to Israel and becoming Israeli citizens. In 1970, this legal provision was even widened. Ever since, children and grandchildren descended from Jewish ancestors and having at least one Jewish grandparent, along with spouses of Jews, enjoy the same right: They can immigrate to Israel and claim Israeli citizenship on the basis of their descent (or marriage). The enlarged Law of Return allows for descent to be traced through both mothers and fathers, thus going beyond religious law (*Halakha*), according to which belonging to the Jewish community can only be passed on by the mother.

By way of both the *Grundgesetz,* or Basic Law, of 1949 and separate legal provisions, such as the *Bundesvertriebenen-und Flüchtlingsgesetz,* or Federal Expellees' and Refugees' Law, of 1953, West Germany granted members of ethnic German minorities in Central and Eastern Europe and the Soviet Union the ability to immigrate and be naturalized. Application of the law depended upon proving German descent. The combination of ethnocultural belonging to the German nation ("practice of Germannness") and the proof of German descent thus became crucial to the process of recognition and naturalization. The latter could be traced back to distant generations that had emigrated from the German territories in the eighteenth century, and sometimes even in medieval times.

These ius sanguinis legal provisions of Israel and Germany allowed the immigration of a total of 2.8 million Jews to Israel and more than 4 million ethnic Germans to Germany. They all received Israeli or German citizenship on the basis of descent, though it cannot be claimed that naturalization was a direct outcome of ius sanguinis, since these immigrants were not born into Israeli or German citizenship by parents already holding the same citizenship. The underlying logic privileging these immigrants over others, however, follows the same principle as ius sanguinis: It is based on the assumption that the nation of citizens shares common descent, as well as a common experience of persecution, and thus should be entitled to the same rights which the nation-state of the ethno-nation provides. Israel has maintained this system until the present, whereas Germany made decisive legal changes in the 1990s that restricted the scope of ethnic German immigration and will eventually put an end to it.

Similar legal provisions of admitting and naturalizing coethnic populations on the basis of ethnocultural commonalities and descent can also be found in the Russian Federation since 1992 and in other post-Communist countries such as Hungary or Poland. In all three cases, coethnic minorities enjoy privileged access to the respective citizenship.

Ius Sanguinis, Citizenship, and New State Formations

Ius sanguinis (and ius soli) played an important role in the formation of new states following decolonization and the implosion of multiethnic empires. Regulating access to the citizenship of the new state is a key element in the formation of the new citizenry. The most inclusive provision in these cases is the so-called zero option, whereby all persons residing on the territory of the state on a particular day are granted citizenship automatically. Thus the zero option follows the principle of ius soli (or rather is an analogous construction, since the question of granting citizenship to the residents of the new state is not linked to descent, but residence). This inclusion into the new citizenship, however, does not necessarily mean that the citizenship law follows the principle of ius soli, as the case of newly established states in the twentieth century make clear. Most states founded after 1918, after 1945, and after 1989 followed a zero-option model but nevertheless based their citizenship law on ius sanguinis, thus excluding children of migrants from easily gaining citizenship.

In this context, the two Baltic states Estonia and Latvia were notorious exceptions after the fall and demise of the Soviet Union. Neither state followed the zero option; rather, each made access to citizenship dependent on proving Estonian or Latvian descent, respectively, thus restrospectively implementing the principle of ius sanguinis. It was stipulated that Estonian or Latvian citizenship could only be claimed by those individuals who could track it back to parents or grandparents who already had this citizenship during the time of national independence in the interwar period. This legal construction led to the exclusion of ethnic Russians who had immigrated to the Baltic republics after 1945 when the region was part of the Soviet Union.

Impact of Ius Sanguinis on Integration

Ius sanguinis and ius soli formally regulate the means by which membership in a state can be acquired. Though citizenship does not directly regulate how relations between state and individual are materially shaped, indirectly it does, since civic and political rights are derived from the status of being a full citizen. Thus access to citizenship is crucial. This is particularly true for those residents of a state who do not automatically have citizenship, namely immigrants (and their children). For them, the practical consequences of having or not having citizenship exercise tremendous influence on their social, economic, and cultural position. Access or nonaccess to citizenship determines their chances to participate in the polity and also, to a certain extent, in the society.

Citizenship laws based on ius sanguinis limit these opportunities for children of immigrants (unless they become naturalized). This legal exclusion built into the structure of a state can have certain unintended social and political consequences, such as marginalization of ethnic-minority migrants, disadvantages in the labor market, spatial segregation, below average educational attainment and careers, and not least of all, a lack of political voice and representation. All of these factors can hinder social integration. In the worst cases, exclusion is mirrored on the side of the receiving population and manifested through xenophobia, nationalist tendencies, and the closure of society vis-à-vis immigrants and foreigners. Thus it is a matter of controversy as to whether strict ius sanguinis regulations are compatible with modern societies, which necessarily experience a high degree of mobility and migration across state borders and depend on their ability to integrate immigrants.

Rainer Ohliger

See also: Citizenship; Ethnic Germans; Germany; Israel; Ius Soli; Law of Return; Migrant Rights; Naturalization; Return Migration; Russian Diaspora

References and further reading:

Aleinikoff, T. Alexander, and Douglas Klusmeyer, eds. 2000. *From Migrants to Citizens: Membership in a Changing World.* Washington, DC: Brookings Institution Press.

Brubaker, Rogers. 1992. *Citizenship and Nationhood in France and Germany.* Cambridge: Harvard University Press.

Cesarani, David, and Mary Fulbrook, eds. 1996. *Citizenship, Nationality, and Migration in Europe.* London and New York: Routledge.

Favell, Adrian. 1997. *Philosophies of Integration: Immigration and the Idea of Citizenship in France and Britain.* London: Macmillan.

Gosewinkel, Dieter. 2001. *Einbürgern und Auschließen. Die Nationalisierung der Staatsangehörigkeit vom Deutschen Bund bis zur Bundesrepublik Deutschland* [Naturalizing and Excluding: The Nationalization of Citizenship from the German Federation to the Federal Republic of Germany]. Göttingen: Vandenhoek and Ruprecht.

Hammar, Tomas. 1990. *International Migration, Citizenship and Democracy.* Aldershot: Gower.

Jacobsen, David. 1996. *Rights across Borders: Immigration and the Decline of Citizenship.* Baltimore and London: Johns Hopkins University Press.

Joppke, Christian. 1999. *Immigration and the Nation-State: The United States, Germany, and Great Britain.* Oxford: Oxford University Press.

Soysal, Yasemin N. 1994. *Limits of Citizenship: Migrants and Postnational Membership in Europe.* Chicago: University of Chicago Press.

Weil, Patrick. 2002. *Qu'est-ce qu'un Français? Histoire de la nationalité française depuis la Révolution* [What is a Frenchman? History of French Nationality since the Revolution]. Paris: Grasset.

Ius Soli

Ius soli is one of the three main mechanisms (along with descent and naturalization) through which citizenship is acquired. Deriving from the Latin term for "law of the soil," it refers to the acquisition of citizenship through birth on the national territory. It is the standard means of acquiring citizenship in the classic countries of immigration—Canada, the United States, and New Zealand—and in one classic country of emigration—Ireland.

Ius soli has come to be viewed as a liberal and progressive conception of nationality. Historically, this was not the case: Its origins were in fact monarchical and imperial. It has its oldest antecedents in the feudal principle of allegiance owed to the nobleman or church because of residence on their territory. The concept was formalized in the seventeenth century, during a fight about property. In 1608, the English courts heard a case brought on behalf of a Scottish child, Robert Calvin, over the Scottish possession of English lands. Before 1608, Scots were not subjects under English law (the closest thing Britain had then to citizenship) but foreigners ("aliens") even if they were born after King James I became King of England in 1604. Under the pressure of the House of Commons, which had its eye on Scottish taxes, the courts ruled in Calvin's favor: All Scots born within King James's realms were English subjects, while those born outside it were not.

Calvin v. Smith is recognized by constitutional historians as the origin of allegiance as the cornerstone of English common law. It also established the basic mechanism of citizenship by birth: People became British subjects by being born on the territory of the king. When Britain acquired an empire, the principle was extended to its colonies, leading to the inclusion of hundreds of millions of people under a nascent form of British nationality. The principle was later extended to the English-speaking countries using the Common Law.

As a mark of ius soli's originally reactionary undertones, postrevolutionary France rejected it in favor of *ius sanguinis*, or citizenship by descent. The concept only came to have liberal implications in an age of migration: Granting citizenship at birth helps ease the integration of the children of migrants. France eventually adopted a variant of ius soli, "double ius soli," through which citizenship is granted to one born in France or to one with a parent born in France. In the main, however, it is more a matter of a historical coincidence than policy design that the main immigration countries use ius soli. It was luck, but useful luck.

Despite, or because of, its liberality, pure ius soli remains an exception, and an increasingly rare one. Britain ended its own use of pure ius soli in 1981, and both Ireland and Australia have debated following suit. In Ireland, a sort of birth tourism emerged in which non-EU nationals sought to give birth there to secure citizenship for their children and exemption from deportation for themselves. Nonetheless, all citizenship regimes are based on some mix of descent and birth, and ius soli will remain a fundamental cornerstone of citizenship.

Randall Hansen

See also: Citizenship; Ius Sanguinis; Law of Return

References and further reading:

Brubaker, Rogers. 1992. *Citizenship and Nationhood in France and Britain.* Cambridge: Harvard University Press.

Dummet, Ann, and Andrew Nicol. 1990. *Subjects, Citizens, Aliens and Others.* London: Weidenfeld and Nicolson.

Hansen, Randall. 1999. "The Politics of Citizenship in 1940s Britain: The British Nationality Act." *Twentieth Century British History* 10, no. 1: 67–95.

Jones, Mervyn V. 1956. *British Nationality Law.* Oxford: Clarendon.